CONFORMITY AND CONFLICT

CONFORMITY
AND CONFLICT
Readings in cultural anthropology

THIRD EDITION

Edited by
JAMES P. SPRADLEY
DAVID W. McCURDY
Macalester College

Little, Brown and Company   Boston   Toronto

Library of Congress Catalog Card No. 76–46799

Second Printing

Published simultaneously in Canada
by Little, Brown & Company (Canada) Limited

Printed in the United States of America

To Barbara Spradley and Carolyn McCurdy

Contents

vii

"Rapping," "shucking," "signifying," and several other
verbal forms represent not only traditional speech styles
of urban black people, but also the ways in which they
can show respect for power, establish their personalities,
and manipulate others.

Bodily adornment among the Tchikrin of Brazil is not
merely decorative, but functions as a complexly coded
communications medium.

Even clothing and footwear of the long-distance runner
can communicate something about the runner: his or her
aspirations, place in the local world of runners, and
self-identity.

A Marshallese Islander uses his knowledge of his society's
matrilineal kinship system to reestablish himself with
relatives and to secure land, a household, and power.

From the perspective of a Chinese woman, the traditional
patrilineal family looks quite different; to succeed there
she must form her own informal uterine family inside
her husband's household.

CONFORMITY AND CONFLICT

I

Culture and the contemporary world

Many students associate cultural anthropology with the study of primitive peoples. They picture the anthropologist as that slightly peculiar person who, dressed in khaki shorts and pith helmet, lives among some exotic tribe in order to record the group's bizarre and not altogether pleasant customs. Like most stereotypes, this one is not completely true but it does reflect anthropology's traditional interest in describing the culture of less complex societies. In the last century, when anthropology became a recognized discipline, its members collected and analyzed the growing number of reports on non-Western peoples by missionaries, travelers, and colonial administrators. This tradition continued into the twentieth century, although the collection of data was refined by actual fieldwork. Impressed by the variety of human behavior, anthropologists sought to record these cultures that were vanishing before the onslaught of Western civilization. Such studies continue among remote groups, and reports of this research are regularly found in professional journals.

During recent decades, however, anthropologists have developed wider interests. As primitive groups have been obliterated or assimilated, anthropologists have increasingly studied subcultures within more complex societies. Certainly World War II and the Cold War stimulated this trend. The United States government employed anthropologists to

1

describe societies in whose territories we fought. The Cold War years, marked by competition with the Russians for influence in developing nations, led to studies of peasant life-styles and culture change.

Today, however, our position in the world has changed. Americans are less welcome in developing nations. Concurrently, problems in our own country have multiplied and taken the center stage of national concern. It is not surprising that anthropologists have extended their attention to subcultures within our own society.

But what can anthropology contribute to an understanding of American life? After all, other social scientists have been doing research in this country for years. Is there anything special about anthropology? In many ways the answer to this question is no. The various social sciences often share the same interests. Yet, as a result of their intensive cross-cultural experience, anthropologists have developed a unique perspective on the nature and the significance of *culture*. This view has emerged from over a century of fieldwork among populations whose behavior was dramatically different from the anthropologists' own. Why, for example, did Iroquois women participate with apparent relish in the gruesome torture of prisoners? How could Bhil tribesmen put chili powder in the eyes of witches, blindfold them, and swing them over a smoky fire by their feet? What possessed Kwakiutl chiefs to destroy their wealth publicly at potlatch ceremonies? Why did Rajput widows cast themselves upon their husbands' funeral pyres? Why did Nagas engage in raids to acquire human heads? In every case, anthropologists were impressed by the fact that this "bizarre" behavior was intentional and meaningful to the participants. Bhils wanted to swing witches; to them it was appropriate. Kwakiutl chiefs made careful investments to increase the wealth they destroyed. These acts were planned; people had a notion of what they were going to do before they did it, and others shared their expectations.

CULTURE

The acquired knowledge that people use to interpret their world and generate social behavior is called *culture*. Culture is not behavior itself, but the knowledge used to construct and understand behavior. It is learned as children grow up in society and discover how their parents, and others around them, interpret the world. In our society we learn to distinguish objects such as cars, windows, houses, children, and food; to recognize attributes like sharp, hot, beautiful, and humid; to classify and perform different kinds of acts; to evaluate what is good and bad and to judge when an unusual action is appropriate or inappropriate. How often have you heard parents explain something about life to a child? Why do you think children are forever asking why? During socialization children learn a culture, and because they learn it from others, they share it with others, a fact that makes human social existence possible.

Culture is thus the system of knowledge by which people design their own actions and interpret the behavior of others. It tells an American that eating with one's mouth closed is proper, while an Indian knows that to be polite one must chew with one's mouth open. There is nothing preordained about cultural categories; they are arbitrary. The same act can have different meanings in various cultures. For example, when adolescent Hindu boys walk holding hands, it signifies friendship, while to Americans the same act may suggest homosexuality. This arbitrariness is particularly important to remember if we are to understand our own complex society. We tend to think that the norms we follow represent the "natural" way human beings do things. Those who behave otherwise are judged morally wrong. This viewpoint is *ethnocentric*, which means that people think their own culture represents the best, or at least the most appropriate, way for human beings to live.

Although in our complex society we share many cultural norms with everyone, each of us belongs to a number of groups possessing exclusive cultural knowledge. We share some categories and plans with family members alone. And our occupational group, ethnic group, voluntary society, and age group each has its distinctive culture. Instead of assuming that another's behavior is reasonable to him, that it is motivated by a different set of cultural norms, we frequently assume that he has intentionally violated accepted conventions. In their attempt to build bridges of understanding across cultural barriers, anthropologists have identified the universality of ethnocentrism many years ago. The study of subcultures in our own society is another attempt to further mutual understanding, as some of the selections in this volume indicate.

How do anthropologists discover and map another culture? Are their methods applicable in the United States? Typically anthropologists live among the people of the society that interests them. They learn the culture by observing, asking questions, and participating in daily activities — a process resembling childhood socialization or enculturation. Obviously, the anthropologist cannot become a child, and must try to learn the norms in a strange group despite his or her foreign appearance and advanced age. Those who study in the United States have followed a similar procedure.

More than anything else, the study of culture separates anthropologists from other social scientists. Other scholars do not ignore culture; they assume their subjects have it, but their main interest is to account for human behavior by plotting correlations among variables. Some social scientists have explained the rise in the American divorce rate as a function of industrialization; this hypothesis can be tested by seeing if higher divorce rates are associated with industrialization and mobility. Anthropologists share a concern for this kind of explanation; for example, many have employed the Human Relations Area Files, a collection of ethnographies describing several hundred societies, as data for testing more general hypotheses. Almost every anthropologist starts with an *ethnography*, the description of a particular culture, and such studies are required to understand the complexity within American society.

As anthropologists have encountered, studied, and compared the world's societies, they have learned more about the concept of culture itself. As we have seen, culture is the knowledge people use to generate behavior, not behavior itself; it is arbitrary, learned, and shared. In addition, culture is adaptive. Human beings cope with their natural and social environment by means of their traditional knowledge. Culture allows for rapid adaptation because it is flexible and permits the invention of new strategies — although change often appears to be painfully slow to those who are in a hurry for it. By the same token, the adaptive nature of culture accounts for the enormous variety of the world's distinct societies.

Culture is a system of interrelated parts. If Americans were to give up automobiles, then other modes of travel, places for courtship, marks of status, and sources of income would have to be found. Culture meets personal needs; through it, people seek security and a sense of control over experience. Indeed, every tradition includes ways to cure the sick, to prepare for the unexpected, and to support the individual. In a complex society with many ways of life in contact with each other, change is persistent. It may be illusion to think that people can control the course of change, or can modify the resulting culture conflict. But if we can understand human cultures — including our own — the illusion may become reality.

CULTURE AND VALUES

It is easy for people to feel that their own way of life is natural and God-given. One's culture is not like a suit of clothing that can be discarded easily or exchanged for each new life-style that comes along. It is rather like a security blanket, and though to some it may appear worn and tattered, outmoded and ridiculous, it has great meaning to its owner. Although there are many reasons for this fact, one of the most important is the value-laden nature of what we learn as members of society. Whether it is acquired in a tribal band, a peasant village, or an urban neighborhood, each culture is like a giant iceberg. Beneath the surface of rules, norms, and behavior patterns there is a system of values. Some of these premises are easily stated by members of a society, while others are outside their awareness. Because many difficulties in the modern world involve values, we must examine this concept in some detail.

A value is an arbitrary conception of what is *desirable* in human experience. During socialization every child is exposed to a constant barrage of evaluations — the arbitrary "rating system" of his culture. Nearly everything he learns is labeled in terms of its desirability. The value attached to each bit of information may result from the pain of a hot stove, the look of disapproval from a parent, the smile of appreciation from a teacher, or some specific verbal instruction. When a parent tells a child, "You should go to college and get a good education," he is expressing a value. Those who do not conform to society's rating system are identified with derogatory labels or are punished in a more severe way. When a Tlingit Indian says to his nephew, "You should marry your father's sister," he is expressing one of the core values of his culture. When a young couple saves income for future emergencies, they are conforming to the American value that the future is more important than the present. When a tramp urinates in an alley, he is violating the value attached to privacy. All these concepts of what is desirable combine cognitive and affective meanings. Individuals internalize their ideas about right and wrong, good and bad, and invest them with strong feelings.

Why do values constitute an inevitable part of all human experience? That human potential is at odds with the requirements of social life is well known. Behavior within the realm of possibility is often outside the realm of necessity. There are numerous ways to resolve the conflict between what people *can do* by themselves, and what they *must do* as members of society. It is a popular notion that prisons and other correctional institutions are the primary means by which our society enforces conformity, but this is not the case. Socialization may be ineffective for a few who require such drastic action, but for the vast majority in any society, conformity results from the internalization of values. As we learn through imitation, identification, and instruction, values are internalized. They provide security and contribute to a sense of personal and social identity. For this reason, individuals in every society cling tenaciously to the values they have acquired and feel threatened when confronted with others who live according to different conceptions of what is desirable.

CULTURAL RELATIVISM

A misconception about values has been spawned by science and, in particular, by the anthropological doctrine of cultural relativism. Some have maintained that it is possible to separate values from facts, and since science is limited to facts, it is possible to do "value-free" research.

By an exercise in mental gymnastics, the very scholars who admit the influence of values in the behavior of others sometimes deny it for themselves. Preferences operate whenever an individual must *select* one action from a multitude of possible courses. Anyone who decides to observe one thing and not another is making that decision on the basis of an implicit or explicit conception of desirability. Science is an activity that makes many value judgments — including which approaches to information gathering are the best. When biologists decide to examine the structure of the DNA molecule using an empirical approach, rather than a mystical, intuitive, or religious one, they are doing so with reference to their sense of what is desirable. Even the decision to study DNA rather than some other substance involves an exercise of values. When doing research on human behavior, the influence of one's values is undeniable. The "objective observer" who is detached from the subject matter, who refrains from allowing values to influence observations, is a myth. This fact does not suggest a retreat from the *quest for objectivity*. It does not mean that social scientists are free to disparage the customs encountered in other societies, or to impose their morals on those being studied. Skilled anthropologists are aware of their own values and then approach other cultures with tolerance and respect. They *identify* rather than *deny* the influence of their own viewpoints. They strive to achieve the ideal of value-free research but realize that it would be naive to assume such a goal possible.

Cultural relativism rests on the premise that it is possible to remain aloof and free from making value judgments. Put simply, this doctrine is based on four interrelated propositions.

1. Each person's value system is a result of his or her experience, i.e., it is learned.
2. The values that individuals learn differ from one society to another because of different learning experiences.
3. Values, therefore, are relative to the society in which they occur.
4. There are no universal values but we should respect the values of each of the world's cultures.

Cultural relativism has enabled the uninformed to understand what appears to be strange and immoral behavior. Although we may not believe it is good to kill infants, for example, we have found it intelligible in the context of a native Australian band. Although Americans generally believe in the desirability of monogamous marriage (or at least serial monogamy), we have found the practice of polygamy in other societies to be comprehensible when related to their cultures. This view presents numerous difficulties. Does one respect a society that believes it best to murder six million of its members who happen to be Jewish? How do anthropologists respect the values of a headhunting tribe when their own heads are at stake?

Moreover, all the statements in this doctrine of relativism are either based on implicit values (i.e., empiricism), or they are outright statements of desirability. The belief that it is good to *respect* the ideals of each of the world's cultures is itself a "relative" value. An extreme relativism is based on the philosophy that it is best to "let everyone do his or her own thing." Given unlimited resources and space this might have been possible, but in the modern world this philosophy represents a retreat from the realities facing us. It absolves the believer from the responsibility of finding some way to resolve conflicts among the world's different value systems. What is needed today is not a "live and let live" policy but a commitment to a higher, more inclusive, value system, and this requires changes that are extremely difficult to achieve.

CONFORMITY AND CONFLICT

Every social system is a moral order; shared values act as the mortar binding together the structure of each human community. Rewards and punishments are based on commonly held values; those persons achieving high status do so in terms of cultural rating systems. These values are expressed in symbolic ways — through food, clothing, wealth, language, behavior — all of which carry implicit messages about good and bad. The pervasiveness of values gives each person a sense of belonging, a sense of being a member of a community, the feeling of joining other human beings who share a commitment to the good life. But the moral nature of every culture has two sides — it facilitates adaptation and survival on the one hand, but it often generates conflict and destruction on the other. Let us examine each of these possibilities.

For almost a million years, people have successfully adapted to a variety of terrestrial environments. From the frozen tundra to the steaming jungle, people have built their homes, reared their children, performed their rituals, and buried their dead. In recent years we have escaped the thin layer of atmosphere surrounding the earth to live, if only for a few days, in outer space and beneath the ocean. All these achievements have been possible because of a unique endowment, our capacity for culture. Wherever people wandered, they developed patterns for organizing behavior, using natural resources, relating to others, and creating a meaningful life. A genetic inheritance did not channel behavior into specialized responses but instead provided a reservoir of plasticity that was shaped by values into one of the many ways to be human. Children in every society do not learn the entire range of potential human behavior — they are taught to *conform* to a very limited number of behavior patterns that are appropriate to a particular society. Human survival depends on cultural conformity, which requires that every individual become a specialist, be committed to a few values, and acquire knowledge and skills of a single society.

This very specialization has led to diversity, resulting in a myriad of contrasting cultures. This volume contains only a small sample of the different symbolic worlds created by people in their attempt to cope with the common problems of human existence. We will see how the generosity of the American Christmas spirit stands in contrast to the daily sharing among the Bushmen. Chicago suburbanites and natives of the Brazilian jungle both adorn their bodies with paint, clothing, and rings, but neither can comprehend how the other defines these symbols. All elements of human experience — kinship, marriage, age, race, sexuality, food, warfare — are socially defined and valued. The difficulty of moving from one cultural world to another is immense.

Cultural diversity has fascinated people for centuries. The study of strange and exotic peoples has attracted the curious for many generations. In the isolation of a remote jungle village or South Sea island, anthropologists found a natural laboratory for carrying out research. Their research reports often seemed more like novels than scientific studies and were read by both professionals and laymen; seldom did any reader feel threatened by the strange behavior of far-off "savages."

But isolation rapidly disappeared, sometimes by virtue of the anthropologists' intrusion! Exploration gave way to colonization, trade, and the massive troop movements of modern warfare. Today it is impossible to find groups of people who are isolated from the remainder of the world. Instead we have a conglomeration of cultures within a single nation, and often within a single city. Anthropologists need only walk down the street from the university to encounter those who have learned a culture unlike their own. Individuals with different language styles, sexual practices, religious rituals, and a host of other strange behavior patterns sit in their classrooms or play with their children on the urban playgrounds. Anthropology today is a science concerned with understanding how people can survive in a world where village, hamlet, city, and nation are all *multicultural.* In isolation, each value system was interesting. Crowded into close and intimate contact, these distinct culture patterns often lead to conflict, oppression, and warfare. Barbara Ward has eloquently summed up our situation:

> In the last few decades, mankind has been overcome by the most change in its entire history. Modern science and techology have created so close a network of communication, transport, economic interdependence — and potential nuclear destruction — that planet earth, on its journey through

infinity, has acquired the intimacy, the fellowship, and the vulnerability of a spaceship.[1]

In a sense, our greatest resource for adapting to different environments — the capacity to create different cultures — has become the source of greatest danger. Diversity is required for survival in the ecological niches of earth, but it can be destructive when all people suddenly find themselves in the same niche. Numerous species have become extinct because of their inability to adapt to a changing *natural* environment. Culture was the survival kit that enabled us to meet fluctuating natural conditions with flexibility, but now we are faced with a radically altered *human* environment. Successful adaptation will require changes that fly in the face of thousands of years of cultural specialization. Our ingenuity has been used to develop unique cultures, but thus far we have failed to develop satisfactory patterns and rules for articulating these differences. Can we survive in a world where our neighbors and even our children have different cultures? Can we adapt to the close, intimate fellowship of a spaceship when each group of passengers lives by different values?

TOWARD A MULTICULTURAL SOCIETY

What is required? In the first place, instead of suppressing cultural diversity by stressing assimilation into the mainstream of American life, we must recognize the extent to which our culture is pluralistic. We must accept the fact that groups within our society are committed to disparate and sometimes conflicting values. The second requirement for a truly multicultural society is that we continuously examine the *consequences* of each value system. What is the long-range effect of our commitment to a "gospel of growth"? What are the results of a belief in male superiority? How do our values of privacy affect those without homes? What is the consequence for minority groups when all students are taught to use "standard English"? As we study American culture we must discover the effect of our dominant values on every sector of life. The ideals that have made this country what it is have also been destructive to some citizens. In our efforts to assimilate ethnic groups, we have destroyed their pride and self-identity. In our attempt to offer the advantages of education to American Indians, we have induced them to become failures because our schools are not able to educate for diversity. In order to demonstrate the tolerance built into American values, we have created the "culturally deprived," but the sophistication of labels does not conceal our prejudice. The absence of men in the

[1] Barbara Ward, *Spaceship Earth* (New York: Columbia University Press, 1966), p. vii.

families of the urban poor is a logical consequence of welfare institutions created from a single value system. The consumer suffers from dangerous products because in our culture productive enterprise is more important than consumer protection. We have only begun to understand some of the consequences of our values, and during the next few decades our survival will demand that the study of values be given top priority.

Finally, the most difficult task for the contemporary world is to induce people to relinquish those values with destructive consequences. This will not be simple, and it probably will not occur without a better understanding of the nature and the function of the world's many value systems. People's capacity to learn has not yet reached its full potential. In every society, children learn to shift from *egocentric* behavior to *ethnocentric* behavior. In deference to desirable community standards, individuals give up those things they desire, and life in a particular society becomes secure and meaningful, with conventional values acting as warp and woof of social interaction.

Can we now learn to shift from *ethnocentric* to *homocentric* behavior? Can we relinquish values desirable from the standpoint of a single community but destructive to the wider world? This change will require a system of ideals greater than the conventions of any localized culture. The change will necessitate a morality that can articulate conflicting value systems and create a climate of tolerance, respect, and cooperation. Only then can we begin to create a culture that will be truly adaptive in today's world.

II

Culture

Culture is learned. At the moment of birth, the human being lacks a culture — a system of beliefs, knowledge, patterns of customary behavior. But from that moment until we die, each of us participates in a kind of universal schooling that teaches us our native culture. Laughing and smiling are genetic responses, but the infant soon learns when to smile, when to laugh, and even how to laugh. Crying is an inborn behavior, but every infant soon learns the rules for crying in a particular culture.

During the first few years of life, cultural learning proceeds at an intense and rapid rate. Informally, without thinking about it, children in every society learn their native language, kinship terms, family structure, how and when to eat, etiquette for everyday life, what goals are worth achieving, and hundreds of other things. Culture is a kind of social heredity: passed on from one generation to the next, it is acquired through learning.

The customs we acquire as members of a society have a curious effect on us. Though we find them difficult to learn, with practice we conform and eventually we come to feel that these customs are right and natural. In time, the explicit rules for customary behavior fade from awareness. Most people are not conscious of the culture that guides their behavior. Conformity is effortless; it feels comfortable and secure.

For example, each of us speaks a native language fluently, yet we are usually unable to state the rules of its grammar. Similarly, people abide by the rest of their culture with confidence, yet they lack a knowledge of its structure. We say then that culture has a tacit, taken-for-granted quality.

It is no accident that anthropologists, interested in understanding culture, have sought out groups with very different life-styles. They have purposely chosen to study in these natural laboratories because they realize that conformity to their own culture acts as a blinder to the study of its patterns. Even the nonconformist rejects little — perhaps a few words, the prevalent style of clothing, the length of hair, or the spending patterns. But when compared with members of non-Western cultures, it is evident that even the most blatant nonconformist thinks, talks, and acts according to our cultural rules. Furthermore, those who withdraw from America's cultural mainstream in an attempt to achieve a radically different life-style only create a new kind of conformity within their special groups.

When people learn about another culture's way of life, its practices seem strange, curious, even bizarre. The first two articles in this section describe the experience of anthropologists who had intense personal encounters with cross-cultural misunderstanding. It is only as we take on the native's point of view and enter into another culture that we begin to make sense of what once appeared strange. Misunderstanding is an inevitable consequence of cultural differences, and leads to bewilderment, anxiety, and sometimes despair — a condition called *culture shock*. But this shock of recognition can also produce insight into a universal phenomenon — conformity to culture. As anthropologists increase their study of complex societies, they should be reminded of the lessons they learned by studying cultures that differ radically from their own.

1

Shakespeare in the bush
LAURA BOHANNAN

Cultural anthropologists are all concerned with meaning, with the difficult task of translation from one language to another. In this classic of anthropology, Laura Bohannan shows the difficulty of translating the meaning of Hamlet to the Tiv in West Africa. She forcefully demonstrates the way in which different cultures provide distinct and separate worlds of meaning for those who have learned to live by them.

Just before I left Oxford for the Tiv in West Africa, conversation turned to the season at Stratford. "You Americans," said a friend, "often have difficulty with Shakespeare. He was, after all, a very English poet, and one can easily misinterpret the universal by misunderstanding the particular."

I protested that human nature is pretty much the same the whole world over; at least the general plot and motivation of the greater tragedies would always be clear — everywhere — although some details of custom might have to be explained and difficulties of translation might produce other slight changes. To end an argument we could not conclude, my friend gave me a copy of *Hamlet* to study in the African bush: it would, he hoped, lift my mind above its primitive surroundings, and possibly I might, by prolonged meditation, achieve the grace of correct interpretation.

It was my second field trip to that African tribe, and I thought myself ready to live in one of its remote sections — an area difficult to cross even on foot. I eventually settled on the hillock of a very knowledgeable old man, the head of a homestead of some hundred and forty people, all of whom were either his close relatives or their wives and children. Like

the other elders of the vicinity, the old man spent most of his time performing ceremonies seldom seen these days in the more accessible parts
of the tribe. I was delighted. Soon there would be three months of enforced isolation and leisure, between the harvest that takes place just
before the rising of the swamps and the clearing of new farms when the
water goes down. Then, I thought, they would have even more time to
perform ceremonies and explain them to me.

I was quite mistaken. Most of the ceremonies demanded the presence of elders from several homesteads. As the swamps rose, the old
men found it too difficult to walk from one homestead to the next, and
the ceremonies gradually ceased. As the swamps rose even higher, all
activities but one came to an end. The women brewed beer from maize
and millet. Men, women, and children sat on their hillocks and drank it.

People began to drink at dawn. By midmorning the whole homestead was singing, dancing, and drumming. When it rained, people had
to sit inside their huts: there they drank and sang or they drank and told
stories. In any case, by noon or before, I either had to join the party or
retire to my own hut and my books. "One does not discuss serious matters when there is beer. Come, drink with us." Since I lacked their capacity for the thick native beer, I spent more and more time with *Hamlet*.
Before the end of the second month, grace descended on me. I was quite
sure that *Hamlet* had only one possible interpretation, and that one universally obvious.

Early every morning, in the hope of having some serious talk before
the beer party, I used to call on the old man at his reception hut — a
circle of posts supporting a thatched roof above a low mud wall to keep
out wind and rain. One day I crawled through the low doorway and
found most of the men of the homestead sitting huddled in their ragged
cloths on stools, low plank beds, and reclining chairs, warming themselves against the chill of the rain around a smoky fire. In the center
were three pots of beer. The party had started.

The old man greeted me cordially. "Sit down and drink." I accepted
a large calabash full of beer, poured some into a small drinking gourd,
and tossed it down. Then I poured some more into the same gourd for
the man second in seniority to my host before I handed my calabash
over to a young man for further distribution. Important people shouldn't
ladle beer themselves.

"It is better like this," the old man said, looking at me approvingly
and plucking at the thatch that had caught in my hair. "You should sit
and drink with us more often. Your servants tell me that when you are
not with us, you sit inside your hut looking at a paper."

The old man was acquainted with four kinds of "papers": tax receipts, bride price receipts, court fee receipts, and letters. The messenger who brought him letters from the chief used them mainly as a badge of office, for he always knew what was in them and told the old man. Personal letters for the few who had relatives in the government or mission stations were kept until someone went to a large market where there was a letter writer and reader. Since my arrival, letters were brought to me to be read. A few men also brought me bride price receipts, privately, with requests to change the figures to a higher sum. I found moral arguments were of no avail, since in-laws are fair game, and the technical hazards of forgery difficult to explain to an illiterate people. I did not wish them to think me silly enough to look at any such papers for days on end, and I hastily explained that my "paper" was one of the "things of long ago" of my country.

"Ah," said the old man. "Tell us."

I protested that I was not a storyteller. Storytelling is a skilled art among them; their standards are high, and the audiences critical — and vocal in their criticism. I protested in vain. This morning they wanted to hear a story while they drank. They threatened to tell me no more stories until I told them one of mine. Finally, the old man promised that no one would criticize my style "for we know you are struggling with our language." "But," put in one of the elders, "you must explain what we do not understand, as we do when we tell you our stories." Realizing that here was my chance to prove *Hamlet* universally intelligible, I agreed.

The old man handed me some more beer to help me on with my storytelling. Men filled their long wooden pipes and knocked coals from the fire to place in the pipe bowls; then, puffing contentedly, they sat back to listen. I began in the proper style, "Not yesterday, not yesterday, but long ago, a thing occurred. One night three men were keeping watch outside the homestead of the great chief, when suddenly they saw the former chief approach them."

"Why was he no longer their chief?"

"He was dead," I explained. "That is why they were troubled and afraid when they saw him."

"Impossible," began one of the elders, handing his pipe on to his neighbor, who interrupted, "Of course it wasn't the dead chief. It was an omen sent by a witch. Go on."

Slightly shaken, I continued. "One of these three was a man who knew things" — the closest translation for scholar, but unfortunately it also meant witch. The second elder looked triumphantly at the first. "So he spoke to the dead chief saying, 'Tell us what we must do so you may rest in your grave,' but the dead chief did not answer. He vanished, and they could see him no more. Then the man who knew things — his

name was Horatio — said this event was the affair of the dead chief's
son, Hamlet."

There was a general shaking of heads round the circle. "Had the
dead chief no living brothers? Or was this son the chief?"

"No," I replied. "That is, he had one living brother who became the
chief when the elder brother died."

The old men muttered: such omens were matters for chiefs and
elders, not for youngsters; no good could come of going behind a chief's
back; clearly Horatio was not a man who knew things.

"Yes, he was," I insisted, shooing a chicken away from my beer. "In
our country the son is next to the father. The dead chief's younger
brother had become the great chief. He had also married his elder brother's widow only about a month after the funeral."

"He did well," the old man beamed and announced to the others, "I
told you that if we knew more about Europeans, we would find they
really were very like us. In our country also," he added to me, "the
younger brother marries the elder brother's widow and becomes the
father of his children. Now, if your uncle, who married your widowed
mother, is your father's full brother, then he will be a real father to you.
Did Hamlet's father and uncle have one mother?"

His question barely penetrated my mind; I was too upset and
thrown too far off balance by having one of the most important elements
of *Hamlet* knocked straight out of the picture. Rather uncertainly I said
that I thought they had the same mother, but I wasn't sure — the story
didn't say. The old man told me severely that these genealogical details
made all the difference and that when I got home I must ask the elders
about it. He shouted out the door to one of his younger wives to bring
his goatskin bag.

Determined to save what I could of the mother motif, I took a deep
breath and began again. "The son Hamlet was very sad because his
mother had married again so quickly. There was no need for her to do so,
and it is our custom for a widow not to go to her next husband until she
has mourned for two years."

"Two years is too long," objected the wife, who had appeared with
the old man's battered goatskin bag. "Who will hoe your farms for you
while you have no husband?"

"Hamlet," I retorted without thinking, "was old enough to hoe his
mother's farms himself. There was no need for her to remarry." No one
looked convinced. I gave up. "His mother and the great chief told Hamlet not to be sad, for the great chief himself would be a father to Hamlet.

Furthermore, Hamlet would be the next chief: therefore he must stay to learn the things of a chief. Hamlet agreed to remain, and all the rest went off to drink beer."

While I paused, perplexed at how to render Hamlet's disgusted soliloquy to an audience convinced that Claudius and Gertrude had behaved in the best possible manner, one of the younger men asked me who had married the other wives of the dead chief.

"He had no other wives," I told him.

"But a chief must have many wives! How else can he brew beer and prepare food for all his guests?"

I said firmly that in our country even chiefs had only one wife, that they had servants to do their work, and that they paid them from tax money.

It was better, they returned, for a chief to have many wives and sons who would help him hoe his farms and feed his people; then everyone loved the chief who gave much and took nothing — taxes were a bad thing.

I agreed with the last comment, but for the rest fell back on their favorite way of fobbing off my questions: "That is the way it is done, so that is how we do it."

I decided to skip the soliloquy. Even if Claudius was here thought quite right to marry his brother's widow, there remained the poison motif, and I knew they would disapprove of fratricide. More hopefully I resumed, "That night Hamlet kept watch with the three who had seen his dead father. The dead chief again appeared, and although the others were afraid, Hamlet followed his dead father off to one side. When they were alone, Hamlet's dead father spoke."

"Omens can't talk!" The old man was emphatic.

"Hamlet's dead father wasn't an omen. Seeing him might have been an omen, but he was not." My audience looked as confused as I sounded. "It *was* Hamlet's dead father. It was a thing we call a 'ghost.'" I had to use the English word, for unlike many of the neighboring tribes, these people didn't believe in the survival after death of any individuating part of the personality.

"What is a 'ghost?' An omen?"

"No, a 'ghost' is someone who is dead but who walks around and can talk, and people can hear him and see him but not touch him."

They objected. "One can touch zombis."

"No, no! It was not a dead body the witches had animated to sacrifice and eat. No one else made Hamlet's dead father walk. He did it himself."

"Dead men can't walk," protested my audience as one man.

I was quite willing to compromise. "A 'ghost' is the dead man's shadow."

But again they objected. "Dead men cast no shadows."

"They do in my country," I snapped.

The old man quelled the babble of disbelief that arose immediately and told me with that insincere, but courteous, agreement one extends to the fancies of the young, ignorant, and superstitious, "No doubt in your country the dead can also walk without being zombis." From the depths of his bag he produced a withered fragment of kola nut, bit off one end to show it wasn't poisoned, and handed me the rest as a peace offering.

"Anyhow," I resumed, "Hamlet's dead father said that his own brother, the one who became chief, had poisoned him. He wanted Hamlet to avenge him. Hamlet believed this in his heart, for he did not like his father's brother." I took another swallow of beer. "In the country of the great chief, living in the same homestead, for it was a very large one, was an important elder who was often with the chief to advise and help him. His name was Polonius. Hamlet was courting his daughter, but her father and her brother . . . [I cast hastily about for some tribal analogy] warned her not to let Hamlet visit her when she was alone on her farm, for he would be a great chief and so could not marry her."

"Why not?" asked the wife, who had settled down on the edge of the old man's chair. He frowned at her for asking stupid questions and growled, "They lived in the same homestead."

"That was not the reason," I informed them. "Polonius was a stranger who lived in the homestead because he helped the chief, not because he was a relative."

"Then why couldn't Hamlet marry her?"

"He could have," I explained, "but Polonius didn't think he would. After all, Hamlet was a man of great importance who ought to marry a chief's daughter, for in his country a man could have only one wife. Polonius was afraid that if Hamlet made love to his daughter, then no one else would give a high price for her."

"That might be true," remarked one of the shrewder elders, "but a chief's son would give his mistress's father enough presents and patronage to more than make up the difference. Polonius sounds like a fool to me."

"Many people think he was," I agreed. "Meanwhile Polonius sent his son Laertes off to Paris to learn the things of that country, for it was the homestead of a very great chief indeed. Because he was afraid that Laertes might waste a lot of money on beer and women and gambling, or get into trouble by fighting, he sent one of his servants to Paris secretly, to spy out what Laertes was doing. One day Hamlet came upon Polonius's daughter Ophelia. He behaved so oddly he frightened her. Indeed" — I was fumbling for words to express the dubious quality of Hamlet's madness — "the chief and many others had also noticed that when Hamlet talked one could understand the words but not what they meant. Many people thought that he had become mad." My audience suddenly became much more attentive. "The great chief wanted to know what was wrong with Hamlet, so he sent for two of Hamlet's age mates [school friends would have taken long explanation] to talk to Hamlet and find out what troubled his heart. Hamlet, seeing that they had been bribed by the chief to betray him, told them nothing. Polonius, however, insisted that Hamlet was mad because he had been forbidden to see Ophelia, whom he loved."

"Why," inquired a bewildered voice, "should anyone bewitch Hamlet on that account?"

"Bewitch him?"

"Yes, only witchcraft can make anyone mad, unless, of course, one sees the beings that lurk in the forest."

I stopped being a storyteller, took out my notebook and demanded to be told more about these two causes of madness. Even while they spoke and I jotted notes, I tried to calculate the effect of this new factor on the plot. Hamlet had not been exposed to the beings that lurk in the forest. Only his relatives in the male line could bewitch him. Barring relatives not mentioned by Shakespeare, it had to be Claudius who was attempting to harm him. And, of course, it was.

For the moment I staved off questions by saying that the great chief also refused to believe that Hamlet was mad for the love of Ophelia and nothing else. "He was sure that something much more important was troubling Hamlet's heart."

"Now Hamlet's age mates," I continued, "had brought with them a famous storyteller. Hamlet decided to have this man tell the chief and all his homestead a story about a man who had poisoned his brother because he desired his brother's wife and wished to be chief himself. Hamlet was sure the great chief could not hear the story without making a sign if he was indeed guilty, and then he would discover whether his dead father had told him the truth."

The old man interrupted, with deep cunning, "Why should a father lie to his son?" he asked.

I hedged: "Hamlet wasn't sure that it really was his dead father." It was impossible to say anything, in that language, about devil-inspired visions.

"You mean," he said, "it actually was an omen, and he knew witches sometimes send false ones. Hamlet was a fool not to go to one skilled in reading omens and divining the truth in the first place. A man-who-sees-the-truth could have told him how his father died, if he really had been poisoned, and if there was witchcraft in it; then Hamlet could have called the elders to settle the matter."

The shrewd elder ventured to disagree. "Because his father's brother was a great chief, one-who-sees-the-truth might therefore have been afraid to tell it. I think it was for that reason that a friend of Hamlet's father — a witch and an elder — sent an omen so his friend's son would know. Was the omen true?"

"Yes," I said, abandoning ghosts and the devil; a witch-sent omen it would have to be. "It was true, for when the storyteller was telling his tale before all the homestead, the great chief rose in fear. Afraid that Hamlet knew his secret he planned to have him killed."

The stage set of the next bit presented some difficulties of translation. I began cautiously. "The great chief told Hamlet's mother to find out from her son what he knew. But because a woman's children are always first in her heart, he had the important elder Polonius hide behind a cloth that hung against the wall of Hamlet's mother's sleeping hut. Hamlet started to scold his mother for what she had done."

There was a shocked murmur from everyone. A man should never scold his mother.

"She called out in fear, and Polonius moved behind the cloth. Shouting, 'A rat!' Hamlet took his machete and slashed through the cloth." I paused for dramatic effect. "He had killed Polonius!"

The old men looked at each other in supreme disgust. "That Polonius truly was a fool and a man who knew nothing! What child would not know enough to shout, 'It's me!'" With a pang, I remembered that these people are ardent hunters, always armed with bow, arrow, and machete; at the first rustle in the grass an arrow is aimed and ready, and the hunter shouts "Game!" If no human voice answers immediately, the arrow speeds on its way. Like a good hunter Hamlet had shouted, "A rat!"

I rushed in to save Polonius's reputation. "Polonius did speak. Hamlet heard him. But he thought it was the chief and wished to kill him to avenge his father. He had meant to kill him earlier that evening. . . ." I broke down, unable to describe to these pagans, who had no belief in individual afterlife, the difference between dying at one's prayers and dying "unhousell'd, disappointed, unaneled."

This time I had shocked my audience seriously. "For a man to raise his hand against his father's brother and the one who has become his father — that is a terrible thing. The elders ought to let such a man be bewitched."

I nibbled at my kola nut in some perplexity, then pointed out that after all the man had killed Hamlet's father.

"No," pronounced the old man, speaking less to me than to the young men sitting behind the elders. "If your father's brother has killed your father, you must appeal to your father's age mates; *they* may avenge him. No man may use violence against his senior relatives." Another thought struck him. "But if his father's brother had indeed been wicked enough to bewitch Hamlet and make him mad that would be a good story indeed, for it would be his fault that Hamlet, being mad, no longer had any sense and thus was ready to kill his father's brother."

There was a murmur of applause. *Hamlet* was again a good story to them, but it no longer seemed quite the same story to me. As I thought over the coming complications of plot and motive, I lost courage and decided to skim over dangerous ground quickly.

"The great chief," I went on, "was not sorry that Hamlet had killed Polonius. It gave him a reason to send Hamlet away, with his two treacherous age mates, with letters to a chief of a far country, saying that Hamlet should be killed. But Hamlet changed the writing on their papers, so that the chief killed his age mates instead." I encountered a reproachful glare from one of the men whom I had told undetectable forgery was not merely immoral but beyond human skill. I looked the other way.

"Before Hamlet could return, Laertes came back for his father's funeral. The great chief told him Hamlet had killed Polonius. Laertes swore to kill Hamlet because of this, and because his sister Ophelia, hearing her father had been killed by the man she loved, went mad and drowned in the river."

"Have you already forgotten what we told you?" The old man was reproachful. "One cannot take vengeance on a madman; Hamlet killed Polonius in his madness. As for the girl, she not only went mad, she was drowned. Only witches can make people drown. Water itself can't hurt anything. It is merely something one drinks and bathes in."

I began to get cross. "If you don't like the story, I'll stop."

The old man made soothing noises and himself poured me some more beer. "You tell the story well, and we are listening. But it is clear that the elders of your country have never told you what the story really means. No, don't interrupt! We believe you when you say your marriage customs are different, or your clothes and weapons. But people are the same everywhere; therefore, there are always witches and it is we, the elders, who know how witches work. We told you it was the great chief who wished to kill Hamlet, and now your own words have proved us right. Who were Ophelia's male relatives?"

"There were only her father and her brother." Hamlet was clearly out of my hands.

"There must have been many more; this also you must ask of your elders when you get back to your country. From what you tell us, since Polonius was dead, it must have been Laertes who killed Ophelia, although I do not see the reason for it."

We had emptied one pot of beer, and the old men argued the point with slightly tipsy interest. Finally one of them demanded of me, "What did the servant of Polonius say on his return?"

With difficulty I recollected Reynaldo and his mission. "I don't think he did return before Polonius was killed."

"Listen," said the elder, "and I will tell you how it was and how your story will go, then you may tell me if I am right. Polonius knew his son would get into trouble, and so he did. He had many fines to pay for fighting, and debts from gambling. But he had only two ways of getting money quickly. One was to marry off his sister at once, but it is difficult to find a man who will marry a woman desired by the son of a chief. For if the chief's heir commits adultery with your wife, what can you do? Only a fool calls a case against a man who will someday be his judge. Therefore Laertes had to take the second way: he killed his sister by witchcraft, drowning her so he could secretly sell her body to the witches."

I raised an objection. "They found her body and buried it. Indeed Laertes jumped into the grave to see his sister once more — so, you see, the body was truly there. Hamlet, who had just come back, jumped in after him."

"What did I tell you?" The elder appealed to the others. "Laertes was up to no good with his sister's body. Hamlet prevented him, because the chief's heir, like a chief, does not wish any other man to grow rich and powerful. Laertes would be angry, because he would have killed his sister without benefit to himself. In our country he would try to kill Hamlet for that reason. Is this not what happened?"

"More or less," I admitted. "When the great chief found Hamlet was still alive, he encouraged Laertes to try to kill Hamlet and arranged a fight with machetes between them. In the fight both the young men were wounded to death. Hamlet's mother drank the poisoned beer that the chief meant for Hamlet in case he won the fight. When he saw his mother die of poison, Hamlet, dying, managed to kill his father's brother with his machete."

"You see, I was right!" exclaimed the elder.

"That was a very good story," added the old man, "and you told it with very few mistakes. There was just one more error, at the very end. The poison Hamlet's mother drank was obviously meant for the survivor of the fight, whichever it was. If Laertes had won, the great chief would have poisoned him, for no one would know that he arranged Hamlet's death. Then, too, he need not fear Laertes' witchcraft; it takes a strong heart to kill one's only sister by witchcraft.

"Sometime," concluded the old man, gathering his ragged toga about him, "you must tell us some more stories of your country. We, who are elders, will instruct you in their true meaning, so that when you return to your own land your elders will see that you have not been sitting in the bush, but among those who know things and who have taught you wisdom."

2

Eating Christmas in the Kalahari
RICHARD BORSHAY LEE

*What happens when an anthropologist living among the bushmen
of Africa decides to be generous and to share a large animal
with everyone at Christmastime? This compelling account
of the misunderstanding and confusion that resulted takes the
reader deeper into the nature of culture. Richard Lee carefully traces how the natives perceived his generosity and taught
the anthropologist something about his own culture.*

The !Kung Bushmen's knowledge of Christmas is thirdhand. The London Missionary Society brought the holiday to the southern Tswana
tribes in the early nineteenth century. Later, native catechists spread
the idea far and wide among the Bantu-speaking pastoralists, even in the
remotest corners of the Kalahari Desert. The Bushmen's idea of the
Christmas story, stripped to its essentials, is "praise the birth of white
man's god-chief"; what keeps their interest in the holiday high is the
Tswana-Herero custom of slaughtering an ox for his Bushmen neighbors
as an annual goodwill gesture. Since the 1930's, part of the Bushmen's
annual round of activities has included a December congregation at the
cattle posts for trading, marriage brokering, and several days of trance-
dance feasting at which the local Tswana headman is host.

As a social anthropologist working with !Kung Bushmen, I found
that the Christmas ox custom suited my purposes. I had come to the
Kalahari to study the hunting and gathering subsistence economy of
the !Kung, and to accomplish this it was essential not to provide them
with food, share my own food, or interfere in any way with their food-
gathering activities. While liberal handouts of tobacco and medical supplies were appreciated, they were scarcely adequate to erase the glaring

Reprinted with permission from *Natural History* Magazine, December, 1969.
Copyright © The American Museum of Natural History, 1969.

disparity in wealth between the anthropologist, who maintained a two-month inventory of canned goods, and the Bushmen, who rarely had a day's supply of food on hand. My approach, while paying off in terms of data, left me open to frequent accusations of stinginess and hard-heartedness. By their lights, I was a miser.

The Christmas ox was to be my way of saying thank you for the cooperation of the past year; and since it was to be our last Christmas in the field, I determined to slaughter the largest, meatiest ox that money could buy, insuring that the feast and trance dance would be a success.

Through December I kept my eyes open at the wells as the cattle were brought down for watering. Several animals were offered, but none had quite the grossness that I had in mind. Then, ten days before the holiday, a Herero friend led an ox of astonishing size and mass up to our camp. It was solid black, stood five feet high at the shoulder, had a five-foot span of horns, and must have weighed 1,200 pounds on the hoof. Food consumption calculations are my specialty, and I quickly figured that bones and viscera aside, there was enough meat — at least four pounds — for every man, woman, and child of the 150 Bushmen in the vicinity of /ai/ai who were expected at the feast.

Having found the right animal at last, I paid the Herero £20 ($56) and asked him to keep the beast with his herd until Christmas day. The next morning word spread among the people that the big solid black one was the ox chosen by /ontah (my Bushman name; it means, roughly, "whitey") for the Christmas feast. That afternoon I received the first delegation. Ben!a, an outspoken sixty-year-old mother of five, came to the point slowly.

"Where were you planning to eat Christmas?"

"Right here at /ai/ai," I replied.

"Alone or with others?"

"I expect to invite all the people to eat Christmas with me."

"Eat what?"

"I have purchased Yehave's black ox, and I am going to slaughter and cook it."

"That's what we were told at the well but refused to believe it until we heard it from yourself."

"Well, it's the black one," I replied expansively, although wondering what she was driving at.

"Oh, no!" Ben!a groaned, turning to her group. "They were right." Turning back to me she asked, "Do you expect us to eat that bag of bones?"

"Bag of bones! It's the biggest ox at /ai/ai."

"Big, yes, but old. And thin. Everybody knows there's no meat on that old ox. What did you expect us to eat off it, the horns?"

Everybody chuckled at Ben!a's one-liner as they walked away, but all I could manage was a weak grin.

That evening it was the turn of the young men. They came to sit at our evening fire. /gaugo, about my age, spoke to me man-to-man.

"/ontah, you have always been square with us," he lied. "What has happened to change your heart? That sack of guts and bones of Yehave's will hardly feed one camp, let alone all the Bushmen around /ai/ai." And he proceeded to enumerate the seven camps in the /ai/ai vicinity, family by family. "Perhaps you have forgotten that we are not few, but many. Or are you too blind to tell the difference between a proper cow and an old wreck? That ox is thin to the point of death."

"Look, you guys," I retorted, "that is a beautiful animal, and I'm sure you will eat it with pleasure at Christmas."

"Of course we will eat it; it's food. But it won't fill us up to the point where we will have enough strength to dance. We will eat and go home to bed with stomachs rumbling."

That night as we turned in, I asked my wife, Nancy: "What did you think of the black ox?"

"It looked enormous to me. Why?"

"Well, about eight different people have told me I got gypped; that the ox is nothing but bones."

"What's the angle?" Nancy asked. "Did they have a better one to sell?"

"No, they just said that it was going to be a grim Christmas because there won't be enough meat to go around. Maybe I'll get an independent judge to look at the beast in the morning."

Bright and early, Halingisi, a Tswana cattle owner, appeared at our camp. But before I could ask him to give me his opinion on Yehave's black ox, he gave me the eye signal that indicated a confidential chat. We left the camp and sat down.

"/ontah, I'm surprised at you: you've lived here for three years and still haven't learned anything about cattle."

"But what else can a person do but choose the biggest, strongest animal one can find?" I retorted.

"Look, just because an animal is big doesn't mean that it has plenty of meat on it. The black one was a beauty when it was younger, but now it is thin to the point of death."

"Well I've already bought it. What can I do at this stage?"

"Bought it already? I thought you were just considering it. Well, you'll have to kill it and serve it, I suppose. But don't expect much of a dance to follow."

My spirits dropped rapidly. I could believe that Ben!a and /gaugo just might be putting me on about the black ox, but Halingisi seemed to be an impartial critic. I went around that day feeling as though I had bought a lemon of a used car.

In the afternoon it was Tomazo's turn. Tomazo is a fine hunter, a top trance performer . . . and one of my most reliable informants. He approached the subject of the Christmas cow as part of my continuing Bushman education.

"My friend, the way it is with us Bushmen," he began, "is that we love meat. And even more than that, we love fat. When we hunt we always search for the fat ones, the ones dripping with layers of white fat: fat that turns into a clear, thick oil in the cooking pot, fat that slides down your gullet, fills your stomach and gives you a roaring diarrhea," he rhapsodized.

"So, feeling as we do," he continued, "it gives us pain to be served such a scrawny thing as Yehave's black ox. It is big, yes, and no doubt its giant bones are good for soup, but fat is what we really crave and so we will eat Christmas this year with a heavy heart."

The prospect of a gloomy Christmas now had me worried, so I asked Tomazo what I could do about it.

"Look for a fat one, a young one . . . smaller, but fat. Fat enough to make us //gom ('evacuate the bowels'), then we will be happy."

My suspicions were aroused when Tomazo said that he happened to know of a young, fat, barren cow that the owner was willing to part with. Was Tomazo working on commission, I wondered? But I dispelled this unworthy thought when we approached the Herero owner of the cow in question and found that he had decided not to sell.

The scrawny wreck of a Christmas ox now became the talk of the /ai/ai water hole and was the first news told to the outlying groups as they began to come in from the bush for the feast. What finally convinced me that real trouble might be brewing was the visit from u!au, an old conservative with a reputation for fierceness. His nickname meant spear and referred to an incident thirty years ago in which he had speared a man to death. He had an intense manner; fixing me with his eyes, he said in clipped tones:

"I have only just heard about the black ox today, or else I would have come here earlier. /ontah, do you honestly think you can serve meat like that to people and avoid a fight?" He paused, letting the implications sink in. "I don't mean fight you, /ontah; you are a white man. I mean a fight between Bushmen. There are many fierce ones here, and with such a small quantity of meat to distribute, how can you give everybody a fair share? Someone is sure to accuse another of taking too much or hogging all the choice pieces. Then you will see what happens when some go hungry while others eat."

The possibility of at least a serious argument struck me as all too real. I had witnessed the tension that surrounds the distribution of meat from a kudu or gemsbok kill, and had documented many arguments that sprang up from a real or imagined slight in meat distribution. The owners of a kill may spend up to two hours arranging and rearranging the piles of meat under the gaze of a circle of recipients before handing them out. And I also knew that the Christmas feast at /ai/ai would be bringing together groups that had feuded in the past.

Convinced now of the gravity of the situation, I went in earnest to search for a second cow; but all my inquiries failed to turn one up.

The Christmas feast was evidently going to be a disaster, and the incessant complaints about the meagerness of the ox had already taken the fun out of it for me. Moreover, I was getting bored with the wise-cracks, and after losing my temper a few times, I resolved to serve the beast anyway. If the meat fell short, the hell with it. In the Bushmen idiom, I announced to all who would listen:

"I am a poor man and blind. If I have chosen one that is too old and too thin, we will eat it anyway and see if there is enough meat there to quiet the rumbling of our stomachs."

On hearing this speech, Ben!a offered me a rare word of comfort. "It's thin," she said philosophically, "but the bones will make a good soup."

At dawn Christmas morning, instinct told me to turn over the butchering and cooking to a friend and take off with Nancy to spend Christmas alone in the bush. But curiosity kept me from retreating. I wanted to see what such a scrawny ox looked like on butchering, and if there *was* going to be a fight, I wanted to catch every word of it. Anthropologists are incurable that way.

The great beast was driven up to our dancing ground, and a shot in the forehead dropped it in its tracks. Then, freshly cut branches were heaped around the fallen carcass to receive the meat. Ten men volunteered to help with the cutting. I asked /gaugo to make the breast bone cut. This cut, which begins the butchering process for most large game, offers easy access for removal of the viscera. But it also allows the hunter to spot-check the amount of fat on the animal. A fat game animal carries a white layer up to an inch thick on the chest, while in a thin one, the knife will quickly cut to bone. All eyes fixed on his hand as /gaugo, dwarfed by the great carcass, knelt to the breast. The first cut opened a pool of solid white in the black skin. The second and third cut widened and deepened the creamy white. Still no bone. It was pure fat; it must have been two inches thick.

"Hey /gau," I burst out, "that ox is loaded with fat. What's this about the ox being too thin to bother eating? Are you out of your mind?"

"Fat?" /gau shot back, "You call that fat? This wreck is thin, sick, dead!" And he broke out laughing. So did everyone else. They rolled on the ground, paralyzed with laughter. Everybody laughed except me; I was thinking.

I ran back to the tent and burst in just as Nancy was getting up. "Hey, the black ox. It's fat as hell! They were kidding about it being too thin to eat. It was a joke or something. A put-on. Everyone is really delighted with it!"

"Some joke," my wife replied. "It was so funny that you were ready to pack up and leave /ai/ai."

If it had indeed been a joke, it had been an extraordinarily convincing one, and tinged, I thought, with more than a touch of malice as many jokes are. Nevertheless, that it was a joke lifted my spirits considerably, and I returned to the butchering site where the shape of the ox was rapidly disappearing under the axes and knives of the butchers. The atmosphere had become festive. Grinning broadly, their arms covered with blood well past the elbow, men packed chunks of meat into the big cast-iron cooking pots, fifty pounds to the load, and muttered and chuckled all the while about the thinness and worthlessness of the animal and /ontah's poor judgment.

We danced and ate that ox two days and two nights; we cooked and distributed fourteen potfuls of meat and no one went home hungry and no fights broke out.

But the "joke" stayed in my mind. I had a growing feeling that something important had happened in my relationship with the Bushmen and that the clue lay in the meaning of the joke. Several days later, when most of the people had dispersed back to the bush camps, I raised the question with Hakekgose, a Tswana man who had grown up among the !Kung, married a !Kung girl, and who probably knew their culture better than any other non-Bushman.

"With us whites," I began, "Christmas is supposed to be the day of friendship and brotherly love. What I can't figure out is why the Bushmen went to such lengths to criticize and belittle the ox I had bought for the feast. The animal was perfectly good and their jokes and wisecracks practically ruined the holiday for me."

"So it really did bother you," said Hakekgose. "Well, that's the way they always talk. When I take my rifle and go hunting with them, if I miss, they laugh at me for the rest of the day. But even if I hit and bring one down, it's no better. To them, the kill is always too small or too old or too thin; and as we sit down on the kill site to cook and eat the liver, they keep grumbling, even with their mouths full of meat. They say things like, 'Oh this is awful! What a worthless animal! Whatever made me think that this Tswana rascal could hunt!' "

"Is this the way outsiders are treated?" I asked.

"No, it is their custom; they talk that way to each other too. Go and ask them."

/gaugo had been one of the most enthusiastic in making me feel bad about the merit of the Christmas ox. I sought him out first.

"Why did you tell me the black ox was worthless, when you could see that it was loaded with fat and meat?"

"It is our way," he said smiling. "We always like to fool people about that. Say there is a Bushman who has been hunting. He must not come home and announce like a braggard, 'I have killed a big one in the bush!' He must first sit down in silence until I or someone else comes up to his fire and asks, 'What did you see today?' He replies quietly, 'Ah, I'm no good for hunting. I saw nothing at all [pause] just a little tiny one.' Then I smile to myself," /gaugo continued, "because I know he has killed something big.

"In the morning we make up a party of four or five people to cut up and carry the meat back to the camp. When we arrive at the kill we examine it and cry out, 'You mean to say you have dragged us all the way out here in order to make us cart home your pile of bones? Oh, if I had known it was this thin I wouldn't have come.' Another one pipes up, 'People, to think I gave up a nice day in the shade for this. At home we may be hungry but at least we have nice cool water to drink.' If the horns are big, someone says, 'Did you think that somehow you were going to boil down the horns for soup?'

"To all this you must respond in kind. 'I agree,' you say, 'this one is not worth the effort; let's just cook the liver for strength and leave the rest for the hyenas. It is not too late to hunt today and even a duiker or a steenbok would be better than this mess.'

"Then you set to work nevertheless; butcher the animal, carry the meat back to the camp and everyone eats," /gaugo concluded.

Things were beginning to make sense. Next, I went to Tomazo. He corroborated /gaugo's story of the obligatory insults over a kill and added a few details of his own.

"But," I asked, "why insult a man after he has gone to all that trouble to track and kill an animal and when he is going to share the meat with you so that your children will have something to eat?"

"Arrogance," was his cryptic answer.

"Arrogance?"

"Yes, when a young man kills much meat he comes to think of himself as a chief or a big man, and he thinks of the rest of us as his servants or inferiors. We can't accept this. We refuse one who boasts, for someday his pride will make him kill somebody. So we always speak of his meat as worthless. This way we cool his heart and make him gentle."

"But why didn't you tell me this before?" I asked Tomazo with some heat.

"Because you never asked me," said Tomazo, echoing the refrain that has come to haunt every field ethnographer.

The pieces now fell into place. I had known for a long time that in situations of social conflict with Bushmen I held all the cards. I was the only source of tobacco in a thousand square miles, and I was not incapable of cutting an individual off for noncooperation. Though my boycott never lasted longer than a few days, it was an indication of my strength. People resented my presence at the water hole, yet simultaneously dreaded my leaving. In short I was a perfect target for the charge of arrogance and for the Bushmen tactic of enforcing humility.

I had been taught an object lesson by the Bushmen; it had come from an unexpected corner and had hurt me in a vulnerable area. For the big black ox was to be the one totally generous, unstinting act of my year at /ai/ai, and I was quite unprepared for the reaction I received.

As I read it, their message was this: There are no totally generous acts. All "acts" have an element of calculation. One black ox slaughtered at Christmas does not wipe out a year of careful manipulation of gifts given to serve your own ends. After all, to kill an animal and share the meat with people is really no more than Bushmen do for each other every day and with far less fanfare.

In the end, I had to admire how the Bushmen had played out the farce — collectively straight-faced to the end. Curiously, the episode reminded me of the *Good Soldier Schweik* and his marvelous encounters with authority. Like Schweik, the Bushmen had retained a thoroughgoing skepticism of good intentions. Was it this independence of spirit, I wondered, that had kept them culturally viable in the face of generations of contact with more powerful societies, both black and white? The thought that the Bushmen were alive and well in the Kalahari was strangely comforting. Perhaps, armed with that independence and with their superb knowledge of their environment, they might yet survive the future.

3

Culture and adaptation in the desert
WILLIAM I. TORRY

*Culture is an adaptive mechanism. People have used it to adjust
to a remarkable range of natural and social environments. In
this article, William I. Torry describes how the Gabra, African
nomads, have culturally adapted to the barren plains and hills of
their habitat along the border between Kenya and Ethiopia. To
survive in this dry land, the Gabra herd camels and small animals such as goats and sheep, which can withstand the lack of
water and forage. But camel herding requires cultural adjustments. The Gabra must move camp regularly, divide their
families for most of the year, put up with their evil-tempered
animals, and constantly seek out better places to forage.*

The Gabra dwell in a harsh terrain on both sides of the Kenya-Ethiopia
border. Along with their neighbors, the Rendille, they are the southern-
most of the world's camel-herding tribes, and the two groups may well
be the only surviving non-Muslim, camel-raising societies. Approximately two-thirds of the Gabra's 24,000 members live a nomadic life
within Kenya's isolated Marsabit district. But the tribe's total territory
encompasses a 20,000-square-mile tract bracketed by Lake Rudolf on
the west, the Marsabit mountain range to the east, the torrid Chalbi
Desert to the south, and the Megado escarpment of Ethiopia to the
north. Lava rubble, volcanic ridges, and shallow craters interspersed by
gravel patches, salt flats, and palm-fringed sand dunes attest to the
region's volcanic origin, and the drabness of the terrain's light cover of
acacia trees, bush, and assorted parched grasses adds to its forbidding
appearance.

Originally published as "Life in the Camel's Shadow." Reprinted with permission from *Natural History* Magazine, May, 1974. Copyright © The American
Museum of Natural History, 1974. Illustrations are omitted.

The amount of available water in this land is the factor that most influences how these nomads live. Sweltering plains cover almost three-quarters of the area and receive an annual rainfall of less than eight inches. Annual precipitation in the mountain zones such as Marsabit and the Huri Hills rarely exceeds thirteen inches. Most of the rain falls in sporadic and localized downpours from March to May and from September to November.

There is sufficient water to meet the needs of humans and animals, but it is often difficult to obtain. The water is confined to a small number of wells, commonly separated from each other by distances of more than twenty miles. Regular movements to Lake Rudolf, the only permanent body of water in the territory, are restricted by its remoteness and proximity to the borders of enemy tribes — Turkana, Dassenitch, and Samburu. Changing forage conditions occasion frequent movements of camps and their herds, usually within an annual circuit of less than 100 miles, and ordinarily, camps shift between the wet season hillsides and the dry season plains. Each movement is accompanied by a flurry of activity, with the women dismantling the tents, which they then load, along with domestic goods and small children, on pack camels. The members of each camp usually leave the site together, but shortly thereafter, individuals or smaller groups may relocate with other camps.

A population the size of the Gabra would not be able to subsist without the use of camels, sheep, and goats. Tilling the soil is considered ritually polluting and conjures up an image in the nomad's mind of the uneventful and unmanly existence associated with sedentary farming. And over-all aridity discourages cultivation. Even cattle husbandry, the most efficient and commonly practiced system of sub-Saharan stock management, could have only limited success here.

The variety of livestock the Gabra breed reflects the diversity of their background. As far back as the eighteenth century, Somali and Rendille tribesmen emigrated with their camels, sheep, and goats to Kenya's Marsabit district and north into Ethiopia. There they joined Borana and Samburu tribesmen who had migrated from their traditional lands with their cattle. Over the years, the four ethnic groups intermixed to form the Gabra tribe. Because of the diversity of livestock under their control, the Gabra were able to exploit almost every niche of their habitat.

Too cool and tick-infested for camels and small stock, the grassy slopes of the highlands now support herds of cattle. But good cattle country is limited, so that Gabra cannot keep large herds of these animals. The dry season milk yield of cattle scarcely covers one-tenth of a herding unit's daily milk budget. Camels, sheep, and goats prefer the hot, salt-rich plains, which lack the abundant grasses and water required by cattle. Camels form the cornerstone of the native economy and adapt well to their habitat, feeding on small shrubs and grasses and navigating nimbly over the stony land.

One important index of the importance of camels to the Gabra is the animals' association with the main camps throughout the year. These mobile residential units, each averaging more than seventy persons and seventeen tents, are the tribe's ritual and political nuclei. For much of the year the camps are occupied by older married persons and young children. Camp residents are frequently related through multiple ties of kinship and marriage. During the dry season, youths drive the bulk of the sheep, goats, and cattle to satellite camps as far as 200 miles away. Here the animals pasture on lusher forage during the long dry season. Camels, however, are kept close to the main camps because their milk is the mainstay of the dry season diet.

Such dispersion of the tribe can lead to many problems. For example, with youths scattered over the territory at the satellite camps for much of the year, the Gabra are at a disadvantage in defending themselves in intertribal fighting. Many Gabra have been killed and thousands of head of livestock have been taken from them during raids by such powerful adversaries as the Somali to the east and the Dassenitch, who live north of Lake Rudolf.

An estimated 40 percent of the camels owned by the Gabra from 1969 to 1971 were adult females. Their total milk yield was sufficient to provide approximately one quart per day for each person in the tribe. A camel in this region seldom produces more than ten quarts of milk daily and then only at the earliest stages of lactation, shortly after the rains begin.

Each Gabra family owns an average of 25 camels, 9 cows, and 125 goats and sheep. Camel holdings of this size are not very impressive by Somali or Bedouin standards, but they do include enough animals to furnish the Gabra upward of 60 percent of their dry season milk supply — the margin of survival during frequent droughts.

The Gabra also subsist through a small amount of trade. Some prosperous merchants have now opened small stores in the few outpost towns within Gabra country. Most traders, however, trek through the country with their wares packed on camels. Through trade, the Gabra can purchase maize meal, tea, coffee beans, and sugar. Although selling camels and their products to outsiders is considered sacrilegious, droughts within the past five years have forced tribesmen to adopt this practice. Camel meat and blood are also important in the Gabra diet. Most of their meat comes from livestock, and about 80 percent of this is camel meat. The meat from one large ox camel is enough to supply an entire camp for two to three days. The young men who live at the distant camel and cattle camps rely for nourishment almost entirely on a mixture of blood and milk.

The Gabra rely on camels for their brute strength as well as for their products. By exploiting the beast's ability to travel long distances burdened with heavy loads, vast stretches of otherwise uninhabitable dry plains lands can be crossed.

During the dry season, the few available water sources — wells, dams, and streams — are heavily taxed. As a result of the scarcity of water, animals overgraze the areas surrounding water sources to a radius of some nine miles, thus forcing the settlements to locate at least this distance from such sites. The Gabra avoid making daily trips to the wells by using their camels to haul large containers of water back to the camp. Each container, woven from wild asparagus roots, can hold five or six gallons of water, and two containers can provide a three- to five-day supply of water for an average family.

Camels are also used to carry the Gabra's leather and mat tents. This gives a family unit the mobility required to respond to suddenly changing pasture conditions.

Without exploiting the milk, meat, blood, and strength of the camel, the nomads would not be able to sustain themselves in the harsh desert environment. But camel husbandry has many drawbacks. For instance, there are breeding problems. Compared to other livestock, camels mature slowly and are incapable of conceiving before their fifth to eighth year. They can continue to bear into their mid-twenties, but few survive beyond twenty. A long gestation period — twelve months — irregular mating patterns, and up to twelve months of lactation stretch birth intervals between twelve to forty months. Even healthy females seldom bear more than eight offspring during their lifetimes.

Actual mating patterns add to the herder's economic woes. When the rains fail, as they often do for several months, the bulls will not rut, so the birthrate is low.

The eating habits of camels pose another set of management problems. The animals do not enthusiastically feed in pastures containing high concentrations of their dung. Except in lush ranges, camels avoid areas visited during preceding days and instead seek patches unspoiled by their droppings.

To determine if a shift of camp is more a consequence of forage depletion than of high dung concentrations is not always easy. Even where forage on unspoiled tracts abounds, camels, unlike cattle, do not remain at one spot long enough to exhaust it. They prefer moving about, sampling scattered shrubs and grasses. Perhaps this exploratory zeal accounts for a herd's highly scattered grazing formations. Cattle often form compact grazing groups, but camels tend to fan out into clusters easily covering one-third of a square mile of open country. This habit makes them easy prey for lions and hyenas and makes a camel herder's work far more difficult than that of a cattle herder. The largest manageable camel herds rarely exceed seventy beasts, and in dense thicket, herds comprise fewer than forty individuals. In contrast, in areas with a thicker grass cover, cattle herds of more than 100 animals are not unusual.

Other camel habits force their keepers to work hard. Whereas a nomadic cattle-herding settlement may be stationary for several months at a time, the Gabra must move an average of once each month because of a number of ecological factors. The most important is the tick *Rhipicephalus pulchellus*, which carries a disease lethal to camels. As the dung levels in the corrals build up, the ticks infest the excreta. They cannot be eliminated by sweeping out the corrals, since they spend part of their life cycle beneath the soil. When dung concentrations reach a certain point the family must move its tent and build a corral on a fresh spot, often no more than three or four hundred yards away.

Although these monthly moves appear minor, the whole camp undergoes the same arduous preparations involved in long-distance migrations. Hence, even though surrounding pastures are only partially grazed, the camp might find it as expedient to move to an ungrazed range three or four miles away as to relocate a mere three or four hundred yards. The tick factor is thus responsible for longer moves, which increase work loads.

Camel anatomy also forces Gabra camps to move frequently during the rainy seasons. A camel's flat, padded feet have little traction on a slippery surface such as a wet corral. The camels must therefore be relocated in areas with more porous soil. Muddy enclosures can so disturb the animals that they attempt to break out unless promptly moved. Also during the wet season, the camps must move because eating water-soaked plants gives camels diarrhea and drinking surface water bloats them.

The behavioral dispositions as well as the physical needs of camels pose serious management problems for the herder. The Gabra often dramatize the vile, unpredictable temper of the camel when zoomorphizing human traits. Whereas stupid, lazy men are equated with cattle and the irrational person is compared to a goat, the solitary or cantankerous individual is associated with the camel. Because it is less habituated to captivity than other livestock, the camel's relationship with man is strained; for the herder this means more work and, occasionally, bodily harm.

Herding is made difficult by the camel's reluctance to return unaided to the camp in the evenings, together with a proclivity for concealing newly born young in the bush. After going without water for several days during the dry season, the beasts occasionally escape the herder's vigil and break away to distant wells. This is one reason why strong young men or elders join the herdboys at sunset to drive the stock home. During the height of the dry seasons or shortly after the rains, herders can often be encountered searching for lost camels. The detective work involved in retrieving stray beasts is both time consuming and irritating. Gabra herders claim that a camel becomes unapproachable after it has been alone in the bush for several days. The herders must often overwhelm such an animal with smoke from an encircling fire. More than half the male camels are gelded so they will be docile enough to carry heavy loads throughout the year. Nonlactating females are also used as beasts of burden, as are bulls on occasion. Pack trains are made up of one or several lines of camels, each numbering up to eight individuals linked tail and mouth by lead ropes. When traveling with loaded beasts, the herder must stay very close to his charges, supervising their movements and guarding against the constant possibility that one or two will step out of tandem, break away, and cause the others to disperse. Catastrophes of this kind result in lost animals and damaged water containers, hides, and domestic utensils.

I was told that one caravan lost seventeen pack camels because a herder did not closely watch his charges. Reports of these disasters, although normally involving fewer beasts, are a frequent topic of conversation in Gabra camps. Tribes using oxen or donkeys for transport have far fewer difficulties of this kind; but these animals are not well adapted to the Gabra's environment.

Camels can inflict nasty bites, even though they do not normally attack people. Herders are quick to show off a scar or two sustained from a sharp incisor or hoof. Bulls become very unruly during the rut, or musth. An early twentieth-century British veterinarian named Legge has vividly described this behavior as follows:

> The animal is constantly grinding his teeth and often froths at the mouth. He is seen to swallow air like a windsucking horse, and . . . he belches it all out again in what seems to be an involuntary effort, in which the head is drawn back and the eyeballs squint downwards. . . . In addition . . . the animal shows a marked pugnacity to strange male camels, or to those which are also musth, and severe, sometimes fatal injuries are often inflicted in the fight which ensues. . . . Musth camels are often affected with diarrhea, and are certainly unpleasant animals to deal with. . . . A camel's bite is severe; he can tear out a muscle or take the top of one's head off with ease.

Milking and mating routines place additional demands on the herder's attention and energy. Cattle are easily milked by one person, but camels are far less cooperative. The animal must first be hobbled and then milked by two boys. At least one other person must stand by with a stick to prevent the more temperamental cows from biting anyone.

The herder also plays a role when camels mate. Experienced bulls can copulate successfully without human assistance, but coitus occurs more quickly if handlers are present to insure that penetration takes place. Whenever I have witnessed this act, a herder has been on hand to couple the animals. Several other persons are pressed into service to keep curious female camels away from the excited couple.

Another important characteristic of camels is their ability to abstain from drinking for long periods. After a series of downpours, a camel can acquire most of its water from moist forage, but during the dry seasons, the animals must be watered every few weeks, and their appetites decline to the point where they show little inclination to feed except in the cool morning hours or later in the afternoon. Cattle must drink every second to third day, and small stock, every third to fifth day. This does not mean, however, that camel watering is a less arduous operation; quite the contrary.

Camels can consume several gallons of water at one time. Water sources are restricted to a few wells and springs located in the Chalbi desert of Kenya and at Gorai in Ethiopia. Once every ten to fifteen days, strong youths drive the camels an average of twenty miles to be watered.

After a one- or two-day walk to the wells through the boulder-strewn hot plains, the herders often encounter long lines of other thirsty herds waiting to be watered. Wells draw all types of stock, and the watering follows an established drinking order. The herders must restrain the camels until the more fragile sheep and goats, and then the cattle, have finished drinking. On very busy days the camels do not get to drink until late afternoon or early evening. But waiting does not mean idleness — far from it. The beasts mill nervously about. If they are not held back, they stampede to the wells, destroying troughs and trampling small stock in the process.

Drawing water from the deeper wells is back-breaking work. A chain of workers stationed at various levels inside the well conveys the water in giraffe-hide buckets to the troughs where at least one person stands ready with a stick to drive back the more aggressive camels. Camels drink their fill in as many as three or four spells, resting between each interval. Each time the animals return, workers must struggle to keep the troughs full of water. Nursing mothers, restless to rejoin their young who have been left behind, look about for an opportunity to make a break for home. The watering process often lasts several hours. Afterward the exhausted herders face a long, hot trek back to the camp.

Raising camels permits survival in this arid land, but camel husbandry is a complicated and difficult enterprise. Local Gabra groups display three types of fluidity in response to the requirements of their stock. The main camp is mobile, for camel ecology precludes fixed residence. Secondly, members of individual families that make up the main camp are widely dispersed for much of the year. Younger persons spend several months away from home at distant camps with the dry stock thereby relieving local grazing pressures. Thirdly, economic opportunism, born from the variable productivity of the camels, limits the time a family spends at any one camp. Local droughts, stock raids, disease, animal shortages, or any of several other factors prompt the homestead to try its fortunes with neighboring kith and kin.

In the process of meeting these requirements, the human community incurs heavy costs in time and energy. The result is that little social activity occurs independent of the actions of camels. Settlement patterns, the division of labor, and community organization all reflect the demanding nature of camel herding as a subsistence mode.

4

Cultural rules for cities: Standing in line
LEON MANN

It is a mistake to believe that only people with strange and exotic customs have culture. Cultural rules govern all our actions, including our mode of encountering strangers in modern cities. A common feature of city life is standing in line, forming queues. Although we usually think of standing in line as a mere transitory phenomenon, an unimportant prelude to some more important activity, lines involve a rather sophisticated knowledge of culture. We learn to stand in line from our earliest years, yet this practice would seem strange and perhaps exotic to an Eskimo or a Bushman unacquainted with Western culture. In this article, Leon Mann describes different kinds of lines and the typical behavior of persons waiting in line. He shows the prevalence of the culture pattern that governs the behavior of people standing in line in Western cities.

Chances are that today you spent a few frustrating minutes standing in line to get a seat in a cafeteria, to buy a train ticket, or to get tickets for a popular movie. If you did not actually stand while waiting for service you probably were in your car waiting to get through the tollbooths, off the freeway, and into the crowded parking lot near your university. Perhaps you queued to make a telephone call or waited in line at the check-out counter of the library. With the growth of large cities and the growing demand for all kinds of services, queues have become commonplace, unavoidable, and for some, a way of life. For some years mathematicians in the field of queuing theory have been describing queues in terms of their causes, the special form they take and the interesting way

Originally published as "Learning to Live with Lines" in *Urbanman: The Psychology of Urban Survival,* John Helmer and Neil A. Eddington, eds. (New York: The Free Press, 1973). Reprinted by permission of the author. References and bibliographic citations are omitted.

they build up and shrink. Opera'ions researchers concerned more with the problem of shortening queues have tried to control them with an eye to improving economy and efficiency of service. And social scientists, always interested in the way in which man adapts to his changing environment, have begun to investigate how city dwellers learn to live with them.

FOUR KINDS OF QUEUES

The common or garden variety of queue, *a single line with a single server,* can be found in almost every cafeteria, greasy spoon, and airport. Its strength lies in the sense of camaraderie which sometimes develops between adjacent queuers as they complain about the slow service. For the cafeteria owner, its advantage lies in the customer with the big eyes and the "smorgasbord" appetite. Restaurateurs believe the big line-up will eventually disappear; the hungry customer will punch a series of buttons, the orders will be dispensed automatically and will be ready and waiting by the time he manages to find his wallet. It is possible, of course, to have queues for which there is no actual service. For example, in waiting lines for washrooms and water fountains "self-service" is the rule.

A variation on the single line–single server theme is to be found in large supermarkets, airport check-in counters, and small-town banks, where a *series of lines* are routed to a number of different servers. This system can produce a great deal of frustration. The real loser is the unwary customer who has yet to recognize the slow tellers in the bank and the tortoises at the check-ins and check-outs. People in other lines come and go while the checker searches for his supply of nickels, or tries to figure out where he left his pencil. This system is at its worst when the person up front produces a piggy bank full of pennies or the lady at the head of the line suddenly drops a dozen eggs on the check-out conveyor belt. Then there is nothing you can do except fume while people in other lines smirk at your misfortune. But there is some advantage in a system which includes a diversified series of lines. It permits the setting up of one or two express lines which provide quick service to customers who are fortunate enough to have only a few items to check out.

The frustrations of the multiple line–multiple server system can be combatted by the more efficient *one line–multiple server* system. This system already exists in barbershops with four chairs, British banks, and their larger Manhattan counterparts. There is a single "feeder" line which branches at the service counter to each of four or five clerks. As each clerk finishes serving a customer he cries "next please!" and the next one in the "feeder" line steps up to take his turn. The basic system is sometimes elaborated by installation of a "Take-A-Check" or a "Take-A-Tab" number dispenser. On arriving at the store the customer takes a number, takes a seat, and waits patiently until his number is called. The system works well in the Eastern Airlines office in San Francisco, but poorly at the photography supplies counter of the Harvard Coop (it seems that Coop clerks abhor numbers). The system can also be a little tough on the worst barber in the barbershop; if his hoarse cry of "next please!" evokes no visible response from customers waiting for a hair cut, his future in the shop is very uncertain.

Exotic *station-to-station* lines, sometimes called "interconnected" queues, are to be found in most hospitals and some Moscow stores. The customer moves from one line to the next in an ever mounting crescendo of impatience and frustration. For example, a shopper for pickled herring in *Gastronom*, the Moscow food store, must work her way through a queue to the counter where they sell herring. A clerk tells her the price, and she walks across the store to the appropriate cashier's window, tells the cashier she wants herring, pays for it, and receives a receipt slip. Then back to the counter, receipt in hand, all set to pick up the wrapped herring, praying that they have not sold out.

Patients at Manhattan's Metropolitan Hospital are constantly exposed to the rigors of station-to-station queuing. This is what happened to Mason Roberts when he appeared at the Metropolitan's outpatient clinic one afternoon in March, 1969, and complained of stomach pains (*New York Times*, March 26, 1969). First he lined up at the central registration window to get forms for the window 6 line, which permitted him to join the chest x-ray line, which set up a wait for the doctor. Somewhere along the line he also queued to pay his bill and to make another appointment. The six different lines took over an hour; the visit with the doctor — who told Roberts he was eating too many spicy foods — took exactly 9 seconds. Roberts' experience is fairly typical of what happens in most large city hospitals. Much worse queues can be found both inside and outside the welfare centers of large cities. On a normal day a welfare applicant or recipient can expect to wait in a series of lines for at least two hours before getting to see a case-worker at Manhattan's Grammercy Welfare Center (*New York Times*, April 25, 1970).

NEW YORK, CITY OF QUEUES

Beyond a shadow of a doubt, New York is the uncrowned queuing capital of the U.S. Over the years there have been some memorable lines on Broadway, outside the Met Opera and the Metropolitan Museum, at Madison Square Garden, and outside Yankee Stadium.

New Yorkers turn out in force when there is an astronaut to be greeted or a hero to be farewelled. During the twenty-four hours when the body of Senator Robert Kennedy lay in St. Patrick's Cathedral (June, 1968), thousands of New Yorkers in lines over one mile long waited patiently to file past the casket. The average wait in line was seven hours, but many who could stay only the one hour of their lunch break, and knew they had no chance of viewing the casket, stood in line as a mark of respect for the slain leader.

On February 7, 1963, despite rain, slush, and bone-chilling cold, a crowd of 23,872 New Yorkers queued up at the Metropolitan Museum of Art to get a glimpse of the *Mona Lisa*. The lines that day stretched over three city blocks. During its three and one-half week sojourn at the Metropolitan, half a million people passed in front of the *Mona Lisa*. When *I am Curious* (*Yellow*) opened at the Rendezvous theater on West 57th Street on March 10, 1969, it quickly drew large crowds and long queues; people were queuing six deep for one and a half blocks for the evening sessions and lines for the 10:00 A.M. session were forming at 7:00 o'clock in the morning. Waiting lines for Broadway hit shows are often themselves smash hits. *South Pacific*, *My Fair Lady*, and *Hello Dolly* drew remarkably long lines during their record runs. When the box office for the musical *Coco* opened on November 3, 1969, the line stretched along 51st Street, turned the corner onto Broadway, headed uptown, and finally came to an end half way up 52nd Street.

It would appear that theater owners have caught onto the idea that a long line of customers in front of their movie house can be good for business. In *Esquire* magazine (December, 1969), movie critic Jacob Brackman observed that many Manhattan movie houses, especially the ones screening "art" movies, were deliberately creating lines on the sidewalk out front, although half the seats inside were still empty. In this age of popular causes a long visible line of eager customers is undeniable evidence of success and provides a free advertisement to any passerby. Even if the movie line is somewhat out in the suburbs, well-removed from the public eye, a shrewd distributor can bring it to the public's attention. The ad for the movie *Monterey Pop*, when it was running on Long Island, featured a large, compact photograph of three bulging lines of teenagers standing outside the theater.

How does the interminable wait to get inside affect the long-suffering moviegoer? Here too the theater owners have modern psychology on their side. Several years ago Leon Festinger, a Stanford social psychologist, carried out a series of studies to test his theory of cognitive dissonance. Festinger and his colleagues found that people who become entangled in a dull, boring task, and for no good reason, tend to reduce their feelings of dysphoria (called "cognitive dissonance") by rationalizing that the task was really quite interesting. This can be applied to the customer who has waited for two hours in a long, cold movie line only to find himself viewng a dull, boring movie. Unless he decides to ask for his money back, the best way to throw off a painful bout of cognitive dissonance is to start believing that the movie really was rich in hidden meanings and stunning in its visual effects. If the customer can enlist some social support for his marathon wait by convincing friends and neighbors about the greatness of the movie, cognitive dissonance can be reduced even further.

Not everyone is sensitive to cognitive dissonance, and those who are do not always attempt to reduce it in a way which drums up business for the theater. Even then, a long wait on the sidewalk need not be harmful for business. For some customers, the relief of getting out of the cold and finding a seat is well worth the price of a ticket.

THE OPTIMISTIC QUEUER

Why do people stand in line when their chances of getting to see a hit play or movie range from poor to hopeless? This puzzle is of more than academic interest for it involves a strange quirk of human behavior. When *My Fair Lady* opened at the Mark Hellinger Theater in 1956, a line would appear nightly outside the theater to wait for the box office to open at 10 o'clock in the morning. Then thirty standing-room tickets for that night's performance would go on sale. But invariably at dawn, four hours before the opening of the ticket box, there would be many more people in line than tickets available. For some peculiar reason the hopeful failed to appreciate that their chances were really hopeless.

Together with Keith Taylor, a psychologist at the University of Melbourne, I decided to investigate why latecomers in long queues are optimistic about their chances of success.

Our first study involved twenty-two queues of football fans outside the Melbourne Football Stadium, in August, 1966. Going on the official notices about the number of tickets on sale, only the first 140 in each queue were likely to get tickets. But, in some of the lines, there were well over 200 people. We decided to interview every tenth person and ask each one to estimate how many people stood ahead of him in line. People in the very first part of the line, as we expected, estimated the length of the queue and their chances of success quite accurately. Then, after the thirtieth person in line, there was a consistent tendency to *over*estimate the number in front, and this occurred all the way up to person 130, almost exactly the point at which the supply of tickets was likely to run out. After the "critical point" the mood of the queuers began to change; people consistently *under*estimated the size of the crowd in front. In other words, they started getting optimistic precisely at the point where they should have given up and gone home. The latecomers' unwarranted optimism seemed to us like a desperate subconscious maneuver to justify standing in line, a case of unintentionally deluding oneself that the line is shorter than it really is. We called this interpretation of the latecomers' optimism, the wish fulfilment hypothesis.

We decided to investigate whether this same phenomenon could be found in very long and very short lines. Observation of a single queue at the Collingwood Football Ground several weeks later showed that the point at which the supply of tickets was likely to run out — position 500 — again marked the point at which unjustified optimism began. Next we interviewed 66 small boys in a line for free Batman shirts, outside a movie house in downtown Melbourne. To attract a large juvenile audience the management had announced that 25 Batman shirts would be given away to the first 25 queuers at the morning matinee. Once again, queuers after the critical point tended to underestimate their position in line.

An alternate explanation for this unbridled optimism is the self-selection interpretation. It holds that a difference might exist between the kinds of people who are found in queues before and after the critical point. Early comers are by nature cautious and pessimistic, while late-comers are adventurous and optimistic. A frivolous variant of the self-selection hypothesis is that the people who join a line after a critical point must be either myopic or psychotic, since normal people give up and go home.

For our final foray into the psychology of latecomers we arranged to take over a high school for a morning and form the 521 students into two parallel lines. This feat was managed with the cooperation of the Principal and Staff of Wattle Park High School, Victoria, Australia. Both lines were told that the experiment was a study of attitudes toward queuing, but our hidden purpose was much more devious. We wanted to create an "experimental" line, in which all of the members knew that a valued commodity (chocolate bars) would be distributed to the first half of the line, and a "control" line, in which the members had no idea that chocolate, indeed any commodity, would be made available. We reasoned that if the wish-fulfilment hypothesis is the correct explanation for the latecomers' optimism, then any tendency to give optimistic estimates should be confined almost entirely to the experimental line, and only after the critical point. While there was a tendency for "late-comers" in the chocolate line to underestimate numbers in front, our findings were not nearly so impressive as in the earlier studies.

But we were not inclined to feel pessimistic about this turn of events. We concluded that "latecomers" in the chocolate line do not experience much pressure to justify standing in line since, in the first place, they were coerced into this hopeless cause by a pair of psychologists. Moreover, in comparison to football tickets and Batman T-shirts, a ten-cent chocolate bar is not quite the stuff delusional fantasies are made of. . . . When the study was over, we fully debriefed the school about the real purpose of our experiment, and for good measure treated every student to a well-earned chocolate bar.

SERVING TIME IN QUEUES

First-come first-served, the basic principle of queuing, is an example of what George Homans, a Harvard sociologist, calls the rule of distributive justice. If a person is willing to invest large amounts of time and suffering in an activity, people who believe there should be an appropriate fit between effort and reward will respect his right to priority. In most queues there is a direct correspondence between inputs (time spent waiting) and outcomes (preferential service). The rule of distributive justice is modified in marathon queues, however, because the queuers need to absent themselves from the line from time to time. Continuous residence in a long, overnight line would impose terrible hardship on the queuers, and so they come to an informal understanding about the minimum inputs of time they must spend to validate occupancy of a position. From our observations of football queues in Melbourne, and from anecdotal evidence, it is clear that rules regarding the serving of time constitute the core of queue culture.

Every August in Melbourne, thousands of football fans form mammoth lines outside the Melbourne Stadium to buy tickets for the equivalent of the "World Series" of Australian rules football. Over the past few years, the social psychology students of the University of Melbourne have descended on the lines to make observations and ask questions. From our interviews and observations we have learned that although arrangements made to control behavior in the queue are informal, they are clearly identifiable. Brief "time outs" or leaves of absence from the queue are accomplished by two universally recognized procedures. One technique is the "shift" system, in which the person joins the queue as part of a small group and takes his turn in spending one hour "on" to every three hours "off." The second technique is designed specially for people who come alone and who for various reasons need to leave the line briefly. They "stake a claim" by leaving some item of personal property such as a labeled box, folding chair, or sleeping bag. The rule in leaving position markers is that one must not be absent for longer than periods of two to three hours. If the norm is broken the person cannot gain re-entry into the queue, and many return to find their property smashed or thrown aside. This actually happened in August, 1966, when irate latecomers noticed that many people in the middle of the queue had not made an appearance for most of the day, and spontaneously seized their boxes and burnt them.

In some marathon queues, "time-outs" are regulated by an ingenious roll call system. The weekly line for tickets at the Metropolitan Opera House in New York is notable for this kind of arrangement. According to a story in the *New Yorker* (January 14, 1967), the lines begin to form the day before the box office opens. The first person in line is the unofficial "keeper of the list," who registers applicants in order of arrival and assigns numbers. Ordinarily, queuers are required to report for "roll call" every two hours throughout the day and night, although the keeper of the list can and does vary this requirement. Otherwise they are free to wander about or go home. Anyone who misses a roll call has his name struck off the list and must start again from the end of the line. Although the Metropolitan security men keep an eye on the proceedings, it is the "keeper of the list" who keeps order, calls off names, pushes people into place, and hands out numbered tags which are recognized at the ticket office. Nobody seems to know how one gets to be appointed "keeper of the list," or if they know they are not saying. Apparently the system works well, because most people know the rules and there are very few attempts to jump the queue.

For the 1968 season the Metropolitan people decided to do away with the overnight part of the queue (as a precaution against the possibility of nocturnal violence and robbery), and the system was modified to cut the amount of time actually spent in line while an increase was made in the frequency of the roll calls. The new system, as described by one of my students (a devoted opera buff), consisted of a series of weekend queue reunions. "People check in on Friday night and their names are taken and they are given numbers. They come back on Saturday and check in again with the head of the line. On Sunday the people meet in a park across the street from Lincoln Center at about 7:00 A.M. and check in again. At 8:00 they cross the street to the Met and wait there until 9:00 when the Met hands out its own tags. Then everyone breaks for breakfast and comes back sometime before 11:00 to wait for the box office to open." . . . In 1969, much to the sorrow of opera buffs and queue addicts, there was no Metropolitan Opera season and no opera queues.

The Metropolitan Opera line is a good example of the principle of keeping the queue "honest" by ensuring that only the dedicated, determined few who are prepared to sacrifice sleep and comfort qualify for the privilege of buying tickets. The imposition of hardship ensures that the casual passerby or the less devoted opera fan cannot claim priority on the basis of order of arrival alone, and so cannot gain an advantage over the genuine opera buff. The "roll call" system illustrates the basic principle that a place in line must be "earned," and to earn it inputs of time and effort are necessary.

Japanese queues for the purchase of home sites provide another example of the roll call system at work. In Tokyo, where home sites are in chronic short supply, mammoth lines form outside real estate company offices whenever it is announced that a parcel of land is about to go on sale. These lines, numbering hundreds of people, will sometimes last for more than two weeks. The *Melbourne Age* (November 11, 1969) has described how the Japanese organize a roll call system. Soon after they arrive the queuers elect a committee from among their numbers. This committee acts as a kind of Queue Self-Government Association which compiles a list of people in order of their arrival and fixes the number of roll calls to be held each day. The president of the Queue Association calls the roll — sometimes three times, occasionally seven times a day. Anyone who misses the roll call loses his place. Similar arrangements for regulating time spent in and out of line are to be found in marathon queues in many large cities.

PRE-QUEUES

But mammoth queues which last for a week or two tend to be frowned upon by city authorities. Such queues tend to clutter sidewalks, pose a health hazard, and sometimes require continual surveillance by police and officials to prevent outbreaks of violence.

In the Melbourne football queues of 1965, thousands of people waited for tickets, some of them for over a week, in mud and drizzling rain. Queuers erected a shanty town of tents and caravans and conditions rapidly became squalid and unhygienic. The following year, to prevent a recurrence of the shanty town, the mayor of Melbourne banned queues outside the stadium until twenty hours before ticket sales started. But football fans, anxious to be sure of getting tickets, spontaneously formed an unofficial pre-queue several hundred yards away from the stadium many hours before the official line was allowed to start. When the barricades were lowered by officials and queuing began, people folded their camp chairs and, keeping the line intact, filed in perfect order to the ticket windows to commence the official twenty-hour wait. The formation of a pre-queue meant that people did not have to converge on the ticket boxes all at the same time, thus preventing chaos and the possibility of violence.

In Havana, lines at the post office, outside ice cream parlors, and in front of restaurants are commonplace. Sometimes the police will not allow a line to form too much in advance in order to keep the sidewalks clear. The Cubans meet this challenge by forming a pre-queue. They station themselves across the street or down the block from the ice cream parlor and check as they arrive as to who preceded them. When formal lining up becomes permitted, the underground line emerges and takes up its official wait.

Pre-queues represent an ingenious solution to the problem of how to maintain order when a large throng gathers before the official starting time.

QUEUE JUMPING

One of the biggest headaches associated with life in a queue is safeguarding it against the activities of would-be queue jumpers.

Before we discuss how people actually deal with queue jumpers, try answering this question, an item from the Allport test of Ascendance-Submission:

> Someone tries to push ahead of you in line. You have been waiting for some time, and can't wait much longer. Suppose the intruder is the same sex as yourself; do you usually
>
> > remonstrate with the intruder . . . ?
> > "look daggers" at the intruder or make clearly audible comments to your neighbor . . . ?
> > decide not to wait and go away . . . ?
> > do nothing . . . ?

The word "remonstrate" sounds a little archaic these days, but in 1928, when Gordon Allport devised the Ascendance-Submission test, it was a perfectly fashionable word. Scores on the A-S scale enabled Allport to decide whether a person was ascendant or submissive, whether he would try to control or dominate a situation, or prefer to yield the right of way.

Several years ago the Ascendance-Submission test was given to 60 Harvard men and a similar number of male students at the University of Melbourne, Australia. Responses to the item about the queue jumper make for some interesting comparisons.

> 42% of Harvards and 55% of Melburnians said they would "remonstrate"
> 32% of Harvards and 27% of Melburnians said they would "look daggers"
> 2% of Harvards and 1% of Melburnians said they would be inclined to "go away"
> and 3% of both Harvards and Melburnians said they would probably "do nothing"

It is apparent that the Harvard and the Melbourne response is rather passive. What emerges from responses to the test items is evidence perhaps that many young people prefer Gandhian non-violence over physical aggression as a *modus vivendi* in waiting lines.

Interviews we have carried out with students from colleges in the Boston area tend to support this preference for non-violence in dealing with queue jumpers. In November 1969, we spent a morning at Boston Garden surveying the line for tickets to a Rolling Stones concert. There were about 600 long-haired, bearded, and beaded college students waiting for tickets to go on sale at 10 A.M. One of the questions we asked was, "What would you do if someone tried to push in front of you?" The answers that morning spoke mainly of peace. "If they want it that bad, let them get in front of me." But some of the queuers seemed ambivalent in their attitudes. One Tufts student, trying to be magnanimous, asserted, "I would tell him to leave, and make it sound serious enough so he wouldn't want to stand around . . . but if he didn't leave, I'd let him stay, because then he'd be spiting himself. But knowing myself, I might just push him out."

Generations of psychologists have long agonized over the apparent discrepancy between people's statements of what they think they will do in a situation and what they actually do. Nowhere is this discrepancy more apparent than in the football waiting line. When quizzed about their preferred ways of handling queue jumpers, football fans, unlike college students, almost always vow they would resort to physical violence to throw out the intruder. But when the queue jumper actually makes his move, it is painfully obvious that the offended victim is more inclined to do nothing.

Why do queuers fail to act together to kick out the queue jumper? The answer to this knotty question lies partially in the varying interests and characteristics of people in different parts of the queue. Naturally, people at the front don't care much about the people who push in behind them, unless queue jumping is so widespread that the entire line becomes vulnerable. For others there is the thought that the intruder might be so desperate that a struggle might bring about injury and damage. There is the fear, too, that if everyone resorts to physical violence, the illusion that the queue is for the most part well-controlled and orderly is quickly shattered; once this happens, there is a danger of complete disintegration.

But, if queuers are reluctant to use physical force to discourage intruders, they have other techniques available for guarding their positions. A barricade of strategically placed barriers, camp cots, and boxes can be effective protection. Keeping close interpersonal distance helps keep people warm and also serves to maintain the "territory" against would-be infiltrators. At times of maximum danger, and in the few moments before the ticket box opens, there is always a visible bunching together, or shrinkage, in the length of a line — literally a closing of the ranks. At the head of the line suspicious-looking outsiders are intimidated by loud catcalls and jeering. Ordinarily this works best during daylight; the sight and sound of fifty jeering people usually inhibits even the boldest queue jumper. But in the dark, when the queue relaxes its vigilance, social pressure tends to be less effective.

It seems puzzling but it is a fact that the favorite hunting ground for the queue jumper lies somewhere near the tail of the queue. If someone is going to risk pushing in, why not try at the front, where the rewards are greater and the wait is shorter? Here we must bear in mind that the people at the front almost always belong to a strong, well-knit clique and are ready for police action, either because they came together at the outset, or because they have had time to establish a strong sense of community. The latecomers at the end, alienated and disorganized, are far less able to defend themselves against predators. Then, again, the queue jumper risks a lot less toward the end of the line, as fewer people are put out by the violation.

Another reason for the high incidence of queue crashing toward the back is the difficulty the latecomers have in spotting an illegal act of entry from the somewhat more acceptable act of *place keeping*. It is always hard to decide whether a person who marches confidently into a line is attempting to crash the queue, or is merely joining his group. Thus, latecomers are usually reluctant to challenge anyone who walks into a line, unless a furtive manner and a pair of shifty eyes mark the person as a nervous, inexperienced queue jumper. Then the queue rarely acts together to expel the violator, but the onus for kicking him out falls squarely on the shoulders of the person who "let him in"; those further back may jeer, catcall, and whistle, but the immediate victim is expected to get rid of the crasher. The reasoning seems to be that the victim was careless in guarding his territory, so it is up to him to handle the situation, quietly and efficiently.

QUEUE BUSINESSES

Whenever demand exceeds supply, it is almost inevitable that businesses associated with ticket speculation will crop up and flourish both inside and outside the queue.

Two major kinds of professional activity can be observed in queues for hard-to-get tickets. Big-time operators are super-efficient entrepreneurs who hire dozens of people to buy up tickets for the black market. This kind of business has been going on for a long time. When Charles Dickens toured America in 1842 to read from his works, enterprising speculators made a fortune scalping tickets to an insatiable public. Speculators engaged teams of up to fifty people to take places in the $2 ticket queue; then, having bought up the choice tickets, resold them for as much as $26 each. Small-time operators, the amateur scalpers, are often university students who resell their two or three tickets to the highest bidder before a football game. A wealthy patron who neglects to buy his seat through regular channels sometimes commissions a small-time operator to stand in line for tickets. Speculation in the physical position itself, rather than in tickets, has been known to occur in waiting lines for Broadway hit shows. For example, in the overnight lines for *My Fair Lady* in 1956, some people made a business of getting in line early in order to sell their advanced positions to latecomers for as much as $20.

In mammoth football queues, another kind of business, queue counting, tends to flourish. Concerned at the number of tickets left, some people want to know where they stand in line. Queue counters are boys who run up and down the length of the line at regular intervals; for a fee (usually 10¢) they give customers up-to-date information on the numbers ahead and behind, as well as topical news and gossip.

As far as we know, there are no records of professional place-keepers, people who *mind* places in queues for a fee, but the existence of such a business would not be surprising in the least.

QUEUES INTERNATIONAL

How widespread is queue culture, and how typical are the kinds of behavior observed in New York opera lines, Tokyo real estate lines, and Melbourne football queues? Although lines for sporting events tend to be unique in their atmosphere and makeup, queues for all kinds of services in practically every country have a great deal in common. In most queues, there is a concern with the problem of safeguarding order, a desire to keep the queue "honest," and the emergence of ingenious systems to balance hardship and "time out." The anthropologist E. T. Hall, in *The Silent Language*, has suggested that a cultural value of egalitarianism is responsible for the manner in which queues and queuing are treated with deference in Western society. In his book, *The Human Dimension*, Hall asserts that respect for queues can also be attributed to a cultural value of orderliness. Presumably the English are high on both egalitarianism and orderliness, because in England democratic queuing is a way of life.

A friend living in England told me she was once waiting for a London bus at a rarely used stop. Since there was only one other person waiting, an elderly lady, she felt no need to bother about a line. Much to my friend's surprise, the matron began to mutter darkly and, unable to contain herself any longer, snapped out "Can't you read the sign? You're supposed to get into a queue!"

Queuing is a traditional part of the Soviet way of life. Commenting on Soviet lines, fifty years after the Revolution, I. Korzhinevsky, head of the consumption department at the Ukrainian Institute of Trade Research, was moved to observe: "We have simply resigned ourselves to the existence of lines." When he visited Russia in the summer of 1954, Henri Cartier-Bresson, the French photographer, was enchanted by the ubiquitous Moscow lines. His camera recorded lines in front of fruit stores, bookshops, groceries, and butcher shops. He was impressed with the orderliness of the long lines outside Lenin's mausoleum and the patience of shoppers in GUM, the large department store. If Cartier-Bresson were to revisit Moscow today, he would probably find that very little has changed. Moscow, like New York, is still a city of queues.

Of course every large city, and a few not so large ones, are plagued by queues, but it is interesting to note what people are queuing for, since this tells us something about their everyday needs and how cities are failing to cope with them. Outside Havana's ice cream parlors, called *coppelias,* Cubans stand in line for two hours for a dish of six-flavor ice cream, while in Mexico City, committees wait patiently in line to catch a *pesero,* a shared, fixed-route taxicab. In Tokyo, people wait in lines outside real estate development offices for as long as two weeks hoping to buy a block of land for a home site. Queues of shoppers form at dawn in Rangoon, Burma to buy rice, bread, and soap at the "People's Store." And somewhere in Nigeria, long lines of Biafrans wait patiently for a turn to wash their clothes at a primitive outdoor laundry.

Queuing is a truly international phenomenon and, in most countries, a culture of the waiting line has developed to regulate order and to control such matters as time outs and place keeping.

LEARNING TO LOVE QUEUES

One of the most disconcerting findings in our research on football queues is that people are beginning to accept them, almost as a kind of cherished tradition or ritual. During the regular football season, although it is possible to get choice seats two hours before the start of most Saturday games, long queues form outside stadiums on Friday afternoons. The new attitude is exemplified by a woman who was heard to say, outside the Melbourne stadium, "People are always knocking queues — what I would like to know is what people like myself would do without them?" In 1966, on a mild afternoon before the World Series football tickets went on sale, we interviewed 122 queuers and discovered that 47 per cent were happy with the queue system. In 1967, after a dreadfully cold, wet night, we interviewed the all-nighters and found that even then 26 percent reported satisfaction.

Perhaps these statistics should not be regarded as surprising since life in a mammoth queue can be in many ways quite pleasant and relaxing, even though time consuming. The enterprising queuers of

Melbourne have learned to cope with the harsh environment outside their stadium by tying tarpaulins to the side of barricades, sleeping on stretchers, and consuming large quantities of liquor. In August, 1966, when we went down to Collingwood, a working-class suburb of Melbourne, to interview the football queuers, we were impressed with the successful adjustment they had made to queue living. The first three families in line, numbering approximately thirty men, women and children, pitched a tent on the sidewalk fronting the ticket box and settled down to a six-day wait around a blazing campfire. Some enthusiasts moved out of their homes and took up formal residence in the queue. Five days before tickets went on sale the general secretary of Collingwood Football Club, Gordon Carlyon, received a letter addressed to "Mr. Alfred McDougall, c/o Queue outside Collingwood Football Ground, Collingwood, 3066." The Melbourne *Herald* reported that Mr. Carlyon threaded his way through beds and tents on the sidewalk outside the stadium to deliver the letter.

It would appear, then, that urban man with his remarkable capacity to put up with continual delays and irritations is not only learning to adapt to queues but is actually beginning to value them as social occasions. The social value of queues is borne out by George Nash, a sociologist at Columbia University, who has carried out surveys of people in movie lines on New York's East Side. He has found that 73 percent of those who wait in movie lines are under thirty and that these young people, rather than complaining about the waste of time (the wait to get in is frequently between one and two hours) regard it as a very rewarding experience. The *New York Times* (April 25, 1970), in reporting Nash's findings, made the following observations:

> Noticing — and getting noticed — is what makes waiting to see a popular "in" movie not just another deadening urban plague to be endured but instead a tolerable and, for many, even pleasurable pastime in itself. The longer the line, the younger, more modish it is likely to be, and the more bemused — and thus not bored — by itself. Almost invariably the predominant conversational gambit has to do with similar evenings at the movies: not remembered great films, but remembered great lines.

In our survey of ticket lines for the Rolling Stones concert at Boston Garden, we obtained further evidence of the social function of queues. When we arrived at the Garden to conduct our interviews, there were approximately 600 college students communing together on blankets and sleeping bags. The sweet smell of marijuana hung in the air. During the night, many of the kids had met up with old friends or made new ones. To one of our questions, "How do you feel about having to wait in line?" a Radcliffe girl answered, "I'm really excited. It's a kind of social event." A Boston University student told us, "It's a groovy way to meet people." These were fairly typical responses. The evidence suggests that queues for concerts, movies, and sporting events have emerged as occasions for socializing and as opportunities for sociability.

GETTING RID OF QUEUES

But queues at airports, and in banks, hospitals, and stores are rarely treated as an occasion for meeting people and conducting sociability. The emotional cost of waiting in such lines is formidable (consider the frustrations, fights, and aggravation generated by a long, tiring wait). And their economic cost is incalculable (consider the waste in man-hours and loss of goodwill for the store).

With the proliferation of queues and queuing, it has become increasingly important to formulate measures to reduce the number and length of lines, to reduce the cost in boredom and misery, and to eliminate, wherever possible, their attendant friction and hostility. What can be done about reducing the number and length of lines?

The application of the computer to ticket selling is one possible solution. Only recently two companies, *Ticketron* and *Computicket*, began to offer instant ticketing to scores of sporting and theatrical events. The system is engagingly simple. The buyer goes to a ticket sales outlet in a department store, railroad station, or supermarket, and tells the clerk the events he wants to see and when. The clerk pushes buttons on a computer console and quizzes a regional memory bank about the best seats available at the preferred price. From its bank of data, the computer provides an instant reading of the best seats at each price level. If the customer decides to buy, the clerk pushes another button and the computer instantaneously delivers a printed ticket for the show.

With the advent of the jumbo 747 jets, computers are being used to speed up airline reservation systems. At the Eastern Airlines terminal in New York passengers check in baggage and receive their seat numbers in a single quick transaction, without having to wait in long lines during the loading of the aircraft. But even though it is not always economical to install a computer ticketing system, it is still possible to introduce more efficient methods of organization to curtail needless waiting.

We all have experienced interminable delays caused by organizational negligence and inefficiency. My pet story stems from a visit to Mexico in the summer of 1969. We wanted to take a bus from Mexico City to Taxco, a journey of 130 miles. Although there were only twenty people ahead of us in line, it was over ninety minutes before we were served. The clerk required five minutes to locate the bus log book, write the destination, date, time of departure and seat number of each ticket, enter the traveler's name and address in another book, and finally exchange the ticket for money. Since the bus company refused to make return reservations in advance, we had to go through the same ordeal the next day in Taxco. In case the manager of the bus company is reading this, here is some (unsolicited) advice. Introduce pre-stamped tickets (it will reduce service time by one-half); hire a second clerk to help out at peak hours (i.e., always); have the two clerks work from a single common queue (both will be occupied constantly and no customer will complain about belonging to a slower line); and finally, put on more buses.

What about friction and fighting in lines caused by queue jumping, disputes about rightful position, and so on? A line which is vaguely defined or poorly regulated is extremely stressful for its members. In such lines the responsibility for safeguarding his place falls entirely on the person. He must remain constantly vigilant and therefore cannot relax for a moment. If a dispute arises, and it is inevitable that one will, he must choose to settle it by force, which is unpleasant, or back down, which is humiliating.

Often these problems arise because the seller neglects to decide where and how people should queue, and there are no police or other officials on the scene to adjudicate. Understandably, the seller is reluctant to intercede in disputes about priority of service. But such disputes need not arise if there is a recognized system for registering order of arrival, such as a *Take-A-Check* or *Take-A-Tab* dispenser. A number system of this kind helps reduce tension in the queue, because if a dispute erupts the victimized person can appeal directly to the authority of the number. Number dispensers are not always feasible, but even then, the strategic erection of barriers to force customers into a single line on arrival (as in the rambling, serpentine lines at Disneyland) can help prevent bitterness and bloodshed. Of course, no method of protecting the line is foolproof. The only way to discourage queue jumping (short of making it a capital offense) is to improve speed and certainty of service.

Finally, what can be done to reduce the boredom, tension, and weariness associated with waiting in lines? A look at recent World's Fairs is instructive. Queues were a common sight during New York's World's Fair of 1964, but Fair officials solved the problem outside Michelangelo's *Pieta* by putting visitors on three tiers of conveyor belts and drawing them slowly past the sculpture. Expo '67, the World's Fair in Montreal, came up with some novel ideas. Twenty-four computerized electronic signboards flashed facts about the most crowded exhibits and restaurants, and urged fairgoers to visit the less-crowded sites. A typical message read: "Lots of room and no waiting at the Cuban pavilion; why not go there now?" Inevitably there were long delays outside the most popular pavilions (at Labyrinth, the wait was sometimes as long as eight hours, rarely less than three hours). To cope with boredom and irritation, strolling troubadours, jazz combos, clowns, and even ice-skaters on a movable rink were dispatched to entertain the longest queues. Then someone decided it would be better to draw crowds away from the congested areas, not to them, and so the entertainers were directed to perform outside the less-popular exhibits.

That is all very well for World's Fairs, but what about the typical large city and its labyrinth of waiting lines? We can see it even now. Strolling troubadours, jazz combos, and clowns entertaining the folks waiting to be seen in hospitals, unemployment agencies, and welfare centers. Meantime, joining an urban queue can be a long, boring, and frustrating experience unless, of course, the queue happens to be for football or cinema tickets.

III

Fieldwork and ethics

To understand and describe an alien culture, anthropologists engage in fieldwork. Because culture is so all-inclusive, because it involves every area of life, anthropologists seek to immerse themselves in the culture they want to study. Fieldwork means living with people, eating their food, learning their language, listening to gossip, watching them discipline children, and seeing them work in traditional occupations. The researchers make observations, record interviews, and chart genealogies. All these activities can be done with detachment and scientific objectivity — but a gap will remain in the researchers' data. Anthropologists identify with, participate in, and imaginatively enter into the lives of those studied. To achieve an understanding of experience from the natives' point of view, to see life from the perspective of another culture, anthropologists themselves become a kind of research instrument. The essence of fieldwork is immersion in an alien way of life, as insider yet outsider, as stranger yet friend.

Anthropologists employ many strategies during field research to understand another culture better. But all strategies and all research ultimately rest on the cooperation of informants. An informant is neither a subject in a scientific experiment nor a respondent who answers the investigator's questions. An informant is a teacher who has a special kind of pupil — a professional anthropologist. In this unique relationship a transformation occurs in the anthropologist's understanding of an alien culture. As Miles Richardson says in one of the selections that follow, it is the informant who transforms the anthropologist from a tourist into an ethnographer. The informant may be a child who explains how to play hopscotch, a cocktail waitress who teaches the anthropologist to serve drinks and to encourage customers to leave tips, an elderly man who teaches the anthropologist to build an igloo, or a grandmother who explains the intricacies of Zapotec kinship. Almost any individual who has acquired a repertoire of cultural behavior can become an informant.

Because fieldwork requires involvement in the lives of people, because it depends on intimate personal relationships, it always raises important ethical issues. Informants often confide personal matters to the anthropologist. And the anthropologist may acquire information that could bring harm to those studied if outsiders learned of it. What is the anthropologist's responsibility to informants? How much should the anthropologist tell the people about the purposes of the study? What if the anthropologist discovers illegal activities? What if military authorities ask the anthropologist for information about population size or political leadership in the village? When publishing reports, should the anthropologist keep the name of the village and the names of informants anonymous? These are only some of the ethical issues involved in carrying out a fieldwork project.

In 1971, The Council of the American Anthropological Association adopted principles of professional responsibility to guide anthropologists. The following nine principles deal specifically with the anthropologist's relations with those people being studied. Examine them carefully and then keep them in mind as you read the following selections, which deal with fieldwork and with ethical dilemmas that developed during field research.

In research, an anthropologist's paramount responsibility is to those he studies. When there is a conflict of interest, these individuals must come first. The anthropologist must do everything within his power to protect their physical, social and psychological welfare and to honor their dignity and privacy.

   a. Where research involves the acquisition of material and information transferred on the assumption of trust between persons, it is axiomatic that the rights, interests, and sensitivities of those studied must be safeguarded.

   b. The aims of the investigation should be communicated as well as possible to the informant.

   c. Informants have a right to remain anonymous. This right should be respected both where it has been promised explicitly and where no clear understanding to the contrary has been reached. These strictures apply to the collection of data by means of cameras, tape recorders, and other data-gathering devices, as well as data collected in face-to-face interviews or in participant observation. Those being studied should understand the capacities of such devices; they should be free to reject them if they wish; and if they accept them, the results obtained should be consonant with the informant's right to welfare, dignity and privacy.

d. There should be no exploitation of individual informants for personal gain. Fair return should be given them for all services.

e. There is an obligation to reflect on the foreseeable repercussions of research and publication on the general population being studied.

f. The anticipated consequences of research should be communicated as fully as possible to the individuals and groups likely to be affected.

g. In accordance with the association's general position on clandestine and secret research, no reports should be provided to sponsors that are not also available to the general public and, where practicable, to the population studied.

h. Every effort should be exerted to cooperate with members of the host society in the planning and execution of research projects.

i. All of the above points should be acted upon in full recognition of the social and cultural pluralism of host societies and the consequent plurality of values, interests, and demands in those societies. This diversity complicates choice-making in research, but ignoring it leads to irresponsible decisions.[1]

---

[1] From "Principles of Professional Responsibility," American Anthropological Association, May 1971.

5

Kapluna daughter: Adopted by the Eskimo

JEAN L. BRIGGS

*Initially, the anthropologist is a stranger, often a threatening
one, to the people she wants to live with and study. One
step toward gaining acceptance is achieved when the anthropologist assumes a role defined as believable and nonthreatening
in the eyes of the people she wishes to study. Jean Briggs
found acceptance in the form of fictive kinship — by playing
the role of daughter. Although playing this role had its
frustrations and limitations, it allowed for her assimilation into
the Eskimo community, and taught her aspects of their culture
which could be learned in no other way.*

"It's very cold down there — *very cold*. If I were going to be at Back
River this winter, I would like to adopt you and try to keep you alive."

My Eskimo visitor, Uunai, dramatized her words with shivers as
we sat drinking tea in the warm nursing station in Gjoa Haven. It was
only mid-August, but already the wind that intruded through the cracks
in the window frame was bitter, and the ground was white with a dust-
ing of new snow. Last winter's ice, great broken sheets of it, still clogged
the harbor, so that the plane I was waiting for was unable to get through
to us. I was on my way to spend a year and a half with the Utkuhikhalingmiut, a small group of Eskimos who lived in Chantrey Inlet at the
mouth of the Back River on the northern rim of the American continent.
They were the most remote group of Eskimos that I could find on the
map of the Canadian Arctic, a people who in many ways lived much
as they had in the days before *kaplunas* (white men) appeared in the
north. They were nomadic; they lived in snowhouses in winter, in tents

in summer; and their diet consisted very largely of fish — trout and whitefish — supplemented now and again by a few caribou.

Uunai's words presaged the most important influence on the course of my life at Back River, namely my adoption as a "daughter" in the household of an Utkuhikhalingmiut family. I want to describe an aspect of that relationship here, with the aim of illustrating some of the difficulties that a host community or family may encounter in its hospitable efforts to incorporate a foreigner.

I arrived in Chantrey Inlet at the end of August 1963 on a plane that the Canadian government sent in once a year to collect the three or four schoolchildren who wished to go to Inuvik. I had with me letters of introduction from the Anglican deacon and his wife in Gjoa Haven. Nakliguhuktuq and Ikayuqtuq were Eskimos from the eastern Arctic who served as missionaries not only to the Anglican Eskimos in Gjoa Haven, but also to the Utkuhikhalingmiut. The letters — written in the syllabic script in which the Utkuhikhalingmiut, like most other Canadian Eskimos, are literate — noted that I would like to live with the Utku- hikhalingmiut for a year or so, learning the Eskimo language and skills: how to scrape skins and sew them, how to catch fish and preserve them or boil the oil out of them for use in lighting and heating the winter iglus. They asked the Eskimos to help me with words and fish and prom- ised that in return I would help them with tea and kerosene. They told the people that I was kind and that they should not be shy and afraid of me — "She's a little bit shy herself" — and assured them that they need not feel (as they often do feel toward kaplunas) that they had to comply with my every wish. They said, finally, that I wished to be adopted into an Eskimo family and to live with them in their iglu as a daughter.

Choosing a father

I had a number of reasons for wishing to be adopted, and there were several precedents for adoption as well: four other kaplunas of my ac- quaintance, both scholars and laymen, who had wintered with Eskimos had done so as "sons," sharing the iglus of their Eskimo families. Living in the iglu would be warmer than living alone, I thought (Ikayuqtuq and Nakliguhuktuq agreed); and I thought vaguely that it might be "safer" if one family had specific responsibility for me. The idea had romantic appeal too; I saw it as a fulfillment of a childhood wish to "be" an Eskimo, and I expected no rapport problems, since on two previous trips to the Alaskan Arctic I had identified strongly with the Eskimo villagers with whom I had lived. To be sure, there were also arguments against adoption: I had qualms concerning the loss of an "objective" position in the community, drains on my supplies that would result from contributing to the maintenance of a family household and loss of privacy with resultant difficulties in working. Still, when the moment of decision came, the balance lay in favor of adoption.

There were two suitable fathers among the Utkuhikhalingmiut (that is, two household heads who had wives alive and at home), and these two were both more than eager to adopt me. One, however — an intelligent, vigorous man named Inuttiaq — far outdid the other in the imagination and persistence with which he "courted" me as a daughter. Not only were he and his family extremely solicitous, but he was also a jolly and ingenious language teacher. Most gratifying of all, both he and his wife, Allaq, were astonishingly quick to understand my halting attempts to communicate. There was no question which family I preferred. Fortunately, Inuttiaq also occupied a much more central position among the Utkuhikhalingmiut than did Nilak, the other possible father. He had many more close kin and was also the Anglican lay leader of the group. I was convinced that both anthropology and I would benefit more if I were adopted by Inuttiaq.

WINTER

From the moment that the adoption was settled, I was "Inuttiaq's daughter" in the camp. Inuttiaq and his relatives with much amusement drilled me in the use of kin terms appropriate to my position, just as they drilled his three-year-old daughter, who was learning to speak. They took charge of my material welfare and of my education in language and skills. Allaq also to some extent took charge of my daily activities, as it was proper that a mother should. She told me what the day's job for the women of the family was going to be: gathering birch twigs for fuel, scraping caribou hides in preparation for the making of winter clothing or skinning the fish bellies out of which oil was to be boiled. The decision to participate or not was left to me, but if I did join the women — and I usually did — she made sure that my share of the work was well within the limits of my ability and stamina. "We will be walking very far tomorrow to get birch twigs," she would say. "You will be too tired." If I went anyway, it was always silently arranged that my load should be the lightest, and if I wandered out of sight of the other women in my search for birch bushes, someone always followed behind — sent by Allaq, as I discovered months later — to make sure that I didn't get lost.

I felt increasingly comfortable with my family and found their solicitude immensely warming. At the same time, I dreaded the loss of privacy that the winter move into their iglu would bring. Curiously, the effect of the move when it came in October was the opposite of what I had expected. I basked in the protectiveness of Inuttiaq's household; and what solitude I needed I found on the river in the mornings, when I jigged for salmon trout through the ice with Inuttiaq, or, to my surprise, in the iglu itself in the afternoons, when the room was full of visitors and I retired into myself, lulled and shielded by the flow of quiet, incomprehensible speech.

BEHAVING

The family's continuing graciousness was very seductive. I came to expect the courtesies that I received and even to resent it a bit when they were not forthcoming, though at the same time I told myself that such feelings were shameful. However, as time passed and I became an established presence in the household, I was less and less often accorded special privileges, except insofar as my ineptitude made services necessary. Allaq still mended my skin boots for me and stretched them when they shrank in drying; my stitches were not small enough and my jaws not strong enough. She continued to fillet my fish when it was frozen nearly as hard as wood. But in other respects Allaq, and especially Inuttiaq — who was far less shy than his wife — more and more attempted to assimilate me into a proper adult parent-daughter relationship. I was expected to help with the household work to the best of my ability — to make tea or bannock and to fetch water — and I was expected to obey unquestioningly when Inuttiaq told me to do something or made a decision on my behalf.

Unfortunately, I found it impossible to learn to behave in every respect like an Utkuhikhalingmiut daughter. Inuttiaq lectured me in general terms on the subject of filial obedience, and once in a while I think he tried to shame me into good behavior by offering himself as a model of virtue — volunteering, for example, to make bannock for me if I were slow in making it for him — but to little avail. Sometimes I was genuinely blind and deaf to his lessons, unaccustomed as I was to Utkuhikhalingmiut subtlety. At other times I saw what was wanted but resisted for reasons I will describe in a moment. Inevitably, conflicts, covert but pervasive, developed, both regarding the performance of household chores and regarding the related matter of obedience to Inuttiaq.

ASSUMPTIONS IN CONFLICT

The causes of the conflicts were three. First was the fact that some feminine skills were hard for me to learn. Overtly my Utkahikhalingmiut parents were very tolerant of the lack of skill that they rightly attributed to kapluna ignorance and perhaps also to kapluna lack of intelligence, or *ihuma*. However, perhaps because of an assumption that kaplunas were unable to learn, if I was at all slow to understand Allaq's instructions and demonstrations, she easily gave up trying to teach me, preferring instead to continue to serve me. And though she stretched my boots and cut my fish in the most cheerful manner, after a while her added chores may well have been burdensome to her.

A second cause of the conflicts was that some of Inuttiaq's and Allaq's assumptions about the nature of parental and daughterly virtue were at variance with mine; in consequence not only did I have to learn new patterns, I also had to unlearn old ones. Hardest of all to learn was unquestioning obedience to paternal authority. Sometimes I could not help resisting, privately but intensely, when Inuttiaq told me to "make tea," to "go home," to "hurry up" or to "pray." I was irritated even by the fact that after the first weeks of gracious formality had passed he began to address me in the imperative form, which is often used in speaking to women, children and young people. Rationally I knew that I should have welcomed this sign of "acceptance," but I could not be pleased. My irritation was due partly to the fact that subordination threatened my accustomed — and highly valued — independence, but it was aggravated by a fear that the restrictions placed on me interfered with my work.

And herein lay the third cause of the conflicts: I found it hard sometimes to be simultaneously a docile and helpful daughter and a conscientious anthropologist. Though Allaq appeared to accept my domestic clumsiness as inevitable, she may have felt less tolerant on the occasions when it was not lack of skill that prevented me from helping her, but anxiety over the pocketful of trouser-smudged, disorganized field notes that cried out to be typed. A number of times, when I could have helped to gut fish or to carry in snow to repair the sleeping platform or floor or could have offered to fetch water or make tea, I sat and wrote instead or sorted vocabulary — tiny slips of paper spread precariously over my sleeping bag and lap. It was sometimes professional anxiety that prompted me to disobey Inuttiaq too; and I am sure that on such occasions, as on others, he must have found my insubordination not only "bad," but completely incomprehensible. My behavior at moving time is an example. My gear, minimal though it was by kapluna standards, placed a severe strain on Inuttiaq when we moved camp. Whereas the sleds of others were loaded to little more than knee height, the load on Inuttiaq's sled was shoulder-high. From his point of view it was only reasonable that he should instruct me to leave my heavy tape recorder and my metal box of field notes on the top of a small knoll, as the Utkuhikhalingmiut cached their own belongings, while we moved downstream, not to return until after the flood season. I, however, questioned whether the water might rise over the knoll, and Inuttiaq's silent scrutiny seemed to say that he considered my inquiry a reflection on his judgment.

I do not mean to create the impression that life in Inuttiaq's household during that first winter was continuous turmoil. There were many days, even weeks, when I, at least, felt the situation to be very peaceful and enjoyable. I was grateful for the warmth of my parents' company and care; it was good to feel that I belonged somewhere, that I was part of a family, even on a make-believe basis. But the rewards of my presence for Inuttiaq and his real family were of a different, and probably of a lesser, order. Because Innutiaq's purchases in Gjoa Haven were supplemented by mine, our household was richer than others in store goods: tea, tobacco, flour, jam, dry milk, raisins and kerosene. But apart from these material benefits, and at first perhaps the novelty (and prestige?) of having a kapluna daughter, it is hard to see what Inuttiaq's family gained in return for the burden they carried. I played "Tavern in the Town" and "Santa Lucia" on my recorder; Innutiaq enjoyed that and once in a while asked me to play for guests. I helped inefficiently in the mornings to remove the whitefish from the family nets and to drag them home, harnessed with Allaq to the sled. I assisted — erratically, as I have mentioned — with the other domestic chores; and in late winter, when the sun returned and Inuttiaq began again to jig for salmon trout, I usually fished with him. That is all that occurs to me, and a trivial contribution it must have been from my family's point of view.

SATAN AND SELF-CONTROL

It was hard for me to know at the time, however, just what their reactions to me were, because the tensions that existed were nearly all covert. Hostility among Utkuhikhalingmiut is ignored or turned into a joke; at worst it becomes the subject of gossip behind the offender's back. I, too, did my best to smother my annoyance with frustration, but my attempts were not wholly successful. My training in self-control was less perfect than theirs, and at the same time the strains were greater than those I was accustomed to dealing with in my own world. Moreover, the most potentially gratifying of the outlets utilized by the Utkuhikhalingmiut — gossip — was not open to me as an anthropologist. I did my best to learn with the children when they were taught to turn annoyance into amusement, but laughter didn't come easily.

The Utkuhikhalingmiut are acutely sensitive to subtle indications of mood. They heard the coldness in my voice when I said, "I don't understand," noted the length of a solitary walk I took across the tundra or the fact that I went to bed early and read with my back turned to the others. Later, Inuttiaq might give me a lecture — phrased, as always, in the most general terms — about the fate of those who lose their tempers: Satan uses them for firewood. Or he might offer me an especially choice bit of fish — whether to shame me or to appease me I don't know. The contrast between my irritability and the surface equanimity of others gave me many uncomfortable moments, but I persuaded myself that the effects of my lapses were shortlived. When I laughed again and heard others laugh with me, or when they seemed to accept the generous gestures with which I tried to make amends, I was reassured that no damage had been done. I was wrong. But it was only when I returned to Gjoa Haven on my way home a year later that I learned how severe the tensions had become between November and January of that first winter. Then the deacon's wife, Ikajuqtuq, told me of the report Inuttiaq had made of me in January when he went in to Gjoa Haven to trade: "She is not happy. She gets angry very easily, and I don't think she likes us anymore." Shortly after Inuttiaq's return from Gjoa Haven in January, conflict erupted into the open.

"THE IGLUS ARE COLD"

The two weeks of Inuttiaq's absence in Gjoa Haven had been an especially trying period for me. I had looked forward to them as a much needed interlude in which to type and organize my swelling pile of penciled notes. When Inuttiaq was at home, it was often difficult to maintain the iglu temperature within the range of 27 to 31 degrees at which typing was feasible. If I tried to type during the daylight hours of the morning, when the outdoor work was done, my fingers and carbon paper froze as a result of Inuttiaq's drafty comings and goings at jobs that seemed to necessitate propping the door open. But in the sociable afternoon and evening hours the snow dome dripped in the heat and occasionally deposited lumps of slush into my typewriter, and the iglu steamed so that my work was lost in a wet fog as a result of Inuttiaq's demands for tea, boiled fox, bannock and soup in rapid succession. Many were the frustrated moments when I heartily wished him gone; but it was only when he *was* gone that I discovered how completely our comfort depended on his presence. "When the men are away the iglus are cold," the women said; and it was true. The morning drafts that had plagued me before were nothing compared with the chill that resulted when nobody came and went at all. It was partly, of course, that Inuttiaq had taken with him one of our two primus stoves and one of the two kerosene storm lanterns, which ordinarily heated the iglu. But Allaq's behavior during her husband's absence intensified the cold. She never boiled fish, rarely brewed tea and never lit the lamp to dry clothes — any of which activities would have warmed the iglu. She merely sat in her corner of the sleeping platform, blew on her hands and remarked that the iglu was cold. It was; it was 20 degrees colder than when Inuttiaq was at home. I fretted and fumed in silent frustration and determined that when he came back I would take drastic steps to improve my working conditions.

I broached the subject to Inuttiaq a few days after his return to camp. He listened attentively to my explanation. I told him that I had thought about going to live for a while in the empty wooden building that stood on a peninsula a few miles from camp. The government had built it as a nursing station, but it had never been used except by me as a cache for my useless belongings. It had a kerosene stove, which would make it luxuriously comfortable — unless the stove was as erratic as the one in the similar nursing station in Gjoa Haven, with which I had once had an unfortunate experience. Inuttiaq agreed that the stove was unpredictable. Instead, he suggested that he take me to the nursing station every morning and fetch me again at night, so that I would not freeze. As often before, he reassured me: "Because you are alone here, you are someone to be taken care of." And, as often before, his solicitude warmed me. "Taking me to the nursing station every day will be a lot of work for you," I said. The round trip took an hour and a half by dog sled, not counting the time and effort involved in harnessing and unharnessing the team. He agreed that it would be a lot of work. "Could you perhaps build me a small iglu?" I asked. It would take only an hour or two to build a tiny iglu near our own, which I could use as an "office"; then he need concern himself no further. Lulled by the assurance he had just given me of his desire to take care of me and by the knowledge that the request I made was not time-consuming, I was the more disagreeably startled when he replied with unusual vigor, "I build no iglus. I have to check the nets."

A DAUGHTER'S TENT

The rage of frustration seized me. He had not given me the true reason for his refusal. It only took two hours to check the nets every second or third day; on the other days, Inuttiaq did nothing at all except eat, drink, visit and repair an occasional tool. He was offended, but I could not imagine why. Whether Inuttiaq read my face I do not know, but he softened his refusal immediately: "Shall Ipuituq or Tutaq" — he named two of the younger men — "build an iglu for you?" Perhaps it would be demeaning for a man of Inuttiaq's status, a mature householder, to build an iglu for a mere daughter. There was something in Inuttiaq's reaction that I did not understand, and a cautioning voice told me to contain my ethnocentric judgment and my anger. I thought of the small double-walled tent that I had brought with me for emergency use. It was stored in the nursing station. "They say my tent is very warm in winter," I said.

Inuttiaq smoked silently. After a while he asked, "Shall they build you an iglu tomorrow?" My voice shook with exasperation: "Who knows?" I turned my head, rummaging — for nothing — in my knapsack until the intensity of my feeling should subside.

Later, when Inuttiaq was smoking his last pipe in bed, I raised the subject again, my manner, I hoped, a successful facsimile of cheerfulness and firmness. "I would like to try the tent and see whether it's warm, as I have heard. We can bring it here, and then if it's not warm, I won't freeze; I'll come indoors." Allaq laughed, Inuttiaq accepted my suggestion, and I relaxed with relief, restored to real cheer by Inuttiaq's offer to fetch the tent from the nursing station the following day — if it stormed — so that he could not go on the trapping trip he had planned.

My cheer was premature. Two days later the tent had still not been fetched, though Inuttiaq had not gone trapping. I decided to walk to the nursing station. I had no intention of fetching the tent myself — it would have been impossible; but I needed a few hours alone, and vaguely I knew that the direction of my walk would be to Inuttiaq a sign, however futile, that I was in earnest about my tent.

But I did not dream that he would respond as charitably as he did. I had just arrived at the nursing station and was searching among my few books for a novel to comfort me in my frustration when I heard the squeak of sled runners on the snow outside and a familiar voice speaking to the dogs: "*Hoooo* [whoa]." Inuttiaq appeared in the doorway. I smiled. He smiled. "Will you want your tent?"

Gratitude and relief erased my anger as Inuttiaq picked up the tent and carried it to the sled. "You were walking," he said, in answer to my thanks. "I felt protective toward you."

It was a truce we had reached, however, not a peace, though I did not realize it at once. Since it was nearly dark when we reached camp, Inuttiaq laid the tent on top of the iglu for the night, to keep it from the dogs. Next morning I went with Inuttiaq to jig for trout up-river, and when we returned I thought that finally the time was ripe for setting up the tent. Not wanting to push Inuttiaq's benevolence too far, and remembering the force of his response to my query about iglu-building, I asked, "Shall I ask Ipuituq to help me put up my tent?" "Yes," said Inuttiaq. There was no warmth in his face; he did not smile, though he did tell me to keep my fur trousers on for warmth while I put up the tent. I obeyed, but the wind had risen while we drank our homecoming tea, so that even in fur trousers tent-raising was not feasible that day or the next.

When the wind died two days later, Inuttiaq and I went fishing again, most companionably. Relations seemed so amicable, in fact, that this time on our return I was emboldened to say directly, without mention of Ipuituq, "I would like to put up my tent."

Naïvely I thought that Inuttiaq would offer to help. He did not. His face was again unsmiling as he answered, "Put it up."

My anger was triggered again. "By myself?" I inquired rudely.

"Yes," said Inuttiaq, equally rudely.

"Thank you very much." I heard the coldness in my voice but did not try to soften it.

Inuttiaq, expressionless, looked at me for a moment then summoned two young men who were nearby and who came, with a cheer that was in marked contrast to his own manner, to help me set up the tent.

Although Inuttiaq thought it ridiculous anyway to set up a tent in winter, I think now that he was also personally affronted by my request. One clue to his reaction I find in a question that I hardly heard at the time: he had wanted to know, after the tent was up, whether I planned to sleep in it or only to work there, and I think he may have felt that my demand for a tent was a sign that I was dissatisfied with him as a father, with his concern for my welfare.

In any case, his behavior was a curious blend of opposites. He chose the site for my tent with care, correcting my own choice with a more practiced eye to prowling dogs and prevailing wind. He offered advice on heating the tent, and he filled my primus stove so that it would be ready for me to use when my two assistants and I had finished setting up the tent. And when I moved my writing things out of his iglu, he told me that if I liked, I might write instead of going fishing. "If I catch a fish, you will eat," he assured me. But he turned his back on the actual raising of the tent and went home to eat and drink tea.

NEVER IN ANGER

On the following day I saw his displeasure in another form. It was Sunday morning and storming; our entrance was buried under drifting snow. Since there could be no church service, Inuttiaq and Allaq had each, separately and in mumbling undertones, read a passage from the Bible. Then Inuttiaq began to read from the prayer book the story of creation, and he asked if I would like to learn. I agreed, the more eagerly because I feared that he had perceived my skepticism toward his religious beliefs and that this was another hidden source of conflict between us. He lectured me at length. The story of creation was followed by the story of Adam and Eve (whose sin was responsible for the division of mankind into kaplunas and Eskimos), and this story was in turn followed by an exposition of proper Christian behavior: the keeping of the

Sabbath — and of one's temper. "God is loving," said Inuttiaq, "but only to believers. Satan is angry. People will go to heaven only if they do not get angry or answer back when they are scolded." He told me that one should not be attached to earthly belongings, as I was: "One should devote himself only to God's word." Most striking of all was the way Inuttiaq ended his sermon to me. "Nakliguhuktuq made me king of the Utkuhikhalingmiut," he said. "He wrote that to me. He told me that if people — including you — don't want to believe what I tell them and don't want to learn about Christianity, then I should write to him, and he will come quickly and scold them. If people don't want to believe Nakliguhuktuq either, then . . . a bigger leader, a kapluna, the king in Cambridge Bay [the government center for the central Arctic], will come in a plane with a big and well-made whip and will whip people. It will hurt a lot."

Much of this I had heard before, but this version was more dramatic than previous ones. It made me see more clearly than I had before something of Inuttiaq's view of kaplunas generally. I heard the hostility directed against myself as well, but again he had softened the latter by blending it with warmth, in the manner that I found so confusing. He knew that I believed in God, he said, because I helped people, I gave things to people — not just to one or two, which God doesn't want, but to everybody.

The rest of the winter passed more peacefully, at least on the surface. I spent much of the time working in my tent, and there was no more overt hostility. But I am no longer sure that my peace of mind was justified. In retrospect, it seems possible that the warm and solicitous acts my family continued to perform were neither rewards for improved behavior on my part nor evidence of a generous willingness to accept me in spite of my thorny qualities, but, rather, attempts to extract or blunt some of the thorns. If I knew I was cared for, I might not get angry so easily. I thought I heard similar logic in the admonition Inuttiaq once in a while gave his six-year-old daughter when she sulked: "Stop crying, you are loved." Another possible motive may have been a desire to shame me, by virtuous example, into reforming. Perhaps these kind acts even had the effect of nullifying Inuttiaq's and Allaq's own prickly feelings, permitting them to prove to themselves that — as Inuttiaq once said — they didn't get angry, only I did.

INCORRIGIBLE

But whatever the interpretation of these incidents, it is clear to me now that there existed more of an undercurrent of tension in my relationship with Inuttiaq and Allaq than I perceived at the time. I began to suspect its presence in the spring, when our iglu melted and I moved — at Inuttiaq's order — back into my own tent; Allaq almost never visited me, as she had done the first days after my arrival in Chantrey Inlet. More important, these winter tensions, I think, added their residue of hostility to a crisis situation that developed at the end of the summer. This introduced a new phase in my relations, not merely with Inuttiaq and Allaq, but with all the other Utkuhikhalingmiut as well — a phase in which I ceased to be treated as an educable child and was instead treated as an incorrigible offender, who had unfortunately to be endured but who could not be incorporated into the social life of the group.

The crisis was brought about by the visit to Chantrey Inlet of a party of kapluna sports fishermen. Every July and August in recent years Chantrey Inlet has been visited by sportsmen from the provinces and from the United States who charter bush planes from private sports airlines and fly up to the Arctic for a week's fishing. Every year the sportsmen ask permission to borrow the Eskimos' canoes, which were given to them by the Canadian government after the famine of 1958 and are indispensable to their economy. In 1958 the disappearance of the caribou herds from the Chantrey Inlet area forced the Eskimos to begin to rely much more completely on fish than they had formerly done. This meant accumulating and storing quantities of fish during seasons when they were plentiful, and to facilitate this, the government introduced fish nets and canoes. Originally there had been six canoes, one for each of the Utkuhikhalingmiut families, but by the time I arrived in Chantrey Inlet only two of these remained in usable condition.

In anger

The first parties that came asked, through me, if they might borrow both canoes, and the Utkuhikhalingmiut, who for various reasons rarely, if ever, refuse such requests, acquiesced, at some cost to themselves. They sat stranded on the shore, unable to fish, unable to fetch the occasional bird that they shot on the water, unable to fetch a resupply of sugar for their tea from the cache on the nearby island and worst of all, perhaps, unable to visit the odd strangers who were camped out of sight across the river. Ultimately these kaplunas left and were replaced by another group, which asked to borrow only one canoe. But relief was short-lived; trolling up and down the unfamiliar river in the late twilight, the kaplunas were unfortunate enough to run the canoe on a rock and tear a large hole in the canvas, whereupon they returned the canoe and announced to the men through sign language that since that craft was unusable they were now obliged to borrow the other — Inuttiaq's. When I arrived on the scene, the kaplunas were attaching their outboard to the canoe as Inuttiaq and the other Utkuhikhalingmiut men watched.

I exploded. Unsmilingly and in a cold voice I told the kaplunas' guide some of the hardships that I foresaw if his men damaged the second canoe. Then, armed with the memory that Innutiaq had earlier, before the arrival of this party of kaplunas, instructed me in vivid language never again to allow anyone to borrow his canoe, I told the kaplunas that the owner of that second canoe did not wish to lend it.

The kapluna guide was not unreasonable; he agreed at once that the loan of the boat was the owner's option: "It's his canoe, after all." Slightly mollified, I turned to Inuttiaq who stood nearby, expressionless like the other Utkuhikhalingmiut. "Do you want me to tell him you don't want to lend your canoe?" I asked in Eskimo. "He will not borrow it if you say you don't want to lend it."

Inuttiaq's expression dismayed me, but I didn't know how to read it. I knew only that it registered strong feeling, as did his voice, which was unusually loud: "Let him have his will!"

"WE WISH SHE WOULD LEAVE"

That incident brought to a head months of uneasiness on the part of the Utkuhikhalingmiut concerning my volatility. I had spoken unbidden and in anger; that much the Eskimos knew. The words they couldn't understand, but it didn't matter; the intrusion and the anger itself were inexcusable. The punishment was so subtle a form of ostracism that I would have continued to think that my difficulties were all of my own imagining had I not come into possession of a letter that Allaq's father, Pala, had written to the deacon, Nakliguhuktuq, the day after the kaplunas left. Pala had intended to send it out on the plane that was daily expected to come and pick up the schoolchildren; he had kept it for a time, but then — fearing that when the plane finally came, he would forget the letter — he had given it to me to hold along with my own correspondence. The letter was in syllabics, of course; in an amoral spirit I decided to read it, to test my skill in reading Eskimo. I did not anticipate the contents: "Yiini [that was my name] lied to the kaplunas. She gets angry very easily. She ought not to be here studying Eskimos. She is very annoying; because she scolds and one is tempted to scold her. She gets angry easily. Because she is so annoying, we wish more and more that she would leave."

But it was not until October, when the autumn iglus were built, that the change in the Eskimos' feelings really became apparent. I was not at all sure that Inuttiaq would invite me to move in with his family again as he had done the year before, but I need not have worried; his hostility did not take such a crass form. However, the quality of life in the iglu was in striking contrast with the previous year. Whereas then Inuttiaq's iglu had been the social center of the camp, now family and visitors congregated next door, in Allaq's father's iglu. Inuttiaq and Allaq — the children too — spent the better part of every day at Pala's. Even in the early mornings, when the family awoke, and at night when we were preparing for bed, I was isolated. It was as though I were not there. If I made a remark to Inuttiaq or Allaq, the person addressed responded with his usual smile, but I had to initiate almost all communication. As a rule, if I did not speak, no one spoke to me. If I offered to fetch water or make tea (which I seldom did), my offer was usually accepted, but no one ever asked me to perform these services. The pointedness of this avoidance was driven home one day when we were cooking. I do not recall what was being made or who had initiated the cooking; I think it likely that I had done so, since the primus stood on the floor in front of me, instead of in its usual place near Allaq. Nevertheless, when the pressure began to run down, unnoticed by me, Inuttiaq turned not to me but to Allaq to order her to pump up the primus. And she had to get up and come over to my side of the iglu to pump up the stove! Had he spoken to me, I would only have had to lean over to do it. Too late I realized the dignity inherent in the Utkuhikhalingmiut pattern of authority, in which the woman is obedient to the man. I envied Allaq the satisfaction of knowing that she was appreciated because she did well and docilely what Inuttiaq told her to do.

One day, about a week after we had moved into the autumn iglus, Inuttiaq suggested that when we moved into winter iglus later on, I should be physically walled off to a degree. Often when Utkuhikhalingmiut build their permanent winter iglus, they attach to one side a small chamber, called a *hiqluaq*, in which to store the fish they net. The hiqluaq opens into the interior of the iglu by way of a hole just big enough to crawl through. Inuttiaq's idea was to build such a chamber for me to live in; after I left, he would use it in the orthodox manner, for fish storage.

But in spite of all these tensions, I was still treated with the most impeccable semblance of solicitude. I was amazed that it should be so — that although my company was anathema, nevertheless people still took care to give me plentiful amounts of the foods I liked best, to warn me away from thin ice and to caution me when my nose began to freeze. The Utkuhikhalingmiut saw themselves — and wanted me to see them — as virtuously solicitous, no matter what provocations I might give them to be otherwise. Allaq's sister expressed this ethos of concern explicitly in a letter to Ikayuqtuq in Gjoa Haven: "Because she is the only kapluna here and a woman as well, we have tried to be good to her . . . and though she is sometimes very annoying . . . we still try to help her."

It was at the end of August that the incident with the kapluna fishermen occurred, and it was the end of November before I was finally able to explain myself to the Utkuhikhalingmiut. I had wanted from the beginning, of course, to confront them with an explanation of my behavior, but I had feared that such un-Eskimo directness would only shock them the more. Instead, I had written my version of the story to Ikayuqtuq, had told her about my attempt to protect the Utkuhikhalingmiut from the impositions of the kaplunas and asked her if she could help to explain my behavior to the Eskimos. My letter went out to Gjoa Haven, along with Pala's, when the school plane came in September. Unfortunately there was no way in which Ikayuqtuq could reply until the strait froze in November, enabling the men to make the long trip out to Gjoa Haven to trade. But when Inuttiaq, accompanied as usual by Allaq's brother, Mannik, finally went out, they brought back from the deacon and his wife a response that surpassed my most sanguine expectations. Inuttiaq reported to his family: "Nakliguhuktuq says that the kaplunas almost shot us when Yiini wasn't there." The exaggeration was characteristic of Inuttiaq's lurid style of fantasy. He turned to me: "Did you write that to Nakliguhuktuq?" I denied it — and later, in Gjoa Haven, Nakliguhuktuq denied having made such a statement to Inuttiaq — but I did confirm the gist of Inuttiaq's report: that I had tried to protect the Eskimos. I described what it was that I had written to Ikayuqtuq, and I explained something of the reasons for my anger at the kaplunas.

WALL OF ICE

The effect was magical. The wall of ice that had stood between me and the community suddenly disappeared. I became consultant on the moral qualities of fishing guides; people talked to me voluntarily, offered me vocabulary, included me in their jokes and in their anecdotes of the day's activities; and Inuttiaq informed me that the next day he and I were going fishing. Most heartwarming of all is the memory of an afternoon soon after the men had returned. The iglu was filled with visitors, and the hum of the primus on which tea was brewing mingled with the low voices of Inuttiaq and his guests. I knew every detail of the scene even as I bent over my writing, and I paid no attention until suddenly my mind caught on the sound of my name: "I consider Yiini a member of my family again." Was that what Inuttiaq had said? I looked up, inquiring. "I consider you a family member again," he repeated. His diction was clear, as it was only when he wanted to be sure that I understood. And he called me "daughter," as he had not done since August.

Not that I had suddenly become a wholly acceptable housemate;

that could never be. I was not and could never become an Utkuhik-halingmiutaq, nor could I ever be a "daughter" to Inuttiaq and Allaq as they understood that role. Inuttiaq made this quite clear one day about this time when we were both sitting, silently working, in the iglu. "I think you're a leader in your country," he said suddenly. The remark had no obvious context; it must mean, I thought, that he had never reconciled himself to my intractable behavior. There was also the slightly wild look that I caught in his eye when I said I thought that I might someday return to Chantrey Inlet. The look vanished when Allaq explained that I meant to return after I had been to my own country, not merely to Gjoa Haven. "Yes," he said then, "We will adopt you again, or others may want to — Nilaak, perhaps, or Mannik, if he marries." And later, when we were talking about the possibility of other "learners" coming to Chantrey Inlet, Inuttiaq said, "We would be happier to have a woman come than a man — a woman like you, who doesn't want to be a wife. Maybe *you* are the only acceptable kapluna."

But it was the letters that Allaq and Inuttiaq wrote me when I left Chantrey Inlet in January that expressed most vividly and succinctly what it meant to them to have a kapluna daughter. They both said, "I didn't think I'd care when you left, but I did."

STRANGER, CHILD, SIMPLETON

I observed three more or less distinct phases in the Utkuhikhalingmiut's view of me. During the first period I was a stranger and a guest, and I was treated with the formal courtesy and deference that the Utkuhik-halingmiut ordinarily accord to such persons. I was referred to as a kapluna, a white person, and addressed by my personal name — "Yiini" in the Eskimos' speech. Much of the time during this period the Eskimos must have been at a loss what to make of my behavior, and often when I did something that under other circumstances they might have defined as reprehensible — when I went to bed early, nursing a bad humor, or when I was silent in depression — they gave me the benefit of the doubt; they asked me if I were tired and considerately lessened my work load or withdrew so that I might "sleep."

Gradually, however, this first phase gave way to a second, in which my immediate family (though not others in the community) treated me in some respects as a daughter and a child. My parents replaced the name "Yiini" with the term "daughter" when speaking, and sometimes when referring to me; and my two small sisters called me "elder sister." Inuttiaq — though never Allaq — also began to use the imperative forms of speech that he used in addressing his other daughters and his wife. Even an appropriate age was invented for me: I had to be younger than Allaq — if only by one season — though all the evidence pointed to my being in fact slightly older than she was. Both parents directed my daily activities, and I was expected to obey them as a daughter should. When I did not, efforts were made to teach me better behavior through lecturing or shaming, the former a technique that was otherwise only used in teaching small children. My moodiness was no longer interpreted charitably, and efforts were made to educate me out of that behavior too.

Categorization of me as a "child" was probably determined by a combination of factors: I had introduced myself as one who wanted to "learn" from the Utkuhikhalingmiut, and I had asked to be adopted as a "daughter"; I was also obviously ignorant of Utkuhikhalingmiut proprieties and skills. The fact that I am a woman may also have facilitated my categorization as a child in several respects. For one thing, among the Utkuhikhalingmiut a woman's technical skill — skin-sewing — is very difficult to learn. I never mastered more than the most rudimentary, clumsy stitching; my work was so poor that when I mended my skin boots, Allaq considered it necessary to redo the job. Moreover, in order to be considered properly adult, a woman must have children, and I had none. For these reasons the role of an adult woman was virtually closed to me, whereas had I been a man, I might have earned an adult role as a fisherman and hunter, as some male kaplunas who have lived among Eskimos appear to have done. Finally, the fact that I am physically weaker than a man and thus unthreatening may have made it easier for the Utkuhikhalingmiut to view my ill temper, as I think they did, like that of a child. Had I been a man, I think they might have seen my temper as dangerous, even potentially lethal — anything but childish.

The third phase, in which I was treated as an incorrigible offender, replaced the "child" phase, I think, when it became apparent to the Utkuhikhalingmiut that I was uneducable. Inuttiaq no longer lectured me or used any other method to teach me. I was called "Yiini" again instead of "daughter," and daughterly services were no longer asked of me. In fact, nothing at all was demanded of me. Though my physical needs for warmth, food and protection from danger were still taken care of, socially I was simply "not there." There was one other person in the community who was similarly ostracized: a woman of about my age, who appeared to be of subnormal intelligence. Almost all of her personal qualities — her imperfect speech, clumsy gestures and domestic incompetence — were subject to comment behind her back, but hostility in her case, as in mine, centered on her volatility — the fact that she was easily upset and was unable to exercise proper restraint in the expression of her feelings. She too was considered uneducable, and I am sure that, like her, I was privately labeled simpleminded.

Hosts and Anthropologists

In more general terms the sequence of judgments passed on me seemed to be: strange; educable; uneducable in important ways. And each phase, each judgment, was associated with a role familiar to the Utkuhikhaling-miut: stranger; child; simpleton — each role being identifiable in terms of the way I was addressed, the kinds of behavior that were expected of me, the interpretations that were placed on my misbehavior and the methods that were used to control that misbehavior.

Although an anthropologist must have a recognized role or roles in order to make it possible to interact with him sensibly and predictably, nevertheless it will be evident from what I have described of my own case that the assignment of a role may create as many problems as it solves for both the anthropologist and his hosts. When Inuttiaq under-took to adopt me, I think he assumed that I would naturally behave as he was accustomed to having daughters behave. He knew, of course, that as a kapluna I was ignorant of the Eskimo skills that adult daughters have usually mastered, but it is easier to recognize cross-cultural differ-ences in technology and language than differences in the structuring of interpersonal relations; one is far more inclined to think of the latter as given in "human nature."

He was wrong, of course, in assuming that my behavior would be that of an Utkuhikhalingmiut daughter. Consequently his first hypothe-sis was replaced by a second: that kaplunas don't (or Yiini doesn't) know how to behave correctly but can learn. For various reasons, none of which were, I think, recognized by Inuttiaq, I didn't learn easily. The first reason why learning must be difficult is that the intruder faces a double task. On the one hand he must discover what has to be learned — that is, what exactly is wrong with his "normal" behavior and what the proper behavior should be. And on the other hand he must overcome resistance to doing what is required — resistance caused by the interfer-ence of his old patterns of role behavior. Such interference may be ex-pected to be particularly marked when the role to be learned bears the same name ("daughter") as a role one is accustomed to playing in one's own culture.

Learning will also be difficult and imperfect because the anthropolo-gist is not completely committed to the role he is playing vis-à-vis his hosts. For one thing, he must try to learn all kinds of facts about the community, many of which it may be inappropriate for someone in his assumed native role to know. He must try to maintain sufficient distance from the culture he is studying and from himself so that he can record "objectively" and, hopefully, use his reactions to his experiences as sources of data. And he must try to record and participate simultaneously. The latter problem has been amply illustrated in my case as I have described it above.

It was because of these difficulties and others that Inuttiaq's second hypothesis — that I was educable — proved to a large extent wrong. And so he arrived at his third hypothesis (shared, as I have said, by the rest of the community), to the effect that I was a defective person: "bad" and "simpleminded."

This analysis of the relationship between my Eskimo family and me is, of course, far from complete. It is obvious that difficulties of conceptualization are only one of the problems that beset relationships of any kind. It is obvious also that most relationships — and the one described here is no exception — have strongly positive features as well, or they would cease to exist. Nevertheless, the account that I have presented here may serve as a basis for discussion of the general issues of anthropological role-playing.

6

The medicine man: Doctoring informants
DAVID W. McCURDY

*Anthropologists often possess skills, knowledge, and equipment
that informants find attractive and useful. The ability to write
may lead to work as a scribe. Mechanical expertise may mean
hours spent repairing machinery. Ownership of a jeep may require the frequent running of errands. Time spent providing
services is time lost to research, but requests for help are often
difficult to ignore. In this article David McCurdy, who once
served in the U.S. Medical Service Corps, describes how he was
gradually drawn into treating the inhabitants of a tribal village
in Central India. Demands on his time become so great that, in
order to continue with research, he was forced to employ several
strategies including hiding, limiting treatment to regular "office
hours," interviewing informants outside the village, and training
a medical staff.*

The morning of May 6, 1962 dawned bright and clear. The village
was already awake, its householders moving quietly to finish their
chores before 100° temperatures overtook the day. I rose at 7 A.M.,
sleepily pulled the mosquito net from the side of my cot, and stood
stretching in the north room of my mud-and-dung-plastered bamboo
house. Searching for a clean shirt in an old and battered green metal
trunk, I could hear, for the first time, the low murmur of voices in the
front yard. "It sounds like some people are out there," I thought to
myself. "I wonder who it can be so early?"

It didn't take long to find out. I dressed quickly and pushed open
the front door. To my astonishment I looked out on a crowd. People
filled the compound, women with infants, men smoking and talking on

Reprinted by permission from *Ethics and Anthropology: Dilemmas in Fieldwork* by Michael A. Rynkiewich and James P. Spradley, pp. 4–16. Copyright © 1976
John Wiley & Sons, Inc.

the verandah, an assortment of children sitting or playing quietly in the warmth of the early morning sun. "Rām, Rām," I said to them automatically. "Rām, Rām, Sāb (sahib)," they answered pleasantly.

Just then Kānjī Pārgī entered the yard, straining under the heavy weight of the water pot he had just filled and carried up from the village well. I had hired Kānjī two months earlier to look after the house. His work freed my time for research, and he proved to be an invaluable informant. "Yē koi hai, Kānjī (What is this, Kānjī)?" I said, gesturing toward the crowd. "Are all these people sick?"

"Yes, Sāb," he replied. "They are troubled with sore eyes and yesterday many people in the village came down with diarrhea. That is why so many have come today."

"But why have they arrived so early?" I said, thinking of the late night I had just put in typing field notes.

"That is bad, Sāb," Kānjī replied apologetically. "People don't know you sleep late. I will warn them to come later tomorrow."

It wasn't really the early hour that bothered me but the large number of villagers who had come for treatment. There must have been 25 people in the compound at that moment, and 5 or 10 more were likely to show up before the rush was over. If Kānjī's estimate was correct, a majority of them suffered from conjunctivitis, an often severe inflamation of the eye, or from diarrhea. Neither condition took too long to treat provided there were no complications. On the other hand there were always hard cases — an infected axe cut, a mysterious chest pain, weight loss, a sore liver, "fever" — and these required more time to diagnose and treat if, indeed, they could be dealt with at all. How much of the morning would I have to devote to these people?

To make matters worse, I had scheduled an interview for about 8:00 A.M. that day. A household head named Vākājī Kātārā had agreed to tell me about his son's wedding, which was now taking place. Bhil weddings are long affairs; they involve a series of rites culminating in the "walk around the fire" at the bride's house. Today Vākājī's son would exchange clothing with his affinal kin, collect money from relatives and friends who live in Ratakote, and set off for the bride's village with his wedding party. I wanted to learn more detail about the wedding and to understand its significance better. Vākājī warned me to come early, however, explaining that once the clothing exchange started that morning, he would be unable to talk again until after his son was married. He would be too busy. I thought of the time it would take to treat all the people in my compound and doubted that I could make it. "How in hell am I going to do research around here if this keeps up?" I muttered to myself.

Research was also on my mind in the fall of 1960. I was sitting with my feet propped up on a chair in the cluttered office that served as the lounge for graduate students in the Department of Sociology and Anthropology at Cornell University. The mahogany doors and wood-work spoke of the room's earlier elegance, part of a suite that once belonged to the president of Cornell University. Now, filled with odd pieces of cast-off furniture, littered with an assortment of old tests and papers, unwashed coffee cups, and overflowing ashtrays, graduate students came here to relax or study. On this day I sat talking with a friend whose graduate career was at the same stage as mine.

"Am I relieved," I said. "Smith and Opler approved my research proposal. I have been working on that thing for six weeks and I didn't think they would ever like it."

"Where are you going to send it?" he asked.

"To Ford, NIMH, and NSF, but I really wrote it for the Ford Foundation. I'm going to have to change it a little for NSF. They should be more interested in the design than in the usefulness of the results. I don't really know what to do for NIMH, I'll have to ask around about that. I hope one of these foundations takes it."

Such talk was common during the fall. We were putting in late nights in preparation for our comprehensive examinations, reading extensively about the region in which we hoped to do fieldwork, studying a language, and trying to generate an acceptable field research proposal. The final task was particularly important. Without an attractive proposal no foundation would provide funds, and without funds, there would be no field trip. Fieldwork was essential to us. Faculty members and senior graduate students frequently spoke about "the field." Students who returned from the field seemed changed; they were somehow more mature as though working in another society gave them more confidence about themselves and their relationship to anthropology.

But fieldwork meant much more than residence in a community with an alien culture. Once there, we all knew that one task held highest priority: gathering of large amounts of high quality data for a thesis and several publications. Those of us who prepared for fieldwork that fall felt some anxiety about our ability to meet this requirement. We knew of students who had returned with less than adequate field notes and we heard statements like, "They say that Jack didn't get much material in the field. They aren't sure he has enough for a thesis. He may have to go back." On the other hand there were also dramatic successes. One student had extended his fieldwork to almost three years, returning home with more than 30,000 note cards filled with data! Stored on their sides, the cards were reputed to line an entire wall of his apartment and to contain the finest information ever collected by an anthropology student at Cornell. The message in both cases seemed clear; the more good material we collected in the field, the better.

The quality of the research proposal and the ties with a foundation it established also underscored the importance of field research. All of us had worked hard on our proposals; they seemed like the distilled efforts of lecture courses, seminar papers, and countless conferences with a graduate committee. Everyone knew that the foundations were selective; they regularly turned down some of the research proposals submitted to them. "Did you hear?" someone would say. "Harry has just been turned down by NSF. He didn't even get as far as the interview. That makes three rejections." We all believed that for some reason foundations didn't have confidence in Harry and his research design, which meant that they *did* have faith in those of us who received support. When we accepted a grant, we accepted a responsibility to the foundation. And with the grant came stronger pressures to pursue fieldwork successfully.

This sense of urgency was uppermost in my mind as I surveyed the villagers who waited for me to treat them that morning in 1962. I had come to India for one purpose: to conduct a study of acculturation among the Bhils of southern Rajasthan. "I'm not here to become a doctor or start a medical practice," I had said to myself again and again during the first months of research. I chose to work in Ratakote, a Bhil village in the Aravalli Hills, because a road had recently opened it up to outside contract, not because its people were sickly or needed medical attention. But now I faced the dilemma more clearly than ever before. One man waited to be interviewed, a strategically important informant. Twenty-five others waited to be treated, people plagued by illness and disease. In the back of my mind a larger question kept surfacing: "What was I going to be for the next year, be an anthropologist or a para-medic?"

Kānjī made a hot cup of Staines instant coffee laced with goat's milk and sugar as I asked my guests if I might "take food" before turning to their ailments. Local customs were on my side for a few minutes at least. As I sat on the verandah waiting for my coffee to cool, J. K. Doshi joined me. He was my Indian assistant whom I had asked to join the project almost immediately upon arrival in southern Rajasthan. "Davidjī," he said quizzically, "Just see all these people. What has brought so many today?"

"Well, Doshijī, it's because we're very popular here in Ratakote," I answered him wryly, for he knew why the villagers had come as well as I did. But his question made me recall the events of the past few months, the decisions I had made to help people, and the increasing tempo of involvement that eventually led to a demand for my services so evident today. Had I done something to cause the dilemma? Surely this did not happen to every anthropologist.

Or did it? Anthropological fieldwork is unique in at least one respect. It creates a close social relationship between anthropologist and informant. I think that for many of us this intimacy and involvement with people was an important drawing card into anthropology. I had not come to India to define people like so many laboratory specimens or subjects for observation. Furthermore, the relationships that had developed even during these early months had facilitated my research. They involved obligations, responsibilities, mutual respect, and a willingness to assist. And I gladly accepted the fact that it was not a one-way street. But now something was happening in the way people defined my role in the village. I had unwittingly acquired an obligation to treat illness in this community. I had become a local healer without knowing it!

Perhaps it had been Amarnāth's headache that started it all. I met Amarnāth for the first time on the evening of my second day in Ratakote. He came with some other people to absorb the heat given off by my kerosene pressure lamp as it burned in the school room where Doshi and I temporarily resided. We had come to our present lodging through the good offices of Nārājī, the village headman. "As long as you behave yourselves you can stay in this village," he had said to us. "Until your new house is finished you will sleep in the school." Amarnāth said little this first evening. He sat with the others and listened to the steady stream of questions and my halting, interpreted, answers. "Where are you from?" "How did you travel here?" "Why did you come to Ratakote?" On subsequent nights I came to know Amarnāth better for he began to talk more openly, and I learned much from him during my first few weeks in the village.

One morning Amarnāth arrived at my door. "I have had a terrible headache for three days, Sāb," he said. "The pain is very sharp here below my eye and here, right over it. It comes up and goes down with the sun. Do you have any medicine that might help?"

I hesitated and thought to myself, "That sounds like a sinus infection. Aspirin would help the pain although I doubt that it would attack the infection."

"Sāb is not a doctor you know," Doshi interjected. Like many high-status Indians, he had seen many requests from others who needed aid, and was on guard against long-term obligations. He tried to protect me now.

On the other hand Amarnāth was already a friend. He had been more willing than any other villager to spend his time answering my questions. He was also in real pain; sinus infections that "come up and go down with the sun" are famous for their ferocity in southern Rajasthan. I took out the bottle of Bayer's aspirin I had brought to India with me, unscrewed the cap, and shook out four tablets. "Here," I said, handing them to Amarnāth, "Take two of these with some water now and two more later this afternoon. You had better rest today, too."

Amarnāth thanked me, turned around, and walked painfully down the path toward his house. But the next morning he returned again. "Sāb, the medicine you gave me was very good," he said. "I would like some more."

"Well, Doshi was right," I thought to myself with some annoyance. "Once you start this kind of thing it is hard to stop." With resignation I gave Amarnāth six more aspirin tablets and wondered if he would be back again the next day. But that was the end of the incident. Later I learned that Amarnāth had divided each of the six tablets in half so that they would last longer, and that he claimed even this smaller dose worked well. In the future his strategy would be copied by other villagers who cut each aspirin tablet I gave them in four parts, hoarded the pieces, and even offered them as gifts to relatives in other Bhil communities.

No one asked me for anything during the next three weeks. Doshi and I continued to live in the school and as the time went by, we became better known to the people who lived near us. Research progressed nicely; I mapped the village, began a census, and participated in several events including a memorial feast for an important man who had died six months earlier. My house, which had been rising slowly during this period, was finally completed in the middle of January. The headman had chosen the location for me, a hill in a central part of one of the village wards, and arranged for three men to do the work. The structure, itself, consisted of two rooms approximately 10 feet square and a covered verandah. Although it could not compare in elegance to the stone houses of other villagers, it was perfect for my needs and we wasted no time in moving in. That evening I gave a party for the men who had worked on the project, and, along with some neighbors who heard what was going on and invited themselves, we drank, talked, and sang late into the night. Most of us got drunk, and we paid for it with a severe hangover the next morning.

One man, Haujī, paid more dearly than the rest, as I learned from his brother about 10 A.M. "Sāb," he shouted as he hurried up to my house. "Haujī is very sick."

"What is the trouble with him?" I asked.

"He can hardly breathe and he is very hot. He felt bad after the party last night and he has been getting worse and worse. He is really bad. Can you come and look at him?"

I had known Haujī almost as long as Amarnāth. He had directed the men who built my house and I often sat with him talking about such things as the size of the rooms, the pitch of the roof, and the possibility of windows. As I spoke with him from day to day I also learned something of the misfortune that could so easily strike Bhil families.

Haujī was born 40 years earlier in a house that stood only 300 yards from my own. When he was 18 years old he was married and continued to live with his parents, a Bhil custom for the youngest son. Over the years his parents died and his wife bore him four children, a boy and three girls. Then, only a year earlier fever struck the family, first afflicting his oldest, a daughter who would have married the next year, and eventually all the children. Haujī tried everything he could to restore their health. He brought them to the village *dēvrā* or god's house where the deity, Bhērōjī, agreed, speaking through a shaman, to cure the children. But this and later shamanistic rituals failed and the children grew worse. Haujī sacrificed a goat to his house god and he held a special ceremony to the goddess Sikōtrī, fearing that she might be to blame for the illness. In the end two daughters and his son died and, in despair, he abandoned his unlucky house for a new one he constructed in the hills. Now his brother's tone of voice seemed to imply that Haujī might be on the verge of death. I left immediately to see if I could help.

I found Haujī lying on the ground under a pile of dirty quilts. He moaned and shook and hardly recognized anybody. He was flushed and feverish and his lungs both sounded congested. "I bet it's pneumonia," I said to Doshi who stood next to me. "There is nothing we can do here. He is going to die unless we get him to the government hospital in Udaipur fast. See if that is O.K. with his brother."

Haujī suffered terribly during the long bumpy ride to the district capital. Once there, he was admitted to a medical ward and eventually given a shot of penicillin. Within two hours his temperature dropped from 106 to 99° and he felt well enough to smile. With things apparently in hand, I left him in the company of his wife and brother and drove back to Ratakote.

The next day Nārājī, the headman, paid me a visit. "The whole village is talking about what you did yesterday, Sāb," he told me. "They say you must be kind to do a thing like that. They say you saved Haujī's life and that you must truly be a man of *pārēm* (love) to give up your own comfort for Haujī." Indeed, people I had never met came to see me during the next few days and more than once I was asked to describe Haujī's condition and how I had made the doctors at the hospital admit him and give him an injection. Some asked directly why I had been so kind as to do a thing like that.

Five days after his trip to the hospital, a very sick Haujī appeared at my door. He had "escaped" from the hospital because "people were dying in there." He had walked back to Ratakote, a distance of over 20 miles, and felt very weak. He was lucky to have received a shot of penicillin that was intended to last for a long period of time. I judged that he would recover with rest and a diet strong in protein and vitamins. I suggested that he eat some eggs, drink whole milk, and kill and eat a chicken now and then. I also promised to get him a bottle of vitamin tonic the next time I made a trip to Udaipur.

Although he complained about weakness for several months, Haujī felt well enough to resume normal activities within two weeks. Much to my surprise, he attributed his cure to the eggs he had eaten. "He does not like eggs very well," his wife explained to me later. "When you said that he must eat them it was like medicine. He told me that you must know about some power in the eggs. After he ate them for a few days he felt so much better that he wanted even more. Our chickens did not lay enough and I had to look for more at other houses. Haujī says you surely know the power of medicines but you hesitate to tell because you are modest."

From then on people tried to tap this hidden power. One day shortly after Haujī's recovery, a woman stopped me as I was walking toward the shrine of Mangra Bābā (hill god) to watch a ceremony. "Sāb, my baby is sick with fever, would you look at her? She just lies there." I stopped by her house but knew that there was little I could do. Fever was a disease to the people of Ratakote. People got fever, suffered with fever, and died from fever. For me, it was a symptom of other diseases, and by itself, it usually told me very little. I looked at the child, asked if anything else were wrong with it, and puzzled, had to claim ignorance about the little girl's affliction. "The baby is certainly sick," I told her. "I don't know what she has and I have no medicine that would do her any good. You should show her to the malaria control worker when he visits the village this week and if she gets worse, you could take her to the hospital in Udaipur."

Other inquiries followed this one over the next few weeks. I saw my first cases of conjunctivitis and diarrhea. I was asked what to do about a painful boil, angina pains, a burning sensation during urination, fever, stomach pains, weakness, lack of appetite, sexual impotency, and a variety of other conditions people suffered from. I responded with courtesy and sympathy and with advice if I could think of any. But I felt frustrated by a lack of medicine; there was nothing concrete I could do to help them.

March was the turning point. Amarnāth, whose house was close to mine, paid me a visit one evening. He favored one leg as he approached and I asked why he limped.

"It's the sore on my shin, Sāb," he replied. "It hurts more than usual tonight."

"What do you mean, more than usual?" I asked. "How long have you had it?"

"Oh, about seven years," he said. "It nearly healed once but I knocked it open again."

The sore was large, over an inch and a half in diameter and so obvious that I wondered how I had missed it before. An area of rough scar tissue surrounded the lesion, indicating a larger area of involvement sometime in the past. It seemed inflamed, which probably explained Amarnāth's present distress. "I bet it won't heal because the circulation is gone," I said looking at the wound. "I wonder how you could get a thing like that to close up? Look Amarjī, why don't you soak a clean cloth in some hot water and put that on the sore? It might help a little. Beyond that I don't know what you could do about it. I don't have anything for it here."

"That's all right, Sāb," Amarnāth told me. "I am used to it. After all, I have had it for a long time now."

I thought about his wound a few days later as the jeep lurched and jounced toward Udaipur over a road that traversed an endless series of rock outcroppings. "What would it be like to have an open sore that would not heal for seven years?" The road smoothed out a bit on the outskirts of the city, then became rougher as the bumpy blacktop started. Soon I could see the house in which my wife, Carolyn, and baby daughter, who had accompanied me to India, lived. They stayed with me from time to time in the village, but found life there difficult. We had rented a room with a porch and kitchen shed soon after arriving. I drove in from the village once each week to see them, buy supplies, clean up, and catch up on typing notes and other work. As I pulled up to the front door, I could see Carolyn talking with a Westerner dressed in a high-necked Indian coat and loose fitting pants. I kissed her and turned to meet the stranger. "This is Arthur Banks, the mission doctor from Kherewara we heard about," she said. "Vickie and I found him in the bazaar today and asked him home for tea while he waits for his bus to Kherewara."

I had heard of Dr. Banks from other acquaintances in the city. He had been on home leave in England when we first arrived in India, but had returned and was hard at work now at what he liked best, public health projects and general clinic work. I liked him immediately. It was not long before my concern about Amarnāth surfaced. "Seven years," he asked. "That's a long time. Why don't you try soaking his foot in a tub of hot water to start with and add some epsom salts. Then try penicillin ointment on it and keep it covered. If there is any circulation left you should be able to get some tissue to form." Before I could ask, he took out his pen and wrote a prescription for penicillin skin ointment. "Do you need anything else?" he asked, looking up from his small prescription pad.

Without hesitation, I said, "Could you give me something that would help with conjunctivitis? I see so much of that in the village. And is there anything that I could use to treat dysentery? People complain to me about that all the time too. I ought to warn you though, I don't feel too secure about giving drugs. I did spend some time in the Army Medical Service Corps but except for one course, I don't know much about tropical diseases."

"I can give you some things you can use safely," he replied assuringly. "Aureomycin eye ointment would be good for conjunctivitis. No telling what is causing the trouble and the ointment should get almost any kind of bacteria. But make sure you continue treatment for a few days after the infection is gone. If you don't you may grow a strain of bacteria that is resistant to the drug. As for dysentery the safest thing you could use would be insoluble sulfa. Just give them enough to do the job and impress on them the need to take it regularly."

The doctor finished his tea and left to catch the Kherewara bus. I visited a drugstore I had shopped at once before and had the prescriptions filled. I also bought surgical gauze, some antiseptic, adhesive tape, aspirin, and epsom salts. Returning to Ratakote, I stopped by Amarnāth's house and asked him to come by and let me look at the sore on his leg again. That evening he soaked his shin for an hour and received his first application of penicillin ointment.

I was pleased and Amarnāth was dumfounded when his wound healed completely in two weeks. But it was just the first in a series of cures I could now effect. The day after I began work on Amarnāth's shin I treated my first case of conjunctivitis. The afflicted person could barely open his swollen eyes in daylight and complained of a constant painful ache at night. The next day after only one treatment I could see no sign of infection. He felt no pain and claimed to be cured. Diarrhea turned out to be a more difficult disease to treat, but sulfa seemed to help.

Word of these successes spread rapidly and patients multiplied. I ran out of medicine in five days and hurried to buy more on my next trip to Udaipur. I was surprised to discover that the druggist now treated me as a medical specialist and would sell me anything I asked for. In fact he seemed to have caught on to my high potential as a customer. "Take sulfa by the 5000-tablet box," he recommended. "It is much less costly that way. And you will be needing much eye ointment this time of year. Why not buy six tubes? Have you got enough penicillin ointment left? You should probably have five or ten more tubes of that as well." Later I would discover that the avaricious druggist was correct. The parade of patients grew longer throughout the spring, and my supply of medicine was often strained.

So was my knowledge of disease. The infections, fevers, pains, and other infirmities that confronted me each day almost always included a mystery or two. Visits to Dr. Banks for advice helped with the diagnosis of some, and the manual he gave me entitled *The Tropical Dispensary Handbook* helped with others. But there would always be a few baffling ailments and I could only advise those afflicted with them to make the long trip to the hospital in Udaipur for tests and, hopefully, better informed opinion.

Most people ignored these limitations and by May, 1962 my future in medicine seemed assured. If I had had any thoughts about extricating myself from paramedical practice, they were dashed by the success of aureomycin, penicillin, sulfa, and the wonderfully fragile local bacteria that had never encountered antibiotics before. These medicines worked too well; village resentment over their denial would have driven me from Ratakote. Instead I continued medical activities, to run what really amounted to a clinic. Villagers marveled at the power of "Sāb's medicine." They bragged about it to their friends and relatives in other communities, and made it and me a status symbol for Ratakote. I found myself sought out by more and more people, strangers, from neighboring villages. One man even walked all the way to Ratakote from Udaipur because someone had told him that, "Sāb cures better than the hospital." If escape from this medical identity was impossible, the preservation of the field research project, to say nothing of my personal commitment to anthropology, graduate committee members, and the Ford Foundation, would require heightened efficiency and a greater degree of control over daily activities. Was there a way to conduct successful fieldwork?

Time was a major part of the problem. Fieldwork takes time. It can easily require four or five hours to type up a day's field notes, even more if one takes particularly long and successful interviews or has observed especially complex events. To complicate matters, the control and scheduling of time is often out of the ethnographer's hands. Informants are busy people; one interviews them at their convenience. Local events schedule themselves.

Treating patients used up valuable time, and the more patients there were the more time treatment took. Even worse, patients interrupted research activity. They arrived at their own convenience, at any time during the day or night that suited them. They would catch me as I hurried to meet an informant for an interview, interrupt as I tried to type field notes, or pull me away from the observation of an interesting religious event. Frustration over time was a constant research companion.

I developed four strategies to deal with this problem. All attempted to schedule time more effectively, to organize daily activity so that there was more time for research. First, I scheduled office hours. Villagers had a tendency to show up for treatment early in the morning, and I formalized their inclination by setting treatment hours in the morning after breakfast, and in the evening around dinner time. I announced this to the headman and village elders, pleading that although I wanted to continue medical assistance, I was a student and needed time for my own work.

Stating hours was easier than enforcing them. I found it difficult to turn people away when they arrived at the wrong time. They had often walked for several miles from some distant part of Ratakote and it seemed heartless to make them wait or ignore their troubles. A second strategy, hiding, seemed to help this difficulty. To hide, I scheduled interviews in distant parts of the village or arranged to observe an event or activity at a place that could not be seen from my house. Since I did research when I was hiding, this strategy directly contributed to field-work. When villagers came for treatment and discovered I was not home, they decided it was better to stop by during morning or evening office hours. Eventually hiding became less necessary as a result.

A third strategy, exporting informants, was closely related to hiding. I discovered this strategy by accident while I was recovering from a bout of dysentery at my residence in Udaipur. Worried about the loss of research time due to illness, I asked Kānjī to pay me a visit for two days. Interviews on this occasion proved so useful, and the time for typing them up so plentiful, that I repeated the process again later.

The fourth strategy, developing a medical staff, was probably most useful of all and turned office hours into work periods on many occasions. Since my arrival in Ratakote, I had worked closely with my research assistant, J. K. Doshi, and my village assistant, Kānjī Pārgī. They shared in research activity and participated in the daily routine of household maintenance. They also helped with the treatment of sick villagers and, before long, learned the questions I asked patients and the treatments I prescribed for common ailments. Gradually they were able to take over much of the outpatient care that I would normally have had to provide. Kānjī inherited "eyes" and "cuts." He developed a gentle skill with patients and his bandages often looked neater, and stayed on longer, than mine. Doshi handled the more sensitive cases, such as diarrhea, colds, and respiratory infections. He became an accomplished diagnostician, treating most cases and sending me the few remaining problems that baffled him. While my associates conducted sick call, I attended to research. I found office hours were an ideal time to catch up on note typing and even managed to schedule interviews, fairly certain that they could be completed without interruption.

The medical training of Kānjī had a side effect that I thought was beneficial. The people of Ratakote were becoming more and more dependent on the relief from suffering that aureomycin, penicillin, and sulfa could provide. Yet I would soon leave the village, depriving them of access to these drugs. Kānjī, I reasoned, now knew enough to treat most common ailments and could continue in medical practice indefinitely. When I asked him about it he readily agreed to the idea, but pointed out one difficulty. He would have to be able to buy drugs in Udaipur and he would have to develop some way to raise the necessary funds in Rata-kote. The first problem was easy to solve. The druggist agreed to sell Kānjī drugs and Dr. Banks lent his authority to the arrangement. The second would be more difficult, because Bhils help each other for nothing as a matter of hospitality. The best we could do while I remained in the village was to extract a promise from people to pay for the cost of Kānjī's medicines.

Time management helped to facilitate research, but it could not cure the basic dilemma. Dealing with patients still took part of my time, and villagers continued to evade the controls I attempted to place on them. There were emergencies that necessitated trips to Udaipur, such as the time a leopard bit a man named Kālāji through the left arm or the occasion when a little girl named Nānī was hemorrhaging from her mucus membranes as the result of a Russel's-viper bite. Some villagers, particularly those who felt themselves to be important, would send for me when someone in their family was ill. Others would try to interrupt me during the day despite efforts to avoid them.

But I came to find time spent treating people was not completely wasted in the context of fieldwork. Curing could generate field data as well. Through medical activity I learned folk classifications of disease and treatment. Since Bhils tied disease so closely to the supernatural, medicine proved to be a gateway to religion. And through the clinic I gained a clear and valued identity in Ratakote. My willingness to help increase their willingness to trust. Through trust emerged more detailed, accurate information. Curing led to the good rapport so necessary to successful fieldwork.

Anthropological fieldwork will always engender conflict between the ethnographer's personal relationships and his research goals. Infor-mants will always make demands on time that are normal from their perspective, and anthropologists will respond to these demands as best they can. In the end fieldwork must involve a compromise, a willingness to recognize that informants are people, too, and that their needs are bound to impinge on research. Yet it may be the anthropologist's re-sponse to these needs that permits research to succeed. It is not clear to me whether curing informants *should* be part of the response. It is evident that medicine and research can mix, and that I would probably find myself in the same dilemma again were I to work in another Indian village.

7

Trouble in the tank:
Ethics in urban fieldwork
JAMES P. SPRADLEY

*All anthropologists fill a double role: anthropologist and citizen.
What should anthropologists do when, in the course of doing
research, they discover patterns of discrimination, inequities,
injustices, or inhumane treatment of the people they study? Because anthropologists have access to information that is hidden
to many other people, do they thereby have a special responsibility? Should they interfere in the operations of the society studied?
And, perhaps most important, how should they make known to the
general public what they discover? All these questions emerged in
the course of studying skid road alcoholics, or tramps, a study
James Spradley carried out in Seattle, Washington. In this article, he
takes us through the experience of research selection and then
through the decision to publish data in a way that most anthropologists avoid. Another report from this urban anthropology
research project appears as article 26 in this volume.*

I

The faculty meeting began promptly at eight o'clock. On that Thursday
morning in early June of 1967, I was beginning to think around the
edges of a decision that would eventually grow into a series of ethical
dilemmas. The chairman took his customary place at the head of the
long seminar table and started the meeting.

"Grand Rounds will meet in Health Sciences 405 this morning at
ten. It's a classic case of schizophrenia. Dr. Johnson will present the case
and I hope you can all come." A moment of silence followed while he

sorted through some papers in front of him. Then, while the other faculty members discussed the Summer Research Training Program for medical students, my thoughts drifted away to my own research program.

I had been on the faculty of the Department of Psychiatry at the University of Washington for nearly a year, yet I still felt somewhat like an outsider. Everyone else seemed to know what was expected of them and I often wished for the security of well-defined responsibilities. My training had not prepared me to give psychological tests or engage in therapy; I had no desire to become a junior psychiatrist. I taught one course in the spring and offered lectures on culture and illness from time to time. Beyond that I was free to become involved in the training of future psychologists, psychiatrists, and physicians. I could participate in patient-related activities such as group therapy. I could also carry out research that was related to mental illness, provided I gathered the data in the greater metropolitan area of Seattle. I felt most comfortable doing research and other faculty understood that role. I was eager to begin a new project since I had recently completed research on a Kwakiutl Indian chief in British Columbia. But, I discovered, the choice to do research only presented me with a new set of alternatives and the necessity to make other choices.

The faculty meeting ended and I edged my way to the door and walked quickly up the long hallway toward the elevator. The Psychiatry Department occupied one wing of the seventh floor of the University Hospital. The two elevators stood opposite the nurses' station and beyond them lay the other wing with patients. The doors opened and a stream of people flowed out; I stepped in, pushed the button for the third floor — Department of Pediatrics — and leaned against the back of the elevator to wait. I knew that whatever I decided to study could easily continue for a number of years. I wanted a project that was interesting, challenging, and thoroughly anthropological. Perhaps a study of the Greek immigrant community in Seattle would meet these criteria; it could even lead someday to research in Greece. I thought of other alternatives like the spiritualist counselors and religious healers who attracted clients from all over the city. I wondered if I studied their methods could I compare them to curing rituals in Africa or Asia? I might study the social structure of a psychiatric ward in any one of a number of hospitals, a project similar to what William Caudill, another anthropologist, had done more than 10 years earlier.

As the elevator stopped at the fourth floor to pick up a nurse I thought about the most likely possibility, a study of urban Indians. Many Native Americans had moved to Seattle from rural reservations and I could investigate their strategies for adapting to city life. A government agency that helped to relocate Native Americans from Alaska had an office near the University of Washington and when I approached the director about a possible study he seemed receptive, even enthusiastic.

But each week brought new ideas, new opportunities. The latest was an alcoholism treatment center. I saw the third floor light come on and when the doors opened I stepped out, went past the waiting area and down the hallway to the Department of Pediatrics. I had decided to see if Jim Oakland, a psychologist who worked there, had time for a cup of coffee in the hospital cafeteria. I wanted to talk to him about the possibilities and problems of studying an alcoholism treatment center.

Jim Oakland and I had taught together at Seattle Pacific College a few years earlier while we both did graduate work in different departments at the University of Washington. We frequently talked about our respective jobs and research interests. He had administered some psychological tests to James Sewid, the Kwakiutl chief whose life history I had recently completed. From time to time I had made suggestions on the social and cultural aspects of his work in developing norms for the Edwards Personality Inventory. His office door was ajar and I pushed it open. "Do you have time for coffee? I want to tell you my latest idea for research." Without a hesitation, he jumped to his feet, reached for his coat, and we were on our way to the first floor of the hospital.

As we sipped coffee in a quiet corner of the busy cafeteria I told him what I knew. "There's a new residential treatment center for skid road alcoholics opening sometime this summer. The King County Sheriff's Department will operate the center; they plan to take drunks arrested in Seattle and keep them at the center for treatment instead of giving them a jail sentence. I don't know much about the details but it would be a chance to get in on the ground floor, the start of the treatment center, and study its culture as it develops."

Jim listened with interest and then asked, "How would you go about doing the research?"

"I would drive out to the treatment center; the buildings are under construction now a few miles outside the city. I'd go maybe three or four days a week, maybe more, to observe and talk with the patients and staff. It would be like studying a small society. The drunks will undergo several months of treatment and I'd want to participate in the various kinds of therapy, observe the work program, eat meals with them, and just hang around to gather data on the informal aspects of the center. I might develop some questionnaires later on and use some personality tests. I'd do an ethnography of the treatment center — my goal would be to describe its culture."

"But why do an ethnography of an alcoholism treatment institution?" he asked. "What kind of contribution will it make? Do you have any larger goals in such a study?" His question went to the heart of my own values and I paused before answering. "Well, in addition to the pure scientific goals, I may be able to learn some things that could improve the treatment milieu and lead to a more effective program. I don't know much about alcoholism but the skid road drunk is the hardest to cure and most approaches haven't worked very well. Maybe I can make some contribution there."

We continued talking for nearly an hour about possible problems, about the goals of such a study, the strategies for collecting data, the ways it might lead to improved treatment, and how I felt about this study in contrast to the others I had considered. We talked again during the next week and by the middle of June all signs pointed toward a study of the alcoholism treatment center.

II

The cool, damp days of June gave way to the bright sun of early summer. Before I made a final decision on the project I tried to find out more about the planned treatment center, reviewed some of the literature on studying institutions, and worked out ideas for gathering data. A colleague in the Department of Psychiatry told me that a Mr. Ron Fagan, newly appointed director of the center, was the kind of person I would find receptive to research. I called Mr. Fagan and made an appointment to meet him. A thin, soft-spoken man in his early fifties, he greeted me warmly; his informal manner put me at ease immediately. He began talking about alcoholics and his hopes for the new facility that he called "Cedar Hills Alcoholism Treatment Center." Although he did not fully understand what approach I would take as an anthropologist, he said that at one time he had collaborated on an alcoholism research project with a sociologist from the university. He believed in the importance of such research. He would welcome the kind of study I wanted to do.

Before we finished talking I knew I would learn a great deal from Mr. Fagan. I also sensed that his work involved far more than a job. He had a lifelong dream to help the alcoholic, especially the "low bottom drunk" from skid road. He recalled his own experiences as we talked, how he had been on skid road in Seattle and San Francisco and other cities around the country, the struggle with drinking, his attempts to stop the vicious cycle, finally hitting bottom and finding help through Alcoholics Anonymous. Since his recovery he had worked in a variety of settings to help alcoholics.

I learned that each year the Seattle police arrested more than 10,000 drunks, sending a steady stream of men to the city jail. After a few weeks or months to dry out, most ended up back on the streets only to find themselves arrested again. It was a revolving door. Ron emphasized that this system did little more than dry out the drunk and keep him away from the bottle for a few weeks. It treated the symptom, not the cause. The men needed help, not punishment. Alcoholism was a disease that could be treated and Cedar Hills would use the best treatment approaches yet developed, everything from medical care and group therapy to Alcoholics Anonymous. Of course they would not have room for all the drunks arrested each year but would select those most likely to respond to treatment. Ron said he would start hiring staff and selecting patients in the next few weeks and I could start my research almost immediately. He offered to let me sit in on interviews with prospective patients and record the development of selection procedures. It would only require the permission of Sheriff Jack Porter, the person ultimately responsible for the center. Confident of the Sheriff's support, Ron said he would arrange for an appointment. I agreed to prepare a brief written proposal.

On July 18 I sent the proposal to Sheriff Jack Porter. It stated my purpose: "This research project will focus on how Cedar Hills functions as a treatment center for alcoholics. A study will be made of the development of the center, the formal and informal organization of staff and patients, the daily activities of each, various types of therapy utilized, and the meaning of the center to the patients, staff, and visitors."

Three days later I sat in a comfortable, overstuffed chair in Sheriff Porter's spacious office with Ron Fagan. He agreed with Ron that my study of Cedar Hills was a good idea and thought it could add to developing an effective treatment program. I pointed out that such a study could add to our understanding of new institutions, provide a basis for evaluating various therapeutic approaches, and that publications on the study could help to inform the community about the center. I then asked him what kind of institution he had in mind at Cedar Hills.

"I feel we must have a custodial type rehabilitation center. Successful treatment of alcoholics demands an institution," he said, leaning forward slightly in his chair. "What do you mean by *custodial* rehabilitation center?" I asked. "There are many other types of institutions but it is necessary to have one with a controlled environment. As long as you have alcoholics and as long as the police have to handle them — somebody has to do it. We have the alcoholics and because no one else is doing it we felt we should attempt some type of rehabilitation program."

As he talked I sensed his deep commitment to reshaping the lives of repeated offenders, to changing the archaic system that only dispensed punishment. My image of a tough cop who had risen to the top in Washington State's most populated county began to fade. He talked of the work release program he had developed for county jail prisoners so they could continue on regular jobs while serving time. He expanded on his ideas for the treatment center: "I think our treatment at Cedar Hills should be as sophisticated as possible. A work program is important in therapy. A work program is also important for returning money to the taxpayer. But work is secondary; cure is the most important. I feel there is value in Alcoholics Anonymous, various therapeutic approaches, and that vocational rehabilitation is very important. If Cedar Hills hasn't changed in six months," he said, emphasizing each word, "we will have to take another good look at it. It must keep changing. We must have some follow-up. If we can follow up on 50 percent of the men who go through Cedar Hills, that is better than others are doing."

I left that meeting deeply impressed with these men who were working to make the effective treatment of chronic alcoholics a reality. I felt exhilarated, filled with anticipation of the research about to begin. Confusion over too many alternatives had given way in a few short weeks to a firm decision to study Cedar Hills Alcoholism Treatment Center. I felt good because I had selected a unique cultural milieu for research. I knew it was a project that could have direct application to a social science problem of immense proportions. At the same time I did not plan to become an applied anthropologist; I would not try to change institutions or individuals. I had even told Ron Fagan that in order to keep from influencing the development of Cedar Hills I would have to withhold much of what I observed until after the study was completed. During the next two years I was to become more deeply involved with transients and drunks from skid road than I could ever have imagined on that warm summer afternoon as I left Sheriff Jack Porter's office.

III

Before July ended I was deep into fieldwork. The treatment center, now nearing completion, still had no patients. In the mornings I visited the criminal court in Seattle to watch the daily parade of drunks, to hear their pleas of "Guilty," and to record the sentences handed out by the judge. Ron Fagan and a newly hired counselor were there to watch and select patients. I interviewed them both to learn their reasons for selecting some men and rejecting others. I visited Cedar Hills and gathered information on the history of the new center. My field notes grew as I wrote down everything I could from my observations and interviews.

By the end of the first week in August a group of men had been selected; they waited in the city jail for their transfer to the county treatment center. Each would receive a six-month sentence; those who responded to treatment quickly could expect an early release. I sensed an air of anticipation among the staff because, at last, the waiting would end and they could get down to the hard task of rehabilitating these derelicts from skid road. But then, at the last minute, a bureaucratic snarl developed over the source of funds to purchase food for the men taken from the Seattle city jail to the King County treatment center. I talked with the staff and others, listened to their frustrations, and recorded their reactions to the news that these first patients would never arrive at Cedar Hills. Some felt the delay was due to the long-time rivalry between the city and county police departments. Another month passed before the problem was solved and a new group of patients selected.

On the morning of September 14, I left home earlier than usual. I drove to the Public Safety Building in downtown Seattle where I met Bill Adams, a police officer who had recently joined the treatment center staff; together we would transport the first six patients to Cedar Hills. At last I could talk to patients, find out the reasons they volunteered for treatment, listen to how they felt about the new center, and hopefully come to understand their lives as alcoholics. The elevator brought the men from the jail on the seventh floor to the basement where they were escorted into a paddy wagon. We drove out of the police garage and headed south. More than 30 minutes later we pulled into the grounds of Cedar Hills. The new buildings and landscaping seemed a sharp contrast to the adjacent county dump, the acres of surrounding woods, and the six transients from skid road.

I still vividly remember one small incident that happened about ten o'clock that morning, although at the time it seemed almost too insignificant to record. Standing around in the basement of the multipurpose building trying to appear unobtrusive, I talked with these patients as they checked-in their meager belongings and received green uniforms to wear while at the center. Several talked about the city jail: "Sure is crowded in there, lotta men are sleeping on the floor," one said. "The food was really terrible," added an older man. "I haven't had coffee in two weeks because I haven't been able to drink the coffee in there." Then two of the others began complaining that the police officers who arrested them had stolen their money. For an instant I felt vaguely uncomfortable, aware that Bill Adams and Sergeant Ron Colvin were listening to these complaints. One patient recalled: "I had a $20 bill when I was arrested and when I asked for the money in my property there was none." The other man claimed he had $22 when picked up for drunk but it also had disappeared. As the discussion ended and the men began to leave for their dormitory, Sergeant Colvin assured me that the money probably hadn't been taken. "These men are drunk when arrested and don't really know what they have in the way of money. This kind of complaint is rather common."

The days that followed brought more patients and Cedar Hills came alive with activity. I interviewed informants and participated in staff meetings, patient orientations, meals, card games, informal bull sessions, and always I made long and detailed notes on what I learned. Late in September I joined a group of new patients for coffee in the dining room. They were discussing the laws in some states that protected alcoholics from repeated arrests for drunkenness; the topic shifted to conditions in drunk tanks in various jails around the country. One man said bitterly, "I don't see how any judge could ever go to bed at night without a guilty conscience after sentencing these men." Another spoke with deep resentment: "Throwing a man in jail over and over again just makes him that much more bitter each time." An hour later I overheard two of these same men talking about their own arrest a few days earlier. It had occurred at the same time and they had gone to jail together. The police officer had ordered them to turn their pockets inside out, ostensibly looking for knives and any items of personal property. One had $17, the other $23, but when they were released from jail to come to Cedar Hills they got nothing back. They noticed I had overheard their complaints and one said, "You'd better not tell on us!" I assured them that I did not work for Cedar Hills and would not tell anyone. Then he said, "In this jail they don't even give you a receipt for the money they take." Only later would I come to fully appreciate the significance of this statement.

During the next few weeks my role as neutral but interested observer became accepted; more and more patients sought me out to talk — and almost always their concern focused on conditions in the jail. If a staff member approached during such a conversation, the subject changed or became very general. But when I was alone with individuals or groups of men, they talked freely, expressing their deep resentment of the power of the police. They spoke from long years of experience; many had served "life sentences on the installment plan," as one man called it. They told me about thefts and beatings, about policemen who roamed around skid road waiting and looking for drunks to pick them up on the least provocation. Out of deep and angry feelings older men decried the drunk tank that they found almost unbearable, often forced to sleep there for several nights at a time on the cold cement floor. Others had witnessed drunks being robbed and beaten by policemen on skid road and in the jail. They stressed the impossibility of ever "beating a drunk charge" so that nearly everyone entered guilty pleas even when innocent. One man recalled, "I was picked up one time for panhandling or begging; I asked a man for a cigarette and they arrested me and brought me in to be booked but the officer in charge just said, 'Well, you haven't been picked up in this jail before, we'll just put down you were drunk.' "

About this time I went to one of the counselors at Cedar Hills, a recovered alcoholic himself who, in years past, had spent many weeks in jail on drunk arrests. One morning in late September we drove together from Seattle to Cedar Hills. "When you were drinking and running and in jail," I asked, "were you ever mistreated by the police? I'm wondering if we can believe the stories the men report." I knew he would willingly tell me of his own experience; he also knew personally hundreds of other men he had worked with in Alcoholics Anonymous. After a moment he replied: "Yes, one time I was in an elevator and I said something that wasn't nice and the policeman started to beat me up. And as to getting rolled, that is very true, drunks are rolled by the police all the time." We talked for some time about the difficult problems these men faced with the police in Seattle and in other cities. And as we continued to drive the last few miles to Cedar Hills I began to feel vaguely unsure about the direction of my research.

IV

October brought a warm Indian summer to Seattle; the trees turned from green to red to gold and the university came alive again with returning students. I continued to gather data on Cedar Hills but now I struggled almost daily with the question I had comfortably resolved during the previous summer: "What should I study?" Should I go on investigating this new institution for the treatment and rehabilitation of alcoholics? Or should I study the much older system for the arrest and incarceration of drunks? Would it be right to use Cedar Hills as a base for interviewing informants about life in jail? If I did change the focus of my research and study the experiences of drunks with the Seattle Police, would it be right to hide this fact from Sheriff Jack Porter? Ron Fagan might accept this shift in my research goals but the Sheriff could hardly allow it. If I began systematic interviews about the jail I would still have to continue some research on Cedar Hills so as not to arouse suspicion among the security officers who worked at the treatment center. On the other hand, maybe I should ignore the stories about the police and stick to my original research goals. After all, I couldn't study everything; sooner or later I had to draw the line and exclude some things that could be investigated.

Jim Oakland knew of what I had learned during those first months of research and one day over lunch I told him, "I'm wondering if I should focus on interviews with patients about the jail, concentrating on their experiences there rather than on the treatment center? Or should I ignore the jail? I don't think I can study both and do justice to my original proposal." I half expected the next question for it was one I had thought about often. "How do you know these stories about the police and the jail are true?" he asked. "Most people would see your informants as merely bums and derelicts who can't be taken seriously."

"I'm not sure they *are* true," I told him. "In fact, up to now I've only thought of them as complaints that would have to be investigated. But I feel sure that something is going on at the jail that few people in Seattle know about. The whole system of arresting drunks seems to breed injustice. They make nearly 12,000 arrests each year and some men spend as much as six months in jail simply for appearing drunk in public. They could bail out for $20 every time if they only had the money. If conditions are half as bad as some men say, then it's a hell of a place. Almost all the men who come for treatment have spent years in and out of jail and they seem far more concerned about the police and doing time in jail than about their drinking. Some of them aren't alcoholics; they volunteer for Cedar Hills just to escape doing hard time in jail. It can't help but have a profound influence on any treatment program. It may be true, as one informant told me, 'After 30 days in jail, you owe yourself a drunk.' I wonder if there's some way to change the laws or something; I don't know, but as long as they keep arresting these men, any kind of treatment program will fight a losing battle." Jim agreed and as we left he encouraged me to seriously consider more concentrated research on the collective experience of these men with the police and in jail.

An unexpected event occurred a few days later to help me decide. On Tuesday, October 31, I sat in court waiting for things to begin. The bailiff rapped his gavel loudly several times; everyone stood in silence. "The Municipal Court Number One of Seattle is now in session. The Honorable James Noe presiding." I knew the procedure by heart and sat down to begin taking notes as I had done on many other mornings. I heard the city attorney begin the process: "Delmar Luden, you have been charged with drunk in public, how do you plead?" "Guilty." After a quick review of his previous record the judge announced, "Thirty days committed." It took 10 seconds from start to finish for Mr. Luden to have his day in court. Stephen Brady followed with a two-day suspended sentence. I wrote rapidly as the tempo picked up — the same charge, the same plea, and always the sentences. Suddenly the fourteenth name caught my attention — Charles Roberts. I looked more closely and saw a former patient from Cedar Hills walk from the holding tank into the courtroom and stand before the judge. Only a few days earlier I had talked with this man about the jail, his past, the treatment program, and his hopes for the future. I avoided looking directly at him for fear he might recognize me sitting there in the audience as a spectator watching him. Judge Noe asked a clerk to notify Cedar Hills and then said, "Mr. Roberts, we are going to continue your case until Thursday morning for sentencing. $500 bail." Charles Roberts walked dejected from the courtroom.

In the months to come other patients would follow like a steady stream going from the treatment center back to skid road, picked up there by the paddy wagon, and taken back to the drunk tank. I knew I could never sit in court again as a detached observer; I would never again see only faceless drunks pleading guilty and receiving their sentences. I could not view these men as merely candidates for an alcoholism treatment center. From now on they would stand there as individuals, men I had listened to, laughed with, shared meals together. Most important, now I knew some of the conditions they would suffer as they took their sentences, turned away from the judge, and walked back into the jail in quiet desperation. As I left the courtroom that day I wondered more than ever about the sign that had stared down at me for months from high over the judge's bench: EQUAL JUSTICE FOR ALL UNDER THE LAW.

V

Almost a year had passed when, one warm September afternoon in 1968, I returned to my office to find a message: "Call Dr. Fred Anderson, Associate Dean of the Medical School." I dialed the number and a secretary answered. "This is Jim Spradley in Psychiatry," I said. "I'm returning Dr. Anderson's call." She sounded as if she expected my voice and said, "Oh, yes, Dr. Spradley, could you come in tomorrow morning at 9:30?" "Yes," I said, "I probably could, what is it about?" She said she would check if I could hold a moment. I'd never met the Associate Dean and I thought it must be some general meeting or perhaps a committee. The secretary's voice came back on the line, "It's about the problems with the police department." I hung up the phone, leaned back in my chair, and picked up an old issue of the Seattle *Post-Intelligencer* that lay on my desk. "I wonder what he'll have to say?" I thought to myself as my eyes scanned the three-week-old headlines: SEATTLE'S DRUNK TANK: A PLACE OF FILTH, STENCH, HUMAN DEGRADATION. I started reading again that paper of August 13, 1968.

> Seen through the eyes of a Skid Road alcoholic, Seattle's City Jail is an overcrowded jungle of concrete and steel.
> It is a place of filth, stench, sleeplessness and human degradation.
> It is a place where you are lucky to get enough to eat or adequate medical attention.

It is a place where the poor stay longer and suffer more.

This is the sordid picture drawn in an 88-page report just completed by Dr. James P. Spradley, assistant professor of psychiatry and anthropology at the University of Washington.

The report is based on interviews during the past year with 101 Skid Road men who have been arrested at least once for public drunkenness.

Spradley undertook the research project to find out if there is any therapeutic value in arresting an alcoholic and throwing him in jail.

He found that the men he questioned looked on their jail experience as much more detrimental than therapeutic. Of the alcoholics he surveyed:

— 83 percent said they had spent at least one night in the jail's drunk tank when it was so crowded they couldn't lie down.

— 93 percent reported that there is only one cup in the drunk tank from which those confined there may drink.

— 98 percent said they had never been given a receipt for money or property taken from them when they were booked into the jail, and 40 percent said police had taken money from their effects while they were in jail.

— 56 percent rated medical care they received in jail as very poor and 46 percent said they had not been able to get medical attention they needed while they were in the drunk tank. . . .

The article continued with more statistics and quotes from the men interviewed. I skipped to the second page of the paper and scanned the other stories: POLICE ABUSE ON SKID ROAD? read one. Another said, SOME ALCOHOLICS THINK POLICE ARREST THEM TO GET TRUSTIES. At the top of the page a small item gave me the most satisfaction. It read,

New emphasis on rehabilitation

The survey of Skid Road alcoholics by Dr. James P. Spradley was made public yesterday only four days after the City Council's Public Safety Committee recommended establishment of a detoxification center for handling public drunks.

Councilman Tim Hill said the purpose of the proposed ordinance is to change the handling of indigent alcoholics from a police matter to a public health procedure.

"The new emphasis," he said, "is on treatment and rehabilitation."

I folded the paper, placed it with a stack of others at the back of my desk, picked up my briefcase and headed for my car, thinking all the while about Dr. Anderson and my appointment the following day.

It was shortly after nine o'clock the next morning when I drove into the staff parking lot at the University Hospital. As I headed for the

Dean's office I thought about the repetitious courtroom drama being enacted at that very moment in downtown Seattle. I wondered how many of the men I would recognize if I had been there this morning. I smiled to myself as I thought about Judge James Noe's recent comment: "Immediately following the news story of your research report the number of drunks on the court docket dropped off significantly," he had said, and then added with a twinkle in his eye, "Maybe that was the only way they could keep the jail clean enough for all the visitors coming through."

Dr. Anderson's secretary showed me to his office and he rose to shake my hand; a soft-spoken physician in his middle fifties, he seemed friendly and interested. "Well," he said, getting right to the point, "I'd like to discuss with you your study of the alcoholic. I've read it and I think it's quite a good study, but I'd be interested in discussing with you how this might be handled in the future to prevent this kind of thing that took place." My pulse quickened and I asked him, "What do you mean, *prevent*?" I tried to appear calm and unconcerned but I was beginning to feel warm and my voice sounded defensive. "Well," he answered, "I mean, perhaps there is some other way it could be handled that might have made it better, perhaps it would have been better to have it delivered at a scientific meeting and then it would have gotten out that way."

By this time I was angry but I tried not to show it. "I can't agree," I said, my voice rising slightly. "If I'd presented the report at a scientific meeting or published it in some journal hardly anyone would have read it and it wouldn't have done much good." I could see the next question coming. "By the way, how did the papers get your report?" Calmly, without hesitating, I looked directly at him and said, "I gave it to them." His mouth dropped open and he looked at me in disbelief.

And so I told him how I had been a member of the Ad Hoc Committee for the Indigent Public Intoxicant set up by Councilman Tim Hill who wanted me to contribute the perspective of the Skid Road Alcoholic. We had met for months to plan a detoxification center as an alternative to jailing men found drunk in public. Judge James Noe was a member of the committee; so was an inspector from the police department, one or two physicians, and others involved in work with alcoholics. We had met for months to plan a detoxification center as an alternative to jailing men found drunk in public. I explained how the committee had been under the pressure of a possible Supreme Court ruling, the case of *Powell* v. *Texas*, how everyone expected the decision would make all drunk laws unconstitutional, and how they agreed that Seattle should set up a detoxification program to prepare for the coming change. Then, early in the summer, the Supreme Court had ruled against Powell, leaving all the state and local drunk laws intact. When our committee had met after that, many members voiced the opinion that now we did not have to plan a detoxification center. Even the physicians on the committee agreed; one man from the University Medical School had said, "I find it hard put to think that any other facility is going to be able to offer better care, other than the bar bit, than the jail." That meeting had convinced me that I should finish up my report and release it. I gave copies to the members of the committee, sent one to the Mayor of Seattle, to the Police Department, to the criminal court, and to members of the Seattle City Council. I had then called the editor of the Seattle *Post-Intelligencer* and gave him a copy.

He listened with interest to my long explanation and then zeroed in on the report itself. "I read the report and I used to work in King County emergency ward. I know the conditions, a lot of men dying in the drunk tank, and I learned quite a bit from your paper, especially about the bail system, and that sort of thing. But I noticed you always commented, even though the statistics might be that only 20 percent experienced some negative feature, you still make a comment in your paper. The bias is toward the negative side of the picture."

By now I was more relaxed and I agreed with him. "That very likely is true," I said, "but no one can do scientific research completely free from bias. I attempted to be impartial but I certainly don't feel that I achieved it fully. I'm willing to take the responsibility for that. But you have to understand that this report was prepared to shed light on a specific issue. The argument today is over whether the jail is therapeutic or not; the Supreme Court decision was based, in part, on the view that jailing a drunk has a therapeutic value for him. In view of this opinion and the fact that many people contend that jails *are* therapeutic, I felt we should hear from those who had repeatedly experienced being jailed for public drunkenness. I presented my data in terms of this issue and I say that in the report."

We talked on for some time about the report and the problem of alcoholics. Dr. Anderson said he was sympathetic with my approach in many ways and that it had not been his idea to call me in. As we drew near the end of our discussion I asked him, "How do you think it might have been handled differently?" He thought for a moment and then said, "Well, perhaps not releasing it to the press as you did. If you could have allowed it to slip out to the press through the subcommittee, then you would have preserved your own kind of scholarly identity in the University."

VI

As people who devote their professional lives to understanding man, anthropologists bear a positive responsibility to speak out publicly, both individually and collectively, on what they know and what they believe as a result of their professional expertise gained in the study of human beings. That is, they bear a professional responsibility to contribute to an "adequate definition of reality" upon which public opinion and public policy may be based.

> — Principles of Professional Responsibility
> American Anthropological Association

8

Anthropologist — the myth teller
MILES RICHARDSON

*Field research in cultural anthropology has always been different
from other kinds of social science investigation, and has a human quality that cannot be reduced to a technique or method.
And that human quality involves informants, individuals from
every culture who become teachers to visiting anthropologists.
In this article Miles Richardson explores this relationship between anthropologists and informants. He writes with insight
and feeling about how the relationship has shaped this discipline
in the past, how it has changed in the modern world, and how
it still lies at the core of our mission as anthropologists.*

I was lying in the sack, staring at the walls, trying to fight the boredom
of my last year in the United States Air Force.[1] It's a hard job, fighting
boredom, especially the military kind. I had tried just about everything:
the bars, the hobby shop, the NCO club, the base library, even the TV in
the dayroom. And the job got harder as the time for my discharge
became shorter. So I was there, waiting, with a mind as empty as I could

Reprinted by permission of the author and the American Anthropological
Association from *American Ethnologist* 2(3), 1975. References are omitted.

[1] I completed the first draft of this article while on sabbatical leave, fall
semester, 1973, and I thank Dr. Irwin A. Berg, Dean of the College of Arts and
Sciences, and the administration of Louisiana State University for granting the
sabbatical. Sam Hilliard, Joyce Rockwood Hudson, Valerie Richardson, and Donald
Vermeer made helpful comments. I particularly thank Ward Goodenough and
Charles Hudson for their encouragement and Charles for his sharp editorial eye.
Illusions do not elude him. Of course, I am solely responsible for this attempt to
write about anthropology.
Because being an anthropologist is an intense thing, I have tried to write
intensely, and, I hope, skillfully. Maybe I'm a frustrated novelist, but I can't help
but feel that there is a place in professional journals for articles that make the
reader grunt and say goddamn. If I were still a Southern Baptist, I would say that
I was writing an inspirational piece, somewhere between Billy Graham's "The Hour
of Decision" and Martin Luther King's "I Have a Dream."

get it. Then it was there. Fresh. Immediate. Complete. It was almost frightening, almost unbelievable, but it became bigger, more exhilarating, more definite. Then it was me, and I decided. I was going to be an anthropologist.

My decision to be an anthropologist continues to amaze me. Even now, twenty years later, I'm still not sure where that idea came from. Certainly my background was not an intellectual one. My father had found his fourth grade education sufficient to move him from a tenant farm to the railroad shops. He read the newspaper and the Bible, and that's all. And I had his scorn for intellectual things. I did read a lot, more than my friends, and the closest I came to an academic award was being second to the top most user of the library at David Crockett High School in Palestine, Texas. Of course, I wasn't reading Shakespeare. I liked historical and frontier novels, but my favorites were westerns — ones by Max Brand, Peter Field, Luke Short, Zane Grey, and especially Will James. Among my classes in school, I liked vocational agriculture. I sent off for extension pamphlets and taught myself how to recognize crazy chick disease and to grow lespedeza. Otherwise I was content to copy term papers, make up book reports, and pester my English teacher, a sweet lady who talked about *Gone with the Wind* with tears in her eyes. So perhaps it is not surprising that in my senior year, having finished my football eligibility and with nothing else to live for, I quit high school and joined the Air Force.

Yet I know that in this background were the reasons why I became an anthropologist. The principal reason was that I was raised as a Southern Baptist. You would think that a person with an intense religious upbringing would become someone compatible with that background, like a school teacher maybe, or a minister, or best of all, a football player. And people often do. One of my brothers was a preacher, and my sister married one. But it didn't work out that way with me. Actually, that's not too uncommon either. I suspect that for every minister the Southern Baptists have produced, they have turned out five atheists. Pound for pound, the Baptists have probably put more souls in hell than has any other religion. And I'm one of them.

It was in my early adolescence that I discovered I was evil. Because I was evil, I was going to die. Those people who had placed their trust in their personal Savior, those who believed in him and were saved, would live forever. Not me; I was going to die. I tried hard not to be evil. I did not swear, I did not smoke, and certainly I did not drink. I didn't play dominoes nor go to the movies on Sunday. I went to church twice on Sunday plus attending the morning Sunday School and the evening Training Union. I tried to think pure thoughts, and that's what really counted: what you were inside. In the Baptist doctrine good works don't save you; it is your inner surrender to Jesus, placing yourself totally in his hands, that brings you peace and everlasting life. No matter how often you go to church, how frequently you pray, or how much money you put in the collection plate, you are not saved until you turn yourself over to Jesus. The only way you know you are saved is that you know. But how could I be sure of such a thing? Surely a saved person always thought clean thoughts, and here I was, looking at girls with lust on my mind and even stealing glances at the big-bosomed preacher's wife. How could I be saved? What could I do to escape death?

"Look to Jesus," the preacher said. But Jesus was a Lévi-Strauss paradox. Jesus-Christ-God was perfect femininity. He was kind, sweet, and full of love. Safe on his gentle breast I would lie. He so loved me that he bled and died on Calvary's tree; he was the gentle Savior who would hear my humble cry. Jesus-Christ-God was perfect masculinity. He was Father, King, Lord, and Master. He was Victor over death and his blood was full of power. He taught gentleness and peace; he sent people to burn forever in hell. How could I touch such a figure? How could I get him to respond? I tried. I searched for a way that I could feel this God and know that I was not abandoned, and alone, and apart, and dead. I have never tried anything harder nor wanted anything more. But I did not succeed, and then I knew I hated God.

My discovery was my salvation. Moved by the bright joy of perfect hate, I put aside Will James and began to read to find out why people were what they were (and why I was what I was). I read erratically, bits and pieces of this and that, stumbling, giving up, and then going in different directions, burning with conflicting emotions, and most of all, alone. Early in my search, I read Thomas Paine's *Age of Reason*, and his challenge to established religion thrilled me. Somewhere along the line I tried E. B. Tylor's *Primitive Culture*, but its nineteenth-century sentence structure was too much. Later I found a list of definitions that I had carefully taken from it: "Animism: the belief in spirits; Fetichism: the worship of stone and objects." Just before I decided to become an anthropologist, I was reading travel-adventure books by Dana and Ginger Lamb, husband and wife, who struggled through deserts, bandits, and inhospitable jungles to find lost cities in Latin America. The picture of myself paddling up a tropical river with some pretty blonde thing on the bow of my dugout was irresistible.

If my idea of anthropology was limited to flashes of myself in romantic situations, my feelings about it and what I wanted from it were full and strong. I wanted freedom. To me, anthropology was liberation. It was going to free me from the view of man groveling before a God that, on the one hand was sweetly sissy and on the other remotely brutal, from a religion that makes the gentle touching between a man and a woman evil, and from a culture that wants to destroy all who read and question. It was going to free me from the memory of seeing families scratching out a living on a half acre of scrub cotton and of hearing my father say to a neighbor, "You know Will, the principal over at Swanson's Springs? He's one of them. He comes to the front door. He doesn't go around to the back, like a good nigger."

Although anthropology was my way out, my freedom would come not from forgetting these things, nor would it come from being a part of movements to change them. I would never be a joiner. After the First Baptist Church, I had had it with formal organizations. Later, in graduate school, when my best friend asked if I would join CORE and the sit-ins that were beginning in New Orleans in the early 1960s, I told him no, that I was going to finish my dissertation. My freedom from the things that nearly destroyed me (and that continue to haunt me) would come from studying them, from wrestling with them in order to expose their secret. At that point, just short of stomping on them and destroying them, for some reason my private battle stops. Today, I have no love for the Southern Baptists, but I can almost say "Billy Graham" without sneering.

After having decided to be an anthropologist and after being discharged, I took my Korean GI Bill and started to get an education. I knew Harvard didn't want no high school dropout from Palestine, Texas, so I enrolled in a local junior college. I worked my way up from there, through undergraduate college and into graduate school. I went into the field, not with a blonde thing, but with a beautiful, brown-haired wife from England, and together we made it through. I struggled with a dissertation, and there I was, some ten years after it had happened, an anthropologist.

Now that I was one, now that I am one, what is it, being an anthropologist?

Being an anthropologist is to be critical, critical of one's self, of one's profession, and of one's society. Critical and suspicious, almost paranoiac. The anthropologist is an academician. He is nearly always located in a university, and the nature of university life, isolated to a degree from the rest of society but dependent in large measure for its existence on that society, each year coming to grips with a new set of students, naive and sophisticated, demanding and apathetic, produces an individual drawn tight with contradictions: a person who arrogantly attacks ignorance but wistfully pleads with the state legislature or the board of trustees, who teaches the love of learning but jealously erects walls between academic departments, and who believes that the search of knowledge is an end in itself but worries at night that his colleagues are advancing faster, gaining more prestige, and earning more money than he. But the critical sensitivity of the anthropologist seems to go beyond that of the academician. You have only to attend the annual meetings of the American Anthropological Association to realize that in the anthropologist you have more than just your ordinary, run-of-the-classroom professor.

Each year, at the time of Thanksgiving, anthropologists in the United States gather together in order to reexamine their collective soul. In search of expiation, individuals stand before their colleagues and accuse each other of exploiting the people whom they study for their own selfish advancement, of being unwitting tools of neocolonial powers, and worse, of being committed counter-subversives employed by the CIA or the Defense Department to study ways in which the United States can continue to maintain control over its client countries. Strong stuff for a boy from east Texas. To be sure, such self-vilification is not restricted to anthropologists; other professional societies also annually lay out their reason for being and pick it apart, looking for defects. And there are anthropologists, perhaps the confident minority, who feel no need for self-analysis and attend the meetings in order to exchange ideas with their friends. Yet the accusations that anthropologists hurl at each other contrast so sharply with the image of the anthropologist as a sympathetic spokesman for the small, the weak, and the forgotten that I have to try to explain it.

That's a big order. Such an explanation would have to examine the makeup of academia and of American society. Like everyone else, anthropologists are part and parcel of the society in which they move about. No more than their informants can anthropologists escape the biases of their home culture. Also, anthropologists vary, so their discontent varies. Do the physical anthropologist (the solid scientist), the archeologist (the dirt scientist), and the linguist (the elegant scientist) share the same discontent of the enthnologist (the uncertain scientist)? Perhaps in a way they do; they are all concerned about the future of anthropology. Yet probably because I am one, I can't escape the feeling that the ethnologist is at least more vocal about what worries him. Indeed, the ethnologist occupies a key position in the science. Because he considerably outnumbers anthropologists in the other specialities and because he has the general knowledge necessary to teach the introductory course, the ethnologist is frequently the person through whom the student meets anthropology. The student may specialize in one of the other fields, but he will enter that field with an ethnological notion of what anthropology is about. So although my partial explanation of anthropological self-criticism will limit itself to the ethnologist, it should be applicable to a degree to the rest of anthropology.

The distinguishing feature of ethnological research is ethnographic fieldwork. In the field the relationship most critical to the ethnographer, the one that actually changes him from tourist to ethnographer, is the relationship with his informant. Whenever you think of the ethnologist in the field, you think of him as an ethnographer talking long hours with his informant. The ethnographer does many other things. He collects figures about rainfall, crop yield, population density, migration, educational levels, and per capita income; he scans newspaper articles about local issues, important persons, and recent events; and he reads historical accounts about past patterns of kinship, religious life, social stratification, and livelihoods. He watches to see how busy the market is, how friends behave, what happens at the soccer match, if men drink on Sunday, and whether the devout are always women. But sooner or later the ethnographer feels that he must spend more time with his informant, for the informant has the type of knowledge that the ethnographer must have in order to understand this community.

Who is this person who defines, even creates, the ethnographer?[2] First, he is an informant, not an informer. An informer squeals to the cops. He passes on information about the activities of criminals to the police, and then the police arrest the criminals. An informant may pass on information about illegal activity to the ethnographer, but the ethnographer never arrests anyone. The informant is not an informer partly because the ethnographer is not a cop. This means that the ethnographer defines the informant. How can that be? If the informant defines the ethnographer, and the ethnographer the informant, how do they ever find each other? Sometimes they don't. Only after considerable trial and error does the ethnographer-informant relationship emerge.

The informant is not a subject. A subject is a person, or an animal, perhaps even a plant, that the experimenter takes out of its natural surroundings and puts into a laboratory so that the experimenter is better able to control the variables that may influence the subject's responses. In order to avoid subject bias, the experimenter sometimes tells the subject — when it is a person — that the experimenter is testing one response when in reality he is testing another. An informant is always a person, never an animal, who cannot exist apart from his natural surroundings. The ethnographer may deceive the informant, but he does so at his peril, for the informant is free to reciprocate and deceive the ethnographer.

The informant is not an interviewee. An interviewee answers questions, frequently highly structured, that an investigator asks, or frequently reads, from a form. This exchange, the interview, may last for as

[2] The description of the informant and of the ethnographer-informant relationship draws on the literature and on my fieldwork, a year and a half in Colombia (1962–1963) and three summers in Costa Rica (1967, 1972, 1973).

long as two or three hours, but often it is shorter, and when it is finished so is the tie between the interviewee and the investigator. Only the single strand of the interview connects them, but several strands tie the ethnographer and the informant together. An informant talks with the ethnographer about a wide range of topics, wandering here, backtracking there. The ethnographer listens more than he talks. When the conversation gradually ends, the ethnographer may ask the informant who in the local community is a good doctor, what is the best day to go to the market, and could he keep an eye on the ethnographer's house while the ethnographer goes to the capital for the next two days. The informant may ask does the United States still have the death penalty, why are so many black people poor in America, and could the ethnographer give him a ride to the city.

The informant is not necessarily a friend. The ties that bind the ethnographer and the informant may create a friendship, and it is difficult to see how an ethnographer or an informant could work with someone they hate. Yet the relationship in itself is not one of friendship. The ethnographer must ask probing questions; he cannot, as one does with friends, accept the informant as the person he is, but the ethnographer must find out, he has to find out, why the informant believes what he does. He goes to the informant seeking knowledge, and the informant becomes his instructor.

The informant is the teacher of the ethnographer. His job is to teach this stranger all that he knows. He explains the strategy of building a house, the characteristics of an extended family, and the meaning of the festival of the dead; he details how he makes pottery, how he reckons kin, and how he confronts sorrow; and he ponders with the ethnographer why cattle are sacred, why brothers are loyal, and why flowers are evil. For his job as teacher, the informant may be paid, not only in favors but also in cash. But he is not an employee; the ethnographer cannot fire him. With the informant as his teacher, the ethnographer struggles to comprehend the details and the meanings of a culture in which he is a student. In the concrete facts of this particular culture, in the knowledge of this particular informant, there is somewhere, if only the ethnographer were wise enough to see it, a key to the whole human story.

Without the informant, the ethnographer cannot carry out his task. The ethnographer can go only so far with figures, newspapers, and histories, and even with observations. To complete his work, he has to turn to the informant; without the informant, he cannot be an ethnographer. Because the informant is so central to the ethnographer's reason for being, any change in the informant or in his relationship to the ethnographer, and any change in his society's relationship to the ethnographer's, will create anxiety in the ethnographer, and through him stress in ethnology, and ultimately conflict in anthropology. This is what has happened, and this is why anthropology's self-criticism is at its present strident pitch.

The traditional pattern of relationships between the informant and the ethnographer, like so many of our activities, grew out of the nineteenth century. This was a vigorous period of development for Western civilization. Externally, it was characterized by renewed expansion, by a rejuvenated colonialism; internally it was marked by the development of academic disciplines, one of which was anthropology. As anthropology developed into a science, it became more and more conscious of the need to collect hard data against which it could check its various theories about the biological and cultural development of men. Because Western civilization was only one array of data among many, only one culture in a world of cultures, anthropologists needed data outside of Western civilization. Earlier, they had relied on the accounts of travelers and missionaries; now they began to collect the data themselves. Because of the state of the world (the ordered relationships among societies, the facilities that the growing number of anthropologists had access to, and the development of transportation) the ethnographers were now able to go to other societies and to study their ways of life. Many of these societies were subordinate to one or another of those that comprised Western civilization, and so at its very beginnings ethnography was the study of subjected people controlled by the ethnographer's society. It was in this environment that the pattern of ethnographic fieldwork developed.

The setting in which the ethnographer and the informant came together was polarized by power and cultural differences. The two societies, the ethnographer's and the informant's, were asymmetrically paired: the ethnographer's was powerful, the informant's weak. The two cultures were likewise different: the ethnographer's literate, massive, and complex; the informant's often preliterate, delicate, and direct. The two individuals were equally dissimilar: the ethnographer was white, spoke an Indo-European language, and was highly educated; the informant was black, red, or yellow, spoke Ibo, Sioux, or Yapese, and was illiterate. However, the ethnographer-informant relationship was structured opposite to the thrust of their setting. The informant occupied the higher, dominant position and the ethnographer the lower, subordinate one. As a member of a distinct, exotic culture, the informant was a man of wisdom, schooled in the traditions of his people. The ethnographer was a trained student; his education had keyed him to discover, to find out, to learn the things that the informant knew.

The ethnographer was in the field to gather data in order to test out different theories about the biological and cultural development of men. Although these theories were most fully expressed in Western civilization, the theories — evolutionary, diffusionist, historical — were not models for Western neocolonialism. On the contrary. Seen in the context of their times, the earlier theorists were caught up in the effort to document the march of mankind, and with their theories they did battle against religious dogmatism, degeneration, and racism. Who can match their record? You have only to read the last sentence of Tylor's *Primitive Culture* to learn that anthropology is a "reformer's science," that the study of culture is a way to combat absolutism and is a path to freedom. The ideology in late nineteenth- and early twentieth-century anthropology was not the ideology of colonial oppression, but of scientific humanism.

As a result of the interplay between the ethnographer, as a scientific humanist, and the informant, as a man of wisdom, striving to communicate across the structural gap that separated their societies, the pattern of fieldwork developed. As time moved, as the early years of the twentieth century came and went, as the colonial powers fought each other for dominance over the informants' societies, the ethnographer tried to find a niche for himself. Guided internally by the need for scientific objectivity, he self-consciously defined himself as different from other whites — from the trader, the missionary, the bureaucrat — and as a person dedicated not to exploiting, not to converting, not to administering, but to understanding the informant's culture. Although in some cases heavily modified by the impact of Western civilization, the informant's culture was still complete, still with its own tools, houses, kinsmen, and religious festivals. The great myths that glorified the history of his people were still fresh on his tongue; the deeds of the great heroes, men and women who fought for their culture, still sparkled in his eyes. The ethnographer took on the task of studying this culture, of describing it in all of its richness before it began to crumble and die. This task led the ethnographer into the interior of the culture, and he began to see it as an elegant balance of technology, kinship, and religion, as a work of art whose beauty lay in the way in which the parts were counterbalanced and interrelated. Yet, the ethnographer's own society, powerful, aggressive, commercial (but also humane), was ripping apart this centuries' old portrait of harmony. Caught between his humanistic appreciation of the informant's culture and his membership in a society destroying that culture, between life and death, the ethnographer searched for understanding, and perhaps forgiveness.

The ethnographer sought understanding in the theories of cultural holism and in the methodology of cultural relativism. The holistic theories viewed particular cultures as forming patterns or configurations in which cultural traits were interrelated in either a value-thematic sense or in a functional-causal one. These theories emerged as a reaction against the "shreds and patches" view of culture in which cultural traits, such as the tipi, the travois, the circular shield were independent units that diffused across the landscape (and sometimes across oceans). Ethnologists of the earlier schools had been using cultural traits to reconstruct the history of cultures. With the exception of the Olympian figure of Kroeber, ethnologists of the holistic school had little interest in the native past and were downright hostile to the idea of cultural evolution. They also seemed uninterested in the ways in which the informant's culture responded to its position at the bottom of the asymmetrical power structure. When they did write about change, it was into the specific past of particular cultures that they looked, as in the case of Africanisms; or it was how individuals in the subordinate society were becoming members of the superordinate society, as in the case of acculturation. This was true of the value-thematic-configurationist school in the United States; the British functionalist approach had even less use for history. "Pseudo-history" was what Radcliffe-Brown called the efforts of the cultural historians. Working at a time when their own society was everywhere penetrating into the societies of their informants, the holistic ethnologists paradoxically adopted a timeless view of culture. A particular culture was a beautiful monad, a configuration of balanced interrelationships, vibrant, delicate, but contained.

Given such a view of culture, the methodological premise of cultural relativism was a logical development. As a tool for research, cultural relativism said that in order to understand any one particular aspect of a culture, you had to see how it was related to the other aspects. In order to understand the Plains Indians' response to death, the gashing of heads and legs, the cutting off of fingers, the destruction of the dead person's lodge, the reluctance of the widow to leave the grave, you had to see how these traits were related to the overall pattern of Dionysian individualism in Plains Indian culture. And in order to understand the Pueblo Indians' reaction to death, the somber funeral feast, the ceremonial closing of the lodge door prohibiting the dead from reentering his home, the firm speech of the chief telling the bereaved that the dead is gone and "They shall not remember any more," you have to view these traits against the Apollonian harmony of Pueblo culture.

As a tool for research, cultural relativism was a significant advance in ethnography. And it remains so today. It belongs to that set of ethnographic core values that says to take cultures as they come, don't prejudge them, don't impose your own ethnocentric categories upon them. In order to comprehend any item of a people's culture, you have to view that item in its sociocultural context. Cultural relativism is as much a part of the ethnographer's tool kit as are field notes, tape recorders, and cameras.

But cultural relativism was more than a methodological tool for research; it was a moral justification for being an anthropologist. Caught in the interplay between scientific humanism, the drive for human freedom, and the encounter with a living, exotic culture threatened by the same civilization that produced the drive, the ethnographer found a sense of mission in cultural relativism. His mission was to preach the doctrine of cultural differences, to lecture to his own society that there is no one path to the solution of human problems. He spoke clearly, "Here is a way of life that through the centuries has found some of the secrets of human existence. The way of our society is not the only way. Look upon this culture and be humble." This was the ethnographer's reason for being: a sort of cultural interpreter who sought to bring the intricate beauty of a fully integrated culture to the notice of his people, so that they would be less arrogant and would administer their power with more sympathy.

The cultural relativists did not study how the power of their society structured the cultures of their informants; rather, they attacked the problem of power obliquely. Horrified by the ethnocentrism of their own colonialist society, the cultural relativists protested that all cultures express equally valid solutions to the human problem and that people (and especially ethnographers) cannot be God and decide which culture is the best. Since the cultures that they studied were still whole, distinct cultures (or could be so reconstructed from the accounts of older informants), they felt strong in their arguments. Perhaps they were naive. But they were the first people in history to immerse themselves systematically, consciously, into a totally foreign culture for the explicit purpose of understanding that culture on its own terms, without any official purpose other than being an ethnographer, without any cultural hull they could hide in when the going got rough — naked, exposed, raw. Reborn by the field experience they returned from that experience as a new breed of humans. Their hope, their mission, lay in convincing other people of the validity of that experience.

So were the ethnographers before World War II and before the Nazis. Out of the spread of Western neocolonialism and from the development of anthropology as a discipline, they evolved a new method of learning: fieldwork. Fieldwork began as a means of gathering data in order to prove or disprove theories of biological and cultural evolution. In time it developed into a fixed pattern with a theory of cultures, with a methodological tool, and with a moral justification. Practiced most brilliantly by Margaret Mead, it was described most romantically by Bronislaw Malinowski:

Soon after I had established myself in Omarakana (Trobriand Islands), I began to take part, in a way, in the village life, to look forward to the important or festive events, to take personal interest in the gossip and the developments of the small village occurrences; to wake up every morning to a day, presenting itself to me more or less as it does to the native. I would get out from under my mosquito net, to find around me the village life beginning to stir, or the people well advanced in their working day according to the hour and also to the season, for they get up and begin their labours early or late, as work presses. As I went on my morning walk through the village, I could see intimate details of family life, of toilet, cooking, taking of meals; I could see the arrangements for the day's work, people starting on their errands, or groups of men and women busy at some manufacturing tasks. Quarrels, jokes, family scenes, events usually trivial, sometimes dramatic but always significant, formed the atmosphere of my daily life, as well as of theirs. It must be remembered that as the natives saw me constantly every day, they ceased to be interested or alarmed, or made self-conscious by my presence, and I ceased to be a disturbing element in the tribal life which I was to study, altering it by my very approach, as always happens with a new-comer to every savage community. In fact, as they knew that I would thrust my nose into everything, even where a well-mannered native would not dream of intruding, they finished by regarding me as part and parcel of their life, a necessary evil or nuisance, mitigated by donations of tobacco.

The traditional pattern of fieldwork, the asymmetrical pairing of the two societies, the great differences between the two cultures, the informant as a man of wisdom and the ethnographer as his student, and the moral justification for being an anthropologist became a part of the subculture of ethnography and of anthropology. This became the image of the ethnographer in the field and the model he used to guide his activities. This was the notion that I carried into the field, and like many of my contemporaries, I found it archaic.

I was just beginning to wake up when a great voice boomed into the patio and blasted me into my mosquito net. "People of San Pedro. Arise! Men to the fields. Children to school. And come to mass Sunday. If you don't, you will turn into Communists or Protestants." A nice guy in other ways, the new priest enjoyed hearing his voice amplified to godlike proportions by the loud speaker located on top of the church steeple, a block from my house. I fought my way through the mosquito net and got my feet on the floor. I leaned down and pulled my machete out from under the mattress. I looked at it a minute, vaguely wondering what I would do if some of the thieves that supposedly lived in San Pedro ever decided to rob me. Doña Leonor had warned me about them, "Listen

mister, you've got to be more careful. Yesterday I passed by your house
and saw that your window was open. The thieves will look in and see
all your things, and at night they will climb over the patio wall and cut
your throat." I hung the machete up and let my dog out into the back
yard. He was a big, black, but very friendly Labrador that in a period of
homesickness, I had named "Tex." He had a loud, deep bark that Doña
Leonor approved of. I belched up last night's *aguardiente* and almost
threw up as the sweet, sticky taste of white rum spread into my mouth.
I turned on my water faucet and looked with dismay at the brown sludge
that came out of it. With my teeth still furry, I went down the street to
buy the morning bread. "The bread hasn't come yet, *mister,*" snapped
the store lady. She turned to another customer, "Look at this, would
you." She spread the newspaper out before his disbelieving eyes.
"Colombia! What a rotten country!" she exclaimed. I peeked over their
shoulders at the front page photograph of a naked body with its head
by its feet. The caption explained that a bandit group, led by *capitán
Tarzán,* had murdered peasants in a mountain village and had mutilated
the bodies. The store lady went on several minutes about how the rich
were hiring the bandits to drive peasants away from their land, so that
the rich could buy the property at a bargain price.

Later that morning, I thought I would be like Malinowski and walk
through the village, etc., so I got Tex and went out. The men had left for
their work, the women were cleaning house behind closed doors and
windows, and the kids were in school. But at least Tex enjoyed it. Being
a Labrador, he couldn't resist jumping into a large spring boxed in with
concrete. As I called him out, a man walking by muttered, *"Gringos!*
Washing their dogs in water that people bathe in." Back at my house, I
was writing field notes, when Seneca came. "I can't go with you today
to visit the tobacco factory. I've got to go to Tuluá and get some medicine
for my mother. We're out of money. Look, *doctor,* could you loan me
two hundred pesos. Thanks. Look, *doctor,* could you speak to your *jefe,*
to the chief of your organization, about me. I know that if you will do
that, he'll hire me. You'll do that, will you? That's all it will take. Just
a word on your part. You are out of cigarettes? Here, I've got one."
Seneca left. For a minute I stood at the doorway and looked at the deserted plaza and across the plaza to the valley and then at the Andes
mountains, rising up to meet the clouds. I shut the door, picked up my
guitar, and thought about Hank Williams and Palestine, Texas.

The traditional model of fieldwork, up in the clouds of Malinowskian romanticism, did not signify when applied to the reality of the
world emerging in the 1950s and the 1960s. The traditional pattern grew
out of the neocolonialism of the late nineteenth century; the new pattern
of fieldwork struggles to take form in the revolutionary turbulence of
the second half of the twentieth century.

The setting in which the ethnographer and the informant work today is still polarized by cultural and power differences. However, these differences are far less sharp than before. The two societies remain asymmetrically paired, but the informant's society has gained considerable power while the ethnographer's society has lost some. The society of the informant is now at least nominally free of the ethnographer's, and, in some cases, it may exercise considerable independence for varying lengths of time. The Arab oil embargo of 1973–1974 is one example. How much real power and true freedom the developing societies have is difficult to assess. Yet in comparison with their status in the traditional pattern of fieldwork, the societies of the informants have gained power.

Moreover, the ethnographer of today comes from a background considerably different from that traditionally associated with anthropology in the United States. At least according to anthropological folklore, ethnographers of the older tradition were largely from the upper classes. Their families were families of solid substance, or they were connected to ones that were. Several had wealthy patrons. The environment in which they grew up was an intellectual one; their relatives were people who valued learning. Nearly all were born in the great cities of the northeast, and ethnically they often were Jewish, German, or Old American. Frequently, they were close, personal friends or close, personal enemies. Beginning after World War II and especially since the Korean War, changes in American society, the rising standard of living, more governmental support for education, and increased urbanization have widened the recruiting base for anthropology. No doubt many continue to come from the upper classes, but also many emerge from the lower levels. They come from backgrounds that ordinarily do not supply academicians. While probably few are ex-Southern Baptists, many are children of parents who earned modest incomes and who placed little faith in education. A substantial number were born in smaller cities and towns in different parts of the country, and while still predominantly white, they are more ethnically diverse than were previous anthropologists. Compelled by the contradictory forces within them, they break the ties with their background and look for a style of life to replace the one of their rough and ready fathers. They adopt the academic style, but it wears unevenly. They overcompensate here, undercompensate there. They are what they scorn in others; they are status-aspiring; they are Archie Bunkers with PhDs. When they go into the field, they carry these scars with them. Insecure in themselves, perhaps they find insecure people to study.

The same changes that have broadened the recruiting base for anthropologists have also popularized anthropology. Earlier, general knowledge about anthropology was restricted to a few who believed that anthropology was to the social sciences what physics was to the natural sciences: intellectual, competent, cool. Currently, while still retaining some of its elitist charm and derring-do, anthropology, like the submarine sandwich, is becoming massified. It seems to be on its way to becoming just another social studies requirement that freshmen have to take, with the anthropologist just another vague, gray figure, barely perceptible against the backdrop of blackboard and chalk dust.

Similarly, the informant — the embodiment of a culture that through the centuries has worked out its deep, smooth solutions to the problems of human existence — is now a tarnished figure barely visible against the backdrop of television, rock music, Charlton Heston, and beer bottles. Even though his race is often different, culturally the informant and his society resemble more and more the ethnographer and his society. While in *recent* times, the ethnographer's society may have secured special forms of music, new types of literature, and new clothing styles from the informant's society, these are small in comparison to the current massive export of cultural items, from computers to Bat Man, from the ethnographer's society to the informant's. The ethnographer is finding that the informant's culture contains the very attributes that he tried to avoid by leaving his own small town: getting ahead even if it means walking on people; forgetting kinship ties with the poor and maximizing those with the rich; ranking men on how well they can fight and fuck, and ranking women on how empty-headed they can pretend to be; and damning all who study and question.

Either because of the wholesale incorporation of cultural traits or because of the more subtle but effective process of modernization, the informant's culture becomes an impoverished version of the ethnographer's. The sphere of the informant's knowledge is less and less distinctive and more and more restricted. It becomes more difficult for the pair to perform the roles of the man of wisdom instructing his most talented student. Occasionally the structure collapses, and the pair find themselves playing out the farce of the ethnographer as patron and the informant as the unfortunate, who begs favors. The proud primitive now whines; the sensitive student now commands. The massification of the ethnographer. The proletarianization of the informant. Disillusion. Bitterness.

The collapse of the traditional pattern of fieldwork against the reality of the contemporary field experience is a major cause of the feeling of disaster and guilt that permeates ethnology, and through ethnology, American anthropology. The traditional pattern justified the ethnographer's being an ethnographer through the message of cultural relativism which rested on the theory of cultures, of shining monads, intricate, complete, dazzlingly crystal against the black sky of nature.

Once these monads began to merge into a uniform, brown sameness, how could the doctrine of cultural differences have any appeal? Once the informant was a man who fought with Geronimo. Now he is a Saturday drunk in the white man's jail. How can the ethnographer profess that every culture has equally valid solutions to the human problem? How can the ethnographer find a special niche for himself in the informant's society? He bumps into others seeking the same niche, sociologists, political scientists, and local ethnographers (the last, exasperated by the constant demands of foreign social scientists, wish that they all would take their problems and go elsewhere). How can the ethnographer be reborn by immersing himself in a truly different culture, when nearly all cultures are becoming the same and the informant looks more and more like the people from across the tracks? How can he handle the guilt generated by seeing how his society exploits the informant's society, when there is no flash of exotic culture to lure his attention away from shacks built from cardboard and lives built from braggadocio and abnegation?

He can't. The collapse of the traditional model of fieldwork, with its moral justification grounded on the theory and experience of cultural differences, against the uncompromising reality of the contemporary structure has left the ethnographer, ethnology, and to a degree, anthropology without a sense of mission. Without an implicit, shared sense of doing what is right, anthropology in the United States has become unhooked from itself. Different anthropologists race each other in their willingness to accept the most devastating criticism. Some happily agree with the sociologists that we should stop trying to be novelists and become scientists (people who wear white smocks and hire interviewers). Others are painfully delighted with the assertion from minority groups that only a Black can understand the soul of the Black (a statement tediously similar to that of the white supremists who say that only the Southerner can understand the South). Still others suicidally rejoice when one of their fellow anthropologists proclaims that the end of anthropology is at hand.

Currently, anthropologists are at each other's throats with three competing justifications for being an anthropologist: (1) Anthropology is a science and needs no other justification. It seeks to broaden and deepen human knowledge about humans through a search for general principles that are applicable to the study of any particular sociocultural system. Anthropologists as anthropologists should stay clear of political matters, such as passing resolutions about racial injustice or genocide. This is the traditional justification, and today's critics swarm around it like oilmen around sheiks. It is toy-playing in the ivory tower, or worse, its neutral stance is a front for the establishment. (2) Anthropology

should be an applied science. While there is nothing wrong with studying baboons, Folsom points, Adena pottery, and cross-cousin marriage,
the basic purpose of anthropology is the application of its knowledge to
easing the pain of transition from the primitive-peasant condition to the
complex-modern one. At one time the applied approach was the radical
one. Indeed, if another bit of anthropological folklore is accurate, the
Society for Applied Anthropology was formed in protest to the failure
of the American Anthropological Association to take the applied field
seriously. Today, however, the daring young men of yesterday are the
gray beards of the establishment. The best that an applied anthropologist can hope for from his critics is to be called a liberal lackey — a
person whose heart bleeds for the underdog but whose pocketbook is
filled with establishment paychecks. (3) Anthropology should be in the
service of the revolution. This recent justification (which like relevance
and streaking is already at the what-else-is-new level) argues that not
only did anthropology grow out of colonialism, but that it is also
colonialistic. To regain its soul, anthropology must place itself at the
service of the society it studies. It should be prepared to fight for the
informant and his society — even if the informant doesn't feel like
fighting. Critics quickly point to the arrogance of the revolutionary
anthropologist — a person who *knows* what *his* people need. Labels like
bourgeois adventurer and radical chic fly around his head and bug him
constantly.

Where do we go from here? As an ethnologist, I'm not sure. Maybe
that is the best way to be. I like what Dell Hymes says:

> I would hope to see the consensual ethos of anthropology move from a
> liberal humanism, defending the powerless, to a socialist humanism,
> confronting the powerful and seeking to transform the structure of
> power. Yet one can have no illusion of unanimity on all issues. In World
> War I, as Norman Thomas once put it, socialists were killing each other
> as cheerfully as Christians. . . . In a given country three conscientious
> anthropologists might choose three different loyalties — one to a govern-
> ment, one to a group seeking to overthrow it or to secede from its con-
> trol, and one to a village that wished to be left alone by both. . . . Nor
> can we ignore obligations to our families, which we might put ahead of
> all others.

We can begin by saying goodby to Malinowskian primitive anthropology. Once we have purged ourselves of the traditional model, we are
ready to accept the contemporary world on its own terms — a basic
anthropological notion. When we do this, something magical happens.
The real world shifts a bit, and there he is — the informant — the man

of wisdom, clear and distinct, ready, if we will but listen, to instruct us once again in the old, old lesson of being human. Maybe he can't tell us everything there is to know about his culture, but he can tell us something of the mystery of the human enterprise. He is no subject or interviewee, but a person — man or woman — who knows that this is the way life is. All we need to do is to listen.

But how to listen, that's the question. As a scientist, as an applied anthropologist, as a revolutionary? What stance should the ethnographer take, not only as an ethnographer listening to his informant, but also as an anthropologist with a mission? That is a decision that each anthropologist must make for himself. But we must expect tension among ourselves, between us and American society, and even between us and our informants and their societies — particularly their elites. As long as ethnographers continue to occupy the precarious junction between superordinate and subordinate societies, we are going to have the stomachaches of contradictions and ambiguities. These contradictions and ambiguities will make us dissatisfied, and restless, and critical, so that being an anthropologist is like being the marshal of Dodge City back in the rough days of radio drama: "It's a chancy job. It makes a man watchful — and a little lonely."

There is another stance that the anthropologist might take. It is older, much older than being a pure scientist, applied scientist, or revolutionary. That is the stance of the myth teller. The myth teller, the epic poet, stood on the fringes of his society and told of the great struggles between gods and humans, how they fought and how they loved. The poet knew these experiences; he felt their heat and pull, but something within him drove him to the margins of society where he could see all that was happening. There he recorded in his head what took place. What he saw moved him. Before him stood the great hero. Two-thirds god, the hero wanted to do everything, learn everything, and understand everything. Because of the god-part that was in him, he could not accept death and strove to conquer it; but because of the human-part, he failed. He was the tragic hero, magnificent in strength, splendid in appearance, courageous in heart, but with one fatal flaw: he was one-third man. The myth teller saw in the struggles of the hero the lot of man. Man's lot is that he question; but it is equally his lot that he receive no answer.

Being human is being heroic. Back at the time when ice chilled the air and when great mammals trembled the earth with their tread, the human epic began. Out of the turbulence of the Pleistocene we arose. Firm of foot, skillful of hand, quick of thought, and with images dazzling in our eyes, we moved out of Africa and out of the Pleistocene, until now we have explored the earth, walked on the moon, and touched

Jupiter and beyond. We are a biological success. We have made our mark for all to see. Who can challenge what we have done?

The reason for our success is our ability to symbolize experience, to dream of what might be and then to act as if the dreams were real. In us all the flow, and crash, and thunder of the primate experience has become externalized and objectified. We have taken the private learning, the inward emotions, the life experience of the individual primate and through the magic of symbols have externalized it onto our behavior, our sounds, and our tools. What once was mating is now marriage, what once were calls are now words, and what once were termite sticks are now atomic bombs.

The ability to symbolize, to have culture, has made us what we are. We know the world because of culture; because of culture we also know fear. The fear that we humans know is not solely the fear of imminent danger: it is the fear of being evil, of being dead, of being alone. While culture allows us to talk to each other, it also prohibits us from being with one another. We can no longer reach out and touch our other selves; we can only encounter what we imagine others to be. We can't approach our other selves directly, but only as we symbolize the others to be: man, woman, black, white, friend, enemy. No matter how hard we try we cannot escape labeling and being labeled. Labeling is as much a part of us as shells are a part of turtles. Shells allow turtles to exploit a niche in the environment; culture allows us to do the same. No more than the turtle can take off his shell can humans stop symbolizing. Only when the turtle becomes extinct and we blow ourselves up will we both be free of shells and culture. Culture is our blessing; it is also our curse, our fatal flaw.

Like the hero seeking after eternal life, we seek to escape loneliness. Walled in by our prison of culture, we can't reach others. We try, we struggle, we stick out our hands, but find nothing. But we try again, and again find nothing. What made us human, the power to envision a better world, won't let us rest. We push ourselves to the limit of our individual cells and try once more, but again there is nothing. What made us human, the ability to label and to act on those labels, guarantees that we fail.

Reality eludes us since we left the warm comfort of the primate troop. As we struggle to cope with the problem of being human, as we try to adapt to the human condition, we evolve cultural patterns that go in contradictory directions. *We are cruel.* We wage war on our own kind, shooting other people with arrows, cutting their bodies with obsidian swords, blasting them apart with land mines. We starve members of our own societies, building economic systems that produce fat billionaires and thin babies, crying in the night. We grind psyches in the grist mill of religion, tearing apart souls for the Glory of God, in the Highest. *We are magnificent.* With a digging stick and a pebble tool we beat the African savanna at its own game. With torch and red ochre we drew on the cave walls of Europe delicate pictures of wild beasts. With shining metal and finely tuned instruments we went to the moon. Before our story ends, perhaps we will feel Mars beneath us and even walk under the light of a new star. *We are love.* We are brothers; we are sisters. Listen to those of us who speak for all: "As a man I work for the party; as a poet I work for man," César Vallejo, Peruvian Marxist. "From where the sun now stands I will fight no more forever," Chief Joseph, American Indian. "Free at last! Free at last! Thank God Almighty, I'm free at last!" Martin Luther King, Jr., Southern Black. We are these things and more. How can a single species do and be so many contradictory things? The ability to symbolize makes us what we are. It accounts for our successes; it is the reason for our failures. Being a human is an impossible task, but it is our task.

The anthropologist's job is to tell of that task, to glorify man by composing and reciting with skill and passion the human myth. Like the poet recording the exploits of the epic hero, the anthropologist mythicizes the human record. He takes the discrete bits of human data, the pelvic girdle, Acheulean handaxes, Eskimo kinship, and phonemic contrasts, and narrates the human story, how we came to be, how we fought in the past, how we live today. As teller of the human story, the anthropologist cannot falsify what we are. He seeks to find the full range of human variation, the cruelty, the magnificence, the love that is in us all and in all of our cultures. But the anthropologist is not a passive recorder of human data; he searches for the human secret.

As myth teller, the anthropologist feels the heat and pull of human effort. As an ethnographer, he stands between the juncture of superordinate and subordinate societies, and he experiences the contradictory stresses of that position. He must not isolate himself from those stresses by putting on a white smock and directing interviewers from the sterile atmosphere of an air-conditioned office. If children consider him just another village idiot, if adults laugh at his childlike mistakes, if he is a consistent victim of Montezuma's Revenge (or the Old World variant, the Pharaoh's Curse), at least he lives in the world of people. Nor can the ethnographer be principally occupied with directing cultural traffic from the superordinate to the subordinate society. Neither can he forget in his anxiety to speak for the poor that the rich also fall within the range of human variation. To recite the human epic, the anthropologist needs the passion of the radical, the practicality of the liberal, and the detachment of the scientist. But in the end, he must remain a teller, perhaps a revolutionary teller, but a poet and not a change agent.

In telling the human myth, of how men wrestle with the problem of being human, of how people envision a society of love but live in a society of hate, of how they conceive of a collective soul but live in individual cells, the anthropologist may find his own salvation. In writing of the struggles of others, he may find ways to cope with his own demons that torture him at night. In reciting the heroism of humans, he may learn to live heroically, to know that Gods live forever, but humans die bravely.

If the anthropologist does not tell the human myth, then who will?

Who will see human gentleness in a Ramapithecus jaw?
Who will look with wonder at the Sorcerer of Les Trois Frères?
Who will hunt meat with the Siriono and weep when a Sánchez dies?

Who will see a verb in a pebble tool, or fight for Papiamentu, or learn the lesson of he be gone?
Who will watch the ghosts dance?

Who will defend the Neanderthal?
Who will argue about the pre-Columbian chicken, or pre-Clovis man, or maize in Africa?
Who will believe in the bifid penis?

Who will watch the birds glide over New Guinea highlands?
Who will feast with the Yanomamö or go north with Nanook?
Who will journey with Don Juan?

Who will record these things and more?
Who will search for the human secret? Who will tell the human myth?
Who will, damn it, who will?

IV

Language and communication

Culture is a system of symbols that allow us to represent and communicate our experience. We are surrounded by symbols — the flag, a new automobile, a diamond ring, billboard pictures, and, of course, spoken and written words. Each symbol has a special meaning in our society.

A symbol is anything that stands for something else. Almost anything we experience can come to have symbolic meaning. Every symbol has a referent that it calls to our attention. The term *mother-in-law* refers to a certain kind of relative, the mother of a person's spouse. When we communicate with symbols, we call attention not only to the referent but also to numerous connotations of the symbol. In our culture *mother-in-law* connotes a person who is difficult to get along with, who meddles in the affairs of her married daughter or son, and who is to be avoided. Human beings have the capacity to assign meaning to anything in our experience in an arbitrary fashion. This fact gives rise to limitless possibilities for communication.

Symbols greatly simplify the task of communication. Once we learn that a word like *barn*, for example, stands for a certain type of building, we can communicate about a whole range of specific buildings that fit into the category. And we can communicate about barns in their absence; we can even invent flying barns and dream about barns. Symbols make it possible to communicate the immense variety of human experience, whether past or present, tangible or intangible, good or bad.

Many channels are available to human beings for symbolic communication — sound, sight, touch, and smell. Language, our most highly developed communication system, uses the channel of sound (or for some deaf people, sight). Linguists have developed techniques for discovering the rules for the formation of sound symbols (phonology), their combination (grammar), and their interpretation (semantics).

To think that language is the only means for communication would be a mistake. In every society people use a wide range of things for communication — clothes, gestures, artifacts, the arrangement of space. In their study of language and communication, anthropologists are going beyond descriptions of sound and grammar to study meaning and style. Beneath the surface of language are hidden meanings built into the very structure of linguistic communication. A person's manner of speaking communicates as well as the words. In the following selections we examine the way that culture, language, and bodily adornment communicate in different cultural settings.

9

The sounds of silence
EDWARD T. HALL
MILDRED REED HALL

*People communicate with more than just words. An important
part of every encounter are the messages we send with our
bodies and faces: the smile, the frown, the slouch of the shoulders, or the tightly crossed legs are only a few gestures which
add another dimension to our verbal statements. These gestures as well as their social meaning change from one culture
to another. In this article, the Halls describe and explain the
function of nonverbal behavior in social encounters.*

Bob leaves his apartment at 8:15 A.M. and stops at the corner drugstore
for breakfast. Before he can speak, the counterman says, "The usual?"
Bob nods yes. While he savors his Danish, a fat man pushes onto the
adjoining stool and overflows into his space. Bob scowls and the man
pulls himself in as much as he can. Bob has sent two messages without
speaking a syllable.

Henry has an appointment to meet Arthur at 11 o'clock; he arrives
at 11:30. Their conversation is friendly, but Arthur retains a lingering
hostility. Henry has unconsciously communicated that he doesn't think
the appointment is very important or that Arthur is a person who needs
to be treated with respect.

George is talking to Charley's wife at a party. Their conversation
is entirely trivial, yet Charley glares at them suspiciously. Their physical
proximity and the movements of their eyes reveal that they are powerfully attracted to each other.

José Ybarra and Sir Edmund Jones are at the same party and it is important for them to establish a cordial relationship for business reasons. Each is trying to be warm and friendly, yet they will part with mutual distrust and their business transaction will probably fall through. José, in Latin fashion, moved closer and closer to Sir Edmund as they spoke, and this movement was miscommunicated as pushiness to Sir Edmund, who kept backing away from this intimacy, and this was miscommunicated to José as coldness. The silent languages of Latin and English cultures are more difficult to learn than their spoken languages.

In each of these cases, we see the subtle power of nonverbal communication. The only language used throughout most of the history of humanity (in evolutionary terms, vocal communication is relatively recent), it is the first form of communication you learn. You use this preverbal language, consciously and unconsciously, every day to tell other people how you feel about yourself and them. This language includes your posture, gestures, facial expressions, costume, the way you walk, even your treatment of time and space and material things. All people communicate on several different levels at the same time but are usually aware of only the verbal dialog and don't realize that they respond to nonverbal messages. But when a person says one thing and really believes something else, the discrepancy between the two can usually be sensed. Nonverbal-communication systems are much less subject to the conscious deception that often occurs in verbal systems. When we find ourselves thinking, "I don't know what it is about him, but he doesn't seem sincere," it's usually this lack of congruity between a person's words and his behavior that makes us anxious and uncomfortable.

Few of us realize how much we all depend on body movement in our conversation or are aware of the hidden rules that govern listening behavior. But we know instantly whether or not the person we're talking to is "tuned in" and we're very sensitive to any breach in listening etiquette. In white middle-class American culture, when someone wants to show he is listening to someone else, he looks either at the other person's face or, specifically, at his eyes, shifting his gaze from one eye to the other.

If you observe a person conversing, you'll notice that he indicates he's listening by nodding his head. He also makes little "Hmm" noises. If he agrees with what's being said, he may give a vigorous nod. To show pleasure or affirmation, he smiles; if he has some reservations, he looks skeptical by raising an eyebrow or pulling down the corners of his mouth. If a participant wants to terminate the conversation, he may start shifting his body position, stretching his legs, crossing or uncrossing them, bobbing his foot or diverting his gaze from the speaker. The more he fidgets, the more the speaker becomes aware that he has lost his audience. As a last measure, the listener may look at his watch to indicate the imminent end of the conversation.

Talking and listening are so intricately intertwined that a person cannot do one without the other. Even when one is alone and talking to oneself, there is part of the brain that speaks while another part listens. In all conversations, the listener is positively or negatively reinforcing the speaker all the time. He may even guide the conversation without knowing it, by laughing or frowning or dismissing the argument with a wave of his hand.

The language of the eyes — another age-old way of exchanging feelings — is both subtle and complex. Not only do men and women use their eyes differently but there are class, generation, regional, ethnic and national cultural differences. Americans often complain about the way foreigners stare at people or hold a glance too long. Most Americans look away from someone who is using his eyes in an unfamiliar way because it makes them self-conscious. If a man looks at another man's wife in a certain way, he's asking for trouble, as indicated earlier. But he might not be ill-mannered or seeking to challenge the husband. He might be a European in this country who hasn't learned our visual mores. Many American women visiting France or Italy are acutely embarrassed because, for the first time in their lives, men really look at them — their eyes, hair, nose, lips, breasts, hips, legs, thighs, knees, ankles, feet, clothes, hairdo, even their walk. These same women, once they have become used to being looked at, often return to the United States and are overcome with the feeling that "No one ever really looks at me anymore."

Analyzing the mass of data on the eyes, it is possible to sort out at least three ways in which the eyes are used to communicate: dominance vs. submission, involvement vs. detachment and positive vs. negative attitude. In addition, there are three levels of consciousness and control, which can be categorized as follows: (1) conscious use of the eyes to communicate, such as the flirting blink and the intimate nose-wrinkling squint; (2) the very extensive category of unconscious but learned behavior governing where the eyes are directed and when (this unwritten set of rules dictates how and under what circumstances the sexes, as well as people of all status categories, look at each other); and (3) the response of the eye itself, which is completely outside both awareness and control — changes in the cast (the sparkle) of the eye and the pupillary reflex.

The eye is unlike any other organ of the body, for it is an extension of the brain. The unconscious pupillary reflex and the cast of the eye have been known by people of Middle Eastern origin for years — although most are unaware of their knowledge. Depending on the context, Arabs and others look either directly at the eyes or deeply *into* the eyes of their interlocutor. We became aware of this in the Middle East several years ago while looking at jewelry. The merchant suddenly started to push a particular bracelet at a customer and said, "You buy this one." What interested us was that the bracelet was not the one that had been consciously selected by the purchaser. But the merchant, watching the pupils of the eyes, knew what the purchaser really wanted to buy. Whether he specifically knew *how* he knew is debatable.

A psychologist at the University of Chicago, Eckhard Hess, was the first to conduct systematic studies of the pupillary reflex. His wife remarked one evening, while watching him reading in bed, that he must be very interested in the text because his pupils were dilated. Following up on this, Hess slipped some pictures of nudes into a stack of photographs that he gave to his male assistant. Not looking at the photographs but watching his assistant's pupils, Hess was able to tell precisely when the assistant came to the nudes. In further experiments, Hess retouched the eyes in a photograph of a woman. In one print, he made the pupils small, in another, large; nothing else was changed. Subjects who were given the photographs found the woman with the dilated pupils much more attractive. Any man who has had the experience of seeing a woman look at him as her pupils widen with reflex speed knows that she's flashing him a message.

The eye-sparkle phenomenon frequently turns up in our interviews of couples in love. It's apparently one of the first reliable clues in the other person that love is genuine. To date, there is no scientific data to explain eye sparkle; no investigation of the pupil, the cornea or even the white sclera of the eye shows how the sparkle originates. Yet we all know it when we see it.

One common situation for most people involves the use of the eyes in the street and in public. Although eye behavior follows a definite set of rules, the rules vary according to the place, the needs and feelings of the people, and their ethnic background. For urban whites, once they're within definite recognition distance (16–32 feet for people with average eyesight), there is mutual avoidance of eye contact — unless they want something specific: a pickup, a handout or information of some kind. In the West and in small towns generally, however, people are much more likely to look at and greet one another, even if they're strangers.

It's permissible to look at people if they're beyond recognition distance; but once inside this sacred zone, you can only steal a glance at strangers. You *must* greet friends, however; to fail to do so is insulting. Yet, to stare too fixedly even at them is considered rude and hostile. Of course, all of these rules are variable.

A great many blacks, for example, greet each other in public even if they don't know each other. To blacks, most eye behavior of whites has the effect of giving the impression that they aren't there, but this is due to white avoidance of eye contact with *anyone* in the street.

Another very basic difference between people of different ethnic backgrounds is their sense of territoriality and how they handle space. This is the silent communication, or miscommunication, that caused friction between Mr. Ybarra and Sir Edmund Jones in our earlier example. We know from research that everyone has around himself an invisible bubble of space that contracts and expands depending on several factors: his emotional state, the activity he's performing at the time and his cultural background. This bubble is a kind of mobile territory that he will defend against intrusion. If he is accustomed to close personal distance between himself and others, his bubble will be smaller than that of someone who's accustomed to greater personal distance. People of North European heritage — English, Scandinavian, Swiss and German — tend to avoid contact. Those whose heritage is Italian, French, Spanish, Russian, Latin American or Middle Eastern like close personal contact.

People are very sensitive to any intrusion into their spatial bubble. If someone stands too close to you, your first instinct is to back up. If that's not possible, you lean away and pull yourself in, tensing your muscles. If the intruder doesn't respond to these body signals, you may then try to protect yourself, using a briefcase, umbrella or raincoat. Women — especially when traveling alone — often plant their pocketbook in such a way that no once can get very close to them. As a last resort, you may move to another spot and position yourself behind a desk or a chair that provides screening. Everyone tries to adjust the space around himself in a way that's comfortable for him; most often, he does this unconsciously.

Emotions also have a direct effect on the size of a person's territory. When you're angry or under stress, your bubble expands and you require more space. New York psychiatrist Augustus Kinzel found a difference in what he calls Body-Buffer Zones between violent and nonviolent prison inmates. Dr. Kinzel conducted experiments in which each prisoner was placed in the center of a small room and then Dr. Kinzel slowly walked toward him. Nonviolent prisoners allowed him to come quite close, while prisoners with a history of violent behavior couldn't tolerate his proximity and reacted with some vehemence.

Apparently, people under stress experience other people as looming larger and closer than they actually are. Studies of schizophrenic patients have indicated that they sometimes have a distorted perception of space, and several psychiatrists have reported patients who experience their body boundaries as filling up an entire room. For these patients, anyone who comes into the room is actually inside their body, and such an intrusion may trigger a violent outburst.

Unfortunately, there is little detailed information about normal people who live in highly congested urban areas. We do know, of course, that the noise, pollution, dirt, crowding and confusion of our cities induce feelings of stress in most of us, and stress leads to a need for greater space. The man who's packed into a subway, jostled in the street, crowded into an elevator and forced to work all day in a bull pen or in a small office without auditory or visual privacy is going to be very stressed at the end of his day. He needs places that provide relief from constant overstimulation of his nervous system. Stress from overcrowding is cumulative and people can tolerate more crowding early in the day than later; note the increased bad temper during the evening rush hour as compared with the morning melee. Certainly one factor in people's desire to commute by car is the need for privacy and relief from crowding (except, often, from other cars); it may be the only time of the day when nobody can intrude.

In crowded public places, we tense our muscles and hold ourselves stiff, and thereby communicate to others our desire not to intrude on their space and, above all, not to touch them. We also avoid eye contact, and the total effect is that of someone who has "tuned out." Walking along the street, our bubble expands slightly as we move in a stream of strangers, taking care not to bump into them. In the office, at meetings, in restaurants, our bubble keeps changing as it adjusts to the activity at hand.

Most white middle-class Americans use four main distances in their business and social relations: intimate, personal, social and public. Each of these distances has a near and a far phase and is accompanied by changes in the volume of the voice. Intimate distance varies from direct physical contact with another person to a distance of six to eighteen inches and is used for our most private activities — caressing another person or making love. At this distance, you are overwhelmed by sensory inputs from the other person — heat from the body, tactile stimulation from the skin, the fragrance of perfume, even the sound of breathing — all of which literally envelop you. Even at the far phase, you're still within easy touching distance. In general, the use of intimate distance in public between adults is frowned on. It's also much too close for strangers, except under conditions of extreme crowding.

In the second zone — personal distance — the close phase is one and a half to two and a half feet; it's at this distance that wives usually stand from their husbands in public. If another woman moves into this zone, the wife will most likely be disturbed. The far phase — two and a half to four feet — is the distance used to "keep someone at arm's length" and is the most common spacing used by people in conversation.

The third zone — social distance — is employed during business transactions or exchanges with a clerk or repairman. People who work together tend to use close social distance — four to seven feet. This is also the distance for conversation at social gatherings. To stand at this distance from someone who is seated has a dominating effect (e.g., teacher to pupil, boss to secretary). The far phase of the third zone — seven to twelve feet — is where people stand when someone says, "Stand back so I can look at you." This distance lends a formal tone to business or social discourse. In an executive office, the desk serves to keep people at this distance.

The fourth zone — public distance — is used by teachers in classrooms or speakers at public gatherings. At its farthest phase — 25 feet and beyond — it is used for important public figures. Violations of this distance can lead to serious complications. During his 1970 U.S. visit, the president of France, Georges Pompidou, was harassed by pickets in Chicago, who were permitted to get within touching distance. Since pickets in France are kept behind barricades a block or more away, the president was outraged by this insult to his person, and President Nixon was obliged to communicate his concern as well as offer his personal apologies.

It is interesting to note how American pitchmen and panhandlers exploit the unwritten, unspoken conventions of eye and distance. Both take advantage of the fact that once explicit eye contact is established, it is rude to look away, because to do so means to brusquely dismiss the other person and his needs. Once having caught the eye of his mark, the panhandler then locks on, not letting go until he moves through the public zone, the social zone, the personal zone and, finally, into the intimate sphere, where people are most vulnerable.

Touch also is an important part of the constant stream of communication that takes place between people. A light touch, a firm touch, a blow, a caress are all communications. In an effort to break down barriers among people, there's been a recent upsurge in group-encounter activities, in which strangers are encouraged to touch one another. In special situations such as these, the rules for not touching are broken with group approval and people gradually lose some of their inhibitions.

Although most people don't realize it, space is perceived and distances are set not by vision alone but with all the senses. Auditory space is perceived with the ears, thermal space with the skin, kinesthetic space with the muscles of the body and olfactory space with the nose. And, once again, it's one's culture that determines how his senses are programmed — which sensory information ranks highest and lowest. The important thing to remember is that culture is very persistent. In this country, we've noted the existence of culture patterns that determine distance between people in the third and fourth generations of some families, despite their prolonged contact with people of very different cultural heritages.

Whenever there is great cultural distance between two people, there are bound to be problems arising from differences in behavior and expectations. An example is the American couple who consulted a psychiatrist about their marital problems. The husband was from New England and had been brought up by reserved parents who taught him to control his emotions and to respect the need for privacy. His wife was from an Italian family and had been brought up in close contact with all the members of her large family, who were extremely warm, volatile and demonstrative.

When the husband came home after a hard day at the office, dragging his feet and longing for peace and quiet, his wife would rush to him and smother him. Clasping his hands, rubbing his brow, crooning over his weary head, she never left him alone. But when the wife was upset or anxious about her day, the husband's response was to withdraw completely and leave her alone. No comforting, no affectionate embrace, no attention — just solitude. The woman became convinced her husband didn't love her and, in desperation, she consulted a psychiatrist. Their problem wasn't basically psychological but cultural.

Why has man developed all these different ways of communicating messages without words? One reason is that people don't like to spell out certain kinds of messages. We prefer to find other ways of showing our feelings. This is especially true in relationships as sensitive as courtship. Men don't like to be rejected and most women don't want to turn a man down bluntly. Instead, we work out subtle ways of encouraging or discouraging each other that save face and avoid confrontations.

How a person handles space in dating others is an obvious and very sensitive indicator of how he or she feels about the other person. On a first date, if a woman sits or stands so close to a man that he is acutely conscious of her physical presence — inside the intimate-distance zone — the man usually construes it to mean that she is encouraging him. However, before the man starts moving in on the woman, he should be sure what message she's really sending; otherwise, he risks bruising his ego. What is close to someone of North European background may be neutral or distant to someone of Italian heritage. Also, women sometimes use space as a way of misleading a man and there are few things that put men off more than women who communicate contradictory messages — such as women who cuddle up and then act insulted when a man takes the next step.

How does a woman communicate interest in a man? In addition to such familiar gambits as smiling at him, she may glance shyly at him, blush and then look away. Or she may give him a real come-on look and move in very close when he approaches. She may touch his arm and ask for a light. As she leans forward to light her cigarette, she may brush him lightly, enveloping him in her perfume. She'll probably continue to smile at him and she may use what ethologists call preening gestures — touching the back of her hair, thrusting her breasts forward, tilting her hips as she stands or crossing her legs if she's seated, perhaps even exposing one thigh or putting a hand on her thigh and stroking it. She may also stroke her wrists as she converses or show the palm of her hand as a way of gaining his attention. Her skin may be unusually flushed or quite pale, her eyes brighter, the pupils larger.

If a man sees a woman whom he wants to attract, he tries to present himself by his posture and stance as someone who is self-assured. He moves briskly and confidently. When he catches the eye of the woman, he may hold her glance a little longer than normal. If he gets an encouraging smile, he'll move in close and engage her in small talk. As they converse, his glance shifts over her face and body. He, too, may make preening gestures — straighening his tie, smoothing his hair or shooting his cuffs.

How do people learn body language? The same way they learn spoken language — by observing and imitating people around them as they're growing up. Little girls imitate their mothers or an older female. Little boys imitate their fathers or a respected uncle or a character on television. In this way, they learn the gender signals appropriate for their sex. Regional, class and ethnic patterns of body behavior are also learned in childhood and persist throughout life.

Such patterns of masculine and feminine body behavior vary widely from one culture to another. In America, for example, women stand with their thighs together. Many walk with their pelvis tipped slightly forward and their upper arms close to their body. When they sit, they cross their legs at the knee or, if they are well past middle age, they may cross their ankles. American men hold their arms away from their body, often swinging them as they walk. They stand with their legs apart (an extreme example is the cowboy, with legs apart and thumbs tucked into his belt). When they sit, they put their feet on the floor with legs apart and, in some parts of the country, they cross their legs by putting one ankle on the other knee.

Leg behavior indicates sex, status and personality. It also indicates whether or not one is at ease or is showing respect or disrespect for the other person. Young Latin-American males avoid crossing their legs. In their world of *machismo*, the preferred position for young males when with one another (if there is no older dominant male present to whom they must show respect) is to sit on the base of their spine with their leg muscles relaxed and their feet wide apart. Their respect position is like our military equivalent; spine straight, heels and ankles together — almost identical to that displayed by properly brought up young women in New England in the early part of this century.

American women who sit with their legs spread apart in the presence of males are *not* normally signaling a come-on — they are simply (and often unconsciously) sitting like men. Middle-class women in the presence of other women to whom they are very close may on occasion throw themselves down on a soft chair or sofa and let themselves go. This is a signal that nothing serious will be taken up. Males, on the other hand, lean back and prop their legs up on the nearest object.

The way we walk, similarly, indicates status, respect, mood and ethnic or cultural affiliation. The many variants of the female walk are too well known to go into here, except to say that a man would have to be blind not to be turned on by the way some women walk — a fact that made Mae West rich before scientists ever studied these matters. To white Americans, some French middle-class males walk in a way that is both humorous and suspect. There is a bounce and looseness to the French walk, as though the parts of the body were somehow unrelated. Jacques Tati, the French movie actor, walks this way; so does the great mime, Marcel Marceau.

Blacks and whites in America — with the exception of middle- and upper-middle-class professionals of both groups — move and walk very differently from each other. To the blacks, whites often seem incredibly stiff, almost mechanical in their movements. Black males, on the other hand, have a looseness and coordination that frequently makes whites a little uneasy; it's too different, too integrated, too alive, too male. Norman Mailer has said that squares walk from the shoulders, like bears, but blacks and hippies walk from the hips, like cats.

All over the world, people walk not only in their own characteristic way but have walks that communicate the nature of their involvement with whatever it is they're doing. The purposeful walk of North Europeans is an important component of proper behavior on the job. Any male who has been in the military knows how essential it is to walk properly (which makes for a continuing source of tension between blacks and whites in the Service). The quick shuffle of servants in the Far East in the old days was a show of respect. On the island of Truk, when we last visited, the inhabitants even had a name for the respectful walk that one used when in the presence of a chief or when walking past a chief's house. The term was *sufan*, which meant to be humble and respectful.

The notion that people communicate volumes by their gestures, facial expressions, posture and walk is not new; actors, dancers, writers and psychiatrists have long been aware of it. Only in recent years, however, have scientists begun to make systematic observations of body motions. Ray L. Birdwhistell of the University of Pennsylvania is one of the pioneers in body-motion research and coined the term kinesics to describe this field. He developed an elaborate notation system to record both facial and body movements, using an approach similar to that of the linguist, who studies the basic elements of speech. Birdwhistell and other kinesicists such as Albert Sheflen, Adam Kendon and William Condon take movies of people interacting. They run the film over and over again, often at reduced speed for frame-by-frame analysis, so that they can observe even the slightest body movements not perceptible at normal interaction speeds. These movements are then recorded in notebooks for later analysis.

To appreciate the importance of nonverbal-communication systems, consider the unskilled inner-city black looking for a job. His handling of time and space alone is sufficiently different from the white middle-class pattern to create great misunderstandings on both sides. The black is told to appear for a job interview at a certain time. He arrives late. The white interviewer concludes from his tardy arrival that the black is irresponsible and not really interested in the job. What the interviewer doesn't know is that the black time system (often referred to by blacks as C. P. T. — colored people's time) isn't the same as that of whites. In the words of a black student who had been told to make an appointment to see his professor: "Man, you *must* be putting me on. I never had an appointment in my life."

The black job applicant, having arrived late for his interview, may further antagonize the white interviewer by his posture and his eye behavior. Perhaps he slouches and avoids looking at the interviewer; to him, this is playing it cool. To the interviewer, however, he may well look shifty and sound uninterested. The interviewer has failed to notice the actual signs of interest and eagerness in the black's behavior, such as the subtle shift in the quality of the voice — a gentle and tentative excitement — an almost imperceptible change in the cast of the eyes and a relaxing of the jaw muscles.

Moreover, correct reading of black-white behavior is continually complicated by the fact that both groups are comprised of individuals — some of whom try to accommodate and some of whom make it a point of pride *not* to accommodate. At present, this means that many Americans, when thrown into contact with one another, are in the precarious position of not knowing which pattern applies. Once identified and analyzed, nonverbal-communications systems can be taught, like a foreign language. Without this training, we respond to nonverbal communications in terms of our own culture; we read everyone's behavior as if it were our own, and thus we often misunderstand it.

Several years ago in New York City, there was a program for sending children from predominantly black and Puerto Rican low-income neighborhoods to summer school in a white upper-class neighborhood on the East Side. One morning, a group of young black and Puerto Rican boys raced down the street, shouting and screaming and overturning garbage cans on their way to school. A doorman from an apartment building nearby chased them and cornered one of them inside a building. The boy drew a knife and attacked the doorman. This tragedy would not have occurred if the doorman had been familiar with the behavior of boys from low-income neighborhoods, where such antics are routine and socially acceptable and where pursuit would be expected to invite a violent response.

The language of behavior is extremely complex. Most of us are lucky to have under control one subcultural system — the one that reflects our sex, class, generation and geographic region within the United States. Because of its complexity, efforts to isolate bits of nonverbal communication and generalize from them are in vain; you don't become an instant expert on people's behavior by watching them at cocktail parties. Body language isn't something that's independent of the person, something that can be donned and doffed like a suit of clothes.

Our research and that of our colleagues has shown that, far from being a superficial form of communication that can be consciously manipulated, nonverbal-communication systems are interwoven into the fabric of the personality and, as sociologist Erving Goffman has demonstrated, into society itself. They are the warp and woof of daily interactions with others and they influence how one expresses oneself, how one experiences oneself as a man or a woman.

Nonverbal communications signal to members of your own group what kind of person you are, how you feel about others, how you'll fit into and work in a group, whether you're assured or anxious, the degree to which you feel comfortable with the standards of your own culture, as well as deeply significant feelings about the self, including the state of your own psyche. For most of us, it's difficult to accept the reality of another's behavioral system. And, of course, none of us will ever become fully knowledgeable of the importance of every nonverbal signal. But as long as each of us realizes the power of these signals, this society's diversity can be a source of great strength rather than a further — and subtly powerful — source of division.

10

"Rapping" in the black ghetto
THOMAS KOCHMAN

*Although the urban subcultures in the United States often use
the sounds and the grammar of English, their styles of speaking are different. Achievement in the ghetto involves the verbal
abilities of "rapping," "shucking," "jiving," "running it down,"
"gripping," "copping a plea," "signifying," and "sounding."
With vivid examples, each of these verbal styles is described.
Thomas Kochman also shows how individuals establish their
personalities, show their respect for power, and stir up excitement by careful manipulation of these verbal abilities.*

"Rapping," "shucking," "jiving," "running it down," "gripping," "copping a plea," "signifying," and "sounding" are all part of the black ghetto
idiom and describe different kinds of talking. Each has its own distinguishing features of form, style, and function; each is influenced by, and
influences, the speaker, setting, and audience; and each sheds light on
the black perspective and the black condition — on those orienting
values and attitudes that will cause a speaker to speak or perform in
his own way within the social context of the black community.

I was first introduced to black idiom in New York City, and, as a
professional linguist interested in dialects, I began to compile a lexicon
of such expressions. My real involvement, however, came in Chicago,
while preparing a course on black idiom at the Center for Inner City
studies, the southside branch of Northeastern Illinois State College.

Here I began to explore the full cultural significance of this kind of
verbal behavior. My students and informants within black Chicago,
through their knowledge of these terms, and their ability to recognize
and categorize the techniques, and to give examples, gave me much

Published by permission of Transaction, Inc., from *Transaction*, Vol. 6, #4,
copyright © 1969, by Transaction, Inc.

reliable data. When I turned for other or better examples to the literature — such as the writings of Malcolm X, Robert Conot, and Iceberg
Slim — my students and informants were able to recognize and confirm
their authenticity.

While often used to mean ordinary conversation, rapping is distinctively a fluent and a lively way of talking, always characterized by a
high degree of personal style. To one's own group, rapping may be descriptive of an interesting narration, a colorful rundown of some past
event. An example of this kind of rap is the answer from a Chicago gang
member to a youth worker who asked how his group became organized:

> Now I'm goin to tell you how the jive really started. I'm going to tell
> you how the club got this big. 'Bout 1956 there used to be a time when
> the Jackson Park show was open and the Stony show was open. Sixty-
> six street, Jeff, Gene, all of 'em, little bitty dudes, little bitty . . . Gene
> wasn't with 'em then. Gene was cribbin (living) over here. Jeff, all of
> 'em, real little bitty dudes, you dig? All of us were little.
>
> Sixty-six (the gang on sixty-sixth street), they wouldn't allow us in
> the Jackson Park show. That was when the parky (?) was headin it.
> Everybody say, If we want to go to the show, we go! One day, who was
> it? Carl Robinson. He went up to the show . . . and Jeff fired on him.
> He came back and all this was swelled up 'bout yay big, you know. He
> come back over to the hood (neighborhood). He told (name unclear)
> and them dudes went up there. That was when mostly all the main
> sixty-six boys was over here like Bett Riley. All of 'em was over here.
> People that quit gang-bangin (fighting, especially as a group), Marvell
> Gates, people like that.
>
> They went on up there, John, Roy and Skeeter went in there. And
> they start humbuggin (fighting) in there. That's how it all started. Sixty-
> six found out they couldn't beat us, at *that* time. They couldn't *whup*
> seven-o. Am I right Leroy? You was cribbin over here then. Am I
> right? We were dynamite! Used to be a time, you ain't have a passport,
> Man, you couldn't walk through here. And if didn't nobody know you
> it was worse than that. . . .

Rapping to a woman is a colorful way of "asking for some pussy."
"One needs to throw a lively rap when he is 'putting the make' on a
broad." (John Horton, "Time and Cool People," *trans*action, April, 1967.)

According to one informant the woman is usually someone he has
just seen or met, looks good, and might be willing to have sexual intercourse with him. My informant says the term would not be descriptive
of talk between a couple "who have had a relationship over any length
of time." Rapping then, is used at the beginning of a relationship to
create a favorable impression and be persuasive at the same time. The
man who has the reputation for excelling at this is the pimp, or mack
man. Both terms describe a person of considerable status in the street

hierarchy, who, by his lively and persuasive rapping ("macking" is also used in this context) has acquired a stable of girls to hustle for him and give him money. For most street men and many teenagers he is the model whom they try to emulate. Thus, within the community you have a pimp walk, pimp style boots and clothes, and perhaps most of all "pimp talk," is a colorful literary example of a telephone rap. One of my informants regards it as extreme, but agrees that it illustrates the language, style and technique of rapping. "Blood" is rapping to an ex-whore named Christine in an effort to trap her into his stable:

> Now try to control yourself baby. I'm the tall stud with the dreamy bedroom eyes across the hall in four-twenty. I'm the guy with the pretty towel wrapped around his sexy hips. I got the same hips on now that you X-rayed. Remember that hump of sugar your peepers feasted on?
>
> She said, "Maybe, but you shouldn't call me. I don't want an incident. What do you want? A lady doesn't accept phone calls from strangers."
>
> I said, "A million dollars and a trip to the moon with a bored, trapped, beautiful bitch, you dig? I'm no stranger. I've been popping the elastic on your panties ever since you saw me in the hall. . . ."

Rapping between men and women often is competitive and leads to a lively repartee with the women becoming as adept as the men. An example follows:

> A man coming from the bathroom forgot to zip his pants. An un-escorted party of women kept watching him and laughing among themselves. The man's friends "hip" (inform) him to what's going on. He approaches one woman — "Hey baby, did you see that big black Cadillac with the full tires? ready to roll in action just for you." She answers — "No, mother-fucker, but I saw a little gray Volkswagen with two flat tires." Everybody laughs. His rap was "capped" (excelled, topped).

When "whupping the game" on a "trick" or "lame" (trying to get goods or services from someone who looks like he can be swindled), rapping is often descriptive of the highly stylized verbal part of the maneuver. In well established "con games" the rap is carefully prepared and used with great skill in directing the course of the transaction. An excellent illustration came from an adept hustler who was playing the "murphy" game on a white trick. The "murphy" game is designed to get the *trick* to give his money to the hustler, who in this instance poses as a "steerer" (one who directs or steers customers to a brothel), to keep the whore from stealing it. The hustler then skips with the money.

> Look Buddy, I know a fabulous house not more than two blocks away. Brother you ain't never seen more beautiful, freakier broads than are in that house. One of them, the prettiest one, can do more with a

swipe than a monkey can with a banana. She's like a rubber doll; she can take a hundred positions."

At this point the sucker is wild to get to this place of pure joy. He entreats the con player to take him there, not just direct him to it.

The "murphy" player will prat him (pretend rejection) to enhance his desire. He will say, "Man, don't be offended, but Aunt Kate, that runs the house don't have nothing but highclass White men coming to her place. . . . You know, doctors, lawyers, big-shot politicians. You look like a clean-cut White man, but you ain't in that league are you? (Iceberg Slim, *Pimp: The Story of My Life.*)

After a few more exchanges of the "murphy" dialogue, "the mark is separated from his scratch."

An analysis of rapping indicates a number of things.

For instance, it is revealing that one raps *to* rather than *with* a person supporting the impression that rapping is to be regarded more as a performance than verbal exchange. As with other performances, rapping projects the personality, physical appearance and style of the performer. In each of the examples given, the intrusive "I" of the speaker was instrumental in contributing to the total impression of the rap.

The combination of personality and style is usually best when "asking for some pussy." It is less when "whupping the game" on someone or "running something down."

In "asking for some pussy" for example, where personality and style might be projected through nonverbal means: stance, clothing, walking, looking, one can speak of a "silent rap." The woman is won here without the use of words, or rather, with words being implied that would generally accompany the nonverbal components.

As a lively way of "running it down" the verbal element consists of personality and style plus information. To someone *reading* my example of the gang member's narration, the impression might be that the information would be more influential in directing the listener's response. The youth worker might be expected to say "So that's how the gang got so big," instead of "Man, that gang member is *bad* (strong, brave)" in which instance he would be responding to the personality and style of the rapper. However, if the reader would *listen* to the gang member on tape or could have been present when the gang member spoke he more likely would have reacted more to personality and style as my informants did.

Remember that in attendance with the youth worker were members of the gang who *already knew* how the gang got started (e.g., "Am

I right Leroy? You was cribbin' over here then") and for whom the information itself would have little interest. Their attention was held by the *way* the information was presented.

The verbal element in "whupping the game" on someone, in the preceding example, was an integral part of an overall deception in which information and personality-style were skillfully manipulated for the purpose of controlling the "trick's" response. But again, greater weight must be given to personality-style. In the "murphy game" for example, it was this element which got the trick to trust the hustler and leave his money with him for "safekeeping."

The function of rapping in each of these forms is *expressive*. By this I mean that the speaker raps to project his personality onto the scene or to evoke a generally favorable response. When rapping is used to "ask for some pussy" or to "whup the game" on someone its function is *directive*. By this I mean that rapping becomes an instrument to manipulate and control people to get them to give up or to do something. The difference between rapping to a "fox" (pretty girl) for the purpose of "getting inside her pants" and rapping to a "lame" to get something from him is operational rather than functional. The latter rap contains a concealed motivation where the former does not.

"Shucking," "shucking it," "shucking and jiving," "S-ing" and "J-ing" or just "jiving," are terms that refer to language behavior practiced by the black when confronting "the Man" (the white man, the establishment, or *any* authority figure), and to another form of language behavior practiced by blacks with each other on the peer group level.

In the South, and later in the North, the black man learned that American society had assigned to him a restrictive role and status. Among whites his behavior had to conform to this imposed station and he was constantly reminded to "keep his place." He learned that it was not acceptable in the presence of white people to show feelings of indignation, frustration, discontent, pride, ambition, or desire; that real feelings had to be concealed behind a mask of innocence, ignorance, childishness, obedience, humility and deference. The terms used by the black to describe the role he played before white folks in the South was "tomming" or "jeffing." Failure to accommodate the white Southerner in this respect was almost certain to invite psychological and often physical brutality. A description related by a black psychiatrist, Alvin F. Poussaint, is typical and revealing:

> Once last year as I was leaving my office in Jackson, Miss., with my Negro secretary, a White policeman yelled, "Hey, boy! Come here!" Somewhat bothered, I retorted: "I'm no boy!" He then rushed at me,

inflamed, and stood towering over me, snorting "What d'ja say, boy?" Quickly he frisked me and demanded, "What's your name boy?" Frightened, I replied, "Dr. Poussaint. I'm a physician." He angrily chuckled and hissed, "What's your first name, boy?" When I hesitated he assumed a threatening stance and clenched his fists. As my heart palpitated, I muttered in profound humiliation, "Alvin."

He continued his psychological brutality, bellowing, "Alvin, the next time I call you, you come right away, you hear? You hear?" I hesitated. "You hear me, boy?" My voice trembling with helplessness, but *following my instincts of self-preservation*, I murmured, "Yes, sir." *Now fully satisfied that I had performed and acquiesced to my "boy" status*, he dismissed me with, "Now, boy, go on and get out of here or next time we'll take you for a little ride down to the station house!" (Alvin F. Poussaint, "A Negro Psychiatrist Explains the Negro Psyche," *The New York Times Magazine*, August 20, 1967 [emphasis mine]).

In the northern cities the black encountered authority figures equivalent to Southern "crackers": policemen, judges, probation officers, truant officers, teachers and "Mr. Charlies" (bosses), and soon learned that the way to get by and avoid difficulty was to shuck. Thus, he learned to accommodate "the Man," to use the total orchestration of speech, intonation, gesture and facial expression for the purpose of producing whatever appearance would be acceptable. It was a technique and ability that was developed from fear, a respect for power, and a will to survive. This type of accommodation is exemplified by the Uncle Tom with his "Yes sir, Mr. Charlie," or "Anything you say, Mr. Charlie."

Through accommodation, many blacks became adept at concealing and controlling their emotions and at assuming a variety of postures. They became competent actors. Many developed a keen perception of what affected, motivated, appeased or satisfied the authority figures with whom they came into contact. Shucking became an effective way for many blacks to stay out of trouble, and for others a useful artifice for avoiding arrest or getting out of trouble when apprehended. Shucking it with a judge, for example, would be to feign repentance in the hope of receiving a lighter or suspended sentence. Robert Conot reports an example of shucking in his book, *Rivers of Blood, Years of Darkness:* Joe was found guilty of possession of narcotics. But he did an excellent job of shucking it with the probation officer.

The probation officer interceded for Joe with the judge: "His own attitude toward the present offense appears to be serious and responsible and it is believed that the defendant is an excellent subject for probation."

Some field illustrations of shucking to get out of trouble came from some seventh-grade children from an inner-city school in Chicago. The children were asked to talk their way out of a troublesome situation.

You are cursing at this old man and your mother comes walking down the stairs. She hears you.
To "talk your way out of this":
"I'd tell her that I was studying a scene in school for a play."

What if you were in a store stealing something and the manager caught you?
"I would start stuttering. Then I would say, 'Oh, Oh, I forgot. Here the money is.' "

A literary example of shucking comes from Iceberg Slim's autobiography. Iceberg, a pimp, shucks before "two red-faced Swede rollers (detectives)" who catch him in a motel room with his whore. My italics identify which elements of the passage constitute the shuck.

> I put my shaking hands into the pajama pockets . . . *I hoped I was keeping the fear out of my face. I gave them a wide toothy smile.* They came in and stood in the middle of the room. Their eyes were racing about the room. Stacy was open mouthed in the bed.
> I said, *"Yes, gentlemen, what can I do for you?"*
> Lanky said, "We wanta see your I.D."
> I went to the closet and got the phony John Cato Fredrickson I.D. I put it in his palm. I felt cold sweat running down my back. They looked at it, then looked at each other.
> Lanky said, "You are in violation of the law. You signed the motel register improperly. Why didn't you sign your full name? What are you trying to hide? What are you doing here in town? It says here you're a dancer. We don't have a club in town that books entertainers."
> I said, *"Officers, my professional name is Johnny Cato. I've got nothing to hide. My full name had always been too long for the marquees. I've fallen into the habit of using the shorter version.*
> *"My legs went out last year. I don't dance anymore: My wife and I decided to go into business. We are making a tour of this part of the country. We think that in your town we've found the ideal site for a Southern fried chicken shack. My wife has a secret recipe that should make us rich up here."* (Iceberg Slim, *Pimp: The Story of My Life.*)

Another example of shucking was related to me by a colleague. A black gang member was coming down the stairway from the club room with seven guns on him and encountered some policemen and detectives coming up the same stairs. If they stopped and frisked him he and others would have been arrested. A paraphrase of his shuck follows: "Man, I gotta get away from up there. There's gonna be some trouble and I don't want no part of it." This shuck worked on the minds of the policemen. It anticipated their questions as to why he was leaving the club room, and why he would be in a hurry. He also gave *them* a reason for wanting to get up to the room fast.

It ought to be mentioned at this point that there was not uniform agreement among my informants in characterizing the above examples as shucking. One informant used shucking only in the sense in which it is used among peers, e.g., bull-shitting, and characterized the above examples as jiving or whupping game. Others however, identified the above examples as shucking, and reserved jiving and whupping game for more offensive maneuvers. In fact, one of the apparent features of shucking is that the posture of the black when acting with members of the establishment be a *defensive* one.

Frederick Douglass, in telling of how he taught himself to read, would challenge a white boy with whom he was playing, by saying that he could write as well as he. Whereupon he would write down all the letters he knew. The white boy would then write down more letters than Douglass did. In this way, Douglass eventually learned all the letters of the alphabet. Some of my informants regarded the example as whupping game. Others regarded it as shucking. The former were perhaps focusing on the maneuver rather than the language used. The latter may have felt that any maneuvers designed to learn to read were justifiably defensive. One of my informants said Douglass was "shucking *in order to* whup the game." This latter response seems to be the most revealing. Just as one can rap to whup the game on someone, so one can shuck or jive for the same purpose; that is, assume a guise or posture or perform some action in a certain way that is designed to work on someone's mind to get him to give up something.

"Whupping game" to con whitey

The following examples from Malcolm X illustrate the shucking and jiving in this context though jive is the term used. Today, whupping game might also be the term used to describe the operation. Whites who came at night got a better reception; the several Harlem nightclubs they patronized were geared to entertain and jive (flatter, cajole) the night white crowd to get their money. (Malcolm X, *The Autobiography of Malcolm X.*)

The maneuvers involved here are clearly designed to obtain some benefit or advantage.

> Freddie got on the stand and went to work on his own shoes. Brush, liquid polish, brush, paste wax, shine rag, lacquer sole dressing . . . step by step, Freddie showed me what to do.

"But you got to get a whole lot faster. You can't waste time!" Freddie showed me how fast on my own shoes. Then because business was tapering off, he had time to give me a demonstration of how to make the shine rag pop like a firecracker. "Dig the action?" he asked. He did it in slow motion. I got down and tried it on his shoes. I had the principle of it. "Just got to do it, faster," Freddie said. *"It's a jive noise, that's all. Cats tip better, they figure you're knocking yourself out!"* (Malcolm X, *The Autobiography of Malcolm X.*)

An eight-year-old boy whupped the game on me one day this way:

My colleague and I were sitting in a room listening to a tape. The door to the room was open and outside was a soda machine. Two boys came up in the elevator, stopped at the soda machine, and then came into the room.

"Do you have a dime for two nickels?" Presumably the soda machine would not accept nickels. I took out the change in my pocket, found a dime and gave it to the boy for two nickels.

After accepting the dime, he looked at the change in my hand and asked, "Can I have two cents? I need carfare to get home." I gave him the two cents.

At first I assumed the verbal component of the maneuver was the rather weak, transparently false reason for wanting the two cents. Actually, as was pointed out to me later, the maneuver began with the first question which was designed to get me to show my money. He could then ask me for something that he knew I had, making my refusal more difficult. He apparently felt that the reason need not be more than plausible because the amount he wanted was small. Were the amount larger, he would no doubt have elaborated on the verbal element of the game. The form of the verbal element could be in the direction of rapping or shucking and jiving. If he were to rap the eight-year-old might say, "Man, you know a cat needs to have a little bread to keep the girls in line." Were he to shuck and jive he might make the reason for needing the money more compelling, look hungry, etc.

The function of shucking and jiving as it refers to blacks and "the Man" is designed to work on the mind and emotions of the authority figure for the purpose of getting him to feel a certain way or give up something that will be to the other's advantage. Iceberg showed a "toothy smile" which said to the detective, "I'm glad to see you" and "Would I be glad to see you if I had something to hide?" When the maneuvers seem to be *defensive* most of my informants regarded the language behavior as shucking. When the maneuvers were *offensive* my informants tended to regard the behavior as "whupping the game."

Also significant is that the first form of shucking described, which developed out of accommodation, is becoming less frequently used today by many blacks, because of a new-found self-assertiveness and pride, challenging the system. The willingness on the part of many blacks to accept the psychological and physical brutality and general social consequences of not "keeping one's place" is indicative of the changing self-concept of the black man. Ironically, the shocked reaction of some whites to the present militancy of the black is partly due to the fact that the black was so successful at "putting Whitey on" via shucking in the past. This new attitude can be seen from a conversation I recently had with a shoe-shine attendant at O'Hare Airport in Chicago.

I was having my shoes shined and the black attendant was using a polishing machine instead of the rag that was generally used in the past. I asked whether the machine made his work any easier. He did not answer me until about ten seconds had passed and then responded in a loud voice that he "never had a job that was easy," that he would give me "one hundred dollars for any *easy* job" I could offer him, that the machine made his job "faster" but not "easier." I was startled at the response because it was so unexpected and I realized that here was a new "breed of cat" who was not going to shuck for a big tip or ingratiate himself with "Whitey" anymore. A few years ago his response probably would have been different.

The contrast between this "shoe-shine" scene and the one illustrated earlier from Malcolm X's autobiography, when "shucking Whitey" was the common practice, is striking.

Shucking, jiving, shucking and jiving, or S-ing and J-ing, when referring to language behavior practiced by blacks, is descriptive of the talk and gestures that are appropriate to "putting someone on" by creating a false impression. The terms seem to cover a range from simply telling a lie, to bullshitting, to subtly playing with someone's mind. An important difference between this form of shucking and that described earlier is that the same talk and gestures that are deceptive to "the Man" are often transparent to those members of one's own group who are able practitioners at shucking themselves. As Robert Conot has pointed out, "The Negro who often fools the White officer by 'shucking it' is much less likely to be successful with another Negro. . . ." Also, S-ing and J-ing within the group often has play overtones in which the person being "put on" is aware of the attempts being made and goes along with it for enjoyment or in appreciation of the style.

"Running it down" is the term used by speakers in the ghetto when it is their intention to give information, either by explanation, narrative, or giving advice. In the following literary example, Sweet Mac is "running this Edith broad down" to his friends:

Edith is the "saved" broad who can't marry out of her religion . . . or do anything else out of her religion for that matter, especially what I wanted her to do. A bogue religion, man! So dig, for the last couple weeks I been quoting the Good Book and all that stuff to her; telling her I am now saved myself, you dig. (Woodie King, Jr., "The Game," *Liberator*, August, 1965.)

The following citation from Claude Brown uses the term with the additional sense of giving advice:

If I saw him (Claude's brother) hanging out with cats I knew were weak, who might be using drugs sooner or later, I'd run it down to him.

It seems clear that running it down has simply an informative function, that of telling somebody something that he doesn't already know.

"Gripping" is of fairly recent vintage, used by black high school students in Chicago to refer to the talk and facial expression that accompanies a *partial* loss of face or self-possession, or showing of fear. Its appearance alongside "copping a plea," which refers to a total loss of face, in which one begs one's adversary for mercy, is a significant new perception. In linking it with the street code which acclaims the ability to "look tough and inviolate, fearless, secure, 'cool,' " it suggests that even the slightest weakening of this posture will be held up to ridicule and contempt. There are always contemptuous overtones attached to the use of the term when applied to the others' behavior. One is tempted to link it with the violence and toughness required to survive on the street. The intensity of both seems to be increasing. As one of my informants noted, "Today, you're *lucky* if you end up in the hospital" — that is, are not killed.

REACTION TO FEAR AND SUPERIOR POWER

Both gripping and copping a plea refer to behavior produced from fear and a respect for superior power. An example of gripping comes from the record *"Street and Gangland Rhythms"* (Band 4 Dumb Boy). Lennie meets Calvin and asks him what happened to his lip. Calvin says that a boy named Pierre hit him for copying off him in school. Lennie, pretending to be Calvin's brother, goes to confront Pierre. Their dialogue follows:

Lennie: "Hey you! What you hit my little brother for?"
Pierre: "Did he tell you what happen man?"
Lennie: "Yeah, he told me what happened."
Pierre: "But you . . . but you . . . but you should tell your people to teach him to go to the school, man." (Pause) "I, I know, I know I didn't have a right to hit him."

Pierre, anticipating a fight with Lennie if he continued to justify his hitting of Calvin, tried to avoid it by "gripping" with the last line.

Copping a plea originally meant "to plead guilty to a lesser charge
to save the state the cost of a trial" (with the hope of receiving a lesser
or suspended sentence), but is now generally used to mean "to beg,"
"plead for mercy," as in the example "Please cop, don't hit me. I give."
(*Street and Gangland Rhythms*, Band 1 "Gang Fight.") This change of
meaning can be seen from its use by Piri Thomas in *Down These Mean
Streets*.

> The night before my hearing, I decided to make a prayer. It had to be
> on my knees, 'cause if I was gonna cop a plea to God, I couldn't play
> it cheap.

The function of gripping and copping a plea is obviously to induce
pity or to acknowledge the presence of superior strength. In so doing,
one evinces noticeable feelings of fear and insecurity which also result
in a loss of status among one's peers.

Signifying is the term used to describe the language behavior that,
as Abrahams has defined it, attempts to "imply, goad, beg, boast by
indirect verbal or gestural means." (Roger D. Abrahams, *Deep Down in
the Jungle*.) In Chicago it is also used as a synonym to describe language
behavior more generally known as "sounding" elsewhere.

Some excellent examples of signifying as well as of other forms of
language behavior come from the well known "toast" (narrative form)
"The Signifying Monkey and the Lion" which was collected by Abrahams from Negro street corner bards in Philadelphia. In the above toast
the monkey is trying to get the lion involved in a fight with the elephant:

> Now the lion came through the jungle one peaceful day,
> When the signifying monkey stopped him, and that is what he started
>   to say:
> He said, "Mr. Lion," he said, "A bad-assed mother-fucker down your
>   way,"
> He said, "Yeah! The way he talks about your folks is a certain shame.
> I even heard him curse when he mentioned your grandmother's name."
> The lion's tail shot back like a forty-four
> When he went down that jungle in all uproar.

Thus the monkey has goaded the lion into a fight with the elephant
by "signifying," that is, indicating that the elephant has been "sounding
on" (insulting) the lion. When the lion comes back, thoroughly beaten
up, the monkey again "signifies" by making fun of the lion:

> . . . lion came back through the jungle more dead than alive,
> When the monkey started some more of that signifying jive.

He said, "Damn, Mr. Lion, you went through here yesterday, the jungle
   rung.
Now you come back today, damn near hung."

The monkey, of course, is delivering this taunt from a safe distance
away on the limb of a tree when his foot slips and he falls to the ground,
at which point,

Like a bolt of lightning, a stripe of white heat,
The lion was on the monkey with all four feet.

In desperation the monkey quickly resorts to "copping a plea":

The monkey looked up with a tear in his eyes,
He said, "Please, Mr. Lion, I apologize."

His "plea" however, fails to move the lion to show any mercy so the
monkey tries another verbal ruse, "shucking":

He said, "You lemme get my head out of the sand,
Ass out the grass, I'll fight you like a natural man."

In this he is more successful as,

The lion jumped back and squared for a fight.
The mother-fucking monkey jumped clear out of sight.

A safe distance away again, the monkey returns to "signifying":

He said, "Yeah, you had me down, you had me at last,
But you left me free, now you can still kiss my ass."

This example illustrates the methods of provocation, goading and
taunting artfully practiced by a signifier.

Interestingly, when the *function* of signifying is *directive* the *tactic*
employed is *indirection*, i.e., the signifier reports or repeats what someone else has said about the listener; the "report" is couched in plausible
language designed to compel belief and arouse feelings of anger and hostility. There is also the implication that if the listener fails to do anything about it — what has to be "done" is usually quite clear — his
status will be seriously compromised. Thus the lion is compelled to vin-
dicate the honor of his family by fighting or else leave the impression
that he is afraid, and that he is not "king" of the jungle. When used for
the purpose of directing action, "signifying" is like "shucking" in also
being deceptive and subtle in approach and depending for success on
the naiveté or gullibility of the person being "put on."

When the function of signifying is to arouse feelings of embarrassment, shame, frustration or futility, to diminish someone's status, the

tactic employed is direct in the form of a taunt, as in the example where the monkey is making fun of the lion.

"SOUNDING" TO RELIEVE TENSIONS

Sounding is the term which is today most widely known for the game of verbal insult known in the past as "Playing the Dozens," "The Dirty Dozens" or just "The Dozens." Other current names for the game have regional distribution: Signifying or "Sigging" (Chicago), Joning (Washington, D.C.), Screaming (Harrisburg), etc. In Chicago, the term "sounding" would be descriptive of the initial remarks which are designed to sound out the other person to see whether he will play the game. The verbal insult is also subdivided, the term "signifying" applying to insults which are hurled directly at the person and "the dozens" applying to results hurled at your opponent's family, especially the mother.

Sounding is often catalyzed by signifying remarks referred to earlier such as "Are you going to let him say that about your mama" to spur an exchange between members of the group. It is begun on a relatively low key and built up by verbal exchanges. The game goes like this:

> One insults a member of another's family; others in the group make disapproving sounds to spur on the coming exchange. The one who has been insulted feels at this point that he must reply with a slur on the protagonist's family which is clever enough to defend his honor (and therefore that of his family). This, of course, leads the other (once again, more due to pressure from the crowd than actual insult) to make further jabs. This can proceed until everyone is bored with the whole affair, until one hits the other (fairly rare), or until some other subject comes up that interrupts the proceedings (the usual state of affairs). (Roger D. Abrahams, "Playing the Dozens," *Journal of American Folklore*, July–September, 1962.)

Mack McCormick describes the dozens as a verbal contest:

> . . . in which the players strive to bury one another with vituperation. In the play, the opponent's mother is especially slandered. . . . Then, in turn fathers are identified as queer and syphilitic. Sisters are whores, brothers are defective, cousins are "funny" and the opponent is himself diseased. (Mack McCormick, "The Dirty Dozens," book jacket in the record album *The Unexpurgated Folksongs of Men*, Arhoolie Records.)

An example of the "game" collected by one of my students goes:

> Frank looked up and saw Leroy enter the Outpost.
> Leroy walked past the room where Quinton, "Nap," "Pretty Black," "Cunny," Richard, Haywood, "Bull" and Reese sat playing cards. As Leroy neared the T.V. room, Frank shouted to him.

Frank: "Hey Leroy, your mama — calling you man."

Leroy turned and walked toward the room where the sound came from. He stood in the door and looked at Frank.

Leroy: "Look mother-fuckers, I don't play that shit."

Frank (signifying): "Man, I told you cats 'bout that mama jive" (as if he were concerned about how Leroy felt).

Leroy: "That's all right Frank; you don't have to tell these funky mother-fuckers nothing; I'll fuck me up somebody yet."

Frank's face lit up as if he were ready to burst his side laughing. "Cunny" became pissed at Leroy.

"Cunny": "Leroy, you stupid bastard, you let Frank make a fool of you. He said that 'bout your mama."

"Pretty Black": "Aw, fat ass head 'Cunny' shut up."

"Cunny": "Ain't that some shit. This Black slick head motor flicker got nerve 'nough to call somebody 'fat-head.' Boy, you so black, you sweat Permalube Oil."

This eased the tension of the group as they burst into loud laughter.

"Pretty Black": "What 'chu laughing 'bout 'Nap,' with your funky mouth smelling like dog shit."

Even Leroy laughed at this.

"Nap": "Your mama mother-fucker."

"Pretty Black": "Your funky mama too."

"Nap" (strongly): "It takes twelve barrels of water to make a steamboat run; it takes an elephant's dick to make your Grandmammy come; she been elephant fucked, camel fucked and hit side the head with your Grandpappy's nuts."

Reese: "Godorr-damn; go on and rap mother-fucker."

Reese began slapping each boy in his hand, giving his positive approval of "Nap's" comment. "Pretty Black" in an effort not to be outdone, but directing his verbal play elsewhere stated:

"Pretty Black": "Reese, what you laughing 'bout? You so square, you shit bricked shit."

Frank: "Whooooowee!"

Reese (sounded back): "Square huh, what about your nappy ass hair before it was stewed; that shit was so bad till, when you went to bed at night, it would leave your head and go on the corner and meddle."

The boys slapped each other in the hand and cracked up.

"Pretty Black": "On the streets meddling, bet Dinky didn't offer me no pussy and I turned it down."

Frank: "Reese scared of pussy."

"Pretty Black": "Hell, yeah; the greasy mother rather fuck old ugly, funky cock Sue Willie than get a piece of ass from a decent broad."

Frank: "Godorr-damn! Not Sue Willie."

"Pretty Black": "Yeah, ol meat-beating Reese rather screw that cross-eyed, clapsy bitch, who when she cry, tears rip down her ass."

Haywood: "Don't be so mean, Black."

Reese: "Aw shut up, you half-White bastard."

Frank: "Wait, man, Haywood ain't gonna hear much more of that half-White shit; he's a brother too."

Reese: "Brother, my Black ass; that White ass landlord gotta be this mother-fucker's paw."

"Cunny": "Man, you better stop foolin with Haywood; he's turning red."

Haywood: "Fuck yall" (as he withdrew from the "sig" game).

Frank: "Yeah, fuck yall; yet's go to the stick hall."

The group left enroute to the billiard hall. (James Maryland, "Signifying at the Outpost," unpublished term paper for the course *Idiom of the Negro Ghettos*, January 1967.)

The above example of sounding is an excellent illustration of the "game" as played by 15–17-year-old Negro boys, some of whom have already acquired the verbal skill which for them is often the basis for having a high "rep." Ability with words is apparently as highly valued as physical strength. In the sense that the status of one of the participants in the game is diminished if he has to resort to fighting to answer a verbal attack, verbal ability may be even more highly regarded than physical ability.

The relatively high value placed on verbal ability must be clear to most black boys at early age. Most boys begin their activity in sounding by compiling a repertoire of "one liners." When the game is played the one who has the greatest number of such remarks wins. Here are some examples of "one liners" collected from fifth- and sixth-grade black boys in Chicago:

Yo mama is so bowlegged, she looks like the bit out of a donut.

Yo mama sent her picture to the lonely hearts club, and they sent it back and said, "We ain't that lonely!"

Your family is so poor the rats and roaches eat lunch out.

Your house is so small the roaches walk single file.

I walked in your house and your family was running around the table. I said, "Why you doin that?" Your mama say, "First one drops, we eat."

Real proficiency in the game comes to only a small percentage of those who play it. These players have the special skill in being able to turn around what their opponents have said and attack them with it. Thus, when someone indifferently said "fuck you" to Concho, his retort was immediate and devastating: "Man, you haven't even kissed me yet."

The "best talkers" from this group often become the successful street-corner, barber shop, and pool hall story tellers who deliver the long, rhymed, witty, narrative stories called "toasts." They are, as Roger D. Abrahams has described, the traditional "men of words" and have become on occasion entertainers such as Dick Gregory and Redd Foxx, who are virtuosos at repartee, and preachers, whose verbal power has been traditionally esteemed.

The function of the "dozens" or "sounding" is to borrow status from an opponent through an exercise of verbal power. The opponent feels compelled to regain his status by "sounding" back on the speaker or other group member whom he regards as more vulnerable.

The presence of a group seems to be especially important in controlling the game. First of all, one does not "play" with just anyone since the subject matter is concerned with things that in reality one is quite sensitive about. It is precisely *because* "Pretty Black" has a "black slick head" that makes him vulnerable to "Cunny's" barb, especially now when the Afro-American "natural" hair style is in vogue. Without the control of the group "sounding" will frequently lead to a fight. This was illustrated by a tragic epilogue concerning Haywood, when Haywood was being "sounded" on in the presence of two girls by his best friend (other members of the group were absent), he refused to tolerate it. He went home, got a rifle, came back and shot and killed his friend. In the classroom from about the fourth grade on fights among black boys invariably are caused by someone "sounding" on the other person's mother.

Significantly, the subject matter of sounding is changing with the changing self-concept of the black with regard to those physical characteristics that are characteristically "Negro," and which in the past were vulnerable points in the black psyche: blackness and "nappy" hair. It ought to be said that for many blacks, blackness was always highly esteemed and it might be more accurate to regard the present sentiment of the black community toward skin color as reflecting a shifted attitude for only a *portion* of the black community. This suggests that "sounding" on someone's light skin color is not new. Nevertheless, one can regard the previously favorable attitude toward light skin color and "good hair" as the prevailing one. "Other things being equal, the more closely a woman approached her white counterpart, the more attractive she was considered to be, by both men and women alike. 'Good hair' (hair that is long and soft) and light skin were the chief criteria." (Elliot Liebow, *Tally's Corner.*)

"The dozens" has been linked to the overall psycho-social growth of the black male. McCormick has stated that a "single round of a dozen or so exchanges frees more pent-up aggressions than will a dose of sodium pentothal." The fact that one permits a kind of abuse within the rules of the game and within the confines of the group which would otherwise not be tolerated, is filled with psychological import. It seems also important, however, to view its function from the perspective of the nonparticipating members of the group. Its function for them may be to incite and prod individual members of the group to combat for the purpose of energizing the elements, of simply relieving the boredom of just "hanging around" and the malaise of living in a static and restrictive environment.

A summary analysis of the different forms of language behavior which have been discussed above permit the following generalizations:

The prestige norms which influence black speech behavior are those which have been successful in manipulating and controlling people and situations. The function of all of the forms of language behavior discussed above, with the exception of "running it down," was to project personality, assert oneself, or arouse emotion, frequently with the additional purpose of getting the person to give up or do something which will be of some benefit to the speaker. Only running it down has as its primary function to communicate information and often here too, the personality and style of the speaker in the form of rapping is projected along with the information.

The purpose for which language is used suggests that the speaker views the social situations into which he moves as consisting of a series of transactions which require that he be continually ready to take advantage of a person or situation or defend himself against being victimized. He has absorbed what Horton has called "street rationality." As one of Horton's respondents put it: "The good hustler . . . conditions his mind and must never put his guard too far down, to relax, or he'll be taken."

I have carefully avoided limiting the group within the black community of whom the language behavior and perspective of their environment is characteristic. While I have no doubt that it is true of those who are generally called "street people" I am uncertain of the extent to which it is true of a much larger portion of the black community, especially the male segment. My informants consisted of street people, high school students, and blacks, who by their occupation as community and youth workers, possess what has been described as a "sharp sense of the streets." Yet it is difficult to find a black male in the community who has *not* witnessed or participated in "the dozens" or heard of signifying, or rapping, or shucking and jiving at some time during his growing up. It would be equally difficult to imagine a high school student in a Chicago inner-city school not being touched by what is generally regarded as "street culture."

In conclusion, by blending style and verbal power, through rapping, sounding and running it down, the black in the ghetto establishes his personality; through shucking, gripping and copping a plea, he shows his respect for power; through jiving and signifying he stirs up excitement. With all of the above, he hopes to manipulate and control people and situations to give himself a winning edge.

11

Cosmetics: The language of bodily adornment

TERENCE S. TURNER

*Bodily adornment among the Tchikrin of Brazil includes elaborate
painting, earplugs, lip plugs, and various styles of clothing.
Terence Turner not only describes these practices, but deciphers
their complex code to reveal their meaning. He suggests that
body decorations have similar functions in all societies.*

Something profound in the nature of man, in his role as a member
of a society or culture, seems to be bound up with his universal urge to
decorate or transform the surface of his body. We might well ask if the
boundaries and appendages of the body carry some universal symbolic
significance, and if so, whether their adornment is a way of focusing and
expressing this symbolic meaning. In other words, bodily adornment may
be a kind of symbolic language. But if it is, how can we decipher its
"message"?

The Tchikrin, one of the least-known peoples of the central Brazilian wilderness (a region virtually unpenetrated by Brazilian settlers), are
among the world's most exotic body adorners. Their elaborate body
painting, their penis sheaths and earplugs, and their spectacular lip plugs
raise the question of the symbolic significance of bodily adornment in a
uniquely compelling way.

The Tchikrin are the northernmost group of the large Kayapo tribe,
a member of the Ge-speaking linguistic family. Their villages are built in
a circle around a large central plaza, each house the residence of an ex-

Originally published as "Tchikrin: A Central Brazilian Tribe and Its Symbolic
Language of Bodily Adornment." Reprinted with permission from *Natural History*
Magazine, October, 1969. Copyright © The American Museum of Natural History,
1969. Illustrations are omitted.

tended family. Throughout their lives the women remain in the households of their birth. Men, however, leave their maternal houses at about the age of eight, when they move to the men's house, which is usually built in the center of the plaza. Only after consummating their marriages by fathering a child do men move into their wives' houses.

The pattern of a man's life cycle focuses on his movement from his maternal household, to the men's house, to his wife's household. Before, during, and after these moves, he is classified according to named age grades, each with its distinctive social properties, styles of body painting and hair cutting, and bodily ornaments. There is a separate and rather different system of age grades for women.

Newborn and nursing infants of both sexes are classified in a category whose name means "little ones." They are the most elaborately ornamented Tchikrin of any age. A few days after a baby's birth, its ear lobes — and if it is a boy, its lower lip — are pierced, usually by its father. Cigar-shaped earplugs of reddened wood are inserted in the ear lobes and replaced from time to time with larger ones until the holes in the lobes have become quite large. A narrow dowel or string of beads is also inserted in a boy's lower lip, but this ornament is not enlarged until much later in life. At the same time, the mother crochets cotton bands, reddens them with paint, and fastens them around the infant's wrists, ankles, and knees. When these grow too tight they are cut away and replaced with larger ones.

The cast-off arm and leg bands and the discarded sets of earplugs are saved by the mother in a special pouch, together with the baby's desiccated umbilical cord. The bands and plugs constitute a sort of record of the baby's growth — analogous, in a way, to a modern mother's "baby book." When the baby grows older the father takes its pouch and hangs it on, or buries it at the root of, a hardwood tree in the savanna. This gives the child a magical infusion of strength and well-being, symbolically neutralizing the weakness and vulnerability of its infancy, for hardwood trees are potent sources of strength, endurance, and health in Kayapo ritual symbolism. The red color of the earplugs and cotton bands serves much the same symbolic function — the fostering of growth and strength — for red is associated with health, energy, and vitality.

Body painting is an outstanding feature of the decoration of both male and female babies. Mothers, grandmothers, or other kinswomen, using a stylus made of the center rib of a leaf, draw complex linear patterns over the entire body of the child. Women also paint each other in this complex style, but except for rare ceremonial occasions, they are not allowed to paint men and older boys. Since only women use the stylus method, the men paint each other in a rougher, simpler pattern.

When a boy is weaned, learns to talk well, and can walk easily, which usually happens between the ages of three and four, he "graduates" from the age grade of little ones to that of "boys about to enter the men's house." This transition, like most changes from one major age category to the next, is accompanied by changes in bodily adornment and features of grooming such as hair style. The boy is now stripped of his infantile ornaments (earplugs and cotton arm and leg bands) and his hair is cut short. Boys of this age spend little time with their mothers and sisters; they already form a quasi-independent masculine play group, a precursor of the age sets and societies of the men's house. Their semi-independence of their maternal families and passage out of infancy are expressed not only by doffing their infantile ornaments and long hair but also by the infrequency with which their mothers paint them in the time-consuming linear "stylus" fashion. Boys of this age are far more apt to be painted with broad areas or bands of black and red, applied directly with the hand.

At about the age of eight (the Tchikrin do not reckon age by number of years, but by broad criteria of physical size and maturity) a decisive event occurs in a boy's life. In a brief but solemn ceremony, an unrelated man called a "substitute father" comes to the boy's maternal house, where he sits waiting silently with his wailing father and mother. The substitute father leads him out into the plaza and paints his body solid black. He then takes the boy by the hand into the men's house, which becomes his home.

He is now cut off from the world of family and blood relationships. The painting ritual thus marks the end of childhood for the boy and he enters a new age grade called "the painted ones." From this time on the boy will never again (except for rare ceremonial occasions) be painted by a woman. Henceforth, he will be painted only by other men, in the rough hand style or with a stamp made of a fruit rind that is cut in a simple pattern.

At puberty, boys go through a brief ceremony in which they are given penis sheaths to wear. After this they may replace their beaded lip ornaments with small versions of the mature men's lip plugs. They also let their hair grow long again, in the style of adult men and women.

Hair is associated with sexual powers. Long hair connotes full participation in sexually based relationships. However, since infants as well as mature adults have long hair, it is evident that the Kayapo notion of participation in sexual relations is considerably different and more complex than our own. For the Kayapo, there are two modes of sexual participation. One, like our own culture's conception, consists of the mature individual's active exercise of his sexual powers, above all in the relationship between husband and wife. The other, for which our culture has no counterpart, consists of the infant's passive biological (and social) dependence on the family, a dependence founded upon its parents' procreative sexual relationship. The Kayapo think of an infant before it is weaned more as an extension of its parents' biological being than as an independent individual. It is conceived as still participating in the biological communion with its parents that it enjoyed in the womb. This is understandable in view of the Kayapo notion of pregnancy — that the fetus grows by nursing inside the mother. Birth, therefore, does not fundamentally change the relationship between mother and infant; it merely transfers its locus from inside her body to outside. The father is also involved in this biological connection, for while the child is still in the womb, his semen — like the mother's milk — is thought to nourish the fetus. The birth of the baby terminates this direct physical link with the father, a rupture that renders the father's relation to his newborn child extremely delicate and fraught with danger. In order to minimize this danger, for several days the father abstains from physical exertions or "strong" and "dangerous" acts, such as killing animals, that might otherwise have a deleterious impact on the child's health.

Because weaning marks the end of full physical communion between mother and child, a child's hair is cut at this time. Short hair symbolizes the attenuation of his direct biological connection with others, a connection that is restored when the child grows to physical maturity and is ready to exercise his own sexual powers. The same principle underlies the custom of cutting the hair as a gesture of mourning for the death of a spouse, sibling, or child. The effect of such a kinsman's death is equivalent to weaning, since it suppresses ties, which the Kayapo conceive as based on an intimate biological bond, between the person who has died and the survivor.

A distinction is made between hair of the head and hair of the face and body. Facial hair is customarily plucked as a matter of ordinary grooming of both sexes and all ages. Here again, however, the sexual significance of hair emerges in one of the more stereotyped forms of Kayapo love-play — it is considered to impart a special *frisson* for lovers to pluck a stray eyebrow or eyelash from each other's faces with their teeth.

The Kayapo recognize, in ritual and other ways, the correlation between the development of sexual maturity and the weakening of family ties. They attempt to offset this tendency toward the isolation of the individual from social control by developing alternate forms of communal integration of the individual's developing sexual powers. Public recognition of the individual's steps toward sexual and social maturity is ritually associated with changes in his social status that move him inexorably toward marriage and the founding of his own family.

The penis sheath is the symbolic expression of the social control and regulation of mature male sexual powers. It is bestowed at puberty, and only after the sheath-bestowing ceremony is a youth's hair allowed to grow long again. Sheath and coiffure are thus complementary aspects of the public recognition of the growing boy's biological sexuality and, at the same time, of its integration into the social order.

Penis sheath, lip plug, and long hair symbolize the community's recognition of a boy's physical maturity, but they do not confer on him the right to put his newly recognized powers into practice. He only wins this right by going through the initiation ceremony, which is completely distinct from the penis-sheath rite and centers around the ceremonial "marriage," or betrothal, of the boy. This ritual marriage is not considered binding: it only establishes in principle the boy's ability to have sexual relations and marry any girl he chooses. Going through the initiation ceremony entitles a boy to move up into the age grade of "bachelor youths."

Bachelor youths eventually become engaged in earnest. Engagement, a private arrangement with a girl and her parents, culminates in the girl's pregnancy and the birth of a child. This event marks the climax of the youth's transition from boyhood to mature manhood, and he thereupon passes from the symbolic tutelage of his substitute father, who has presided over the successive stages of the long initiation process. Having founded his own family, he is definitively free of his lingering childhood bonds to his maternal family. He is entitled to move out of the men's house into his wife's house, and simultaneously to graduate to the age grade of mature men, significantly called "fathers." Fathers make up the membership of the men's societies, which meet (but do not reside) in the men's house and conduct the political affairs of the community.

These vital transitions in a man's life are expressed by a final transformation in bodily ornamentation — the replacement of the youth's small lip plug by a saucerlike plate, which may reach a diameter of four inches, or an alternative form, a long cylinder of rock crystal or wood. As an expression of mature manhood, this extraordinary ornament has a complex significance.

One aspect of its symbolism is implicit in the contrast between the lip plug and earplug. Both hearing and speaking have specific social associations for the Kayapǫ, and these associations relate to each other as complementary passive and active values. Hearing is a passive activity. The word *mari* "hearing" signifies understanding in the passive sense of knowing about something. Hearing in this sense is used in the common idiomatic expression of affirmation of specific relationships. If a man has good relations with his father's side of the family, for example, he says, "I hear them strongly" (*mari taytch*). Speaking, on the other hand, is perhaps the most fundamental social act of self-assertion, and its assertive connotations are highly elaborated and associated with mature masculinity. Flamboyant oratory is one of the major activities of Kayapo men.

The huge lip plugs of the father's age grade are consciously associated with this flamboyant oral assertiveness. The dynamism and oral aggressiveness of adult male public behavior rests on a foundation of sexual assertiveness: graduation to father status depends on a man's actually siring a child. The fulfillment of male sexual powers in paternity and the resulting integration of men in specific family units are, in other words, what earn men the right to aggressive, oral self-assertion in the men's house. The full-size lip plug, in its double character as the badge of paternity and the symbol of mature male oral aggressiveness, precisely embodies this relationship between the phallic and oral components of adult masculinity, and by the same token, of the family and communal levels of men's social relations.

If paternity is the criterion for communal recognition of male maturity, then infants assume a reciprocal importance as the "objective correlatives" of manhood in both its biological and social aspects (phallic power and family membership). Infants, then, are the passive extensions, or corroborations, of the father's sexual powers and social position as *paterfamilias*. The relation of the infant to its father is in fact analogous to that between hearing (in its Kayapo sense of passive affirmation of social relations) and speaking (considered as social self-assertion). The symbolic complementarity of infantile earplug and paternal lip plug neatly expresses this social complementarity, especially when the phallic connotations of the cigar-shaped earplugs are taken into account. The same considerations explain why women do not wear lip plugs and why neither adult men nor women wear earplugs.

In contrast to the man's pattern of life, for the Tchikrin woman there is no dramatic transformation in social relations involved in biological parenthood. The residence rule dictates that women spend their entire life cycle in the households into which they are born. The contrasts between female and male body decoration reflect the difference in social pattern.

Girls, like boys, dispense with their earplugs and have their hair cut upon weaning. They continue, however, to wear crocheted red cotton arm and leg bands — in recognition of their continuing membership in their parental families — until they are judged ready for childbearing.

At about the age of eight — the same age that a boy leaves home to enter the men's house — a girl is initiated into sexual relations under the aegis of a special ceremonial guardian. This event marks her graduation into the age grade of "given ones." In all probability the name indicates (the Kayapo have no explicit explanation for it) that girls of this age grade are considered to be "bestowed" upon the initiated men of the village for

sexual purposes. Given ones are expected to take an active and enthusiastic part in communal dances; dancing in groups during communal rituals
is, in fact, their chief collective activity.

The rite that recognizes that a girl has reached the stage of potential
motherhood bears many resemblances to the boy's ceremony of induction
into the men's house, and has the same purpose of formally dissolving
the childhood bond to the parental family. In the girls' ceremony, a
"substitute mother" paints the girls' thighs, breasts, and upper arms
with broad black stripes, and cuts off their arm and leg bands (the symbols of parental ties). Henceforth, they are known as "black-thighed
ones," and are considered ready to consummate their courtships with
one of their suitors in marriage by giving birth to a child. Only this event
differentiates women in a social sense from their parental families, since
it enables them to set up distinct families of their own within the household they share with their parents. Independence from the parental family (established much earlier for boys by their move to the men's house)
is the prerequisite for social recognition of their reproductive powers as
fully developed, autonomous, and "adult." This recognition, as we have
seen, is symbolized for both sexes by long hair. For this reason, a woman
is allowed to wear her hair long only upon the birth of her first child.

After attaining black-thighed status, a girl is qualified to join one
of the mature women's societies, whose members gather regularly, every
few weeks or so, to paint each other. It is interesting that while adult
women often use the hand technique of the mature men to paint each
other, they may equally well employ the stylus method used by mothers
to paint their infants. Men and boys are almost never painted in this
style after they leave home for the men's house; the use of it by adult
women is another mark of their greater continuity with the social circumstances of childhood.

The typical daily routine of a Tchikrin mother, however, has relatively little place for collective activities. She must nurse her baby and
care for her younger children. One of the most frequent maternal chores
is delousing, which, interestingly enough, conforms to a sexually asymmetrical pattern partially similar to that of body painting. Women delouse children, other women, and men (usually their husbands), but men
do not delouse women.

A woman's day usually includes a trip to her garden or perhaps an
expedition to gather firewood, normally cut by women. She is likely to
return from either heavily burdened. She must cook for her husband and
children (each nuclear family within the household gardens and cooks for
itself). The Tchikrin, like other members of the Ge linguistic group, lack
pottery. They cook by baking bundles of food wrapped in leaves, in a
temporary earth "oven" composed of heated stones, leaves, and earth.

At the end of the day a woman may get a little time to relax with her husband on the family bed, a mat-covered platform of split logs.

Lip plug, earplugs, penis sheath, hair style, cotton leg and arm bands, and body painting make up a symbolic language that expresses a wide range of information about social status, sex, and age. As a language, however, it does more than merely communicate this information from one individual to another: at a deeper level, it establishes a channel of communication *within* the individual between the social and biological aspects of his personality.

The social and psychological "message" of bodily adornment is coded and transmitted on an even more basic level by the colors used in body painting, and the symbolic associations of the parts of the body to which each color is applied. The colors of Tchikrin body painting are red (made from the seeds of the urucú plant), black (made from the juice of the genipa fruit), and, rarely, white (made from white clay), and these are used in determinate ways. Red is always applied on the extremities of the body — the forearms and hands, lower legs and feet, and the face. Black is always used on the trunk and upper parts of the limbs, as well as for the square cheek patches and borders along the shaved area of the forehead. The black face paintings, executed with painstaking care, are often covered immediately after they are finished with a heavy coat of red, which renders them almost invisible. The explanation for this peculiar practice lies in the symbolic values of the colors involved.

Red always connotes energy, health, and "quickness," both in the sense of swiftness and of heightened sensitivity (which the Kayapo conceive of as "quickness" or "lightness" of skin). Black, on the other hand, is associated with transitions between clearly defined states or categories, with "borderline" conditions or regions where normal clear-cut structures of ideas and rules of behavior are "blacked out."

It is interesting that the word for black, *tuk*, also means "dead," and is the adjective used for the zone of land just outside the village, which separates it from the completely wild forest and savanna country. The graveyard and the secluded camps used by groups going through "transitional" rites, such as initiation, are located in this interstitial area. Death itself is conceived of by the Tchikrin as a transitional phase between life and total extinction. The ghosts of the dead live on for one generation in the village of the dead, after which they "die" once more, this time passing into total oblivion.

White, which occurs only in relatively infrequent ceremonial decorations, is associated less with transition than with the pure, "terminal" state of complete transcendence of the normal social world. It is, for example, the color of ghosts. White clay is the food of ghosts, and the vil-

lages of the ghosts are always located near outcroppings of white clay
or rocks.

Body painting for both ordinary social and ritual occasions seems to
be a means of expressing heightened integration and participation in the
social order as well as a means of heightening individual biological and
psychological powers. Red is applied on the parts of the body most immediately associated with swiftness, agility, and sensory contact with the
outside world (feet, hands, and face). This seems logical enough from
what we have seen of the symbolic values of the color red. Black is used
for the parts of the body most intimately associated with the individual's
biological being, his inner self as contrasted with his faculties of relating to the world (the trunk, upper parts of the limbs, and certain areas of
the head).

Why should black, which symbolizes the marginal, transitional, or
imperfectly integrated aspects of the social order, be thus associated with
the individual's presocial (biological) being in those situations where integration into society is being dramatized and reaffirmed?

To answer this question adequately we must start from an understanding of the symbolic significance of the skin in Kayapo culture. The
skin, for the Kayapo, is the boundary of the individual on several levels
of meaning. In the obvious physical sense, it separates the individual from
the external environment, which includes other people. But in a more
subtle sense, the skin symbolizes the boundary between two levels of
the human personality: the lower level, based on presocial drives emanat-
ing from the individual's biological constitution, and the higher level of
moral conscience and intellectual consciousness based on cultural principles derived from social sources outside the individual. More simply, this
inner, psychological boundary corresponds to the boundary between the
physical individual and his society.

The proper balance of relations between the levels of the individual's
personality, like proper relations between individuals in society, depends
in Kayapo thought on the right sort of communication taking place across
these two correlated boundaries. They must be crossed in both directions,
for society needs the biological energies of individuals, but it also needs
to control them to prevent disruption and chaos. The individual subsists
through his biological energies, but he needs the steadying influence of
social values, cognitive categories, and moral principles or he will "go
berserk" (a recognized condition in Kayapo, known as *aybanh*). Disease,
death, the breaking of certain taboos, and going berserk are all conceived
as improper forms of eruption of the biological level of existence into the
social, orderly level.

The interesting point for our purposes is that all of these "erup-
tions" are associated with disorders or treatments of the skin: sick peo-

ple are painted red, dead people either red or black, taboo-breakers get hives or other skin diseases, the skin of berserks becomes alternately overheated and then cold and insensitive, etc. When black, the color associated with transition between the social and asocial worlds, is painted on the skin of the central parts of the body, it expresses the transcendence of the boundary between individual and society and thus reaffirms the mutual integration of the biological individual and the "body social."

It becomes easy to understand, then, why the Tchikrin paint over the black designs of the face with red: They are concerned not so much with esthetic results as with a symbolic statement, in which both colors have complementary "messages" to transmit. The overpainting with red serves to energize, to charge with biological and psychic life-force, the sensory and intelligent part of the person whose socialization has been asserted by the black designs below.

Body painting at this general level of meaning really amounts to the imposition of a second, social "skin" on the naked biological skin of the individual. This second skin of culturally standardized patterns symbolically expresses the "socialization" of the human body — the subordination of the physical aspects of individual existence to common social values and behavior.

It would be misleading to lay too much emphasis on the superficial differences between Tchikrin body adornment and our own culture's elaborate array of clothing and hair styles, makeup, and jewelry. Among the Tchikrin, as among ourselves, the decoration of the surface of the body serves as a symbolic link between the "inner man" and some of his society's most important values.

12

Decoding the runner's wardrobe
JEFFREY E. NASH

Body painting and ornaments of the Tchikrin, described in the last article may seem exotic and uncommon. The symbolic language may appear foreign, something outside of our daily experience. But the basic cultural process exists in every society: clothes communicate. How we adorn our bodies carries a multitude of messages about what we think is important in life. In this article Jeffrey Nash brings us closer to home. He shows how long-distance runners, those who pursue it as an avocation, learn what clothes to wear when running. And their clothes do more than protect their feet and keep them warm. The wardrobe of long-distance runners has meaning. It says something about individuals, their aspirations, their places in the local world of runners, and their self-identities. This article decodes that message; it is an ethnography of the silent language of clothes.

Somewhere in the dim prehistory of humankind, our ancestors began to adorn their bodies. A momentous transition occurred: from reliance on biology, humans moved to reliance on culture. Clothing replaced hair and fur to protect from the cold or to shield from the heat. Most of us think of clothes as primarily functional — they cover our bodies to protect us from the elements. But this commonsense view is naive. In fact, the earliest Neanderthal graves produced artifacts which suggest that body adornment may have been first used for symbolic purposes rather than practical ones. Human beings in every culture employ the language of body adornment — using animal skins, paint, cloth, metal, plastic, rubber, canvas, wood, leaves, nylon, feathers, and bark. All people communicate important information by the way they decorate their bodies.

This article was written especially for this volume and has never before been published.

There is a popular myth, reinforced by the type of pictures found in *National Geographic Magazine,* that so-called "primitive peoples" are preoccupied with decorating their bodies. We marvel at their intricately painted bodies, lip plugs, ornate feather headdresses, penis sheaths, and strange types of clothing. Such adornment *must* have symbolic meaning. Otherwise why would they take such pains to decorate their bodies?

At the same time we view our own body adornment practices in much more pragmatic terms. We assume that our clothing is simple, tasteful, and used primarily for protection from the elements. A small amount of paint on the lips, efforts to curl or to wave hair, earrings, finger rings, shoes, hats, and other paraphernalia add to our attractiveness — but certainly they do not communicate anything. We do not "speak" to one another by the way we clothe and decorate our bodies. But are we, after all, really so different? Do the clothes we wear function as a silent language? And if so, how can we decode their meaning?

It is my contention that body decoration is even more important for people who live in cities than for tribal hunters. Size and density of urban populations have created a world of strangers. Each day we encounter dozens of people we do not know; clothing and other forms of body adornment allow us to communicate with strangers without speaking. How we dress tells other people about our values, our identities, our political views, our age, and dozens of other important things. Our clothing may pave the way for verbal communication or signal that we do not want to interact.

The businessman who wears a Brooks Brothers suit, low-cut leather shoes, white shirt, and tie, and who heads for the commuter train in a London Fog coat with briefcase in hand communicates a whole range of messages. The construction worker in overalls and hard hat is doing more than wearing clothes that protect his body; he is saying something to the world. The college student in faded jeans, construction boots, flannel shirt, puffy down jacket, and backpack is doing much more than dressing comfortably and practically; he or she is communicating in the language of body adornment.

RUNNERS

This article examines how clothes and posture serve a communications function. In it, I want to decode the messages in the wardrobe of one urban subculture, a group of people who identify themselves as "runners." By the term *runner,* I do not refer to people who merely run, for whatever purpose. Runners are people who have acquired a body of cultural knowledge about running. They use this knowledge to order their lives; they think of themselves as runners. The *runner* may be a business person, a housewife, a teacher, or a minister who sets aside a portion of each day for the purpose of running. They share a culture that is quite distinct from that of others who merely run, whether as members of a high school or college track team, as track coaches, or as joggers who go out occasionally to lose weight or improve their health. Perhaps the most important distinguishing characteristic of runners is the clothes they wear; this subculture has a well-developed language of clothes and body movement.

The culture of runners is preserved, generated, and disseminated in two ways: through personal contacts and through running clubs or associations. The first usually involves two persons discovering that they are both interested in running. They meet at their place of work, at the local high school track, or on the pathways at the city park. They discuss mutual habits and problems with running. Knowledge about articles of clothing, shoes in particular, and running lore in general are exchanged.

However, running clubs play the major role in producing and maintaining this cultural knowledge. These clubs typically have many members, with a small cadre of race organizers, newsletter editors, and others who volunteer significant amounts of time to the organization. Most organizations are based in urban areas and serve a local membership. There are, however, nationwide organizations and publications that cater to the runners and their need for knowledge. Publications of both local and national organizations provide a wealth of information to the runner. For instance, the next issue of *Runner's World* is frequently awaited in anxious anticipation; it may contain an article on the problems of shoe wear, an announcement about training schedules, or a personal account from another reader.

As an individual is socialized into this culture, he or she learns to recognize the runner's appearance. Elsewhere[1] I have discussed this socialization and how one experiences an identity change in becoming a runner. Unquestionably, this culture borrows from the world of professional and amateur track, and individual members may participate in both worlds. Unlike their athlete counterparts, runners have no season for training and receive no glory or adulation. The runner's motivation to run daily, yearly, even for a lifetime, is based on a particular self-identity. The runner thinks of himself or herself as a special type of person. This identity may not be the primary one in life, but it does represent a commitment to a way of life that includes constant training. This identity, the knowledge commensurate with it, and the person's

---

[1] Jeffrey Nash, "The Short and Long of It: Legitimizing Motives for Running," in Jeffrey Nash and James P. Spradley (eds.), *Sociology: A Descriptive Approach* (Chicago: Rand McNally, 1976).

place in the world of runners is communicated clearly by dress and even by running posture.

Consider the following example. Early in the morning a solitary figure runs down the middle of the street in a residential section of a large midwestern city. He passes another man running in the opposite direction. Each individual keeps his eyes straight ahead or on the path in front of him; although they see each other, neither acknowledges the presence of the other. A few miles farther, near the park, the runner spots another figure just over the top of the next hill. Their routes appear to cross but soon the other will be out of sight. The runner speeds up, moving to within hearing range. The other figure turns, raises a hand in a waving gesture. The runner returns the gesture calling out, "Looks good." The other person replies, "Yeah, great day." Each continues running; within a few seconds they are out of each other's sight.

A casual observer might infer that the first encounter was between strangers, the second between friends. But such is not the case. Both were strangers; our runner has never seen either person before. In the first case, communication occurred, but it was by means of a silent language alone. Our runner quickly decoded the message in the other's clothes, which said, "I'm not a runner but only someone who jogs before breakfast, probably for my health." In the second encounter, the silent message was, "I'm a runner," and led quickly to the verbal exchange. But how did this communication occur? What silent grammar did the runner employ to interpret the clothing and the posture of these strangers? To answer these questions we must look at runners' cultural attitudes toward shoes, shirts, shorts, other paraphernalia, and posture. We need to understand also how these adornments are influenced by the weather. The answers to these questions will provide a guide to the cultural rules by which a runner's wardrobe can be decoded.

THE PRIMACY OF SHOES

Without doubt, it is shoes that make the runner. Their primacy derives in part from the physical punishment that the feet must endure in long runs over hard city pavement. The "good shoe" protects the foot; it is also light and well suited for the purposes of the run.

But runners do not simply go out and purchase a shoe. There are at present more than 150 models of running shoes and approximately 25 manufacturers of these shoes. The runner selects a particular kind of shoe that he or she considers best. At home, the runner may have a closet for special gear, which may contain several pairs of shoes. But how does the runner decide which shoes to purchase? Function, durability, price, and weight are all important; however, overriding those considerations is the meaning of each style of shoe. Shoes communicate a message; runners select the pair that communicates the right message.

There are two basic types of shoes the runner knows about: spikes and flats. Spikes are used primarily for tracks. Occasionally a race will be conducted over a gravel or dirt road and spikes may be used, but they are not used for the daily run on city streets. Therefore, we will focus on the second type of shoe, the flat.

Flats may be divided into two subtypes, the training flat and the racing flat. The latter is generally much lighter with less padding to absorb shock, less support in heels and uppers; the training shoe is designed for daily wear and generally provides more support and shock absorption.

The characteristics of each shoe type are numerous and the typical runner will not be able to articulate all details of shank, heel, toe, support, durability, etc. However, a runner will have a minimal level of knowledge that includes ability to recognize the manufacturer's logo. Manufacturers emboss this symbol on all the different kinds of shoes they make — from ultra-light spikes to heavy training flats. When our runner spots the figure at the top of the hill and suspects a runner, he moves close enough to see the Nike logo, the bold white stripe in the shape of a check mark with a rounded point; then he knows that a greeting is appropriate. This is not to say that only runners wear Nike shoes. Rather, the Nike logo is consistent with the total configuration that the runner presents. It completes the picture and may well be the definitive mark of a runner.

The same process applies for the three-striped logo of the Adidas, the distinctive double-crossed lines of the Tiger, or the muted belt with two oblong holes of the New Balance. A person running down the street wearing blue jeans and a pair of four-striped Kinney sneakers is simply not a runner, though the sneakers look much like the three-striped Adidas. A runner knows that although the cost of the Adidas, Nike, Puma, or Tiger shoes may be three times that of a discount store's "running shoe," a person who is serious about running would never use "discounted" shoes. In fact, so important is the right shoe that some shoe manufacturers have struggled to acquire a runner's reputation for their shoe. For example, the American-made Brooks 270, much cheaper than the imported shoes, has been advertised extensively. The promotion stresses its quality as a running shoe — its light weight, sole design, heel support, and the like — to convince buyers that despite the shoe's low price, it is a genuine running shoe. Nevertheless, few Brooks 270s are seen on the feet of weekend racers, although most know the upside-down check logo.

If one wears a shoe known to be a runner's shoe, those knowledgeable in these matters can recognize another of their kind. Shoes are ranked in terms of status in the runner's culture, but for the purpose of achieving recognition as a member, it is sufficient merely to be sporting a running shoe; an Interval 3:05 New Balance or a Brooks 270 will do the job.

Although any running shoe suffices to communicate "I am a runner," the kind of shoe worn does articulate the message further. For example, a person sporting a pair of Eugen Brutting Marathons, a shoe with a distinctive diamond embossed with the letters EB, communicates that his or her commitment to running is serious. These shoes cost approximately $12 more than other popular running shoes. They are known for their ultralight yet substantive construction. A person wearing them communicates that he or she knows a great deal about shoes, that he or she trains long and hard and for fast times.

The exotic shoe may indicate that the wearer has some special need in footwear. The serious runner runs long and hard. With increased distance comes worry about the possibility of injury. The nagging knee pain or the strained tendon in the foot can interfere with preparation for racing. Runners believe that improper footwear can contribute to knee and leg problems by placing stress on these parts of the anatomy with repeated and peculiar foot-pavement contact. Thus, a runner wearing Karhu 2323s may have a knee problem that is alleviated by the high heel design of this shoe. These orange and black shoes communicate that the wearer has a special need and that this shoe fits the need. This runner knows shoes. It is not that the runner wants to acquire high status by displaying the special shoe; instead, the special shoe means that despite pain or discomfort the runner continues to run. Special shoes, then, indicate dedication toward running, and mark their wearers as the most conscientious members of the runner's culture.

SHIRTS AS BILLBOARDS

Shoes may make runners, but shirts advertise their messages. The shirt is the second most important article of clothing for communicating a runner's identity. The message shirt may be displayed even in cold weather by wearing it over warm sweats or warmups. This is by no means a widespread practice, but when it is done, it is regarded as meaningful by other runners.

There are two types of shirt: the T-shirt and the tank top. T-shirts have a special significance since they are often used as prizes in races. Such shirts are embossed in letters proclaiming the name of the event — for example, Bay City 25k, AAU State Championship 10k, or the Berry City 5-Mile Open. Runners know these races. Some are very popular and attract many runners, while others are highly competitive and attract only the most committed.

Races are held in the evenings and on weekends. Some races are open to all who can pay the minimal entrance fee; others are open only to members of the local running association; and still others require qualifying performances in other races. From this array of races, a runner can find someone of equal or similar ability and training with whom competition can be close and mutually rewarding. Any run that involves competition among runners can be a race. It is the terms of the competition that vary. Races range from the short 2-miler to the 26-mile, 385-yard marathon. The prestige accorded a runner from participation in a race is associated with the terms of the race. Short races are for beginners. If accomplished racers run a short race it is usually for time, i.e., to determine how fast these short distances can be covered. This enables them to know whether they can train for faster times in longer races. Races of five miles and more are for the accomplished runner; they are the objectives of training.

Runners generally rank all races; hence, those who wear shirts proclaiming their participation in them are likewise rated. The marathons, of course, have the highest prestige. A Lake City Marathon shirt on a person running in the park is a definite sign that the person is a runner. A Berry City 5-Mile Open shirt, however, may or may not signify a runner. The Berry City race is popular and is short enough to attract the casual jogger and many part-time runners. Thus, wearers of the shirt may race only once a year; they may simply have walked across the finish line to get the shirt. Even a nonparticipant could pick up such a shirt as a discarded item from some runner's collection. Thus, decoding the runner's wardrobe requires not only an awareness of the custom of awarding shirts at races but also familiarity with the ranking of races within the runner's world.

Probably the most communicative badge of a serious runner is the tank-top shirt. This shirt has no sleeves and exposes arms and shoulders. The tank-top shirt may be so important to the runner's appearance that even cold weather will not deter him from wearing it. A popular custom is to don the tank top over a regular T-shirt so that one may simultaneously ward off the cold and communicate the message "I am a runner."

In some cases, an unmarked tank top says more than a marked T-shirt. For example, a race held early in the spring designs divisions of competitors: joggers, or those who do not compete year round; and runners, those who do. A local sporting goods store donates shirts of two different colors to be worn during the race, one color for the joggers and the other for the runners. It is customary in most races to award the T-shirt only to those who finish the race. In this race, however, custom is flaunted. A shirt from this race has little power to communicate a person's identity as a runner.

Other runners know that a blue shirt with the lettering "Stolen from Kotter's" on the back is a shirt worn by those in the jogger's category at the first and least taxing race of the season, sponsored by a civic group, not by the local running association. A person serious about competition will prefer to be identified with a race in which distances are carefully marked, in which sponsorship is from the runner's culture, and to which only serious runners are attracted. In these "runner's races" one can mingle with better runners on an equal basis. A shirt proclaiming the AAU State Championship 10k meet does not tell whether the runner is fast or slow. However, it does tell that the wearer chose to compete in a race in which most other participants were competitive, dedicated runners. In the absence of a marked tank top, the unmarked variety is preferable to the blue "Stolen from Kotter's" shirt.

There is still more to the tank top's message. Serious runners know that many prestigious marathons, like the Boston Marathon, do not award shirts. Those competing in such big-time races are often affiliated with a local track club. Even if the runner has never run in the Boston, wearing a shirt that bears the name of the club that sponsors a few serious runners will give him high status among fellow runners. A tank top with the words "Tri-Cities Track" says of the wearer, "I am a runner." It is more convincing than a T-shirt from a local marathon, but this is something that only experienced runners would know.

Other message shirts popular among runners communicate a commitment to running but stress a philosophical position or opinion about it. A T-shirt with Run for Fun indicates that the wearer is a runner, but not one of the competitive types. Shirts may advertise insider or runners' jokes, such as Athlete's Foot. This message has a double meaning since Athlete's Foot is also the name of a nationally known supplier of athletic goods for runners.

Our runner's journey through the park could bring him in contact with a serious runner adorned in Interval 3:05 shoes and a Tri-Cities Track shirt, or he could encounter a more casual but nevertheless committed runner sporting Brooks 270s and wearing a Berry City 5-Mile Open shirt. Both encounters would signal the presence of a runner and both could appropriately trigger greetings. Perhaps a hand wave would be in order to the 3:05 wearer out of deference to high accomplishment, while a conversation would be appropriate with the wearer of Brooks 270s.

Of course, the type of exchange will depend upon the relative status of the two runners. In the example above, we are assuming that our runner does not regard himself in a class with the Tri-Cities Track shirt wearer, but instead feels more comfortable around the Berry City man. Equals in the runners' world exchange greetings, whereas unequals merely acknowledge each other's identity. The higher status runner's acknowledgement demonstrates that the lower status runner is "within" the dress code of the runner, and the lower status runner's acknowledgement of the higher confirms standards for dress and appearance of the serious runner.

SHORTS

In moderate to warm weather most runners wear shorts. The meaning of shorts is less complicated than that of shoes and shirts. Nevertheless, shorts do carry a message. Shorts purchased from a discount store and designed with splits on the legs, presumably to allow unimpeded leg movement, dignify the runner's appearance. However, the true runner does not buy shorts from a discount store. He or she will procure shorts from the sporting goods store that has acquired a reputation as a store for runners. There may be several such stores and of course their inventory will include other sports equipment. What distinguishes these stores is their large selection of shoes and array of colored and light-weight silk and synthetic runners' shorts. The fanciest shorts, of course, are saved for racing and are not worn for daily training. For training, the runner will use an old pair and may even wear them over long under-wear in the winter months.

Like their shirts, runners' shorts may bear lettering. Runners with track club affiliations may don a pair of shorts with the club's name or symbol. For training runs and for races of lesser importance, i.e., those used for preparation for a target or primary race, shorts with identifying markings of some university or college are often worn. These shorts may not have been stolen from the athletic department of the university. They could have been purchased, or they may be rejects, or more likely they are for sale at local shops. Nevertheless, wearing these shorts communicates at least a sympathy with "big-time" college racing. They say, "I belong to, or sympathize with, organized running."

Another way to communicate a message is to wear shorts bearing the name of some distant university. For instance, if one lives, works, and runs in Texas, shorts with colors and markings of the University of Illinois worn with shoes and a shirt with the name of an AAU race on it indicate a dedicated runner. These shorts communicate that the wearer not only participates in local events, but also possesses an impressive record as a runner, one that spans several states.

OTHER PARAPHERNALIA

Shoes, shirts, and shorts comprise the fundamental elements in the runner's wardrobe. However, other paraphernalia accent the runner's identity. These paraphernalia are much like exclamation points in a sentence. They exclaim an identity; for communications purposes, they are redundant. A person in New Balance shoes, a Lake City Marathon shirt, and lightweight, leg split shorts is most assuredly a runner. To add to this couture a small band of elastic material fitted tightly over the forehead merely punctuates identity.

Such paraphernalia for the head includes the sweatband, the bill, and the hat. Sweatbands come in many colors. They may be white or a solid color, or they may be designed with stripes of alternating colors or with red stars on a white field. Less commonly used is the bill, which is a hat without a top. A bill consists of a visor and a strap that fastens around the head. The bill shades the eyes and is used during summer months by some runners. Hats, the final item, come in a variety of shapes and colors. For example, there is the billed hat, identical to the bill except that it has a top, and the beer hat, a floppy, short-brimmed cloth hat imprinted with the name of some beer manufacturer. Wearing headgear is optional and may depend on such practical matters as keeping long hair out of the eyes during a run. However, the type of hat selected can communicate a message. A beer hat communicates a more casual attitude than the billed hat. The billed hat which was made famous by an Olympic runner says, "I am out to win, I take myself seriously in these affairs," while the hat brightly decorated in Budweiser red and white says, "I'm not so dedicated that I won't take a beer in training."

In addition to headgear, there are watches — not ordinary wristwatches. They are sophisticated stopwatches that the runner uses to time himself. Other watches, such as electronic timers, are carried in the hand or are sometimes worn around the neck (anchored, of course), or require an assistant. For the purpose of identification, the wristwatch is very useful. It is larger than an ordinary watch, and when worn by an appropriately garbed person, signifies a runner concerned about improving his "times." The watch says, "I run for times. I want to improve and am willing to train to achieve my goal."

VARIATIONS ON THE THEME

Naturally, the amount of clothing worn depends somewhat on weather conditions. The shoes, shirt, shorts combinations manifest themselves differently in winter, but they remain part of the wardrobe of the winter runner. In fact, in winter, we can refer to the shoes, shirt, shorts configuration as an "overlaid identifying appearance." In other words, the three elements that are important in warm weather retain their significance, because they are often worn over clothing added to protect the body from the cold. The additional clothing is called the sweats.

Sweats is the word used to refer to cotton or synthetic two-piece suits worn for warmth. Sweats are often combined with shorts and shirts and may be a substitute for them, while the shoes remain a constant.

Neither rain, nor snow, nor ice can dissuade the runner from wearing favorite Tigers, Nikes, or Pumas. When we see a person out in subzero weather in lightweight nylon and rubber shoes, we may assume he or she is a runner. But other hardy or foolish souls have been observed at this practice. To know whether or not the person fearless of frostbite is a runner, we need more information. Does the person wear a T-shirt over a sweat shirt? . . . shorts over thermal longwear? . . . a pair of Adidas sweats in a solid color with white stripes down the legs? . . . a ski cap?

According to running folklore headgear is the most important practical item for winter running. Runners believe that a major portion of body heat is lost through the top of the head. Therefore, we will never observe a dedicated runner in winter with an uncovered head. Whereas a nonrunner may have on a heavy coat and no hat, a runner may wear a T-shirt, shorts, and a ski cap. An extreme, but nevertheless common, example is the runner who wears two shirts including his T-shirt of the day, layered leg wear, a sweats bottom with shorts, and a ski cap, while on his feet are running shoes *without socks*. Many runners believe that they have fewer blisters without socks. They become accustomed to sockless shoe wear in the warm months, and they simply continue the practice into the cold months. Thus, we know that the person in Tigers without socks running in the snow is a self-identified runner.

BODY IMAGE AND POSTURE

The final communicative component in the appearance of runners is the body image and the posture projected. First, runners present a slim profile. Their faces appear drawn and gaunt; double chins and pot bellies are generally absent. A maxim in the runner's folklore maintains that a runner's ideal weight should equal twice the height in inches. Thus, a 6-foot-tall man should weigh about 144 pounds. Not all runners conform to this prescription, but the runner's folklore extols the light body and most runners are slim.

In addition to the thin profile, running postures may convey messages. Runners run erect, with head upright and eyes straight ahead, and strive for a steady, unhurried gait. Runners want long strides and smooth foot–pavement contact, and do not jolt or jog along with an up-and-down movement. They do not breathe hard in an uncontrolled fashion, and run "within themselves," which means they can run faster or slower. They seek a plateau of performance at which they feel the body is transformed into a running machine, methodically moving through the city, smoothly gliding over curbs and rough footing, around cars and up and over hills.

Thus, clothes interact with body image and posture to form the runner's appearance, an appearance that is known by others who are themselves runners. A person running with head down, breathing hard, moving with arms in front of the body and with fists clenched is not a runner, regardless of what he or she may be wearing. The runner glides along, arms moving in the direction of the run, hands cupped in a relaxed posture. The runner must learn to relax all muscles except those used in locomotion. Such relaxation is demonstrated in the appearance of effortless running and communicates the message, "I know how to run properly."

In the opening example, our runner sees a silhouette moving in the fashion characteristic of a runner. He moves closer, sees identifying clothes, and then knows that this other person, this stranger, is one of his kind, at least in this specialized and temporary sense. The two runners possess, for the moment, a consciousness of kind, and they greet each other in ritualistic fashion.

THE RITUAL OF GREETING

The ritual of the greeting is flexible; it assumes many forms. The simplest form is the hand wave. Here runners recognize and acknowledge each other by a hand movement that is not part of the running posture. For example, a raised open hand or an away-from-the-body jerking motion can signify a greeting. These movements may be performed with élan by the novice runner, while they may be only slightly perceptible in the accomplished master.

Runners often develop their own version of the nonverbal greeting. They may raise a few fingers and nod their heads, nod the head only, or wave the palms in an outward position. As long as the movements contrast with the regular movements of running, they serve as a greeting.

The nonverbal greeting is used when runners intend to communicate to each other that they wish to continue their own pace, that they do not wish to converse. Two runners of equal appearance and of equal commitment to running will recognize the nonverbal greeting to mean, "Pass on, I'm training." On occasion a novice will misread these signals and attempt to engage the wearer of a Lake City Marathon shirt and a wrist timer in conversation. That the marathoner is in interval training — fast running alternated with slow — is communicated to any accomplished runner through dress, timer, breathing, and appearance of fatigue. Upon recognition, a nonverbal greeting is appropriate, not an extended verbal greeting that would disrupt the spacing of intervals.

When a novice fails to recognize interval training behavior, he or she may attempt to converse with the runner by asking, "How long have you been running?" or "Hard work, huh? You race a lot?" The marathoner must either interrupt the schedule and answer, or greet the novice in a nonverbal fashion and continue training.

Extended conversations are appropriate as a part of a ritual greeting on certain occasions: when both runners are out for a long, slow run, and when both are new to running and can provide each other with vital information about race organization or equipment. For example, two runners start to pass each other with nonverbal greetings. One turns to the other and says, "You like your Tigers?" The other replies, "Yes, but they don't hold up very well." The first runner agrees, "I had a pair of Pumas that had that problem, then I switched to New Balance. I'm getting much better mileage now." The other says, "That's great. Where did you get the New Balances?" The first answers, "Down at Kotter's. They're about $20.00." The other says, "I'll look into that. See you around." They part, each continuing in the original direction.

In this example, the two runners are dressed alike. Neither is wearing a track club shirt or lightweight shorts. Both have golfing hats, one a bill and the other a roll-up beer hat. Each correctly reads the other's appearance to mean: here is a runner like myself, about the same in conditioning and commitment. Of course, the conversation might have revealed that the original assumptions were incorrect, with one runner better conditioned and faster than the other. But the point is that each accepted the other's appearance as sufficient grounds for an extended conversational greeting. The runner must display an intention for a casual training run to the other to indicate that an extended greeting is appropriate.

Conclusion

The existence of a runner's culture allows its members to recognize one another and to convey messages. This communication process is accomplished by adorning the body in appropriate articles of clothing, which can be decoded to give specific meanings. Shoes function to identify the runner, and special or exotic shoes may convey specific messages about the wearer. Likewise, shirts vary from those with the high prestige of the track club and the marathon to the casual runner's "I love jogging" shirt. Shorts also range from the discount store's gym shorts to the runner's silks. Body image and posture interact with clothing to produce an appearance clearly recognizable to the runner. The extent of recognition varies from the simple ability to detect a fellow runner to the appreciation of training habits and commitment to running. Greetings between runners may be verbal or nonverbal, depending upon the display of intention found in the runner's dress and posture. Openness to conversation is associated with long, slow runs or less arduous daily treks, while the serious trainer requires the nonverbal exchange.

We have thus seen that runners may engage in specialized forms of communication. Each runner learns to read the appearance of the other and judges on the basis of that appearance the appropriateness of passing in silence, of passing with a nonverbal greeting, or of joining for extended conversation while running.

V

Kinship and family

Social life is essential to human existence. We remain in the company of other people from the day we are born to the time of our death. People teach us to speak. They show us how to relate to our surroundings. They give us the help and the support we need to achieve personal security and mental well-being. Alone, we are relatively frail, defenseless primates; in groups we are astonishingly adaptive and powerful. Yet despite these advantages, well-organized human societies are difficult to achieve. Some species manage to produce social organization genetically. But people are not like bees or ants. We lack the genetically coded directions for behavior that make these insects successful social animals. Although we seem to inherit a general need for social approval, we also harbor individual interests and ambitions that can block or destroy close social ties. To overcome these divisive tendencies, human groups organize around several principles designed to foster cooperation and group loyalty. Kinship is among the strongest of these.

What underlies the strength of kinship bonds? The answer appears to lie in the strong emotional content of the relationships established by birth and marriage, for these associations are the building blocks of kinship. The birth of a child sets up a particularly durable social bond. A child's appearance is announced by an increasingly uncomfortable pregnancy and is accompanied by danger and pain during birth. A mother already feels close to someone she has worked so hard to produce. The helpless infant draws strong feelings of support from its parents and others who happen to be near. As a child grows to adulthood, it may receive more or less support from its parents, depending on the child-training customs of the society into which it is born. In every society, however, children tend to be loyal to their parents, and parents feel responsibility and love for their children. The relationship automatically creates the beginning of a kinship system.

Marriage is neither as durable or intense an association as the bond between parent and child. But it is nonetheless a universal feature of social organization and a basic relationship capable of generating strong loyalty. Mating is an intimate feature of the tie as is coparenthood and often, economic cooperation. Marriage links lines of blood-related relatives together and permits the birth of legitimate children.

Based on birth and marriage, kinship systems may include hundreds of relatives in various kinds of groups. Although distantly related people may feel less loyalty and obligation toward each other, large kinship systems work remarkably well as the primary basis of organization in many societies.

Whether large or small, kinship systems always include families. Usually these consist of at least an adult couple and their children. This nuclear family, as it is called, is characteristic of American society, and it lasts only as long as its members continue to remain at home. In a great many societies the ideal family size is much larger than this. The Chinese family described by Margery Wolf in this section often consists of a couple, their sons and their sons' wives, and their grandchildren and any other unattached children. Extended families of this sort provide a very different style of life than do our small families. As we see in the following selections, family life is different from one society to the next and for different family members within the same household. And larger kinship systems are easier to understand once we see how people use them.

13

Matrilineal kinship: Coming home to Bokelab
MICHAEL A. RYNKIEWICH

A kinship system is much more than a set of formal rules defining identities, roles, and groups. It is a personal guide used by individuals to meet their own needs and aspirations. Michael Rynkiewich uses this theme to show how a Marshallese Islander, Benjinij, uses his knowledge of kinship to reestablish himself on Bojalablab Atoll. Arriving in ignorance after a prolonged absence, Benjinij learns to identify his kinsmen, treat them properly, and use his relationships with them to secure land, a household, and power.

One of the most important ways people all over the world are alike is the fundamental basis on which they organize their social lives. To relate effectively to each other, people must identify themselves and those around them, behave according to roles composed of specific rules for action, and participate in clearly defined groups. Although all of us use information about identity, role, and groups to guide our daily social behavior, the specific knowledge used by different peoples to accomplish this end varies. For example, if you were to live with the people of a Highland New Guinea community, you would quickly discover that their social organization was so different from yours that you would have to learn about a new set of identities, system of roles, and collection of groups. Only after gathering such information would you be able to get along properly with the members of the community in the context of their social system. Even in our own society many small groups have

This article was written especially for this volume. The research on which it is based was carried out in the Marshall Islands between June, 1969 and December, 1970. Bojalablab Atoll and the people in the story are fictional, but the account is an accurate recording of form, meaning, and functions of Marshallese kinship.

such different organizations that a new language of social behavior must be learned to fit acceptably within them.

Take a football team, for example. Suppose that you were pulled from the stands by a coach at a professional football game, dressed in a uniform, and sent on the field. As you run toward the players whose uniforms are the same color as yours, the coach yells these instructions: "Tell the quarterback to run a sixty series option down, out and down, to the split end." Unless you had played football before, you might not even realize that the term *quarterback* labels a kind of identity for one player. Even if you did understand what a quarterback was, you might not know about any of his identifying attributes, for example, that he wears a number between 10 and 19 on his back. You might also miss the fact that you are the split end (your number is 88, a sign of your position), that you should talk to the quarterback outside the huddle, and that you should line up ten to fifteen yards from the tackle on the line of scrimmage. In addition, you would not understand the instructions for action contained in the phrase "sixty series option" so you would have little idea about what your teammates planned to do or how your opponents might react. Without such information about identities, expectations for behavior, and group composition, you could not begin to play football in a socially organized manner as part of a team. The same principles govern people's behavior in every social situation.

Social organization can be achieved in several basic ways. The structure of the football team, for example, reflects a need to meet particular characteristics inherent in the game itself. As a consequence, the team has a limited and specialized social organization. On the other hand, most societies use a more general approach to achieve systematic social interaction. Instead of the exigencies of a particular game, they face such wider needs as sustenance and defense that must be met if the members of the group are to survive. Thus, their organization is often based on more general human characteristics such as age, sex, and rank. Of these, however, by far the most common and important is kinship.

Kinship provides a way of defining identities, roles, and groups for people everywhere. In many societies kinship is the dominant principle for social organization. The term *kinship* is not as simple as it sounds. Americans tend to think of kinsmen as blood relatives, but in many parts of the world this definition is too limited. In such cases kinship is a complex language of social relationships that includes not only those who are related genealogically through blood and marriage, but also people who share no blood connection but who somehow come to be identified as kinsmen. This extension of the system is possible because individuals determine the identity of kinsmen not only by genealogical linkage, but by behavior as well. Thus, when someone acts like a kinsman, he is often treated as one. Conversely, some people may not be called relatives although they are related by blood ties. They simply do not behave as kinsmen should.

This emphasis on the importance of social organization and the stress on identity, role, and group should not be allowed to obscure the place of the individual in social interaction. People do use kinship rules to structure and interpret behavior, but they also manipulate their knowledge of kinship to serve their own interests. Just as a quarterback uses his knowledge of football and the many plays and options open to him to move his offense and win the game, so the individual uses his understanding of his kinship system to meet his own requirements and aspirations. Like every set of cultural rules, kinship is a flexible and ever-changing system.

To better understand the importance and the meaning of kinship, it is useful to look at a society — Bokelab islet of Bojalablab Atoll in the Marshall Islands — in which it plays a dominant role. By taking the perspective of one man, Benjinij, from this society, we can consider some of the problems he solves by the judicious use of his knowledge about kinship. Benjinij is returning to Bojalablab after a long absence. To re-establish himself there among his kinsmen, he must identify and relate to his relatives and demonstrate and manipulate his membership rights in a landholding kinship group.

GOING HOME

Benjinij steadied himself at the bow as the ship left the calm lagoon water and met the jolting ocean waves. His mind was not on the trade goods in the ship's hold nor on the copra the ship would buy. He was a passenger getting off at the first stop, Bokelab islet. He could not see it yet, but it was just over the horizon and his mind dwelt on his situation.

Benjinij's mother had been born on Bojalablab Atoll, the ship's destination. His father was from another atoll, and his mother had gone with her husband to live there. When Benjinij was quite young, the Japanese had sent his father to Palau island for training as a carpenter. Benjinij and his mother went along. However, both of Benjinij's parents were killed in air raids during World War II. When peace returned, the now mature Benjinij became a sailor, and at age 30, ten years after the conflict had ended, he was coming to live with his mother's people.

Bojalablab Atoll stood against the red of the late afternoon sky, like a pencil line marked on the horizon. As the ship drew nearer, the line differentiated into beach, brush, and coconut trees. Benjinij watched the waves, hypnotized by their motion. As he watched, a wave rose to four feet at the edge of the reef, then flattened as it raced over the barrier, its surface reflecting the vivid colors of the coral below. Then the wave's leading edge, white with foam, flung itself on the beach.

The ship slowed and the noise of its small boat being raised from the deck brought Benjinij back from his reverie. When the ship had anchored, Benjinij climbed in the small boat so that he could be first ashore. The steersman caught a wave, then alternately throttled and accelerated the boat's engine to keep just behind the crest. Just as it seemed that it would be smashed on the shore, the boat swerved sharply to the left in response to the steersman's hand and settled down in the lee of the wave, coming gently to rest on the sandy beach. Benjinij walked onto Bokelab islet, home at last.

As he stood on the beach of his mother's home for the first time, Benjinij's thoughts turned to the problems that confronted him. He could see several people coming toward the shore and others standing near bags of dried coconut meat. Many of them were his kinsmen whom he would eventually have to identify by determining their relationship to him. Only then would he know how to behave toward them and what to expect they would do in return. His parents had taught him what every Marshallese child should know about kinsmen, but he was not very practiced in relating to these particular kin nor did he know their particular histories or the instances of cooperation and conflict. In addition, he did not know to which groups he or they belonged. He had much to learn to establish himself here, to be socially, economically, and politically successful. His key to the network of relationships on Bokelab islet was something his mother had told him years earlier, that her brother's name was Tibnil and if he ever returned to Bokelab he should depend on him for help.

Benjinij asked for directions to Tibnil's household, and started off down the road that ran parallel to the lagoon. He found Tibnil sitting in his cookhouse talking with two younger men of the household as they waited for the women to finish baking the breadfruit and fish collected that afternoon. They exchanged greetings and Benjinij was enjoined to come in the cookhouse and sit. Though Tibnil would not have recognized him, an old man on the ship had sent word that Benjinij was coming. Consequently, as is the custom, no questions were asked about the other's name. Tibnil did speak at length about his joy at Benjinij's arrival, lamenting the death of his sister and brother-in-law. Benjinij would eat, sleep, and work within this household because he had the kinship right to stay with his mother's brother as long as he liked. Thus, a bond was renewed and through Tibnil, Benjinij began to find his way into the complex network formed by kinsmen.

KINDS OF KIN

The few basic terms Benjinij used to identify his kinsmen are presented in Figure I. He calls everyone in his grandfather's generation either *jimau* (male) or *jibu* (female); as he grows old, all kin of his grandchildren's generation he will term *jibu* for either sex. (This differs from our own system in which we mark off grandfather from great-uncle and first cousin twice-removed, and grandson from grand-nephew and first cousin twice-removed.)

In general, Benjinij calls everyone of his father's generation *jinu* (female) or *jema* (male), and everyone in his children's generation, *neju* (either sex). Two exceptions are his mother's brothers, only Tibnil in this case, whom he calls *uleba*, and his sister's sons, whom he would call *mangeru*.

In Benjinij's own generation, he refers to anyone born before him as *jeu* (either sex) and everyone born later *jetu* (either sex). Again, this includes kinsmen we would call brother, sister, first cousin, second cousin, and so on. These ten basic terms, though they can be modified somewhat, enable him to identify all his relatives except his brothers-in-law.

All these terms are used to address kinsmen. However, Benjinij must make one other distinction, though it is usually not used in address, but only to refer to a particular group of relatives. In Benjinij's own generation, female parallel cousins and female cross-cousins differ. The children of Benjinij's father's brother and his mother's sister are called parallel cousins because the sex of the two connecting relatives is the same: mother and her sister, father and his brother. Female parallel cousins are classed with Benjinij's own sister and are referred to by a combination of terms; *jeu jinu* if older than Benjinij and *jetu jinu* if younger. On the other hand, cross-cousins, the children of Benjinij's father's sister and his mother's brother, are referred to as *jeu reliku* if older and *jetu reliku* if younger. The significance of this distinction will become clear in the discussion of proper kinship behavior.

Knowing possible classes of kinsmen did not tell Benjinij which kin fit into each category. To make this discovery, he had to depend partly on genealogical information. For example, his mother had told him that Tibnil was her brother, so he was to be called *uleba*. But the genealogical links for many people he met were never entirely clear to him. To place them, he listened to what Tibnil and other known relatives called such kin. For example, when Benjinij arrived at Tibnil's house he was greeted by two pretty girls and some other children. Benjinij did not know who they were, but during his first few days there he heard what they called Tibnil. When one of the girls, LiNana, called

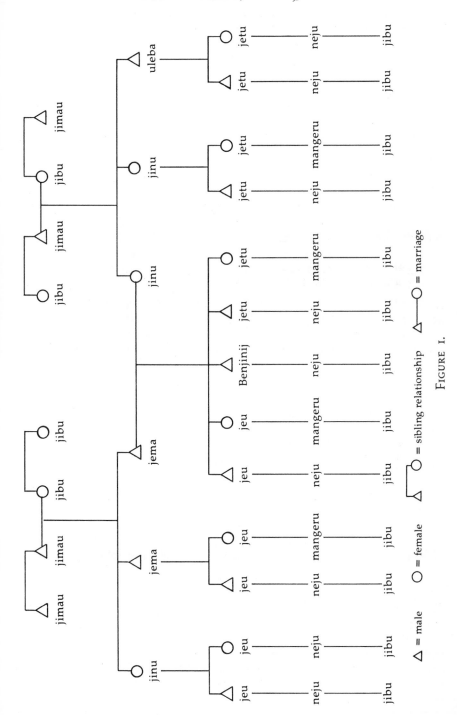

FIGURE I.

Tibnil "father," Benjinij knew that she stood in the relationship of younger cross-cousin to him because she was female, younger than him, and a child of his mother's brother.

When the other girl called Tibnil "mother's brother," Benjinij knew that she was an elder sister and parallel cousin. Benjinij quickly figured out the kinship identities of most people on the islet, and from this knowledge he was able to behave in a proper way toward them.

Kinship roles

To produce such behavior Benjinij needed to know what to call his kinsmen. He would not, for example, act the same way toward Tibnil, his mother's brother, as he would toward a man he called "father." The former relationship involves both authority and some degree of permitted disrespect. Marshallese sayings give the expectation that the mother's brother will be a hard taskmaster while the sister's son is often mischievous. On the other hand, the relationship between father and child has little authority but a lot of respect, so that a child would never be mischievous with his father.

Although each kinsman requires special forms of behavior, with little exception all may be classified into two groups based on opposite forms of action. One kind of relationship can be called reserved. In the context of Marshallese culture, in the presence of certain kinsmen Benjinij cannot refer to such bodily functions as defecation, urination, bathing, and sexual intercourse. The relationship implies respect and some degree of social distance.

As illustrated in Table I, the most reserved relationship exists between Benjinij and anyone he calls sister and parallel cousin. He is careful never to be alone with such kinswomen for fear of fostering the idea that a sexual interest exists between them. These kinswomen often make requests of Benjinij and he does all he can to meet such demands. Moreover, he is careful that no one else should behave improperly when he is in their presence. Once Benjinij and a "sister," a parallel cousin, sat with a group of young people by the road. A boy began to tell about a fight in which one man was kicked in the groin. Benjinij quickly disappeared. The next day he took the young storyteller aside and told him in annoyed tones to be more careful about ascertaining the relationship of those in his audience before he started talking about such private matters. Relatives called mother, father, and child must also be treated with respect (Table I).

The other major relationship is marked by joking. In many ways, it is the opposite of the reserved relationship because any kind of joking is permitted with no hint of respect or authority. People in these relationships need not hide from each other knowledge of when and where they

TABLE I. *Basic Marshallese kinship roles*

Reserved behavior	Joking behavior
Sister (parallel cousin)	Cross-cousin
Mother	Grandmother
Father	Grandfather
Child	Grandchild
Mother's brother or sister's child	

perform bodily functions. Sexual intercourse between such relatives is permitted, except in the case of genealogical grandparents and grandchildren. The joking relationship provides some of the most interesting and humorous exchanges between kinsmen, often taking the form of a game with one relative trying to outdo another in the grossness of his references to sexual parts and functions.

For example, Benjinij might be expected to engage in such a discussion of private parts with his cross-cousin, LiNana, if he met her on the road. First, he would likely pretend not to notice her and walk by without a greeting. But she would not allow such a challenge to go unmet, and might open with a comment like, "Your penis!" He could reply, "You have no pubic hair!" to which she might respond, "The hair of your anus!" The conversation would likely escalate with such assertions and retorts as, "Nothing is larger than the lips of your vagina." "Your little penis is half-baked." "Why is there mud in your vagina?" (implying promiscuity in the sense that she will lie anywhere, even in the mud), and the parting and winning shout, "Go masturbate yourself!" Such joking behavior is also enjoyed with kin called grandfather, grandmother, and grandchild. Thus, by knowing kinship terms, Benjinij can identify people and use appropriate behavior with them. In only a few months, Benjinij had become part of an ongoing social system which gave him support for his new life on Bokelab.

DESCENT GROUPS

Although Benjinij had managed to establish himself in the islet's social network of kinsmen, he also wanted a household of his own, a place to work, a family, and the respect of the community. To acquire these things he needed land. The place he had in mind was a plot located near the middle of the islet rising quickly from the lagoon shore to 10 feet above high tide, then dropping off to a densely wooded interior with several taro pits before ending on the side facing the ocean. The strip was only three quarters of a mile long, but like most plots of land, it touched both shores to give the people access to the whole range of the islet's microenvironments. Benjinij suspected that he might have some claim to the land because Tibnil had often sent him there to work. He determined to see if he could get permission to live there.

Benjinij sat with Tibnil one evening, intent on asking him about the land, but he avoided doing so directly. Instead, he asked about Marshallese custom with respect to group membership and inheritance. He knew that both Americans and Japanese placed great importance on their fathers, even taking the paternal name as their own. He also knew from such sayings as "the children of women are most important" that the Marshallese way was different. When he asked about the meaning of that saying, Tibnil replied with this story:

> An old woman, Likatunger, promised the chieftainship to whichever of her sons would win a canoe race. As each of them departed she entreated him to take her along. But when she cried, "*Ekatuke iu!*" each son from the eldest on down replied, "*Kattar wut jetu*" (wait for my younger brother). Only her youngest son, Jabrau, stopped long enough to take her on board. She then gave him the paraphernalia with which to sail and Jabrau easily overtook his brothers. As he broke into the lead his eldest brother asked permission to ride along. Jabrau took him on board, but he knew his brother intended to jump off the canoe first when it reached shore and claim the chieftainship. Therefore, on the last tack, Jabrau allowed the boom to swing, knocking his brother overboard and breaking his back in the process. Jabrau won the chieftainship *kinke e jela kataike ngan jinen* (because he knew how to submit to his mother).

Tibnil stressed that land and authority came through mothers, not fathers. Benjinij had suspected as much and asked Tibnil where the latter got his authority to manage the land. Tibnil said the rights were not his alone, that they were passed down over many generations. Then he began to list all those people who had had a right in the land he controlled, beginning with the name of the oldest woman he could remember, and then her brother. He named her children, both male and female, her daughter's male and female children, and her daughter's daughter's male and female children. On and on he went, naming only the children of women, finally arriving at Benjinij's mother, and then Benjinij himself (their genealogical positions are shown in Figure II).

Benjinij now knew he was on the right track. The group whose members Tibnil had named is called *bwij* or matrilineage. Matrilineages are formed by the descent ideology that "the children of women are most important," their new members including only the children of each group's female members. The matrilineage is the major landholding unit

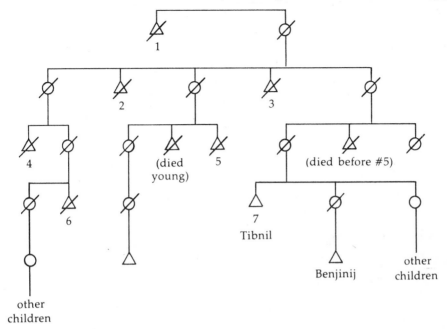

Lineage heads are numbered in succession.
Deceased relatives are shown with a diagonal line through them.

FIGURE II. *Benjinij's matrilineage*

on Bojalablab atoll and like corporations, no one of its members may dispose of any matrilineage land rights or be denied the use of matrilineage land, except when he has gravely insulted his fellow lineage mates. A matrilineage does have a leader called an *alab*, meaning land manager or lineage head. He handles lineage affairs and represents the kin group in its dealings with other members of the community. He does not own the land; no individual does. Rather, it belongs to the whole group, including the dead and those not yet born. However, the lineage head can allocate specific pieces of land to lineage members and sometimes others, for their own temporary use.

To affirm the source of his rights as lineage head, Tibnil recited the order of succession. He went from the brother of the oldest woman, to his sister's son, and on through brothers and cousins, skipping only those who had died before their chance for succession came (marked on Figure II by numbers). When he had finished, Benjinij knew he had come to the right place. His mother's words, "Go to my brother and he will take care of you," came back to him. He asked for and received permission to build a house on the land he wanted.

ESTABLISHING A HOUSEHOLD

Planning the house and organizing the work was left to Tibnil, who told the women of his own and other households of the lineage to begin collecting pandanus leaves to make thatch and mats. The men of the lineage and other male members of their households cut down pandanus trees and sawed them up to make posts and rafters. Benjinij worked for cash to buy plywood for the walls and, although normally he had to give Tibnil a small percentage of the profits from the sale of any coconut meat derived from lineage land, Tibnil helped Benjinij by not requiring this share. The land was cleared, coral pebbles brought for the floor and yard, walls erected, and roof thatched in about three weeks.

When the house was finished, Benjinij moved in, but not by himself. For several months he had been keeping company in secret with his cross-cousin, LiNana. They had decided to live together for a while, and her father, Tibnil, had agreed. She was pregnant so one of her younger sisters came along to help keep their house. Benjinij had land to work and a household to support.

GAINING POWER

Benjinij had successfully achieved his initial goals because he became adept at manipulating the systems of kinship and descent. However, a year after he moved into his new house, he faced a problem that he could not have envisioned on his arrival. He had to struggle against his kinsmen to protect his position in the matrilineage and the community.

The problem started when Tibnil became ill and died and his sister asserted that she would succeed him as lineage head. Her claim was based on the rule that says the successor should come from the senior generation of the lineage, and she was the only living member of that generation. Benjinij was close to her and knew he would enjoy her favor if she were the leader. However, two others were contending for the position. An old woman of another branch of the lineage claimed that she should become Tibnil's successor, although she was part of the next lower generation. She cited another rule of succession to back her claim, that lineage heads should come from the oldest branch of the lineage, the one to which she belonged. A man from the middle branch of the lineage also claimed Tibnil's position. Although he was in a generation junior to Tibnil's sister and in a lineage branch less old than that of the second claimant, he was a male and entitled to hold power over women. Each contender had a valid claim to leadership, but the rules were contradictory. Naturally, each cited only those rules which demonstrated the priority of his or her claim.

Benjinij vociferously defended the right of Tibnil's sister to succeed. The second woman had the support of her children, and to Benjinij's surprise, the man from the middle branch of the lineage was supported by his sons. True, he was the only living member of the middle branch and had no other supporters, but his sons did not even belong to the lineage, holding membership in their mother's group instead. Benjinij asked Tibnil's sister why these sons would dare argue their father's case. She explained:

> You know that the branches of a matrilineage sometimes split away from each other. Each one takes some of the lineage land and selects its own lineage head. Each branch then becomes a separate matrilineage. Look at our matrilineage. We own three pieces of land, and we have three branches. Many generations have gone by since we were all real siblings. His sons want him to be lineage head in the hope that as the leader he will force our matrilineage to split into three separate ones. If that happened, their father would be the sole member of his matrilineage, and the sole owner of one of the pieces of land. Then, because he is the last of his branch, his sons would inherit his land when he died. That is why we must oppose him, because our land could be stolen away by people who are not in our lineage.

Benjinij had learned a lesson: kinsmen not only cooperate on matters, but they also dispute over the rights they share. If he did not resist the claims of the old man, his plot of land might be taken from the lineage. After this talk, Benjinij argued more earnestly than ever for the succession of Tibnil's sister.

The sons of the old man talked against Benjinij, but their father did not cooperate. Less than a year after the dispute began, he died. A short time later the woman from the oldest branch of the lineage also died and Tibnil's sister was left as undisputed leader of the lineage.

With Tibnil's sister in firm control, Benjinij was assured of control over his own affairs within the framework of the lineage, for he was its oldest living male. Tibnil's sister, embarrassed to go to the islet's council because of her sex, sent Benjinij in her stead. Though she kept the title, he did the work and gained experience representing his lineage to the community. Years later, when Tibnil's sister died, Benjinij's succession as lineage head was not disputed.

THE MEANING OF KINSHIP

When Benjinij stepped ashore on Bokelab islet, he had to establish himself in an ongoing, socially organized community. The cultural knowledge he used to enter the social network is different from the information we would use if we moved to a different town in the United States. Although he had to refine this knowledge by attempting to apply it in many new social situations, Benjinij succeeded because he understood the basic features of the Marshallese kinship and descent systems. Because he knew the proper kinship terms and the appropriate ways to behave, he became part of a household and a member of the community. He was able to claim his position as a member of a landholding group and eventually gain an allocation of land because he understood the principles of matrilineal descent. Through the complexities and conflicts of a dispute among lineage members, Benjinij emerged in a strong position because he had backed a winner. In sum, Benjinij's basic needs — food, sex, shelter, power, and meaning — were at least partially satisfied through the Marshallese systems of kinship and descent.

14

Uterine families and the women's community
MARGERY WOLF

Is the meaning of the family the same for men and women?
Margery Wolf answers "no" in this article based on field-
work in a rural Taiwanese village. For men living in the
community, the patrilineal family extends in an unbroken line
of ancestors and descendants. Membership is permanent; loyalty
assured. For women, the patrilineal family is temporary. Born
into one family and married into another, women discover that
their happiness and interests depend on their membership in an
informal uterine family that grows up inside the household.
Family relationships can only be understood if we take the
women's as well as the men's views into account.

Few women in China experience the continuity that is typical of the lives of the menfolk. A woman can and, if she is ever to have any economic security, must provide the links in the male chain of descent, but she will never appear in anyone's genealogy as that all-important name connecting the past to the future. If she dies before she is married, her tablet will not appear on her father's altar; although she was a temporary member of his household, she was not a member of his family. A man is born into his family and remains a member of it throughout his life and even after his death. He is identified with the family from birth, and every action concerning him, up to and including his death, is in the context of that group. Whatever other uncertainties may trouble his life, his place in the line of ancestors provides a permanent setting. There is no such secure setting for a woman. She will abruptly leave the household into which she is born, either as an infant or as an adult bride, and enter another whose members treat her with suspicion or even hostility.

A man defines his family as a large group that includes the dead, the not-yet-born, and the living members of his household. But how does a woman define her family? This is not a question that China specialists often consider, but from their treatment of the family in general, it would seem that a woman's family is identical with that of the senior male in the household in which she lives. Although I have never asked, I imagine a Taiwanese man would define a woman's family in very much those same terms. Women, I think, would give quite a different answer. They do not have an unchanging place, assigned at birth, in any group, and their view of the family reflects this.

When she is a child, a woman's family is defined for her by her mother and to some extent by her grandmother. No matter how fond of his daughter the father may be, she is only a temporary member of his household and useless to his family — he cannot even marry her to one of his sons as he could an adopted daughter. Her irrelevance to her father's family in turn affects the daughter's attitude toward it. It is of no particular interest to her, and the need to maintain its continuity has little meaning for her beyond the fact that this continuity matters a great deal to some of the people she loves. As a child she probably accepts to some degree her grandmother's orientation toward the family: the household, i.e., those people who live together and eat together, including perhaps one or more of her father's married brothers and their children. But the group that has the most meaning for her and with which she will have the most lasting ties is the smaller, more cohesive unit centering on her mother, i.e., the uterine family — her mother and her mother's children. Father is important to the group, just as grandmother is important to some of the children, but he is not quite a member of it, and for some uterine families he may even be "the enemy." As the girl grows up and her grandmother dies and a brother or two marries, she discovers that her mother's definition of the family is becoming less exclusive and may even include such outsiders as her brother's new wife. Without knowing precisely when it happened, she finds that her brother's interests and goals have shifted in a direction she cannot follow. Her mother does not push her aside, but when the mother speaks of the future, she speaks in terms of her son's future. Although the mother sees her uterine family as adding new members and another generation, her daughter sees it as dissolving, leaving her with strong particular relationships, but with no group to which she has permanent loyalties and obligations.

When a young woman marries, her formal ties with the household of her father are severed. In one of the rituals of the wedding ceremony the bride's father or brothers symbolically inform her by means of spilt water that she, like the water, may never return, and when her wedding sedan chair passes over the threshold of her father's house, the doors are slammed shut behind her. If she is ill-treated by her husband's family, her father's family may intervene, but unless her parents are willing to bring her home and support her for the rest of her life (and most parents are not), there is little they can do beyond shaming the other family. This is usually enough.

As long as her mother is alive, the daughter will continue her contacts with her father's household by as many visits as her new situation allows. If she lives nearby she may visit every few days, and no matter where she lives she must at least be allowed to return at New Year. After her mother dies her visits may become perfunctory, but her relations with at least one member of her uterine family, the group that centered on her mother, remain strong. Her brother plays an important ritual role throughout her life. She may gradually lose contact with her sisters as she and they become more involved with their own children, but her relations with her brother continue. When her sons marry, he is the guest of honor at the wedding feasts, and when her daughters marry he must give a small banquet in their honor. If her sons wish to divide their father's estate, it is their mother's brother who is called on to supervise. And when she dies, the coffin cannot be closed until her brother determines to his own satisfaction that she died a natural death and that her husband's family did everything possible to prevent it.

With the ritual slam of her father's door on her wedding day, a young woman finds herself quite literally without a family. She enters the household of her husband — a man who in an earlier time, say fifty years ago, she would never have met and who even today, in modern rural Taiwan, she is unlikely to know very well. She is an outsider, and for Chinese an outsider is always an object of deep suspicion. Her husband and her father-in-law do not see her as a member of their family. But they do see her as essential to it; they have gone to great expense to bring her into their household for the purpose of bearing a new generation for their family. Her mother-in-law, who was mainly responsible for negotiating the terms of her entry, may harbor some resentment over the hard bargaining, but she is nonetheless eager to see another generation added to *her* uterine family. A mother-in-law often has the same kind of ambivalence toward her daughter-in-law as she has toward her husband — the younger woman seems a member of her family at times and merely a member of the household at others. The new bride may find that her husband's sister is hostile or at best condescending, both attitudes reflecting the daughter's distress at an outsider who seems to be making her way right into the heart of the family.

Chinese children are taught by proverb, by example, and by experience that the family is the source of their security, and relatives the only people who can be depended on. Ostracism from the family is one of the harshest sanctions that can be imposed on erring youth. One of the reasons mainlanders as individuals are considered so untrustworthy on Taiwan is the fact that they are not subject to the controls of (and therefore have no fear of ostracism from) their families. If a timid new bride is considered an object of suspicion and potentially dangerous because she is a stranger, think how uneasy her own first few months must be surrounded by strangers. Her irrelevance to her father's family may result in her having little reverence for descent lines, but she has warm memories of the security of the family her mother created. If she is ever to return to this certainty and sense of belonging, a woman must create her own uterine family by bearing children, a goal that happily corresponds to the goals of the family into which she has married. She may gradually create a tolerable niche for herself in the household of her mother-in-law, but her family will not be formed until she herself forms it of her own children and grandchildren. In most cases, by the time she adds grandchildren, the uterine family and the household will almost completely overlap, and there will be another daughter-in-law struggling with loneliness and beginning a new uterine family.

The ambiguity of a man's position in relation to the uterine families accounts for much of the hostility between mother-in-law and daughter-in-law. There is no question in the mind of the older woman but that her son *is* her family. The daughter-in-law might be content with this situation once her sons are old enough to represent her interests in the household and in areas strictly under men's control, but until then, she is dependent on her husband. If she were to be completely absorbed into her mother-in-law's family — a rare occurrence unless she is a *sim-pua* — there would be little or no conflict; but under most circumstances she must rely on her husband, her mother-in-law's son, as her spokesman, and here is where the trouble begins. Since it is usually events within the household that she wishes to affect, and the household more or less overlaps with her mother-in-law's uterine family, even a minor foray by the younger woman suggests to the older one an all-out attack on everything she has worked so hard to build in the years of her own loneliness and insecurity. The birth of grandchildren further complicates their relations, for the one sees them as new members for her family and the other as desperately needed recruits to her own small circle of security.

In summary, my thesis contends . . . that because we have heretofore focused on men when examining the Chinese family — a reasonable approach to a patrilineal system — we have missed not only some of the system's subtleties but also its near-fatal weaknesses. With a male focus we see the Chinese family as a line of descent, bulging to encompass all the members of a man's household and spreading out through his descendants. With a female focus, however, we see the Chinese family not as a continuous line stretching between the vague horizons of past and future, but as a contemporary group that comes into existence out of one woman's need and is held together insofar as she has the strength to do so, or, for that matter, the need to do so. After her death the uterine family survives only in the mind of her son and is symbolized by the special attention he gives her earthly remains and her ancestral tablet. The rites themselves are demanded by the ideology of the patriliny, but the meaning they hold for most sons is formed in the uterine family. The uterine family has no ideology, no formal structure, and no public existence. It is built out of sentiments and loyalties that die with its members, but it is no less real for all that. The descent lines of men are born and nourished in the uterine families of women, and it is here that a male ideology that excludes women makes its accommodations with reality.

Women in rural Taiwan do not live their lives in the walled courtyards of their husbands' households. If they did, they might be as powerless as their stereotype. It is in their relations in the outside world (and for women in rural Taiwan that world consists almost entirely of the village) that women develop sufficient backing to maintain some independence under their powerful mothers-in-law and even occasionally to bring the men's world to terms. A successful venture into the men's world is no small feat when one recalls that the men of a village were born there and are often related to one another, whereas the women are unlikely to have either the ties of childhood or the ties of kinship to unite them. All the same, the needs, shared interests, and common problems of women are reflected in every village in a loosely knit society that can when needed be called on to exercise considerable influence.

Women carry on as many of their activities as possible outside the house. They wash clothes on the riverbank, clean and pare vegetables at a communal pump, mend under a tree that is a known meetingplace, and stop to rest on a bench or group of stones with other women. There is a continual moving back and forth between kitchens, and conversations are carried on from open doorways through the long, hot afternoons of summer. The shy young girl who enters the village as a bride is examined as frankly and suspiciously by the women as an animal that is up for sale. If she is deferential to her elders, does not criticize or compare her new world unfavorably with the one she has left, the older residents will gradually accept her presence on the edge of their conversations and stop changing the topic to general subjects when she brings the family laundry to scrub on the rocks near them. As the young bride meets other girls in her position, she makes allies for the future, but she must also develop relationships with the older women. She learns to use considerable discretion in making and receiving confidences, for a girl who gossips freely about the affairs of her husband's household may find herself labeled a troublemaker. On the other hand, a girl who is too reticent may find herself always on the outside of the group, or worse yet, accused of snobbery. I described in *The House of Lim* the plight of Lim Chui-ieng, who had little village backing in her troubles with her husband and his family as the result of her arrogance toward the women's community. In Peihotien the young wife of the storekeeper's son suffered a similar lack of support. Warned by her husband's parents not to be too "easy" with the other villagers lest they try to buy things on credit, she obeyed to the point of being considered unfriendly by the women of the village. When she began to have serious troubles with her husband and eventually his family, there was no one in the village she could turn to for solace, advice, and most important, peacemaking.

Once a young bride has established herself as a member of the women's community, she has also established for herself a certain amount of protection. If the members of her husband's family step beyond the limits of propriety in their treatment of her — such as refusing to allow her to return to her natal home for her brother's wedding or beating her without serious justification — she can complain to a woman friend, preferably older, while they are washing vegetables at the communal pump. The story will quickly spread to the other women, and one of them will take it on herself to check the facts with another member of the girl's household. For a few days the matter will be thoroughly discussed whenever a few women gather. In a young wife's first few years in the community, she can expect to have her mother-in-law's side of any disagreement given fuller weight than her own — her mother-in-law has, after all, been a part of the community a lot longer. However, the discussion itself will serve to curb many offenses. Even if the older woman knows that public opinion is falling to her side, she will still be somewhat more judicious about refusing her daughter-in-law's next request. Still, the daughter-in-law who hopes to make use of the village forum to depose her mother-in-law or at least gain herself special privilege will discover just how important the prerogatives of age and length of residence are. Although the women can serve as a powerful protective force for their defenseless younger members, they are also a very conservative force in the village.

Taiwanese women can and do make use of their collective power to lose face for their menfolk in order to influence decisions that are ostensibly not theirs to make. Although young women may have little or no influence over their husbands and would not dare express an unsolicited opinion (and perhaps not even a solicited one) to their fathers-in-law, older women who have raised their sons properly retain considerable influence over their sons' actions, even in activities exclusive to men. Further, older women who have displayed years of good judgment are regularly consulted by their husbands about major as well as minor economic and social projects. But even men who think themselves free to ignore the opinions of their women are never free of their own concept, face. It is much easier to lose face than to have face. We once asked a male friend in Peihotien just what "having face" amounted to. He replied, "When no one is talking about a family, you can say it has face." This is precisely where women wield their power. When a man behaves in a way that they consider wrong, they talk about him — not only among themselves, but to their sons and husbands. No one "tells him how to mind his own business," but it becomes abundantly clear that he is losing face and by continuing in this manner may bring shame to the family of his ancestors and descendants. Few men will risk that.

The rules that a Taiwanese man must learn and obey to be a successful member of his society are well developed, clear, and relatively easy to stay within. A Taiwanese woman must also learn the rules, but if she is to be a successful woman, she must learn not to stay within them, but to *appear* to stay within them; to manipulate them, but not to appear to be manipulating them; to teach them to her children, but not to depend on her children for her protection. A truly successful Taiwanese woman is a rugged individualist who has learned to depend largely on herself while appearing to lean on her father, her husband, and her son. The contrast between the terrified young bride and the loud, confident, often lewd old woman who has outlived her mother-in-law and her husband reflects the tests met and passed by not strictly following the rules and by making purposeful use of those who must. The Chinese male's conception of women as "narrow-hearted" and socially inept may well be his vague recognition of this facet of women's power and technique.

The women's subculture in rural Taiwan is, I believe, below the level of consciousness. Mothers do not tell their about-to-be-married daughters how to establish themselves in village society so that they may have some protection from an oppressive family situation, nor do they warn them to gather their children into an exclusive circle under their own control. But girls grow up in village society and see their mothers and sisters-in-law settling their differences to keep them from a public airing or presenting them for the women's community to judge. Their mothers have created around them the meaningful unit in their fathers' households, and when they are desperately lonely and unhappy in the households of their husbands, what they long for is what they have lost. . . . [Some] areas in the subculture of women . . . mesh perfectly into the main culture of the society. The two cultures are not symbiotic because they are not sufficiently independent of one another, but neither do they share identical goals or necessarily use the same means to reach the goals they do share. Outside the village the women's subculture seems not to exist. The uterine family also has no public existence, and appears almost as a response to the traditional family organized in terms of a male ideology.

15

Family and kinship among black Americans
CHARLES V. WILLIE

The family is the primary unit of social organization in most
societies. The family unites its members in economic cooperation;
it socializes children, cares for the aged, and provides an expres-
sive outlet. But the family exists as part of a larger, more com-
plex society. The roles that people play at home are inevitably
affected by their association with outsiders. In this article,
Charles V. Willie describes three forms of the black family in
America, showing how each reflects the experience of its mem-
bers as they adapt to social constraints and opportunities thrust
on them by external circumstances.

It has been difficult to understand the black family in America because
most writers fail to deal with it on its own terms. Usually the black
family is compared to or contrasted with the white family.

Scholars who follow this approach do so, they say, because racism
is a pervasive experience in the United States which none can escape.
But the author's upbringing, in a black community in Dallas, Texas,
taught him that all blacks did was not necessarily a reaction to the
actions of whites.

Indeed, reference groups for many blacks consisted of other blacks
— black family members, black neighbors, black friends, black church
members, and black club members. Social sanctions, norms, and behavior standards were generated by these groups.

The Sunday School Superintendent of the church attended by the
family of orientation of the author organized Christmas parties at the
church for the children and Labor Day picnics in the country for
the teenagers and young adults. He gave neckties to boys who graduated

Originally published as "The Black Family and Social Class," *American Journal*
of Orthopsychiatry 44, no. 1 (January 1974): 50–60. Copyright © 1974 the American
Orthopsychiatric Association, Inc. Reproduced by permission.

from high school and went on to college and saved cereal box tops for the young. He delivered chicken dinners, which were prepared by the women of the church, to the homes of neighbors. He was a janitor in a building where automobiles were sold and serviced. He was an ordained clergyman with limited training of less than a high school education. His limited education and unskilled occupation were probably a manifestation of racism. But in Oak Cliff, a black community in Dallas, he was never looked upon as a victim. To the children in the author's community he was the Reverend J. I. Farrar — a decent, kind, and courteous gentleman, a man interested in children, and a man to whom one could always turn for help. It was the Reverend Farrar's love for the church, community, and children that was partly responsible for teaching them how to love others, despite the presence of racism. The interaction between the Reverend Farrar and his community is a common story about local black leaders throughout this nation; it is not necessarily a reaction to whites.

My interest in understanding the way of life of blacks independent of any reference to the way of life of whites is due to a desire (1) to extricate the social and behavioral sciences from a white ethnocentric perspective, and (2) to increase their contribution to the understanding of social change. Innovations in life-styles, including family life-styles, often develop among minority populations in the society before they are adopted by the majority. Such innovations may not be recognized when the way of life of the majority is looked upon as the "ideal type" and the behavior of others is considered deviant.

METHOD

During the past few years we have compiled approximately 200 case studies of black families, many southern migrants or descendants of southern migrants who now live in the northeastern region of the United States. The case studies were obtained as an assignment for students enrolled in a course on "The Black Family." The responsibility for locating a black family was that of each student. Many students interviewed families in their home towns scattered throughout the region. They interviewed families who were friends, referred to them by friends, referred by an agency, or selected at random by knocking on the door of a stranger. Students were provided with an interview schedule that requested specific information about economic, social and demographic characteristics, family customs, aspirations of parents for children, and patterns of authority within the family. Interviewers were black and white undergraduate students.

Out of the 200 or more case studies, nine were selected for detailed analysis in this paper as a composite representation of three income groups. Household income was the primary basis for more or less arbitrarily selecting three families each for middle-income, marginal-income, and lower-income groups. Utilized in this study were the student reports that contained the most complete and detailed descriptions. We cannot claim to have randomly selected the families for analysis. But we can say that the bias of the investigator was not the basic factor that determined whether or not a family was included among the nine for intensive study. The income groups studied ranged from $3,000 to $6,000 (low-income), $6,000 to $10,000 (marginal-income), and $10,000 to $20,000 (middle-income). Essentially, this study is an example of inductive analysis. Two variables — race and economic status — were used. Since blacks often are referred to as if they were a homogeneous group, nine families of the same race but of different income groups were studied to determine if, in fact, their way of life, customs, and practices were similar. Probability sampling, of course, would be necessary if the goal had been to make generalizations about the frequency of certain behavior forms within the total black population. This was not our goal. Thus, less rigor in the process of selecting the families for intensive analysis was possible.

Social class refers to style of life as well as economic resources. No operational definition of social class was developed for this study. The middle-class, working-class, and lower-class categories referred to later in this paper were derived from the analysis. The composite picture for the three families in each of the income groups was different from the style of life of black families in other income groups. Only the composite picture of the style of life for a social class is given. Detailed information on each of the nine families is presented elsewhere in a book-length manuscript.[1] The three social classes included in this study represent about 75% of all blacks. Not included are the upper-middle class and the upper class, probably few in number, and at the other end of the stratification hierarchy, the under class — 20% to 25% of all blacks.

FINDINGS

Middle class: The affluent conformists. Middle-class status for most black families is a function of dual employment of husband and wife. Black men and women have relied heavily on the public sector for employment at livable wages.

The public school has been an employment haven for black working wives. It has provided steady and continuous work and often has been the one occupational role in the family which has enabled it to lay

---

[1] C. Willie, *A New Look at Black Families* [Bayside, N.Y.: General Hall Publishers, 1976].

claim to a professional style of life. Because of educational requirements, black female teachers of middle-class families are likely to be more highly educated than their male spouses. The length of employment of professional working wives is likely to be as long as that of their husbands, with only brief interruptions for childbearing. The numbers of children in black middle-class families tend to be small, ranging from one to three, but more often two or less. Thus, the black woman, in a public sector job with prescribed yearly increments and retirement benefits and with only a few interruptions in her labor force status, tends to draw a decent income by the time she reaches middle age.

Continuity in employment also is a characteristic of black men in middle-class families. Public sector jobs, especially in the postal service, have been a source of support and security over the years. Some black men have, however, received financially rewarding professional positions in industry.

The economic foundation for middle-class black families is a product of the cooperation of the husband and wife. Their way of life is a genuine illustration of a team effort. Few, if any, family functions, including cooking, cleaning, and buying, are considered to be the exclusive prerogative of the husband or wife. Probably the best example of the liberated wife in American society is the wife in the black middle-class family. She and her husband have acted as partners out of necessity and thus have carved out an equalitarian pattern of interaction in which neither husband nor wife has ultimate authority. He or she alone could not achieve a comfortable style of life, because of racial discrimination and the resulting income limitations of the kinds of jobs available to most blacks. Together they are able to make it, and this they have done. In the 1970s middle-class black families earned $10,000 to $20,000 a year — the joint income of husband and wife.

Such income is lavishly spent on a home and on the education of children. Unless restricted by racial discrimination, middle-class black families tend to trade in older homes for new structures as their income and savings increase. Thus, families in the income range mentioned above are likely to be found in houses valued from $25,000 to $35,000. The real expense in housing, however, is in the up-to-date furnishings and modern appliances. For most middle-class black families, their home is their castle and it is outfitted as such.

Because work is so consuming for the husband and wife, little time is left for socializing. Most families have nearby relatives — usually the reason for migrating to a particular city. They visit relatives occasionally, may hold membership in a social organization, participate regularly in church activities, and spend the remainder of their free time in household upkeep and maintenance chores.

In most middle-class black families, one member almost always has attended college. Often both have attended college. The husband and wife struggled and made great sacrifices to complete their formal education. Not infrequently, college and graduate school are completed on a part-time basis after adulthood and while the husband or wife, who also may be a parent, is employed full-time. Parents who have experienced these struggles and hardships know that their middle-class status, which usually is not achieved until middle age, is directly correlated with their increased education. New jobs, especially public school teaching, and salary increments can be traced directly to the added schooling. Education has been a major contributor to upward mobility for blacks.

Because education and, consequently, economic affluence are so closely tied together for middle-class black households, parents tend to go all out for their offspring. Particularly do they wish their children to go to college immediately after graduating from high school so that they will not have to struggle as long as did their parents whom middle-class status eluded during young-adult years. An ambition of most parents is to give to their children opportunities they did not have.

As a starter, almost all children in middle-class households are given music lessons. Daughters, in particular, are expected to learn to play a musical instrument, usually the piano. Recreational skills are developed, too. Most children in middle-class black families are expected to work around the house for an allowance. Families try to inculcate in their children positive attitudes toward work and thrift.

Active involvement in community affairs that take on the characteristics of a movement is not the cup of tea for most black middle-class, middle-aged adults. Their adolescent children may be deeply involved in various liberation movements but seldom are the parents.

Middle-class black families in America, probably more so than any other population group in this society, manifest the Puritan orientation toward work and success that is characteristic of our basic values. For them, work is a consuming experience. Little time is left for recreation and other kinds of community participation, except regular involvement in church affairs. The way of life of black middle-class Americans is a scenario patterned after Weber,[2] except that most blacks have little capital other than the house they own, which, of course, is their primary symbol of success.

Working class: The innovative marginals. Family life in the black working class is a struggle for survival that requires the cooperative efforts of all — husband, wife, and children. Income for black working-class families ranged from $6,000 to $10,000 during the 1970s. This is hardly enough for luxury living when the family size is considered.

[2] M. Weber, *The Protestant Ethic and the Spirit of Capitalism* (London: George Allen and Unwin, 1948).

Black working-class families tend to be larger families, consisting of five or more children.

There is some indication that the size of the family is a source of pride for the parents, especially the father and maybe the mother too. The bearing and rearing of children are considered to be an important responsibility, so much so that black working-class parents make great personal sacrifices for their families. They tend to look upon children as their unique contribution to society, a contribution they are unable to make through their work roles, which at best are semi-skilled. The family size of the black working class also may be a function of age at marriage, usually before twenty-one for the wife and mother and often during the late teens. Husbands tend to assume parenthood responsibilities early too; often they are only one or two years older than their spouses.

The cohesion of the black working-class family results not so much from understanding and tenderness shown by one for the other as from the joint and heroic effort to stave off adversity. Without the income of either parent or the contributions of children from part-time employment, the family would topple back into poverty.

The parents in black working-class families are literate but of limited education. Most have completed elementary school but may be high school drop-outs. Seldom do any have more than a high school education. This is the educational level they wish their children to achieve, although some families hope that one or two of the smarter children in their brood will go on to college. The jobs they wish for their children also are those that require only a high school or junior college education, like work as a secretary, nurse, mechanic, or bank messenger.

Racial discrimination, on the one hand, and insufficient education, on the other, have teamed up to delimit the employment opportunities for black working-class families. Their mobility from rural to urban areas and from the South to the North usually has been in search for a better life. Families tend to be attracted to a particular community because of the presence of other relatives who sometimes provided temporary housing.

In general, the moves have opened up new opportunities and modest advancement such as from gas station attendant to truck driver, or from farm laborer to dairy tanker. The northern migration has resulted in some disappointments, too. On balance, new employment opportunities have resulted from the move from South to North, particularly for wives who have found work in institutional settings, such as hospitals, more profitable than private household work. Nursing aide and cooking jobs have been outlets for women and have enabled them to supplement the family income.

One sacrifice that the members of black working-class families have made so as to pull out of and stay beyond the clutches of poverty is to give up on doing things together as a family. Long working hours and sometimes two jobs leave little time for the father to interact with family members. In some households, the husband works during the daytime and the wife works during the evening hours. In other families, children work up to twenty hours a week after school and on weekends. These kinds of work schedules mean that the family as a unit is not able to share any meals together, except possibly on Sunday.

Despite the hardships, there is a constancy among the members of black working-class families that tends to pull them through. Some husbands and wives have been married more than two decades; they tend to have been residents of their neighborhoods for ten or more years and to have worked for the same employer over a long period of time. Though their earnings are modest, this continuity in area of residence and in other experiences has stabilized these families and enabled their members to accumulate the makings of a tolerable existence without the losses that come from frequent stops and starts.

Another stabilizing experience is the home that some black working-class families own. Rather than renting, many are paying mortgages. Their homes may range in value from $10,000 to $15,000, may be located in isolated rural or unsightly urban areas, and may be in a poor state of exterior repair but neat and clean on the inside. Home owner-ship for black working-class families is not so much a symbol of success as an indicator of respectability.

Black working-class parents boast of the fact that their children are good and have not been in trouble with the police. They also have a strong sense of morality, which emphasizes "clean living." The home they own is part of their claim to respectability. The owned home is one blessing that can be counted. It is a haven from the harsh and sometimes unfriendly world.

There is little time for community activities for black working-class families. Most spare time is devoted to associating with household members or with nearby relatives. Religion is important; but participa-tion in church activities is limited to regular or occasional attendance at Sunday worship services. The mother in such families tries to maintain tenuous contacts with at least one community institution, such as the school. She even may be a member of the Parent-Teachers Association but is not deeply involved in organizational maintenance work as a volunteer.

Black working-class parents do well by their children if no special problems are presented. Their comprehension of psychological maladap-tion, however, is limited. These problems are dealt with by a series of intended remedial actions that seem to be of little assistance in solving the child's real problem and usually result in frustration both for the parent and for the offspring. Black working-class families have learned to endure; and so they bear with the afflictions of their members — those they do not understand as well as those with obvious sources of causation.

Cooperation for survival is so basic in black working-class families that relationships between the husband and wife take on an equalitarian character. Each knows that his or her destiny is dependent upon the actions of the other. Within the family, however, husbands and wives tend to have assigned roles, although in time of crisis, these roles can change. The husband tends to make decisions about financial expenditures, including the spending of money for furniture. He also has basic responsibility for household upkeep. The father is the chief advisor for the boys. The mother tends to be responsible for the cooking and cleaning, although she may delegate these chores to the children. She is the chief advisor for the girls. She also maintains a liaison relationship with the school and may be the adult link between the family and the church if the father is not inclined to participate.

We tend to think in terms of upward mobility in American society. Indeed, this is what many working-class families are — households moving out of poverty into respectability; households that emphasize mobility, goal, and purpose; households committed to making a contribution to society by raising and maintaining a family of good citizens. This, of course, involves a struggle. But the struggle may be a function of the ending of good times rather than the overcoming of adversity. A black working-class family may be of a lower-income household on its way up or a middle-income household on its way down. A middle-income family beset with illness, for example, could slip into the working-class status due to reduction in income and the requirement for change in style of living. How often this occurs, we do not know. It does occur often enough to keep the working class from becoming a homogeneous lot. For this and other reasons, one should not expect to find a common philosophical orientation within the working class.

Lower class: The struggling poor. The most important fact about black lower-class families is their low-income status; it forces them to make a number of clever, ingenious, and sometimes foolish arrangements to exist. These range from extended households consisting of several generations under one roof to taking in boarders or foster children for pay. Boyfriend-girlfriend relationships between adults often assume some parental functions when children are involved, while the participants maintain their autonomy unfettered by marital bonds. Because every penny counts, poor households often do whatever they must do to bring money in. Conventional practices of morality may be set aside for expedient arrangements that offer the hope of a livable existence. The struggle among poor families is a struggle for existence. All else is secondary. Family income tends to vary from $3,000 to $6,000, and more often than not the household does not receive public welfare.

The struggle is severe and there is little margin for error. Black low-income families learn to live with contingency. They hope for little and expect less. Parents love their children but seldom understand them. Men and women become sexually involved but are afraid to entrust their futures to each other. There is much disappointment. The parents in broken families often have broken spirits — too broken to risk a new disappointment. For this reason, black lower-class parents often appear to be uncommitted to anyone or to anything when in actuality they are afraid to trust.

Movement is constant, as if one were afraid to stay put and settle down. Jobs, houses, and cities are changed; so are spouses and boyfriends and girlfriends. Unemployment is a constant specter. The womenfolk in the household usually find employment as maids or private household workers. The males are unskilled factory workers or maintenance men between periods of no work at all.

Marriage may occur at an early age, as early as sixteen years for some girls. The first child is sometimes born before the first marriage. Others tend to come in rapid succession. Some families have as many as eight or more children, while others are smaller. When the burdens of child care, illness, and unemployment strike at the same time, they often are overwhelming. Drinking, gambling, and other escape behavior may increase. A fragile love and capacity for endurance are shattered, and the man in the house moves out, no longer able to take it. One more failure is experienced.

The parents in black lower-class families are grade school or high school dropouts. Neither spouse has more education than the other. Thus, parents in lower-class families sometimes hold themselves up to their children as failures, as negative images of what not to do. There is only limited ability to give guidance concerning what ought to be done. Thus, children are advised not to marry early, not to drop out of school, and not to do this and not to do that. There is admonition but little concrete effort at prevention.

Scapegoating is a common way of explaining deviant behavior in children. Juvenile delinquency may be attributed to the disreputable parent. The mother on location seldom knows what to do. Although little love may exist between parents, there is fierce loyalty between mothers and offspring, and between grandmothers and children. The children come first. Mothers will extend every effort to take care of their sons and daughters, even into adulthood. Grandparents are excellent babysitters. They are expected to teach their grandchildren good manners and other fundamentals.

A strong custom of brothers and sisters helping each other exists in the lower class. The problem is that siblings are struggling too. About the most one can do for the other is share already overcrowded living quarters when a new member comes to town or when a two-parent family breaks down. The move from one city to another often is for the purpose of being near kinsmen. There is strong loyalty between siblings and a standing obligation to help.

Little participation in any community association is seen. Religion is important for some black lower-class families. But for others, it is no more than a delusion. Those who attend church regularly tend to engulf their lives with religion and especially with affirmations about its saving grace and reward system after death. Some shy away from the church as one more disappointing promise that has copped out on the poor without really helping. Black lower-class people are seldom lukewarm about religion. They are either all for it or all against it, although the latter are reluctant to deny their children religious experience, just in case there is more to it than was realized.

It is hard for a poor black family to overcome poverty; so much is lined up against it. If illness or unemployment does not drain away resources, there is a high probability that old age will.

Conclusion

We turn now to a theoretical discussion of the differences that have been observed. In his classical article, "Social Structure and Anomie," Robert Merton[3] identified five kinds of adaptations by individuals to social organizations: conformity, innovation, ritualism, retreatism, and rebellion. We shall discuss three of the adaptations to explain the way of life of the three different social classes. The conformist acknowledges the legitimacy of societal values and goals and also accepts the means that are sanctioned and prescribed for achieving them. The innovationist believes in the socially sanctioned goals but must improvise new and different means. The retreatist gives up on the socially sanctioned values and goals as well as the means and, therefore, is declared to be in a state of anomie or normlessness. This theoretical formulation provides a helpful way for conceptually approaching an understanding of the differences between middle-class, working-class, and lower-class black families.

[3] R. Merton, *Social Structure and Social Theory* (New York: Free Press, 1949), p. 133.

Middle-class black families subscribe to the basic values and goals in American society and utilize appropriately prescribed means for their achievement. Its members are success-oriented, upwardly mobile, materialistic, and equalitarian. They consume themselves in work and leave little time for leisure. Education, hard work, and thrift are accepted as the means for the achievement of success. Property, especially residential property, is a major symbol of success. This is the American way and the prevailing way of life to which the middle-class black family in America conforms. Thus, its members may be called conformists.

Black working-class families also have internalized the basic values and goals of this nation. They too are success-oriented and upwardly mobile. However, their symbol of success differs from that of the black middle class. The welfare of the total family is the principal measure of effective functioning. A black working-class family is successful if it is respectable. A family is respectable when its members are well-fed, well-clothed, and well-housed, and do not get into trouble with the police.

The location and value of a house is not so important. Home ownership is important but home value is something else. In the latter respect, the black working class differs from the black middle class, in which an expensive home is the symbol of success.

Almost everything that the black working-class parents do to achieve success and respectability is extraordinary, compared with the black middle class. Their education is limited; their occupations are unskilled; their income is modest; and their families are relatively larger. Yet they dream the impossible dreams about doing for their children what they could not do for themselves. By hook or crook, they — the parents — manage to do it when others said it couldn't be done. The members of the working class are the creative innovationists of our times. They strive to achieve the societal values and goals, are deficient in the possession of socially sanctioned means, but somehow overcome.

The black lower class is fatalistic. No note of hope does it sing. Failure and disappointment recur repeatedly, as if they were a refrain. Unable to deal with the difficulties presented, black lower-class families withdraw. The parents appear to be uninvolved with anyone or anything. They have retreated from social organizations but not necessarily from all social relations for we know of their loyalty to their children.

The retreatist behavior of black lower-class families is sometimes described as being in opposition to the basic values and goals of social organization — a rejection of that which is socially sanctioned. This may not be the case, however, but only the way it appears. Presumably, lower-class households, like the working class, wish for family cohesion. The tie between mother and offspring is a residual family relationship indicative of this desire. Presumably, also, lower-class families, like the middle class, wish for material comforts and new experiences. Spending sprees and impulse traveling are indicative of these desires.

Because of inadequate resources, lower-class families dare not hope for the fulfillment of their wishes in a systematic and regularized way. To protect themselves from more disappointment, denial of the wish for improvement is one approach and poking fun at the struggle for social mobility is another.

A fuller explanation of the retreatist behavior of the lower class requires examination of the interaction between objective and subjective dimensions of social structure. Despite the rhetoric about self-reliance and self-sufficiency, the family members of the working class and the middle class did not make it on their own unassisted by the social system. They acknowledged their interdependence, and asked for and received help when they needed it. Upward social mobility involves giving and receiving from others. The poor are given precious little in our society and so their capacity to receive is underdeveloped. In the giving of help, we learn to love. In the receiving of assistance, we learn to trust. Because the poor have been given so little in society, the poor have not learned how to receive — which is to say, the poor have not learned how to trust.

We learn to trust before we learn to love. Love involves commitment to persons, social groups, and social organizations. The members of lower-class families can commit themselves to persons, especially the mothers to their offspring and the siblings to each other; but they cannot commit themselves to a society they have never learned to trust. Thus, the retreatist behavior of the lower class may be a manifestation of the absence of trust rather than a rejection of social organization in favor of social disorganization.

This paper clearly demonstrates that it is inappropriate to say, "a black family is a black family is a black family." Styles of life do vary among blacks by social class. Recognition of this should serve as a corrective against stereotyping black ways of life.

The neat way in which the different black family life-styles by social class fit into the theoretical model developed by Robert Merton for explaining variation in adaptations to the social organization also suggests that all black families, including the middle-class, the working-class, and the lower-class, participate in a common system of values shared by all families, including blacks and whites in the United States.

Finally, there was evidence of limited opportunities available to blacks due largely to racial discrimination. This was a common experience of most black families of all social classes. A frequent manifestation of racial discrimination was the delimitation of economic opportunity. Inadequate financial resources frequently resulted in the joint participation of husband and wife in the labor force — a circumstance more or less pervasive among black families, especially those who were upwardly mobile.

On the basis of this analysis, one may conclude (1) that black and white families in America share a common value system, (2) that they adapt to the society and its values in different ways, largely because of racial discrimination, and (3) that the unique adaptation by blacks is further differentiated by variations in style of life by social class.

Our initial assumption that the way of life of blacks in America can be understood independent of their involvement with whites appears to be unwarranted. Moreover, the life-styles of different social classes cannot be understood apart from the rest of society.

Referring to the interdependence of blacks and whites in America, this paper ends with the statement of a modified version of the wisdom of Eliza Doolittle, created by George Bernard Shaw. She said that she discovered the difference between a flower girl and a lady is not so much how she acts but how she is treated. Our revised version emphasizes *both* personal action *and* social reaction. We assert that the difference between the families of racial groups in the United States, and the difference between the families of various social classes within the racial groups are a result of how each family acts *as well as* how each family is treated.

16

Sororities and the husband game
JOHN FINLEY SCOTT

Every society has norms governing marriage. In American
society, as in many others, class differences are maintained by
our marriage rules. The structure and function of the university
sorority are analyzed by John Finley Scott for their effect upon
class structure.

> Marriages, like births, deaths, or initiations at puberty, are rearrange-
> ments of structure that are constantly recurring in any society; they are
> moments of the continuing social process regulated by custom; there
> are institutionalized ways of dealing with such events. — A. R. Radcliffe-
> Brown, *African Systems of Kinship and Marriage.*

In many simple societies, the "institutionalized ways" of controlling
marriage run to diverse schemes and devices. Often they include special living quarters designed to make it easy for marriageable girls to
attract a husband: the Bontok people of the Philippines keep their girls
in a special house, called the *olag,* where lovers call, sex play is free,
and marriage is supposed to result. The Ekoi of Nigeria, who like their
women fat, send them away to be specially fattened for marriage. Other
peoples, such as the Yao of central Africa and the aborigines of the
Canary Islands, send their daughters away to "convents" where old
women teach them the special skills and mysteries that a young wife
needs to know.

Accounts of such practices have long been a standard topic of anthropology lectures in universities, for their exotic appeal keeps the
students, large numbers of whom are sorority girls, interested and alert.
The control of marriage in simple societies strikes these girls as quite
different from the freedom that they believe prevails in America. This

is ironic, for the American college sorority is a pretty good counterpart in complex societies of the fatting houses and convents of the primitives.

Whatever system they use, parents in all societies have more in mind than just getting their daughters married; they want them married to the *right* man. The criteria for defining the right man vary tremendously, but virtually all parents view some potential mates with approval, some with disapproval, and some with downright horror. Many ethnic groups, including many in America, are *endogamous*, that is, they desire marriage of their young only to those within the group. In *shtetl* society, the Jewish villages of eastern Europe, marriages were arranged by a *shatchen*, a matchmaker, who paired off the girls and boys with due regard to the status, family connections, wealth, and personal attractions of the participants. But this society was strictly endogamous — only marriage within the group was allowed. Another rule of endogamy relates to social rank or class, for most parents are anxious that their children marry at least at the same level as themselves. Often they hope the children, and especially the daughters, will marry at a higher level. Parents of the *shtetl*, for example, valued *hypergamy* — the marriage of daughters to a man of higher status — and a father who could afford it would offer substantial sums to acquire a scholarly husband (the most highly prized kind) for his daughter.

The marriage problem, from the point of view of parents and of various ethnic groups and social classes, is always one of making sure that girls are available for marriage with the right man while at the same time guarding against marriage with the wrong man.

THE UNIVERSITY CONVENT

The American middle class has a particular place where it sends its daughters so they will be easily accessible to the boys — the college campus. Even for the families who worry about the bad habits a nice girl can pick up at college, it has become so much a symbol of middle-class status that the risk must be taken, the girl must be sent. American middle-class society has created an institution on the campus that, like the fatting house, makes the girls more attractive; like the Canary Island convent, teaches skills that middle-class wives need to know; like the *shtetl*, provides matchmakers; and without going so far as to buy husbands of high rank, manages to dissuade the girl from making alliances with lower-class boys. That institution is the college sorority.

A sorority is a private association which provides separate dormitory facilities with a distinctive Greek letter name for selected female college students. Membership is by invitation only, and requires recommendation by former members. Sororities are not simply the feminine counterpart of the college fraternity. They differ from fraternities because marriage is a more important determinant of social position for women than for men in American society, and because standards of conduct associated with marriage correspondingly bear stronger sanctions for women than for men. Sororities have much more "alumnae" involvement than fraternities, and fraternities adapt to local conditions and different living arrangements better than sororities. The college-age sorority "actives" decide only the minor details involved in recruitment, membership, and activities; parent-age alumnae control the important choices. The prototypical sorority is not the servant of youthful interests; on the contrary, it is an organized agency for controlling those interests. Through the sorority, the elders of family, class, ethnic, and religious communities can continue to exert remote control over the marital arrangements of their young girls.

The need for remote control arises from the nature of the educational system in an industrial society. In simple societies, where children are taught the culture at home, the family controls the socialization of children almost completely. In more complex societies, education becomes the province of special agents and competes with the family. The conflict between the family and outside agencies increases as children move through the educational system and is sharpest when the children reach college age. College curricula are even more challenging to family value systems than high school courses, and children frequently go away to college, out of reach of direct family influence. Sometimes a family can find a college that does not challenge family values in any way: devout Catholic parents can send their daughters to Catholic colleges; parents who want to be sure that daughter meets only "Ivy League" men can send her to one of the "Seven Sisters" — the women's equivalent of the Ivy League, made up of Radcliffe, Barnard, Smith, Vassar, Wellesley, Mt. Holyoke and Bryn Mawr — if she can get in.

The solution of controlled admissions is applicable only to a small proportion of college-age girls, however. There are nowhere near the number of separate, sectarian colleges in the country that would be needed to segregate all the college-age girls safely, each with her own kind. Private colleges catering mostly to a specific class can still preserve a girl from meeting her social or economic inferiors, but the fees at such places are steep. It costs more to maintain a girl in the Vassar dormitories than to pay her sorority bills at a land-grant school. And even if her family is willing to pay the fees, the academic pace at the elite schools is much too fast for most girls. Most college girls attend large, tax-supported universities where the tuition is relatively low and where admissions policies let in students from many strata and diverse ethnic backgrounds. It is on the campuses of the free, open, and competitive state universities of the country that the sorority system flourishes.

When a family lets its daughter loose on a large campus with a heterogenous population, there are opportunities to be met and dangers to guard against. The great opportunity is to meet a good man to marry, at the age when the girls are most attractive and the men most amenable. For the girls, the pressure of time is urgent; though they are often told otherwise, their attractions are in fact primarily physical, and they fade with time. One need only compare the relative handicaps in the marital sweepstakes of a thirty-eight-year-old single male lawyer and a single, female teacher of the same age to realize the urgency of the quest.

The great danger of the public campus is that young girls, however properly reared, are likely to fall in love, and — in our middle-class society at least — love leads to marriage. Love is a potentially random factor, with no regard for class boundaries. There seems to be no good way of preventing young girls from falling in love. The only practical way to control love is to control the type of men the girl is likely to encounter; she cannot fall dangerously in love with a man she has never met. Since kinship groups are unable to keep "undesirable" boys off the public campus entirely, they have to settle for control of counter-institutions within the university. An effective counter-institution will protect a girl from the corroding influences of the university environment.

There are roughly three basic functions which a sorority can perform in the interest of kinship groups:

It can ward off the wrong kind of men.

It can facilitate moving-up for middle-status girls.

It can solve the "Brahmin problem" — the difficulty of proper marriage that afflicts high-status girls.

Kinship groups define the "wrong kind of man" in a variety of ways. Those who use an ethnic definition support sororities that draw an ethnic membership line; the best examples are the Jewish sororities, because among all the ethnic groups with endogamous standards (in America at any rate), only the Jews so far have sent large numbers of daughters away to college. But endogamy along class lines is even more pervasive. It is the most basic mission of the sorority to prevent a girl from marrying out of her group (exogamy) or beneath her class (hypogamy). As one of the founders of a national sorority artlessly put it in an essay titled "The Mission of the Sorority":

There is a danger, and a very grave danger, that four years' residence in a dormitory will tend to destroy right ideals of home life and substitute in their stead a belief in the freedom that comes from community living . . . culture, broad, liberalizing, humanizing culture, we cannot get too much of, unless while acquiring it we are weaned from home and friends, from ties of blood and kindred.

A sorority discourages this dangerous weaning process by introducing the sisters only to selected boys; each sorority, for example, has dating relations with one or more fraternities, matched rather nicely to the sorority on the basis of ethnicity and/or class. (A particular sorority, for example, will have dating arrangements not with all the fraternities on campus, but only with those whose brothers are a class-match for their sisters.) The sorority's frantically busy schedule of parties, teas, meetings, skits, and exchanges keep the sisters so occupied that they have neither time nor opportunity to meet men outside the channels the sorority provides.

Marrying up

The second sorority function, that of facilitating hypergamy, is probably even more of an attraction to parents than the simpler preservation of endogamy. American society is not so much oriented to the preservation of the *status quo* as to the pursuit of upward mobility.

In industrial societies, children are taught that if they study hard they can get the kind of job that entitles them to a place in the higher ranks. This incentive actually is appropriate only for boys, but the emphasis on using the most efficient available means to enter the higher levels will not be lost on the girls. And the most efficient means for a girl — marriage — is particularly attractive because it requires so much less effort than the mobility through hard work that is open to boys. To the extent that we do socialize the sexes in different ways, we are more likely to train daughters in the ways of attracting men than to motivate them to do hard, competitive work. The difference in motivation holds even if the girls have the intelligence and talent required for status climbing on their own. For lower-class girls on the make, membership in a sorority can greatly improve the chances of meeting (and subsequently marrying) higher-status boys.

Now we come to the third function of the sorority — solving the Brahmin problem. The fact that hypergamy is encouraged in our society creates difficulties for girls whose parents are already in the upper strata. In a hypergamous system, high status *men* have a strong advantage; they can offer their status to a prospective bride as part of the marriage bargain, and the advantages of high status are often sufficient to offset many personal drawbacks. But a *woman's* high status has very little exchange value because she does not confer it on her husband.

This difficulty of high status women in a hypergamous society we may call the Brahmin problem. Girls of Brahmin caste in India and Southern white women of good family have the problem in common. In order to avoid the horrors of hypogamy, high status women must compete for high status men against women from all classes. Furthermore, high status women are handicapped in their battle by a certain type of vanity engendered by their class. They expect their wooers to court them in the style to which their fathers have accustomed them; this usually involves more formal dating, gift-giving, escorting, taxiing, etc., than many college swains can afford. If upperstratum men are allowed to find out that the favors of lower class women are available for a much smaller investment of time, money, and emotion, they may well refuse to court upper-status girls.

In theory, there are all kinds of ways for upper-stratum families to deal with surplus daughters. They can strangle them at birth (female infanticide); they can marry several to each available male (polygyny); they can offer money to any suitable male willing to take one off their hands (dowries, groom-service fees). All these solutions have in fact been used in one society or another, but for various reasons none is acceptable in our society. Spinsterhood still works, but marriage is so popular and so well rewarded that everybody hopes to avoid staying single.

The industrial solution to the Brahmin problem is to corner the market, or more specifically to shunt the eligible bachelors into a special marriage market where the upper stratum women are in complete control of the bride-supply. The best place to set up this protected marriage-market is where many suitable men can be found at the age when they are most willing to marry — in short, the college campus. The kind of male collegians who can be shunted more readily into the specialized marriage-market that sororities run, are those who are somewhat uncertain of their own status and who aspire to move into higher strata. These boys are anxious to bolster a shaky self-image by dating obviously high-class sorority girls. The fraternities are full of them.

How does a sorority go about fulfilling its three functions? The first item of business is making sure that the girls join. This is not as simple as it seems, because the values that sororities maintain are more important to the older generation than to the college-age girls. Although the sorority image is one of membership denied to the "wrong kind" of girls, it is also true that sororities have quite a problem recruiting the "right kind." Some are pressured into pledging by their parents. Many are recruited straight out of high school, before they know much about what really goes on at college. High school recruiters present sorority life to potential rushees as one of unending gaiety; life outside the sorority is painted as bleak and dateless.

A membership composed of the "right kind" of girls is produced by the requirement that each pledge must have the recommendation of, in most cases, two or more alumnae of the sorority. Membership is often passed on from mother to daughter — this is the "legacy," whom sorority actives have to invite whether they like her or not. The sort of headstrong, innovative, or "sassy" girl who is likely to organize a campaign inside the sorority against prevailing standards is unlikely to receive alumnae recommendations. This is why sorority girls are so complacent about alumnae dominance, and why professors find them so bland and uninteresting as students. Alumnae dominance extends beyond recruitment, into the daily life of the house. Rules, regulations, and policy explanations come to the house from the national association. National headquarters is given to explaining unpopular policy by an available stratagem; a favorite device (not limited to the sorority) is to interpret all nonconformity as sexual, so that the girl who rebels against wearing girdle, high heels, and stockings to dinner two or three times a week stands implicitly accused of promiscuity. This sort of argument, based·on the shrewdness of many generations, shames into conformity many a girl who otherwise might rebel against the code imposed by her elders. The actives in positions of control (house manager, pledge trainer, or captain) are themselves closely supervised by alumnae. Once the right girls are initiated, the organization has mechanisms that make it very difficult for a girl to withdraw. Withdrawal can mean difficulty in finding alternative living quarters, loss of prepaid room and board fees, and stigmatization.

Sororities keep their members, and particularly their flighty pledges, in line primarily by filling up all their time with house activities. Pledges are required to study at the house, and they build the big papier-mâché floats (in collaboration with selected fraternity boys) that are a traditional display of "Greek Row" for the homecoming game. Time is encompassed completely; activities are planned long in advance, and there is almost no energy or time available for meeting inappropriate men.

The girls are taught — if they do not already know — the behavior appropriate to the upper strata. They learn how to dress with expensive restraint, how to make appropriate conversation, how to drink like a lady. There is some variety here among sororities of different rank; members of sororities at the bottom of the social ladder prove their gentility by rigid conformity in dress and manner to the stereotype of the sorority girl, while members of top houses feel socially secure even when casually dressed. If you are born rich you can afford to wear Levi's and sweatshirts.

PRELIMINARY EVENTS

The sorority facilitates dating mainly by exchanging parties, picnics, and other frolics with the fraternities in its set. But to augment this the "fixer-uppers" (the American counterpart of the *shatchen*) arrange dates with selected boys; their efforts raise the sorority dating rate above the independent level by removing most of the inconvenience and anxiety from the contracting of dates.

Dating, in itself, is not sufficient to accomplish the sorority's purposes. Dating must lead to pinning, pinning to engagement, engagement to marriage. In sorority culture, all dating is viewed as a movement toward marriage. Casual, spontaneous dating is frowned upon; formal courtship is still encouraged. Sorority ritual reinforces the progression from dating to marriage. At the vital point in the process, where dating must be turned into engagement, the sorority shores up the structure by the pinning ritual, performed after dinner in the presence of all the sorority sisters (who are required to stay for the ceremony) and attended, in its classic form, by a choir of fraternity boys singing outside. The commitment is so public that it is difficult for either partner to withdraw. Since engagement is already heavily reinforced outside the sorority, pinning ceremonies are more elaborate than engagements.

The social columns of college newspapers faithfully record the successes of the sorority system as it stands today. Sorority girls get engaged faster than "independents," and they appear to be marrying more highly ranked men. But what predictions can we make about the system's future?

All social institutions change from time to time, in response to changing conditions. In the mountain villages of the Philippines, the steady attacks of school and mission on the immorality of the *olag* have almost demolished it. Sororities, too, are affected by changes in the surrounding environment. Originally they were places where the few female college students took refuge from the jeers and catcalls of men who thought that nice girls didn't belong on campus. They assumed their present, endogamy-conserving form with the flourishing of the great land-grant universities in the first half of this century.

ON THE BRINK

The question about the future of the sorority system is whether it can adapt to the most recent changes in the forms of higher education. At present, neither fraternities nor sororities are in the pink of health. On some campuses there are chapter houses which have been reduced to taking in nonaffiliated boarders to pay the costs of running the property. New sorority chapters are formed, for the most part, on new or low-prestige campuses (where status-anxiety is rife); at schools of high prestige fewer girls rush each year and the weaker houses are disbanding.

University administrations are no longer as hospitable to the Greeks as they once were. Most are building extensive dormitories that compete effectively with the housing offered by sororities; many have adopted regulations intended to minimize the influence of the Greeks on campus activities. The campus environment is changing rapidly: academic standards are rising, admission is increasingly competitive and both male and female students are more interested in academic achievement; the proportion of graduate students seriously training for a profession is increasing; campus culture is often so obviously pluralist that the Greek claim to monopolize social activity is unconvincing.

The sorority as it currently stands is ill-adapted to cope with the new surroundings. Sorority houses were built to provide a setting for lawn parties, dances, and dress-up occasions, and not to facilitate study; crowding and noise are severe, and most forms of privacy do not exist. The sorority songs that have to be gone through at rushing and chapter meetings today all seem to have been written in 1915 and are mortifying to sing today. The arcane rituals, so fascinating to high school girls, grow tedious and sophomoric to college seniors.

But the worst blow of all to the sorority system comes from the effect of increased academic pressure on the dating habits of college men. A student competing for grades in a professional school, or even in a difficult undergraduate major, simply has not the time (as he might have had in, say, 1925) to get involved in the sorority forms of courtship. Since these days almost all the "right kind" of men *are* involved in demanding training, the traditions of the sorority are becoming actually inimical to hypergamous marriage. Increasingly, then, sororities do not solve the Brahmin problem but make it worse.

One can imagine a sorority designed to facilitate marriage to men who have no time for elaborate courtship. In such a sorority, the girls — to start with small matters — would improve their telephone arrangements, for the fraternity boy in quest of a date today must call several times to get through the busy signals, interminable paging, and lost messages to the girl he wants. They might arrange a private line with prompt answering and faithfully recorded messages, with an unlisted number given only to busy male students with a promising future. They would even accept dates for the same night as the invitation, rather than, as at present, necessarily five to ten days in advance, for the only thing a first-year law student can schedule that far ahead nowadays is his studies. Emphasis on fraternity boys would have to go, for living in a fraternity and pursuing a promising (and therefore competitive) major field of study are rapidly becoming mutually exclusive. The big formal dances would go (the fraternity boys dislike them now); the football floats would go; the pushcart races would go. The girls would reach the hearts of their men not through helping them wash their sports cars but through typing their term papers.

But it is inconceivable that the proud traditions of the sororities that compose the National Panhellenic Council could ever be bent to fit the new design. Their structure is too fixed to fit the changing college and their function is rapidly being lost. The sorority cannot sustain itself on students alone. When parents learn that membership does not benefit their daughters, the sorority as we know it will pass into history.

VI

Roles and groups

For most people, social interaction is unconscious and automatic. We associate with other people from the time we are born. Of course we experience moments when we feel socially awkward and out of place, but generally we learn to act toward others with confidence. Yet our unconscious ease masks an enormously complex process. When we enter a social situation, how do we know what to do? What should we say? How are we supposed to act? Are we dressed appropriately? Are we talking to the right person? Without knowing it, we have learned a complex set of cultural categories for social interaction that enable us to estimate the social situation, identify the people in it, act appropriately, and recognize larger groups of people.

Identity and role are basic to social intercourse. Social identity refers to the cultural knowledge necessary for categorizing different kinds of interacting people. The old saying, "You can't tell the players without a program," goes for our daily associations as well. Instead of a program, however, we identify the actors by a range of signs from the way they dress to the claims they make about themselves. Most identities are stated, so we may be heard to say things like, "That's President Davis," or "She's a lawyer," when we explain social situations to others. This identification of actors is a prerequisite for appropriate social interaction.

Social roles are the rules for action associated with particular identities. We use them to interpret and generate social behavior. For example, a professor plays a role in the classroom. Although unaware of this role, the professor will stand, use the blackboard, look at notes, and speak with a slightly more formal air than usual. The professor does not wear blue jeans and a T-shirt, chew gum, sit cross-legged on the podium, or sing. These actions might be appropriate for this person when assuming the identity of "friend" at a party, but they are out of place in the classroom.

In the following selections we see the importance of identity and role, particularly as they pertain to rank and deference. We also catch a glimpse of relationships between groups that maintain a dominant–subordinate association. In every case, social interaction turns out to be more complex than we may imagine.

17

Male and female: The doctor-nurse game
LEONARD I. STEIN

*The characteristics of sex and occupational role are related
in this article to inequality. Leonard Stein describes the game
played between doctor and nurse in American hospitals, the
object of which is for the nurse to transmit recommendations for
the treatment of patients to the doctor without appearing to
challenge his authority as a male and a physician. Using rules
of behavior defined for this purpose in American culture, the
nurse must be indirect and deferential as she advises on treatment, while the doctor must be positive and accepting. If either
breaks the rules, interaction becomes strained, and effective
working relations in the hospital break down.*

The relationship between the doctor and the nurse is a very special one.
There are few professions where the degree of mutual respect and cooperation between co-workers is as intense as that between the doctor and
nurse. Superficially, the stereotype of this relationship has been dramatized in many novels and television serials. When, however, it is observed carefully in an interactional framework, the relationship takes
on a new dimension and has a special quality which fits a game model.
The underlying attitudes which demand that this game be played are
unfortunate. These attitudes create serious obstacles in the path of meaningful communications between physicians and nonmedical professional
groups.

The physician traditionally and appropriately has total responsibility for making the decisions regarding the management of his patients'
treatment. To guide his decisions he considers data gleaned from several

From "The Doctor-Nurse Game," *Archives of General Psychiatry* 16 (June
1967) : 699–703. Copyright 1967, American Medical Association. Reprinted by
permission of the author and the publisher.

234

sources. He acquires a complete medical history, performs a thorough physical examination, interprets laboratory findings, and at times, obtains recommendations from physician-consultants. Another important factor in his decision-making is the recommendations he receives from the nurse. The interaction between doctor and nurse through which these recommendations are communicated and received is unique and interesting.

THE GAME

One rarely hears a nurse say, "Doctor, I would recommend that you order a retention enema for Mrs. Brown." A physician, upon hearing a recommendation of that nature, would gape in amazement at the effrontery of the nurse. The nurse, upon hearing the statement, would look over her shoulder to see who said it, hardly believing the words actually came from her own mouth. Nevertheless, if one observes closely, nurses make recommendations of more import every hour and physicians willingly and respectfully consider them. If the nurse is to make a suggestion without appearing insolent and the doctor is to seriously consider that suggestion, their interaction must not violate the rules of the game.

Object of the game. The object of the game is as follows: the nurse is to be bold, have initiative, and be responsible for making significant recommendations, while at the same time she must appear passive. This must be done in such a manner so as to make her recommendations appear to be initiated by the physician.

Both participants must be acutely sensitive to each other's nonverbal and cryptic verbal communications. A slight lowering of the head, a minor shifting of position in the chair, or a seemingly nonrelevant comment concerning an event which occurred eight months ago must be interpreted as a powerful message. The game requires the nimbleness of a high wire acrobat, and if either participant slips the game can be shattered; the penalties for frequent failure are apt to be severe.

Rules of the game. The cardinal rule of the game is that open disagreement between the players must be avoided at all costs. Thus, the nurse must communicate her recommendations without appearing to be making a recommendation statement. The physician, in requesting a recommendation from a nurse, must do so without appearing to be asking for it. Utilization of this technique keeps anyone from committing themselves to a position before a sub rosa agreement on that position has already been established. In that way open disagreement is avoided. The greater the significance of the recommendation, the more subtly the game must be played.

To convey a subtle example of the game with all its nuances would require the talents of a literary artist. Lacking these talents, let me give you the following example which is unsubtle, but happens frequently. The medical resident on hospital call is awakened by telephone at 1:00 A.M. because a patient on a ward, not his own, has not been able to fall asleep. Dr. Jones answers the telephone and the dialogue goes like this:

> This is Dr. Jones.
> (An open and direct communication.)
> Dr. Jones, this is Miss Smith on 2W — Mrs. Brown, who learned today of her father's death, is unable to fall asleep.
> (This message has two levels. Openly, it describes a set of circumstances, a woman who is unable to sleep and who that morning received word of her father's death. Less openly, but just as directly, it is a diagnostic and recommendation statement; i.e., Mrs. Brown is unable to sleep because of her grief, and she should be given a sedative. Dr. Jones, accepting the diagnostic statement and replying to the recommendation statement, answers.)
> What sleeping medication has been helpful to Mrs. Brown in the past?
> (Dr. Jones, not knowing the patient, is asking for a recommendation from the nurse, who does know the patient, about what sleeping medication should be prescribed. Note, however, his question does not appear to be asking her for a recommendation. Miss Smith replies.)
> Pentobarbital mg 100 was quite effective night before last.
> (A disguised recommendation statement. Dr. Jones replies with a note of authority in his voice.)
> Pentobarbital mg 100 before bedtime as needed for sleep; got it?
> (Miss Smith ends the conversation with the tone of a grateful supplicant.)
> Yes, I have, and thank you very much doctor.

The above is an example of a successfully played doctor-nurse game. The nurse made appropriate recommendations which were accepted by the physician and were helpful to the patient. The game was successful because the cardinal rule was not violated. The nurse was able to make her recommendation without appearing to, and the physician was able to ask for recommendations without conspicuously asking for them.

The scoring system. Inherent in any game are penalties and rewards for the players. In game theory, the doctor-nurse game fits the nonzero sum game model. It is not like chess, where the players compete with each other and whatever one player loses the other wins. Rather, it is the kind of game in which the rewards and punishments are shared by both players. If they play the game successfully they both win rewards, and if they are unskilled and the game is played badly, they both suffer the penalty.

The most obvious reward from the well-played game is a doctor-nurse team that operates efficiently. The physician is able to utilize the nurse as a valuable consultant, and the nurse gains self-esteem and professional satisfaction from her job. The less obvious rewards are no less important. A successful game creates a doctor-nurse alliance; through this alliance the physician gains the respect and admiration of the nursing service. He can be confident that his nursing staff will smooth the path for getting his work done. His charts will be organized and waiting for him when he arrives, the ruffled feathers of patients and relatives will have been smoothed down, and his pet routines will be happily followed, and he will be helped in a thousand and one other ways.

The doctor-nurse alliance sheds its light on the nurse as well. She gains a reputation for being a "damn good nurse." She is respected by everyone and appropriately enjoys her position. When physicians discuss the nursing staff it would not be unusual for her name to be mentioned with respect and admiration. Their esteem for a good nurse is no less than their esteem for a good doctor.

The penalties for a game failure, on the other hand, can be severe. The physician who is an unskilled gamesman and fails to recognize the nurses' subtle recommendation messages is tolerated as a "clod." If, however, he interprets these messages as insolence and strongly indicates he does not wish to tolerate suggestions from nurses, he creates a rocky path for his travels. The old truism "If the nurse is your ally you've got it made, and if she has it in for you, be prepared for misery" takes on life-sized proportions. He receives three times as many phone calls after midnight as his colleagues. Nurses will not accept his telephone orders because "telephone orders are against the rules." Somehow, this rule gets suspended for the skilled players. Soon he becomes like Joe Bfstplk in the "Li'l Abner" comic strip. No matter where he goes, a black cloud constantly hovers over his head.

The unskilled gamesman nurse also pays heavily. The nurse who does not view her role as that of consultant, and therefore does not attempt to communicate recommendations, is perceived as a dullard and is mercifully allowed to fade into the woodwork.

The nurse who does see herself as a consultant but refuses to follow the rules of the game in making her recommendations has hell to pay. The outspoken nurse is labeled a "bitch" by the surgeon. The psychiatrist describes her as unconsciously suffering from penis envy and her behavior is the acting out of her hostility towards men. Loosely translated, the psychiatrist is saying she is a bitch. The employment of the unbright outspoken nurse is soon terminated. The outspoken bright nurse whose recommendations are worthwhile remains employed. She is, however, constantly reminded in a hundred ways that she is not loved.

Genesis of the game

To understand how the game evolved, we must comprehend the nature of the doctors' and nurses' training which shaped the attitudes necessary for the game.

Medical student training. The medical student in his freshman year studies as if possessed. In the anatomy class he learns every groove and prominence on the bones of the skeleton as if life depended on it. As a matter of fact, he literally believes just that. He not infrequently says, "I've got to learn it exactly; a life may depend on me knowing that." A consequence of this attitude, which is carefully nurtured throughout medical school, is the development of a phobia: the over-determined fear of making a mistake. The development of this fear is quite understandable. The burden the physician must carry is at times almost unbearable. He feels responsible in a very personal way for the lives of his patients. When a man dies leaving young children and a widow, the doctor carries some of her grief and despair inside himself; and when a child dies, some of him dies too. He sees himself as a warrior against death and disease. When he loses a battle, through no fault of his own, he nevertheless feels pangs of guilt, and he relentlessly searches himself to see if there might have been a way to alter the outcome. For the physician a mistake leading to a serious consequence is intolerable, and any mistake reminds him of his vulnerability. There is little wonder that he becomes phobic. The classical way in which phobias are managed is to avoid the source of the fear. Since it is impossible to avoid making some mistakes in an active practice of medicine, a substitute defensive maneuver is employed. The physician develops the belief that he is omnipotent and omniscient, and therefore incapable of making mistakes. This belief allows the phobic physician to actively engage in his practice rather than avoid it. The fear of committing an error in a critical field like medicine is unavoidable and appropriately realistic. The physician, however, must learn to live with the fear rather than handle it defensively through a posture of omnipotence. This defense markedly interferes with his interpersonal professional relationships.

Physicians, of course, deny feelings of omnipotence. The evidence, however, renders their denials to whispers in the wind. The slightest mistake inflicts a large narcissistic wound. Depending on his underlying personality structure the physician may be obsessed for days about it, quickly rationalize it away, or deny it. The guilt produced is unusually exaggerated and the incident is handled defensively. The ways in which physicians enhance and support each other's defenses when an error is made could be the topic of another paper. The feeling of omnipotence becomes generalized to other areas of his life. A report of the Federal Aviation Agency (FAA), as quoted in *Time Magazine* (August 5, 1966), states that in 1964 and 1965 physicians had a fatal-accident rate four times as high as the average for all other private pilots. Major causes of the high death rate were risk-taking attitudes and judgments. Almost all of the accidents occurred on pleasure trips, and were therefore not necessary risks to get to a patient needing emergency care. The trouble, suggested an FAA official, is that too many doctors fly with "the feeling that they are omnipotent." Thus, the extremes to which the physician may go in preserving his self-concept of omnipotence may threaten his own life. This overdetermined preservation of omnipotence is indicative of its brittleness and its underlying foundation of fear of failure.

The physician finds himself trapped in a paradox. He fervently wants to give his patient the best possible medical care, and being open to the nurses' recommendations helps him accomplish this. On the other hand, accepting advice from nonphysicians is highly threatening to his omnipotence. The solution for the paradox is to receive sub rosa recommendations and make them appear to be initiated by himself. In short, he must learn to play the doctor-nurse game.

Some physicians never learn to play the game. Most learn in their internship, and a perceptive few learn during their clerkships in medical school. Medical students frequently complain that the nursing staff treats them as if they had just completed a junior Red Cross first-aid class instead of two years of intensive medical training. Interviewing nurses in a training hospital sheds considerable light on this phenomenon. In their words they said,

> A few students just seem to be with it, they are able to understand what you are trying to tell them, and they are a pleasure to work with; most, however, pretend to know everything and refuse to listen to anything we have to say and I guess we do give them a rough time.

In essence, they are saying that those students who quickly learn the game are rewarded, and those that do not are punished.

Most physicians learn to play the game after they have weathered a few experiences like the one described below. On the first day of his internship, the physician and nurse were making rounds. They stopped at the bed of a fifty-two-year-old woman who, after complimenting the young doctor on his appearance, complained to him of her problem with constipation. After several minutes of listening to her detailed description of peculiar diets, family home remedies, and special exercises that have helped her constipation in the past, the nurse politely interrupted the patient. She told her the doctor would take care of the problem and that he had to move on because there were other patients waiting to see him. The young doctor gave the nurse a stern look, turned toward the patient, and kindly told her he would order an enema for her that very afternoon. As they left the bedside, the nurse told him the patient has had a normal bowel movement every day for the past week and that in the twenty-three days the patient has been in the hospital she has never once passed up an opportunity to complain of her constipation. She quickly added that *if* the doctor wanted to order an enema, the patient would certainly receive one. After hearing this report the intern's mouth fell open and the wheels began turning in his head. He remembered the nurse's comment to the patient that "the doctor had to move on," and it occurred to him that perhaps she was really giving him a message. This experience and a few more like it, and the young doctor learns to listen for the subtle recommendations the nurses make.

Nursing student training. Unlike the medical student who usually learns to play the game after he finishes medical school, the nursing student begins to learn it early in her training. Throughout her education she is trained to play the doctor-nurse game.

Student nurses are taught how to relate to physicians. They are told he has infinitely more knowledge than they, and thus he should be shown the utmost respect. In addition, it was not many years ago when nurses were instructed to stand whenever a physician entered a room. When he would come in for a conference the nurse was expected to offer him her chair, and when both entered a room the nurse would open the door for him and allow him to enter first. Although these practices are no longer rigidly adhered to, the premise upon which they were based is still promulgated. One nurse described that premise as, "He's God almighty and your job is to wait on him."

To inculcate subservience and inhibit deviancy, nursing schools, for the most part, are tightly run, disciplined institutions. Certainly there is great variation among nursing schools, and there is little question that the trend is toward giving students more autonomy. However, in too many schools this trend has not gone far enough, and the climate remains restrictive. The student's schedule is firmly controlled and there is very little free time. Classroom hours, study hours, mealtime, and bedtime with lights out are rigidly enforced. In some schools meaningless chores are assigned, such as cleaning bedsprings with cotton applicators. The relationship between student and instructor continues this military flavor. Often their relationship is more like that between recruit and drill sergeant than between student and teacher. Open dialogue is inhibited by attitudes of strict black and white, with few, if any, shades of gray. Straying from the rigidly outlined path is sure to result in disciplinary action.

The inevitable result of these practices is to instill in the student nurse a fear of independent action. This inhibition of independent action is most marked when relating to physicians. One of the students' greatest fears is making a blunder while assisting a physician and being publicly ridiculed by him. This is really more a reflection of the nature of their training than the prevalence of abusive physicians. The fear of being humiliated for a blunder while assisting in a procedure is generalized to the fear of humiliation for making any independent act in relating to a physician, especially the act of making a direct recommendation. Every nurse interviewed felt that making a suggestion to a physician was equivalent to insulting and belittling him. It was tantamount to questioning his medical knowledge and insinuating he did not know his business. In light of her image of the physician as an omniscient and punitive figure, the questioning of his knowledge would be unthinkable.

The student, however, is also given messages quite contrary to the ones described above. She is continually told that she is an invaluable aid to the physician in the treatment of the patient. She is told that she must help him in every way possible, and she is imbued with a strong sense of responsibility for the care of her patient. Thus she, like the physician, is caught in a paradox. The first set of messages implies that the physician is omniscient and that any recommendation she might make would be insulting to him and leave her open to ridicule. The second set of messages implies that she is an important asset to him, has much to contribute, and is duty-bound to make those contributions. Thus, when her good sense tells her a recommendation would be helpful to him she is not allowed to communicate it directly, nor is she allowed not to communicate it. The way out of the bind is to use the doctor-nurse game and communicate the recommendation without appearing to do so.

FORCES PRESERVING THE GAME

Upon observing the indirect interactional system which is the heart of the doctor-nurse game, one must ask the question, "Why does this inefficient mode of communication continue to exist?" The forces mitigating against change are powerful.

Rewards and punishments. The doctor-nurse game has a powerful innate self-perpetuating force — its system of rewards and punishments. One potent method of shaping behavior is to reward one set of behavioral patterns and to punish patterns which deviate from it. As described earlier, the rewards given for a well-played game and the punishments meted out to unskilled players are impressive. This system alone would be sufficient to keep the game flourishing. The game, however, has additional forces.

The strength of the set. It is well recognized that sets are hard to break. A powerful attitudinal set is the nurse's perception that making a suggestion to a physician is equivalent to insulting and belittling him. An example of where attempts are regularly made to break this set is seen on psychiatric treatment wards operating on a therapeutic community model. This model requires open and direct communication between members of the team. Psychiatrists working in these settings expend a great deal of energy in urging for and rewarding openness before direct patterns of communication become established. The rigidity of the resistance to break this set is impressive. If the physician himself is a prisoner of a set and therefore does not actively try to destroy it, change is near impossible.

The need for leadership. Lack of leadership and structure in any organization produces anxiety in its members. As the importance of the organization's mission increases, the demand by its members for leadership commensurately increases. In our culture human life is near the top of our hierarchy of values, and organizations which deal with human lives, such as law and medicine, are very rigidly structured. Certainly some of this is necessary for the systematic management of the task. The excessive degree of rigidity, however, is demanded by its members for their own psychic comfort rather than for its utility in efficiently carrying out its mission. The game lends support to this thesis. Indirect communication is an inefficient mode of transmitting information. However, it effectively supports and protects a rigid organizational structure with the physician in clear authority. Maintaining an omnipotent leader provides the other members with a great sense of security.

Sexual roles. Another influence perpetuating the doctor-nurse game is the sexual identity of the players. Doctors are predominately men and nurses are almost exclusively women. There are elements of the game which reinforce the stereotyped roles of male dominance and female passivity. Some nursing instructors explicitly tell their students that their femininity is an important asset to be used when relating to physicians.

THE COMMUNITY

The doctor and nurse have a shared history and thus have been able to work out their game so that it operates more efficiently than one would expect in an indirect system. Major difficulty arises, however, when the physician works closely with other disciplines which are not normally considered part of the medical sphere. With expanding medical horizons encompassing cooperation with sociologists, engineers, anthropologists, computer analysts, etc., continued expectation of a doctor-nurselike interaction by the physician is disastrous. The sociologist, for example, is not willing to play that kind of game. When his direct communications are rebuffed the relationship breaks down.

The major disadvantage of a doctor-nurselike game is its inhibitory effect on open dialogue which is stifling and anti-intellectual. The game is basically a transactional neurosis, and both professions would enhance themselves by taking steps to change the attitudes which breed the game. . . .

18

Only on Sundays: Women's place in Greece
MURIEL DIMEN-SCHEIN

*In many societies the avenue to status and prestige is closely
linked to the work one does. Americans, for example, take
pride in their work, and different degrees of status are allotted
to different types of jobs. In the Greek community described
in this article, labor is clearly divided according to sex. Muriel
Schein describes the few means women have to achieve status
in the eyes of their community and exposes some discontents
within the system.*

The 430 inhabitants of Kriovrisi, a remote village high in the Pindus
Mountains of northwestern Greece, belong to an ethnic minority known
as Koutsovlachs. They are Greek in religion and other major cultural
characteristics, not the least of which is the position of women.

Residing in stone houses clustered on a steep mountain slope, the
people of Kriovrisi eke out a living from small, barely arable plots in
the shallow valley below the village and from overgrazed pastures and
pine forests on the surrounding mountainsides. The majority of the
men are shepherds, keeping flocks of sheep and goats; the rest farm or
engage in miscellaneous occupations. Their work requires a multiplicity
of skills, entrepreneurship, travel, and contacts. In contrast, the lives
of the women are similar; all perform the basic tasks of cooking, cleaning, clothes making, and child rearing.

The contrast between the diversity of men's labors and the similarity of the women's was brought home to me when my husband and
I spent a year studying the lives of the people of Kriovrisi. Despite my
urban American background and my specialized training for ethnographic research, I could immediately empathize with the women and

Originally published as "Only on Sundays," *Natural History* Magazine, April,
1971. Copyright © 1974 Muriel Dimen-Schein. Reprinted by permission of the
author. Illustrations are omitted.

discuss problems of household management with them; whereas my husband found that the men's routine activities were not at all like any work he knew, and he had to learn about them from scratch. In both cultures, all females are taught household skills early in their lives; males, however, may have one of a variety of jobs, choosing a specific occupation and learning the requisite skills much later.

Like many others, I have long been interested in this widespread contrast between the lives of men and women. My own concern with women's liberation led me to observe the lives of women in Kriovrisi and to compare them with our own. In my opinion, the conditions underlying women's lives in villages like Kriovrisi and in cities like New York lead ultimately to feelings of discontent among women. Yet I know that Kriovrisi women are content with their lives, and I recognize the validity and appropriateness of their feelings. Current thought tempts one to say that the position of Kriovrisi women results from male oppression. However, although male chauvinism indeed exists in the daily life of Kriovrisi (and of New York City), it is nowhere the cause of female oppression. Seen from afar, the activities and prestige of each sex form parts of a total system. Here, then, we can examine the lives of women in one small village and perhaps understand one part of this system.

In Kriovrisi, a man's achievements — the type of work he does, the degree of financial success, his largesse toward other men — partly determine his own and his wife's social rank. Nonmanual labor is more prestigious than manual labor. The wife of a shepherd or a farmer will at times have to work in the fields or the pastures. Based on this criterion the wives of the village stock merchant, of the village cheese merchant, and of the village secretary rank highest. Most occupations, however, involve manual labor, so that the rest of the villagers are then judged according to their earnings. The merchants are the wealthiest, and shepherds tend to be wealthier than any others.

A further consideration is independence. It is preferable to work for oneself, but a wealthy hired herder will receive more prestige than a poor independent shepherd. The uses to which a man puts his income also affect his rank and, therefore, that of his wife. These uses include meat once a week, wine and liquor for guests, urban-style clothing, a house in good repair, and a secondary school education for his sons. In addition, he must be generous outside his household, treat other men to coffee or drinks in a cafe, and publicly pay large sums to the bands of musicians who come to Kriovrisi on festival days.

The behavior and demeanor of her children, their progress in school, and their prospects for marriage and work also contribute to a woman's position. It is a great disappointment if a woman is childless, but it is considered foolish and animallike to have more than four children. When children are below school age, they are their mother's special responsibility. Our landlady, Evanthia, told of a time during the Greek civil war (1947–49) when she was alone in her home with her young son when the enemy arrived. She feared for her son's life not only because she loved him but also because if anything had happened to him, "my husband would have killed me."

If children attend school regularly, learn to read, write, and count, and win prizes on the annual day of promotion in June, both they and their parents receive praise. Passing the examination to attend secondary school located in the county seat brings even more honor to parents, especially to mothers. As they mature, children must behave respectfully toward their elders. A well-behaved child, on entering a room or store where people are sitting, always says, "Good-day to you," and "good-bye" on leaving; to omit this will bring forth comments on the child's upbringing. Thus, the low opinion that the village women had of one woman, who was poor and who, with her husband, had once held unpopular political views, was ameliorated somewhat by the educational achievements and good manners of her three sons.

The marriages parents arrange for their children can also bring prestige. If a mother has raised her daughter to be a skilled housekeeper and if a father has amassed a dowry of $2,000 or more, they can find a suitable husband for her, say, a clerk in a town bank. Such a marriage means upward mobility for the daughter and is a tribute to her parents' farsightedness.

A woman's household skills, the final criterion of prestige, also bear on the other criteria, for her children's behavior and her husband's business success depend to some extent on how well she feeds and clothes them. Her house must always be presentable; indeed, cleaning and decoration are frequently done with the thought that "someone might drop in." This standard requires daily airing of rugs and blankets, sweeping, polishing of the glass shades from the kerosine lamps (Kriovrisi has no electricity), and two or three trips to one of the 13 village springs for water. Women take pride in this hard work.

Daily household work includes food preparation. The housewife provides coffee and bread for breakfast, the main meal at noon or one o'clock, and a supper of leftovers and salad at seven or eight o'clock. Because the midday meal is the most important, providing the most nourishment, it requires planning and creativity. As one woman put it after we had finished the midday meal, "Well, that's another day taken care of." A good housewife can feed unexpected guests, and can offer sweets, coffee, and liqueurs to afternoon and Sunday visitors.

In addition to the daily routine, there are other occasional but essential tasks. Women bake all the bread, which constitutes half the diet, a dozen or so loaves at a time. They are very critical of their own and others' bread, often comparing lightness, texture, and taste. Periodically, clothes, blankets, and rugs must be washed and clothing ironed. The industrious housewife collects brushwood to burn in the oven and chops the firewood that her husband or son has brought from the forest. The most fastidious and admired housewives clean their houses thoroughly once a year, usually in June. This can take two or three weeks and involves not only scrubbing and repairing furnishings but also covering the walls with lime, which makes them white and bright and "kills germs."

When all of these maintenance tasks are done, women devote their time to other, more creative work in which they take a great deal of interest, and which provides a more durable basis for prestige. In May or June they begin to wash and dye wool gathered from their own sheep or purchased from shepherds. They spend all their free time spinning. Once the wool is spun, the women knit underwear, socks and sweaters, or weave blankets and rugs. The older women sometimes make original patterns while the younger women copy designs of rugs that they see in urban magazines. They discuss and compare each other's rugs, most of which are for household use. Only a few of these are sold at the annual bazaar held in the county seat. Married women work on items for their own houses, while unmarried women make their trousseaux.

In part, then, women derive their identity from their work. Men do certain things, women do others. Women take pride in their ability to do necessary work that men and children cannot do for themselves. When Evanthia's sons were leaving on their winter migration with their flocks, her daughter, Amalia, packed their clothes and set aside food. I suggested that the men could do that themselves. Amalia said, "They're men and they don't know how," then added that men are not inclined to do this work and do not want to learn, for it would be inappropriate for them.

A woman gains her identity and prestige primarily from family and household activities. A woman's personal creations, represented, for example, by woven woolen articles, can be worked on only when the major and most time-consuming treadmill tasks of household maintenance are done. Her only other products are her children. It is not surprising, then, that a woman's prestige derives, not from her own achievements, but from those of other members of her household and family line. Even the name that many people know her by is not her own, but her husband's. She takes not only his last name but also his first; if his name is Takis, she is known to his relatives and friends as (Mrs.) Takina.

In contrast, men engage in various business pursuits, and have personal transactions with men from other households, as well as with merchants and government officials outside of Kriovrisi. Their prestige and rank are not limited to household and family, although these are important.

In Kriovrisi, this situation exists because there is no alternative role for women. Not only would few men and women seriously consider other activities as appropriate for women, but the village's economic and social structure does not permit other possibilities. Females are brought up solely to perform the combined role of wife and mother. When a girl is born, the joy at her birth is tinged with disappointment. Although all children are valued, sons affirm their fathers' masculinity. Furthermore, daughters are an economic burden. Sons bring in money in the form of a wife's dowry, daughters take it away for their dowries.

Young girls are encouraged to perform womanly tasks. By the time they are six, they learn to spin, using a stick and a bit of old wool their mothers have given them. Two or three will stand on a pathway, in perfect imitation of their mothers, spinning and talking. Both boys and girls begin school at age six, but six grades are considered sufficient for girls. They will, after all, marry; secondary education is not necessary for that. In Kriovrisi only 4 girls out of 62 unmarried girls of the appropriate age were attending secondary school or a university in 1967–68. It is a different matter for boys, who are encouraged to go on to the six-year high school if they can. Since not all boys can make a decent living in the village, an education is important for it may lead to economic and social mobility outside the village. Although schooling is free, the student must pay for room and board in the town. While some return on this investment can be expected for males, this expense would be a waste for females who need the money for dowries. In addition, the income an educated boy can earn helps to dower his sister.

So girls finish school at age 12. Having learned to sweep, fetch water, and care for young children, they now begin to weave and knit. They practice by knitting heavy sweaters or weaving saddle blankets and pack bags from coarse wool. After a year or so, they start to use finer wool to weave the rugs, blankets, and pillow covers that will form part of their trousseaux. At 13 or 14, they begin to take over the heavier household tasks, while their mothers do the cooking.

During these years, girls spend most of their time with other girls, a pattern that will continue for the rest of their lives. In Kriovrisi, the separation of space into male and female worlds is not as sharp as in some Greek villages, where women are forbidden to enter cafes, but it exists. Males, when not working, relax in cafes or near the village office with other males. A female spends any free moment she has with other females in or near the house. This leisure is always busy leisure. On most occasions, a woman's hands are occupied with some useful work. As Evanthia said, "If I sit with my hands empty, I feel I've done nothing; but if I spin, at least I've eked out a few cents." Friends will spin or weave together, they may help each other work, or they may bake a cake together. It is only on Sundays that their hands are free from labor for an hour or two; then after church, they will walk around the village together, dressed in their finest.

Public contacts between young men and women are limited. Again, on Sundays, they may meet, perhaps during their stroll. On festival occasions, when a gypsy band visits the village, boys and girls do traditional dances together.

At this time, the parents are arranging the girls' marriages. Only recently have a few girls begun to choose their mates. Parents look first among the best families of Kriovrisi, thus insuring that their daughters will remain nearby, and that the bride and her in-laws will not be strangers to each other. More and more often, however, because of the population decline in Kriovrisi, they must ask friends and relatives outside the village to find mates. When a suitable mate is found, both sets of parents negotiate the dowry, and the marriage ceremony takes place soon afterward.

After marriage, the male-female separation may continue, depending on the type of household that the bride and groom establish. There are two major kinds of households: the nuclear family, composed of a married couple and their children; and the stem family, composed of a married couple, their son, and his wife and children. Most households begin as stem families, becoming nuclear if the two couples quarrel and separate or if the elders die. In such households the division of labor between males and females tends to have more daily importance than the conjugal ties.

In 1968, Ioannis, a young shepherd from Kriovrisi, married Sophia, a girl from another village. She moved into his household, comprised of his parents and his four sisters. After the wedding, Sophia and Ioannis rarely appeared together. He was either in the pastures with the sheep or in a cafe with other young men. She was always in the company of at least one sister-in-law or other female relative.

The bride begins a second phase of her education when she marries. Sophia's mother-in-law, Anna, and sisters-in-law were, for example, teaching Sophia how to spin, a skill that for some reason she had never acquired. At first Sophia did the heavy work and only such minor cooking tasks as making salad, while Anna did most of the cooking.

The bride gradually learns the finer aspects of cooking. This is considered wise and proper, for there is an old story about a woman who wanted her daughter-in-law to do all the cooking. The daughter-in-law did, but because she came from a wealthier household, she used only butter and no oil in her cooking. Soon the woman discovered that there was no butter left, and from then on she did all her own cooking.

In her new household, the bride is subject to the authority of her husband and of her in-laws, both male and female. Among the women, a division of labor and a hierarchy of authority develops. In this particular household, Anna was in charge; of her four daughters, the eldest (20 years old) was second in command and directed the other three, as well as Sophia, in their tasks.

The relationship between mother-in-law and daughter-in-law tends to be fraught with tensions, as attested to by the many jokes that women tell. It seems that daughters-in-law are expected to be lazy. Once when I was standing with my arms folded, our landlady, Evanthia, said to me, "Why are you standing with your arms like that? Do you think you're a new daughter-in-law?" The bride must learn to perform household tasks in a way that pleases her mother-in-law. If she is strong-willed, then fights are likely to ensue.

The newly married woman may also have to deal with the contradictions between her roles as wife and as daughter-in-law. As a wife, her status complements that of her husband; as a daughter-in-law, her status supplements and competes with that of her mother-in-law. This may cause severe conflicts in some households, as when mother-in-law and daughter-in-law disagree on how money should be spent. Women have a great deal of control over economic matters within the household. In Kriovrisi, the mother-in-law can retain this control even after her son has married and, in some cases, even after her own husband, the nominal household head, has relinquished his power or has died.

A few households in Kriovrisi were notorious for fights between mother-in-law and daughter-in-law. In one of them, Argorou, the mother-in-law, who was 78 years old and half-blind, ended the argument by gratuitously proclaiming, "All right, I'll leave. Just give me some bread and cheese and I'll go away. Don't worry about me." Her daughter-in-law, Olga, was put in the position of having asked Argorou to leave, which she had not done. Olga came to tell our landlady the story of the fight. After she left, I asked Evanthia why these fights happened. Smiling slyly, she said, "Her husband likes his mother too much." We talked some more about the problem, and it emerged that Olga had no choice, for village women view a bad husband or mother-in-law as just the luck of the game and feel they can do nothing about it. Evanthia sat silent for a moment, then said, "But, still, it's not right. Olga should be treated better than that. Even a daughter-in-law is human."

In many cases, the women live together amicably and provide company for each other in a way that prevents their work from becoming the alienating experience it can be for women living in nuclear families like our own. The division of labor among females also permits the multitude of tasks to be done efficiently. In addition, within the context of her role, a woman has much to look forward to, for one day her life will be easier; she will have a daughter or daughter-in-law to do the heavy work, she will cook, she will play with her grandchildren, and she will have the right, as a mother-in-law, to sit and do nothing, if she wishes, but talk with old friends for an afternoon hour.

There are many resemblances between this situation and that of other societies, including our own industrialized, urban society. The sexual division of labor, based on the long maturation period of human offspring, is a social adaptation, probably as old as human society, that has enabled human groups to survive. Since females must care for the young, their mobility is restricted. While males can range farther afield, females stay fairly close to the place of residence, caring for it and also engaging in food-getting activities that do not take them far away. A division of labor among females, such as described for Kriovrisi, allows greater efficiency in the pursuit of these activities. Likewise, among males who engage in various means of livelihood, cooperation and specialization between two or more males also renders food-getting more efficient.

Changes are slow to take place in this division of labor, which underlies so many other social patterns. Despite time- and energy-saving devices, such as wood-burning stoves and, more recently, propane gas burners instead of fireplaces, liquid dish detergent (as Evanthia said, "Things are much easier with 'Thrill' "), and ready-made clothes instead of homespun, the role of women seems to have changed little since the nineteenth century, at least as it is portrayed by the old women of Kriovrisi today. A woman's basic tasks are the same, the separation of male and female worlds continues, and the working of wool continues to absorb any excess time or energy.

It is only in cities that change can occur. There are girls, whose parents were born in Kriovrisi and later emigrated to a city, who now go to secondary school and the university. One such girl, the daughter of an Athens cheese merchant, went to a French private school there and attended law school. Another attends the university in Ioannina. The urban environment provides jobs suitable for women, such as teaching positions, secretarial jobs, or sales positions. In Kriovrisi, there is room for only one teacher (a male) and no business concern needs women.

In the city, major technological changes enable women to spend much less time and energy at household tasks. All clothes are ready-made. Running water and electricity, laundromats and prepared foods decrease much of the household labor. These changes permit the nuclear family to predominate, for one woman can do all the necessary tasks with time to spare.

In Greece, as in the United States, women in cities are beginning to be discontent with, and to question, traditional roles. Maria, a 45-year-old woman from Kriovrisi, lived with her husband in Ioannina, a city of some 40,000 people, and had a 15-year-old daughter studying to be a French teacher. Maria felt that "in Greece, women have no value; their work is considered to be worthless, and the work itself is hard." Her husband disagreed, adding that "perhaps village women have to work hard, but it is different in the city." Perhaps the difficulty Maria felt, living in the city, was the loneliness of solitary household work; perhaps it was also her awareness of the increased opportunities that were open to her daughter.

Urban women, however, feel pressure not to work outside the household. Many men feel dishonored if their wives work, and women feel that once they have children they would be neglecting their duties if they went to work. These attitudes reflect both an economy unable to provide adequate work even for its male population and the prevailing ideology of appropriate male and female roles. In 1967 a popular song, "The Girls Who Go Two by Two," dramatized the confined role of Greek women:

> Young girls in pairs
> passing by,
> shy and embarrassed
> the young girls hurry by.
>
> Young girls looking in the
> mirror, the mirror.
> Every night secretly they watch
> themselves getting older
> with fear in their hearts.
>
> Young girls are so so pretty,
> so so unlucky.
> You see the ugliness of
> their parents.
> They'll pay for it very dearly.

One day, dejected, they'll
stand before the altar.
Their mothers will cry,
relatives, in-laws.
The unlucky girls have
nothing more to say.

In Kriovrisi, what little questioning there is does not go far. Zoe, 23 years old, lives with her husband, her mother-in-law, and a year-old daughter. She is much put-upon by both her husband and her mother-in-law. Her husband yells at her at the slightest excuse and continually gives her orders. Her mother-in-law constantly criticizes her work. One winter day after a heavy snowfall, the stove, for some reason, would not work. We were all cold and uncomfortable. Zoe's brother had been married a few days before, and she wanted to visit him and his bride on the other side of the village. But her mother-in-law forbade her to go. Her baby was crying a lot because she had just been weaned. In exasperation, Zoe said to me, "Don't ever become a mother. It's not worth it." Six months later, when the weather was warm, I went to visit her. Zoe's daughter was playing on the floor of a sunny room in a new house. Zoe told me she was pregnant, and although she would have preferred to wait another year, she was very happy about it. "You should have children," she said. "But you told me never to become a mother," I reminded her. "I didn't mean it," she said. "We should marry, have children, and raise them. What else are we put on earth for?"

19

Reciprocal exploitation
in an Indian-white community
NIELS WINTHER BRAROE

*In a small town on the western Canadian prairie live two groups:
Indians and whites. Everyone recognizes their existence, and
members from both groups interact. Niels Winther Braroe sets
out to examine the process of interaction. He deftly shows how
each group has stereotypes of the other — Indians for whites,
whites for Indians — and how they relate to each other in terms
of these stereotypes. He demonstrates further how the interactions of the two groups confirm their views of each other. And
in so doing he reveals how a complex social structure operates
in this Canadian town.*

In this paper I shall examine the manner in which conceptions of self
and other held by Indians and whites contribute stability to a community structure of roles and values which is riddled with apparent inconsistency and contradiction.[1] As a point of departure, I shall focus on a
recurrent type of behavior: the practice by Indians and whites alike of
"victimizing" one another, of misrepresenting the self and self-motiva-
tions in social and economic transactions. The insight gleaned from
consideration of these performances will be offered in support of the

Reprinted by permission of the author and publisher from *Southwestern
Journal of Anthropology* 21, no. 2 (1965): 166–178. Bibliography and bibliographic
citations are omitted.

[1] The research upon which this paper is based was done in the summer of 1963,
and was supported by the University of Illinois and in part by the Saskatchewan
Cultural Ecology Research Program, NSF Grant G23815, administered by the Social
Science Institute of Washington University, and directed by John W. Bennett. I am
indebted to Edward M. Bruner, Joseph R. Gusfield, and George L. Hicks for critical
comments and suggestions.

hypothesis that these misrepresentations allow both Indians and whites to resolve value and role contradictions which might otherwise engender social conflict or personal disorganization.

I

The perspective adopted in this paper draws on the work of Rose, Goffman, Berreman, and others relating to the nature of the self and human interaction. Human beings are categorized according to the major roles they enact in society, roles being a "cluster of related meanings and values that guide and direct an individual's behavior in a given social setting. . . ." Roles and the self are seen as growing out of continuous social symbolic interaction in which individuals present and express themselves in ways intended to influence a shared definition of the situation. A large portion of this interaction is concerned with crediting or discrediting the selves thus presented: "this imputation — this self — is a *product* of the scene that comes off. . . ."

Two aspects of this perspective are prominent in the following pages. The first deals with the tendency of the participants in a community or a social setting to arrive at a working consensus, an agreement about how they will behave toward one another and upon the symbols and meanings which will guide this action. Secondly, people generally work to support consensus and devise means of avoiding its disintegration and the associated failure of self-validations.

> A person is an individual who becomes involved in a value of some kind . . . and then makes a public claim that he is to be defined and treated as someone who possesses the value or property in question. The limits to his claims, and hence the limits to his self, are primarily determined by the objective facts of his social life and secondarily determined by the degree to which a sympathetic interpretation of these facts can bend them in his favor. Any event which demonstrates that someone has made a false claim, defining himself as something which he is not, tends to destroy him.

This paper explores self and other images of white and Indian persons vis-à-vis one another. Attention is directed to the ways in which each credits or validates the roles and self of the other in the context of a community "working consensus" that provides the framework of day-to-day interaction. One question is central to this discussion: how do Indians adapt to circumstances of economic and social deprivation? How do they adapt to membership in the lowest category of a rigidly hierarchical status system?

II

Jasper is a town of about 2400 persons on the western prairie of Saskatchewan.[2] Small-scale cattle ranching and mixed farming are the predominant economic activities of whites in this region; they come to Jasper for goods and services, and often move there after retirement. In Jasper there are two general stores, a movie theatre, two small hotels, a pub, three Chinese-owned restaurants, several auto and farm equipment stores, and so on. The town, however, is no longer the isolated focus of patterns of leisure and consumption, as area residents now make frequent trips to a shopping center in a small city about sixty miles away.

Twenty miles from town is a small non-treaty Indian reserve which is the home of about a hundred and ten Plains Cree. The Indians make their living by the sale of poplar posts to ranchers and to the lumber yard in town, and by seasonal agricultural labor. All receive government relief, their most stable source of income. Jasper Indians do not identify with whites to the extent that white cultural goals and values are outwardly accepted and Indian ones entirely rejected. They revere generosity and sharing, for example, and ridicule white ideas about the dignity of work, the accumulation of material goods, punctuality, and the like. The fact that so few of them are acculturated — that is, display their selves as white — is not difficult to understand given the nature of their relations with the dominant society; these relations impede the communication of white culture and limit the participation of Indians in white institutional activities. Until six years ago there was no school for Indian children; even now their school is segregated on the reserve. Since most parents do not value education, class attendance is poor. Children do not learn to speak English until they are six or seven years old. Jasper Indians uniformly profess belief in "Indian" religion and emphatically call attention to their participation in it. None of the Indians are even nominally Christian, and there is no record of any effort in the past generation to convert them. No one among them has ever served in the military.

While Indians go to town frequently, even in the worst weather, the reserve itself is isolated. Whites seldom visit it and never live there. A policeman said, "We don't really know what goes on up there, and don't really care as long as they don't make trouble in town." Lacking electricity, reserve Indians have no radios or television sets, and hence are further isolated by minimal exposure to mass media.[3] Occupational

_____

[2] The name Jasper, and the names of all informants mentioned in this paper, are pseudonyms.

[3] Several families have quite recently acquired small transistor radios.

opportunities in town do not exist. None of the merchants or business-men questioned said that they were willing to hire Indians, even for the most menial tasks.

Similarly, the legal status of Indians and their dependence on pater-nalistic government relief are important factors in their marginal in-volvement in the local economy. They do not have the capital resources to increase the income from communally-owned reserve holdings. They have not learned skills that would bring them regular employment in the Jasper community or allow them to emigrate to a more favorable urban location.[4]

Attitudes of whites toward Indians are obstacles to Indian assimila-tion. The common denominator of nearly all of these attitudes is that Indians are childish and irresponsible. For some, such as the man to whom Indians bring their dilapidated cars for repair, this is mixed with pity. He knows that his work will likely go unpaid, but he says, "They can't help it, they're just kids with money. They got nothing, and whenever they do get a little money they can't wait to spend it." At the other extreme there are people who share this appraisal of Indian char-acter as childlike, but who express a spare-the-rod-spoil-the-child opin-ion. They insist that Indians should be compelled to behave responsibly and that they ought to be given no social privileges or aid until they do so. Others, including many ranchers, think that the Indians should be allowed to rot. "I can make a living off this land," they say, "why can't they? It's because we help them so much that they're so lazy."

Jasper whites not only consider Indians to be irresponsible, but speak of them as worthless. Some see them circumstantially so, others consider Indians worthless as human beings. For the latter, Indians are innately without value, and no amount of "help" by white society will ever make Indians self-sufficient. They are regarded as parasites, a liability inherited from the past. Few whites, however, display active hostility toward Indians, not excluding those who consider them little more than superfluous appendages to white society. The absence of malice on the part of whites is one of the most remarkable aspects of Indian-white relations. Even those white men who have been involved in brawls with Indians do not bear animosity toward them. In fact, both Indians and whites describe these events with the greatest amusement.

The conception which whites have of Indians differs dramatically from whites' image of themselves. They extol responsibility, indepen-dence, and self-sufficiency. The residents of Jasper and its surroundings feel themselves close to the western frontier era — indeed this part of

---

[4] One family of Jasper Indians does travel to Alberta each summer to work on the beet farms there. They return at the end of each season to spend the winter on the reserve.

North America was the scene of the closing days of the "Old West." A sentiment commonly expressed by Jasper whites is one of confidence in the face of adversity, of dauntlessness in the confrontation of nature. Town-dwelling men speak with pride of the ability to "take care of myself." Only Indians go on relief. The image of the strong, silent cowboy is taken seriously in Jasper. With it go the attributes of unwavering integrity, fairness, and helpfulness. Jasper is a particularistic community, where people applaud the man who is willing to help others without demanding repayment; but they believe that a man must not accept a hand unless he intends to reciprocate someday. These values pervade the complex, reticulate cooperative work groups among ranchers.

III

The whites' emphasis upon the values of integrity and charity are often not discernible in their day-to-day behavior toward Indians. Indians who have cut and cured poplar posts near the reserve, and who do not have trucks, persuade whites to haul the posts to town. For his small investment of time, the white charges as much as 25 percent of the load's value; customarily he goes into the lumber yard office to collect his money from the manager while the Indian unloads the posts in the yard. Whites say that one has to pocket one's money before the Indian "gets his hands on it," or risk never being paid. Again, whites frequently take advantage of the restrictions placed upon Indians in disposing of reserve resources. The law forbids Indians to sell cattle or hay without permission from the Indian agent, and the money from such sales is supposed to go to a common reserve fund rather than to individual Indians. To circumvent this, Indians sell these things to whites, but for only a fraction of their value.[5] Similarly, a few ranchers take advantage of the Indians' desire for spending money, by arranging to place cattle on reserve pasture for much less than it would cost if legal channels were used. In this way a small "grazing fee" is collected by an Indian who needs money for a trip to a Sun Dance on another reserve, and the white is enabled to feed his cattle for a pittance. Indians are overcharged for merchandise and services in town, and they are paid less for their labor than a white man would be. Indian women are not infrequently objects of white sexual gratification.

White belief in the irresponsibility of Indians is demonstrated continuously. For example, at the suggestion of some Jasper residents, the

---

[5] Six years ago, the Indian Affairs Branch supplied reserve families with a total of about seventy cows: today there are only about twenty-five. They have been sold (illegally), eaten and allowed to starve or freeze to death.

Indian department no longer gives relief money directly to the Indians. Instead, a local general store receives these funds, which are credited to Indian families to whom supplies of food and clothing are doled out on a weekly basis.

While not all whites engage in these practices, those who do are neither publicly nor privately censured by those who do not have such dealings with Indians. Neither do white members of the Jasper community comment upon the less direct deprivation of Indians. The legal and political status of Indians is, of course, a matter of national governmental policy. But whites make no effort to bring about policy changes which might lead to Indian self-sufficiency, nor do they take action at the local community level to provide Indians with occupational skills or agricultural training which would improve Indian standards of living.

In a particularistic community where standards of honesty and humaneness are prized, the exploitation and deprivation of a segment of that community stands out as a manifest anomaly. It is not out of place to ask how the conceptions of self which incorporate these values also incorporate behavior and attitudes which contradict them. One way to minimize this conflict is to insist upon maintaining social distance between whites and Indians. This amounts to ignoring that a conflict exists. To a certain extent, the white members of the Jasper community take this solution. For instance, an examination of back issues of the weekly Jasper newspaper for its sixty-year history revealed that, apart from mentions of Indians in the "Police Court" column, there has been no recognition that an Indian reserve exists near Jasper. Not even editorial notice has been taken of the Indian members of the community.

It is impossible, nonetheless, for Jasper whites always to ignore the presence and condition of Indians. There are other features of white deportment toward Indians which lend understanding of how apparent value contradictions are resolved. To identify these, it is useful to consider some of the ways that Indians, in turn, "con" white men.

Jasper Indians find one source of income in the poplar posts which they cut from reserve lands and (illegally) from the nearby forest preserve. Ordinarily, these are soaked in a "bluestone" preservative for about a day. Sometimes an impatient Indian will paint the posts with laundry blueing instead and then sell them to an unsuspecting white man. Another quick way of getting money is to sell a quantity of posts sight unseen, telling the buyer that they are stacked at some spot on the reserve. When the white man returns later, having found no posts, the Indian innocently conjectures that "somebody musta stole 'em." Again, Indians are able to stack posts for white buyers in such a way that there appear to be more than there actually are.

The "con game" played by Indians against whites is often carried out in the context of enduring relationships. For example, one Indian, John Sweet Grass, receives a monthly disability check from the government for about seventy dollars. Each month, he takes part of it to the owner of an appliance store in Jasper to "hold" for him, with the understanding that he may request small amounts of it at any time. By the end of every month John has overdrawn his allowance, and the financial state of affairs between him and his "banker" is hopelessly confused, as it has been for years. In effect, John has a reliable, permanent source of spending money. The storekeeper laments, "I really don't know anymore *how* much he owes me, I probably never will. What can I do? If I don't take care of him, he'll probably starve."

At every turn, Indians act the part of con artists in their dealings with whites. An Indian will call at the home of an absent white man and tell his wife that her husband instructed him to get from her several dollars due him for some work done. When the husband returns, his wife discovers that the payment was for an imaginary task — *he* hasn't seen this Indian in weeks.

Incidents of Indians duping whites occur with persistent, almost monotonous regularity: an Indian persuades a white to transport him and his family home from town in sub-zero weather for some agreed-upon price. When they arrive at the reserve, the Indian proclaims that he "hasn't got the money now, but I'll pay you later," which means never. A common way for Indians to borrow money is to offer some useless, worthless item as security — a piece of clothing or household utensil — and then never return to claim it, nor to pay the debt.

One of the most celebrated recent coups concerned the illegal sale of a water pump and windmill by several Indians to a neighboring rancher. This man paid for the machinery and steel tower on which it was mounted without a permit from the Indian agent, whose office is more than a hundred miles from Jasper. The rancher and his son disassembled the purchase and took it home. That night, the same Indians collected the tower and pump, hauled it into town, and resold it the next day to a junk dealer. In these transactions, whites do not hold Indians guilty for their behavior. They do not complain to the police when they suffer losses, even in cases where there is proof that Indians are the malefactors. A rancher, from whom Indians regularly poach chickens, says, "They know that all they have to do is ask me for 'em if they were really hungry, but they'd rather steal 'em."

Why, one may ask, does a white man, whom we should expect to know better, buy a pig-in-a-poke? Why, in their relations with Indians, do whites keep coming back for more? Why is an Indian lent money when all past experience must teach that it probably will never be returned? One outcome of the usual sequence of events in a con is that the "mark" learns his lesson; he is presumably a poorer but a more cautious man. We must look elsewhere for the source of white gullibility than in some sort of "mass stupidity" or failure to learn from experience. In fact, Jasper whites *expect* to be conned by Indians; storekeepers extend credit to Indians knowing that the accounts will never be settled.[6] It may be suggested that whites allow Indians to con them in order that Indian irresponsibility and childishness may be demonstrated and confirmed. A rancher pays an Indian in advance for his labor in stacking bales of hay. When the Indian does not show up to fulfill his part of the bargain, the rancher's image of the Indian as irresponsible is validated. His tolerance of the social deprivation of Indians can then be justified: "They *are* children and irresponsible. They are not really men, so they cannot be expected to participate in the adult world." Similarly, those whites who directly exploit Indians are provided a means of preserving a defensible image of self: "Sure, he takes advantage of me, but then, that is to be expected of children. I graze my cattle on the reserve, but then I'm the one who takes care of him, who gives him money, and sees that he does not starve." Not a few whites are persuaded that Indians have no desire to adopt white roles. A veterinarian claimed, "The last thing they want is to live like white men — they're no more than unemployed buffalo hunters, and happy just like they are."

IV

Looking at these transactions from an Indian point of view, an arresting feature is disclosed. Most Indians do not accept white judgments of their role, their self, or their personal worth. Still, they seldom openly dispute white conceptions of Indian character — in fact, as we have seen, they behave in such a way to validate the white image of themselves.

Indians do not regard themselves as foolish children; on the contrary they consider themselves rather artful and successful exploiters of white men. What they do is to represent themselves to white audiences as the sort of persons whites take them to be, and represent themselves to other Indians as something different. In their performances before whites, Indians acknowledge irresponsibility, but they perform for a dual audience; to other Indians they are seen as turning to account (mistaken) white imputations of themselves.

Backstage, in Goffman's terminology, Indians "drop the front." In

---

[6] White residents of Jasper, especially those who have fewest contacts with Indians, and who are the most literate members of the community, point to a novel as an accurate portrayal of Indian character. *Stay Away, Joe,* by Dan Cushman, describes the slapstick adventures of a young Indian in his con game with white society. "If you want to know what Indians are *really* like," they advise, "read that book, it's a scream."

this region, "the impression fostered by the performance is knowingly contradicted as a matter of course." Jokes are made about the stupidity of whites and the ease with which they are taken in. Fine points of strategy are discussed. "The way to get off easy," according to one informant, "is to act like a dumb Indian in front of the magistrate." This way, the punishment for being drunk and disorderly will be lighter than a white man would receive, and "credit" can even be arranged — the magistrate will give the guilty Indian months to pay his fine.

Much of this backstage activity resembles that reported by Berreman for the Aleut. Aleuts, though they identify with whites as a *valuation group*, respond to the denial of entrance into white institutional activities by valuation group alienation. They have come to look more appreciatively at white society, but, deprived of acceptance by whites, they orient themselves negatively towards those people toward whose cultural values and goals they are drawn. "Role segregation" and "role distance" are two of the means Aleuts employ to cope with their ambivalence.

Earlier, we observed that Jasper Indians are excluded from playing white roles, and that structural barriers prevent Indian participation in the larger society. It was noted that, to a greater or lesser extent, most Jasper Indians do not perform in the presence of a white audience in a fashion which suggests that they embrace white cultural goals. The impression of them was that they are relatively "unacculturated." Nevertheless, it is evident that Jasper Indians too have begun to identify positively with white culture. In spite of the barriers to acculturation, they show signs of having recognized the taking of white roles as desirable. Perhaps one of the facilitating circumstances of this process has been the similarity between some of the principal values of traditional Plains Indian culture and those of the Anglo-American Jasper community. Standards of masculinity, competitiveness, a dual standard of sex behavior, qualities of leadership, and the like are features of value orientations among Jasper whites which are remarkably like value orientations of the formerly more autonomous Plains Cree. We may expect that a group of one cultural heritage will identify with a group of another with greater ease when their conceptions of the male role contain analogous properties.

Many aspects of the structural relations between whites and Indians have worked toward acceptance by Indians of white cultural goals and meanings. For one, the extermination of the buffalo and the demise of the traditional pattern of Plains subsistence forced Indians to search elsewhere for means of livelihood. Formerly, Indians were spatially less isolated from whites than today: in the last ten years all of the white families but one which lived in the hills near the reserve have moved away because of the cold, lonely winters. Today also, with modern mechanized agriculture, the demand for Indian labor has declined. In the early reserve period, after the turn of the century, it was common for Indian families to live for long periods on the property of ranchers for whom they worked. Some Jasper adults, in fact, were born on ranches where their parents lived permanently, in familiar interaction with their white employers.

Indians have other opportunities for exposure to white culture. All Indian women now go to the hospital in Jasper to have their children; Indian men mix with whites in the pub; Indian children now have a white schoolteacher; Jasper Indians maintain close relations with members of other reserves who are more acculturated than they.

Continuous face-to-face interaction over generations leads to some consensual definition of the situation, and it is reasonable to expect that the subordinate Indians should have incorporated into their conceptions of self some of the content of white roles. One piece of evidence indicating that Indians have come to regard whites as a positive reference group is that they frequently judge their own behavior by white standards. It is not uncommon for Indians to show remorse about excessive drinking, for example. Most Indians express a desire to be self-supporting, and to own land and cattle the same as their white neighbors. An excerpt from the author's field diary is illustrative:

> Saturday nite: Charlie Running Calf, his wife and I strolled around town this evening. Charlie, who had been hauling bales on Newcomb's ranch for the past two days, had just come from the pub and was a little tight. We passed Roger McDougal. Charlie said, "Hiya Roger, how you been," in an expansive tone. Charlie's wife said, *"Charlie,* you can't talk to those people like that." He replied, "Whatdya mean, I'm a *workin'* man, ain't I?"

However much Indians embrace white culture, they are refused the privilege of playing white roles. They cannot go into business for themselves, as has been indicated, because their legal status prohibits the accumulation of the capital necessary to engage in full-scale farming or ranching. Nor have they skills which would allow wage employment off the reserve. Consequently, Jasper Indians are alienated from their valuation group just as Berreman's Aleuts were. If they cannot be white, however, it is necessary for them to define the self ". . . along defensible lines." This must furthermore be done in a way that permits validation of this self by whites. To the Indian, then, his "irresponsible" performances declare: "Because I can trick white men so easily, they are not as smart as they think they are. *I'm* the one who's taking advantage of them. I can make a living by my wits."

V

We have looked at some of the ways whites and Indians in a small community portray the self in the ordinary course of daily life. We have seen also how the actions of each group validate the claims of the other. Indians and whites successfully predict one another's behavior, in a manner which mutually credits images of Indian and white selves. Among the consequences of this exchange, two are selected here for discussion.

In his article, "On Cooling the Mark Out," Erving Goffman addresses himself to the problem of adaptations which people make to failure, to the ways that individuals deal with repudiations of the self which are implied by the unsuccessful fulfillment of some role. It often becomes necessary that a person whose self has suffered failure be "consoled" by some other person. He is helped to adjust to his loss, he is "cooled out." This is particularly important when a person is deeply engaged in this self, and where its loss reflects upon him negatively. It sometimes occurs, Goffman adds, that the various participants in a network of interaction take measures to avoid altogether the troublesome procedure of cooling out; they attempt to cover up the fact that a person has failed or that his value as an individual is negligible.

Such processes may be recognized in transactions between Jasper whites and Indians. Indians do not have the liberty of playing white roles, but at the same time they increasingly identify with these roles and with white cultural values. They are accordingly in the plight of people whose worth is denied. Indians cannot salvage much of their value in the estimation of whites, but they do have means of saving face in the eyes of other Indians. This is accomplished, we have noted, when the Indian subcommunity observes one of its members making a fool of a white man, bringing off some deception with impunity. In effect, the validation of this transaction by whites serves to "cool out" Indians. Now, few Jasper Indians show evidence of serious personal disorganization, a consequence, it is proposed, of whites and Indians having found a way of avoiding a confrontation. Whites, at the same time, are spared the malaise of recognizing moral inconsistency in their own behavior.

Routines of self-presentation and identification in Jasper have consequences for stability at the structural as well as at the personal level.[7]

---

[7] Both Indians and whites are, of course, largely unaware of the social and personal consequences of their behavior. It is likely that this ignorance is requisite to the achievement of these results. See Schneider for a discussion of the *structural* necessity for keeping "failures" ignorant of their status.

The successful cooling out of a failure means that he will be less likely to protest or to threaten the established system of social relationships. The position of Indians in Jasper is one of subordination and deprivation. The social-psychological dynamics of role-playing and identification take place in a manner which contributes to the perpetuation of a caste-like status system. Indians are provided an "out," entailing adjustment to a place in their social environment which would otherwise be intolerable. The alternative to acquiescence, of course, would be for Indians to try to alter their environment, to challenge white superordination. Support for this assertion can be found in historical data, and in the examination of instances where the customary validations of Indian and white images of self fail.

Nearly a hundred years ago, not far from Jasper, a group of white traders "massacred" a small band of Indian horse-thieves. The expedition was organized by a white man whose horse had been stolen by an Indian, sold back to him, and then stolen again by the same Indian; the whites attacked a camp where they believed the culprit was hiding. The significant aspect of white ideas about Indians at that time was that they were held responsible for their behavior and punishable for their deceptions. In this and numerous other instances, whites were not indulgently disposed to treat Indians as irresponsible, and the outcome was frequently violent.

Today, when representations of Indian and white selves fail, persons are embarrassed, insulted, or provoked. An Indian, for example, inopportunely asked a white man in town for several dollars. He was refused, and told that he was a worthless beggar, incapable of properly supporting his wife and children. The Indian was affronted, enraged, and the two men exchanged blows in the street. It was not so much the refusal that brought violence, as the white's rejection of the self presented by the Indian. The normal course of interaction was disrupted when the white man withheld agreement to a definition of the situation including an image of the Indian as uncommitted to white values and unobligated by white standards of responsibility.

In this paper, I have described something of the tenor of Indian-white interaction, employing the social-psychological perspective which stresses role-taking, performances, and the self. It was suggested that a social structure including the superordination of whites over Indians is supported through a consensual definition of the situation embodying images of self which Indians and whites present to one another. The analysis was not exclusively concerned with the *results* of acculturation, or the extent to which Indians overtly embrace white values, but considered as well the kinds of involvement of these values in selves identified with whites and Indians vis-à-vis one another. In other words, the emphasis has been on the *mechanisms* of acculturative processes rather than upon the conditions of culture contact or the larger, more abstract, results of contact. As much space has been devoted to the "how" of persistence of Indian segregation — the complimentary presentation of diverse self-images — as to the "why."

A final comment is in order. Looking at the results of acculturation rather than at the daily interplay between whites and Indians, one might conclude that differences in cultural values expressed in the different presentations of self represent points of tension or potential conflict between whites and Indians. The evidence presented above suggests that such a view is not entirely accurate. The different sets of values embodied in Indian and white roles constitute an accommodation or a *solution* to certain conflicts and not merely a source of them. It is, in fact, because of the contrasting images of Indian and white man that interaction proceeds with as little conflict as actually occurs.

20

Men at home: Urban neighbors
RUTH HILL USEEM
JOHN USEEM
DUANE L. GIBSON

*In small tribal societies, relationships between people tend to be
personal, face-to-face. The web of kinship and common residence binds people together in a kind of intimacy seldom
experienced in cities. To people who live in large cities or their
suburbs, strangers are an ordinary part of life. Urban dwellers
are joined to numerous groups by social bonds, but not all of
these are ties of kinship or common residence. One type of social
relationship familiar to urban dwellers is that of "neighbors."
How do neighbors act toward each other? What are the rights
and duties of this social relationship? And how does it function
for men who live in an urban area? These are some of the questions discussed in this article.*

INTRODUCTION

The popular literature on man in a modern urban civilization presents
the image of persons divested of enduring social ties, caught between
conflicting pressures, and vulnerable to a depersonalized social world.
This imagery of man accommodating to a new kind of human environment needs careful appraisal before it can be assumed that structural
tensions have a one-to-one relationship with tensions experienced by
individuals or that the passing of older norms has left vacuums.

In a society characterized by the nuclear family, high mobility,
urban habitats, and subtle types of social stratification, how does a
reasonably "normal," successful man put together the varied facets of

Originally published as "The Function of Neighboring for the Middle-Class
Male." Reprinted by permission of the authors and the Society for Applied Anthropology from *Human Organization* 19(2), 1960.

his life and maintain his equilibrium? To examine this problem, an empirical study was made of the social and cultural resources of contemporary American society which are available to and used by middle-class men in coping with and preventing stress.[1] An earlier report[2] dealt with the stresses and resources in the world of work; the present one is concerned with the patterns of neighboring which have significance for the mental health of the male.

The data for this paper were secured in open-ended interviews with seventy-five men holding middle-management positions within bureaucratic structures, ranging between 25 and 50 years of age, currently residing in the midwest, all having family responsibilities — 74 of the 75 are married, the one not married has children from a previous marriage residing with him, and 70 of the 75 have children. The group is highly mobile both geographically speaking (sixty percent have lived in their present neighborhoods less than two years) and occupationally speaking (sixty percent have held their present occupational role less than one year, 88 percent less than three years).

In exploring the meaning of their residential areas with the men of the sample, we found some illuminating material on the definition of the neighborhood and neighbors, the cultural norms and principles of neighboring, the ways in which these are resources or sources of stress, the extent to which the neighborhood serves as a network of personal support in lieu of that traditionally supplied by extended kin, and the way in which the neighborhood helps or hinders a man in establishing his self-identity in contemporary life.

NEIGHBORS AND NEIGHBORHOOD: A DISTINCTION

In research on neighborhoods, particularly urban neighborhoods, some confusion has been precipitated by defining neighbors as people who live in a neighborhood or, the reverse, that a neighborhood is composed of neighbors.[3] Perhaps this confusion arises from the fact that a rural

---

[1] Supported by a grant from the National Institute of Mental Health, United States Public Health Service, administered by the Social Research Service of the Department of Sociology and Anthropology of Michigan State University.

[2] John and Ruth Useem, "Social Stresses and Resources Among Middle Management Men" in E. Gartly Jaco (ed.), *Patients, Physicians and Illness*, The Free Press, Glencoe, Ill., 1958.

[3] See, for example, Paul Wallin who found that, although the interviewees were instructed to define a neighbor as a person living "within one block in any direction from the block where you live," the sample utilized a more restricted definition of neighbors. Wallin assumed that the interviewees were also restricting the definition of neighborhood. "A Guttman Scale for Measuring Neighborliness," *American Journal of Sociology*, LIX (November, 1953), 243–246. Peter Mann has helped to clarify this point by observing that: "The people who inhabit [neighborhoods] should therefore be called neighbors, but here, at once, a problem arises. In ordinary conversation, if we refer to our 'neighbors,' we normally mean a small

neighborhood was composed of one's neighbors, but changes in the spatial arrangements of, and social relationships between, people have meant that these terms are no longer coterminous. At any rate, we shall use here the definitions of neighbors and neighborhood which emerge from the data gathered from our sample.

Neighbors, as designated by the men of our sample, are the adult occupants of households in close proximity to themselves. Each man conceived of himself and his wife as the center of his neighbors; and thus those immediately surrounding him are denoted as "my" neighbors, "our" neighbors, or the people living "next to us." Such persons are usually spatially and visibly accessible to the man and his wife. This would imply that, unless there is ecological separation of a small number of home units from other units, each contiguous household in a densely settled area will have an overlapping but slightly different set of neighbors.

Neighborhood is used by our informants in two ways. One is to refer to the locality of one's close neighbors; when so used it is either clear in the context of this discussion, or the term is modified by some adjective such as my "immediate" neighborhood. The second and more common usage is to refer to a geographical area distinguished by the characteristics and style of its inhabitants, including the type and arrangement of their housing. The crucial item in delineating the neighborhood in this sense is not the number of people but the "reputation" of the neighborhood — what it is known for. In the present trend toward large, residential settlements of persons similar in social and economic status and living in homes of comparable size and arrangement, the neighborhood can be composed of thousands of residents and coincide with a section, development, subdivision, school district, political entity, etc.

To keep these two meanings clear, we shall call the first the immediate neighborhood and the second the larger neighborhood, remembering that for some few who live in an isolated settlement of a few homes the two senses of neighborhoods may be synonymous.

Neighbors and the larger neighborhood have different although related functions in the lives of the men of our sample, and we shall take them up separately.

THREE ASPECTS OF NEIGHBORING WITH NEIGHBORS

There are three distinguishable but interrelated aspects of neighboring — the cultural norms of neighboring, the overt behavior between

---

number of people who live very near to us; rarely would we mean from five to ten thousand people living in the same neighborhood unit as ourselves." "The Concept of Neighborliness," *American Journal of Sociology*, LX (September, 1954), 163–168.

neighbors, and the individual's emotional assessment of both the norms and the overt behavior.

By *cultural norms* we shall mean here what Goffman calls "rules of conduct."

> A rule of conduct may be defined as a guide for action, recommended not because it is pleasant, cheap or effective, but because it is suitable or just. . . . Rules of conduct impinge upon the individual in two general ways: directly as *obligations*, establishing how he is morally constrained to conduct himself; indirectly, as *expectations*, establishing how others are morally bound to act in regard to him.[4]

The *overt behavior* between neighbors includes "manifest neighborliness,"[5] that is, behavior which is in keeping with the cultural norms, acts which are in the form of violations of the rules (feuding with one's neighbor, for example, is interaction between neighbors but is not an expression of the rules), and behavior which falls under other rules (for example, close friendships).

The third aspect of neighboring is the *meanings* which both the norms and the overt behavior have for the individual. He may feel satisfaction in his neighboring relationships or he may feel stressed; he may be aware of the norms but dislike conforming to them; he may feel stressed by not being able to conform to the norms, etc. This is an important dimension, for it is only persons who feel stress or experience satisfaction.

We shall try to keep these three threads woven together in the following discussion.

UNDERLYING PRINCIPLES OF NEIGHBORING

There are subcultural variations in the specific content of behavior which is enjoined by the social rules of neighboring; but underlying all these variations are several basic principles which the men recognize implicitly or explicitly as the yardsticks by which overt behavior is assessed.

1. Neighboring should be *categorical*. That is, obligations should be felt towards and certain types of behavior expected from any person who is an instance of the category, neighbor. Persons living close by the

---

[4] Erving Goffman, "The Nature of Deference and Demeanor," *American Anthropologist*, LVIII (June, 1956), 473–502. This is a very insightful article, and the authors are indebted to it for a number of provocative leads.

[5] See: Peter Mann, "The Concept of Neighborliness," *op. cit.*, 164. Sylvia Fleis Fava, "Suburbanism as a Way of Life," *American Sociological Review*, XXI (February, 1956), 34–37, states, "Thus, neighboring is defined operationally as the practice of certain folkways."

individual are classified as neighbors whether or not close personal interaction, or for that matter, any personal interaction, exists. Thus it is possible to say, as the men do, "I just moved in two months ago and have not yet met my neighbors"; or, "I don't do anything with my neighbors"; or, "Regardless of who the person is, if he were a close neighbor, I would feel free to ask him for help." Children are not categorized as neighbors because these obligations and expectations are not applied to them; they are classified by some such terms as "my neighbor's children," or the "neighborhood kids." There are cultural rules for children in neighboring relationships, but they are different. Aged parents likewise are not considered neighbors but "my neighbor's parents."

2. Neighboring should be *symmetrical*. Neighboring is presumed to be between persons who are equals — at least in their status capacity of neighbors. Sometimes persons will underplay or overplay their other statuses in order to maintain the fiction that "they are just like their neighbors." One of the men described it thus:

> I'm much better off than my neighbors. I have this big, old house with quite an acreage around it; the other houses around me are nice, new ranch houses; but they're the kind foremen and junior executives just coming up have. They're not younger than me necessarily, but younger in business ways. I am sure there are many people in our neighborhood that *don't know that I make any more money than they do*. They just think he's the guy that gets out and mows his lawn on Sunday afternoon *like everybody else*.

Neighboring should be symmetrical also along sex and age lines. Thus, neighboring occurs male with male, female with female, couple with couple, family with family, or female with young child(ren) with female with young child(ren).[6]

3. Neighboring should be *reciprocal*. This is closely related to the principle of symmetry. To some extent, neighboring relationships are reciprocal to the particular person ("If our neighbor has helped us out,

[6] The one interesting exception to this mentioned by several of the men was that of a relationship established with a neighbor widower. Such widowers were often included in parties for couples which the men gave and were occasionally invited to family dinners (a rare occurrence with other neighbors). In these cases the relationship was asymmetrical. As we shall see later, close neighborliness is primarily female initiated; and since widowers do not have this avenue of inclusion in the social network, special efforts were made to involve them by social acts not ordinarily expected between neighbors. No mention was made of widows for, if they existed, it is presumed that they were seen when the husband was not present and fell into the category of "female with female" and hence, the husband was not involved.

we would do it in turn for him"), but neighboring relations are also reciprocal to persons as instances of the category, neighbor. For example, a person feels obligated to help a neighbor who has a death in the family, whether or not he has had such experience in his own family — "That's just being nice people."

RESOURCE AND STRESS

When those who categorize each other as neighbors meet the conditions of symmetry and reciprocity, agree on the substantive rules of neighboring, and act overtly in keeping with the rules, patterns of neighboring are resources both for the prevention of and alleviation of stress for the individual.

If, however, the conditions of symmetry and reciprocity do not obtain between those categorized as neighbors, or if there is not agreement between neighbors as to the substantive expectations which they have of each other, or if overt behavior deviates from expectations, or if obligations are fulfilled but are considered onerous, or some combination of these, neighboring precipitates stress in the individual.

ON BEING A GOOD NEIGHBOR

The cultural norms of neighboring can be stated in answer to the question, "What is being a good neighbor?," in contrast, say, to being a good friend, or a good colleague, etc.

1. Emergency aid. A good neighbor is one who can be *counted on for help in times of crises.* Giving aid in an emergency is one of the most compelling obligations which one has to anyone in the category of neighbor.[7] Ordinarily, however, these obligations are performed "spontaneously" and unthinkingly. The most common of these emergency circumstances are accidents, sudden illnesses, births, deaths, and breakdown of mechanical equipment, particularly automobiles.

Help is limited to *action* (to be sure given in a friendly and sympathetic manner) and is confined to meeting the emergency directly or meeting the on-going demands of the family (caring for children, preparing food, emergency nursing aid, etc.). It does not involve lending money, or giving advice, or even knowing all the details of the emergency situation. Sometimes overt aid is not needed, but the neighbor is expected to at least offer to "do something" ("Let me know if there is anything I can do").

---

[7] This is a reflection of the general cultural pattern found in Western society, and particularly in American society, that proximity to persons involved in critical situations obligates the individual to offer aid. This is quite in contrast to India, where such obligations are not felt to the same extent. Even in the United States, these obligations are not as compelling in urban situations.

However, the actions called for are limited to a period which can be labeled an emergency. If, for example, an illness persists, the neighbor is expected to routinize the need and make arrangements for it. It is all right to push once the car for a neighbor whose car battery is dead, but then it is expected that he will either get it charged or get a new one and not call on his neighbor day after day.

> Assume that something happened, say, to my wife which necessitated hospitalization or something like that. I think the neighbors, *for a matter of day or two*, would step in and take over the children in a very friendly way *until such time as arrangements could be made*, like having a nurse or a relative come in.

Although the male may receive many benefits, a large share of the actual emergency aid is carried out by the wives. Men will be expected, if they are home, to provide transportation in emergencies, do chores connected with the outside of the house, help repair mechanical appliances or make arrangements for their repair (e.g., call a plumber if the neighbor husband is out of town and the sewer is stopped up). Most of the aid extended in critical situations, however, is connected with picking up the wife's responsibilities, and this is done by neighbor women. The man, however, feels that if his wife has performed these acts, he in a sense has performed them. As unwittingly stated by one man:

> If somebody dies in the neighborhood, *we* cook pies, take care of their children, everything else, sure. My wife is very good, to a fault. (Would you say that your wife does most of these things?) What can I do except offer to drive somebody?

Ninety-five percent of the men feel they can depend on their neighbors for emergency aid in unexpected situations which precipitate disruptions in the normal routine of family life. Knowing they can rely on neighbors is an important resource for men who spend the major portion of their daytime hours (and for some, evenings, occasional nights, and weekends) away from their families. Especially is this true for the American family which is separated from extended kin and has in the home for many hours of the day but one adult, the wife, upon whom falls the major share of family responsibilities. In this sense, the pattern of emergency aid is a resource which prevents stress from arising during the time the male is performing his occupational role. He can be at work without having the worry of his family on his mind, and he is less likely to be interrupted in the performance of his occupational duties. The pattern is also a resource which is utilized for the alleviation of stress when it is translated into manifest neighborliness during actual emergencies.

To say that reliance on neighbors is a type of crisis insurance does not mean that men necessarily recognize this function explicitly. People live their culture rather than intellectualize it. As put so aptly by one of the men:

> That's a funny thing, you know. I've never thought of neighbors along the lines that you've been questioning me this morning. For example, when my wife was on the verge of going to the hospital, several neighbors came over to volunteer their help. They said that if we were caught in the middle of the night before we could get hold of the nurse, they would come in and take care of things. Four or five neighbors volunteered their help. I said before that I don't do anything with my neighbors, which is true, I don't. But they're very good neighbors, very friendly; and in an emergency I am sure that I could count on them. But I just never thought about it in quite that way before.

There were four cases of men who do not rely on their neighbors in times of crises. Two felt they could but would not want to. One is a man who has members of his wife's extended family residing near them. ("I suppose we could go to our neighbors, but we wouldn't. My wife has a brother in town, and her parents are living here.") The other is a person who feels he could not fulfill the condition of reciprocity. ("I feel I could, but I certainly would not want to. We have young children, and we live in a neighborhood of people much older than ourselves; and we would not be able to reciprocate.") The other two cases are instances which do not meet the principle of symmetry for both rent living quarters in immediate neighborhoods of homeowners. One is stressed by this fact for his wife feels all alone with the children, whereas the other is not stressed for he is without children and finds anonymous living quite satisfactory. (Those who rented in all rental or predominantly rental neighborhoods felt they could rely on their neighbors in emergency situations).

2. *Mutual aid.* A good neighbor is one with whom *mutual aid* patterns can be established. In emergency aid, time is of the essence, and anyone in the category of neighbor can be called upon for help and should be rendered assistance. In mutual aid, time is less imperative, and greater selectivity is exercised in choosing among those persons labeled neighbors as to with which ones mutual aid patterns are established. In other words, the selection is less categorical and more emphasis is put upon the relationship being symmetrical and reciprocal to the particular person.

> You can ask them to watch the kids *if you can watch theirs*, get something from the store *if you've done the same for them. The same things you're willing to do for them, you can ask them to do for you.*

With whom mutual aid patterns can be established and the substantive content of the patterns vary with a number of factors. In general, the lower the socioeconomic status, the earlier the couples are in the family cycle, and the newer the neighborhood, the more extensive are the patterns of mutual aid; the higher the socioeconomic status, the later the couples are in the family cycle, and the older the neighborhood, the more the patterns of mutual aid are confined to protecting the property investments of the neighbors.

We are not interested here in delineating the full range of the variations, but several instances will illustrate the point. New neighborhoods of young couples with young children and modest incomes have a number of "do it yourself" programs which require the cooperation of more than one man to get the jobs done. The men aid each other in solving their common problems of maintaining homes — painting houses, building garages, seeding lawns, putting in shrubbery, etc.

> There's not a lot of running around together socially, but out there [new suburban development] if one's got a job, we all pitch in and do it together. I've helped them paint the inside of their houses, and they've helped me. When we needed fences, why we all pitched in and put up the fences. If I'm fixing something at the house and need a little help on it, why I've always gone to them to see if they can give me a hand on it — and they usually do. And it's the same with them. If they've got something they need help on, they come to one or another of us.

All the men with young children who lived in this type of immediate neighborhood mentioned the common mutual aid which went on between their wives with respect to child care, e.g., babysitting for each other.

In contrast with the above are older neighborhoods of higher income status and people later in the family cycle. In such areas the home and lawn problems either have already been taken care of or the men pay to have such jobs done and, hence, these projects do not become the source of neighborly cooperation. However, they do have mutual aid patterns of "keeping an eye on" each other's properties, particularly during vacations. This mutual aid pattern is commonly symbolized by the phrase, "the neighbor we leave our key with."

If those who fall into the category of neighbors meet the principles of symmetry and reciprocity, mutual aid patterns are established which are a resource for enabling families to fulfill their functions. All but seven of the men have established some mutual aid patterns with particular neighbors. Four of the seven who did not have any mutual aid patterns were renters in homeowner areas, two had recently moved into neighborhoods and had not yet established relationships, and in one case both the man and his wife worked and had little interaction with neighbors in any sphere. Only two of those who did not have mutual aid patterns, however, felt stressed by their absence.

Of the 68 who reported some type of mutual aid patterns nine still experienced stress because, although they could depend on their neighbors for some things, they could not establish some desired mutual aid relationship. These fell into two groups — those who were not symmetrically related to any neighbors in the family cycle stage (e.g., a couple with young children none of whose neighbors had young children) or in socioeconomic status (e.g., being considerably above the neighbors in income level and wishing to establish a different set of mutual aid patterns consonant with that income level).

3. *Borrowing.* A good neighbor is one from whom one can *borrow* and to whom one can *lend.* The men gave us little information concerning the borrowing which goes on among women neighbors, although most mentioned that it does exist. For males, borrowing is confined to items connected with male-oriented activities around the home — tools, ladders, lawn equipment — and follows the principles of symmetry and reciprocity; you should not borrow unless you have an equivalent item to lend. For example, if a man in the neighborhood "has everything" and the other men have modest amounts of equipment, borrowing will be between those having modest holdings and not from the man to whom you can lend nothing — for it is impossible to reciprocate.

Items which are borrowed are those for which the person has only one time or occasional use and not things which are required regularly, unless some informal arrangements have been made for the exchange of large items. Items should be returned immediately after their use, and in good condition (perhaps better condition than they were in when borrowed, but at least not worse).

Nothing should be borrowed which, according to the standards of the neighbors, should be within the income bracket of people who live in that type of neighborhood. Paint brushes and lawn mowers are borrowable items in a neighborhood of young people just getting established, but they are not borrowable in established upper-income neighborhoods. If a person cannot afford the equipment which goes with the type of neighborhood in which he is living, the men feel that he shouldn't be living in that neighborhood.

As in emergency aid and mutual aid, borrowing is a resource for meeting family needs — particularly for young couples just establishing their homes. Only four of the men were non-borrowers and all four were renters in predominantly home-owned areas. The most commonly mentioned source of stress for the men in this area was neighbors who broke the rules of borrowing by borrowing too often, too much, and by not returning in good condition. This was not, however, a major source of stress for the men of the sample, for they reported that they took indirect steps to "put a stop to" such borrowing.

4. *Perimeter of privacy.* Good neighbors *respect the privacy of each other.* Around each neighbor there is a perimeter of privacy (having both spatial and psychological dimensions) which should not be invaded. One man states: "We have a very congenial group of neighbors; they mind their own business." What is a neighbor's own business or the zone which is considered inviolable varies with a number of factors of which the most important are male-female, socioeconomic status, stage in the family cycle, stage in the occupational world.

All the men recognized that their neighboring relationships are quite distinct from those of their wives. Although the males spend a small segment of their life with their neighbors, many of the daytime activities of the distaff side are centered in the neighborhood. Wives are likely to be more personally involved with each other, i.e., their perimeter of privacy is less. The men point out that "there's a lot of stuff going on in the daytime when I'm not there" and "what I talk about [with my neighbors] and what my wife talks about are two different things." When the male comes home, the wife's perimeter of privacy shifts to a family perimeter (e.g., women who visit in each other's homes during the day do not visit each other when the man is at home). "I occasionally see the neighbor lady running out the back door when I walk down the street."

The immediate neighborhood is a major resource to the man to the extent that his wife feels satisfied in her neighboring relationships with other women. The man does not need his neighbors to perform his main occupational task; but women, especially young mothers with young children on modest incomes do need their neighbors for mutual aid and mutual psychological reinforcement. Female neighbors are expected to fulfill many of the needs of the woman for primary group interaction; if these are not met, the woman is thrown on the husband and he, in turn, becomes stressed.[8] This may in turn reverberate into his effectiveness on the job, for his energy is not released for concentrating on what he feels is his primary role, nor can he feel relaxed and revitalized when he comes home to a wife unhappy in her neighboring relationships.

Typical of those who feel stress in this area are the following:

We recently moved, and [my wife's neighboring relationship] is the only sour note in our moving. It didn't bother me particularly to move out of

[8] Whyte implies that the visiting patterns of new suburbia are extensions of the "organization man"; our data would indicate that these patterns are the outgrowth of the needs of wives and children and the stage in the family cycle, rather than the direct needs of the organization man for self-expression. William H. Whyte, Jr., *The Organization Man.*

A, but it did my wife, although I had been in A as long as she had been. In fact, for a time I began to think I was being unfair to the point of cruelty because she was very unhappy, and still is, at being separated from a close group of women with whom she was associated.

Our neighborhood is very old. I think it's one of the things that bothers my wife about living there; there are no young wives in the neighborhood. She puts a lot of pressure on me to take her back to her family [who live in another city] on weekends, and she wants me to try to get a job there so she can be near her family. I don't know what I'm going to do.

To say that the wife's perimeter of privacy is different from the male's does not say, of course, what the male's is. Neighboring between males is primarily an outdoor, daylight activity. In a north temperate climate, this means that men get together usually on weekends in the late spring, summer, and early fall months when they are performing male-oriented home activities — mowing the yard, gardening, painting, etc.

Although there is some variation by social class, for the male, occupational life and family relationships are sacred; they are within the zone considered private and are not open for conversation with neighbors. Common topics of conversation are those which do not infringe on the privacy of the neighbor and which are thought of as male interests — sports, weather, lawns, cars, house improvements. Rated high as a conversation piece is the "crab grass" which gets more mention than any other single item.

Most of the contacts between males are made while they are standing up ("we holler across the fence at each other," "when people are out we call people by their first names and windbag with them") although they occasionally may end with a small gathering sitting down together outside "with a bottle of beer." In neighborhoods of young people, the contacts are increased when on mutual aid projects.

Special note should be made of the significance of containing the man's occupational life within the perimeter of privacy. Confidences are not exchanged in this area, and what the man does at work is "his own business" which should be respected as being private. The higher the person is in his managerial status, the more important it is to segmentalize neighboring relationships from business relationships and the more there is need to make certain that a man's off-work activities do not reverberate into the occupational sphere of his life. For example, the occupational relationship between two men relatively low in an organization might not be seriously affected if they do not get along together or if their wives are feuding with each other in the immediate neighborhood; but for men whose main business is the organizing of men's occupational arrangements, such conflicting roles in the neighborhood might seriously hamper their on-work duties.

And yet the higher the status of the executive, the fewer the appropriate neighborhoods in which he can live and the more likely he is to reside nearer to persons that he contacts in the course of his business world. Especially is this true in smaller cities. For this reason, the restrictions against penetrating the occupational life of one's neighbors are tighter in upper-class neighborhoods than they are in neighborhoods composed of men of lower managerial status — although even here they exist. This taboo applies to the women as well as to the men. Women are expected to not carry tales about their husband's occupational role beyond the confines of the home.

Particularly to be avoided is living next door to — that is, having as a close neighbor — a person with whom one is associated closely in an occupational role.

One further note on the perimeter of privacy. To some extent the psychological privacy is translated into spatial terms. The least private, and hence the area in which one is most accessible to one's neighbors, is the yard surrounding one's house.[9] Entertaining on this semi-private, semi-public property is considered less an invasion of privacy, and hence less personally involving, than entertaining within the house. At backyard cookouts, each family may contribute part of the fare, and in a sense they are entertaining each other on "neighborhood property." The next most accessible spaces are porches and doorsteps. Neighbors will drop by to sit on the porch or stoop who would never drop by to visit in the house.

Similarly, within the house there are different definitions of space privacy. Parties in the recreation room are not as personally involving as

[9] There is a cultural variation of this. In southern California, where considerable family living is carried on outside the patio, the backyard is defined as being as private as the house; and this fact is often recognized by building fences, or walls, or having tall shrubbery which shuts off the backyard from the neighbor. If a person has a right to be in the backyard, then he also has the right to wander on into the contiguous part of the house without knocking. The frontyard, however, is still semi-public. In Western India, the significant perimeter is the wall of the compound which encloses both the front and backyards. If a person has been given permission to invade the privacy of the front gate, then he may step on into the house without indicating that he wishes to invade privacy. In other words, in the midwest the point of challenge is the front and back doors; in southern California it is the front door and back gate; and in India it is the front and back gate. There have been some changes in the midwest as greater emphasis has been put on summer living in the backyard, and patterns have not yet jelled as to whether one is or is not accessible to neighbors when eating in the backyard. In many midwest communities there are prohibitions concerning the height of the fence which can be erected, i.e., the degree to which you can cut off a neighbor from his rights to semi-public living.

are parties in the living section of the house. If a man, for example, has the only recreation room in his immediate neighborhood, this may become the gathering spot for the annual Christmas party; but the neighbors who come do not feel that they have to repay this party, for it is in an area which is defined for this occasion as semi-neighboring public. Meals at the family dining table constitute an invasion of privacy; and we found no cases where neighbors, when acting in the status capacity of neighbors, exchanged dinners with each other. Bedrooms are never entered by neighbors in the ordinary course of neighboring relationships, although there would be exceptions made in times of crises or emergencies.

Greatest stress in this area of privacy maintenance is found among men who cannot translate their conceptions of privacy into spatial terms. They know that their neighbors know their business even though both they and their neighbors act as though they could not hear or see what went on within the sphere of privacy.

5. *Friendly — but not friends.* Good neighbors are *friendly* with each other — but *they are not friends.* Under certain circumstances, persons who start out in the category of neighbors may shift over to a friends basis; in such cases the perimeter of privacy becomes less — both spatially and emotionally. Friends can "run in" without prearrangements, and more of the personal details of life are exchanged. However, only four of the men had neighbors whom they also counted as friends, and with whom they interacted under another set of norms. The rest mention that their wives count some neighbor women as friends, but that they do not.

What is considered "friendly" relationships? It might be stated thus: immediate neighborhoods composed of children-bound, housebound couples who are in modest circumstances have a number of friendly social activities which take place within the immediate neighborhood. The higher the socioeconomic status of the neighbors, the later they are in the family cycle, the more likely is the immediate neighborhood to be the place where the family lives as a separate unit, and recreational pursuits are pursued outside the immediate neighborhood.[10] The following excerpts serve to illustrate the contrast:

[A lives in a new suburban development of young couples.] I live in a very friendly community. We talk about sports, hunting, fishing, and so

[10] Although we do not have any strictly lower-class neighborhoods, evidently this generalization does extend downward. Gottlieb points out that persons in upper income levels go out of their neighborhoods to cocktail lounges, but lower-class areas have taverns located in their midst and draw their clientele from a restricted geographical area. David Gottlieb, "The Neighborhood Tavern and the Cocktail Lounge: A Study of Class Differences," *American Journal of Sociology,* LXII (May, 1957), 559–563.

forth and attempt to make plans for a hunting trip. Sometimes the men will get together to watch the children while women go off to the movies or have one of their showers. And we talk about homes, naturally. You see, everyone down there has just bought a new home, so they're interested in home furnishings and decorations, and what they're going to do — are they going to build a garage, and what kind of grass are they going to put in, and so forth.

[B lives in an older neighborhood of large homes and, as he puts it, the men hold "responsible positions in business or industry or are professional people — doctors and lawyers."] My contacts with my neighbors are coincidental because it so happens I belong to a club that three of our neighbors do. I see them over there quite frequently; but as far as being a real visiting type neighborhood, I don't think we are. People generally stick pretty much to themselves out there.

Children, however, do not stay young and neither do these men remain static in their socioeconomic status. If they move their household as fast as they change their family or socioeconomic status and can, therefore, establish symmetrical and reciprocal friendly relationships with their neighbors, stress does not arise. However, for many of the men of our sample, their occupational mobility (and consequently their expectations for neighborly relationships) outstrips their geographical mobility, and they find themselves with neighbors considerably below themselves. ("I didn't make more income when I went there, but now I am probably more successful than most of the people living there.")

So long as they remain with a particular set of neighbors, there is a strain to be consistent with the norms of the neighbors. ("I have advanced beyond most of them, but I've tried not to let it show or let it interfere.") If the disparity becomes too great, however, and if they no longer wish to maintain the fiction that they are "just like their neighbors," stress does occur.

I want more room in the house; I want land around it. I suppose there is what you would call snob appeal of wanting to live in a bigger house and in a neighborhood with more people of a comparable income bracket than I'm in now. I bought this house when I was making $200 a month, and it wasn't too ambitious a project. But we have outgrown it financially and socially as well as the physical space.

The following instance summarizes some of the changes:

We had much closer social relationships in the neighborhood we lived in before. When we moved into that neighborhood, we had one youngster and another on the way. Most of the couples that moved in were our same age with youngsters coming along, too. And we were all just getting started on our careers. We formed a very close neighborhood unit. Where we are now we are pretty much on our own. Our oldest girl is fourteen, and most of our neighbors are a different age than we are. We go back for social relationships with our old neighbors; the only thing is that they, like us, no longer live in the old neighborhood. They're scattered all over in different suburbs. Some of them live in other cities, and we may look them up on our vacation, or I'll drop in to see the family if I'm in their city on business.

6. Other expectations. Not all rules of neighboring apply to personal interaction. Good neighbors show respect for each other by the *condition in which they keep their property* and the *manner in which they act within their sphere of privacy.* What is expected of neighbors and the obligations felt toward them varies with the reputation which members of the immediate neighborhood wish to maintain, but in any case the rules are both symmetrical and reciprocal. For example, expression of regard for neighbors may take the form of keeping the house in good repair, the lawn mowed, the garage door closed.

Although neighbors are expected to respect the privacy of their neighbors, and although what goes on within their family life is their own business, deviations (e.g., bickering spouses, noisy parties, immoral conduct, slovenly housekeeping) from whatever are the norms of the neighbors do become topics of conversation, particularly between women neighbors who in turn relay these items to their husbands.

However, respect for privacy is shown by not openly acknowledging the deviation to the offender himself or herself. Neighbors should not "tell off" a neighbor or call a deviation in behavior to the attention of the deviant directly.[11] The assumption is that the person should be sensitive to the patterns displayed around him and should control his own behavior. It is, in part, because of this rule that the men are quite aware of the occasions on which others deviate from their expectations or on which their own perimeters of privacy are invaded, but they are not similarly aware of the occasions on which their own behavior affronts their neighbors.

---

[11] It may be that this rule applies only to middle class and above. Lower-class neighbors may be more blunt in their expressions, but we have no data to either affirm or deny this possibility. The rule against calling attention to deviations directly to the deviant is part of a more pervasive American cultural pattern. Students from India studying abroad claimed that the British were quick to tell them when they were not conforming to British customs, but that Americans would neither tell them their *faux pas* nor explicitly state the culture rules they were breaking. See: Useem and Useem, *The Western-Educated Man In India*, Dryden Press, 1954.

A highly sensitive area in the sphere of privacy is child-rearing practices. Theoretically, how neighbors raise their children is "their business" and yet, the way in which children are raised does indicate the regard in which you hold your neighbors. Children, particularly of pre-school and primary grade age, within a neighborhood are dependent upon each other for playmates, learn from each other, and set standards for each other.

If neighbors have common patterns of child rearing, neighbors feel reinforced. If, however, they do not, the men experience stress. Typical of the men who feel stressed is the following:

> The thing I don't like about our neighborhood — and frankly I want to move when I can afford a little better, which shouldn't be too long now — is the philosophy of this neighborhood; it's how quick can I get my kid out of school so he can work in the factory and bring in more money. We plan to send our children to college. God knows we are not snobs, but there has just got to be a feeling of common interest. Those kids are nice and everything, but they get their philosophy from their parents, and it conflicts with the philosophy that ours get from us. There are plenty of areas around here that have more or less areas of mutual interest with us, and we are planning to move.

THE LARGER NEIGHBORHOOD

When asked to "describe the neighborhood in which you live," all of the men employed the larger neighborhood as their reference and used one or more of the following items: one-half used a specific name ("X hills," "R subdivision");[12] almost one-half used social class ("upper-middle class," "middle-class"); one-third employed some adjective with a class meaning ("good neighborhood," "not fashionable at all," "nice but deteriorating"); one-fourth used price range of homes — particularly if they resided in either a new development or in an upper income neighborhood ("$8,000 to $10,000 homes," "$20,000 homes and up"); one-fourth indicated the age of the neighborhood ("new development," "older neighborhood"); one-fifth referred to the occupations of the household heads ("hourly rated people," "junior executives," "professional people"); 6 percent referred specifically to the age of residents ("younger couples," "older people"). There was a scattering of responses such as size of lots, availability of public services, degree of ruralness, etc.

[12] We suspect that an even higher proportion would have used a name to communicate the type of neighborhood in which they lived had the interviewers been from the same city and therefore knowledgeable about the reputation which a name would convey. To be sure, there are some larger neighborhoods without a specific name.

It is significant that not one of these men described their neighborhoods in terms which would refer to the tone of interpersonal interaction, e.g., friendly, cooperative, people interesting to talk to, although these terms were employed when referring to neighbors. Larger neighborhood reputation evidently has a different function in the lives of these men than has interpersonal relationships with neighbors.

The reputation of the larger neighborhood which the resident shares indicates to some extent the type of person he is. In American culture, an individual cannot call attention directly to his achievements, but rather must seek our respect indirectly. Self-esteem is built upon a number of facets, and neighborhood reputation is one of these which a man uses to identify himself both to himself and others. He becomes an instance of the reputation which the larger neighborhood has, i.e., he is the type of person who lives in that type of neighborhood. If the man's self-image is consistent with the neighborhood reputation, he gains a sense of satisfaction; if, however, there is disparity between what he would like his self-image to be and the meaning which the neighborhood reputation conveys to others, he feels stressed.

A related aspect of self-image to which the reputation of the larger neighborhood contributes is his conception of himself as a provider for his family. Part of the reputation of the neighborhood is based on the type of services provided for the members — schools, churches, transportation facilities, shopping areas, etc. The man sees himself as the provider of the neighborhood setting, with its attendant facilities for his wife and children.

> I needed a larger house, but there was also a desire to associate with a better neighborhood, although the neighborhood we lived in before was not a low-class neighborhood. There are so many advantages that I could see that the children would get out of the new neighborhood with their associations in school.

New developments of families in the early part of the family cycle witness greater activities for the establishment of neighborhood reputations than do older developments of families with children later in the life cycle.

> We have a small homeowners association down there [suburban new development] which has been set up to try to promote the area and improve it and its relations to the city. We have a parents club in connection with the school, and a number of other very active organizations — all of which are because the neighborhood is new, because there are so many young couples in it.

Generally speaking, the more urban and anonymous the situation, the greater weight the neighborhood reputation has as a symbol of status, for the man has fewer other avenues for gaining respect (i.e., he is not known personally for what he is to others). Also the higher the socioeconomic status, the more the man's social activities take place outside the immediate neighborhood, and hence the greater the need for having a neighborhood identity which conveys to people outside the neighborhood the type of person he is. Especially stressed in this area are those who have risen fast occupationally but who have been unable to purchase homes in neighborhoods commensurate with their new status.

The reputation of the larger neighborhood is the setting within which relationships are established with close neighbors — for it is presumed that neighbors will share the characteristics of the larger neighborhood. In this sense, one picks his close neighbors by picking the reputation of the larger neighborhood. Residents of the larger neighborhood are considered somewhat interchangeable, and the assumption is that an individual could live any place in the larger neighborhood and expect to establish comparable neighboring relationships with close neighbors.

None of the organizations in which these men were employed put direct pressure on their people to live in particular neighborhoods. Those lower in occupational status categorically denied that where they lived ("as long as it was decent and respectable") had any relevance for their career. Those higher in occupational status felt that the reputation of their neighborhood was irrelevant for their selection for advancement (which they felt was based solely on their competence on the job), but that *after* they had advanced in the organization there was or would be some informal expectations by others (both those higher and lower than themselves) for them to live in neighborhoods with reputations commensurate with their higher positions. However, the men felt this pressure to move as one which was self-imposed rather than imposed by their organizations.

RÉSUMÉ AND IMPLICATIONS

The analysis of the evidence collected in this field study suggests the need for further empirical work on the functional significance of emergent social groupings in modern American civilization. The findings herein depicted obviously do not hold for other segments of American society or for other societies, but they do invite comparisons to highlight their significance.[13]

1. The *nuclear family* in all societies is dependent upon other social structures for fulfilling its functions of socializing and educating the

---

[13] We are indebted to William F. Whyte for a number of pertinent suggestions in this section.

young, for psychological, social and economic support of its members. In most societies, a major structure which has been and still is used is the extended kin group, although many other groupings, such as caste and ethnic enclaves, have performed these functions.

The nuclear family of the segment of American society we have under consideration is a small unit without much of the network of social support supplied by extended kin. This lack of kin support is due to a number of factors of which the most important are: (a) the wide geographical dispersal of kin (only two of our sample had members of their wives' extended kin group near enough to call upon for aid — and these two did use this resource); and (b) the wide divergence of the men in their occupational status and style of life from other members of their kin — successful, individual upward mobility removes the men not only geographically, but also socially and psychologically, from kin members. The men of the sample reported that they had "little in common" except shared memories of childhood with their fathers, mothers and siblings.

2. The *self-identity* of this segment of American society stems primarily from the occupational role, and this status position is the pivot for assessing the relevance and appropriateness of extended family, neighbors, schools, churches, friends and style of life. Viewed world-wide this is a rather unique development, for in societies which are characterized by primary self-identity growing out of family member-ship, class or caste status, the work role is chosen or entered into because of its appropriateness for one's family, social class, or caste status rather than the reverse.

Viewed in this light, the residential neighborhood has become, for upwardly mobile men stripped of kin and whose values stem primarily from the work role, the *locus* for working out the supporting framework for the functioning of their nuclear family and the basis for entrance into other supporting institutions of church, school, clubs, etc. The high preoccupation of the men with the social and status characteristics of their neighbors and neighborhood is understandable, for it stems from their need to have consistency and mutually reinforcing life segments. Residential neighborhoods in other areas of the world which do not serve these purposes also do not precipitate such concern for socioeco-nomic status on the part of their members. For many neighborhoods in the American South (which include widely divergent social classes) this has become a relatively recent preoccupation, since school facilities have been equated with residential areas. In India, a major concern with residential living is not socioeconomic class so much as caste or commu-nity, for the extended kin is the source of support for "untouchables," Brahmins, Parsees, Anglo-Indians. With the emergence of non-caste oriented activities and the breaking up of the joint family in India, there are developing in urban centers certain neighborhoods not unlike those described in this paper, although not as yet with as clearly defined cultural norms for interaction.

Residential mobility, so characteristic of this segment of American life, is not then *per se* a stressful process leading to anomie, as it has sometimes been claimed, but is actually a resource for occupationally upwardly mobile men; for moving enables them to activate the supporting neighborhood functions appropriate for their changing occupational role. If the men can meet the cultural norms of neighboring based on categorical designation, symmetry and reciprocity, neighbors and neighborhoods become limited but tangible resources; if the men and their families cannot meet these norms, they become a potential source of stress.

The findings of this study indicate that there are social strengths inherent in modern American life which help to sustain the individual and his family in the routine stresses of daily living, and that there are resources built into ordinary social groupings which provide persons with means for coping with and alleviating stresses in a complex world. There have been shifts in functions from one institution to another and the development of new activities to fulfill new needs precipitated by modern urban American civilization.

VII

Economic systems

People everywhere must obtain material things and the help of others if they are to meet their biological and social needs. We use clothing and shelter to maintain our body temperature at about 98.6 degrees. We need vegetable and animal products in order to sustain ourselves. We require the services of other people when we are helpless children or oldsters unable to fend for ourselves. Cultural preferences may determine the kind of clothes we wear and the foods we eat, but all people must meet these needs to survive. Similarly, people everywhere have social needs. Human beings are social animals. They associate with each other in complex networks; they assume various identities and play many different roles. Once again, culture dictates a variety of ways for people to conduct their social lives, but in every society social interaction requires the use of material goods and the exchange of services. Providing goods and services people require to meet their biological and social wants is the task of economic systems.

Production is a most important function of any economic system. Production provides people with needed raw materials and allows them to manufacture the many items they require. But production is no simple matter. It demands special units of production, the groups of people who work together. Some productive groups are based on family and kinship; others are specially organized groups like the factory crews of industrialized nations. Production also involves a technology, i.e., the knowledge people employ to make and use tools and extract and refine raw materials. It is easy to underestimate the technological sophistication of nonindustrialized peoples like the hunter-gatherer !Kung Bushmen described in this section. But it is wise to note that people's technology generally works for them, permitting adaptation to an incredible variety of natural environments. From the viewpoint of particular individuals, few technologies are simple. An engineer working in an American steel plant operates using an extremely complex repertoire of technological knowledge. But so does the !Kung hunter as he reads the faint signs left behind by the antelope he is tracking.

Perhaps the largest difference between the !Kung and our own economies lies in the distribution of goods and services. The !Kung exchange things and help each other because they are obliged to do so. They live in a world of relatives, friends, and associates with whom the exchange of goods and assistance is a normal part of interaction. Exchanges associated with role obligation are usually referred to as reciprocal. Reciprocal exchange exists in American society too, for we employ it when we work together in our families, exchange Christmas gifts, or tip waitresses. But we are more reliant on market exchange, which depends more on our present needs and desires, our resources, and the cost of the thing we want. Market exchange is characteristic of complex societies where people must seek fulfillment of their economic needs from strangers. Whether exchange is reciprocal or market, no matter how production is organized and technology developed, all human beings rely on an economy to survive and to live a satisfying life.

21

The hunters: Scarce resources in the Kalahari
RICHARD BORSHAY LEE

*Peoples who hunt and gather wild foods experience an intimate
relationship with their natural environments. A band's size and
structure, the breadth of its territory, and the frequency and
pattern of its movement depend on the abundance of vegetable
foods, game, and water. For many Western anthropologists, the
life of hunter-gatherers seems precarious and fraught with hardship. Yet, according to Richard B. Lee, this picture is largely
inaccurate. In this article he points out that the !Kung Bushmen
who live in the Kalahari Desert of South Africa survive well in
what Westerners would consider a marginal habitat. Depending,
like most hunter-gatherers, on vegetable foods for their sustenance, the !Kung actually spend little time at food collecting,
yet they live long and fruitful lives in their desert home.*

The current anthropological view of hunter-gatherer subsistence rests
on two questionable assumptions. First is the notion that these peoples
are primarily dependent on the hunting of game animals, and second is
the assumption that their way of life is generally a precarious and
arduous struggle for existence.

Recent data on living hunter-gatherers show a radically different
picture. We have learned that in many societies, plant and marine
resources are far more important than are game animals in the diet.
More important, it is becoming clear that, with a few conspicuous
exceptions, the hunter-gatherer subsistence base is at least routine and
reliable and at best surprisingly abundant. Anthropologists have consistently tended to underestimate the viability of even those "marginal
isolates" of hunting peoples that have been available to ethnographers.

Reprinted by permission from Richard Lee and Irvin DeVore, editors, *Man the
Hunter* (Chicago: Aldine Publishing Company); copyright © 1968 Wenner-Gren
Foundation for Anthropological Research, Inc. References and footnotes are omitted.

The purpose of this paper is to analyze the food getting activities of one such "marginal" people, the !Kung Bushmen of the Kalahari Desert. Three related questions are posed: How do the Bushmen make a living? How easy or difficult is it for them to do this? What kinds of evidence are necessary to measure and evaluate the precariousness or security of a way of life? And after the relevant data are presented, two further questions are asked: What makes this security of life possible? To what extent are the Bushmen typical of hunter-gatherers in general?

BUSHMAN SUBSISTENCE

The !Kung Bushmen of Botswana are an apt case for analysis. They inhabit the semi-arid northwest region of the Kalahari Desert. With only six to nine inches of rainfall per year, this is, by any account, a marginal environment for human habitation. In fact, it is precisely the unattractiveness of their homeland that has kept the !Kung isolated from extensive contact with their agricultural and pastoral neighbors.

Field work was carried out in the Dobe area, a line of eight permanent waterholes near the South-West Africa border and 125 miles south of the Okavango River. The population of the Dobe area consists of 466 Bushmen, including 379 permanent residents living in independent camps or associated with Bantu cattle posts, as well as 87 seasonal visitors. The Bushmen share the area with some 340 Bantu pastoralists largely of the Herero and Tswana tribes. The ethnographic present refers to the period of field work: October, 1963–January, 1965.

The Bushmen living in independent camps lack firearms, livestock, and agriculture. Apart from occasional visits to the Herero for milk, these !Kung are entirely dependent upon hunting and gathering for their subsistence. Politically they are under the nominal authority of the Tswana headman, although they pay no taxes and receive very few government services. European presence amounts to one overnight government patrol every six to eight weeks. Although Dobe-area !Kung have had some contact with outsiders since the 1880's, the majority of them continue to hunt and gather because there is no viable alternative locally available to them.

Each of the fourteen independent camps is associated with one of the permanent waterholes. During the dry season (May–October) the entire population is clustered around these wells. Table 1 shows the numbers at each well at the end of the 1964 dry season. Two wells had no camp resident and one large well supported five camps. The number of camps at each well and the size of each camp changed frequently during the course of the year. The "camp" is an open aggregate of cooperating persons which changes in size and composition from day to

TABLE 1. *Numbers and distribution of resident Bushmen and Bantu by waterhole**

Name of waterhole	No. of camps	Population of camps	Other Bushmen	Total Bushmen	Bantu
Dobe	2	37	—	37	—
!angwa	1	16	23	39	84
Bate	2	30	12	42	21
!ubi	1	19	—	19	65
!gose	3	52	9	61	18
/ai/ai	5	94	13	107	67
!xabe	—	—	8	8	12
Mahopa	—	—	23	23	73
Total	14	248	88	336	340

* Figures do not include 130 Bushmen outside area on the date of census.

day. Therefore, I have avoided the term "band" in describing the !Kung Bushman living groups.

Each waterhole has a hinterland lying within a six-mile radius which is regularly exploited for vegetable and animal foods. These areas are not territories in the zoological sense, since they are not defended against outsiders. Rather they constitute the resources that lie within a convenient walking distance of a waterhole. The camp is a self-sufficient subsistence unit. The members move out each day to hunt and gather, and return in the evening to pool the collected foods in such a way that every person present receives an equitable share. Trade in foodstuffs between camps is minimal; personnel do move freely from camp to camp, however. The net effect is of a population constantly in motion. On the average, an individual spends a third of his time living only with close relatives, a third visiting other camps, and a third entertaining visitors from other camps.

Because of the strong emphasis on sharing, and the frequency of movement, surplus accumulation of storable plant foods and dried meat is kept to a minimum. There is rarely more than two or three days' supply of food on hand in a camp at any time. The result of this lack of surplus is that a constant subsistence effort must be maintained throughout the year. Unlike agriculturalists who work hard during the planting and harvesting seasons and undergo "seasonal unemployment" for several months, the Bushmen hunter-gatherers collect food every third or fourth day throughout the year.

Vegetable foods comprise from 60–80 per cent of the total diet by weight, and collecting involves two or three days of work per woman per week. The men also collect plants and small animals but their major contribution to the diet is the hunting of medium and large game. The men are conscientious but not particularly successful hunters; although men's and women's work input is roughly equivalent in terms of man-day of effort, the women provide two to three times as much food by weight as the men.

Table 2 summarizes the seasonal activity cycle observed among the Dobe-area !Kung in 1964. For the greater part of the year, food is locally abundant and easily collected. It is only during the end of the dry season in September and October, when desirable foods have been eaten out in the immediate vicinity of the waterholes that the people have to plan longer hikes of 10–15 miles and carry their own water to those areas where the mongongo nut is still available. The important point is that food is a constant, but distance required to reach food is a variable; it is short in the summer, fall, and early winter, and reaches its maximum in the spring.

This analysis attempts to provide quantitative measures of subsistence status including data on the following topics: abundance and variety of resources, diet selectivity, range size and population density, the composition of the work force, the ratio of work to leisure time, and the caloric and protein levels in the diet. The value of quantitative data is that they can be used comparatively and also may be useful in archeological reconstruction. In addition, one can avoid the pitfalls of subjective and qualitative impressions; for example, statements about food "anxiety" have proven to be difficult to generalize across cultures.

Abundance and variety of resources. It is impossible to define "abundance" of resources absolutely. However, one index of *relative* abundance is whether or not a population exhausts all the food available from a given area. By this criterion, the habitat of the Dobe-area Bushmen is abundant in naturally occurring foods. By far the most important food is the mongongo (mangetti) nut (*Ricinodendron rautanenii* Schinz). Although tens of thousands of pounds of these nuts are harvested and eaten each year, thousands more rot on the ground each year for want of picking.

The mongongo nut, because of its abundance and reliability, alone accounts for 50 per cent of the vegetable diet by weight. In this respect it resembles a cultivated staple crop such as maize or rice. Nutritionally it is even more remarkable, for it contains five times the calories and ten times the proteins per cooked unit of the cereal crops. The average daily per-capita consumption of 300 nuts yields about 1,260 calories and 56 grams of protein. This modest portion, weighing only about 7.5 ounces, contains the caloric equivalent of 2.5 pounds of cooked rice and the protein equivalent of 14 ounces of lean beef.

Furthermore the mongongo nut is drought resistant and it will still

Table 2. *The Bushman annual round*

Season	Jan.	Feb.	Mar.	April	May	June	July	Aug.	Sept.	Oct.	Nov.	Dec.
		Summer Rains		Autumn Dry			Winter Dry			Spring Dry		First Rains
Availability of Water		Temporary summer pools everywhere		Large summer pools				Permanent waterholes only				Summer pools developing
Group Moves		Widely dispersed at summer pools		At large summer pools				All population restricted to permanent waterholes				Moving out to summer pools
Men's Subsistence Activities	1. Hunting with bow, arrows, and dogs (year-round)											
	2.	Running down immatures					Trapping small game in snares				Running down newborn animals	
	3. Some gathering (year-round)											
Women's Subsistence Activities	1. Gathering of mongongo nuts (year-round)											
	2.	Fruits, berries, melons					Roots, bulbs, resins			Roots, leafy greens		
Ritual Activities		Dancing, trance performances, and ritual curing (year-round)			Boys' initiation*							†
Relative Subsistence Hardship			Water-food distance minimal					Increasing distance from water to food			Water-food distance minimal	

* Held once every five years; none in 1963–64.

† New Year's: Bushmen join the celebrations of their missionized Bantu neighbors.

be abundant in the dry years when cultivated crops may fail. The extremely hard outer shell protects the inner kernel from rot and allows the nuts to be harvested for up to twelve months after they have fallen to the ground. A diet based on mongongo nuts is in fact more reliable than one based on cultivated foods, and it is not surprising, therefore, that when a Bushman was asked why he hadn't taken to agriculture he replied: "Why should we plant, when there are so many mongongo nuts in the world?"

Apart from the mongongo, the Bushmen have available 84 other species of edible food plants, including 29 species of fruits, berries, and melons and 30 species of roots and bulbs. The existence of this variety allows for a wide range of alternatives in subsistence strategy. During the summer months the Bushmen have no problem other than to choose among the tastiest and most easily collected foods. Many species, which are quite edible but less attractive, are bypassed, so that gathering never exhausts *all* the available plant foods of an area. During the dry season the diet becomes much more eclectic and the many species of roots, bulbs, and edible resins make an important contribution. It is this broad base that provides an essential margin of safety during the end of the dry season when the mongongo nut forests are difficult to reach. In addition, it is likely that these rarely utilized species provide important nutritional and mineral trace elements that may be lacking in the more popular foods.

Diet selectivity. If the Bushmen were living close to the "starvation" level, then one would expect them to exploit every available source of nutrition. That their life is well above this level is indicated by the data in Table 3. Here all the edible plant species are arranged in classes according to the frequency with which they were observed to be eaten. It should be noted, that although there are some 85 species available, about 90 per cent of the vegetable diet by weight is drawn from only 23 species. In other words, 75 per cent of the listed species provide only 10 per cent of the food value.

In their meat-eating habits, the Bushmen show a similar selectivity. Of the 223 local species of animals known and named by the Bushmen, 54 species are classified as edible, and of these only 17 species were hunted on a regular basis. Only a handful of the dozens of edible species of small mammals, birds, reptiles, and insects that occur locally are regarded as food. Such animals as rodents, snakes, lizards, termites, and grasshoppers, which in the literature are included in the Bushman dietary, are despised by the Bushmen of the Dobe area.

Range size and population density. The necessity to travel long distances, the high frequency of moves, and the maintenance of populations at low densities are also features commonly associated with the

TABLE 3. *!Kung Bushman plant foods*

Food class	Fruit and nut	Bean and root	Fruit and stalk	Root, bulb	Fruit, berry, melon	Resin	Leaves	Seed, bean	Total number of species in class	Estimated contribution by weight to vegetable diet	Estimated contribution of each species
I. Primary Eaten daily throughout year (mongongo nut)	1	—	—	—	—	—	—	—	1	c. 50	c. 50*
II. Major Eaten daily in season	1	1	1	1	4	—	—	—	8	c. 25	c. 3
III. Minor Eaten several times per week in season	—	—	—	7	3	2	2	—	14	c. 15	c. 1
IV. Supplementary Eaten when classes I–III locally unavailable	—	—	—	9	12	10	1	—	32	c. 7	c. 0.2
V. Rare Eaten several times per year	—	—	—	9	4	—	—	—	13	c. 3	c. 0.1
VI. Problematic Edible but not observed to be eaten	—	—	—	4	6	4	1	2	17	nil	nil
Total Species	2	1	1	30	29	16	4	2	85	100	—

* 1 species constitutes 50 per cent of the vegetable diet by weight.

† 62 species constitute the remaining 10 per cent of the diet.

‡ 23 species constitute 90 per cent of the vegetable diet by weight.

hunting and gathering way of life. Density estimates for hunters in western North America and Australia have ranged from 3 persons/ square mile to as low as 1 person/100 square miles. In 1963–65, the resident and visiting Bushmen were observed to utilize an area of about 1,000 square miles during the course of the annual round for an effective population density of 41 persons/100 square miles. Within this area, however, the amount of ground covered by members of an individual camp was surprisingly small. A day's round-trip of twelve miles serves to define a "core" area six miles in radius surrounding each water point. By fanning out in all directions from their well, the members of a camp can gain access to the food resources of well over 100 square miles of territory within a two-hour hike. Except for a few weeks each year, areas lying beyond this six-mile radius are rarely utilized, even though they are no less rich in plants and game than are the core areas.

Although the Bushmen move their camps frequently (five or six times a year) they do not move them very far. A rainy season camp in the nut forests is rarely more than ten or twelve miles from the home waterhole, and often new campsites are occupied only a few hundred yards away from the previous one. By these criteria, the Bushmen do not lead a free-ranging nomadic way of life. For example, they do not undertake long marches of 30 to 100 miles to get food, since this task can be readily fulfilled within a day's walk of home base. When such long marches do occur they are invariably for visiting, trading, and marriage arrangements, and should not be confused with the normal routine of subsistence.

Demographic factors. Another indicator of the harshness of a way of life is the age at which people die. Ever since Hobbes characterized life in the state of nature as "nasty, brutish and short," the assumption has been that hunting and gathering is so rigorous that members of such societies are rapidly worn out and meet an early death. Silberbauer, for example, says of the Gwi Bushmen of the central Kalahari that "life expectancy . . . is difficult to calculate, but I do not believe that many live beyond 45." And Coon has said of the hunters in general:

> The practice of abandoning the hopelessly ill and aged has been observed in many parts of the world. It is always done by people living in poor environments where it is necessary to move about frequently to obtain food, where food is scarce, and transportation difficult. . . . Among peoples who are forced to live in this way the oldest generation, the generation of individuals who have passed their physical peak is reduced in numbers and influence. There is no body of elders to hand on tradition and control the affairs of younger men and women, and no formal system of age grading.

The !Kung Bushmen of the Dobe area flatly contradict this view. In a total population of 466, no fewer than 46 individuals (17 men and 29 women) were determined to be over 60 years of age, a proportion that compares favorably to the percentage of elderly in industrialized populations.

The aged hold a respected position in Bushman society and are the effective leaders of the camps. Senilicide is extremely rare. Long after their productive years have passed, the old people are fed and cared for by their children and grandchildren. The blind, the senile, and the crippled are respected for the special ritual and technical skills they possess. For instance, the four elders at !gose waterhole were totally or partially blind, but this handicap did not prevent their active participation in decision-making and ritual curing.

Another significant feature of the composition of the work force is the late assumption of adult responsibility by the adolescents. Young people are not expected to provide food regularly until they are married. Girls typically marry between the ages of 15 and 20, and boys about five years later, so that it is not unusual to find healthy, active teenagers visiting from camp to camp while their older relatives provide food for them.

As a result, the people in the age group 20–60 support a surprisingly large percentage of non-productive young and old people. About 40 per cent of the population in camps contribute little to the food supplies. This allocation of work to young and middle-aged adults allows for a relatively carefree childhood and adolescence and a relatively unstrenuous old age.

Leisure and work. Another important index of ease or difficulty of subsistence is the amount of time devoted to the food quest. Hunting has usually been regarded by social scientists as a way of life in which merely keeping alive is so formidable a task that members of such societies lack the leisure time necessary to "build culture." The !Kung Bushmen would appear to conform to the rule, for as Lorna Marshall says:

> It is vividly apparent that among the !Kung Bushmen, ethos, or "the spirit which actuates manners and customs," is survival. Their time and energies are almost wholly given to this task, for life in their environment requires that they spend their days mainly in procuring food.

It is certainly true that getting food is the most important single activity in Bushman life. However this statement would apply equally well to small-scale agricultural and pastoral societies too. How much time is *actually* devoted to the food quest is fortunately an empirical question. And an analysis of the work effort of the Dobe Bushmen shows some unexpected results. From July 6 to August 2, 1964, I recorded all the daily activities of the Bushmen living at the Dobe waterhole. Because of the coming and going of visitors, the camp population fluctuated in size day by day, from a low of 23 to a high of 40, with a mean of 31.8 persons. Each day some of the adult members of the camp went out to hunt and/or gather while others stayed home or went visiting. The daily recording of all personnel on hand made it possible to calculate the number of man-days of work as a percentage of total number of man-days of consumption.

Although the Bushmen do not organize their activities on the basis of a seven-day week, I have divided the data this way to make them more intelligible. The work-week was calculated to show how many days out of seven each adult spent in subsistence activities (Table 4, Column 7). Week II has been eliminated from the totals since the investigator contributed food. In week I, the people spent an average of 2.3 days in subsistence activities, in week III, 1.9 days, and in week IV, 3.2 days. In all, the adults of the Dobe camp worked about two and a half days a week. Since the average working day was about six hours long, the fact emerges that !Kung Bushmen of Dobe, despite their harsh environment, devote from twelve to nineteen hours a week to getting food. Even the hardest working individual in the camp, a man named ≠oma who went out hunting on sixteen of the 28 days, spent a maximum of 32 hours a week in the food quest.

Because the Bushmen do not amass a surplus of foods, there are no seasons of exceptionally intensive activities such as planting and harvesting, and no seasons of unemployment. The level of work observed is an accurate reflection of the effort required to meet the immediate caloric needs of the group. This work diary covers the mid-winter dry season, a period when food is neither at its most plentiful nor at its scarcest levels, and the diary documents the transition from better to worse conditions (see Table 2). During the fourth week the gatherers were making overnight trips to camps in the mongongo nut forests seven to ten miles distant from the waterhole. These longer trips account for the rise in the level of work, from twelve or thirteen to nineteen hours per week.

If food getting occupies such a small proportion of a Bushman's waking hours, then how *do* people allocate their time? A woman gathers on one day enough food to feed her family for three days, and spends the rest of her time resting in camp, doing embroidery, visiting other camps, or entertaining visitors from other camps. For each day at home, kitchen routines, such as cooking, nut cracking, collecting firewood, and fetching water, occupy one to three hours of her time. This rhythm of steady work and steady leisure is maintained throughout the year.

TABLE 4. *Summary of Dobe work diary*

Week	(1) Mean group size	(2) Adult-days	(3) Child-days	(4) Total man-days of consumption	(5) Man-days of work	(6) Meat (lbs.)	(7) Average work-week/adult	(8) Index of subsistence effort
I (July 6–12)	25.6 (23–29)	114	65	179	37	104	2.3	.21
II (July 13–19)	28.3 (23–27)	125	73	198	22	80	1.2	.11
III (July 20–26)	34.3 (29–40)	156	84	240	42	177	1.9	.18
IV (July 27–Aug. 2)	35.6 (32–40)	167	82	249	77	129	3.2	.31
4-wk. total	30.9	562	304	866	178	490	2.2	.21
Adjusted total*	31.8	437	231	668	156	410	2.5	.23

* See text.

Key: Column 1: Mean group size = $\dfrac{\text{total man-days of consumption}}{7}$.

Column 7: Work-week = the number of work days per adult per week.

Column 8: Index of subsistence effort = $\dfrac{\text{man-days of work}}{\text{man-days of consumption}}$ (e.g., in Week I, the value of "S" = .21, i.e., 21 days of work/100 days of consumption or 1 work day produces food for 5 consumption days).

The hunters tend to work more frequently than the women, but their schedule is uneven. It is not unusual for a man to hunt avidly for a week and then do no hunting at all for two or three weeks. Since hunting is an unpredictable business and subject to magical control, hunters sometimes experience a run of bad luck and stop hunting for a month or longer. During these periods, visiting, entertaining, and especially dancing are the primary activities of men. (Unlike the Hadza, gambling is only a minor leisure activity.)

The trance-dance is the focus of Bushman ritual life; over 50 per cent of the men have trained as trance-performers and regularly enter trance during the course of the all-night dances. At some camps, trance-dances occur as frequently as two or three times a week and those who have entered trances the night before rarely go out hunting the following day. . . . In a camp with five or more hunters, there are usually two or three who are actively hunting and several others who are inactive. The net effect is to phase the hunting and non-hunting so that a fairly steady supply of meat is brought into a camp.

Caloric returns. Is the modest work effort of the Bushmen sufficient to provide the calories necessary to maintain the health of the population? Or have the !Kung, in common with some agricultural peoples, adjusted to a permanently substandard nutritional level?

During my field work I did not encounter any cases of kwashiorkor, the most common nutritional disease in the children of African agricultural societies. However, without medical examinations, it is impossible to exclude the possibility that subclinical signs of malnutrition existed.

Another measure of nutritional adequacy is the average consumption of calories and proteins per person per day. The estimate for the Bushmen is based on observations of the weights of foods of known composition that were brought into Dobe camp on each day of the study period. The per-capita figure is obtained by dividing the total weight of foodstuffs by the total number of persons in the camp. These results are set out in detail elsewhere and can only be summarized here. During the study period 410 pounds of meat were brought in by the hunters of the Dobe camp, for a daily share of nine ounces of meat per person. About 700 pounds of vegetable foods were gathered and consumed during the same period. Table 5 sets out the calories and proteins available per capita in the !Kung Bushman dietary from meat, mongongo nuts, and other vegetable sources.

This output of 2,140 calories and 93.1 grams of protein per person per day may be compared with the Recommended Daily Allowances (RDA) for persons of the small size and stature but vigorous activity regime of the !Kung Bushmen. The RDA for Bushmen can be estimated at 1,975 calories and 60 grams of protein per person per day. Thus it is

TABLE 5. *Caloric and protein levels in the !Kung Bushman dietary, July–August, 1964*

Class of food	Percentage contribution to diet by weight	Per capita consumption		Calories per person per day	Percentage caloric contribution of meat and vegetables
		Weight in grams	Protein in grams		
Meat	37	230	34.5	690	33
Mongongo nuts	33	210	56.7	1,260	
Other vegetable foods	30	190	1.9	190	67
Total all sources	100	630	93.1	2,140	100

apparent that food output exceeds energy requirements by 165 calories and 33 grams of protein. One can tentatively conclude that even a modest subsistence effort of two or three days work per week is enough to provide an adequate diet for the !Kung Bushmen.

THE SECURITY OF BUSHMAN LIFE

I have attempted to evaluate the subsistence base of one contemporary hunter-gatherer society living in a marginal environment. The !Kung Bushmen have available to them some relatively abundant high-quality foods, and they do not have to walk very far or work very hard to get them. Furthermore this modest work effort provides sufficient calories to support not only the active adults, but also a large number of middle-aged and elderly people. The Bushmen do not have to press their youngsters into the service of the food quest, nor do they have to dispose of the oldsters after they have ceased to be productive.

The evidence presented assumes an added significance because this security of life was observed during the third year of one of the most severe droughts in South Africa's history. Most of the 576,000 people of Botswana are pastoralists and agriculturalists. After the crops had failed three years in succession and over 100,000 head of cattle had died on the range for lack of water, the World Food Program of the United Nations instituted a famine relief program which has grown to include 180,000 people, over 30 per cent of the population. This program did not touch the Dobe area in the isolated northwest corner of the country and the Herero and Tswana women there were able to feed their families only by joining the Bushman women to forage for wild foods. Thus the natural plant resources of the Dobe area were carrying a higher proportion of population than would be the case in years when the Bantu harvested crops. Yet this added pressure on the land did not seem to adversely affect the Bushmen.

In one sense it was unfortunate that the period of my field work happened to coincide with the drought, since I was unable to witness a "typical" annual subsistence cycle. However, in another sense, the coincidence was a lucky one, for the drought put the Bushmen and their subsistence system to the acid test and, in terms of adaptation to scarce resources, they passed with flying colors. One can postulate that their subsistence base would be even more substantial during years of higher rainfall.

What are the crucial factors that make this way of life possible? I suggest that the primary factor is the Bushmen's strong emphasis on vegetable food sources. Although hunting involves a great deal of effort and prestige, plant foods provide from 60–80 per cent of the annual diet by weight. Meat has come to be regarded as a special treat; when available, it is welcomed as a break from the routine of vegetable foods, but it is never depended upon as a staple. No one ever goes hungry when hunting fails.

The reason for this emphasis is not hard to find. Vegetable foods are abundant, sedentary, and predictable. They grow in the same place year after year, and the gatherer is guaranteed a day's return of food for a day's expenditure of energy. Game animals, by contrast, are scarce, mobile, unpredictable, and difficult to catch. A hunter has no guarantee of success and may in fact go for days or weeks without killing a large mammal. During the study period, there were eleven men in the Dobe camp, of whom four did no hunting at all. The seven active men spent a total of 78 man-days hunting, and this work input yielded eighteen animals killed, or one kill for every four man-days of hunting. The probability of any one hunter making a kill on a given day was 0.23. By contrast, the probability of a woman finding plant food on a given day was 1.00. In other words, hunting and gathering are not equally felicitous subsistence alternatives.

Consider the productivity per man-hour of the two kinds of subsistence activities. One man-hour of hunting produces about 100 edible calories, and of gathering, 240 calories. Gathering is thus seen to be 2.4 times more productive than hunting. In short, hunting is a *high-risk, low-return* subsistence activity, while gathering is a *low-risk, high-return* subsistence activity.

It is not at all contradictory that the hunting complex holds a central place in the Bushman ethos and that meat is valued more highly than vegetable foods. Analogously, steak is valued more highly than potatoes in the food preferences of our own society. In both situations the meat is more "costly" than the vegetable food. In the Bushman case, the cost of food can be measured in terms of time and energy expended. By this standard, 1,000 calories of meat "costs" ten man-hours, while the "cost" of 1,000 calories of vegetable foods is only four man-hours. Further, it is to be expected that the less predictable, more expensive food source would have a greater accretion of myth and ritual built up around it than would the routine staples of life, which rarely if ever fail.

Conclusions

Three points ought to be stressed. First, life in the state of nature is not necessarily nasty, brutish, and short. The Dobe-area Bushmen live well today on wild plants and meat, in spite of the fact that they are confined to the least productive portion of the range in which Bushman peoples were formerly found. It is likely that an even more substantial subsistence base would have been characteristic of these hunters and gatherers in the past, when they had the pick of African habitats to choose from.

Second, the basis of Bushman diet is derived from sources other than meat. This emphasis makes good ecological sense to the !Kung Bushmen and appears to be a common feature among hunters and gatherers in general. Since a 30 to 40 per cent input of meat is such a consistent target for modern hunters in a variety of habitats, is it not reasonable to postulate a similar percentage for prehistoric hunters? Certainly the absence of plant remains on archeological sites is by itself not sufficient evidence for the absence of gathering. Recently-abandoned Bushman campsites show a similar absence of vegetable remains, although this paper has clearly shown that plant foods comprise over 60 per cent of the actual diet.

Finally, one gets the impression that hunting societies have been chosen by ethnologists to illustrate a dominant theme, such as the extreme importance of environment in the molding of certain cultures. Such a theme can be best exemplified by cases in which the technology is simple and/or the environment is harsh. This emphasis on the dramatic may have been pedagogically useful, but unfortunately it has led to the assumption that a precarious hunting subsistence base was characteristic of all cultures in the Pleistocene. This view of both modern and ancient hunters ought to be reconsidered. Specifically I am suggesting a shift in focus away from the dramatic and unusual cases, and toward a consideration of hunting and gathering as a persistent and well-adapted way of life.

22

Penny capitalism on an urban streetcorner
ELLIOT LIEBOW

*In our complex Western economy, the job a man has and the
value the society places on it determine his productive capability
and measure his worth. Elliot Liebow examines the cultural
meaning of jobs to men in the black ghetto. Given the limitations
placed on him by his immediate society, the black "corner
man" cannot hope to fill a job valued by the larger society. As
a result his pay is low, his future dim, and his self-esteem diminished; he is unable to provide for the needs of his family or
himself.*

A pickup truck drives slowly down the street. The truck stops as it
comes abreast of a man sitting on a cast-iron porch and the white driver
calls out, asking if the man wants a day's work. The man shakes his
head and the truck moves on up the block, stopping again whenever
idling men come within calling distance of the driver. At the Carry-out
corner, five men debate the question briefly and shake their heads no
to the truck. The truck turns the corner and repeats the same performance up the next street. In the distance, one can see one man, then another, climb into the back of the truck and sit down. It starts and stops,
the truck finally disappears.

What is it we have witnessed here? A labor scavenger rebuffed by
his would-be prey? Lazy, irresponsible men turning down an honest
day's pay for an honest day's work? Or a more complex phenomenon
marking the intersection of economic forces, social values, and individual
states of mind and body?

Let us look again at the driver of the truck. He has been able to
recruit only two or three men from each twenty or fifty he contacts. To

Reprinted from *Tally's Corner* by Elliot Liebow, pp. 29–71, by permission of
Little, Brown and Co. Copyright © 1967 by Little, Brown and Company (Inc.).

him, it is clear that the others simply do not choose to work. Singly or in groups, belly-empty or belly-full, sullen or gregarious, drunk or sober, they confirm what he has read, heard and knows from his own experience: these men wouldn't take a job if it were handed to them on a platter.[1]

Quite apart from the question of whether or not this is true of some of the men he sees on the street, it is clearly not true of all of them. If it were, he would not have come here in the first place; or having come, he would have left with an empty truck. It is not even true of most of them, for most of the men he sees on the street this weekday morning do, in fact, have jobs. But since, at the moment, they are neither working nor sleeping, and since they hate the depressing room or apartment they live in, or because there is nothing to do there,[2] or because they want to get away from their wives or anyone else living there, they are out on the street, indistinguishable from those who do not have jobs or do not want them. Some, like Boley, a member of a trash-collection crew in a suburban housing development, work Saturdays and are off on this weekday. Some, like Sweets, work nights cleaning up middle-class trash, dirt, dishes, and garbage, and mopping the floors of the office buildings, hotels, restaurants, toilets, and other public places dirtied during the day. Some men work for retail businesses such as liquor stores which do not begin the day until ten o'clock. Some laborers, like Tally, have already come back from the job because the ground was too wet for pick and shovel or because the weather was too cold for pouring concrete. Other employed men stayed off the job today for personal reasons: Clarence to go to a funeral at eleven this morning and Sea Cat to answer a subpoena as a witness in a criminal proceeding.

Also on the street, unwitting contributors to the impression taken away by the truck driver, are the halt and the lame. The man on the cast-iron steps strokes one gnarled arthritic hand with the other and says he doesn't know whether or not he'll live long enough to be eligible for Social Security. He pauses, then adds matter-of-factly, "Most times, I don't care whether I do or don't." Stoopy's left leg was polio-withered in childhood. Raymond, who looks as if he could tear out a fire hydrant, coughs up blood if he bends or moves suddenly. The quiet man who

[1] By different methods, perhaps, some social scientists have also located the problem in the men themselves, in their unwillingness or lack of desire to work: "To improve the underprivileged worker's performance one must help him to learn *to want* . . . higher social goals for himself and his children. . . . The problem of changing the work habits and motivation of [lower class] people . . . is a problem of changing the goals, the ambitions, and the level of cultural and occupational aspiration of the underprivileged worker." (Emphasis in original.) Allison Davis, "The Motivation of the Underprivileged Worker," p. 90.

[2] The comparison of sitting at home alone with being in jail is commonplace.

hangs out in front of the Saratoga apartments has a steel hook strapped onto his left elbow. And had the man in the truck been able to look into the wine-clouded eyes of the man in the green cap, he would have realized that the man did not even understand he was being offered a day's work.

Others, having had jobs and been laid off, are drawing unemployment compensation (up to $44 per week) and have nothing to gain by accepting work which pays little more than this and frequently less.

Still others, like Bumdoodle the numbers man, are working hard at illegal ways of making money, hustlers who are on the street to turn a dollar any way they can: buying and selling sex, liquor, narcotics, stolen goods, or anything else that turns up.

Only a handful remains unaccounted for. There is Tonk, who cannot bring himself to take a job away from the corner, because, according to the other men, he suspects his wife will be unfaithful if given the opportunity. There is Stanton, who has not reported to work for four days now, not since Bernice disappeared. He bought a brand new knife against her return. She had done this twice before, he said, but not for so long and not without warning, and he had forgiven her. But this time, "I ain't got it in me to forgive her again." His rage and shame are there for all to see as he paces the Carry-out and the corner, day and night, hoping to catch a glimpse of her.

And finally, there are those like Arthur, able-bodied men who have no visible means of support, legal or illegal, who neither have jobs nor want them. The truck driver, among others, believes the Arthurs to be representative of all the men he sees idling on the street during his own working hours. They are not, but they cannot be dismissed simply because they are a small minority. It is not enough to explain them away as being lazy or irresponsible or both because an able-bodied man with responsibilities who refuses work is, by the truck driver's definition, lazy and irresponsible. Such an answer begs the question. It is descriptive of the facts; it does not explain them.

Moreover, despite their small numbers, the don't-work-and-don't-want-to-work minority is especially significant because they represent the strongest and clearest expression of those values and attitudes associated with making a living which, to varying degrees, are found throughout the streetcorner world. These men differ from the others in degree rather than in kind, the principal difference being that they are carrying out the implications of their values and experiences to their logical, inevitable conclusions. In this sense, the others have yet to come to terms with themselves and the world they live in.

Putting aside, for the moment, what the men say and feel, and looking at what they actually do and the choices they make, getting a job, keeping a job, and doing well at it is clearly of low priority. Arthur will not take a job at all. Leroy is supposed to be on his job at 4:00 P.M. but it is already 4:10 and he still cannot bring himself to leave the free games he has accumulated on the pinball machine in the Carry-out. Tonk started a construction job on Wednesday, worked Thursday and Friday, then didn't go back again. On the same kind of job, Sea Cat quit in the second week. Sweets had been working three months as a busboy in a restaurant, then quit without notice, not sure himself why he did so. A real estate agent, saying he was more interested in getting the job done than in the cost, asked Richard to give him an estimate on repairing and painting the inside of a house, but Richard, after looking over the job, somehow never got around to submitting an estimate. During one period, Tonk would not leave the corner to take a job because his wife might prove unfaithful; Stanton would not take a job because his woman had been unfaithful.

Thus, the man-job relationship is a tenuous one. At any given moment, a job may occupy a relatively low position on the streetcorner scale of real values. Getting a job may be subordinated to relations with women or to other non-job considerations; the commitment to a job one already has is frequently shallow and tentative.

The reasons are many. Some are objective and reside principally in the job; some are subjective and reside principally in the man. The line between them, however, is not a clear one. Behind the man's refusal to take a job or his decision to quit one is not a simple impulse or value choice but a complex combination of assessments of objective reality on the one hand, and values, attitudes and beliefs drawn from different levels of his experience on the other.

Objective economic considerations are frequently a controlling factor in a man's refusal to take a job. How much the job pays is a crucial question but seldom asked. He knows how much it pays. Working as a stock clerk, a delivery boy, or even behind the counter of liquor stores, drug stores, and other retail businesses pays one dollar an hour. So, too, do most busboy, car-wash, janitorial, and other jobs available to him. Some jobs, such as dishwasher, may dip as low as eighty cents an hour and others, such as elevator operator or work in a junk yard, may offer $1.15 or $1.25. Take-home pay for jobs such as these ranges from $35 to $50 a week, but a take-home pay of over $45 for a five-day week is the exception rather than the rule.

One of the principal advantages of these kinds of jobs is that they offer fairly regular work. Most of them involve essential services and are therefore somewhat less responsive to business conditions than are some higher paying, less menial jobs. Most of them are also inside jobs not dependent on the weather, as are construction jobs and other higher-paying outside work.

Another seemingly important advantage of working in hotels, restaurants, office and apartment buildings, and retail establishments is that they frequently offer an opportunity for stealing on the job. But stealing can be a two-edged sword. Apart from increasing the cost of the goods or services to the general public, a less obvious result is that the practice usually acts as a depressant on the employee's own wage level. Owners of small retail establishments and other employers frequently anticipate employee stealing and adjust the wage rate accordingly. Tonk's employer explained why he was paying Tonk $35 for a 55–60 hour workweek. These men will all steal, he said. Although he keeps close watch on Tonk, he estimates that Tonk steals from $35 to $40 a week.[3] What he steals, when added to his regular earnings, brings his take-home pay to $70 or $75 per week. The employer said he did not mind this because Tonk is worth that much to the business. But if he were to pay Tonk outright the full value of his labor, Tonk would still be stealing $35–$40 per week and this, he said, the business simply would not support.

This wage arrangement, with stealing built-in, was satisfactory to both parties, with each one independently expressing his satisfaction. Such a wage-theft system, however, is not as balanced and equitable as it appears. Since the wage level rests on the premise that the employee will steal the unpaid value of his labor, the man who does not steal on the job is penalized. And furthermore, even if he does not steal, no one would believe him; the employer and others believe he steals because the system presumes it.

Nor is the man who steals, as he is expected to, as well off as he believes himself to be. The employer may occasionally close his eyes to the worker's stealing but not often and not for long. He is, after all, a businessman and cannot always find it within himself to let a man steal from him, even if the man is stealing his own wages. Moreover, it is only by keeping close watch on the worker that the employer can control how much is stolen and thereby protect himself against the employee's stealing more than he is worth. From this viewpoint, then, the employer is not in wage-theft collusion with the employee. In the case of Tonk, for instance, the employer was not actively abetting the theft. His estimates of how much Tonk was stealing was based on what he thought Tonk was able to steal despite his own best efforts to prevent him from steal-

[3] Exactly the same estimate as the one made by Tonk himself. On the basis of personal knowledge of the stealing routine employed by Tonk, however, I suspect the actual amount is considerably smaller.

ing anything at all. Were he to have caught Tonk in the act of stealing, he would, of course, have fired him from the job and perhaps called the police as well. Thus, in an actual if not in a legal sense, all the elements of entrapment are present. The employer knowingly provides the conditions which entice (force) the employee to steal the unpaid value of his labor, but at the same time he punishes him for theft if he catches him doing so.

Other consequences of the wage-theft system are even more damaging to the employee. Let us, for argument's sake, say that Tonk is in no danger of entrapment; that his employer is willing to wink at the stealing and that Tonk, for his part, is perfectly willing to earn a little, steal a little. Let us say, too, that he is paid $35 a week and allowed to steal $35. His money income — as measured by the goods and services he can purchase with it — is, of course, $70. But not all of his income is available to him for all purposes. He cannot draw on what he steals to build his self-respect or to measure his self-worth. For this, he can draw only on his earnings — the amount given him publicly and voluntarily in exchange for his labor. His "respect" and "self-worth" income remains at $35 — only half that of the man who also receives $70 but all of it in the form of wages. His earnings publicly measure the worth of his labor to his employer, and they are important to others and to himself in taking the measure of his worth as a man.[4]

With or without stealing, and quite apart from any interior processes going on in the man who refuses such a job or quits it casually and without apparent reason, the objective fact is that menial jobs in retailing or in the service trades simply do not pay enough to support a man and his family. This is not to say that the worker is underpaid; this may or may not be true. Whether he is or not, the plain fact is that, in such a job, he cannot make a living. Nor can he take much comfort in the fact that these jobs tend to offer more regular, steadier work. If he cannot live on the $45 or $50 he makes in one week, the longer he works, the longer he cannot live on what he makes.[5]

[4] Some public credit may accrue to the clever thief but not respect.

[5] It might be profitable to compare, as Howard S. Becker suggests, gross aspects of income and housing costs in this particular area with those reported by Herbert Gans for the low-income working class in Boston's West End. In 1958, Gans reports, median income for the West Enders was just under $70 a week, a level considerably higher than that enjoyed by the people in the Carry-out neighborhood five years later. Gans himself rented a six-room apartment in the West End for $46 a month, about $10 more than the going rate for long-time residents. In the Carry-out neighborhood, rooms that could accommodate more than a cot and a miniature dresser — that is, rooms that qualified for family living — rented for $12 to $22 a week. Ignoring differences that really can't be ignored — the privacy and self-contained efficiency of the multi-room apartment as against the fragmented, public living of the rooming-house "apartment," with a public toilet on a floor al-

Construction work, even for unskilled laborers, usually pays better, with the hourly rate ranging from $1.50 to $2.60 an hour.[6] Importantly, too, good references, a good driving record, a tenth grade (or any high school) education, previous experience, the ability to "bring police clearance with you" are not normally required of laborers as they frequently are for some of the jobs in retailing or in the service trades.

Construction work, however, has its own objective disadvantages. It is, first of all, seasonal work for the great bulk of the laborers, beginning early in the spring and tapering off as winter weather sets in.[7] And even during the season the work is frequently irregular. Early or late in the season, snow or temperatures too low for concrete frequently sends the laborers back home, and during late spring or summer, a heavy rain on Tuesday or Wednesday, leaving a lot of water and mud behind it, can mean a two or three day workweek for the pick-and-shovel men and other unskilled laborers.[8]

The elements are not the only hazard. As the project moves from one construction stage to another, laborers — usually without warning — are laid off, sometimes permanently or sometimes for weeks at a

---

ways different from the one your room is on (no matter, it probably doesn't work, anyway) — and assuming comparable states of disrepair, the West Enders were paying $6 or $7 a month for a room that cost the Carry-outers at least $50 a month, and frequently more. Looking at housing costs as a percentage of income — and again ignoring what cannot be ignored: that what goes by the name of "housing" in the two areas is not at all the same thing — the median income West Ender could get a six-room apartment for about 12 percent of his income, while his 1963 Carry-out counterpart, with a weekly income of $60 (to choose a figure from the upper end of the income range), often paid 20–33 percent of his income for one room. See Herbert J. Gans, *The Urban Villagers*, pp. 10–13.

[6] The higher amount is 1962 union scale for building laborers. According to the Wage Agreement Contract for Heavy Construction Laborers (Washington, D.C., and vicinity) covering the period from May 1, 1963 to April 30, 1966, minimum hourly wage for heavy construction laborers was to go from $2.75 (May 1963) by annual increments to $2.92, effective November 1, 1965.

[7] "Open-sky" work, such as building overpasses, highways, etc., in which the workers and materials are directly exposed to the elements, traditionally begins in March and ends around Thanksgiving. The same is true for much of the street repair work and the laying of sewer, electric, gas, and telephone lines by the city and public utilities, all important employers of laborers. Between Thanksgiving and March, they retain only skeleton crews selected from their best, most reliable men.

[8] In a recent year, the crime rate in Washington for the month of August jumped 18 percent over the preceding month. A veteran police officer explained the increase to David L. Bazelon, Chief Judge, U.S. Court of Appeals for the District of Columbia. "It's quite simple. . . . You see, August was a very wet month. . . . These people wait on the street corner each morning around 6:00 or 6:30 for a truck to pick them up and take them to a construction site. If it's raining, that truck doesn't come, and the men are going to be idle that day. If the bad weather keeps up for three days . . . we know we are going to have trouble on our hands — and sure enough, there invariably follows a rash of purse-snatchings, house-breakings and the like. . . . These people have to eat like the rest of us, you know." David L. Bazelon, Address to the Federal Bar Association, p. 3.

time. The more fortunate or the better workers are told periodically to "take a walk for two, three days."

Both getting the construction job and getting to it are also relatively more difficult than is the case for the menial jobs in retailing and the service trades. Job competition is always fierce. In the city, the large construction projects are unionized. One has to have ready cash to get into the union to become eligible to work on these projects and, being eligible, one has to find an opening. Unless one "knows somebody," say a foreman or a laborer who knows the day before that they are going to take on new men in the morning, this can be a difficult and disheartening search.

Many of the nonunion jobs are in suburban Maryland or Virginia. The newspaper ads say, "Report ready to work to the trailer at the intersection of Rte. 11 and Old Bridge Rd., Bunston, Virginia (or Maryland)," but this location may be ten, fifteen, or even twenty-five miles from the Carry-out. Public transportation would require two or more hours to get there, if it services the area at all. Without access to a car or to a car-pool arrangement, it is not worthwhile reading the ad. So the men do not. Jobs such as these are usually filled by word of mouth information, beginning with someone who knows someone or who is himself working there and looking for a paying rider. Furthermore, nonunion jobs in outlying areas tend to be smaller projects of relatively short duration and to pay somewhat less than scale.

Still another objective factor is the work itself. For some men, whether the job be digging, mixing mortar, pushing a wheelbarrow, unloading materials, carrying and placing steel rods for reinforcing concrete, or building or laying concrete forms, the work is simply too hard. Men such as Tally and Wee Tom can make such work look like child's play; some of the older work-hardened men, such as Budder and Stanton, can do it too, although not without showing unmistakable signs of strain and weariness at the end of the workday. But those who lack the robustness of a Tally or the time-inured immunity of a Budder must either forego jobs such as these or pay a heavy toll to keep them. For Leroy, in his early twenties, almost six feet tall but weighing under 140 pounds, it would be as difficult to push a loaded wheelbarrow, or to unload and stack 96-pound bags of cement all day long, as it would be for Stoopy with his withered leg.

Heavy, backbreaking labor of the kind that used to be regularly associated with bull gangs or concrete gangs is no longer characteristic of laboring jobs, especially those with the larger, well-equipped construction companies. Brute strength is still required from time to time, as on smaller jobs where it is not economical to bring in heavy equipment or where the small, undercapitalized contractor has none to bring in. In many cases, however, the conveyor belt has replaced the wheelbarrow or the Georgia buggy, mechanized forklifts have eliminated heavy, manual lifting, and a variety of digging machines have replaced the pick and shovel. The result is fewer jobs for unskilled laborers and, in many cases, a work speed-up for those who do have jobs. Machines now set the pace formerly set by men. Formerly, a laborer pushed a wheelbarrow of wet cement to a particular spot, dumped it, and returned for another load. Another laborer, in hip boots, pushed the wet concrete around with a shovel or a hoe, getting it roughly level in preparation for the skilled finishers. He had relatively small loads to contend with and had only to keep up with the men pushing the wheelbarrows. Now, the job for the man pushing the wheelbarrow is gone and the wet concrete comes rushing down a chute at the man in the hip boots who must "spread it quick or drown."

Men who have been running an elevator, washing dishes, or "pulling trash" cannot easily move into laboring jobs. They lack the basic skills for "unskilled" construction labor, familiarity with tools and materials, and tricks of the trade without which hard jobs are made harder. Previously unused or untrained muscles rebel in pain against the new and insistent demands made upon them, seriously compromising the man's performance and testing his willingness to see the job through.

A healthy, sturdy, active man of good intelligence requires from two to four weeks to break in on a construction job.[9] Even if he is willing somehow to bull his way through the first few weeks, it frequently happens that his foreman or the craftsman he services with materials and general assistance is not willing to wait that long for him to get into condition or to learn at a glance the difference in size between a rough 2" x 8" and a finished 2" x 10". The foreman and the craftsman are themselves "under the gun" and cannot "carry" the man when other men, who are already used to the work and who know the tools and materials, are lined up to take the job.

Sea Cat was "healthy, sturdy, active and of good intelligence." When a judge gave him six weeks in which to pay his wife $200 in back child-support payments, he left his grocery-store job in order to take a higher-paying job as a laborer, arranged for him by a foreman friend. During the first week the weather was bad and he worked only Wednesday and Friday, cursing the elements all the while for cheating him out of the money he could have made. The second week, the weather was fair but he quit at the end of the fourth day, saying frankly that the

---

[9] Estimate of Mr. Francis Greenfield, President of the International Hod Carriers, Building and Common Laborers' District Council of Washington, D.C., and Vicinity. I am indebted to Mr. Greenfield for several points in these paragraphs dealing with construction laborers.

work was too hard for him. He went back to his job at the grocery store and took a second job working nights as a dishwasher in a restaurant,[10] earning little if any more at the two jobs than he would have earned as a laborer, and keeping at both of them until he had paid off his debts.

Tonk did not last as long as Sea Cat. No one made any predictions when he got a job in a parking lot, but when the men on the corner learned he was to start on a road construction job, estimates of how long he would last ranged from one to three weeks. Wednesday was his first day. He spent that evening and night at home. He did the same on Thursday. He worked Friday and spent Friday evening and part of Saturday draped over the mailbox on the corner. Sunday afternoon, Tonk decided he was not going to report on the job the next morning. He explained that after working three days, he knew enough about the job to know that it was too hard for him. He knew he wouldn't be able to keep up and he'd just as soon quit now as get fired later.

Logan was a tall, two-hundred-pound man in his late twenties. His back used to hurt him only on the job, he said, but now he can't straighten up for increasingly longer periods of time. He said he had traced this to the awkward walk he was forced to adopt by the loaded wheelbarrows which pull him down into a half-stoop. He's going to quit, he said, as soon as he can find another job. If he can't find one real soon, he guesses he'll quit anyway. It's not worth it, having to walk bent over and leaning to one side.

Sometimes, the strain and effort is greater than the man is willing to admit, even to himself. In the early summer of 1963, Richard was rooming at Nancy's place. His wife and children were "in the country" (his grandmother's home in Carolina), waiting for him to save up enough money so that he could bring them back to Washington and start over again after a disastrous attempt to "make it" in Philadelphia. Richard had gotten a job with a fence company in Virginia. It paid $1.60 an hour. The first few evenings, when he came home from work, he looked ill from exhaustion and the heat. Stanton said Richard would have to quit, "he's too small [thin] for that kind of work." Richard said he was doing O.K. and would stick with the job.

At Nancy's one night, when Richard had been working about two weeks, Nancy and three or four others were sitting around talking, drinking, and listening to music. Someone asked Nancy when was Richard going to bring his wife and children up from the country. Nancy said she didn't know, but it probably depended on how long it would take him to save up enough money. She said she didn't think he could stay with the fence job much longer. This morning, she said, the man

---

[10] Not a sinecure, even by streetcorner standards.

Richard rode to work with knocked on the door and Richard didn't answer. She looked in his room. Richard was still asleep. Nancy tried to shake him awake. "No more digging!" Richard cried out. "No more digging! I can't do no more God-damn digging!" When Nancy finally managed to wake him, he dressed quickly and went to work.

Richard stayed on the job two more weeks, then suddenly quit, ostensibly because his pay check was three dollars less than what he thought it should have been.

In summary of objective job considerations, then, the most important fact is that a man who is able and willing to work cannot earn enough money to support himself, his wife, and one or more children. A man's chances for working regularly are good only if he is willing to work for less than he can live on, and sometimes not even then. On some jobs, the wage rate is deceptively higher than on others, but the higher the wage rate, the more difficult it is to get the job, and the less the job security. Higher-paying construction work tends to be seasonal and, during the season, the amount of work available is highly sensitive to business and weather conditions and to the changing requirements of individual projects.[11] Moreover, high-paying construction jobs are frequently beyond the physical capacity of some of the men, and some of the low-paying jobs are scaled down even lower in accordance with the self-fulfilling assumption that the man will steal part of his wages on the job.[12]

Bernard assesses the objective job situation dispassionately over a cup of coffee, sometimes poking at the coffee with his spoon, sometimes staring at it as if, like a crystal ball, it holds tomorrow's secrets. He is twenty-seven years old. He and the woman with whom he lives have a baby son, and she has another child by another man. Bernard does odd jobs — mostly painting — but here it is the end of January, and his last job was with the Post Office during the Christmas mail rush. He would like postal work as a steady job, he says. It pays well (about $2.00 an hour) but he has twice failed the Post Office examination (he graduated

---

[11] The overall result is that, in the long run, a Negro laborer's earnings are not substantially greater — and may be less — than those of the busboy, janitor, or stock clerk. Herman P. Miller, for example, reports that in 1960, 40 percent of all jobs held by Negro men were as laborers or in the service trades. The average annual wage for nonwhite nonfarm laborers was $2,400. The average earning of non-white service workers was $2,500 (*Rich Man, Poor Man*, p. 90). Francis Greenfield estimates that in the Washington vicinity, the 1965 earnings of the union laborer who works whenever work is available will be about $3,200. Even this figure is high for the man on the streetcorner. Union men in heavy construction are the aristocrats of the laborers. Casual day labor and jobs with small firms in the building and construction trades, or with firms in other industries, pay considerably less.

[12] For an excellent discussion of the self-fulfilling assumption (or prophecy) as a social force, see "The Self-Fulfilling Prophecy," Ch. XI, in Robert K. Merton's *Social Theory and Social Structure*.

from a Washington high school) and has given up the idea as an imprac-
tical one. He is supposed to see a man tonight about a job as a parking
attendant for a large apartment house. The man told him to bring his
birth certificate and driver's license, but his license was suspended because of a backlog of unpaid traffic fines. A friend promised to lend him
some money this evening. If he gets it, he will pay the fines tomorrow
morning and have his license reinstated. He hopes the man with the job
will wait till tomorrow night.

A "security job" is what he really wants, he said. He would like to
save up money for a taxicab. (But having twice failed the postal examination and having a bad driving record as well, it is highly doubtful that
he could meet the qualifications or pass the written test.) That would be
"a good life." He can always get a job in a restaurant or as a clerk in a
drugstore but they don't pay enough, he said. He needs to take home at
least $50 to $55 a week. He thinks he can get that much driving a truck
somewhere . . . Sometimes he wishes he had stayed in the army . . .
A security job, that's what he wants most of all, a real security job . . .

When we look at what the men bring to the job rather than at what
the job offers the men, it is essential to keep in mind that we are not
looking at men who come to the job fresh, just out of school perhaps,
and newly prepared to undertake the task of making a living, or from
another job where they earned a living and are prepared to do the same
on this job. Each man comes to the job with a long job history characterized by his not being able to support himself and his family. Each man
carries this knowledge, born of his experience, with him. He comes to
the job flat and stale, wearied by the sameness of it all, convinced of his
own incompetence, terrified of responsibility — of being tested still again
and found wanting. Possible exceptions are the younger men not yet, or
just, married. They suspect all this but have yet to have it confirmed by
repeated personal experience over time. But those who are or have been
married know it well. It is the experience of the individual and the group;
of their fathers and probably their sons. Convinced of their inadequacies,
not only do they not seek out those few better-paying jobs which test
their resources, but they actively avoid them, gravitating in a mass to
the menial, routine jobs which offer no challenge — and therefore pose
no threat — to the already diminished images they have of themselves.

Thus Richard does not follow through on the real estate agent's
offer. He is afraid to do on his own — minor plastering, replacing broken
windows, other minor repairs, and painting — exactly what he had been
doing for months on a piecework basis under someone else (and which
provided him with a solid base from which to derive a cost estimate).

Richard once offered an important clue to what may have gone on
in his mind when the job offer was made. We were in the Carry-out, at a

time when he was looking for work. He was talking about the kind of jobs available to him.

> I graduated from high school [Baltimore] but I don't know anything. I'm dumb. Most of the time I don't even say I graduated, 'cause then somebody asks me a question and I can't answer it, and they think I was lying about graduating. . . . They graduated me but I didn't know anything. I had lousy grades but I guess they wanted to get rid of me.
>
> I was at Margaret's house the other night and her little sister asked me to help her with her homework. She showed me some fractions and I knew right away I couldn't do them. I was ashamed so I told her I had to go to the bathroom.

And so it must have been, surely, with the real estate agent's offer. Convinced that "I'm dumb . . . I don't know anything," he "knew right away" he couldn't do it, despite the fact that he had been doing just this sort of work all along.

Thus, the man's low self-esteem generates a fear of being tested and prevents him from accepting a job with responsibilities or, once on a job, from staying with it if responsibilities are thrust on him, even if the wages are commensurately higher. Richard refuses such a job, Leroy leaves one, and another man, given more responsibility and more pay, knows he will fail and proceeds to do so, proving he was right about himself all along. The self-fulfilling prophecy is everywhere at work. In a hallway, Stanton, Tonk and Boley are passing a bottle around. Stanton recalls the time he was in the service. Everything was fine until he attained the rank of corporal. He worried about everything he did then. Was he doing the right thing? Was he doing it well? When would they discover their mistake and take his stripes (and extra pay) away? When he finally lost his stripes, everything was all right again.

Lethargy, disinterest, and general apathy on the job, so often reported by employers, has its streetcorner counterpart. The men do not ordinarily talk about their jobs or ask one another about them.[13] Although most of the men know who is or is not working at any given time, they may or may not know what particular job an individual man has. There is no overt interest in job specifics as they relate to this or that person, in large part perhaps because the specifics are not especially relevant. To know that a man is working is to know approximately how

---

[13] This stands in dramatic contrast to the leisure-time conversation of stable, working-class men. For the coal miners (of Ashton, England), for example, "the topic [of conversation] which surpasses all others in frequency is work — the difficulties which have been encountered in the day's shift, the way in which a particular task was accomplished, and so on." Josephine Klein, *Samples from English Cultures*, Vol. I, p. 88.

much he makes and to know as much as one needs or wants to know about how he makes it. After all, how much difference does it make to know whether a man is pushing a mop or pulling trash in an apartment house, a restaurant, or an office building, or delivering groceries, drugs, or liquor, or, if he's a laborer, whether he's pushing a wheelbarrow, mixing mortar, or digging a hole. So much does one job look like every other that there is little to choose between them. In large part, the job market consists of a narrow range of nondescript chores calling for nondistinctive, undifferentiated, unskilled labor. "A job is a job."

A crucial factor in the streetcorner man's lack of job commitment is the overall value he places on the job. *For his part, the streetcorner man puts no lower value on the job than does the larger society around him.* He knows the social value of the job by the amount of money the employer is willing to pay him for doing it. In a real sense, every pay day, he counts in dollars and cents the value placed on the job by society at large. He is no more (and frequently less) ready to quit and look for another job than his employer is ready to fire him and look for another man. Neither the streetcorner man who performs these jobs nor the society which requires him to perform them assess the job as one "worth doing and worth doing well." Both employee and employer are contemptuous of the job. The employee shows his contempt by his reluctance to accept it or keep it, the employer by paying less than is required to support a family.[14] Nor does the low-wage job offer prestige, respect, interesting work, opportunity for learning or advancement, or any other compensation. With few exceptions, jobs filled by the streetcorner men are at the bottom of the employment ladder in every respect, from wage level to prestige. Typically, they are hard, dirty, uninteresting, and underpaid. The rest of society (whatever its ideal values regarding the dignity of labor) holds the job of the dishwasher or janitor or unskilled laborer in low esteem if not outright contempt.[15] So does the streetcorner man. He cannot do otherwise. He cannot draw from a job those social values which other people do not put into it.[16]

---

[14] It is important to remember that the employer is not entirely a free agent. Subject to the constraints of the larger society, he acts for the larger society as well as for himself. Child labor laws, safety and sanitation regulations, minimum wage scales in some employment areas, and other constraints, are already on the books; other control mechanisms, such as a guaranteed annual wage, are to be had for the voting.

[15] See, for example, the U.S. Bureau of the Census, *Methodology and Scores of Socioeconomic Status*. The assignment of the lowest SES ratings to men who hold such jobs is not peculiar to our own society. A low SES rating for "the shoeshine boy or garbage man . . . seems to be true for all [industrial] countries." Alex Inkeles, "Industrial Man," p. 8.

[16] That the streetcorner man downgrades manual labor should occasion no surprise. Merton points out that "the American stigmatization of manual labor

Only occasionally does spontaneous conversation touch on these matters directly. Talk about jobs is usually limited to isolated statements of intention, such as "I think I'll get me another gig [job]," "I'm going to look for a construction job when the weather breaks," or "I'm going to quit. I can't take no more of his shit." Job assessments typically consist of nothing more than a noncommittal shrug and "It's O.K." or "It's a job."

One reason for the relative absence of talk about one's job is, as suggested earlier, that the sameness of job experience does not bear reiteration. Another and more important reason is the emptiness of the job experience itself. The man sees middle-class occupations as a primary source of prestige, pride, and self-respect; his own job affords him none of these. To think about his job is to see himself as others see him, to remind him of just where he stands in this society.[17] And because society's criteria for placement are generally the same as his own, to talk about his job can trigger a flush of shame and a deep, almost physical ache to change places with someone, almost anyone, else.[18] The desire to be a person in his own right, to be noticed by the world he lives in, is shared by each of the men on the streetcorner. Whether they articulate this desire (as Tally does below) or not, one can see them position themselves to catch the attention of their fellows in much the same way as plants bend or stretch to catch the sunlight.[19]

Tally and I were in the Carry-out. It was summer, Tally's peak earning season as a cement finisher, a semiskilled job a cut or so above that of the unskilled laborer. His take-home pay during these weeks was well over a hundred dollars — "a lot of bread." But for Tally, who no longer had a family to support, bread was not enough.

. . . *has been found to hold rather uniformly in all social classes*" (emphasis in original; *Social Theory and Social Structure*, p. 145). That he finds no satisfaction in such work should also occasion no surprise: "[There is] a clear positive correlation between the over-all status of occupations and the experience of satisfaction in them." Inkeles, "Industrial Man," p. 12.

[17] "[In our society] a man's work is one of the things by which he is judged, and certainly one of the more significant things by which he judges himself. . . . A man's work is one of the more important parts of his social identity, of his self; indeed, of his fate in the one life he has to live." Everett C. Hughes, *Men and Their Work*, pp. 42–43.

[18] Noting that lower-class persons "are constantly exposed to evidence of their own irrelevance," Lee Rainwater spells out still another way in which the poor are poor: "The identity problems of lower class persons make the soul-searching of middle class adolescents and adults seem rather like a kind of conspicuous consumption of psychic riches" ("Work and Identity in the Lower Class," p. 3).

[19] Sea Cat cuts his pants legs off at the calf and puts a fringe on the raggedy edges. Tonk breaks his "shades" and continues to wear the horn-rimmed frames minus the lenses. Richard cultivates a distinctive manner of speech. Lonny gives himself a birthday party. And so on.

"You know that boy came in last night? That Black Moozlem? That's what I ought to be doing. I ought to be in his place."

"What do you mean?"

"Dressed nice, going to [night] school, got a good job."

"He's no better off than you, Tally. You make more than he does."

"It's not the money. [Pause] It's position, I guess. He's got position. When he finish school he gonna be a supervisor. People respect him. . . . Thinking about people with position and education gives me a feeling right here [pressing his fingers into the pit of his stomach]."

"You're educated, too. You have a skill, a trade. You're a cement finisher. You can make a building, pour a sidewalk."

"That's different. Look, can anybody do what you're doing? Can anybody just come up and do your job? Well, in one week I can teach you cement finishing. You won't be as good as me 'cause you won't have the experience but you'll be a cement finisher. That's what I mean. Anybody can do what I'm doing and that's what gives me this feeling. [Long pause] Suppose I like this girl. I go over to her house and I meet her father. He starts talking about what he done today. He talks about operating on somebody and sewing them up and about surgery. I know he's a doctor 'cause of the way he talks. Then she starts talking about what she did. Maybe she's a boss or a supervisor. Maybe she's a lawyer and her father says to me, 'And what do you do, Mr. Jackson?' [Pause] You remember at the courthouse, Lonny's trial? You and the lawyer was talking in the hall? You remember? I just stood there listening. I didn't say a word. You know why? 'Cause I didn't even know what you was talking about. That's happened to me a lot."

"Hell, you're nothing special. That happens to everybody. Nobody knows everything. One man is a doctor, so he talks about surgery. Another man is a teacher, so he talks about books. But doctors and teachers don't know anything about concrete. You're a cement finisher and that's your specialty."

"Maybe so, but when was the last time you saw anybody standing around talking about concrete?"

The streetcorner man wants to be a person in his own right, to be noticed, to be taken account of, but in this respect, as well as in meeting his money needs, his job fails him. The job and the man are even. The job fails the man and the man fails the job.

Furthermore, the man does not have any reasonable expectation that, however bad it is, his job will lead to better things. Menial jobs are not, by and large, the starting point of a track system which leads to even better jobs for those who are able and willing to do them. The busboy or dishwasher in a restaurant is not on a job track which, if negotiated skillfully, leads to chef or manager of the restaurant. The busboy or dishwasher who works hard becomes, simply, a hard-working busboy or dishwasher. Neither hard work nor perseverance can conceivably carry the janitor to a sitdown job in the office building he cleans up. And it is the apprentice who becomes the journeyman electrician, plumber, steam fitter or bricklayer, not the common unskilled Negro laborer.

Thus, the job is not a stepping-stone to something better. It is a dead end. It promises to deliver no more tomorrow, next month or next year than it does today.

Delivering little, and promising no more, the job is "no big thing." The man appears to treat the job in a cavalier fashion, working and not working as the spirit moves him, as if all that matters is the immediate satisfaction of his present appetites, the surrender to present moods, and the indulgence of whims with no thought for the cost, the consequences, the future. To the middle-class observer, this behavior reflects a "present-time orientation" — an "inability to defer gratification." It is this "present-time" orientation — as against the "future orientation" of the middle-class person — that "explains" to the outsider why Leroy chooses to spend the day at the Carry-out rather than report to work; why Richard, who was paid Friday, was drunk Saturday and Sunday and penniless Monday; why Sweets quit his job today because the boss looked at him "funny" yesterday.

But from the inside looking out, what appears as a "present-time" orientation to the outside observer is, to the man experiencing it, as much a future orientation as that of his middle-class counterpart.[20] The difference between the two men lies not so much in their different orientations to time as in their different orientations to future time or, more specifically, to their different futures.[21]

The future orientation of the middle-class person presumes, among other things, a surplus of resources to be invested in the future and a belief that the future will be sufficiently stable both to justify his investment (money in a bank, time and effort in a job, investment of himself in marriage and family, etc.) and to permit the consumption of his investment at a time, place and manner of his own choosing and to his greater satisfaction. But the streetcorner man lives in a sea of want. He does not, as a rule, have a surplus of resources, either economic or psychological. Gratification of hunger and the desire for simple creature comforts cannot be long deferred. Neither can support for one's flagging self-esteem. Living on the edge of both economic and psychological

[20] Taking a somewhat different point of view, S. M. Miller and Frank Riessman suggest that "the entire concept of deferred gratification may be inappropriate to understanding the essence of workers' lives" ("The Working Class Subculture: A New View," p. 87).

[21] This sentence is a paraphrase of a statement made by Marvin Cline at a 1965 colloquium at the Mental Health Study Center, National Institute of Mental Health.

subsistence, the streetcorner man is obliged to expend all his resources on maintaining himself from moment to moment.[22]

As for the future, the young streetcorner man has a fairly good picture of it. In Richard or Sea Cat or Arthur he can see himself in his middle twenties; he can look at Tally to see himself at thirty, at Wee Tom to see himself in his middle thirties, and at Budder and Stanton to see himself in his forties. It is a future in which everything is uncertain except the ultimate destruction of his hopes and the eventual realization of his fears. The most he can reasonably look forward to is that these things do not come too soon. Thus, when Richard squanders a week's pay in two days it is not because, like an animal or a child, he is "present-time oriented," unaware of or unconcerned with his future. He does so precisely because he is aware of the future and the hopelessness of it all.

Sometimes this kind of response appears as a conscious, explicit choice. Richard had had a violent argument with his wife. He said he was going to leave her and the children, that he had had enough of everything and could not take any more, and he chased her out of the house. His chest still heaving, he leaned back against the wall in the hallway of his basement apartment.

"I've been scuffling for five years," he said. "I've been scuffling for five years from morning till night. And my kids still don't have anything, my wife don't have anything, and I don't have anything.

"There," he said, gesturing down the hall to a bed, a sofa, a couple of chairs and a television set, all shabby, some broken. "There's everything I have and I'm having trouble holding onto that."

Leroy came in, presumably to petition Richard on behalf of Richard's wife, who was sitting outside on the steps, afraid to come in. Leroy started to say something but Richard cut him short.

"Look, Leroy, don't give me any of that action. You and me are

---

[22] And if, for the moment, he does sometimes have more money than he chooses to spend or more food than he wants to eat, he is pressed to spend the money and eat the food anyway since his friends, neighbors, kinsmen, or acquaintances will beg or borrow whatever surplus he has or, failing this, they may steal it. In one extreme case, one of the men admitted taking the last of a woman's surplus food allotment after she had explained that, with four children, she could not spare any food. The prospect that consumer soft goods not consumed by oneself will be consumed by someone else may be related to the way in which portable consumer durable goods, such as watches, radios, television sets, or phonographs, are sometimes looked at as a form of savings. When Shirley was on welfare, she regularly took her television set out of pawn when she got her monthly check. Not so much to watch it, she explained, as to have something to fall back on when her money runs out toward the end of the month. For her and others, the television set or the phonograph is her savings, the pawnshop is where she banks her savings, and the pawn ticket is her bankbook.

entirely different people. Maybe I look like a boy and maybe I act like a boy sometimes but I got a man's mind. You and me don't want the same things out of life. Maybe some of the same, but you don't care how long you have to wait for yours and *I — want — mine — right — now.*"[23]

Thus, apparent present-time concerns with consumption and indulgences — material and emotional — reflect a future-time orientation. "I want mine right now" is ultimately a cry of despair, a direct response to the future as he sees it.[24]

In many instances, it is precisely the streetcorner man's orientation to the future — but to a future loaded with "trouble" — which not only leads to a greater emphasis on present concerns ("I want mine right now") but also contributes importantly to the instability of employment, family and friend relationships, and to the general transient quality of daily life.

Let me give some concrete examples. One day, after Tally had gotten paid, he gave me four twenty-dollar bills and asked me to keep them for him. Three days later he asked me for the money. I returned it and asked why he did not put his money in a bank. He said that the banks close at two o'clock. I argued that there were four or more banks within

---

[23] This was no simple rationalization for irresponsibility. Richard had indeed "been scuffling for five years" trying to keep his family going. Until shortly after this episode, Richard was known and respected as one of the hardest-working men on the street. Richard had said, only a couple of months earlier, "I figure you got to get out there and try. You got to try before you can get anything." His wife Shirley confirmed that he had always tried. "If things get tough, with me I'll get all worried. But Richard get worried, he don't want me to see him worried. . . . He *will* get out there. He's shoveled snow, picked beans, and he's done some of everything. . . . He's not ashamed to get out there and get us something to eat." At the time of the episode reported above, Leroy was just starting marriage and raising a family. He and Richard were not, as Richard thought, "entirely different people." Leroy had just not learned, by personal experience over time, what Richard had learned. But within two years Leroy's marriage had broken up and he was talking and acting like Richard. "He just let go completely," said one of the men on the street.

[24] There is no mystically intrinsic connection between "present-time" orientation and lower-class persons. Whenever people of whatever class have been uncertain, skeptical or downright pessimistic about the future, "I want mine right now" has been one of the characteristic responses, although it is usually couched in more delicate terms: e.g., Omar Khayyam's "Take the cash and let the credit go," or Horace's "*Carpe diem.*" In wartime, especially, all classes tend to slough off conventional restraints on sexual and other behavior (i.e., become less able or less willing to defer gratification). And when inflation threatens, darkening the fiscal future, persons who formerly husbanded their resources with commendable restraint almost stampede one another rushing to spend their money. Similarly, it seems that future-time orientation tends to collapse toward the present when persons are in pain or under stress. The point here is that, the label notwithstanding (what passes for) present-time orientation appears to be a situation-specific phenomenon rather than a part of the standard psychic equipment of Cognitive Lower Class Man.

a two-block radius of where he was working at the time and that he could easily get to any one of them on his lunch hour. "No, man," he said, "you don't understand. They close at two o'clock and they closed Saturday and Sunday. Suppose I get into trouble and I got to make it [leave]. Me get out of town, and everything I got in the world layin' up in that bank? No good! No good!"

In another instance, Leroy and his girl friend were discussing "trouble." Leroy was trying to decide how best to go about getting his hands on some "long green" (a lot of money), and his girl friend cautioned him about "trouble." Leroy sneered at this, saying he had had "trouble" all his life and wasn't afraid of a little more. "Anyway," he said, "I'm famous for leaving town."[25]

Thus, the constant awareness of a future loaded with "trouble" results in a constant readiness to leave, to "make it," to "get out of town," and discourages the man from sinking roots into the world he lives in.[26] Just as it discourages him from putting money in the bank, so it discourages him from committing himself to a job, especially one whose payoff lies in the promise of future rewards rather than in the present. In the same way, it discourages him from deep and lasting commitments to family and friends or to any other persons, places or things, since such commitments could hold him hostage, limiting his freedom of movement and thereby compromising his security which lies in that freedom.

What lies behind the response to the driver of the pickup truck, then, is a complex combination of attitudes and assessments. The street-corner man is under continuous assault by his job experiences and job fears. His experiences and fears feed on one another. The kind of job he can get — and frequently only after fighting for it, if then — steadily confirms his fears, depresses his self-confidence and self-esteem until finally, terrified of an opportunity even if one presents itself, he stands defeated by his experiences, his belief in his own self-worth destroyed and his fears a confirmed reality.

[25] And proceeded to do just that the following year when "trouble" — in this case, a grand jury indictment, a pile of debts, and a violent separation from his wife and children — appeared again.

[26] For a discussion of "trouble" as a focal concern of lower-class culture, see Walter Miller, "Lower Class Culture as a Generating Milieu of Gang Delinquency," pp. 7, 8.

23

The impact of money
on an African subsistence economy
PAUL J. BOHANNAN

*In this article Paul Bohannan describes the early colonial econ-
omy of the Tiv of Nigeria and shows that it contained three
spheres of exchange. These spheres — subsistence, prestige,
and women in marriage — were separated by the rule that goods
from one could not be used to purchase goods in another without loss of prestige to one party in the exchange. When general-
purpose money was introduced from the West, it became
possible to equate the values of each sphere, and radical change
took place. The author discusses in detail the changes resulting
from the introduction of money.*

It has often been claimed that money was to be found in much of the
African continent before the impact of the European world and the
extension of trade made coinage general. When we examine these claims,
however, they tend to evaporate or to emerge as tricks of definition. It is
an astounding fact that economists have, for decades, been assigning
three or four qualities to money when they discuss it with reference to
our own society or to those of the medieval and modern world, yet the
moment they have gone to ancient history or to the societies and economies studied by anthropologists they have sought the "real" nature of
money by allowing only one of these defining characteristics to dominate
their definitions.

All economists learned as students that money serves at least three
purposes. It is a means of exchange, it is a mode of payment, it is a

From "The Impact of Money on an African Subsistence Economy," *The Journal of Economic History* 19 (December 1959) : 491–503. Reprinted by permission
of the publisher and the author. Some footnotes, the bibliographic citations, and
the bibliography are omitted.

standard of value. Depending on the vintage and persuasion of the author of the book one consults, one may find another money use — storage of wealth. In newer books, money is defined as merely the means
of unitizing purchasing power, yet behind that definition still lie the
standard, the payment, and the exchange uses of money.

It is interesting that on the fairly rare occasions that economists discuss primitive money at all — or at least when they discuss it with any
empirical referent — they have discarded one or more of the money
uses in framing their definitions. Paul Einzig,[1] to take one example
from many, first makes a plea for "elastic definitions," and goes on to
point out that different economists have utilized different criteria in
their definitions; he then falls into the trap he has been exposing: he
excoriates Menger for utilizing only the "medium of exchange" criterion and then himself omits it, utilizing only the standard and payment criteria, thus taking sides in an argument in which there was no
real issue.

The answer to these difficulties should be apparent. If we take no
more than the three major money uses — payment, standard, and means
of exchange — we will find that in many primitive societies as well as
in some of the ancient empires, one object may serve one money use
while quite another object serves another money use. In order to deal
with this situation, and to avoid the trap of choosing one of these uses
to define "real" money, Karl Polanyi[2] and his associates have labeled
as "general-purpose money" any item which serves all three of these
primary money uses, while an item which serves only one or two is
"special-purpose money." With this distinction in mind, we can see
that special-purpose money was very common in pre-contact Africa,
but that general-purpose money was rare.

This paper is a brief analysis of the impact of general-purpose
money and increase in trade in an African economy which had known
only local trade and had used only special-purpose money.

The Tiv are a people, still largely pagan, who live in the Benue
Valley in Central Nigeria, among whom I had the good fortune to live
and work for well over two years. They are prosperous subsistence
farmers and have a highly developed indigenous market in which they
exchanged their produce and handicrafts, and through which they carried on local trade. The most distinctive feature about the economy of
the Tiv — and it is a feature they share with many, perhaps most, of

[1] Paul Einzig, *Primitive Money in Its Ethnological, Historical and Economic
Aspects* (London: Eyre and Spottiswoode, 1949), pp. 319–26.

[2] Karl Polanyi, "The Economy as Instituted Process," in Karl Polanyi, Con-
rad M. Arensberg, and Harry W. Pearson, eds. *Trade and Market in the Early Empires* (Glencoe, Ill.: The Free Press and The Falcon's Wing Press, 1957), pp. 264–66.

the pre-monetary peoples — is what can be called a multi-centric economy. Briefly, a multi-centric economy is an economy in which a society's exchangeable goods fall into two or more mutually exclusive spheres, each marked by different institutionalization and different moral values. In some multi-centric economies these spheres remain distinct, though in most there are more or less institutionalized means of converting wealth from one into wealth in another.

Indigenously there were three spheres in the multi-centric economy of the Tiv. The first of these spheres is that associated with subsistence, which the Tiv call *yiagh*. The commodities in it include all locally produced foodstuffs: the staple yams and cereals, plus all the condiments, vegetable side-dishes, and seasonings, as well as small livestock — chickens, goats, and sheep. It also includes household utensils (mortars, grindstones, calabashes, baskets, and pots), some tools (particularly those used in agriculture), and raw materials for producing any items in the category.

Within this sphere, goods are distributed either by gift giving or through marketing. Traditionally, there was no money of any sort in this sphere — all goods changed hands by barter. There was a highly developed market organization at which people exchanged their produce for their requirements, and in which today traders buy produce in cheap markets and transport it to sell in dearer markets. The morality of this sphere of the economy is the morality of the free and uncontrolled market.

The second sphere of the Tiv economy is one which is in no way associated with markets. The category of goods within this sphere is slaves, cattle, ritual "offices" purchased from the Jukun, that type of large white cloth known as *tugudu*, medicines and magic, and metal rods. One is still entitled to use the present tense in this case, for ideally the category still exists in spite of the fact that metal rods are today very rare, that slavery has been abolished, that European "offices" have replaced Jukun offices and cannot be bought, and that much European medicine has been accepted. Tiv still quote prices of slaves in cows and brass rods, and of cattle in brass rods and *tugudu* cloth. The price of magical rites, as it has been described in the literature, was in terms of *tugudu* cloth or brass rods (though payment might be made in other items); payment for Jukun titles was in cows and slaves, *tugudu* cloths and metal rods.[3]

None of these goods ever entered the market as it was institutionalized in Tivland, even though it might be possible for an economist to find the principle of supply and demand at work in the exchanges which

[3] B. Akiga Sai, *Akiga's Story* (London: International Institute of African Languages and Cultures, 1939), p. 382 and passim.

characterized it. The actual shifts of goods took place at ceremonies, at more or less ritualized wealth displays, and on occasions when "doctors" performed rites and prescribed medicines. Tiv refer to the items and the activities within this sphere by the word *shagba*, which can be roughly translated as prestige.

Within the prestige sphere there was one item which took on all of the money uses and hence can be called a general-purpose currency, though it must be remembered that it was of only a *very limited range*. Brass rods were used as means of exchange *within the sphere;* they also served as a standard of value within it (though not the only one), and as a means of payment. However, this sphere of the economy was tightly sealed off from the subsistence goods and its market. After European contact, brass rods occasionally entered the market, but they did so only as means of payment, not as medium of exchange or as standard of valuation. Because of the complex institutionalization and morality, no one ever sold a slave for food; no one, save in the depths of extremity, ever paid brass rods for domestic goods.

The supreme and unique sphere of exchangeable values for the Tiv contains a single item: rights in human beings other than slaves, particularly rights in women. Even twenty-five years after official abolition of exchange marriage, it is the category of exchange in which Tiv are emotionally most entangled. All exchanges within this category are exchanges of rights in human beings, usually dependent women and children. Its values are expressed in terms of kinship and marriage.

Tiv marriage is an extremely complex subject. Again, economists might find supply and demand principles at work, but Tiv adamantly separate marriage and market. Before the coming of the Europeans all "real" marriages were exchange marriages. In its simplest form, an exchange marriage involves two men exchanging sisters. Actually, this simple form seldom or never occurred. In order for every man to have a ward (*ingol*) to exchange for a wife, small localized agnatic lineages formed ward-sharing groups ("those who eat one Ingol" — *mbaye ingol i mom*). There was an initial "exchange" — or at least, distribution — of wards among the men of this group, so that each man became the guardian (*tien*) of one or more wards. The guardian, then, saw to the marriage of his ward, exchanging her with outsiders for another woman (her "partner" or *ikyar*) who becomes the bride of the guardian or one of his close agnatic kinsmen, or — in some situations — becomes a ward in the ward-sharing group and is exchanged for yet another woman who becomes a wife.

Tiv are, however, extremely practical and sensible people, and they know that successful marriages cannot be made if women are not consulted and if they are not happy. Elopements occurred, and sometimes a woman in exchange was not forthcoming. Therefore, a debt existed from the ward-sharing group of the husband to that of the guardian.

These debts sometimes lagged two or even three generations behind actual exchanges. The simplest way of paying them off was for the eldest daughter of the marriage to return to the ward-sharing group of her mother, as ward, thus cancelling the debt.

Because of its many impracticalities, the system had to be buttressed in several ways in order to work: one way was a provision for "earnest" during the time of the lag, another was to recognize other types of marriage as binding to limited extents. These two elements are somewhat confused with one another, because of the fact that right up until the abolition of exchange marriage in 1927, the inclination was always to treat all non-exchange marriages as if they were "lags" in the completion of exchange marriages.

When lags in exchange occurred, they were usually filled with "earnests" of brass rods or, occasionally, it would seem, of cattle. The brass rods or cattle in such situations were *never* exchange equivalents (*ishe*) for the woman. The only "price" of one woman is another woman.

Although Tiv decline to grant it antiquity, another type of marriage occurred at the time Europeans first met them — it was called "accumulating a woman/wife" (*kem kwase*). It is difficult to tell today just exactly what it consisted in, because the terminology of this union has been adapted to describe the bridewealth marriage that was declared by an administrative fiat of 1927 to be the only legal form.

Kem marriage consisted in acquisition of sexual, domestic and economic rights in a woman — but not the rights to filiate her children to the social group of the husband. Put in another way, in exchange marriage, both rights *in genetricem* (rights to filiate a woman's children) and rights *in uxorem* (sexual, domestic and economic rights in a woman) automatically were acquired by husbands and their lineages. In *kem* marriage, only rights *in uxorem* were acquired. In order to affiliate the *kem* wife's children, additional payments had to be made to the woman's guardians. These payments were for the children, not for the rights *in genetricem* in their mother, which could be acquired only by exchange of equivalent rights in another woman. *Kem* payments were paid in brass rods. However, rights in women had no equivalent or "price" in brass rods or in any other item — save, of course, identical rights in another woman. *Kem* marriage was similar to but showed important differences from bridewealth marriage as it is known in South and East Africa. There rights in women and rights in cattle form a single economic sphere, and could be exchanged directly for one another. Among Tiv, however, conveyance of rights in women necessarily involved direct exchange of another woman. The Tiv custom that ap-

proached bridewealth was not an exchange of equivalents, but payment
in a medium that was specifically not equivalent.

Thus, within the sphere of exchange marriage there was no item
that fulfilled any of the uses of money; when second-best types of
marriage were made, payment was in an item which was specifically not
used as a standard of value.

That Tiv do conceptualize exchange articles as belonging to different
categories, and that they rank the categories on a moral basis, and that
most but not all exchanges are limited to one sphere, gives rise to the
fact that two different kinds of exchanges may be recognized: exchange
of items contained within a single category, and exchanges of items
belonging to different categories. For Tiv, these two different types of
exchange are marked by separate and distinct moral attitudes.

To maintain this distinction between the two types of exchanges
which Tiv mark by different behavior and different values, I shall use
separate words. I shall call those exchanges of items within a single category "conveyances" and those exchanges of items from one category to
another "conversions." Roughly, conveyances are morally neutral; conversions have a strong moral quality in their rationalization.

Exchanges within a category — particularly that of subsistence, the
only one intact today — excite no moral judgments. Exchanges between
categories, however, do excite a moral reaction: the man who exchanges
lower category goods for higher category goods does not brag about his
market luck but about his "strong heart" and his success in life. The
man who exchanges high category goods for lower rationalizes his
action in terms of high-valued motivation (most often the needs of his
kinsmen).

The two institutions most intimately connected with conveyance
are markets and marriage. Conveyance in the prestige sphere seems (to
the latter-day investigator, at least) to have been less highly institutionalized. It centered on slave dealing, on curing, and on the acquisition
of status.

Conversion is a much more complex matter. Conversion depends on
the fact that some items of every sphere could, on certain occasions, be
used in exchanges in which the return was *not* considered equivalent
(*ishe*). Obviously, given the moral ranking of the spheres, such a situation leaves one party to the exchange in a good position, and the other
in a bad one. Tiv says that it is "good" to trade food for brass rods, but
that it is "bad" to trade brass rods for food, that it is good to trade your
cows or brass rods for a wife, but very bad to trade your marriage ward
for cows or brass rods.

Seen from the individual's point of view, it is profitable and possible to invest one's wealth if one converts it into a morally superior

category: to convert subsistence wealth into prestige wealth and both into women is the aim of the economic endeavor of individual Tiv. To put it into economists' terms: conversion is the ultimate type of maximization.

We have already examined the marriage system by which a man could convert his brass rods to a wife: he could get a *kem* wife and *kem* her children as they were born. Her daughters, then, could be used as wards in his exchange marriages. It is the desire of every Tiv to "acquire a woman" (*ngoho kwase*) either as wife or ward in some way other than sharing in the ward-sharing group. A wife whom one acquires in any other way is not the concern of one's marriage-ward sharing group because the woman or other property exchanged for her did not belong to the marriage-ward group. The daughters of such a wife are not divided among the members of a man's marriage-ward group, but only among his sons. Such a wife is not only indicative of a man's ability and success financially and personally, but rights in her are the only form of property which is not ethically subject to the demands of his kinsmen.

Conversion from the prestige sphere to the kinship sphere was, thus, fairly common; it consisted in all the forms of marriage save exchange marriage, usually in terms of brass rods.

Conversion from the subsistence sphere to the prestige sphere was also usually in terms of metal rods. They, on occasion, entered the market place as payment. If the owner of the brass rods required an unusually large amount of staples to give a feast, making too heavy a drain on his wives' food supplies, he might buy it with brass rods.

However, brass rods could not possibly have been a general currency. They were not divisible. One could not receive "change" from a brass rod. Moreover, a single rod was worth much more than the usual market purchases for any given day of most Tiv subsistence traders. Although it might be possible to buy chickens with brass rods, one would have to have bought a very large quantity of yams to equal one rod, and to buy an item like pepper with rods would be laughable.

Brass rods, thus, overlapped from the prestige to the subsistence sphere on some occasions, but only on special occasions and for large purchases.

Not only is conversion possible, but it is encouraged — it is, in fact, the behavior which proves a man's worth. Tiv are scornful of a man who is merely rich in subsistence goods (or, today, in money). If, having adequate subsistence, he does not seek prestige in accordance with the old counters, or if he does not strive for more wives, and hence more children, the fault must be personal inadequacy. They also note that they all try to keep a man from making conversions; jealous kinsmen of a rich man will bewitch him and his people by fetishes, in order to make him expend his wealth on sacrifices to repair the fetishes, thus maintain- ing economic equality. However, once a conversion has been made, de- mands of kinsmen are not effective — at least, they take a new form.

Therefore, the man who successfully converts his wealth into higher categories is successful — he has a "strong heart." He is both feared and respected.

In this entire process, metal rods hold a pivotal position, and it is not surprising that early administrators considered them money. Orig- inally imported from Europe, they were used as "currency" in some part of southern Nigeria in the slave trade. They are dowels about a quarter of an inch in diameter and some three feet long; they can be made into jewelry, and were used as a source of metal for castings.

Whatever their use elsewhere, brass rods in Tivland had some but not all of the attributes of money. Within the prestige sphere, they were used as a standard of equivalence, and they were a medium of exchange; they were also a mode for storage of wealth, and were used as payment. In short, brass rods were a general-purpose currency *within the prestige sphere*. However, outside of the prestige sphere — markets and mar- riage were the most active institutions of exchange outside it — brass rods fulfilled only one of these functions of money: payment. We have examined in detail the reasons why equivalency could not exist between brass rods and rights in women, between brass rods and food.

We have, thus, in Tivland, a multi-centric economy of three spheres, and we have a sort of money which was general-purpose money within the limited range of the prestige sphere, and a special-purpose money in the special transactions in which the other spheres overlapped it.

The next question is: what happened to this multi-centric economy and to the morality accompanying it when it felt the impact of the ex- panding European economy in the nineteenth and early twentieth cen- turies, and when an all-purpose money of very much greater range was introduced?

The Western impact is not, of course, limited to economic institu- tions. Administrative organizations, missions and others have been as effective instruments of change as any other.

One of the most startling innovations of the British administration was a general peace. Before the arrival of the British, one did not ven- ture far beyond the area of one's kinsmen or special friends. To do so was to court death or enslavement.

With government police systems and safety, road-building was also begun. Moving about the country has been made both safe and com- paratively easy. Peace and the new road network led to both increased trade and a greater number of markets.

Not only has the internal marketing system been perturbed by the introduction of alien institutions, but the economic institutions of the Tiv have in fact been put into touch with world economy. Northern Nigeria, like much of the rest of the colonial world, was originally taken over by trading companies with governing powers. The close linkage of government and trade was evident when taxation was introduced into Tivland. Tax was originally paid in produce, which was transported and sold through Hausa traders, who were government contractors. A few years later, coinage was introduced; taxes were demanded in that medium. It became necessary for Tiv to go into trade or to make their own contract with foreign traders in order to get cash. The trading companies, which had had "canteens" on the Benue for some decades, were quick to cooperate with the government in introducing a "cash crop" which could be bought by the traders in return for cash to pay taxes, and incidentally to buy imported goods. The crop which proved best adapted for this purpose in Tivland was beniseed (*sesamum indicum*), a crop Tiv already grew in small quantities. Acreage need only be increased and facilities for sale established.

There is still another way in which Tiv economy is linked, through the trading companies, to the economy of the outside world. Not only do the companies buy their cash crops, they also "stake" African traders with imported goods. There is, on the part both of the companies and the government, a desire to build up "native entrepreneurial classes." Imported cloth, enamelware, and ironmongery are generally sold through a network of dependent African traders. Thus, African traders are linked to the companies, and hence into international trade.

Probably no single factor has been so important, however, as the introduction of all-purpose money. Neither introduction of cash crops and taxes nor extended trading has affected the basic congruence between Tiv ideas and their institutionalization to the same extent as has money. With the introduction of money the indigenous ideas of maximization — that is, conversion of all forms of wealth into women and children — no longer leads to the result it once did.

General-purpose money provides a common denominator among all the spheres, thus making the commodities within each expressible in terms of a single standard and hence immediately exchangeable. This new money is misunderstood by Tiv. They use it as a standard of value in the subsistence category, even when — as is often the case — the exchange is direct barter. They use it as a means of payment of bridewealth under the new system, but still refuse to admit that a woman has a "price" or can be valued in the same terms as food. At the same time, it has become something formerly lacking in all save the prestige sphere of Tiv economy — a means of exchange. Tiv have tried to categorize money with the other new imported goods and place them all in a fourth economic sphere, to be ranked morally below subsistence. They have, of course, not been successful in so doing.

What in fact happened was that general-purpose money was introduced to Tivland, where formerly only special-purpose money had been known.

It is in the nature of a general-purpose money that it standardizes the exchangeability value of every item to a common scale. It is precisely this function which brass rods, a "limited-purpose money" in the old system, did not perform. As we have seen, brass rods were used as a standard in some situations of conveyance in the intermediate or "prestige" category. They were also used as a means of payment (but specifically not as a standard) in some instances of conversion.

In this situation, the early Administrative officers interpreted brass rods as "money," by which they meant a general-purpose money. It became a fairly easy process, in their view, to establish by fiat an exchange rate between brass rods and a new coinage, "withdraw" the rods, and hence "replace" one currency with another. The actual effect, as we have seen, was to introduce a general-purpose currency in place of a limited-purpose money. Today all conversions and most conveyances are made in terms of coinage. Yet Tiv constantly express their distrust of money. This fact, and another — that a single means of exchange has entered all the economic spheres — has broken down the major distinctions among the spheres. Money has created in Tivland a uni-centric economy. Not only is the money a general-purpose money, but it applies to the full range of exchangeable goods.

Thus, when semi-professional traders, using money, began trading in the foodstuffs marketed by women and formerly solely the province of women, the range of the market was very greatly increased and hence the price in Tiv markets is determined by supply and demand far distant from the local producer and consumer. Tiv react to this situation by saying that foreign traders "spoil" their markets. The overlap of marketing and men's long-distance trade in staples also results in truckload after truckload of foodstuffs exported from major Tiv markets every day they meet. Tiv say that food is less plentiful today than it was in the past, though more land is being farmed. Tiv elders deplore this situation and know what is happening, but they do not know just where to fix the blame. In attempts to do something about it, they sometimes announce that no women are to sell any food at all. But when their wives disobey them men do not really feel that they were wrong to have done so. Tiv sometimes discriminate against non-Tiv traders in attempts to stop export of food. In their condemnation of the situation which is depriving them of their food faster than they are able to increase production, Tiv elders always curse money itself. It is money which, as the instrument for selling one's life subsistence, is responsible for the worsened situation — money and the Europeans who brought it.

Of even greater concern to Tiv is the influence money has had on marriage institutions. Today every woman's guardian, in accepting money as bridewealth, feels that he is converting down. Although attempts are made to spend money which is received in bridewealth to acquire brides for one's self and one's sons, it is in the nature of money, Tiv insist, that it is most difficult to accomplish. The good man still spends his bridewealth receipts for brides — but good men are not so numerous as would be desirable. Tiv deplore the fact that they are required to "sell" (*te*) their daughters and "buy" (*yam*) wives. There is no dignity in it since the possibility of making a bridewealth marriage into an exchange marriage has been removed.

With money, thus, the institutionalization of Tiv economy has become uni-centric, even though Tiv still see it with multi-centric values. The single sphere takes many of its characteristics from the market, so that the new situation can be considered a spread of the market. But throughout these changes in institutionalization, the basic Tiv value of maximization — converting one's wealth into the highest category, women and children — has remained. And in this discrepancy between values and institutions, Tiv have come upon what is to them a paradox, for all that Westerners understand it and are familiar with it. Today it is easy to sell subsistence goods for money to buy prestige articles and women, thereby aggrandizing oneself at a rapid rate. The food so sold is exported, decreasing the amount of subsistence goods available for consumption. On the other hand, the number of women is limited. The result is that bridewealth gets higher: rights in women have entered the market, and since the supply is fixed, the price of women has become inflated.

The frame of reference given me by the organizer of this symposium asked for comments on the effects of increased monetization on trade, on the distribution of wealth and indebtedness. To sum up the situation in these terms, trade has vastly increased with the introduction of general-purpose money but also with the other factors brought by a colonial form of government. At the same time, the market has expanded its range of applicability in the society. The Tiv are, indigenously, a people who valued egalitarian distribution of wealth to the extent that they believed they bewitched one another to whittle down the wealth of one man to the size of that of another. With money, the degree and extent of differentiation by wealth has greatly increased and will probably continue to increase. Finally, money has brought a new form of indebtedness — one which we know, only too well. In the indigenous system, debt took either the form of owing marriage wards and was hence congruent with the kinship system, or else took the form of decreased prestige. There was no debt in the sphere of subsistence because there was no credit there save among kinsmen and neighbors whose activities were aspects of family status, not acts of money-lenders. The introduction of general-purpose money and the concomitant spread of the market has divorced debt from kinship and status and has created the notion of debt in the subsistence sphere divorced from the activities of kinsmen and neighbors.

In short, because of the spread of the market and the introduction of general-purpose money, Tiv economy has become a part of the world economy. It has brought about profound changes in the institutionalization of Tiv society. Money is one of the shatteringly simplifying ideas of all time, and like any other new and compelling idea, it creates its own revolution. The monetary revolution, at least in this part of Africa, is the turn away from the multi-centric economy. Its course may be painful, but there is very little doubt about its outcome.

24

Reciprocity in the marketplace: Tipping in an urban nightclub
KATHERINE CARLSON

*Economic cooperation underlies the remarkable human ability
to adapt and survive in virtually every part of the world. From
the desert to a Western factory, we have developed our ability
to work together, feel concern for each other's welfare, and meet
our obligations to provide others with things they need. But
occasionally we fail in our economic duty, and others remind us
of our transgressions. In this article Katherine Carlson describes
such a situation. She notes that cocktail waitresses, who depend
largely on tips for a living, often find customers less than willing
to tip. Faced with this problem, waitresses develop strategies to
remind customers of their responsibility, or to confront them
publicly with their economic duty.*

A man and a woman enter a busy Waikiki nightclub. Led to a table by a
doorman, they are soon approached by a waitress who greets them and
takes their order for drinks. The waitress returns in a few minutes with
their order, a bourbon and water and a margarita. After placing the
drinks in front of them, she says, "That will be four dollars, please," and
waits as the man fishes in his wallet for a five-dollar bill. "Here," he
says, handing her the money, "Keep the change." As she takes the cash
she thanks him, knowing the extra dollar is meant for her. She has
received a tip.

This example of tipping is familiar to most Americans. The custom
is an integral part of several economic transactions in which one person
serves another. Whenever we drink at a club, ride in a taxicab, eat at a

This paper was written especially for this volume and has never before been
published.

restaurant, or face a bellman who has just opened the door to our hotel room, we expect to give a gratuity to the person who has served us. For most people, tipping is a regular, though sometimes burdensome, obligation.

To the people who serve others — waitresses, waiters, coat check girls, porters, cab drivers — tips are both a blessing and a curse. They are a blessing because they provide extra, usually undertaxed, income, occasionally in substantial amounts. They are a curse because employers tend to underpay employees who receive tips, assuming that workers can derive an adequate living from gratuities. The end result for service personnel is a potentially large income subject to extreme fluctuation and instability. There are customers who regularly fail to live up to their tipping obligation, or who are at best unpredictable as tippers. There are also seasonal fluctuations, and unlike most salaried workers, the service employee is directly and immediately affected by a decline in business.

The problem is particularly acute for cocktail waitresses who work in busy clubs and have a minimum of contact with their customers. Ideally, a customer should tip the waitress at a rate amounting to no less than 15 percent of his bill. On a good night, many customers will live up to this expectation, and some may even tip as high as 50 percent. When tips are large, the waitress will make far more from them than she does from her wages. A large volume of business should increase tip income.

But many nights are bad. Customers may regularly depart without leaving a tip, or may give an amount far short of the customary sum. Several factors can contribute to a bad night. In Waikiki, where research for this paper was conducted, one of the slowest business periods for both tourists and local tradesmen is between Thanksgiving and Christmas. This season delivers few customers and those who do go to bars seem to be less generous. Accordingly, income from tips is low and the waitress's income drops substantially. The type of tourist is also important. Canadians, for example, are reputed to be heavy drinkers but poor tippers. Canadian tourists appear in large numbers during certain times of year, contributing to the waitress's work load but not to her income.

For the waitress, tips are income; regular wages are "extra." This view may stem from the fact that her working shift is short, usually no more than four or six hours a night. Although she considers herself employed full time, a waitress may work only twenty or thirty hours a week and receive an hourly wage set at the legal minimum. As a consequence, she feels that if she is not tipped, she is not being paid. It is not surprising, therefore, that she resents customers who undertip or fail to leave a tip at all, and that she attempts to do something about them. To obtain a desired minimum level of tipping income, she employs a set of strategies that can be called *tipping practices*.

Tipping practices are a complex set of strategies that play on the customer's personal reputation and sense of obligation. Practices may simply remind someone who has bought drinks that he is a customer and hence should tip, or they may amount to a public confrontation in which the customer loses face if he fails to leave a gratuity. In either case the waitress attempts to heighten the customer's awareness, and sometimes the awareness of those around him, that he has a particular kind of relationship with her that involves tipping. To understand the special nature of tipping practices, it is important to look at the reciprocal nature of tipping itself.

RECIPROCITY

When the couple in our opening example entered the Waikiki nightclub and ordered drinks, they really assumed two kinds of economic obligation. First, they contracted with the waitress for two drinks, a bourbon and water and a margarita, which had stated prices; by doing so they assumed the obligation to pay for the drinks. Anthropologists usually refer to this kind of economic transaction as market exchange. It fits the Western economic model based on price, supply, and demand and resembles the usual kind of buying and selling that Americans are familiar with in the marketplace.

But the couple, or more accurately the man, for it is males who generally pay bills and tip in nightclubs, also assumed a second kind of economic obligation. By ordering drinks he assumed the identity of customer, which is paired with the identity of waitress. One requirement of being a customer is to tip the waitress at the accepted rate. Economic transactions of this sort, which require exchange on the basis of one's role obligations, are called reciprocal exchange. Christmas and birthday gifts, dinner parties for friends, and tipping all fall into this category.

The sense of obligation associated with reciprocal exchange as opposed to that associated with market exchange limits the options open to the waitress who wishes to ensure adequate tips. Failure to pay for something in the market is prohibited by law. If a customer attempts to leave a nightclub without paying for his drinks, he will be stopped by a doorman, asked to pay, and eventually turned over to the police if he refuses to comply.

Reciprocal exchange is a different matter. Because his role obligates him to do so, the customer is expected to tip the waitress. But if he fails in this duty he cannot be arrested or even pressured by a doorman, for his obligation to tip is not buttressed by law. As in so many other roles we play in daily life, proper behavior can be enforced only through public pressure or can result from a sense of personal obligation to follow social norms.

The waitress must act within these limits when attempting to influence her customers. In fact, her approach can never be entirely direct. She is in the same position as the person who wishes to be invited to dinner at a friend's house or the man who wants his wife to buy him an expensive set of golf clubs for his birthday. She cannot simply state her desire for a tip just as these people cannot ask for what they want. To do so would threaten or even destroy the reciprocal relationship. Instead, she must communicate her desires and the customer's duty more subtly, a constraint that sets limits on the tipping practices she may use.

TIPPING PRACTICES

Tipping practices are the strategies used by waitresses to communicate their desire for tips and to ensure that customers leave an acceptably large gratuity. Not all tipping practices carry the same weight; some confront the customer with his duty more directly than others. Let us examine these different tipping strategies.

Personalizing the service. Personalizing the service is the most obvious route open to the waitress who wishes to ensure an acceptably large tip. Theoretically, the waitress's obligation in her relationship with a customer is to provide service. The more personal the service, the more likely the customer will recognize the reciprocal nature of the relationship and feel the need to fulfill his end of the bargain. There are a number of things the waitress can do to make the customer feel that he has received personal and special attention. To begin with, she greets him with a smile and a welcome before she asks for his drink order. She may also ask where he is from or find something else to talk with him about. But the amount of personal conversation is limited by demands on her time when the club is busy. She will probably engage in less small talk when business is heavy, for under busy conditions, stopping to talk to some may lead to unreasonable and resented delays for other customers.

The waitress may also improve the quality of her interaction with customers by being prompt with orders, emptying ashtrays regularly, and being attentive to their needs for new drinks. Again, she must be careful not to cross the line between good service and pushiness. Although the first may be rewarded, the second is likely to cause resentment and decrease the size of her tips. Instead, she combines a personal touch with efficiency, remembering which drink goes to which customer and the entire order for parties of several people who want another round. Although her ability to memorize large drink orders comes primarily from repeating them and inspecting empty glasses from the previous round, it makes each customer feel he is an individual, distinct within the crowd of people the waitress is serving. Her real feelings, of course, may be quite different as summed up by her comment to the bartender, "Here's scotch and water again."

Unfortunately for the waitress, personalized service is not always possible nor does it always work. When this strategy fails, she must resort to other tactics which tell the customer more clearly that he is expected to tip.

Reminders. Reminders symbolize the tipping transaction. To convey their message, all reminders depend in some way on the manipulation of the customer's change. Most customers do not have the correct change when they come to pay their bills. The act of giving the customer his change provides the waitress with an opportunity to remind him of his obligation to her. These reminders fall into three basic categories: laying the money on the table, using a tip tray, and using a tip tray with some change in quarters.

The simplest way to return change is by laying the money on the table. This act may seem relatively innocent but actually it contains some hints for the customer. Instead of placing the money in his hand, the waitress puts it on a surface that is part of her property or is at least her responsibility. She cleans the table, sets it up, and clears it off. Things left on it unclaimed will come to her. When a customer picks up his change from the table and places it in his pocket, he removes the money from her jurisdiction. Thus, he must consciously decide how much money to pick up from the table, a process that reminds him of an obligation to tip.

Knowing this, the waitress will even try to ignore a customer's action when he reaches out to take his change, for experience tells her that once he has his money in hand, he is much less likely to give any of it to her. Placing the money on the table also makes it easier for the customer to tip, because it gives him a surface from which to draw. Otherwise, he has to juggle the change in his hands.

One refinement associated with laying the change on the table involves the order in which the change is returned. The coins are put on the table first, and the bills placed on top of them. To retrieve his change, the customer must use two motions. First he must pick up the bills, and when he does, the coins are left to remind him that he should tip. If he decides to retrieve them, too, he must use a second or even a third motion, each symbolizing his unwillingness to live up to his responsibilities.

Laying the money on the table sometimes has a special advantage. The table top may be messy and wet from the remains of many drinks. Customers do not like to put wet money in their pockets so the waitress may put the money down where she is sure it will become damp. She does not care if her tips are wet and sticky.

In Hawaii, it is the custom in many bars for persons to place a "pool" of money on the table. When the waitress brings drinks, she draws money from this pool to pay for them and returns change to the same spot. On reorders, the waitress continues to draw bills from the pool, but will try to avoid taking any coins. After an evening of drinking, a considerable pile of change will have accumulated. The great number of coins may be seen as a burden by the customer, and because it looks like a minor sum of money, may be left as part of the waitress's tip. However, the pile may add up to a large amount of money.

Use of a tip tray represents a more insistent reminder to the customer. The tray is not only a receptacle designed for the return of change, it is, as its name signifies, an artifact that serves notice on the customer that he is expected to tip. Some hints associated with placing the customer's change on the table can be used with the tip tray as well — for example, change may be returned with the coins under the bills.

The tip tray can also be used with a practice that involves giving the customer ready-made tipping money. Called a *quarter break*, this practice involves dividing one dollar of the change into four quarters. Again, the extra change reminds the customer that he is expected to tip and provides him with the means to do so. The quarters make it easier for the customer by permitting him to tip less than a dollar when that amount would be too much. The practice of breaking change may be extended in the case of large bills. If a bill is fourteen dollars, for example, and the customer gives the waitress a twenty-dollar bill, she will return his change in the form of four quarters and five one-dollar bills. Breaking the five-dollar bill into ones makes a more definite statement that tipping is expected.

Most waitresses feel that the way coins are arranged on the tip tray also works to remind the customer to tip. They often place quarters in each corner of the tray or at least in some regular pattern. By this arrangement the customer is put on notice that the waitress is aware of the money on the tray and that she knows the customer has enough change to tip her. When tips have been especially bad, waitresses may experiment with different arrangements of quarters, trying to hit on the one that yields the best results. In one club, a waitress even bought a bag of Hershey "kisses" and began leaving them on the tip tray along with the change. She hoped that this additional "gift" would lead to larger tips, but she discontinued the practice when customers began to recover their change and leave her the candy.

Use of a tip tray may help counteract other problems. When money is left on the table, the waitress must wait for the customer to leave before she can collect it. Sometimes a prudent wife, more conservative with the family budget and perhaps a bit jealous of a gratuity meant for another woman who is attractive and revealingly dressed, will pick up the coins. As she sees the woman follow her husband out of the club, the waitress can only stand by and watch, helpless as her tip slips away from her. With the use of the tip tray the money is a bit safer. Once the customer has signaled his intention to tip her by taking some of his change, the waitress may be able to pick up the tray before he leaves. Such immediate tipping is preferable in clubs where customers leave the table to dance or where they move from one table to another.

Confrontations. When the waitress lays the money on the table or uses a tip tray, there is still the possibility that a customer will ignore the messages these acts communicate and will fail to tip her. Under these circumstances she may resort to more direct measures by confronting the customer. Confrontation requires the waitress's presence, which renders the customer's tipping behavior public. In using confrontation, the waitress takes full advantage of the customer's presumed uncertainty about tipping and of his embarrassment at being caught failing to reciprocate in his relationship with her. Aware of the customer's possible reluctance, the waitress attempts to convey the consequences of his failure to tip before it is too late. She does this by subjecting him to both visual and verbal embarrassment in the form of four strategies: making a fast pickup, using the cocktail tray, hiding the change, and lowering the cocktail tray.

Making a fast pickup is used in conjunction with the tip tray. If the amount of money on the tray is fairly small and can reasonably be given as a tip, the waitress will wait only a short time before she retrieves it. In one small club, waitresses have been known to make one circle of the room after returning the customers' change, then to return, pick up the tray, thank the customers, and walk off as if the money in the tray is meant for them. Some customers do intend to leave all the money on the tray for the waitress, but many simply have not had time to pick up their change. Once the waitress has left with the money, the only way a customer can retrieve change is by calling her back and publicly announcing that she has gotten away with his money. Should she be called back, the waitress will apologize, saying that she thought the money on the tray was her tip. Unless he wishes to look like a cheapskate the customer will have to let the waitress keep the money.

The cocktail tray is also used to confront the reluctant customer. The waitress uses her cocktail tray as a kind of personal tip tray, holding it out with the change on it for the customer to retrieve. She will complicate this process by using a quarter break and by placing the bills on top of the coins. The customer is faced with the task of picking up a pile of bills and change while the waitress looks on. She watches as he decides how much to tip her, and by her gaze she exerts considerable pressure. If he is uncertain about what is correct or expected, or even if he would prefer to leave a small gratuity, her presence is likely to make him opt for the role of big spender rather than that of cheapskate.

The cocktail tray offers another advantage. It is supported only by a woman's forearm providing a very unstable surface from which to pick up change. As the customer pushes down on the tray to pick up his change, it will move and wobble, giving the impression that he is overanxious to retrieve the money. In addition, the cocktail tray is usually wet. As a result, coins tend to stick to it. If he wants his change, the customer must painstakingly slide each coin off the tray separately, looking and presumably feeling like a penny pincher with each success-ful recovery. Rather than suffer this embarrassment and loss of esteem, which is made worse by the presence of the waitress, the customer will usually leave one or two quarters as a tip. He often does so with a sigh of exasperation, having given up in the battle for the change and waving the waitress away with a surly "Keep it." Again, she politely thanks him.

The waitress can make it even more embarrassing for the customer by lowering the tray, thus effectively exaggerating the instability of the tray's surface. If she moves her tray down just slightly as the customer reaches for his change, he will appear to grab for his money rather than pick it up. This will be apparent to others, and although the customer may suspect the waitress is behind his problem, he will also be affected by the way he has acted. Again, this may be sufficient to convince him that he should leave the change for the waitress.

A final variation in the use of the cocktail tray is a little like the fast pickup described above. Called *hiding the change*, it is a deliberate attempt to coerce the customer. To effect the strategy, the waitress places the coins very close to the lip of the tray under the bills. Because a cocktail tray has an edge that obscures part of its surface, it may be impossible for the customer to see the coins, causing him to retrieve only the bills. The waitress may exaggerate this problem by holding the tray above the seated customer's eye level. After he removes his hand and begins to put his bills away, the waitress dips the tray to show him the coins, says "Thank you," and walks away. By the time the customer realizes that his change amounted to more than just bills, and that the coins he has just seen and for which he has just been thanked have been taken as a tip, the waitress is gone. The only way he can get the money back is to call out to the waitress, announcing his cheapness to her and to everyone else within earshot.

CUSTOMER RESPONSE

Of course, customers are not entirely helpless in their exchanges with waitresses. They have at their disposal several techniques that interfere with the waitress's tipping practices. A customer may, for example, deny the waitress a medium for action by paying with the exact change or by using a credit card. Without the change as an operating tool, the waitress can do very little. Customers with exact change, however, are rare because it requires that their pockets be stuffed with coins.

The customer may also make specific requests to the waitress that deny her the use of tipping practices. He may require her to place the money on the table, for example, when she would like to give it to him on the cocktail tray. Or he may ask that she avoid giving him silver. The waitress can counter this request by claiming that she has no bills with which to make change, but there may be no point in doing so if it is clear that the customer will pick up his money in any form it is given to him. Customers may also ask the waitress to steady her cocktail tray, or more forcefully, reach out and stabilize it themselves. Customers who do this are often impervious to the impression it makes on those around them and will not succumb to any practice the waitress can employ.

In fact, a customer may ignore American cultural rules about tipping and the exchange of money without any sign of embarrassment. He may simply refuse or fail to recognize the existence of tipping practices when they are directed at him by the waitress. A surprising number of customers, for example, will methodically pick quarters off a sticky, unstable tray without worrying about the meaning that others may attribute to their actions. Such resistance may occur relatively frequently; it represents a response to pressure from the waitress. High-pressure techniques often lead to negative feelings between the two, for in using them, the waitress demands that the customer meet his obligations or pay a high social cost.

Finally, a customer may respond to the waitress by putting her off. He may say, "I'll tip you later," in an effort to reassure her that she is in his mind. Waitresses, however, are well aware that people who say this seldom do tip, or tip less than a reasonable amount. All the waitress can do is hope that a tip will come and be as attentive as possible to the customer's needs.

CLUB ATMOSPHERE

In larger perspective, the way tipping practices are employed says something about human relationships in public places. Waitresses do not regularly use all the practices available to them. Instead, certain practices seem to be used by most waitresses in particular nightclubs, indicating that there is something about the club environment itself that favors particular techniques.

The feature of clubs that seems most important in this respect is intimacy. Some nightclubs are felt to be intimate either because they are small, or because their space and activity give an illusion of intimacy.

Other clubs seem impersonal because they are large or crowded. Noise level, busy activity, and sexual display also contribute to the degree of intimacy or impersonality a club achieves. Even small clubs may appear impersonal if they are noisy, frantically busy, or marked by a live sex display, striptease show, or topless waitresses.

Although customers may not be conscious of the quality of their surroundings, their tipping behavior seems to conform to it. In intimate clubs they feel closer to the waitress. A regular relationship between the two is easily established. In impersonal clubs the reverse is true. Customers are likely to think of themselves as part of a faceless crowd. They may hardly notice the waitress, or they think of her merely as an employee of the establishment, paid for her work by the management, and having no special relationship with them.

It is not surprising, therefore, to discover that tipping practices are not usually employed by waitresses in very intimate clubs, or if used at all, they constitute reminders rather than confrontations. In impersonal nightclubs, on the other hand, confrontations are common. In fact, tipping practices may be part of a club's policy. New waitresses are told in some establishments to use their cocktail tray to return change, or engage in some other variety of confrontation with the customer.

Another feature of nightclubs that seems to affect customers is quality of service and entertainment. If a customer feels he is getting his money's worth because the quality of the drinks, the service, and the show is high, he is more likely to tip the waitress. But if the club offers a second-rate show, watery drinks, and poor service, a customer is likely to take his resentment out on the waitress by tipping her poorly or not at all. The situation may be made worse if the management wants waitresses to press drinks on customers or to rush them in any way. This sense of pressure can be found in many Waikiki nightclubs that boast exorbitant prices for drinks and poor shows. When customers are pleased with the nightclub, waitresses generally need not use tipping practices that confront the customer. But in nightclubs that dissatisfy the customer, confrontation practices are common and probably add to the customer's overall dislike of his surroundings.

CONCLUSION

As we have seen, two kinds of economic transaction operate between a waitress and her customer in a nightclub. In one, market exchange, the customer orders and pays for a commodity, the drinks. In the other, reciprocity, he tips the waitress because he must as part of his customer role. The first transaction is underwritten by legal sanctions and is almost always carried on without incident. The second transaction, reciprocity, is maintained only by informal obligation. What the waitress thinks she should receive as a tip may not coincide with what the customer feels he should give her. Because she depends on tips to make her living, the waitress uses tipping practices to remind the customer of his obligations. The simplest of these merely reminds the customer that he is expected to tip; more complex practices confront him with his duty.

The growth of impersonal public settings in the American hotel and entertainment industry may spell the end of tipping altogether. Perhaps because it is impossible to maintain the illusion of personal service and thus reciprocal obligation under these circumstances, there is more and more talk of abolishing tipping. A recent solution, however, has changed the nature of tipping as an economic transaction. In some clubs a service charge is automatically added to the customer's bill, making the tip part of the regular market transaction. In some clubs where the service charge is not included on the bill, a reminder that "tips are not included," is printed instead. In such cases the establishment itself uses a reminder to help the waitress get her tips.

As our mass society becomes less personal, reciprocal exchange becomes something of an anachronism within the larger market economy. In those reciprocal exchanges that remain, the market aspect of goods is downplayed by emphasizing the nonmonetary nature of the exchange and stressing "It's the thought, not the price of the gift, that counts." Although we tend to put a financial value on gifts, and expect to receive gifts of appropriate value in return, we downplay price in favor of emotion.

For tipping there is no such alternative. Travel and dining-out publications may advise customers about the extent of their tipping obligation, and some customers may even laboriously figure out the precise percentage of their bill as a basis for their tip, but the feeling of personal association between the customer and waitress is difficult to sustain. It seems impossible for the custom of tipping to last forever in large, impersonal settings. Nevertheless, waitresses, who are both recipients and enforcers of the reciprocal obligation as it is now defined, will continue to employ and adjust their tipping practices according to the necessities of the situation.

VIII

Law and politics

Every society faces the problem of controlling the behavior of its individual members. This task is accomplished in part by enculturation. As each individual learns the culture into which he or she is born, individual behavior conforms more and more closely to acceptable patterns. But no society has a perfect record of conformity. People do violate the rules of their culture, and choose to go against accepted ways of behavior. No culture can solve all conflicts of interest. Differences of opinion about the allocation of scarce resources arise and must be settled. Disputes break out and must be settled. It is for these reasons that law and politics are required by all societies.

Politics refers to the cultural processes used for making decisions that affect public policy. A band of hunters and gatherers must decide where to make camp for the night — a public policy decision. Citizens of a large city must decide where a new highway will be constructed — a public policy decision. The decisions differ and the political processes in which decisions are made also differ. But in each case politics is involved. Politics always involves power. Once a public policy decision, such as where to camp for the night, has been made, someone or some group has the power to enforce the decision. If a highway is to run through a residential section of a city and if a legitimate decision has been made, someone has the power to destroy or move the houses in the highway's path. In the selections that follow we see different ways that political power is exercised in widely variant cultures.

When disputes occur between individuals or groups within a society, law is needed. Law refers to processes — whether formal or informal — used for settling disputes. Every culture has means of settling disputes and of getting the people to accept the settlement. The legal and political systems cannot be thought of as separate parts of any culture, except for analytical purposes. In practice, both are backed by legitimate power and authority, and in many instances the two systems operate together. As the following selections will demonstrate, politics and law, while having similar functions from one society to the next, appear in a great variety of forms.

25

Yanomamö: The fierce people
NAPOLEON A. CHAGNON

Every society provides a basis for authority and ways to gain
support for such authority. In this article, Napoleon Chagnon
describes the Yanomamö, a group which bases its authority
structure on a continuum of violence and on claims to fierce-
ness or willingness to do violence.

The Yanomamö Indians are a tribe in Venezuela and Brazil who practice a slash-and-burn way of horticultural life. Traditionally, they have
been an inland "foot" tribe, avoiding larger rivers and settling deep in
the tropical jungle. Until about 1950 they had no sustained contact with
other peoples except, to a minor extent, with another tribe, the Carib-
speaking Makiritaris to the northeast.

I recently lived with the Yanomamö for more than a year, doing
research sponsored by the U.S. Public Health Service, with the cooperation of the Venezuela Institute for Scientific Research. My purpose was to study Yanomamö social organization, language, sex practices, and forms of violence, ranging from treacherous raids to chest-
pounding duels.

Those Yanomamö who have been encouraged to live on the larger
rivers (Orinoco, Mavaca, Ocamo, and Padamo) are slowly beginning to
realize that they are not the only people in the world; there is also a
place called Caraca-tedi (Caracas), from whence come foreigners of an
entirely new order. These foreigners speak an incomprehensible language, probably a degenerate form of Yanomamö. They bring malaria
pills, machetes, axes, cooking pots, and *copetas* ("guns"), have curious
ideas about indecency, and speak of a new "spirit."

Reprinted with permission from *Natural History* Magazine, January, 1967.
Copyright © The American Museum of Natural History, 1967. Illustrations are
omitted.

However, the Yanomamö remain a people relatively unadulterated by outside contacts. They are also fairly numerous. Their population is roughly 10,000, the larger portion of them distributed throughout southern Venezuela. Here, in basins of the upper Orinoco and all its tributaries, they dwell in some 75 scattered villages, each of which contains from 40 to 300 individuals.

The largest, most all-embracing human reality to these people is humanity itself; Yanomamö means true human beings. Their conception of themselves as the only true "domestic" beings (those that dwell in houses) is demonstrated by the contempt with which they treat non-Yanomamö, who, in their language, are "wild." For instance, when referring to themselves, they use an honorific pronoun otherwise reserved for important spirits and headmen; when discussing *nabäs* ("non-Yanomamö"), an ordinary pronoun is enough. Again, in one of the myths about their origin, the first people to be created were the Yanomamö. All others developed by a process of degeneration and are, therefore, not quite on a par with the Yanomamö.

In addition to meaning "people," Yanomamö also refers to the language. Their tribal name does not designate a politically organized entity but is more or less equivalent to our concept of humanity. (This, of course, makes their most outstanding characteristic — chronic warfare, of which I shall speak in detail — seem rather an anomaly.) Sub-Yanomamö groupings are based on language differences, historical separation, and geographical location.

For instance, two distinguishable groups, Waika (from *waikaö* — "to kill off") and Shamatari, speak nearly identical dialects; they are differentiated mostly on the basis of a specific event that led to their separation. The Shamatari, the group I know best, occupy the area south of the Orinoco to, and including portions of, northern Brazil. Their differentiation from the Waika probably occurred in the past 75 years.

According to the Indians, there was a large village on a northern tributary of the upper Orinoco River, close to its headwaters. The village had several factions, one of which was led by a man called Kayabawä (big tree). A notably corpulent man, he also had the name Shamatari, derived from *shama*, the "tapir," a robust ungulate found throughout tropical South America. As the story goes, Shamatari's faction got into a fight with the rest of the village over the possession of a woman, and the community split into two warring halves. Gradually the fighting involved more villages, and Shamatari led his faction south, crossed the Orinoco, and settled there. He was followed by members of other villages that had taken his part in the fight.

Those who moved to the south side of the Orinoco came to be called Shamataris by those living on the north side, and the term is now applied to any village in this area, whether or not it can trace its origin to the first supporters of Shamatari.

For the Yanomamö, the village is the maximum political unit and the maximum sovereign body, and it is linked to other villages by ephemeral alliances, visiting and trade relationships, and intermarriages. In essence, the village is a building — a continuous, open-roofed lean-to built on a circular plan and surrounded by a protective palisade of split palm logs. The roof starts at or near ground level, ascends at an angle of about 45 degrees, and reaches a height of some 20 to 25 feet. Individual segments under the continuous roof are not partitioned; from a hammock hung anywhere beneath it one can see (and hear, thanks to the band shell nature of the structure) all that goes on within the village.

The palisade, about three to six feet behind the base of the roof, is some ten feet high and is usually in various stages of disrepair, depending on the current warfare situation. The limited number of entrances are covered with dry palm leaves in the evening; if these are moved even slightly, the sound precipitates the barking of a horde of ill-tempered, underfed dogs, whose bad manners preadapt the stranger to what lies beyond the entrance.

A typical "house" (a segment under the continuous roof) shelters a man, his wife or wives, their children, perhaps one or both of the man's parents, and, farther down, the man's brothers and their families. The roof is alive with cockroaches, scorpions, and spiders, and the ground is littered with the debris of numerous repasts — bird, fish, and animal bones; bits of fur; skulls of monkeys and other animals; banana and plantain peelings; feathers; and the seeds of palm fruits. Bows and arrows stand against housepoles all over the village, baskets hang from roof rafters, and firewood is stacked under the lower part of the roof where it slopes to the ground. Some men will be whittling arrow points with agouti-tooth knives or tying feathers to arrow shafts. Some women will be spinning cotton, weaving baskets, or making hammocks or cotton waistbands. The children, gathered in the center of the village clearing, frequently tie a string to a lizard and entertain themselves by shooting the animal full of tiny arrows. And, of course, many people will be outside the compound, working in their gardens, fishing, or collecting palm fruits in the jungle.

If it is a typical late afternoon, most of the older men are gathered in one part of the village, blowing one of their hallucinatory drugs (ebene) up each other's nostrils by means of a hollow tube and chanting to the forest demons (hekuras) as the drug takes effect. Other men may be curing a sick person by sucking, massaging, and exhorting the evil spirit from him. Everybody in the village is swatting vigorously at the voracious biting gnats, and here and there groups of people delouse each other's heads and eat the vermin.

In composition, the village consists of one or more groups of patrilineally related kinsmen (*mashis*), but it also contains other categories, including people who have come from other villages seeking spouses. All villages try to increase their size and consider it desirable for both the young men and young women to remain at home after marriage. Since one must marry out of his *mashi*, villages with only one patrilineage frequently lose their young men to other villages; they must go to another village to *siohamou* (to "son-in-law") if they want wives. The parents of the bride-to-be, of course, want the young man to remain in their village to help support them in their old age, particularly if they have few or no sons. They will frequently promise a young man one or more of the sisters of his wife in order to make his stay more attractive.

He, on the other hand, would rather return to his home village to be with his own kinsmen, and the tendency is for postmarital residence to be patrilocal (with the father of the groom). If a village is rich in axes and machetes, it can and does coerce its poorer trading partners into permitting their young women to live permanently with the richer village. The latter thus obtains more women, while the poorer village gains some security in the trading network. The poor village then coerces other villages even poorer, or they raid them and steal their women.

The patrilineages that maintain the composition of the villages, rich or poor, include a man and his brothers and sisters, his children and his brothers' children, and the children of his sons and brothers' sons. The ideal marriage pattern is for a group of brothers to exchange sisters with another group of brothers. Furthermore, it is both permissible and desirable for a man to marry his mother's brother's daughter (his matrilateral cross-cousin) and/or his father's sister's daughter (his patrilateral cross-cousin) and, as we have seen earlier, to remain in his parents' village. Hence, the "ideal" village would have at least two patrilineages that exchanged marriageable people.

There is a considerable amount of adherence to these rules, and both brother-sister exchange and cross-cousin marriage are common. However, there are also a substantial number of people in each village who are not related in these ways. For the most part they are women and their children who have been stolen from other villages, segments of lineages that have fled from their own village because of fights, and individuals — mostly young men — who have moved in and attached themselves to the household of one of the lineage (*mashi*) leaders.

Even if the sex ratio is balanced, there is a chronic shortage of women. A pregnant woman or one who is still nursing her children must not have sexual relationships. This means that for as many as three years, even allowing for violations of the taboos, a woman is asexual as far as the men are concerned. Hence, men with pregnant wives, and bachelors too, are potentially disruptive in every village because they constantly seek liaisons with the wives of other men. Eventually such relationships are discovered and violence ensues.

The woman, even if merely suspected of having affairs with other men, is beaten with a club; burned with a glowing brand; shot with a barbed arrow in a non-vital area, such as the buttocks, so that removal of the barb is both difficult and painful; or chopped on the arms or legs with a machete or ax. Most women over thirty carry numerous scars inflicted on them by their enraged husbands. My study of genealogies also indicates that not a few women have been killed outright by their husbands. The woman's punishment for infidelity depends on the number of brothers she has in the village, for if her husband is too brutal, her brothers may club him or take her away and give her to someone else.

The guilty man, on the other hand, is challenged to a fight with clubs. This duel is rarely confined to the two parties involved, for their brothers and supporters join the battle. If nobody is seriously injured, the matter may be forgotten. But if the incidents are frequent, the two patrilineages may decide to split while they are still on relatively "peaceable" terms with each other and form two independent villages. They will still be able to reunite when threatened by raid from a larger village.

This is only one aspect of the chronic warfare of the Yanomamö — warfare that has a basic effect on settlement pattern and demography, intervillage political relationships, leadership, and social organization. The collective aggressive behavior is caused by the desire to accent "sovereignty" — the capacity to initiate fighting and to demonstrate this capacity to others.

Although the Yanomamö are habitually armed with lethal bows and arrows, they have a graded system of violence within which they can express their *waiteri*, or "fierceness." The form of violence is determined by the nature of the affront or wrong to be challenged. The most benign form is a duel between two groups, in which an individual from each group stands (or kneels) with his chest stuck out, head up in the air, and arms held back and receives a hard blow to the chest. His opponent literally winds up and delivers a close-fist blow from the ground, striking the man on the left pectoral muscle just above the heart. The impact frequently drops the man to his knees, and participants may cough up blood for several days after such a contest. After receiving several such blows, the man then has his turn to strike his opponent, while the respective supporters of each antagonist gather around and frenziedly urge their champion on.

All men in the two villages are obliged to participate as village representatives, and on one occasion I saw some individuals take as many as three or four turns of four blows each. Duels of this type usually result from minor wrongs, such as a village being guilty of spreading bad rumors about another village, questioning its generosity or fierceness, or accusing it of gluttony at a feast. A variant of this form of duel is side slapping, in which an open-handed blow is delivered across the flank just above the pelvis.

More serious are the club fights. Although these almost invariably result from cases in which a wife has been caught in an affair with another man, some fights follow the theft of food within the village. The usual procedure calls for a representative from each belligerent group. One man holds a ten-foot club upright, braces himself by leaning on the club and spreading his feet, then holds his head out for his opponent to strike. Following this comes his turn to do likewise to his adversary. These duels, more often than not, end in a free-for-all in which everybody clubs everybody else on whatever spot he can hit. Such brawls occasionally result in fatalities. However, since headmen of the respective groups stand by with bows drawn, no one dares deliver an intentionally killing blow, for if he does, he will be shot. The scalps of the older men are almost incredible to behold, covered as they are by as many as a dozen ugly welts. Yet, most of them proudly shave the top of their heads to display their scars.

Also precipitated by feuds over women are spear fights, which are even more serious than club fights. Members of a village will warn those of the offending village that they are coming to fight with spears. They specify that they are not planning to shoot arrows unless the others shoot first. On the day of the fight, the attackers enter the other village, armed with five or six sharpened clubs or slender shafts some eight feet long and attempt to drive the defenders out. If successful, the invaders steal all the valuable possessions — hammocks, cooking pots, and machetes — and retreat. In the spear fight that occurred while I was studying the tribe, the attackers were successful, but they wounded several individuals so badly that one of them died. The fighting then escalated to a raid, the penultimate form of violence.

Such raids may be precipitated by woman stealing or the killing of a visitor (visitors are sometimes slain because they are suspected of having practiced harmful magic that has led to a death in the host's village). Raids also occur if a man kills his wife in a fit of anger; her natal village is then obliged to avenge the death. Most raids, however, are in revenge for deaths that occurred in previous raids, and once the vendetta gets started, it is not likely to end for a long time. Something else may trigger a raid. Occasionally an ambitious headman wearies of peaceful times — a rarity, certainly — and deliberately creates a situation that will demonstrate his leadership.

A revenge raid is preceded by a feast in which the ground bones of the person to be avenged are mixed in a soup of boiled, ripe plantains (the mainstay of Yanomamö diet) and swallowed. Yanomamö are endocannibals, which means they consume the remains of members of their own group. This ceremony puts the raiders in the appropriate state of frenzy for the business of warfare. A mock raid — rather like a dress rehearsal — is conducted in their own village on the afternoon before the day of the raid, and a life-size effigy of an enemy, constructed of leaves or a log, is slain. That evening all the participants march, one at a time, to the center of the village clearing, while clacking their bows and arrows and screaming their versions of the calls of carnivorous birds, mammals, and even insects.

When all have lined up facing the direction of the enemy village, they sing their war song, "I am a meat-hungry buzzard," and shout several times in unison until they hear the echo return from the jungle. They then disperse to their individual sections of the village to vomit the symbolic rotten flesh of the enemy that they, as symbolic carnivorous vultures and wasps, partook of in the lineup. The same thing, with the exception of the song, is repeated at dawn the following morning. Then the raiders, covered with black paint made of chewed charcoal, march out of the village in single file and collect the hammocks and plantains that their women have previously set outside the village for them. On each night they spend en route to the enemy they fire arrows at a dummy in a mock raid. They approach the enemy village itself under cover of darkness, ambush the first person they catch, and retreat as rapidly as possible. If they catch a man and his family, they will shoot the man and steal the woman and her children. At a safe distance from her village, each of the raiders rapes the woman, and when they reach their own village, every man in the village may, if he wishes, do likewise before she is given to one of the men as a wife. Ordinarily she attempts to escape, but if caught, she may be killed. So constant is the threat of raids that every woman leaves her village in the knowledge that she may be stolen.

The supreme form of violence is the *nomohoni* — the "trick." During the dry season, the Yanomamö do a great deal of visiting. An entire village will go to another village for a ceremony that involves feasting, dancing, chanting, curing, trading, and just plain gossiping.

Shortly after arrival, the visitors are invited to recline in the hammocks of the hosts. By custom they lie motionless to display their fine decorations while the hosts prepare food for them. But now suppose that a village has a grudge to settle with another, such as deaths to avenge. It enlists the support of a third village to act as accomplice. This third village, which must be on friendly terms with the intended victims, will invite them to a feast. While the guests recline defenseless in the hammocks, the hosts descend on them with axes and sharpened poles, treacherously killing as many as they can. Those that manage to escape the slaughter inside the village are shot outside the palisade by the village that instigated the *nomohoni*. The women and children will be shared between the two accomplices.

Throughout all this ferocity there are two organizational aspects of violence. One concerns leadership: A man must be able to demonstrate his fierceness if he is to be a true leader. It is equally important, however, that he have a large natural following — that is, he must have many male kinsmen to support his position and a quantity of daughters and sisters to distribute to other men. Lineage leaders cannot accurately be described as unilateral initiators of activities; rather, they are the vehicles through which the group's will is expressed. For example, when a certain palm fruit is ripe and is particularly abundant in an area some distance from the village, everybody knows that the whole village will pack its belongings and erect a temporary camp at that spot to collect the fruit. The headman does little more than set the date. When his kinsmen see him packing, they know that the time has come to leave for the collecting trip. True, the headman does have some initiative in raiding, but not even this is completely independent of the attitudes of his followers, which dictate that a death must be avenged. However, when the purpose of a raid is to steal women, the headman does have some freedom to act on his own initiative.

As a general rule, the smaller his natural following, the more he is obliged to demonstrate his personal qualities of fierceness and leadership. Padudiwä, the headman of one of the lineages in Bisaasi-tedi, took pains to demonstrate his personal qualities whenever he could; he had only two living brothers and four living sisters in his group. Most of his demonstrations of ferocity were cruel beatings he administered to his four wives, none of whom had brothers in the village to take their part. Several young men who attached themselves to his household admired him for this.

Padudiwä was also responsible for organizing several raids while I lived with the villagers of Bisaasi-tedi. Every one of them was against Patanowä-tedi, a village that was being raided regularly by some seven or eight other villages, so that the danger of being raided in return was correspondingly reduced. On one occasion, when three young men from Patanowä-tedi arrived as emissaries of peace, Padudiwä wanted to kill them, although he had lived with them at one time and they were fairly close relatives. The murder was prevented by the headman of the other — and larger — lineage in the village, who warned that if an attempt were made on the lives of the visitors he himself would kill Padudiwä.

Obviously then, Padudiwä's reputation was built largely on calculated acts of fierceness, which carefully reduced the possibility of personal danger to himself and his followers, and on cunning and cruelty. To some extent he was obliged by the smallness of his gathering to behave in such a way, but he was certainly a man to treat with caution.

Despite their extreme aggressiveness, the Yanomamö have at least two qualities I admired. They are kind and indulgent with children and can quickly forget personal angers. (A few even treated me almost as an equal — in their culture this was a considerable concession.) But to portray them as "noble savages" would be misleading. Many of them are delightful and charming people when confronted alone and on a personal basis, but the greater number of them are much like Padudiwä — or strive to be that way. As they frequently told me, *Yanomamö täbä waiteri!* — "Yanomamö are fierce!"

26

Beating the drunk charge
JAMES P. SPRADLEY

*In the urban American court studied in the following article,
nearly 12,000 men are charged each year with public drunkenness. Though many post bail and go free, most of the poor
appear in court and place themselves at the mercy of the judge.
They are not entirely destitute, however, and have an elaborate
set of strategies for "beating the drunk charge." James Spradley
analyzes these strategies, shows their differential effectiveness,
and demonstrates how they reflect specific values of American
culture.*

It could be Miami, New York, Chicago, Minneapolis, Denver, Los Angeles, Seattle, or any other American city. The criminal court may be in
the basement of a massive public building constructed at the turn of the
century, or high above the city in a modern skyscraper. The judges who
hear the never-ending list of cases may be veterans of the bench or men
whose memories of law school are fresh and clear. But one scene does
not change. Each weekday morning a group of unshaven men file into
court with crestfallen faces, wrinkled clothing, and bloodshot eyes. They
stand before the prosecuting attorney and hear him say, "You have been
charged with public drunkenness, how do you plead?"

The most staggering problem of law and order in America today is
public drunkenness. In 1968 the F.B.I. reported that one and a half million arrests for this crime made up nearly one third of all arrests. This
means that every twenty seconds another person is arrested and charged
with being drunk in public. During 1967, in Seattle, Washington, 51 per-

This article was written especially for this volume. Some data presented here
are also published in a more complete study of this culture, entitled *You Owe Yourself a Drunk: An Ethnography of Urban Nomads,* 1970, Little, Brown and Company, Boston. Those interested in the meaning of various terms not explained here
should consult this ethnographic study.

cent of all arrests and 65 percent of all cases that appeared in the criminal court were for intoxication. In that same year the chief of police stated, "As a public official I have no choice. Whether alcoholism is a disease or not would not affect my official position. Drunkenness is a crime. So we must enforce the law by arresting people. We know in the Police Department that probably right at this moment there are more than two hundred men in the city jail serving sentences for drunkenness who have never posed any threat to the community in any fashion at all."

Who are these men that are repeatedly arrested for drunkenness? Who are the ones who spend much of their lives in jail for their public behavior? The first task in this study was to discover how these men identified themselves. This was necessary because the police, courts, social scientists, and most citizens see them as criminals, homeless men, derelicts, and bums who have lost the ability to organize their behavior in the pursuit of goals. The word these men used to identify their subcultural membership was the term *tramp*. There were several different kinds of tramps recognized by informants; for example, a "mission stiff" is a tramp who frequents the skid-road missions, while a "rubber tramp" travels about in his own car. This category system constitutes one of the major social identity domains in the subculture.

Tramps have other ways to conceptualize their identity when they "make the bucket," or are incarcerated. As an inmate in jail one is either a *drunk*, a *trusty*, a *lockup*, a *kickout*, or a *rabbit*. In the particular jail studied there are over sixty different kinds of trusties. This fact led some tramps to believe they were arrested to provide cheap labor for the police department. In their capacity as trusties, nearly 125 men provide janitorial service for the city hall, outlying police precincts, and the jail. They assist in the preparation of food, maintain the firing range, care for police vehicles, and do numerous other tasks. Most men soon learn that doing time on a drunk charge is not a desirable occupation, so they use many strategies to escape the confines of the jail or to reduce the length of their sentence. When a man is arrested he is placed in the drunk tank where he awaits his arraignment in court. Those sentenced to do time will spend it in close association with other tramps. If a man is not experienced in the ways of this culture, he will learn them while he is in jail, for it is a veritable storehouse of invaluable information for those who are repeatedly arrested for public intoxication. He will learn to think of himself as a tramp and to survive on the street by employing more than a dozen "ways of making it." More important, as he discovers that the jailhouse has a revolving door for drunks, he will do his best to "beat the drunk charge." The casual observer in court may find the arraignment and sentencing of drunk cases to be a cut-and-dried process. From the perspective of these men, however, it is more like a game of skill and chance being played by the tramp and law-enforcement agencies. In this article we shall examine the rules of this game, the strategies employed by tramps, and the underlying American cultural values that make it intelligible to the outsider.

PLANS FOR BEATING THE DRUNK CHARGE

Every culture contains one type of shared knowledge called *plans*. These are related to the achievement of goals. A plan is a set of rules that specifies a goal, conditions under which the goal will be chosen, techniques for the attainment of the goal, and conditions under which a particular technique will be used to attain the goal. The methods of ethnoscience are designed to map culturally shared systems of knowledge, and were used in this study to discover the plans tramps employ in their relationship to law-enforcement agencies.

The goal: Maximize freedom — minimize incarceration. There are many goals which tramps pursue. Most aims are referred to in a specific manner, such as "making a flop," "making a jug," "getting a dime," or "bailing out." Freedom is a general objective that includes such specific goals as rabbiting from jail, concealing one's identity, making a pay-off to a bull, leaving town, avoiding the police, and beating a drunk charge. Men do not always select one of these goals in order to maximize freedom — they sometimes even choose paths leading to *incarceration*. In a sample of a hundred men, 10 percent reported they had gone to jail and asked to be locked up in order to stop drinking. At other times a tramp will go to jail on his own to request a place to sleep or something to eat. Such cases are rare, and most tramps abhor imprisonment because they have learned a life style of mobility and the restrictions in the bucket lead to intense frustration. A testimonial to the fact that men do not seek imprisonment, as some outsiders believe, is the large number of strategies this culture has for avoiding incarceration. Almost every experience in the tramp world is defined, in part, by noting the degree of risk it entails for being jailed.

Techniques for the attainment of the goal. Because of the public nature of their life style, sooner or later most of these men end up in jail. Their specific objective at that time is to "beat the drunk charge." If successful, this could mean freedom in a few hours or at least a sentence of shorter duration than they would otherwise have received. The techniques for reaching this goal were discovered during interviews in which informants were asked: "Are there different ways to beat a drunk charge?" They responded with many specific instances in which they had taken action to beat the charge. These were classified as follows:

1. Bail out.
2. Bond out.

  3. Request a continuance.
  4. Have a good record.
  5. Use an alias.
  6. Plead guilty.
  7. Hire a defense attorney.
  8. Plead not guilty.
  9. Submit a writ of habeas corpus.
  10. Make a statement:
      a. Talk of family ties.
      b. Talk of present job.
      c. Talk of intent to work.
      d. Tell of extenuating circumstances.
      e. Offer to leave town.
  11. Request the treatment center (alcoholic).

Each of these techniques labels a *category* of many different acts that are considered equivalent. For example, a man may bail out by using money he had with him when arrested, by borrowing from another man in jail, by contacting an employer who loans or gives him the money, and so on. There are several ways to "have a good record": a man must stay out of jail for at least six months for his record to begin to affect the length of his jail sentence. In order to do this a man may travel, quit drinking, stay off skid road, or go to an alcoholism treatment center for a long stay. Each kind of statement includes specific instances, varying from one man to another and from one time to the next. This category system is extremely important to tramps. Once they have learned these techniques, they practice them until their skill increases. Judges may consider an old-time tramp as a "con artist," but in this culture he is a man with expertise in carrying out these culturally shared techniques.

Conditions influencing selection. When a man is arrested he must process a great deal of information before he makes a decision to employ one or more of these techniques. He must assess his own resources, the probabilities of success, the risk of doing more time, etc. He needs to know the sentencing practices of the judge, the population of the jail, and the weather conditions. The most important factors that influence his decision are shown in Table I.

AMERICAN CULTURAL VALUES

Every society is based upon shared values — conceptions of the desirable in human experience. They are the basis for rewards and punishments. It is not surprising to most Americans that our culture, like most others, has rules about the undesirability of certain behavior *in public*. We have outlawed nudity, begging, drinking, elimination of wastes, and

TABLE I. *Conditions influencing selection of a way to beat a drunk charge*

Strategy	Risk of outcome?	Risk offending bulls?	Risk getting more time?	Risk doing dead time?	Money needed?
Bail out	No	No	No	No	$20
Bond out	No	No	No	No	$20+
Request a continuance	Yes	Yes	No	Yes	Yes
Have a good record	No	No	No	No	No
Use an alias	Yes	Yes	Yes	No	No
Plead guilty	Yes	No	No	No	No
Hire a defense attorney	Yes	Yes	No	Yes	Yes
Plead not guilty	Yes	Yes	Yes	Yes	No
Submit a writ of habeas corpus	Yes	Yes	Yes	Yes	No
Make a statement	Yes	No	Yes	No	No
Request a treatment center	Yes	Yes	Yes	Yes	No

intoxication in public places. We are offended by many other acts — if they occur in public. Tramps are booked for public intoxication, but they are often arrested because they urinate, sleep, or drink in some public place. Poverty has made it impossible for them to conceal their behavior behind the walls of a home. The extent of these restrictions upon *public* acts are in contrast to many non-Western societies where there is a wider range of acceptable public behavior. Because public drunkenness, which covers a multitude of other public sins, involves more arrests each year than any other crime, we may conclude that *privacy* is an important value in our culture.

Above the judge's bench in the criminal court where this study took place, there is a large wooden plaque inscribed "Equal Justice for All Under the Law." Given the laws prohibiting public behavior of various kinds, we might still expect that the punishment for violation would be distributed *equally*. Thus, if two men with the same criminal record are found guilty of the same crime, they should receive the same punishment. If two men are found drunk in public for the first time, it would be unfair to fine one a few dollars and require the other to pay several hundred dollars. Upon examining the penalties given for public drunkenness, we discover a rather startling fact: *the less a man conforms to other American values, the more severe his punishment* — not because he violates other laws, but because he does not conform to the values of *materialism, moralism,* and *work.* These values are the basis for a set of implicit "punishment rules." Although they are unwritten, those who administer justice in our society have learned to punish the drunk offender on the basis of these rules.

Rule 1: *When guilty of public drunkenness, a man deserves greater punishment if he is poor*. In every society, when individuals violate legal norms they are punished. Physical torture, public humiliation, incarceration, and banishment from the society are some of the forms this punishment takes. It is not surprising that in our society, with its emphasis upon the value of material goods, violators are punished by making them give up some form of property. An individual may be fined after he has been convicted of public drunkenness. Most offenders pay money in the form of a "bail" prior to conviction. A few hours after being arrested, most men are able to be released from jail in a sober condition. They are still innocent before the law and an arraignment is scheduled at which time they may plead guilty or not guilty. If they enter the latter plea, they must appear in court at another time for a trial. In order to insure that a man returns for his arraignment he is asked to deposit bail money with the court, which will be returned to him when he is sentenced or acquitted. In most courts a man may choose to ignore the arraignment and thereby "forfeit" his bail. It is still within the power of the court to issue a warrant for his arrest in this case and compel him to appear in court, but this is seldom done. Instead, much like bail for a traffic violation, forfeiture of the drunk bail is considered as a just recompense to society for appearing drunk in public.

When arrested, tramps are eager to post bail since it means an immediate release from jail. They do not need to wait for the arraignment which may not occur for several days. The bail is $20 and is almost always forfeited. This system of punishment treats offenders equally — *unless a man does not have $20.*

Those who are caught in the grip of poverty are usually convicted, and their punishment is "doing time" instead of "paying money." In America, the rich have money, the poor have time. It might be possible to punish men equitably using these two different commodities but such is not the case. If a man is poor he must be unwilling to expend his energies in the pursuit of materialism, and therefore his punishment should be more severe than that given to those with money. How does this occur? Each time a man is arrested his bail is always twenty dollars, but if he is indigent, his sentences become longer with each conviction. A man can be arrested hundreds of times and bail out for only twenty dollars, but not if he is poor. Consider the case of one man who was arrested in Seattle over one hundred times during a twenty-one-year period. On many arrests he bailed out, but for about seventy convictions he was sentenced to jail, and gradually his sentences grew to the maximum of six months for a single arrest. During this period he was sentenced to nearly fourteen years in jail — a punishment he could have avoided for only a hundred dollars for each of those years. This man was given a life sentence on the installment plan, not for being drunk but for being poor. There are many cases where a rich man and a poor man are arrested and booked for drunkenness on the same night. The rich man is released in a few hours because he had twenty dollars. The poor man is released in a few months because he did not have twenty dollars. One way then to beat a drunk charge is to bail out. If you do not have money, it is still possible to use this strategy by bonding out or asking for a continuance. A bond requires some collateral or assurance that the twenty dollars *plus* a fee to the bondsman will be paid. A continuance enables you to wait a few more days before being sentenced, and during that time, it may be possible to get money from a friend or an employer. Whether he can use these ways to beat a drunk charge or not, the tramp who is repeatedly arrested soon learns he is being punished because he does not conform to the value of materialism.

Rule 2: *When guilty of public drunkenness, a man deserves greater punishment if he has a bad reputation.* Most cultures have a moralistic quality that often leads to stereotyping and generalizing about the quality of a man's character. In our society once a person has been convicted of a crime, he is viewed by others with suspicion. He may never violate legal norms again, but for all practical purposes he is morally reprehensible. Since judges increase the length of a man's sentence with each arrest, he must engage in behavior designed to give him a "good record" if he is to beat the drunk charge. One way to do this is by travelling. For example, if a man stayed out of jail in Seattle for six months, subsequent convictions would begin again with short sentences; thus, when arrested several times, he often decided it would be better if he went to another town. When his arrest record began to grow in this new place, he would move on; after a period of time he would return to Seattle. Men learn to calculate the number of "days hanging" for each city where they are arrested, and their mobility is determined by the magnitude of the next sentence. Some men use an alias when arrested in an attempt to obscure the fact that they have a long record. If this ploy is successful, a man who, because of his record, deserves a sentence of six months, may only be given two or three days. Another way to beat a drunk charge is to volunteer to go to an alcoholism treatment center. A man may not believe that he is an alcoholic or even that he has a "drinking problem," but if he will agree with society's judgment — that his long record of arrests shows he is morally debased — and ask to be helped, his incarceration will be reduced. But not all men are candidates for treatment. Those with the worst records are rejected and must do their time in jail. A man with a bad reputation thus will be given a more severe punishment for the same crime than one with a good reputation.

Rule 3: *When guilty of public drunkenness, a man deserves greater punishment if he does not have a steady job.* American culture places great value on work as an end in itself. Resistance to hippies and welfare programs alike is based, in part, on the value of work. Tramps know that judges punish more severely those who do not have steady employment. If a man cannot beat a drunk charge in some other way, he will make a statement telling the judge that he will find a job, return to a former job, or provide evidence that he is currently employed in a respectable occupation. Tramps often earn a living by "junking" to find things to sell, "spot jobbing," or "panhandling" (begging on the street) — but all these "occupations" are not admired in our society and cannot be used as evidence that one is conforming to the value of work. When a man appears in court with evidence that he is working, the judge will often suspend or shorten his sentence.

Tramps who have been unable to beat the drunk charge before being sentenced may capitalize on this value in another way. One man reported that he had written a letter to himself while in jail. The letter appeared to have been written by an employer in another city offering the man a steady job. The inmate asked another man who was being released from jail to carry the letter to that city and mail it from there. When it arrived, he used it to convince the judge that he should receive an early release in order to accept steady employment. Another inmate, when released from jail, went personally to the judge and pretended to be a contractor; he told him that a man who had worked for him was in jail and he would employ him if he were released. The judge complied with the request, and the two tramps left town together — proud of their achievement, surer than ever that one of the best ways to beat a drunk charge was to understand the value of work in American culture.

The values our culture places upon privacy, materialism, moralism, and work are not the only ones affecting the lives of tramps. These are men who live in a society that holds no place for them. Their life style is offensive to most Americans, and for this reason they are arrested, jailed, and punished by standards that do not apply to the rest of society. In response to these practices they have learned a culture with well-developed plans for survival. They have adopted a nomadic style of life — moving from one urban center to another to maximize their freedom. In spite of their efforts, sooner or later, most tramps find themselves arrested, and it is then that the techniques for beating a drunk charge will be found most useful.

27

Poor man, rich man, big-man, chief
MARSHALL D. SAHLINS

*Melanesia and Polynesia provide an interesting contrast in
political complexity, as Marshall Sahlins describes in the following article. The Melanesian "big-man" is the self-made leader
of his small localized kinship group, whereas the Polynesian
chief is a "born" leader. The Polynesian system, which depends
upon the ascribed right of its chief to lead, attains far larger
proportions than the Melanesian structure, which depends on
the ability of certain individuals to influence others.*

With an eye to their own life goals, the native peoples of Pacific Islands
unwittingly present to anthropologists a generous scientific gift: an extended series of experiments in cultural adaptation and evolutionary development. They have compressed their institutions within the confines
of infertile coral atolls, expanded them on volcanic islands, created with
the means history gave them cultures adapted to the deserts of Australia,
the mountains and warm coasts of New Guinea, the rain forests of the
Solomon Islands. From the Australian Aborigines, whose hunting and
gathering existence duplicates in outline the cultural life of the later
Paleolithic, to the great chiefdoms of Hawaii, where society approached
the formative levels of the old Fertile Crescent civilizations, almost every
general phase in the progress of primitive culture is exemplified.

Where culture so experiments, anthropology finds its laboratories
— makes its comparisons.

In the southern and eastern Pacific two contrasting cultural provinces have long evoked anthropological interest: *Melanesia*, including
New Guinea, the Bismarcks, Solomons, and island groups east to Fiji;

From "Poor Man, Rich Man, Big-Man, Chief: Political Types in Melanesia
and Polynesia," *Comparative Studies in Society and History* 5 (April 1963) : 285–
303. Reprinted by permission of Cambridge University Press. Many footnotes, the
bibliographic citations, and the bibliography are omitted.

and *Polynesia*, consisting in its main portion of the triangular constella-
tion of lands between New Zealand, Easter Island, and the Hawaiian
Islands. In and around Fiji, Melanesia and Polynesia intergrade culturally, but west and east of their intersection the two provinces pose
broad contrasts in several sectors: in religion, art, kinship groupings,
economics, political organization. The differences are the more notable
for the underlying similarities from which they emerge. Melanesia and
Polynesia are both agricultural regions in which many of the same crops
— such as yams, taro, breadfruit, bananas, and coconuts — have long
been cultivated by many similar techniques. Some recently presented
linguistic and archaeological studies indeed suggest that Polynesian cultures originated from an eastern Melanesian hearth during the first millennium B.C. Yet in anthropological annals the Polynesians were to become famous for elaborate forms of rank and chieftainship, whereas
most Melanesian societies broke off advance on this front at more rudimentary levels.

It is obviously imprecise, however, to make out the political contrast
in broad culture-area terms. Within Polynesia, certain of the islands,
such as Hawaii, the Society Islands and Tonga, developed unparalleled
political momentum. And not all Melanesian polities, on the other side,
were constrained and truncated in their evolution. In New Guinea and
nearby areas of western Melanesia, small and loosely ordered political
groupings are numerous, but in eastern Melanesia, New Caledonia and
Fiji for example, political approximations of the Polynesian condition
become common. There is more of an upward west to east slope in political development in the southern Pacific than a step-like, quantum
progression. It is quite revealing, however, to compare the extremes of
this continuum, the western Melanesian underdevelopment against the
greater Polynesian chiefdoms. While such comparison does not exhaust
the evolutionary variations, it fairly establishes the scope of overall
political achievement in this Pacific phylum of cultures.

Measurable along several dimensions, the contrast between developed Polynesian and underdeveloped Melanesian polities is immediately
striking for differences in scale. H. Ian Hogbin and Camilla Wedgwood
concluded from a survey of Melanesian (most western Melanesian) societies that ordered, independent political bodies in the region typically
include seventy to three hundred persons; more recent work in the New
Guinea Highlands suggests political groupings of up to a thousand, occasionally a few thousand, people.[1] But in Polynesia sovereignties of two
thousand or three thousand are run-of-the-mill, and the most advanced

[1] H. Ian Hogbin and Camilla H. Wedgwood, "Local Groupings in Melanesia,"
Oceania 23 (1952–53) : 241–276; 24 (1953–54) : 58–76.

chiefdoms, as in Tonga or Hawaii, might claim ten thousand, even tens of thousands. Varying step by step with such differences in size of the polity are differences in territorial extent: from a few square miles in western Melanesia to tens or even hundreds of square miles in Polynesia.

The Polynesian advance in political scale was supported by advance over Melanesia in political structure. Melanesia presents a great array of social-political forms: here political organization is based upon patrilineal descent groups, there on cognatic groups, or men's club-houses recruiting neighborhood memberships, on a secret ceremonial society, or perhaps on some combination of these structural principles. Yet a general plan can be discerned. The characteristic western Melanesian "tribe," that is, the ethnic-cultural entity, consists of many autonomous kinship-residential groups. Amounting on the ground to a small village or a local cluster of hamlets, each of these is a copy of the others in organization, each tends to be economically self-governing, and each is the equal of the others in political status. The tribal plan is one of politically un-integrated segments — segmental. But the political geometry in Poly-nesia is pyramidal. Local groups of the order of self-governing Melane-sian communities appear in Polynesia as subdivisions of a more inclusive political body. Smaller units are integrated into larger through a system of intergroup ranking, and the network of representative chiefs of the subdivisions amounts to a coordinating political structure. So instead of the Melanesian scheme of small, separate, and equal political blocs, the Polynesian polity is an extensive pyramid of groups capped by the fam-ily and following of a paramount chief. (This Polynesian political up-shot is often, although not always, facilitated by the development of ranked lineages. Called *conical clan* by Kirchhoff, at one time *ramage* by Firth and *status lineage* by Goldman, the Polynesian ranked lineage is the same in principle as the so-called *obok* system widely distributed in Central Asia, and it is at least analogous to the Scottish clan, the Chi-nese clan, certain Central African Bantu lineage systems, the house-groups of Northwest Coast Indians, perhaps even the "tribes" of the Is-raelites. Genealogical ranking is its distinctive feature: members of the same descent unit are ranked by genealogical distance from the common ancestor; lines of the same group become senior and cadet branches on this principle; related corporate lineages are relatively ranked, again by genealogical priority.)

Here is another criterion of Polynesian political advance: historical performance. Almost all of the native peoples of the South Pacific were brought up against intense European cultural pressure in the late eigh-teenth and the nineteenth centuries. Yet only the Hawaiians, Tahitians, Tongans, and to a lesser extent the Fijians, successfully defended them-selves by evolving countervailing, native-controlled states. Complete with public governments and public law, monarchs and taxes, ministers and minions, these nineteenth-century states are testimony to the native Polynesian political genius, to the level and the potential of indigenous political accomplishments.

Embedded within the grand differences in political scale, structure and performance is a more personal contrast, one in quality of leadership. An historically particular type of leader-figure, the "big-man" as he is often locally styled, appears in the underdeveloped settings of Melanesia. Another type, a chief properly so-called, is associated with the Polynesian advance. Now these are distinct sociological types, that is to say, differences in the powers, privileges, rights, duties, and obligations of Melanesian big-men and Polynesian chiefs are given by the divergent societal contexts in which they operate. Yet the institutional distinctions cannot help but be manifest also in differences in bearing and character, appearance and manner — in a word, personality. It may be a good way to begin the more rigorous sociological comparison of leadership with a more impressionistic sketch of the contrast in the human dimension. Here I find it useful to apply characterizations — or is it caricature? — from our own history to big-men and chiefs, however much injustice this does to the historically incomparable backgrounds of the Melanesians and Polynesians. The Melanesian big-man seems so thoroughly bourgeois, so reminiscent of the free-enterprising rugged individual of our own heritage. He combines with an ostensible interest in the general welfare a more profound measure of self-interested cunning and economic calculation. His gaze, as Veblen might have put it, is fixed unswervingly to the main chance. His every public action is designed to make a competitive and invidious comparison with others, to show a standing above the masses that is product of his own personal manufacture. The historical caricature of the Polynesian chief, however, is feudal rather than capitalist. His appearance, his bearing is almost regal; very likely he just *is* a big man — " 'Can't you see he is a chief? See how big he is?' " [2] In his every public action is a display of the refinements of breeding, in his manner always that *noblesse oblige* of true pedigree and an incontestable right of rule. With his standing not so much a personal achievement as a just social due, he can afford to be, and he is, every inch a chief.

In the several Melanesian tribes in which big-men have come under anthropological scrutiny, local cultural differences modify the expression of their personal powers. But the indicative quality of big-man authority

[2] Edward Winslow Gifford, *Tongan Society* (Honolulu: Bernice P. Bishop Museum Bulletin 61, 1926).

is everywhere the same: it is *personal* power. Big-men do not come to office; they do not succeed to, nor are they installed in, existing positions of leadership over political groups. The attainment of big-man status is rather the outcome of a series of acts which elevate a person above the common herd and attract about him a coterie of loyal, lesser men. It is not accurate to speak of "big-man" as a political title, for it is but an acknowledged standing in interpersonal relations — a "prince among men" so to speak as opposed to "The Prince of Danes." In particular Melanesian tribes the phrase might be "man of importance" or "man of renown," "generous rich-man," or "center-man," as well as "big-man."

A kind of two-sidedness in authority is implied in this series of phrases, a division of the big-man's field of influence into two distinct sectors. "Center-man" particularly connotes a cluster of followers gathered about an influential pivot. It socially implies the division of the tribe into political in-groups dominated by outstanding personalities. To the in-group, the big-man presents this sort of picture:

> The place of the leader in the district group [in northern Malaita] is well summed up by his title, which might be translated as "center-man." . . . He was like a banyan, the natives explain, which, though the biggest and tallest in the forest, is still a tree like the rest. But, just because it exceeds all others, the banyan gives support to more lianas and creepers, provides more food for the birds, and gives better protection against sun and rain.[3]

But "man of renown" connotes a broader tribal field in which a man is not so much a leader as he is some sort of hero. This is the side of the big-man facing outward from his own faction, his status among some or all of the other political clusters of the tribe. The political sphere of the big-man divides itself into a small internal sector composed of his personal satellites — rarely over eighty men — and a much larger external sector, the tribal galaxy consisting of many similar constellations.

As it crosses over from the internal into the external sector, a big-man's power undergoes qualitative change. Within his faction a Melanesian leader has true command ability, outside of it only fame and indirect influence. It is not that the center-man rules his faction by physical force, but his followers do feel obliged to obey him, and he can usually get what he wants by haranguing them — public verbal suasion is indeed so often employed by center-men that they have been styled "harangue-utans." The orbits of outsiders, however, are set by their own center-men. " 'Do it yourself. I'm not *your* fool,' " would be the characteristic

[3] H. Ian Hogbin, "Native Councils and Courts in the Solomon Islands," *Oceania* 14 (1943–44) : 258–283.

response to an order issued by a center-man to an outsider among the Siuai.[4] This fragmentation of true authority presents special political difficulties, particularly in organizing large masses of people for the prosecution of such collective ends as warfare or ceremony. Big-men do instigate mass action, but only by establishing both extensive renown and special personal relations of compulsion or reciprocity with other center-men.

Politics is in the main personal politicking in these Melanesian societies, and the size of a leader's faction as well as the extent of his renown are normally set by competition with other ambitious men. Little or no authority is given by social ascription: leadership is a creation — a creation of followership. "Followers," as it is written of the Kapauku of New Guinea, "stand in various relations to the leader. Their obedience to the headman's decisions is caused by motivations which reflect their particular relations to the leader." [5] So a man must be prepared to demonstrate that he possesses the kinds of skills that command respect — magical powers, gardening prowess, mastery of oratorical style, perhaps bravery in war and feud. Typically decisive is the deployment of one's skills and efforts in a certain direction: towards amassing goods, most often pigs, shell monies and vegetable foods, and distributing them in ways which build a name for cavalier generosity, if not for compassion. A faction is developed by informal private assistance to people of a locale. Tribal rank and renown are developed by great public giveaways sponsored by the rising big-man, often on behalf of his faction as well as himself. In different Melanesian tribes, the renown-making public distribution may appear as one side of a delayed exchange of pigs between corporate kinship groups; a marital consideration given a bride's kinfolk; a set of feasts connected with the erection of a big-man's dwelling, or of a clubhouse for himself and his faction, or with the purchase of higher grades of rank in secret societies; the sponsorship of a religious ceremony; a payment of subsidies and blood compensations to military allies; or perhaps the giveaway in a ceremonial challenge bestowed on another leader in the attempt to outgive and thus outrank him (a potlatch).

The making of the faction, however, is the true making of the Melanesian big-man. It is essential to establish relations of loyalty and obligation on the part of a number of people such that their production can be mobilized for renown-building external distribution. The bigger the faction the greater the renown; once momentum in external distribution has been generated the opposite can also be true. Any ambitious man who

[4] Douglas Oliver, *A Solomon Islands Society* (Cambridge: Harvard University Press, 1955).

[5] Leopold Pospisil, *Kapauku Papuans and Their Law* (New Haven: Yale University Press, Yale University Publications in Anthropology, no. 54, 1958).

can gather a following can launch a societal career. The rising big-man necessarily depends initially on a small core of followers, principally his own household and his closest relatives. Upon these people he can prevail economically: he capitalizes in the first instance on kinship dues and by finessing the relation of reciprocity appropriate among close kinsmen. Often it becomes necessary at an early phase to enlarge one's household. The rising leader goes out of his way to incorporate within his family "strays" of various sorts, people without familial support themselves, such as widows and orphans. Additional wives are especially useful. The more wives a man has the more pigs he has. The relation here is functional, not identical: with more women gardening there will be more food for pigs and more swineherds. A Kiwai Papuan picturesquely put to an anthropologist in pidgin the advantages, economic and political, of polygamy: " 'Another woman go garden, another woman go take firewood, another woman go catch fish, another woman cook him — husband he sing out plenty people come kaikai [i.e., come to eat].' " [6] Each new marriage, incidentally, creates for the big-man an additional set of in-laws from whom he can exact economic favors. Finally, a leader's career sustains its upward climb when he is able to link other men and their families to his faction, harnessing their production to his ambition. This is done by calculated generosities, by placing others in gratitude and obligation through helping them in some big way. A common technique is payment of bridewealth on behalf of young men seeking wives.

The great Malinowski used a phrase in analyzing primitive political economy that felicitously describes just what the big-man is doing: amassing a "fund of power." A big-man is one who can create and use social relations which give him leverage on others' production and the ability to siphon off an excess product — or sometimes he can cut down their consumption in the interest of the siphon. Now although his attention may be given primarily to short-term personal interests, from an objective standpoint the leader acts to promote long-term societal interests. The fund of power provisions activities that involve other groups of the society at large. In the greater perspective of that society at large, big-men are indispensable means of creating supralocal organization: in tribes normally fragmented into small independent groups, big-men at least temporarily widen the sphere of ceremony, recreation and art, economic collaboration, of war too. Yet always this greater societal organization depends on the lesser factional organization, particularly on the ceilings on economic mobilization set by relations between center-men and followers. The limits and the weaknesses of the political order in general are the limits and weaknesses of the factional in-groups.

[6] Gunnar Landtman, *The Kiwai Papuans of British New Guinea* (London: Macmillan, 1927).

And the personal quality of subordination to a center-man is a serious weakness in factional structure. A personal loyalty has to be made and continually reinforced; if there is discontent it may well be severed. Merely to create a faction takes time and effort, and to hold it, still more effort. The potential rupture of personal links in the factional chain is at the heart of two broad evolutionary shortcomings of western Melanesian political orders. First, a comparative instability. Shifting dispositions and magnetisms of ambitious men in a region may induce fluctuations in factions, perhaps some overlapping of them, and fluctuations also in the extent of different renowns. The death of a center-man can become a regional political trauma: the death undermines the personally cemented faction, the group dissolves in whole or in part, and the people re-group finally around rising pivotal big-men. Although particular tribal structures in places cushion the disorganization, the big-man political system is generally unstable over short terms: in its superstructure it is a flux of rising and falling leaders, in its substructure of enlarging and contracting factions. Secondly, the personal political bond contributes to the containment of evolutionary advance. The possibility of their desertion, it is clear, often inhibits a leader's ability to forceably push up his followers' output, thereby placing constraints on higher political organization, but there is more to it than that. If it is to generate great momentum, a big-man's quest for the summits of renown is likely to bring out a contradiction in his relations to followers, so that he finds himself encouraging defection — or worse, an egalitarian rebellion — by encouraging production.

One side of the Melanesian contradiction is the initial economic reciprocity between a center-man and his followers. For his help they give their help, and for goods going out through his hands other goods (often from outside factions) flow back to his followers by the same path. The other side is that a cumulative build-up of renown forces center-men into economic extortion of the faction. Here it is important that not merely his own status, but the standing and perhaps the military security of his people depend on the big-man's achievements in public distribution. Established at the head of a sizeable faction, a center-man comes under increasing pressure to extract goods from his followers, to delay reciprocities owing them, and to deflect incoming goods back into external circulation. Success in competition with other big-men particularly undermines internal-factional reciprocities: such success is precisely measurable by the ability to give outsiders more than they can possibly reciprocate. In well delineated big-man polities, we find leaders negating the reciprocal obligations upon which their following had been predicated. Substituting extraction for reciprocity, they must compel their people to "eat the leader's renown," as one Solomon Island group puts it, in return for productive efforts. Some center-men appear more able than others to dam the inevitable tide of discontent that mounts within their factions, perhaps because of charismatic personalities, perhaps because of the particular social organizations in which they operate. But paradoxically the ultimate defense of the center-man's position is some slackening of his drive to enlarge the funds of power. The alternative is much worse. In the anthropological record there are not merely instances of big-man chicanery and of material deprivation of the faction in the interests of renown, but some also of overloading of social relations with followers: the generation of antagonisms, defections, and in extreme cases the violent liquidation of the center-man. Developing internal constraints, the Melanesian big-man political order brakes evolutionary advance at a certain level. It sets ceilings on the intensification of political authority, on the intensification of household production by political means, and on the diversion of household outputs in support of wider political organization. But in Polynesia these constraints were breached, and although Polynesian chiefdoms also found their developmental plateau, it was not before political evolution had been carried above the Melanesian ceilings. The fundamental defects of the Melanesian plan were overcome in Polynesia. The division between small internal and larger external political sectors, upon which all big-man politics hinged, was suppressed in Polynesia by the growth of an enclaving chiefdom-at-large. A chain of command subordinating lesser chiefs and groups to greater, on the basis of inherent societal rank, made local blocs or personal followings (such as were independent in Melanesia) merely dependent parts of the larger Polynesian chiefdom. So the nexus of the Polynesian chiefdom became an extensive set of offices, a pyramid of higher and lower chiefs holding sway over larger and smaller sections of the polity. Indeed the system of ranked and subdivided lineages (conical clan system), upon which the pyramid was characteristically established, might build up through several orders of inclusion and encompass the whole of an island or group of islands. While the island or the archipelago would normally be divided into several independent chiefdoms, high-order lineage connections between them, as well as kinship ties between their paramount chiefs, provided structural avenues for at least temporary expansion of political scale, for consolidation of great into even greater chiefdoms.

The pivotal paramount chief as well as the chieftains controlling parts of a chiefdom were true office holders and title holders. They were not, like Melanesian big-men, fishers of men: they held positions of authority over permanent groups. The honorifics of Polynesian chiefs likewise did not refer to a standing in interpersonal relations, but to their leadership of political divisions — here "The Prince of Danes" *not* "the prince among men." In western Melanesia the personal superiorities and inferiorities arising in the intercourse of particular men largely defined the political bodies. In Polynesia there emerged suprapersonal structures of leadership and followership, organizations that continued independently of the particular men who occupied positions in them for brief mortal spans.

And these Polynesian chiefs did not make their positions in society — they were installed in societal positions. In several of the islands, men did struggle to office against the will and stratagems of rival aspirants. But then they came *to* power. Power resided in the office; it was not made by the demonstration of personal superiority. In other islands, Tahiti was famous for it, succession to chieftainship was tightly controlled by inherent rank. The chiefly lineage ruled by virtue of its genealogical connections with divinity, and chiefs were succeeded by first sons, who carried "in the blood" the attributes of leadership. The important comparative point is this: the qualities of command that had to reside in men in Melanesia, that had to be personally demonstrated in order to attract loyal followers, were in Polynesia socially assigned to office and rank. In Polynesia, people of high rank and office *ipso facto* were leaders, and by the same token the qualities of leadership were automatically lacking — theirs was not to question why — among the underlying population. Magical powers such as a Melanesian big-man might acquire to sustain his position, a Polynesian high chief inherited by divine descent as the *mana* which sanctified his rule and protected his person against the hands of the commonalty. The productive ability the big-man laboriously had to demonstrate was effortlessly given Polynesian chiefs as religious control over agricultural fertility, and upon the ceremonial implementation of it the rest of the people were conceived dependent. Where a Melanesian leader had to master the compelling oratorical style, Polynesian paramounts often had trained "talking chiefs" whose voice was the chiefly command.

In the Polynesian view, a chiefly personage was in the nature of things powerful. But this merely implies the objective observation that his power was of the group rather than of himself. His authority came from the organization, from an organized acquiescence in his privileges and organized means of sustaining them. A kind of paradox resides in evolutionary developments which detach the exercise of authority from the necessity to demonstrate personal superiority: organizational power actually extends the role of personal decision and conscious planning, gives it greater scope, impact, and effectiveness. The growth of a political system such as the Polynesian constitutes advance over Melanesian orders of interpersonal dominance in the human control of human affairs.

Especially significant for society at large were privileges accorded Polynesian chiefs which made them greater architects of funds of power than ever was any Melanesian big-man.

Masters of their people and "owners" in a titular sense of group resources, Polynesian chiefs had rights of call upon the labor and agricultural produce of households within their domains. Economic mobilization did not depend on, as it necessarily had for Melanesian big-men, the *de novo* creation by the leader of personal loyalties and economic obligations. A chief need not stoop to obligate this man or that man, need not by a series of individual acts of generosity induce others to support him, for economic leverage over a group was the inherent chiefly due. Consider the implications for the fund of power of the widespread chiefly privilege, related to titular "ownership" of land, of placing an interdiction, a tabu, on the harvest of some crop by way of reserving its use for a collective project. By means of the tabu the chief directs the course of production in a general way: households of his domain must turn to some other means of subsistence. He delivers a stimulus to household production: in the absence of the tabu further labors would not have been necessary. Most significantly, he has generated a politically utilizable agricultural surplus. A subsequent call on this surplus floats chieftainship as a going concern, capitalizes the fund of power. In certain islands, Polynesian chiefs controlled great storehouses which held the goods congealed by chiefly pressures on the commonalty. David Malo, one of the great native custodians of old Hawaiian lore, felicitously catches the political significance of the chiefly magazine in his well-known *Hawaiian Antiquities*:

> It was the practice for kings [i.e., paramount chiefs of individual islands] to build store-houses in which to collect food, fish, tapas [bark cloth], malos [men's loin cloths] pa-us [women's loin skirts], and all sorts of goods. These store-houses were designed by the Kalaimoku [the chief's principal executive] as a means of keeping the people contented, so they would not desert the king. They were like the baskets that were used to entrap the *hinalea* fish. The *hinalea* thought there was something good within the basket, and he hung round the outside of it. In the same way the people thought there was food in the storehouses, and they kept their eyes on the king. As the rat will not desert the pantry . . . where he thinks food is, so the people will not desert the king while they think there is food in his store-house.[7]

Redistribution of the fund of power was the supreme art of Polynesian politics. By well-planned *noblesse oblige* the large domain of a para-

---

[7] David Malo, *Hawaiian Antiquities* (Honolulu: Hawaiian Gazette Co., 1903).

mount chief was held together, organized at times for massive projects, protected against other chiefdoms, even further enriched. Uses of the chiefly fund included lavish hospitality and entertainments for outside chiefs and for the chief's own people, and succor of individuals or the underlying population at large in times of scarcities — bread and circuses. Chiefs subsidized craft production, promoting in Polynesia a division of technical labor unparalleled in extent and expertise in most of the Pacific. They supported also great technical construction, as of irrigation complexes, the further returns to which swelled the chiefly fund. They initiated large-scale religious construction too, subsidized the great ceremonies, and organized logistic support for extensive military campaigns. Larger and more easily replenished than their western Melanesian counterparts, Polynesian funds of power permitted greater political regulation of a greater range of social activities on greater scale.

In the most advanced Polynesian chiefdoms, as in Hawaii and Tahiti, a significant part of the chiefly fund was deflected away from general redistribution towards the upkeep of the institution of chieftainship. The fund was siphoned for the support of a permanent administrative establishment. In some measure, goods and services contributed by the people precipitated out as the grand houses, assembly places, and temple platforms of chiefly precincts. In another measure, they were appropriated for the livelihood of circles of retainers, many of them close kinsmen of the chief, who clustered about the powerful paramounts. These were not all useless hangers-on. They were political cadres: supervisors of the stores, talking chiefs, ceremonial attendants, high priests who were intimately involved in political rule, envoys to transmit directives through the chiefdom. There were men in these chiefly retinues — in Tahiti and perhaps Hawaii, specialized warrior corps — whose force could be directed internally as a buttress against fragmenting or rebellious elements of the chiefdom. A Tahitian or Hawaiian high chief had more compelling sanctions than the harangue. He controlled a ready physical force, an armed body of executioners, which gave him mastery particularly over the lesser people of the community. While it looks a lot like the big-man's faction again, the differences in functioning of the great Polynesian chief's retinue are more significant than the superficial similarities in appearance. The chief's coterie, for one thing, is economically dependent upon him rather than he upon them. And in deploying the cadres politically in various sections of the chiefdom, or against the lower orders, the great Polynesian chiefs sustained command where the Melanesian big-man, in his external sector, had at best renown.

This is not to say that the advanced Polynesian chiefdoms were free of internal defect, of potential or actual malfunctioning. The large political-military apparatus indicates something of the opposite. So does the recent work of Irving Goldman [8] on the intensity of "status rivalry" in Polynesia, especially when it is considered that much of the status rivalry in developed chiefdoms, as the Hawaiian, amounted to popular rebellion against chiefly despotism rather than mere contest for position within the ruling-stratum. This suggests that Polynesian chiefdoms, just as Melanesian big-man orders, generate along with evolutionary development countervailing anti-authority pressures, and that the weight of the latter may ultimately impede further development.

The Polynesian contradiction seems clear enough. On one side, chieftainship is never detached from kinship moorings and kinship economic ethics. Even the greatest Polynesian chiefs were conceived superior kinsmen to the masses, fathers of their people, and generosity was morally incumbent upon them. On the other side, the major Polynesian paramounts seemed inclined to "eat the power of the government too much," as the Tahitians put it, to divert an undue proportion of the general wealth toward the chiefly establishment. The diversion could be accomplished by lowering the customary level of general redistribution, lessening the material returns of chieftainship to the community at large — tradition attributes the great rebellion of Mangarevan commoners to such cause. Or the diversion might — and I suspect more commonly did — consist in greater and more forceful exactions from lesser chiefs and people, increasing returns to the chiefly apparatus without necessarily affecting the level of general redistribution. In either case, the well-developed chiefdom creates for itself the dampening paradox of stoking rebellion by funding its authority.

In Hawaii and other islands cycles of political centralization and decentralization may be abstracted from traditional histories. That is, larger chiefdoms periodically fragmented into smaller and then were later reconstituted. Here would be more evidence of a tendency to overtax the political structure. But how to explain the emergence of a developmental stymie, of an inability to sustain political advance beyond a certain level? To point to a chiefly propensity to consume or a Polynesian propensity to rebel is not enough: such propensities are promoted by the very advance of chiefdoms. There is reason to hazard instead that Parkinson's notable law is behind it all: that progressive expansion in political scale entailed more-than-proportionate accretion in the ruling apparatus, unbalancing the flow of wealth in favor of the apparatus. The ensuing unrest then curbs the chiefly impositions, sometimes by reducing chiefdom scale to the nadir of the periodic cycle. Comparison of the

[8] Irving Goldman, "Status Rivalry and Cultural Evolution in Polynesia," *American Anthropologist* 57 (1957) : 680–697; "Variations in Polynesian Social Organization," *Journal of the Polynesian Society* 66 (1957) : 374–390.

requirements of administration in small and large Polynesian chiefdoms helps make the point.

A lesser chiefdom, confined say as in the Marquesas Islands to a narrow valley, could be almost personally ruled by a headman in frequent contact with the relatively small population. Melville's partly romanticized — also for its ethnographic details, partly cribbed — account in *Typee* makes this clear enough. But the great Polynesian chiefs had to rule much larger, spatially dispersed, internally organized populations. Hawaii, an island over four thousand square miles with an aboriginal population approaching one hundred thousand, was at times a single chiefdom, at other times divided into two to six independent chiefdoms, and at all times each chiefdom was composed of large subdivisions under powerful subchiefs. Sometimes a chiefdom in the Hawaiian group extended beyond the confines of one of the islands, incorporating part of another through conquest. Now, such extensive chiefdoms would have to be coordinated; they would have to be centrally tapped for a fund of power, buttressed against internal disruption, sometimes massed for distant, perhaps overseas, military engagements. All of this to be implemented by means of communication still at the level of word-of-mouth, and means of transportation consisting of human bodies and canoes. (The extent of certain larger chieftainships, coupled with the limitations of communication and transportation, incidentally suggests another possible source of political unrest: that the burden of provisioning the governing apparatus would tend to fall disproportionately on groups within easiest access of the paramount.) A tendency for the developed chiefdom to proliferate in executive cadres, to grow top-heavy, seems in these circumstances altogether functional, even though the ensuing drain on wealth proves the chiefdom's undoing. Functional also, and likewise a material drain on the chiefdom at large, would be widening distinctions between chiefs and people in style of life. Palatial housing, ornamentation and luxury, finery and ceremony, in brief, conspicuous consumption, however much it seems mere self-interest always has a more decisive social significance. It creates those invidious distinctions between rulers and ruled so conducive to a passive — hence quite economical! — acceptance of authority. Throughout history, inherently more powerful political organizations than the Polynesian, with more assured logistics of rule, have turned to it — including in our time some ostensibly revolutionary and proletarian governments, despite every pre-revolutionary protestation of solidarity with the masses and equality for the classes.

In Polynesia then, as in Melanesia, political evolution is eventually shortcircuited by an overload on the relations between leaders and their people. The Polynesian tragedy, however, was somewhat the opposite of the Melanesian. In Polynesia, the evolutionary ceiling was set by extraction from the population at large in favor of the chiefly faction, in Melanesia by extraction from the big-man's faction in favor of distribution to the population at large. Most importantly, the Polynesian ceiling was higher. Melanesian big-men and Polynesian chiefs not only reflect different varieties and levels of political evolution, they display in different degrees the capacity to generate and to sustain political progress.

Especially emerging from their juxtaposition is the more decisive impact of Polynesian chiefs on the economy, the chiefs' greater leverage on the output of the several households of society. The success of any primitive political organization is decided here, in the control that can be developed over household economies. For the household is not merely the principal productive unit in primitive societies, it is often quite capable of autonomous direction of its own production, and it is oriented towards production for its own, not societal consumption. The greater potential of Polynesian chieftainship is precisely the greater pressure it could exert on household output, its capacity both to generate a surplus and to deploy it out of the household towards a broader division of labor, cooperative construction, and massive ceremonial and military action. Polynesian chiefs were the more effective means of societal collaboration on economic, political, indeed all cultural fronts. Perhaps we have been too long accustomed to perceive rank and rule from the standpoint of the individuals involved, rather than from the perspective of the total society, as if the secret of the subordination of man to man lay in the personal satisfactions of power. And then the breakdowns too, or the evolutionary limits, have been searched out in men, in "weak" kings or megalomaniacal dictators — always, "who is the matter?" An excursion into the field of primitive politics suggests the more fruitful conception that the gains of political developments accrue more decisively to society than to individuals, and the failings as well are of structure not men.

28

Oil in Santa Barbara and power in America
HARVEY MOLOTCH

*Political power exists in every society. When anthropologists
study such power in small tribal societies, they realize that it is
exercised through both formal and informal channels. The same
is true about power in large urban cultures. In this article,
Harvey Molotch examines one critical event that occurred in
January, 1969 — a massive eruption of crude oil that covered the
coastline of Santa Barbara, California. Through this event he
takes us into the culture of political power and shows the informal rules that operate in American society.*

More than oil leaked from Union Oil's Platform A in the Santa Barbara
Channel — a bit of truth about power in America spilled out along with
it. It is the thesis of this paper that this technological "accident," like all
accidents, provides clues to the realities of social structure (in this
instance, power arrangements) not otherwise available to the outside
observer. Further, it is argued, the response of the aggrieved population
(the citizenry of Santa Barbara) provides insight into the more general
process which shapes disillusionment and frustration among those who
come to closely examine and be injured by existing power arrangements.

A few historical details concerning the case under examination are
in order. For over fifteen years, Santa Barbara's political leaders had
attempted to prevent despoilation of their coastline by oil drilling on
adjacent federal waters. Although they were unsuccessful in blocking
eventual oil leasing (in February, 1968) of *federal* waters beyond the
three-mile limit, they were able to establish a sanctuary within *state*
waters (thus foregoing the extraordinary revenues which leases in such
areas bring to adjacent localities — e.g., the riches of Long Beach). It
was therefore a great irony that the one city which voluntarily ex-

Reprinted with permission from *Sociological Inquiry* 40 (Winter, 1969). References and bibliographic citations are omitted.

changed revenue for a pure environment should find itself faced, on January 28, 1969, with a massive eruption of crude oil — an eruption which was, in the end, to cover the entire city coastline (as well as much of Ventura and Santa Barbara County coastline as well) with a thick coat of crude oil. The air was soured for many hundreds of feet inland and the traditional economic base of the region (tourism) was under threat. After ten days of unsuccessful attempts, the runaway well was brought under control, only to be followed by a second eruption on February 12. This fissure was closed on March 3, but was followed by a sustained "seepage" of oil — a leakage which continues, at this writing, to pollute the sea, the air, and the famed local beaches. The oil companies had paid $603,000,000 for their lease rights and neither they nor the federal government bear any significant legal responsibility toward the localities which these lease rights might endanger.

If the big spill had occurred almost anywhere else (e.g., Lima, Ohio; Lompoc, California), it is likely that the current research opportunity would not have developed. But Santa Barbara is different. Of its 70,000 residents, a disproportionate number are upper class and upper middle class. They are persons who, having a wide choice of where in the world they might live, have chosen Santa Barbara for its ideal climate, gentle beauty, and sophisticated "culture." Thus a large number of worldly, rich, well-educated persons — individuals with resources, spare time, and contacts with national and international elites — found themselves with a commonly shared disagreeable situation: the pollution of their otherwise near-perfect environment. Santa Barbarans thus possessed none of the "problems" which otherwise are said to inhibit effective community response to external threat: they are not urban villagers; they are not internally divided and parochial like the Springdalers; nor emaciated with self-doubt and organizational naiveté as is supposed of the ghetto dwellers. With moral indignation and high self-confidence, they set out to right the wrong so obviously done to them.

Their response was immediate. The stodgy *Santa Barbara News-Press* inaugurated a series of editorials, unique in uncompromising stridency. Under the leadership of a former State Senator and a local corporate executive, a community organization was established called "GOO" (Get Oil Out!) which took a militant stand against any and all oil activity in the Channel.

In a petition to President Nixon (eventually to gain 110,000 signatures), GOO's position was clearly stated:

> . . . With the seabed filled with fissures in this area, similar disastrous oil operation accidents may be expected. And with one of the largest faults centered in the channel waters, one sizeable earthquake could mean possible disaster for the entire channel area. . . .

Therefore, we the undersigned do call upon the state of California and the Federal Government to promote conservation by:

1. Taking immediate action to have present offshore oil operations cease and desist at once.
2. Issuing no further leases in the Santa Barbara Channel.
3. Having all oil platforms and rigs removed from this area at the earliest possible date.

The same theme emerged in the hundreds of letters published by the *News-Press* in the weeks to follow and in the positions taken by virtually every local civic and government body. Both in terms of its volume (372 letters published in February alone) and the intensity of the revealed opinions, the flow of letters was hailed by the *News-Press* as "unprecedented." Rallies were held at the beach, GOO petitions were circulated at local shopping centers and sent to friends around the country; a fund-raising dramatic spoof of the oil industry was produced at a local high school. Local artists, playwrights, advertising men, retired executives and academic specialists from the local campus of the University of California (UCSB) executed special projects appropriate to their areas of expertise.

A GOO strategy emerged for a two-front attack. Local indignation, producing the petition to the President and thousands of letters to key members of Congress and the executive would lead to appropriate legislation. Legal action in the courts against the oil companies and the federal government would have the double effect of recouping some of the financial losses certain to be endured by the local tourist and fishing industries while at the same time serving notice that drilling would be a much less profitable operation than it was supposed to be. Legislation to ban drilling was introduced by Cranston in the U.S. Senate and Teague in the House of Representatives. Joint suits by the city and County of Santa Barbara (later joined by the State) for $1 billion in damages was filed against the oil companies and the federal government.

All of these activities — petitions, rallies, court action, and legislative lobbying — were significant for their similarity in revealing faith in "the system." The tendency was to blame the oil companies. There was a muckraking tone to the Santa Barbara response: oil and the profit-crazy executives of Union Oil were ruining Santa Barbara — but once our national and state leaders became aware of what was going on, and were provided with the "facts" of the case, justice would be done.

Indeed, there was good reason for hope. The quick and enthusiastic responses of Teague and Cranston represented a consensus of men otherwise polar opposites in their political behavior: Democrat Cranston was a charter member of the liberal California Democratic Council; Republican Teague was a staunch fiscal and moral conservative (e.g., a strong Vietnam hawk and unrelenting harasser of the local Center for the Study of Democratic Institutions). Their bills, for which there was great optimism, would have had the consequence of effecting a "permanent" ban on drilling in the Channel.

But from other quarters there was silence. Santa Barbara's representatives in the state legislature either said nothing or (in later stages) offered minimal support. It took several months for Senator Murphy to introduce Congressional legislation (for which he admitted to having little hope) which would have had the consequence of exchanging the oil companies' leases in the Channel for comparable leases in the under-exploited Elk Hills oil reserve in California's Kern County. Most disappointing of all to Santa Barbarans, Governor Reagan withheld support for proposals which would end the drilling.

As subsequent events unfolded, this seemingly inexplicable silence of the democratically elected representatives began to fall into place as part of a more general problem. American democracy came to be seen as a much more complicated affair than a system in which governmental officials actuate the desires of the "people who elected them" once those desires come to be known. Instead, increasing recognition came to be given to the "all-powerful oil lobby"; to legislators "in the pockets of Oil"; to academicians "bought" by Oil; and to regulatory agencies which lobby for those they are supposed to regulate. In other words, Santa Barbarans became increasingly *ideological*, increasingly *sociological*, and in the words of some observers, increasingly *"radical."*[1] Writing from his lodgings in the area's most exclusive hotel (the Santa Barbara Biltmore), an irate citizen penned these words in his published letter to the *News-Press:*

> We the people can protest and protest and it means nothing because the industrial and military junta are the country. They tell us, the People, what is good for the oil companies is good for the People. To that I say, Like Hell! . . .
> Profit is their language and the proof of all this is their history (*SBNP*,[2] Feb. 26, 1969, p. A-6).

As time wore on, the editorials and letters continued in their bitterness.

THE EXECUTIVE BRANCH AND THE REGULATORY AGENCIES: DISILLUSIONMENT

From the start, Secretary Hickel's actions were regarded with suspicion. His publicized associations with Alaskan Oil interests did his reputation

---

[1] See the report of Morton Mintz in the June 29, 1969 *Washington Post.* The conjunction of these three attributes is not, in my opinion, coincidental.

[2] *SBNP* will be used to denote *Santa Barbara News-Press* throughout this paper.

no good in Santa Barbara. When, after a halt to drilling (for "review" of procedures) immediately after the initial eruption, Hickel one day later ordered a resumption of drilling and production (even as the oil continued to gush into the channel), the government's response was seen as unbelievingly consistent with conservationists' worst fears. That he backed down within 48 hours and ordered a halt to drilling and production was taken as a response to the massive nationwide media play then being given to the Santa Barbara plight and to the citizens' mass outcry just then beginning to reach Washington.

Disenchantment with Hickel and the executive branch also came through less spectacular, less specific, but nevertheless genuine activity. First of all, Hickel's failure to support any of the legislation introduced to halt drilling was seen as an *action* favoring Oil. His remarks on the subject, while often expressing sympathy with Santa Barbarans[3] (and for a while placating local sentiment) were revealed as hypocritical in light of the action not taken. Of further note was the constant attempt by the Interior Department to minimize the extent of damage in Santa Barbara or to hint at possible "compromises" which were seen locally as near-total capitulation to the oil companies.

Volume of oil spillage. Many specific examples might be cited. An early (and continuing) issue in the oil spill was the *volume* of oil spilling into the Channel. The U.S. Geological Survey (administered by Interior), when queried by reporters, broke its silence on the subject with estimates which struck as incredible in Santa Barbara. One of the extraordinary attributes of the Santa Barbara locale is the presence of a technology establishment among the most sophisticated in the country. Several officials of the General Research Corporation (a local R & D firm with experience in marine technology) initiated studies of the oil outflow and announced findings of pollution volume at a "minimum" of tenfold the Interior estimate. Further, General Research provided (and the *News-Press* published) a detailed account of the methods used in making the estimate. Despite repeated challenges from the press, Interior both refused to alter its estimate or to reveal its method for making estimates. Throughout the crisis, the divergence of the estimates remained at about tenfold.

The "seepage" was estimated by the Geological Survey to have been reduced from 1,260 gallons per day to about 630 gallons. General Research, however, estimated the leakage at the rate of 8,400 gallons per day at the same point in time as Interior's 630 gallon estimate. The lowest estimate of all was provided by an official of the Western Oil

[3] Hickel publicly stated and wrote (personal communication) that the original leasing was a mistake and that he was doing all within discretionary power to solve the problem.

and Gas Association, in a letter to the *Wall Street Journal*. His estimate: "Probably less than 100 gallons a day" (*SBNP*, August 5, 1969:A-1).

Damage to beaches. Still another point of contention was the state of the beaches at varying points in time. The oil companies, through various public relations officials, constantly minimized the actual amount of damage and maximized the effect of Union Oil's cleanup activity. What surprised (and most irritated) the locals was the fact that Interior statements implied the same goal. Thus Hickel referred at a press conference to the "recent" oil spill, providing the impression that the oil spill was over, at a time when freshly erupting oil was continuing to stain local beaches. President Nixon appeared locally to "inspect" the damage to beaches, and Interior arranged for him to land his helicopter on a city beach which had been cleaned thoroughly in the days just before, but spared him a close-up of much of the rest of the County shoreline which continued to be covered with a thick coat of crude oil. (The beach visited by Nixon has been oil stained on many occasions subsequent to the President's departure.) Secret service men kept the placards and shouts of several hundred demonstrators safely out of Presidential viewing or hearing distance.

Continuously, the Oil and Interior combine implied the beaches to be restored when Santa Barbarans knew that even a beach which looked clean was by no means restored. The *News-Press* through a comprehensive series of interviews with local and national experts on wildlife and geology made the following points clear:

1. As long as oil remained on the water and oil continued to leak from beneath the sands, all Santa Barbara beaches were subject to continuous doses of oil — subject only to the vagaries of wind change. Indeed, all through the spill and up to the present point in time, a beach walk is likely to result in tar on the feet. On "bad days" the beaches are unapproachable.

2. The damage to the "ecological chain" (a concept which has become a household phrase in Santa Barbara) is of unknown proportions. Much study will be necessary to learn the extent of damage.

3. The continuous alternating natural erosion and building up of beach sands means that "clean" beaches contain layers of oil at various sublevels under the mounting sands; layers which will once again be exposed when the cycle reverses itself and erosion begins anew. Thus, it will take many years for the beaches of Santa Barbara to be completely restored, even if the present seepage is halted and no additional pollution occurs.

Damage to wildlife. Oil on feathers is ingested by birds, continuous preening thus leads to death. In what local and national authorities called a hopeless task, two bird-cleaning centers were established to cleanse feathers and otherwise administer to damaged wild-fowl. (Oil money helped to establish and supply these centers.) Both spokesmen from Oil and the federal government then adopted these centers as sources of "data" on the extent of damage to wild-fowl. Thus, the number of dead birds due to pollution was computed on the basis of number of fatalities at the wild-fowl centers.[4] This of course is preposterous given the fact that dying birds are provided with very inefficient means of propelling themselves to such designated places. The obviousness of this dramatic understatement of fatalities was never acknowledged by either Oil or Interior — although noted in Santa Barbara.

At least those birds in the hands of local ornithologists could be confirmed as dead — and this fact could not be disputed by either Oil or Interior. Not so, however, with species whose corpses are more difficult to produce on command. Several observers at the Channel Islands (a national wildlife preserve containing one of the country's largest colonies of sea animals) reported sighting unusually large numbers of dead sea-lion pups — on the oil stained shores of one of the islands. Statement and counter-statement followed with Oil's defenders arguing that the animals were not dead at all — but only appeared inert because they were sleeping. Despite the testimony of staff experts of the local Museum of Natural History and the Museum Scientist of UCSB's Biological Sciences Department that the number of "inert" sea-lion pups was far larger than normal and that field trips had confirmed the deaths, the position of Oil, as also expressed by the Department of the Navy (which administers the stricken island) remained adamant that the sea animals were only sleeping (cf. *Life*, June 13, 1969; July 4, 1969). The dramatic beaching of an unusually large number of dead whales on the beaches of Northern California — whales which had just completed their migration through the Santa Barbara Channel — was acknowledged, but held not to be caused by oil pollution. No direct linkage (or non-linkage) with oil could be demonstrated by investigating scientists (cf. *San Francisco Chronicle*, March 12, 1969:1-3).

In the end, it was not simply Interior, its U.S. Geological Survey and the President which either supported or tacitly accepted Oil's public relations tactics. The regulatory agencies at both national and state level, by action, inaction and implication had the consequence of defending Oil at virtually every turn. Thus at the outset of the first big blow, as the ocean churned with bubbling oil and gas, the U.S. Coast Guard (which

[4] In a February 7 letter to Union Oil shareholders, Fred Hartley informed them that the bird refuge centers had been "very successful in their efforts." In fact, by April 30, 1969, only 150 birds (of thousands treated) had been returned to the natural habitat as "fully recovered" and the survival rate of birds treated was estimated as a miraculously high (in light of previous experience) 20 per cent (cf. *SBNP*, April 30, 1969, F-3).

patrols Channel waters regularly) failed to notify local officials of the pollution threat because, in the words of the local commander, "the seriousness of the situation was not apparent until late in the day Tuesday and it was difficult to reach officials after business hours" (*SBNP*, January 30, 1969:A-1, 4). Officials ended up hearing of the spill from the *News-Press*.

The Army Corps of Engineers must approve all structures placed on the ocean floor and thus had the discretion to hold public hearings on each application for a permit to build a drilling platform. With the exception of a single *pro forma* ceremony held on a platform erected in 1967, requests for such hearings were never granted. In its most recent handling of these matters (at a point long after the initial eruption and as oil still leaks into the ocean) the Corps changed its criteria for public hearings by restricting written objections to new drilling to "the effects of the proposed exploratory drilling on *navigation or national defense*" (*SBNP*, August 17, 1969:A-1, 4). Prior to the spill, effects on *fish and wildlife* were specified by the Army as possible grounds for objection, but at that time such objections, when raised, were more easily dismissed as unfounded.

The Federal Water Pollution Control Administration consistently attempted to understate the amount of damage done to waterfowl by quoting the "hospital dead" as though a reasonable assessment of the net damage. State agencies followed the same pattern. The charge of "Industry domination" of state conservation boards was levelled by the State Deputy Attorney General, Charles O'Brien (*SBNP*, February 9, 1969:A-6). Thomas Gaines, a Union Oil Executive, actually sits as a member on the State Agency Board most directly connected with the control of pollution in Channel waters. In correspondence with complaining citizens, N. B. Livermore, Jr., of the Resources Agency of California refers to the continuing oil spill as "minor seepage" with "no major long-term effect on the marine ecology." The letter adopts the perspective of Interior and Oil, even though the state was in no way being held culpable for the spill (letter, undated, to Joseph Keefe, citizen, University of California, Santa Barbara Library, on file).

With these details under their belts, Santa Barbarans were in a position to understand the sweeping condemnation of the regulatory system as contained in a *News-Press* front page, banner-headlined interview with Rep. Richard D. Ottenger (D-NY), quoted as follows: "And so on down the line. Each agency has a tendency to become the captive of the industry that it is to regulate" (*SBNP*, March 1, 1969:A-1).

THE CONGRESS: DISILLUSIONMENT

Irritations with Interior were paralleled by frustrations encountered in dealing with the Congressional establishment which had the responsibility of holding hearings on ameliorative legislation. A delegation of Santa Barbarans was scheduled to testify in Washington on the Cranston bill. From the questions which Congressmen asked of them, and the manner in which they were "handled," the delegation could only conclude that the Committee was "in the pockets of Oil." As one of the returning delegates put it, the presentation bespoke of "total futility."

At this writing, six months after their introduction, both the Cranston and Teague bills lie buried in committee with little prospect of surfacing. Cranston has softened his bill significantly — requiring only that new drilling be suspended until Congress is convinced that sufficient technological safeguards exist. But to no avail.

SCIENCE AND TECHNOLOGY: DISILLUSIONMENT

From the start, part of the shock of the oil spill was that such a thing could happen in a country with such sophisticated technology. The much overworked phrase, "If we can send a man to the moon . . ." was even more overworked in Santa Barbara. When, in years previous, Santa Barbara's elected officials had attempted to halt the original sale of leases, "assurances" were given from Interior that such an "accident" could not occur, given the highly developed state of the art. Not only did it occur, but the original gusher of oil spewed forth completely out of control for ten days and the continuing "seepage" which followed it remains uncontrolled to the present moment, seven months later. That the government would embark upon so massive a drilling program with such unsophisticated technologies, was striking indeed.

Further, not only were the technologies inadequate and the plans for stopping a leak, should it occur, nonexistent, but the area in which the drilling took place was known to be ultrahazardous from the outset. That is, drilling was occurring on an ocean bottom known for its extraordinary geological circumstances — porous sands lacking a bedrock "ceiling" capable of containing runaway oil and gas. Thus the continuing leakage through the sands at various points above the oil reservoir is unstoppable, and could have been anticipated with the data *known to all parties involved.*

Another peculiarity of the Channel is the fact that it is located in the heart of earthquake activity in that region of the country which, among all regions, is among the very most earthquake prone.[5] Santa Barbarans are now asking what might occur in an earthquake: if pipes on the ocean floor and casings through the ocean bottom should be

---

[5] Cf. "Damaging Earthquakes of the United States through 1966," Fig. 2, National Earthquake Information Center, Environmental Science Services Administration, Coast and Geodetic Survey.

sheared, the damage done by the Channel's *thousands* of potential producing wells would be devastating to the entire coast of Southern California.[6]

Recurrent attempts have been made to ameliorate the continuing seep by placing floating booms around an area of leakage and then having workboats skim off the leakage from within the demarcated area.[7] Chemical dispersants, of various varieties, have also been tried. But the oil bounces over the sea booms in the choppy waters; the work boats suck up only a drop in the bucket; and the dispersants are effective only when used in quantities which constitute a graver pollution threat than the oil they are designed to eliminate. Cement is poured into suspected fissures in an attempt to seal them up. Oil on beaches is periodically cleaned by dumping straw over the sands and then raking up the straw along with the oil it absorbs.

This striking contrast between the sophistication of the means used to locate and extract oil compared to the primitiveness of the means to control and clean it up was widely noted in Santa Barbara. It is the result of a system which promotes research and development which leads to strategic profitability rather than to social utility. The common sight of men throwing straw on miles of beaches within sight of complex drilling rigs capable of exploiting resources thousands of feet below the ocean's surface, made the point clear.

The futility of the clean-up and control efforts was widely noted in Santa Barbara. Secretary Hickel's announcement that the Interior Department was generating new "tough" regulations to control off-shore drilling was thus met with great skepticism. The Santa Barbara County Board of Supervisors was invited to "review" these new regulations — and refused to do so in the belief that such participation would be used to provide the fraudulent impression of democratic responsiveness — when, in fact, the relevant decisions had been already made. In previous years when they were fighting against the leasing of the Channel, the Supervisors had been assured of technological safeguards; now, as the emergency continued, they could witness for themselves the dearth of any means for ending the leakage in the Channel. They had also heard the testimony of a high-ranking Interior engineer who, when asked if such safeguards could positively prevent future spills, explained that "no prudent engineer would ever make such a claim" (*SBNP*, February

---

[6] See Interview with Donald Weaver, Professor of Geology, UCSB, *SBNP*, Feb. 21, 1969, p. A-1, 6. (Also, remarks by Professor Donald Runnells, UCSB geologist, *SBNP*, Feb. 23, 1969, p. B-2.) Both stress the dangers of faults in the Channel, and potential earthquakes.

[7] More recently, plastic tents have been placed on the ocean floor to trap seeping oil; it is being claimed that half the runaway oil is now being trapped in these tents.

19, 1969:A-1). They also had the testimony of Donald Solanas, a regional supervisor of Interior's U.S. Geological Survey, who had said about the Union Platform eruption: "I could have had an engineer on that platform 24 hours a day, 7 days a week and he couldn't have prevented the accident."

His "explanation" of the cause of the "accident": "Mother earth broke down on us" (*SBNP*, February 28, 1969:C-12).

Given these facts, as contained in the remarks of Interior's own spokesmen, combined with testimony and information received from non-Interior personnel, Interior's new regulations and the invitation to the County to participate in making them, could only be a ruse to preface a resumption of drilling. In initiating the County's policy of not responding to Interior's "invitation," a County Supervisor explained: "I think we may be falling into a trap" (*SBNP*, April 1, 1969).

The very next day, the Supervisors' suspicions were confirmed. Interior announced a selective resumption of drilling "to relieve pressures." (*News-Press* letter writers asked if the "pressure" was geological or political.) The new tough regulations were themselves seriously flawed by the fact that most of their provisions specified those measures, such as buoyant booms around platforms, availability of chemical dispersants, etc., which had proven almost totally useless in the current emergency. They fell far short of minimum safety requirements as enumerated by UC Santa Barbara geologist Robert Curry who criticized a previous version of the same regulations as "relatively trivial" and "toothless"[8] (*SBNP*, March 5, 1969:C-9).

[8] Curry's criticism is as follows:

"These new regulations make no mention at all about in-pipe safety valves to prevent blowouts, or to shut off the flow of oil deep in the well should the oil and gas escape from the drill hole region into a natural fissure at some depth below the wellhead blowout preventers. There is also no requirement for a backup valve in case the required preventer fails to work. Remember, the runaway well on Union Platform A was equipped with a wellhead blowout preventer. The blowout occurred some 200 below that device.

"Only one of the new guidelines seems to recognize the possible calamitous results of the earthquakes which are inevitable on the western offshore leases. None of the regulations require the minimization of pollution hazards during drilling that may result from a moderate-magnitude, nearby shallow-focus earthquake, seismic sea wave (tsunami) or submarine landslide which could shear off wells below the surface.

"None of the regulations state anything at all about onshore oil and gas storage facilities liable to release their contents into the oceans upon rupture due to an earthquake or seismic sea wave.

"None of the new regulations stipulate that wells must be cased to below a level of geologic hazard, or below a depth of possible open fissures or porous sands, and, as such, none of these changes would have helped the present situation in the Santa Barbara Channel or the almost continuous blowout that has been going on since last year in the Bass Straits off Tasmania, where one also finds porous sands extending all the way up to the sea floor in a tectonically active region — exactly the situation we have here."

On the other hand, the new regulations did specify that oil companies would henceforth be financially responsible for damages resulting from pollution mishaps. (This had been the *de facto* reality in the Union case; the company had assumed responsibility for the clean-up, and advised stockholders that such costs were covered by "more than adequate" insurance.[9]) The liability requirement has been vociferously condemned by the oil companies — particularly by those firms which have failed to make significant strikes on their Channel leases (*SBNP*, March 14, 1969). Several of these companies have now entered suit (supported by the ACLU) against the federal government charging that the arbitrary changing of lease conditions renders Channel exploitation "economically and practically impossible," thus depriving them of rights of due process (*SBNP*, April 10, 1969:A-1).

The weaknesses of the new regulations came not as a surprise to people who had already adapted to thinking of Oil and the Interior Department as the same source. There was much less preparation for the results of the Presidential Committee of "distinguished" scientists and engineers (the DuBridge Panel) which was to recommend means of eliminating the seepage under Platform A. Given the half-hearted, inexpensive, and primitive attempts by Union Oil to deal with the seepage, feeling ran high that at last the technological sophistication of the nation would be harnessed to solve this particular vexing problem. Instead, the panel — after a two-day session and after hearing testimony from no one not connected with either Oil or Interior — recommended the "solution" of drilling an additional 50 wells under Platform A in order to pump the area dry as quickly as possible. The process would require ten to twenty years, one member of the panel estimated.[10]

The recommendation was severely terse, requiring no more than one and a half pages of type. Despite an immediate local clamor, Interior refused to make public the data or the reasoning behind the recommendations. The information on Channel geological conditions was provided by the oil companies; the Geological Survey routinely depends upon the oil industry for the data upon which it makes its "regulatory" decisions. The data, being proprietary, could thus not be released. Totally inexplicable, in light of this "explanation," is Interior's continuing refusal to immediately provide the information given a recent clear-

---

[9] Letter from Fred Hartley, President of Union Oil, to "all shareholders," dated February 7, 1969.

[10] Robert Curry of the geography department of the University of California, Santa Barbara, warned that such a tactic might in fact accelerate leakage. If, as he thought, the oil reservoirs under the Channel are linked, accelerated development of one such reservoir would, through erosion of subterranean linkage channels, accelerate the flow of oil into the reservoir under Platform A, thus adding to the uncontrolled flow of oil through the sands and into the ocean. Curry was not asked to testify by the DuBridge Panel.

ance by Union Oil for public release of all the data. Santa Barbara's local experts have thus been thwarted by the counter-arguments of Oil-Interior that "if you had the information we have, you would agree with us."

Science was also having its non-neutral consequences on the other battlefront being waged by Santa Barbarans. The chief Deputy Attorney General of California, in his April 7 speech to the blue-ribbon Channel City Club of Santa Barbara, complained that the oil industry "is preventing oil drilling experts from aiding the Attorney General's office in its lawsuits over the Santa Barbara oil spill" (SBNP, Aug. 8, 1969). Complaining that his office has been unable to get assistance from petroleum experts at California universities, the Deputy Attorney General further stated:

> The university experts all seem to be working on grants from the oil industry. There is an atmosphere of fear. The experts are afraid that if they assist us in our case on behalf of the people of California, they will lose their oil industry grants.

At the Santa Barbara Campus of the University, there is little Oil money in evidence and few, if any, faculty members have entered into proprietary research arrangements with Oil. Petroleum geology and engineering is simply not a local specialty. Yet it is a fact that Oil interests did contact several Santa Barbara faculty members with offers of funds for studies of the ecological effects of the oil spill, with publication rights stipulated by Oil.[11] It is also the case that the Federal Water Pollution Control Administration explicitly requested a UC Santa Barbara botanist to withhold the findings of his study, funded by that Agency, on the ecological consequences of the spill (SBNP, July 29, 1969:A-3).

Except for the Deputy Attorney General's complaint, none of these revelations received any publicity outside of Santa Barbara. But the Attorney's allegation became something of a statewide issue. A professor at the Berkeley campus, in his attempt to refute the allegation,

---

[11] Verbal communication from one of the faculty members involved. The kind of "studies" which oil enjoys is typified by a research conclusion by Professor Wheeler J. North of Cal Tech, who after performing a one week study of the Channel ecology under Western Oil and Gas Association sponsorship, determined that it was the California winter floods which caused most of the evident disturbance and that (as quoted from the Association Journal) "Santa Barbara beaches and marine life should be back to normal by summer with no adverse impact on tourism." Summer came with oil on the beaches, birds unreturned, and beach motels with unprecedented vacancies.

actually confirmed it. Wilbur H. Somerton, Professor of petroleum engineering, indicated he could not testify against Oil

> because my work depends on good relations with the petroleum industry. My interest is serving the petroleum industry. I view my obligation to the community as supplying it with well-trained petroleum engineers. We train the industry's engineers and they help us. (*SBNP*, April 12, 1969, as quoted from a *San Francisco Chronicle* interview.)

Santa Barbara's leaders were incredulous about the whole affair. The question — one which is more often asked by the downtrodden sectors of the society — was asked: "Whose University is this, anyway?" A local executive and GOO leader asked, "If the truth isn't in the universities, where is it?" A conservative member of the State Legislature, in a move reminiscent of SDS demands, went so far as to ask an end to all faculty "moonlighting" for industry. In Santa Barbara, the only place where all of this publicity was occurring, there was thus an opportunity for insight into the linkages between knowledge, the University, government and Oil and the resultant non-neutrality of science. The backgrounds of many members of the DuBridge Panel were linked publicly to the oil industry. In a line of reasoning usually the handiwork of groups like SDS, a *News-Press* letter writer labeled Dr. DuBridge as a servant of Oil interests because, as a past President of Cal Tech, he would have had to defer to Oil in generating the massive funding which that institution requires. In fact, the relationship was quite direct. Not only has Union Oil been a contributor to Cal Tech, but Fred Hartley (Union's President) is a Cal Tech trustee. The impropriety of such a man as DuBridge serving as the key "scientist" in determining the Santa Barbara outcome seemed more and more obvious.

TAXATION AND PATRIOTISM: DISILLUSIONMENT

From Engler's detailed study of the politics of Oil, we learn that the oil companies combat local resistance with arguments that hurt: taxation and patriotism. They threaten to take their operations elsewhere, thus depriving the locality of taxes and jobs. The more grandiose argument is made that oil is necessary for the national defense; hence, any weakening of "incentives" to discover and produce oil plays into the hands of the enemy.

Santa Barbara, needing money less than most locales and valuing environment more, learned enough to know better. Santa Barbara wanted Oil to leave, but Oil would not. Because the oil is produced in federal waters, only a tiny proportion of Santa Barbara County's budget indirectly comes from oil, and virtually none of the city of Santa Barbara's budget comes from oil. *News-Press* letters and articles disposed of the defense argument with these points: (1) oil companies deliberately limit oil production under geographical quota restrictions designed to maintain the high price of oil by regulating supply; (2) the federal oil import quota (also sponsored by the oil industry) which restricts imports from abroad, weakens the country's defense posture by forcing the nation to exhaust its own finite supply while the Soviets rely on the Middle East; (3) most oil imported into the U.S. comes from relatively dependable sources in South America which foreign wars would not endanger; (4) the next major war will be a nuclear holocaust with possible oil shortages a very low level problem.

Just as an attempt to answer the national defense argument led to conclusions the very opposite of Oil's position, so did a closer examination of the tax argument. For not only did Oil not pay very much in local taxes, Oil also paid very little in *federal* taxes. In another of its front-page editorials the *News-Press* made the facts clear. The combination of the output restrictions, extraordinary tax write-off privileges for drilling expenses, the import quota, and the 27.5 per cent depletion allowance, all created an artificially high price of U.S. oil — a price almost double the world market price for the comparable product delivered to comparable U.S. destinations.[12] The combination of incentives available creates a situation where some oil companies pay no taxes whatever during extraordinarily profitable years. In the years 1962–1966, Standard of New Jersey paid less than 4 per cent of profits in taxes, Standard of California, less than 3 per cent, and 22 of the largest oil companies paid slightly more than 6 per cent (*SBNP*, February 16, 1969:A-1). It was pointed out, again and again to Santa Barbarans, that it was this system of subsidy which made the relatively high cost deep-sea exploration and drilling in the Channel profitable in the first place. Thus, the citizens of Santa Barbara, as federal taxpayers and fleeced consumers, were subsidizing their own demise. The consequence of such a revelation can only be *infuriating*.

[12] Cf. Walter J. Mead, "The Economics of Depletion Allowance," testimony presented to Assembly Revenue and Taxation Committee, California Legislature, June 10, 1969, mimeo; "The System of Government Subsidies to the Oil Industry," testimony presented to the U.S. Senate Subcommittee on Antitrust and Monopoly, March 11, 1969. The ostensible purpose of the depletion allowance is to encourage oil companies to explore for new oil reserves. A report to the Treasury Department by Consad Research Corp. concluded that *elimination* of the depletion allowance would decrease oil reserves by only 3 per cent. The report advised that more efficient means could be found than a system which causes the government to pay $10 for every $1 in oil added to reserves. (Cf. Leo Rennert, "Oil Industry's Favors," *SBNP*, April 27, 1969, pp. A-14, 15 as reprinted from the *Sacramento Bee*.)

THE MOBILIZATION OF BIAS

The actions of Oil and Interior and the contexts in which such actions took place can be reexamined in terms of their function in diffusing local opposition, disorienting dissenters, and otherwise limiting the scope of issues which are potentially part of public controversies. E. E. Schatt-schneider has noted:

> All forms of political organization have a bias in favor of the exploitation of some kinds of conflict and the suppression of others because *organization is the mobilization of bias.* Some issues are organized into politics while others are organized out.

Expanding the notion slightly, certain techniques shaping the "mobilization of bias" can be said to have been revealed by the present case study.

1. *The pseudo-event.* Boorstin has described the use of the pseudo-event in a large variety of task accomplishment situations. A pseudo-event occurs when men arrange conditions to simulate a certain kind of event, such that certain prearranged consequences follow as though the actual event had taken place. Several pseudo-events may be cited. *Local participation in decision making.* From the outset, it was obvious that national actions vis-à-vis Oil in Santa Barbara had as their strategy the freezing out of any local participation in decisions affecting the Channel. Thus, when in 1968 the federal government first called for bids on a Channel lease, local officials were not even informed. When subsequently queried about the matter, federal officials indicated that the lease which was advertised for bid was just a corrective measure to prevent drainage of a "little old oil pool" on federal property adjacent to a state lease producing for Standard and Humble. This "little old pool" was to draw a high bonus bid of $21,189,000 from a syndicate headed by Phillips (*SBNP*, February 9, 1969:A-17). Further, local officials were not notified by any government agency in the case of the original oil spill, nor (except after the spill was already widely known) in the case of any of the previous or subsequent more "minor" spills. Perhaps the thrust of the federal government's colonialist attitude toward the local community was contained in an Interior Department engineer's memo written to J. Cordell Moore, Assistant Secretary of Interior, explaining the policy of refusing public hearings prefatory to drilling: "We preferred not to stir up the natives any more than possible."[13] (The memo

---

[13] Cranston publicly confronted the staff engineer, Eugene Standley, who stated that he could neither confirm nor deny writing the memo. (Cf. *SBNP*, March 11, 1969, p. A-1.)

was released by Senator Cranston and excerpted on page 1 of the *News-Press*.)

Given this known history, the Santa Barbara County Board of Supervisors refused the call for "participation" in drawing up new "tougher" drilling regulations, precisely because they knew the government had no intention of creating "safe" drilling regulations. They refused to take part in the pseudo-event and thus refused to let the consequences (in this case the appearance of democratic decision-making and local assent) of a pseudo-event occur.

Other attempts at the staging of pseudo-events may be cited. Nixon's "inspection" of the Santa Barbara beachfront was an obvious one. Another series of pseudo-events were the Congressional hearings staged by legislators who were, in the words of a local well-to-do lady leader of GOO, "kept men." The locals blew off steam — but the hearing of arguments and the proposing of appropriate legislation based on those arguments (the presumed essence of the Congressional hearing as a formal event) certainly did not come off. Many Santa Barbarans had a similar impression of the court hearings regarding the various legal maneuvers against oil drilling; legal proceedings came to be similarly seen as ceremonious arrangements for the accomplishing of tasks not revealed by their formally-stated properties.

2. *The creeping event.* A creeping event is, in a sense, the opposite of a pseudo-event. It occurs when something *is* actually taking place, but when the manifest signs of the event are arranged to occur at an inconspicuously gradual and piecemeal pace, thus eliminating some of the consequences which would otherwise follow from the event if it were to be perceived all-at-once to be occurring. Two major creeping events were arranged for the Santa Barbara Channel. Although the great bulk of the bidding for leases in the Channel occurred simultaneously, the first lease was, as was made clear earlier, advertised for bid prior to the others and prior to any public announcement of the leasing of the Channel. The federal waters' virginity was thus ended with only a whimper. A more salient example of the creeping event is the resumption of production and drilling after Hickel's second moratorium. Authorization to resume *production* on different specific groups of wells occurred on these dates in 1969: February 17; February 21; February 22; and March 3. Authorization to resume *drilling* of various groups of new wells was announced by Interior on these dates in 1969: April 1, June 12, July 2, August 2, and August 16. (This is being written on August 20.) Each time, the resumption was announced as a safety precaution to relieve pressures, until finally on the most recent resumption date, the word "deplete" was used for the first time as the reason for granting

permission to drill. There is thus no *particular* point in time in which production and drilling was re-authorized for the Channel — and full resumption has still not been officially authorized.

A creeping event has the consequences of diffusing resistance to the event by holding back what journalists call a "time peg" on which to hang "the story." Even if the aggrieved party should get wind that "something is going on," strenuous reaction is inhibited. Non-routine activity has as its prerequisite the crossing of a certain threshold point of input; the dribbling out of an event has the consequence of making each of the revealed inputs fall below the threshold level necessary for non-routine activity. By the time it becomes quite clear that "something *is* going on" both the aggrieved and the sponsors of the creeping event can ask why there should be a response "*now*" when there was none previously to the very same kind of stimulus. In such manner, the aggrieved has resort only to frustration and a gnawing feeling that "events" are sweeping him by.

3. The "neutrality" of science and the "knowledge" producers. I have already dealt at some length with the disillusionment of Santa Barbarans with the "experts" and the University. After learning for themselves of the collusion between government and Oil and the use of secret science as a prop to that collusion, Santa Barbarans found themselves in the unenviable position of having to demonstrate that science and knowledge were, in fact, not neutral arbiters. They had to demonstrate, by themselves, that continued drilling was not safe, that the "experts" who said it was safe were the hirelings directly or indirectly of Oil interests and that the report of the DuBridge Panel recommending massive drilling was a fraudulent document. They had to document that the University *petroleum* geologists were themselves in league with their adversaries and that knowledge unfavorable to the Oil interests was systematically withheld by virtue of the very structure of the knowledge industry. As the SDS has learned in other contexts, this is no small task. It is a long story to tell, a complicated story to tell, and one which pits lay persons (and a few academic renegades) against a profession and patrons of a profession. An illustration of the difficulties involved may be drawn from very recent history. Seventeen Santa Barbara plaintiffs, represented by the ACLU, sought a temporary injunction against additional Channel drilling at least until the information utilized by the DuBridge Panel was made public and a hearing could be held. The injunction was not granted and, in the end, the presiding federal judge ruled in favor of what he termed the "expert" opinions available to the Secretary of the Interior. It was a function of limited time for rebuttal, the disorienting confusions of courtroom procedures, and also perhaps the desire to not offend the Court, that the ACLU lawyer could not make his subtle, complex and highly controversial case that the "experts" were partisans and that their scientific "findings" follow from that partisanship.

4. *Constraints of communication media.* Just as the courtroom setting was not amenable to a full reproduction of the details surrounding the basis for the ACLU case, so the media in general — through restrictions of time and style — prevent a full airing of the details of the case. A more cynical analysis of the media's inability to make known the Santa Barbara "problem" in its full fidelity might hinge on an allegation that the media are constrained by fear of "pressures" from Oil and its allies; Metromedia, for example, sent a team to Santa Barbara which spent several days documenting, interviewing and filming for an hour-long program — only to suddenly drop the whole matter due to what is reported by locals in touch with the network to have been "pressures" from Oil. Such blatant interventions aside, however, the problem of full reproduction of the Santa Barbara "news" would remain problematic nonetheless.

News media are notorious for the anecdotal nature of their reporting; even so-called "think pieces" rarely go beyond a stringing together of proximate "events." There are no analyses of the "mobilization of bias" or linkages of men's actions and their pecuniary interests. Science and learning are assumed to be neutral; regulatory agencies are assumed to function as "watch-dogs" for the public. Information to the contrary of these assumptions is treated as exotic exception; in the manner of Drew Pearson columns, exception piles upon exception without intellectual combination, analysis or ideological synthesis. The complexity of the situation to be reported, the wealth of details needed to support such analyses require more time and effort than journalists have at their command. Their recitation would produce long stories not consistent with space requirements and make-up preferences of newspapers and analogous constraints of the other media. A full telling of the whole story would tax the reader/viewer and would risk boring him.

For these reasons, the rather extensive media coverage of the oil spill centered on a few dramatic moments in its history (e.g., the initial gusher of oil) and a few simple-to-tell "human interest" aspects such as the pathetic deaths of the sea birds struggling along the oil-covered sands. With increasing temporal and geographical distance from the initial spill, national coverage became increasingly rare and increasingly sloppy. Interior statements on the state of the "crisis" were reported without local rejoinders as the newsmen who would have gathered them began leaving the scene. It is to be kept in mind that, relative to other local events, the Santa Barbara spill received extraordinarily extensive national coverage.[14] The point is that this coverage is nevertheless inadequate in both its quality and quantity to adequately inform the American public.

5. *The routinization of evil.* An oft quoted American cliché is that the news media cover only the "bad" things; the everyday world of people going about their business in conformity with American ideals loses out to the coverage of student and ghetto "riots," wars and crime, corruption and sin. The grain of truth in this cliché should not obfuscate the fact that there are *certain kinds of evil* which, partially for reasons cited in the preceding paragraphs, also lose their place in the public media and the public mind. Pollution of the Santa Barbara Channel is now routine; the issue is not whether or not the Channel is polluted, but *how much* it is polluted. A recent oil slick discovered off a Phillips Platform in the Channel was dismissed by an oil company official as a "routine" drilling by-product which was not viewed as "obnoxious." That "about half" of the current oil seeping into the Channel is allegedly being recovered is taken as an improvement sufficient to preclude the "outrage" that a big national story would require.

Similarly, the pollution of the "moral environment" becomes routine; politicians are, of course, on the take, in the pockets of Oil, etc. The depletion allowance issue becomes not whether or not such special benefits should exist at all, but rather whether it should be at the level of 20 or 27.5 per cent. "Compromises" emerge such as the 24 per cent depletion allowance and the new "tough" drilling regulations, which are already being hailed as "victories" for the reformers (cf. *Los Angeles Times*, July 14, 1969:17). Like the oil spill itself, the depletion allowance debate becomes buried in its own disorienting detail, its ceremonious pseudo-events and in the triviality of the "solutions" which ultimately come to be considered as the "real" options. Evil is both banal and complicated; both of these attributes contribute to its durability.[15]

THE STRUGGLE FOR THE MEANS TO POWER

It should (although it does not) go without saying that the parties competing to shape decision-making on oil in Santa Barbara do not have equal access to the means of "mobilizing bias" which this paper has discussed. The same social structural characteristics which Michels has asserted make for an "iron law of oligarchy" make for, in this case, a series of extraordinary advantages for the Oil-government combine. The

---

[14] Major magazine coverage occurred in these (and other) national publications: *Time* (Feb. 14, 1969); *Newsweek* (March 3, 1969); *Life* (June 13, 1969); *Saturday Review* (May 10, 1969); *Sierra Club Bulletin*; *Sports Illustrated* (April 10, 1969). The last three articles cited were written by Santa Barbarans.

[15] The notion of the banality of evil is adapted from the usage of Arendt, 1963.

ability to create pseudo-events such as Nixon's Santa Barbara inspection or controls necessary to bring off well-timed creeping events are not evenly distributed throughout the social structure. Lacking such ready access to media, lacking the ability to stage events at will, lacking a well-integrated system of arrangements for goal attainment (at least in comparison to their adversaries), Santa Barbara's leaders have met with repeated frustrations.

Their response to their relative powerlessness has been analogous to other groups and individuals who, from a similar vantage point, come to see the system up close. They become willing to expand their repertoire of means of influence as their cynicism and bitterness increase concomitantly. Letter writing gives way to demonstrations, demonstrations to civil disobedience. People refuse to participate in "democratic procedures" which are a part of the opposition's event-management strategy. Confrontation politics arise as a means of countering with "events" of one's own, thus providing the media with "stories" which can be simply and energetically told. The lesson is learned that "the power to make a reportable event is . . . the power to make experience."

Rallies were held at local beaches; Congressmen and state and national officials were greeted by demonstrations. (Fred Hartley, of Union Oil, inadvertently landed his plane in the midst of one such demonstration, causing a rather ugly name-calling scene to ensue.) A "sail-in" was held one Sunday with a flotilla of local pleasure boats forming a circle around Platform A, each craft bearing large anti-oil banners. (Months earlier boats coming near the platforms were sprayed by oil personnel with fire hoses.) City-hall meetings were packed with citizens reciting "demands" for immediate and forceful local action.

A City Council election in the midst of the crisis resulted in the landslide election of the Council's bitterest critic and the defeat of a veteran Councilman suspected of having "oil interests." In a rare action, the News-Press condemned the local Chamber of Commerce for accepting oil money for a fraudulent tourist advertising campaign which touted Santa Barbara (including its beaches) as restored to its former beauty. (In the end, references to the beaches were removed from subsequent advertisements, but the oil-financed campaign continued briefly.)

In the meantime, as a Wall Street Journal reporter was to observe "a current of gloom and despair" ran through the ranks of Santa Barbara's militants. The president of Sloan Instruments Corporation, an international R & D firm with headquarters in Santa Barbara, came to comment:

We are so God-damned frustrated. The whole democratic process seems to be falling apart. Nobody responds to us, and we end up doing things progressively less reasonable. This town is going to blow up if there isn't some reasonable attitude expressed by the Federal Government — nothing seems to happen except that we lose.

Similarly, a well-to-do widow, during a legal proceeding in Federal District Court in which Santa Barbara was once again "losing," whispered in the author's ear: "Now I understand why those young people at the University go around throwing things. . . . The individual has no rights at all."

One possible grand strategy for Santa Barbara was outlined by a local public relations man and GOO worker:

> We've got to run the oil men out. The city owns the wharf and the harbor that the company has to use. The city has got to deny its facilities to oil traffic, service boats, cranes and the like. If the city contravenes some federal navigation laws (which such actions would unquestionably involve), to hell with it.
>
> The only hope to save Santa Barbara is to awaken the nation to the ravishment. That will take public officials who are willing to block oil traffic with their bodies and with police hoses, if necessary. Then federal marshals or federal troops would have to come in. This would pull in the national news media (*SBNP*, July 6, 1969, p. 7).

This scenario has thus far not occurred in Santa Barbara, although the use of the wharf by the oil industries has led to certain militant actions. A picket was maintained at the wharf for two weeks, protesting the conversion of the pier from a recreation and tourist facility to a heavy industrial plant for the use of the oil companies.[16] A boycott of other wharf businesses (e.g., two restaurants) was urged. The picket line was led by white, middle-class adults — one of whom had almost won the mayoralty of Santa Barbara in a previous election. Hardly a "radical" or a "militant," this same man was several months later representing his neighborhood protective association in its opposition to the presence of a "Free School" described by this man (somewhat ambivalently) as a "hippie hotel."

Prior to the picketing, a dramatic Easter Sunday confrontation (involving approximately 500 persons) took place between demonstrators and city police. Unexpectedly, as a wharf rally was breaking up, an oil service truck began driving up the pier to make delivery of casing supplies for oil drilling. There was a spontaneous sit-down in front of the truck. For the first time since the Ku Klux Klan folded in the 1930's,

16 As a result of local opposition, Union Oil was to subsequently move its operations from the Santa Barbara wharf to a more distant port in Ventura County.

a group of Santa Barbarans (some young, some "hippie," but many hard-working middle-class adults), was publicly taking the law into its own hands. After much lengthy discussion between police, the truck driver and the demonstrators, the truck was ordered away and the demonstrators remained to rejoice their victory. The following day's *News-Press* editorial, while not supportive of such tactics, found much to excuse — noteworthy given the paper's long standing *bitter* opposition to similar tactics when exercised by dissident Northern blacks or student radicals.

A companion demonstration on the water failed to materialize; a group of Santa Barbarans was to sail to the Union platform and "take it"; choppy seas, however, precluded a landing, causing the would-be conquerors to return to port in failure.

It would be difficult to speculate at this writing what forms Santa Barbara's resistance might take in the future. The veteran *News-Press* reporter who has covered the important oil stories has publicly stated that if the government fails to eliminate both the pollution and its causes "there will, at best, be civil disobedience in Santa Barbara and at worst, violence." In fact, talk of "blowing up" the ugly platforms has been recurrent — and is heard in all social circles.

But just as this kind of talk is not completely serious, it is difficult to know the degree to which the other kinds of militant statements are serious. Despite frequent observations of the "radicalization"[17] of Santa Barbara, it is difficult to determine the extent to which the authentic grievances against Oil have generalized to a radical analysis of American society. Certainly an SDS membership campaign among Santa Barbara adults would be a dismal failure. But that is too severe a test. People, especially basically contented people, change their world-view only very slowly, if at all. Most Santa Barbarans go about their comfortable lives in the ways they always did; they may even help Ronald Reagan to another term in the statehouse. But I do conclude that large numbers of persons have been moved, and that they have been moved in the directions of the radical left. They have gained insights into the structure of power in America not possessed by similarly situated persons in other parts of the country. The claim is thus that some Santa Barbarans, especially those with most interest and most information about the oil spill and its surrounding circumstances, have come to view power in America more intellectually, more analytically, more sociologically — more *radically* — than they did before.

I hold this to be a general sociological response to a series of

<hr/>

[17] Cf. Morton Mintz, "Oil Spill 'Radicalizes' a Conservative West Coast City," *Washington Post*, June 29, 1969, pp. C-1, 5.

concomitant circumstances, which can be simply enumerated (*again!*) as follows:

1. *Injustice.* The powerful are operating in a manner inconsistent with the normatively sanctioned expectations of an aggrieved population. The aggrieved population is deprived of certain felt needs as a result.

2. *Information.* Those who are unjustly treated are provided with rather complete information regarding this disparity between expectations and actual performances of the powerful. In the present case, that information has been provided to Santa Barbarans (and only to Santa Barbarans) by virtue of their own observations of local physical conditions and by virtue of the unrelenting coverage of the city's newspaper. Hardly a day has gone by since the initial spill that the front page has not carried an oil story; everything the paper can get its hands on is printed. It carries analyses; it makes the connections. As an appropriate result, Oil officials have condemned the paper as a "lousy" and "distorted" publication of "lies."[18]

3. *Literacy and leisure.* In order for the information relevant to the injustice to be assimilated in all its infuriating complexity, the aggrieved parties must be, in the larger sense of the terms, literate and leisured. They must have the ability and the time to read, to ponder and to get upset.

My perspective thus differs from those who would regard the radical response as appropriate to some form or another of social or psychological freak. Radicalism is not a subtle form of mental illness (cf. recent statements of such as Bettelheim) caused by "rapid technological change," or increasing "impersonality" in the modern world; radicals are neither "immature," "underdisciplined," nor "anti-intellectual." Quite the reverse. They are persons who most clearly live under the conditions specified above and who make the most rational (and moral) response, given those circumstances. Thus radical movements draw their membership disproportionately from the most leisured, intelligent and informed of the white youth, and from the young blacks whose situations are most analogous to these white counterparts.

THE ACCIDENT AS A RESEARCH METHODOLOGY

If the present research effort has had as its strategy anything pretentious enough to be termed a "methodology," it is the methodology of what could be called "accident research." I define an "accident" as an

---

[18] Union Oil's public relations director stated: "In all my long career, I have never seen such distorted coverage of a news event as the *Santa Barbara News-Press* has foisted on its readers. It's a lousy newspaper." (*SBNP*, May 28, 1969, p. A-1.)

occasion in which miscalculation leads to the breakdown of customary order. It has as its central characteristic the fact that an event occurs which is, to some large degree, unanticipated by those whose actions caused it to occur. As an event, an accident is thus crucially dissimilar both from the pseudo-event and the creeping event. It differs from the pseudo-event in that it bespeaks of an authentic and an unplanned happening; it differs from the creeping event in its suddenness, its sensation, in the fact that it brings to light a series of preconditions, actions and consequences all at once. It is "news" — often sensational news. Thresholds are reached; attentions are held.

The accident thus tends to have consequences which are the very opposite of events which are pseudo or creeping. Instead of being a deliberately planned contribution to a purposely developed "social structure" (or, in the jargon of the relevant sociological literature, "decisional outcome"), it has as its consequence the revelation of features of a social system, or of individuals' actions and personalities, which are otherwise deliberately obfuscated by those with the resources to create pseudo- and creeping events. A resultant convenience is that the media, at the point of accident, may come to function as able and persistent research assistants.

At the level of everyday individual behavior, the accident is an important lay methodological resource of gossipers — especially for learning about those possessing the personality and physical resources to shield their private lives from public view. It is thus that the recent Ted Kennedy accident functioned so well for the purpose (perhaps useless) of gaining access to that individual's private routines and private dispositions. An accident such as the recent unprovoked police shooting of a deaf mute on the streets of Los Angeles provides analogous insights into routine police behavior which official records could never reveal. The massive and unprecedented Santa Barbara oil spill has similarly led to important revelations about the structure of power. An accident is thus an important instrument for learning about the lives of the powerful and the features of the social system which they deliberately and quasi-deliberately create. It is available as a research focus for those seeking a comprehensive understanding of the structure of power in America.

FINALE

Bachrach and Baratz have pointed to the plight of the pluralist students of community power who lack any criteria for the inevitable *selecting* of the "key political decisions" which serve as the basis for their research conclusions. I offer accident as a criterion. An accident is not a decision, but it does provide a basis for insight into whole series of decisions and non-decisions, events and pseudo-events which, taken together, might provide an explanation of the structure of power. Even though the local community is notorious for the increasing triviality of the decisions which occur within it, accident research at the local level might serve as "micro"-analyses capable of revealing the "second face of power," ordinarily left faceless by traditional community studies which fail to concern themselves with the processes by which bias is mobilized and thus how "issues" rise and fall.

The present effort has been the relatively more difficult one of learning not about community power, but about national power — and the relationship between national and local power. The "findings" highlight the extraordinary intransigence of national institutions in the face of local dissent, but more importantly, point to the processes and tactics which undermine that dissent and frustrate and radicalize the dissenters.

The relationship described between Oil, government, and the knowledge industry does not constitute a unique pattern of power in America. All major sectors of the industrial economy lend themselves to the same kind of analysis as Oil in Santa Barbara. Where such analyses have been carried out, the results are analogous in their content and analogous in the outrage which they cause. The nation's defeat in Vietnam, in a sense an accident, has led to analogous revelations about the arms industry and the manner in which American foreign policy is waged.[19] Comparable scrutinies of the agriculture industry, the banking industry, etc., would, in my opinion, lead to the same infuriating findings as the Vietnam defeat and the oil spill.

The national media dwell upon only a few accidents at a time. But across the country, in various localities, accidents routinely occur — accidents which can tell much not only about local power, but about national power as well. Community power studies typically have resulted in revelations of the "pluralistic" squabbles among local sub-elites which are stimulated by exogenous interventions. Accident research at the local level might bring to light the larger societal arrangements which structure the parameters of such local debate. Research at the local level could thus serve as an avenue to knowledge about *national* power. Sociologists should be ready when an accident hits in their neighborhood, and then go to work.

---

[19] I have in mind the exhaustively documented series of articles by I. F. Stone in the *New York Review of Books* over the course of 1968 and 1969, a series made possible, in part, by the outrage of Senator Fulbright and others at the *mistake* of Vietnam.

IX

Religion, magic, and world view

People seem most content when they are confident about themselves and the order of things around them. Uncertainty breeds debilitating anxiety; insecurity saps people's sense of purpose and their willingness to participate in social activity. Most of the time our usual cultural institutions serve as a lens through which we can reliably view and interpret the world and respond to its demands. But from time to time the unexpected or the contradictory intervenes to shake our assurance. A farmer may wonder about his skill when a properly planted and tended crop fails to grow. A wife may feel bewildered when the man she has treated with tenderness and justice for many years runs off with another woman. Death, natural disaster, and countless other forms of adversity strike without warning, eating away at the foundations of our confidence.

At these crucial points in life, we often fill the gap in our knowledge with answers of another kind. We employ a religious dimension to help account for the vagaries of our experience. Religion is cultural knowledge, often associated with the supernatural, that people use to cope with the ultimate problems of their existence. Its use gives us a sense of understanding and control. A crop failure takes on meaning if it can be attributed to the will of God. Unfaithfulness in a spouse makes sense when it is thought to be the outcome of love magic. Adversity, if not controllable, may seem less threatening when we identify the spirit, deity, or witch causing it.

People may deal with misfortune and uncertainty through magic or religious ritual. Magic consists of the strategies used to control supernatural power. Specialists in magic, often referred to as shamans possess their own power or know sayings and rituals that control supernatural force. They seek to produce clearly defined ends, such as the healing of a patient or the growth of a crop. During the ritual, the magician may imitate the desired result, may draw power to effect it from some sacred fetish such as a rabbit's foot, or may minister to a piece of the object or person he wishes to influence.

Religious ritual most often entails the worship of deities or spirits. Supplicants seek to influence supernatural beings through prayer, sacrifice, and several other forms of religious expression. Worshippers do not control the gods, but they do achieve a sense of well-being in the belief that their world is in friendly, or at least trustworthy, hands.

World view refers to a system of comprehensive concepts and often unstated assumptions about life. It usually contains a cosmology about the way things are and a mythology concerning how things have come to be that way. World view presents answers to some of the more general questions and contradictions surrounding our lives. Death, conflicting values, and the meaning of human existence may all find explanation in a group's world view.

Religion, magic, and world view also serve a social function. Human societies are fragile, complex entities, continuously bombarded by disruptive changes and strained by the individual ambitions of their members. Important values are easily forgotten or ignored; significant social conventions may disappear or meet with a variety of interpretations. Religion and magic regularly dramatize important features of the social structure. In our society, preachers of many denominations and faiths regularly remind us of our social responsibilities, emphasize the importance of our relationships by conducting baptisms and weddings, and review what was laudable about us at our funerals. Such social consequences go hand in hand with religion's psychological functions.

29

When technology fails:
Magic and religion in New Guinea
PHILIP L. NEWMAN

All men experience anxiety when confronted with situations they cannot control, and in many societies natural methods of influencing and predicting events work only part of the time. In such instances, supernatural forces are invoked to account for such events and man's relation to them. In this article, Philip Newman describes the use of magic and witchcraft by a highland New Guinea people and shows that they employ such practices throughout their lives whenever faced with uncertainty. He suggests that magical procedures can be ranked according to their ability to release tension, and that the choice of particular magical practices correlates with the degree of anxiety to be reduced.

Man has created many forms in his quest for means of dealing with the world around him. Whether these forms be material tools, social groups, or intangible ideas, they are all, in a sense, "instruments": each is a means to some end; each has a purpose that it fulfills. When we think of such things as magical rites, a belief in ghosts, or accusations of sorcery, however, the matter of purpose becomes less obvious. In the descriptions and in the case history that follow, we will try both to show something of the magical and religious beliefs of a New Guinea people and to demonstrate the purposes that these beliefs have for the men who hold them.

In the mountainous interior of Australian New Guinea, the Asaro

Originally published as "Sorcery, Religion, and the Man." Reprinted with permission from *Natural History* Magazine, February, 1962. Copyright © The American Museum of Natural History, 1962. Illustrations are omitted.

River has its headwaters some thirty miles to the north of Goroka, a European settlement that serves as the administrative center for the Central Highlands District. Near Goroka, the Asaro flows through a wide valley where the ground cover is mostly grasses and reeds. In its upper reaches, this valley narrows into a gorge where steep, heavily forested ridges reach out toward the river from mountain masses on either side. Some 12,000 people live on this part of the river, occupying an area of approximately 200 square miles. While these people are culturally and linguistically similar, they do not form a single political unit. Indeed, before contact with Europeans, the area was characterized by incessant intertribal warfare. Even now, when active warfare is no longer part of their lives, the pattern of alliances and animosities among the tribes is a factor in social intercourse.

Except for the cessation of warfare, life in the valley today is little changed from what it was before the Australian government began active pacification of the area after the end of World War II. Almost daily, the people climb up from the valley floor to enter the dense forest on the mountain slopes. It is here that building wood is gathered; birds and small marsupials are shot for meat, plumage, or fur; plants that provide for many needs are collected.

Below an altitude of some 7,000 feet, the forest has been cut back to make room for gardens that cling to the sides of steep ridges and crowd together in the narrow valley floors. These gardens provide the people's staple foods — sweet potatoes, yams, sugar cane, and a variety of green vegetables. A woman spends most of her time at garden work, preparing new planting areas, weeding the crop, and harvesting the mature plants. In fallow areas nearby she can turn loose the pigs her husband has entrusted to her care. If they wander too far afield by evening, her call will bring them back on the run. They know that a meal awaits them, as well as a snooze by the fire in their "mother's" house.

While each family may have one or more houses near the forest or in their garden, the center of social life is the village. The villages are located on the tops of ridges in spots usually selected with an eye to their defensibility against enemies. The fifteen to twenty houses that compose each village usually march in single file along the narrow ridge. But, if space permits, they are formed into a square. All the houses are much alike — round, about fifteen feet in diameter, made of double rows of five-foot stakes. The space between the stakes is filled with grass and the outside covered with strips of bark. The roof is thatched and topped with a long, tasseled pole.

Two or three houses always stand out. They are larger, they are not in line with the rest, and they may have as many as eight poles protruding through their roofs. These are the men's houses. As a rule, men and women do not live together, for the men fear that too much contact with women is weakening. For this reason, a man builds a house for his wife — or each of them, if he has more than one — and then helps in the construction of the larger house where he and the other men of the village will sleep apart. Ideally, all the men who live together in a single house can trace their descent back to a known, common ancestor. They thus constitute a lineage. Such a lineage is connected to the other village men's houses by descent links, but in many cases the links are so amorphous that no one can actually tell what they are. Similarly, several villages will be linked together into a clan, but genealogical ties may be more imputed than real.

Just as the forest and the garden represent the physical framework within which each individual lives, so too these various orders of grouping — the lineage, the village, the clan, and the tribe — represent the social framework of existence. The members of these groups are the people with whom each individual is in daily contact. They nurture him, teach him, and assist him in times of crisis. It is from these groups that he derives such things as his name, his rights to the land for gardening and hunting, and the financial help that he needs when it is time to purchase a wife. They hail his birth and mourn his death.

In turn, each individual has obligations to the other members of these groups. He acts as a representative of his group when dealing with outsiders. In this way, he enters into a whole series of relationships with individuals and groups outside his own immediate circle. He may visit a neighboring clan to help one of his own clansmen win the admiration of a prospective bride by sitting up all night near the hot fire singing love songs to her. Or a trip may take him to a nearby tribe, where he dances mightily with other men to show that his group is appreciative of the gift of food and valuables they are about to receive. He may walk several days over difficult ground to reach a completely alien group, where he can barter for shells, plumes, or foodstuffs not available in his own group. As in all societies, the groups comprising the society provide for the individual, while the individual, in turn, contributes some of his efforts to the life of the group.

Man not only has his tools and his society to help cope with the world: he also has his ideas. There are some problems presented by the environment for which the people of the upper Asaro have not yet devised a mechanical or technical solution. There are other problems for which a technical solution seems not enough. Finally, there are problems for which an idea seems to be an inherently better solution than a physical or social tool. It is here that we enter the realm of magic and religion.

A great many of the activities among the upper Asaro people have a magical or religious component. When a child is born, it is cleaned, fed, and covered with grease to help protect it from the cool mountain air. It is also protected, nonphysically, by burying its umbilical cord in some secluded spot — so that sorcerers cannot later use this piece of the newformed being to cause illness or death by magical means. During the first few days of life, the infant is also made to accept, via magic, his first social responsibility — not to cry at night and disturb its mother. A small bundle of sweet-smelling grass is placed on the mother's head and her desire for uninterrupted slumber is blown into the grass by an attendant. The grass is then crushed over the head of the child and its pungent odor released so that the infant will breathe in the command along with the scent of the plant.

Throughout an individual's life there will be magical rites to protect him from various dangers, to overcome difficulties, and to assist his growth. When a young boy kills his first animal, his hand will be magically "locked" in the position that first sent an arrow on a true course. When he reaches puberty and moves out of his mother's house to begin his life in the men's house, he will be ritually cleansed of the contamination he has been subjected to during his years of association with women. If he were not so cleansed, he would never become strong enough to engage in men's activities. During the years when a young man is trying to win the favor of a girl, he not only relies on his prowess in singing love songs and his decorations, but on his knowledge of love magic as well. If all the usual spells and potions fail, he may utilize one especially powerful form that is thought to make him appear to his beloved with an entirely new face — the face of someone he knows she likes.

In his mature years, when a man's attention turns to the growth of pigs and gardens, he will have magical as well as technical skills to help him. Gardens are not difficult to grow in this fertile land, but it is still wise to put a certain series of leaves across one's fences, so that any thief will find his arms and legs paralyzed should he decide to raid the garden. It also behooves one whose gardens are near the main trails and settlements to give them magical assistance, for a slow-growing garden in such a conspicuous place could be an embarrassment.

The raising of pigs is a more difficult matter, and it is here that magical and religious rites become greatly elaborated. Some of these rites are performed by an individual for his own pigs. It may be a simple performance, as when smoke is blown into the ear of a wild pig to tame it. The theory is that the smoke cools and dries the pig's "hot" disposition. On the other hand, these individual rites may attain considerable complexity, as in the propitiation of forest spirits called *nokondisi*. These spirits are capricious in nature — sometimes playing malicious tricks on men and sometimes performing acts of kindness. Each man, therefore, maintains a small, fenced enclosure in which he builds a miniature earth oven and a tiny house. By placing food in the earth oven he may be able to entice a *nokondisi* to come live near his pigs and watch after them. In return for the food, the spirit will help bring in lost pigs, protect the herd from thieves, and carry the animals safely across flooded streams during the rainy season.

In addition to the magic performed by an individual on behalf of his own pigs, some rather elaborate rites are performed by the lineage and clan for all the pigs belonging to these groups. The largest of these is the *gerua* ceremony, performed at intervals of from five to seven years. In this ritual, hundreds of pigs are killed and used to pay off various kinds of economic obligations to other clans. It is a time for feasting and dancing, for courting and reunion. It is also a time for propitiating the ghosts of the dead in the hope that they will help the living grow their pigs. All the pigs are killed in the name of particular ghosts. The songs are pleas for ghostly assistance. The wooden *gerua* boards, with their colorful geometric designs, are visible symbols to the ghosts that they have not been forgotten. It is not tender sentiment that motivates this display, however. Rather, it is the fear that failure to do so will engender the wrath of the ever watchful dead.

The magical and religious beliefs that we have so far examined are all used in conjunction with other practices of a nonmagical nature. There are some areas, however, where no purely technical solutions are available, and where magic and religion are the only "tools" available. One such area is sickness. The people of the upper Asaro are not generally aware of modern medical practices, although efforts are being made in that direction. The nonmagical techniques available to them, such as inhaling the steam from fragrant plants to relieve a stopped-up nose, are few. These remedies do not extend to more serious maladies. When serious illness strikes, the only recourse is to magic.

The magical solutions available are many and varied. There are herbs with magical properties that are administered in much the same way as are medicines in our own society. I made a cursory check, however, which seems to show that few of the plants possess any curative value.

Ghosts and forest spirits are frequently thought to be the causes of illness, for they are deemed capable of entering the body and devouring a person's inner organs. Cures for such illnesses usually involve propitiation of the offending supernatural.

Witches and sorcerers are believed to be another major cause of illness, for they are supposedly capable of injecting foreign bodies into a victim, or performing black magic on objects that have been in association with the victim. To cure illness caused in this way involves calling in a magical specialist who can either extract the foreign bodies or retrieve the objects being operated upon.

While the ideas and rites listed here do not exhaust the entire inventory available to the group under discussion, they give some sense of the variety that exists. The notions are interesting in themselves, but the question of how an individual makes use of these notions is even more fascinating. Let us look at a crisis in the life of one of these people, and see how he picks and chooses among the various "tools" at his disposal.

Ombo was a young man in his early thirties. He had been married for about five years, but was childless. Early one April, it was announced in the traditional style that his wife, Magara, was with child. On such an occasion, a food distribution is held in the village and the announcement, along with gifts of food, was sent out to related villages. Ombo was instructed in the food taboos he would have to undergo during the period of his wife's pregnancy to protect himself from her increased contamination.

All went well for the first few weeks and then Magara became ill. It is doubtful that her illness was associated with her pregnancy, for her symptoms were the classic signs of malaria — a rather rare disease in this part of the highlands. The first attempts to cure her involved a variety of highly regarded pseudomedications.

A potion of sweet-smelling leaves was administered. A command to the effect that the illness should depart was blown into the leaves, and the leaves were eaten. It was thought that the command, thus internalized, would drive out the illness.

At various other times, attempts were made to relieve her headaches and body pains by rubbing the afflicted areas with stinging nettles. It was held that when the welts and the pain caused by the nettles subsided, the pains in her body would also leave. On one occasion her husband blew smoke over her during a period of fever because, as we have seen, smoke is held to have a cooling and drying effect. He also painted various parts of her body with mud in an effort to cause the pain to dry up at the same time the mud dried.

This kind of treatment continued until early May without any noticeable improvement in Magara's condition. After almost a month had passed and it became apparent that the illness was not going away, Ombo began to speculate on a possible cause. During the next few weeks he came up with several solutions. While he had been away from the village, working for Europeans in Goroka, he had acquired some charms to help him win at a card game popular among the sophisticated younger men.

One of these charms was fairly new and he was worried that he might not have gained sufficient control over it. Since he kept it hidden in his wife's house, his conclusion was that the charm was exerting its influence on her and causing the illness. He therefore removed it from her house and sent it away to a friend in another tribe. There was no improvement in his wife's condition.

Ombo's next action was to destroy his spirit house. He had not kept it in good repair and had not been diligent in feeding the *nokondisi* that lived there. His father suggested that the angered spirit was taking revenge on Magara. By destroying the house of the spirit, Ombo caused it to retreat to the forest where it could do no harm. Finally, he burned the costly paraphernalia of a potent sorcery technique he had purchased some years before, fearing it affected his wife.

By now it was late in May. Magara had become so ill that she stopped all but the most minimal work in her garden. Concern about her illness began to increase, and people outside the immediate family began to speculate about its cause. Ombo's older brother mentioned one day that a malevolent ghost might be behind it. It was not long after this that a meeting was held in the men's house and Fumai, a member of the lineage, recounted a dream he had had the night before. In it, he had seen the ghost of Ombo's great-grandmother sitting in the forest near the spot where *gerua* boards are displayed for the ancestors. She had covered herself with ashes and, in a fit of self-pity, was wailing loudly because no one had made a *gerua* board in her honor at the last *gerua* ceremony, and no one had killed a pig in her name. Since ashes are put on at the death of a near relative as a sign of mourning, while clay is put on if the deceased is more distantly related, and since ghosts are thought to be capable of causing death, it was concluded that the dream was prophetic. It implied the imminent death of Magara at the great-grandmother's hands unless something were done.

The next day, Ombo and his wife, along with his parents and siblings, set out for the spot where the ghost had been "seen." A pig was killed there in honor of the ghost. It was cooked in an earth oven filled with valued food items — the largest sweet potatoes, the most succulent yams, and the most highly prized varieties of taro. While water was being poured into the oven, a speech was addressed to the ghost. It was pointed out that the food had been prepared and donated in her honor at considerable trouble to those present. The feeling was expressed that she should be satisfied with the amount and the quality of the offering. She was then told to refrain from causing trouble in the future. As the food steamed in the oven, a *gerua* board was made in the ghost's honor and placed among others in a nearby tree. Some of the food was eaten and the rest was later distributed among members of the lineage.

Things seemed to go well for the next few weeks. Magara improved and was able to return to her work in the garden. Discussion of the topic was dropped. Then, late in June, she suddenly became ill again. Ombo was greatly upset. I suggested to him that she might have malaria and should be taken to the medical aid post. But Ombo did not want to do this, for by now he was convinced that his wife was being attacked by a sorcerer. To deal with this threat, a magical specialist had to be called in. It was several days before he arrived, for he lived some distance away in another tribe. As with any good "doctor," his first acts were aimed at relieving his patient's pain and fever. With much physical strain, he literally pulled the pain from her body and cast it into the ground where it could do no further harm. His next task was to find out what was causing her illness. For over two hours he sat chatting with Ombo and Magara, discussing the history of the illness, the treatments that had been used, and their own life histories. All the while, he puffed on a tobacco pipe made of a bamboo tube. The degree of irritation caused by the smoke in his throat signalized the appearance in the conversation of significant diagnostic events. Finally, he announced his conclusion — illness by black magic.

To eliminate the effects of the imputed black magic, the object being manipulated by the sorcerer had to be recovered. To do this, the magical specialist first had a bundle of long, thin leaves prepared. Into the bundle were put cooked pork and a variety of plants with magical properties. The specialist never directly touched the bundle himself, but directed Ombo in its preparation. When the bundle was completed, it and a specially prepared bamboo tube were both carried into Magara's house. She was given the tube to hold and the bundle was hung in the rafters near the center pole. After a rite to protect her from further sorcery, Ombo and Magara were locked together in the house.

The specialist remained outside. He walked round and round the house, reciting spells and whirling a special plant around his head. He was pulling the unknown object away from the sorcerer and bringing it back home. The ceremony became a real struggle: the object would come tantalizingly close, only to slip away. Then the specialist announced that the object had arrived. Magara was instructed to open the bundle in the rafters. Inside, among the bits of meat, were a small spider and a piece of string of the type used to hang ornaments around the neck.

The spider, Magara and Ombo were told, was an assistant to the specialist. It had taken the string out of the sorcerer's house and into the open where the specialist could reach it with his powers. The sorcerer was thought to be a young man who had once wanted to marry Magara. The existence of a disappointed suitor was one fact that had come out during the specialist's long interview. When Magara had married Ombo, the suitor had become angry and cut a bit of her necklace string to use for sorcery. The specialist placed the recovered string in the bamboo tube that Magara had been holding, and the tube was then hidden away among the thatch.

From that time until late September, when I left the area, Magara did not experience any further attacks of illness, although she was not in the best of health. The community considered her cured. Significantly, her child was born prematurely in September and died two days later, but no one saw any connection between this death and her illness.

What, then, can we say about the purpose of such ideas and behavior patterns? A situation such as Magara's creates a great deal of tension in an individual who experiences it. If magic does nothing more, it allows the bearer of this tension to act. Both the patient and those concerned feel that something is being done. The pioneer anthropologist Bronislaw Malinowski long ago made the point: "Magic expresses the greater value for man of confidence over doubt, of steadfastness over vacillation, of optimism over pessimism."

It is a rare man indeed, however, who can maintain his confidence and optimism in the face of repeated failure. The question then arises, why is it that magic is not more readily given up? Three answers have traditionally been given to this question, all of them valid. In the first place, for people such as these, there is no alternative. Secondly, for the believer in the efficacy of magic, the occasional chance successes are more significant than repeated failure. Finally, explanations for failures are always at hand. Inadvertent errors in spells or formulas that must be performed precisely, or imagined countermagic, are ready explanations that are necessarily built into the very nature of magic.

The case history we have seen suggests still a fourth answer. This answer becomes apparent, however, only if we examine the way in which an individual makes use of the magical notions available to him. In the progression of the various magical techniques and explanations employed by Ombo, we can see that they call for behavior patterns allowing for increasingly aggressive release of the tension built up in him by the failure of previously selected techniques.

The simple pseudomedicinal rites, such as rubbing with nettles and painting with mud, were enough to reduce the tension of the initial crisis. The treatment was symptomatic and there was no attempt to identify the cause of the illness. When it became apparent that these techniques had failed, we find Ombo resorting to the more drastic measure of destroying valuable property. The frustration was not yet great enough to cause him to seek outlets in other people: that which he destroyed and removed from his use belonged only to him. In the next phase, we find that a ghost is predicated as the causative agent. One need not be nice to ghosts. They, like the living, are thought to be a mercenary lot who do not much care what is said about them as long as they get their just due. The speech made to the great-grandmother was studded with commands and expressions of anger at the trouble the ghost had caused. This was an excellent mechanism for the release of tension, just as was the physical act of killing the pig.

Finally, we see the most aggressive act of all — accusing a specific individual of sorcery. The accused individual was a member of an enemy tribe and lived some distance away. It was, therefore, unlikely that accuser and accused would often meet. But if the two had come together, a fight would have been inevitable. In former times, this could have led to open warfare. Thus, Ombo not only used magic as a tool against disease, but also selected the magical tools in such an order that his own increasing anxiety was relieved by increasingly aggressive actions. It is thus not only the forms created by man that enable him to cope with the world he meets, but the very way in which he manipulates those forms that are available to him.

30

Baseball magic
GEORGE J. GMELCH

Americans pride themselves on their "scientific" approach to life and problem solving. But as George Gmelch demonstrates in this article, American baseball players, much like the New Guinea Highlanders described earlier in this section by Phillip Newman, also depend to a great extent on supernatural forces to ensure success in their athletic endeavors. He demonstrates that the findings of anthropologists in distant cultures shed light on our own cultural practices.

We find magic wherever the elements of chance and accident, and the emotional play between hope and fear have a wide and extensive range. We do not find magic wherever the pursuit is certain, reliable, and well under the control of rational methods. — Bronislaw Malinowski.

Professional baseball is a nearly perfect arena in which to test Malinowski's hypothesis about magic. The great anthropologist was not, of course, talking about sleight of hand but of rituals, taboos and fetishes that men resort to when they want to ensure that things go their own way. Baseball is rife with this sort of magic, but, as we shall see, the players use it in some aspects of the game far more than in others.

Everyone knows that there are three essentials of baseball — hitting, pitching and fielding. The point is, however, that the first two, hitting and pitching, involve a high degree of chance. The pitcher is the player least able to control the outcome of his own efforts. His best pitch may be hit for a bloop single while his worst pitch may be hit directly to one of his fielders for an out. He may limit the opposition to a single hit and lose, or he may give up a dozen hits and win. It is not uncommon for pitchers to perform well and lose, and vice versa; one has only to

Published by permission of Transaction, Inc., from *Transaction*, Vol. 8, #8, copyright © 1971 by Transaction, Inc.

look at the frequency with which pitchers end a season with poor won-lost percentages but low earned run averages (number of runs given up per game). The opposite is equally true: some pitchers play poorly, giving up many runs, yet win many games. In brief, the pitcher, regardless of how well he performs, is dependent upon the proficiency of his teammates, the inefficiency of the opposition and the supernatural (luck).

But luck, as we all know, comes in two forms, and many fans assume that the pitcher's tough losses (close games in which he gave up very few runs) are eventually balanced out by his "lucky" wins. This is untrue, as a comparison of pitchers' lifetime earned run averages to their overall won-lost records shows. If the player could apply a law of averages to individual performance, there would be much less concern about chance and uncertainty in baseball. Unfortunately, he cannot and does not.

Hitting, too, is a chancy affair. Obviously, skill is required in hitting the ball hard and on a line. Once the ball is hit, however, chance plays a large role in determining where it will go, into a waiting glove or whistling past a falling stab.

With respect to fielding, the player has almost complete control over the outcome. The average fielding percentage or success rate of .975, compared to a .245 success rate for hitters (the average batting average), reflects the degree of certainty in fielding. Next to the pitcher or hitter, the fielder has little to worry about when he knows that better than 9.7 times in ten he will execute his task flawlessly.

If Malinowski's hypothesis is correct, we should find magic associated with hitting and pitching, but none with fielding. Let us take the evidence by category — ritual, taboo and fetish.

RITUAL

After each pitch, ex-major leaguer Lou Skeins used to reach into his back pocket to touch a crucifix, straighten his cap and clutch his genitals. Detroit Tiger infielder Tim Maring wore the same clothes and put them on exactly in the same order each day during a batting streak. Baseball rituals are almost infinitely various. After all, the ballplayer can ritualize any activity he considers necessary for a successful performance, from the type of cereal he eats in the morning to the streets he drives home on.

Usually, rituals grow out of exceptionally good performances. When the player does well he cannot really attribute his success to skill alone. He plays with the same amount of skill one night when he gets four hits as the next night when he goes hitless. Through magic, such as ritual, the player seeks greater control over his performance, actually control over the elements of chance. The player, knowing that his ability is fairly constant, attributes the inconsistencies in his performance to some form of behavior or a particular food that he ate. When a player gets four hits in a game, especially "cheap" hits, he often believes that there must have been something he did, in addition to his ability, that shifted luck to his side. If he can attribute his good fortune to the glass of iced tea he drank before the game or the new shirt he wore to the ballpark, then by repeating the same behavior the following day he can hope to achieve similar results. (One expression of this belief is the myth that eating certain foods will give the ball "eyes," that is, a ball that seeks the gaps between fielders.) In hopes of maintaining a batting streak, I once ate fried chicken every day at 4:00 P.M., kept my eyes closed during the national anthem and changed sweat shirts at the end of the fourth inning each night for seven consecutive nights until the streak ended.

Fred Caviglia, Kansas City minor league pitcher, explained why he eats certain foods before each game: "Everything you do is important to winning. I never forget what I eat the day of a game or what I wear. If I pitch well and win I'll do it all exactly the same the next day I pitch. You'd be crazy not to. You just can't ever tell what's going to make the difference between winning and losing."

Rituals associated with hitting vary considerably in complexity from one player to the next, but they have several components in common. One of the most popular is tagging a particular base when leaving and returning to the dugout each inning. Tagging second base on the way to the outfield is habitual with some players. One informant reported that during a successful month of the season he stepped on third base on his way to the dugout after the third, sixth and ninth innings of each game. Asked if he ever purposely failed to step on the bag he replied, "Never! I wouldn't dare, it would destroy my confidence to hit." It is not uncommon for a hitter who is playing poorly to try different combinations of tagging and not tagging particular bases in an attempt to find a successful combination. Other components of a hitter's ritual may include tapping the plate with his bat a precise number of times or taking a precise number of warm-up swings with the leaded bat.

One informant described a variation of this in which he gambled for a certain hit by tapping the plate a fixed number of times. He touched the plate once with his bat for each base desired: one tap for a single, two for a double and so on. He even built in odds that prevented him from asking for a home run each time. The odds of hitting a single with one tap were one in three, while the chances of hitting a home run with four taps were one in 12.

Clothing is often considered crucial to both hitters and pitchers. They may have several athletic supporters and a number of sweat shirts with ritual significance. Nearly all players wear the same uniform and undergarments each day when playing well, and some even wear the same street clothes. In 1954, the New York Giants, during a 16-game winning streak, wore the same clothes in each game and refused to let them be cleaned for fear that their good fortune might be washed away with the dirt. The route taken to and from the stadium can also have significance; some players drive the same streets to the ballpark during a hitting streak and try different routes during slumps.

Because pitchers only play once every four days, the rituals they practice are often more complex than the hitters', and most of it, such as tugging the cap between pitches, touching the rosin bag after each bad pitch or smoothing the dirt on the mound before each new batter, takes place on the field. Many baseball fans have observed this behavior never realizing that it may be as important to the pitcher as throwing the ball.

Dennis Grossini, former Detroit farmhand, practiced the following ritual on each pitching day for the first three months of a winning season. First, he arose from bed at exactly 10:00 A.M. and not a minute earlier or later. At 1:00 P.M. he went to the nearest restaurant for two glasses of iced tea and a tuna fish sandwich. Although the afternoon was free, he observed a number of taboos such as no movies, no reading and no candy. In the clubhouse he changed into the sweat shirt and jock he wore during his last winning game, and one hour before the game he chewed a wad of Beechnut chewing tobacco. During the game he touched his letters (the team name on his uniform) after each pitch and straightened his cap after each ball. Before the start of each inning he replaced the pitcher's rosin bag next to the spot where it was the inning before. And after every inning in which he gave up a run he went to the clubhouse to wash his hands. I asked him which part of the ritual was most important. He responded: "You can't really tell what's most important so it all becomes important. I'd be afraid to change anything. As long as I'm winning I do everything the same. Even when I can't wash my hands [this would occur when he must bat] it scares me going back to the mound. . . . I don't feel quite right."

One ritual, unlike those already mentioned, is practiced to improve the power of the baseball bat. It involves sanding the bat until all the varnish is removed, a process requiring several hours of labor, then rubbing rosin into the grain of the bat before finally heating it over a flame. This ritual treatment supposedly increases the distance the ball travels after being struck. Although some North Americans prepare their bats in this fashion it is more popular among Latin Americans. One informant admitted that he was not certain of the effectiveness of the treatment. But, he added, "There may not be a God, but I go to church just the same."

Despite the wide assortment of rituals associated with pitching and hitting, I never observed any ritual related to fielding. In all my 20 interviews only one player, a shortstop with acute fielding problems, reported any ritual even remotely connected to fielding.

TABOO

Mentioning that a no-hitter is in progress and crossing baseball bats are the two most widely observed taboos. It is believed that if the pitcher hears the words "no-hitter" his spell will be broken and the no-hitter lost. As for the crossing of bats, that is sure to bring bad luck; batters are therefore extremely careful not to drop their bats on top of another. Some players elaborate this taboo even further. On one occasion a teammate became quite upset when another player tossed a bat from the batting cage and it came to rest on top of his. Later he explained that the top bat would steal hits from the lower one. For him, then, bats contain a finite number of hits, a kind of baseball "image of limited good." Honus Wagner, a member of baseball's Hall of Fame, believed that each bat was good for only 100 hits and no more. Regardless of the quality of the bat he would discard it after its 100th hit.

Besides observing the traditional taboos just mentioned, players also observe certain personal prohibitions. Personal taboos grow out of exceptionally poor performances, which a player often attributes to some particular behavior or food. During my first season of professional baseball I once ate pancakes before a game in which I struck out four times. Several weeks later I had a repeat performance, again after eating pancakes. The result was a pancake taboo in which from that day on I never ate pancakes during the season. Another personal taboo, born out of similar circumstances, was against holding a baseball during the national anthem.

Taboos are also of many kinds. One athlete was careful never to step on the chalk foul lines or the chalk lines of the batter's box. Another would never put on his cap until the game started and would not wear it at all on the days he did not pitch. Another had a movie taboo in which he refused to watch a movie the day of a game. Often certain uniform numbers become taboo. If a player has a poor spring training or a bad year, he may refuse to wear the same uniform number again. I would not wear double numbers, especially 44 and 22. On several occasions, teammates who were playing poorly requested a change of uniform during the middle of the season. Some players consider it so important that they will wear the wrong size uniform just to avoid a certain number or to obtain a good number.

Again, with respect to fielding, I never saw or heard of any taboos being observed, though of course there were some taboos, like the uniform numbers, that were concerned with overall performance and so included fielding.

FETISHES

These are standard equipment for many baseball players. They include a wide assortment of objects: horsehide covers of old baseballs, coins, bobby pins, protective cups, crucifixes and old bats. Ordinary objects are given this power in a fashion similar to the formation of taboos and rituals. The player during an exceptionally hot batting or pitching streak, especially one in which he has "gotten all the breaks," credits some unusual object, often a new possession, for his good fortune. For example, a player in a slump might find a coin or an odd stone just before he begins a hitting streak. Attributing the improvement in his performance to the new object, it becomes a fetish, embodied with supernatural power. While playing for Spokane, Dodger pitcher Alan Foster forgot his baseball shoes on a road trip and borrowed a pair from a teammate to pitch. That night he pitched a no-hitter and later, needless to say, bought the shoes from his teammate. They became his most prized possession.

Fetishes are taken so seriously by some players that their teammates will not touch them out of fear of offending the owner. I once saw a fight caused by the desecration of a fetish. Before the game, one player stole the fetish, a horsehide baseball cover, out of a teammate's back pocket. The prankster did not return the fetish until after the game, in which the owner of the fetish went hitless, breaking a batting streak. The owner, blaming his inability to hit on the loss of the fetish, lashed out at the thief when the latter tried to return it.

Rube Waddel, an old-time Philadelphia Athletic pitching great, had a hairpin fetish. However, the hairpin he possessed was only powerful as long as he won. Once he lost a game he would look for another hairpin, which had to be found on the street, and he would not pitch until he found another.

The use of fetishes follows the same pattern as ritual and taboo in that they are connected only with hitting or pitching. In nearly all cases the player expressed a specific purpose for carrying a fetish, but never did a player perceive his fetish as having any effect on his fielding.

I have said enough, I think, to show that many of the beliefs and practices of professional baseball players are magical. Any empirical connection between the ritual, taboo and fetishes and the desired event is quite absent. Indeed, in several instances the relationship between the cause and effect, such as eating tuna fish sandwiches to win a ball game, is even more remote than is characteristic of primitive magic. Note, however, that unlike many forms of primitive magic, baseball magic is usually performed to achieve one's own end and not to block someone else's. Hitters do not tap their bats on the plate to hex the pitcher, but to improve their own performance.

Finally, it should be plain that nearly all the magical practices that I participated in, observed or elicited, support Malinowski's hypothesis that magic appears in situations of chance and uncertainty. The large amount of uncertainty in pitching and hitting best explains the elaborate magical practices used for these activities. Conversely, the high success rate in fielding, .975, involving much less uncertainty, offers the best explanation for the absence of magic in this realm.

31

Urban witches

EDWARD J. MOODY

*Witchcraft is usually seen as a feature of underdeveloped
societies, but it is also present in the urban centers of the United
States. Edward Moody presents empirical data on the person
who uses black magic, and analyzes the function it has for the
magician. Even in "civilized" societies, some men try to explain
events in their lives and to compensate for personal inadequacies
and anxieties by a belief in witchcraft.*

Every Friday evening just before midnight, a group of men and women
gathers at a home in San Francisco; and there, under the guidance of
their high priest, a sorcerer or magus sometimes called the "Black Pope
of Satanism," they study and practice the ancient art of black magic.
Precisely at midnight they begin to perform Satanic rituals that apparently differ little from those allegedly performed by European Satanists and witches at least as early as the seventh century. By the dim
and flickering light of black candles, hooded figures perform their rites
upon the traditional Satanic altar — the naked body of a beautiful
young witch — calling forth the mysterious powers of darkness to do
their bidding. Beneath the emblem of Baphomet, the horned god, they
engage in indulgences of flesh and sense for whose performance their
forebears suffered death and torture at the hands of earlier Christian
zealots.

Many of these men and women are, by day, respected and responsible citizens. Their nocturnal or covert practice of the black art

This article was written especially for this volume. The research on which the
article is based was conducted from October 1967 to August 1969. Since then,
changes in the institutional structure of the Church have taken place and the composition of the membership has altered slightly. The patterns of behavior, the
therapeutic interactions described remain, in the author's opinion, essentially unchanged.

would, if exposed, make them liable to ridicule, censure, and even punishment. Even though we live in an "enlightened" age, witches are still
made a focus of a community's aggression and anxiety. They are de-
nounced from the pulpit, prosecuted to the limit of the law, and subjected to extralegal harassment by the fearful and ignorant.

Why then do the Satanists persist? Why do they take these risks?
What benefits do they derive from membership in a Satanic church,
what rewards are earned from the practice of witchcraft? What indulgences are enjoyed that they could not as easily find in one of the more
socially acceptable arenas of pleasure available in our "permissive"
society?

The nearly universal allegation of witchcraft in the various cultures of the world has excited the interest of social scientists for years
and the volume of writing on the topic is staggering. Most accounts of
witchcraft, however, share the common failing of having been written
from the point of view of those who do not themselves practice the
black art. Few, if any, modern authors have had contact with witches,
black magicians, or sorcerers, relying instead on either the anguished
statements of medieval victims of inquisition torture, or other types of
secondhand "hearsay" evidence for their data. To further confuse the
issue, authoritative and respected ethnologists have reported that black
magic and witchcraft constitute an imaginary offense because it is impossible — that because witches cannot do what they are supposed
to do, they are nonexistent.

WITCHES AND MAGICIANS

But the witches live. In 1965 while carrying out other research in San
Francisco, California, I heard rumors of a Satanic cult which planned
to give an All-Hallows Eve blessing to a local chamber of horrors. I
made contact with the group through its founder and high priest and
thus began over two years of participant-observation as a member of a
contemporary black magic group. As a member of this group I interacted
with my fellow members in both ritual and secular settings. The following description is based on the data gathered at that time.

The witches and black magicians who were members of the group
came from a variety of social class backgrounds. All shades of political
opinion were represented from Communist to American Nazi. Many
exhibited behavior identified in American culture as "pathological," such
as homosexuality, sadomasochism, and transvestism. Of the many
characteristics that emerged from psychological tests, extensive observations, and interviews, the most common trait, exhibited by nearly all
Satanic novices, was a high level of general anxiety related to low self-
esteem and a feeling of inadequacy. This syndrome appears to be related

to intense interpersonal conflicts in the nuclear family during socialization. Eighty-five percent of the group, the administrative and magical hierarchy of the church, reported that their childhood homes were split by alcoholism, divorce, or some other serious problem. Their adult lives were in turn marked by admitted failure in love, business, sexual, or social relationships. Before entering the group each member appeared to have been battered by failure in one or more of the areas mentioned, rejected or isolated by a society frightened by his increasingly bizarre and unpredictable behavior, and forced into a continuing struggle to comprehend or give meaning to his life situation.

Almost all members, prior to joining the group, had made some previous attempt to gain control over the mysterious forces operating around them. In order to give their environment some structure, in order to make it predictable and thus less anxiety-provoking, they dabbled in astrology, the Tarot, spiritualism, or other occult sciences, but continued failure in their everyday lives drove them from the passive and fatalistic stance of the astrologer to consideration of the active and manipulative role of sorcerer or witch. In articles in magazines such as *Astrology* and *Fate,* the potential Satanist comes into direct contact with magic, both white and black. Troubled by lack of power and control, the pre-Satanist is frequently introduced to the concept of magic by advertisements which promise "Occult power . . . now . . . for those who want to make real progress in understanding and working the forces that rule our Physical Cosmos . . . a self-study course in the practice of Magic." Or, Ophiel will teach you how to "become a power in your town, job, club, etc.," how to "create a familiar [a personal magic spirit servant] to help you through life," how to "control and dominate others." "The Secret Way" is offered free of charge, and the Esoteric Society offers to teach one how herbs, roots, oils, and rituals may be used, through "white magic," to obtain love, money, power, or a peaceful home. They will also teach one self-confidence and how to banish "unwanted forces." The reader is invited to join the Brotherhood of the White Temple, Inc.; the Monastery of the Seven Rays (specializing in sexual magic); the Radiant School; and numerous other groups that promise to reveal the secrets of success in business, sex, love, and life — the very secrets the potential or pre-Satanist feels have eluded him. Before joining the group, the pre-Satanist usually begins to perform magic ceremonies and rituals whose descriptions he receives for a fee from one of the various groups noted above, from magical wholesale houses, or from occult book clubs. These practices reinforce his "magical world view," and at the same time bring him in contact with other practitioners of the magical arts, both white and black.

Although most of the mail-order magic groups profess to practice

"white" magic — benevolent magic designed only to benefit those involved and never aggressive or selfish, only altruistic — as opposed to
"black," malevolent, or selfish magic, even white magic rituals require
ingredients that are rare enough so they can be bought only at certain
specialty stores. These stores, usually known to the public as candle
shops although some now call themselves occult art supply houses, provide not only the raw materials — oils, incenses, candles, herbs, parch-
ments, etc. — for the magical workings, but serve as meeting places for
those interested in the occult. A request for some specific magic in-
gredient such as "John the Conqueror oil," "Money-come" powder,
"crossing" powder, or black candles usually leads to a conversation
about the magical arts and often to introductions to other female witches
and male warlocks. The realization that there are others who privately
practice magic, white or black, supports the novice magician in his
new-found interest in magical manipulation. The presence of other
witches and magicians in his vicinity serves as additional proof that the
problems he has personally experienced may indeed be caused by
witchcraft, for the pre-Satanist has now met, firsthand, witches and
warlocks who previously were only shadowy figures, and if there are a
few known witches, who knows how many there might be practicing
secretly?

Many witches and magicians never go beyond the private practice
of white or black magic, or at most engage in a form of magic "recipe"
swapping. The individual who does join a formal group practicing magic
may become affiliated with such a group in one of several ways. In some
cases he has been practicing black magic with scant success. Perhaps he
has gone no further than astrology or reading the designs on the ancient Tarot cards, a type of socially acceptable magic which the leader
of the Satanic church disparagingly calls "god in sport clothes." But
the potential Satanist has come to think of the cosmos as being ordered,
and ordered according to magical — that is, imperceptible — principles.
He is prompted by his sense of alienation and social inadequacy to try
to gain control of the strange forces that he feels influence or control
him and, hearing of a Satanic church, he comes to learn magic.

Others join because of anxiety and inadequacy of a slightly different nature. They may be homosexual, nymphomaniac, sadist, or maso-
chist. They usually have some relatively blatant behavioral abnormality
which, though they personally may not feel it wrong, is socially mal-
adaptive and therefore disruptive. As in many "primitive" societies,
magic and witchcraft provide both the "disturbed" persons and, in some
cases, the community at large with a ready and consistent explanation
for those "forces" or impulses which they themselves have experienced.
Seeking control, or freedom, the social deviants come ultimately to the

acknowledged expert in magic of all kinds, the head of the Satanic church, to have their demons exorcised, the spells lifted, and their own powers restored.

Others whose problems are less acute come because they have been brought, in the larger religious context, to think of themselves as "evil." If their struggle against "evil" has been to no avail, many of the individuals in question take this to mean that the power of "evil" is greater than the power of "good" — that "God is dead" — and so on. In their search for a source of strength and security, rather than continue their vain struggle with that "evil" force against which they know themselves to be powerless, they seek instead to identify themselves with evil, to join the "winning" side. They identify with Satan — etymologically the "opposition" — and become "followers of the left-hand path," "walkers in darkness."

Finally, there are, of course, those who come seeking thrills or titillation, lured by rumors of beautiful naked witches, saturnalian orgies, and other strange occurrences. Few of these are admitted into the group.

BLACK MAGIC

For the novice, initial contact with the Satanists is reassuring. Those assisting the "Prince of Darkness" who heads the church are usually officers in the church, long-term members who have risen from the rank and file to positions of trust and authority. They are well-dressed, pleasant persons who exude an aura of confidence and adequacy. Rather than having the appearance of wild-eyed fanatics or lunatics, the Satanists look like members of the middle-class, but successful middle-class. The Prince of Darkness himself is a powerfully built and striking individual with a shaven head and black, well-trimmed beard. Sitting among the implements of magic, surrounded by books that contain the "secrets of the centuries," he affirms for those present what they already know: that there is a secret to power and success which can and must be learned, and that secret is black magic.

All magic is black magic according to the Satanists. There is no altruistic or white magic. Each magician intends to benefit from his magical manipulation, even those workings performed at someone else's behest. To claim to be performing magic only for the benefit of others is either hypocrisy — the cardinal sin in Satanic belief — or naiveté, another serious shortcoming. As defined by the Satanists, magic itself is a suprisingly common-sense kind of phenomenon: "the change in situations or events in accordance with one's will, which would, using normally accepted methods, be unchangeable." Magic can be divided into two categories: ritual (ceremonial) and nonritual (manipulative).

Ritual, or "the greater magic," is performed in a specified ritual area and at a specific time. It is an emotional, not an intellectual act. Although the Satanists spend a great deal of time intellectualizing and rationalizing magic power, they state specifically that "any and all intellectual activity must take place *before* the ceremony, not during it." [1]

The "lesser magic," nonritual (manipulative) magic, is, in contrast, a type of transactional manipulation based upon a heightened awareness of the various processes of behavior operative in interaction with others, a Satanic "games people play." The Satanist in ritual interaction is taught to analyze and utilize the motivations and behavioral Achilles' heels of others for his own purposes. If the person with whom one is interacting has masochistic tendencies, for example, the Satanist is taught to adopt the role of sadist, to "indulge" the other's desires, to be dominant, forceful, and even cruel in interaction with him.

Both the greater and the lesser magic is predicated upon a more general "magical" world view in which all elements of the "natural world" are animate, have unique and distinctive vibrations that influence the way they relate to other natural phenomena. Men, too, have vibrations, the principal difference between men and inanimate objects being that men can alter their pattern of vibrations, sometimes consciously and at will. It is the manipulation and the modification of these vibrations, forces, or powers that is the basis of all magic. There are "natural magicians," untrained and unwitting manipulators of magic power. Some, for example, resonate in harmony with growing things; these are people said to have a "green thumb," gardeners who can make anything grow. Others resonate on the frequency of money and have the "Midas touch" which turns their every endeavor into a profit-making venture. Still others are "love magnets"; they automatically attract others to them, fascinate and charm even though they may be physically plain themselves. If one is a "natural magician," he does some of these things unconsciously, intuitively, but because of the intellectual nature of our modern world, most people have lost their sensitivity to these faint vibrations. Such individuals may, if they become witches, magicians or Satanists, regain contact with that lost world just as tribal shamans are able to regain contact with another older world where men communicated with animals and understood their ways. It is this resensitization to the vibrations of the cosmos that is the essence of magical training. It takes place best in the "intellectual decompression chamber" of magic ritual, for it is basically a "subjective" and "non-scientific" phenomenon.

[1] The official doctrine of several Satanic groups within the continental United States is contained in the *Satanic Bible* by Anton Szandor LaVey (New York: Avon Books, 1969), p. 111.

Those who have become members of the inner circle learn to make use of black magic, both greater and lesser in obtaining goals which are the antithesis of Christian dogma. The seven deadly sins of Christian teaching — greed, pride, envy, anger, gluttony, lust, and sloth — are depicted as Satanic virtues. Envy and greed are, in the Satanic theology, natural in man and the motivating forces behind ambition. Lust is necessary for the preservation of the species and not a Satanic sin. Anger is the force of self-preservation. Instead of denying natural instincts the Satanist learns to glory in them and turn them into power.

Satanists recognize that the form of their ritual, its meanings, and its functions are largely determined by the wider society and its culture. The novitiate in the Satanic cult is taught, for example, that the meaning of the word "Satan" etymologically is "the opposition," or "he who opposes," and that Satanism itself arose out of opposition to the demeaning and stultifying institutions of Christianity. The cult recognizes that had there been no Christianity there would be no Satanism, at least not in the form it presently takes, and it maintains that much of the Satanic ritual and belief is structured by the form and content of Christian belief and can be understood only in that larger religious context. The Satanists choose black as their color, not white, precisely because white is the symbol of purity and transcendence chosen by Christianity, and black therefore has come to symbolize the profane earthy indulgences central to Satanic theodicy. Satanists say that their gods are those of the earth, not the sky; that their cult is interested in making the sacred profane, in contrast to the Judeo-Christian cults which seek to make the profane sacred. Satanism cannot, in other words, be understood as an isolated phenomenon, but must be seen in a larger context.

The Satanic belief system, not surprisingly, is the antithesis of Christianity. Their theory of the universe, their cosmology, is based upon the notion that the desired end state is a return to a pagan awareness of the mystical forces inhabiting the earth, a return to an awareness of their humanity. This is in sharp contrast to the transcendental goals of traditional Christianity. The power associated with the pantheon of gods is also reversed: Satan's power is waxing; God's, if he still lives, waning. The myths of the Satanic church purport to tell the true story of the rise of Christianity and the fall of paganism, and there is a reversal here too. Christ is depicted as an early "con man" who tricked an anxious and powerless group of individuals into believing a lie. He is typified as "pallid incompetence hanging on a tree." [2] Satanic novices are taught that early church fathers deliberately picked on those aspects of human desire that were most natural and made them sins, in order

[2] LaVey 1969 : 31.

to use the inevitable transgressions as a means of controlling the popu-
lace, promising them salvation in return for obedience. And finally, their
substantive belief, the very delimitation of what is sacred and what is
profane, is the antithesis of Christian belief. The Satanist is taught to
"be natural; to revel in pleasure and in self-gratification. To emphasize
indulgence and power in this life."

The opposition of Satanists to Christianity may be seen most clearly
in the various rituals of greater magic. Although there are many different types of rituals all aimed at achieving the virtues that are the in-
verted sins of the Christian, we shall examine briefly only two of these:
blasphemy and the invocation of destruction. By far the most famous of
Satanic institutions, the Black Mass and other forms of ritual blasphemy
serve a very real and necessary function for the new Satanist. In many
cases the exhortations and teachings of his Satanic colleagues are not
sufficient to alleviate the sense of guilt and anxiety he feels when engaging in behavior forbidden by Judeo-Christian tradition. The novice
may still cower before the charismatic power of Christian symbols; he
may still feel guilty, still experience anxiety and fear in their presence.
It is here that the blasphemies come into play, and they take many forms
depending on the needs of the individuals involved.

A particular blasphemy may involve the most sacred Christian
rituals and objects. In the traditional Black Mass powerful Christian
symbols such as the crucifix are handled brutally. Some Black Masses
use urine or menstrual flow in place of the traditional wine in an attempt to evoke disgust and aversion to the ritual. If an individual can
be conditioned to respond to a given stimulus, such as the communion
wafer or wine, with disgust rather than fear, that stimulus's power to
cause anxiety is diminished. Sexuality is also used. A young man who
feared priests and nuns was deliberately involved in a scene in which
two witches dressed as nuns interacted with him sexually; his former
neurotic fear was replaced by a mildly erotic curiosity even in the
presence of real nuns. The naked altar — a beautiful young witch — in-
troduces another deliberate note of sexuality into a formerly awe-inspir-
ing scene.

By far the most frequently used blasphemy involves laughter. Awe-
inspiring or fear-producing institutions are made the object of ridicule.
The blasphemous rituals, although still greater magic, are frequently
extremely informal. To the outsider they would not seem to have any
structure; the behavior being exhibited might appear to be a charade,
or a party game. The Satanists decide ahead of time the institution to
be ridiculed and frequently it is a Christian ritual. I have seen a group
of Satanists do a parody of the Christmas manger scene, or dress in
clerical garb while performing a satire of priestly sexual behavior. The

target of blasphemy depends upon the needs of the various Satanists. If the group feels it is necessary for the well-being of one member, they will gladly, even gleefully, blaspheme anything from psychiatry to psychedelics.

In the invocation of destruction black magic reaches its peak. In some cases an individual's sense of inadequacy is experienced as victimization, a sense of powerlessness before the demands of stronger and more ruthless men. The Satanic Bible, in contrast to Christian belief, teaches the fearful novice that "Satan represents vengeance instead of turning the other cheek." In the Third Chapter of the Book of Satan, the reader is exhorted to "hate your enemies with a whole heart, and if a man smite you on one cheek, SMASH him on the other . . . he who turns the other cheek is a cowardly dog." [3]

One of the most frequently used rituals in such a situation is the Conjuration of Destruction, or Curse. Contrary to popular belief, black magicians are not indiscriminately aggressive. An individual must have harmed or hurt a member of the church before he is likely to be cursed. Even then the curse is laid with care, for cursing a more powerful magician may cause one's curse to be turned against oneself. If, in the judgment of the high priest and the congregation, a member has been unjustly used by a non-Satanist, even if the offender is an unaffiliated witch or magician, at the appropriate time in the ritual the member wronged may step forward and, with the aid and support of the entire congregation, ritually curse the transgressor. The name of the intended "sacrifice" is usually written on parchment made of the skin of unborn lamb and burned in the altar flame while the member himself speaks the curse; he may use the standard curse or, if he so desires, prepare a more powerful, individualistic one. In the curse he gives vent to his hostility and commands the legions of hell to torment and sacrifice his victim in a variety of horrible ways. Or, if the Satanist so desires, the High Priest will recite the curse for him, the entire group adding their power to the invocation by spirited responses.

The incidence of harmful results from cursing is low in the church of Satan because of two factors: first, one does not curse other members of the church for fear that their superior magic might turn the curse back upon its user; second, victims outside the congregation either do not believe in the power of black magic or do not recognize the esoteric symbols that should indicate to them they are being cursed.

On only one occasion was I able to see the effect of a curse on a "victim." A member attempted to use the church and its members for publicity purposes without their permission. When the leader of the

[3] LaVey 1969 : 33.

group refused to go along with the scheme, the man quit — an action that would normally have brought no recrimination — and began to slander the church by spreading malicious lies throughout San Francisco social circles. Even though he was warned several times to stop his lies, the man persisted; so the group decided to level the most serious of all curses at him, and a ritual death rune was cast.

Casting a death rune, the most serious form of greater magic, goes considerably beyond the usual curse designed to cause only discomfort or unhappiness, but not to kill. The sole purpose of the death rune is to cause the total destruction of the victim. The transgressor's name is written in blood (to the Satanist, blood is power — the very power of life) on special parchment, along with a number of traditional symbols of ceremonial magic. In a single-minded ritual of great intensity and ferocity, the emotional level is raised to a peak at which point the entire congregation joins in ritually destroying the victim of the curse. In the case in question, there was an orgy of aggression. The lamb's-wool figurine representing the victim was stabbed by all members of the congregation; hacked to pieces with a sword, shot with a small calibre pistol, and then burned.

A copy of the death rune was sent to the man in question, and every day thereafter an official death certificate was made out in his name and mailed to him. After a period of weeks during which the "victim" maintained to all who would listen that he "did not believe in all that nonsense," he entered the hospital with a bleeding ulcer. Upon recovery he left San Francisco permanently.

In fairness, I must add that the "victim" of the curse had previously had an ulcer, was struggling with a failing business, and seemed hypertense when I knew him. His knowledge of the "curse" may have hastened the culmination of his difficulties. The Satanic church, however, claimed it as a successful working, a victory for black magic, and word of it spread among the adherents of occult subculture, enhancing the reputation of the group.

CONCLUSION

Contemporary America is presently undergoing a witchcraft revival. On all levels, from teenagers to octogenarians, interest in, or fear of, witchcraft has increased dramatically over the past two years. It is hardly possible to pass a popular magazine rack without seeing an article about the revival of the black arts. Covens and cults multiply, as does the number of exorcisms and reconsecrations. England, France, Germany, and a host of other countries all report a rebirth of the black art. Why? Those who eventually become Satanists are attempting to cope with the everyday problems of life, with the here and now, rather than with some transcendental afterlife. In an increasingly complex world which they do not fully understand, an anxiety-provoking world, they seek out a group dedicated to those mysterious powers that the sufferers have felt moving them. Fearful of what one witch calls "the dark powers we all feel moving deep within us," they come seeking either *release* or *control*. They give various names to the problems they bring, but all, anxious and afraid, come to the Satanic cult seeking help in solving problems beyond their meager abilities. Whatever their problem — bewitchment, business failure, sexual impotence, or demonic possession — the Satanists, in the ways I have mentioned and many more, *can* and *do* help them. Witchcraft, the witches point out, "is the most practical of all beliefs. According to its devotees, its results are obvious and instantaneous. No task is too high or too lowly for the witch." Above all, the beliefs and practices provide the witch and the warlock with a sense of power, a feeling of control, and an explanation for personal failure, inadequacy, and other difficulties.

Moreover, a seeker's acceptance into the Inner Circle provides a major boost for his self-esteem; he has, for the first time, been accepted into a group as an individual despite his problems and abnormalities. Once within the Inner Circle that support continues. The Satanic group is, according to the cultural standards of his society, amoral, and the Satanist frequently finds himself lauded and rewarded for the very impulses and behavior that once brought shame and doubt.

Each Satanist is taught, and not without reason, that the exposure of his secret identity, of the fact that he is a powerful and adequate black magician, means trouble from a fearful society. Therefore, in keeping with the precepts of lesser magic, he learns to transform himself magically by day (for purposes of manipulation) into a bank clerk, a businessman, or even a college professor. He wears the guise and plays the role expected by society in order to manipulate the situation to his own advantage, to reach his desired goals. Members of society at large, aware only of his "normal" role behavior and unaware of the secret person within, respond to him positively instead of punishing him or isolating him. Then, in the evening, in the sanctity of his home, or when surrounded by his fellow magicians, he reverts to his "true" role, that of Satanic priest, and becomes himself once again. Inadequate and anxious persons, guilty because of socially disapproved impulses, are accepted by the Satanists and taught that the impulses they feel are natural and normal, but must be contained within certain spatial and temporal boundaries — the walls of the ritual chamber, the confines of the Inner Circle.

32

The Maya bonesetter as sacred specialist
BENJAMIN D. PAUL

Religious beliefs and rituals function to provide support in time of crisis. Religious specialists function in the same way at special crisis points within the social life of a community. The midwife, the shaman, and the bonesetter all are sacred specialists in the Guatemalan town discussed in this article. They derive their power from the supernatural; they reduce anxiety and give support and confidence in times of illness and other crises. In this article, Benjamin D. Paul reports on the supernatural summoning of one bonesetter and discusses the function of such specialists in this Mayan community.

Among the dozen Maya communities that ring the shores of Lake Atitlán in the northwestern highlands of Guatemala, the town of San Pedro la Laguna is perhaps the most enterprising and progressive. A few decades ago the Pedranos, with their own labor and initiative, built a road around the steep sides of a huge volcanic mountain, and by now Pedranos own and operate two large buses and a dozen trucks, each representing a capital investment of over $10,000. These vehicles serve San Pedro and the surrounding region by providing efficient transportation to the coastal lowlands and to the capital of Guatemala. For reasons of history and ecology each village in the area has developed distinctive specialties, and it can be said that in recent years modern transport service has become one of San Pedro's specialties.

Another Pedrano specialty of greater antiquity and of quite a different order is the traditional art of bonesetting. In 1941, when we first began fieldwork, a healer named Ventura successfully treated a severe incapacitating ankle sprain sustained by my wife on a rocky San

Reprinted by permission of the author and publisher from *Ethnology* 15, no. 1 (January 1976): 77–82. Bibliography and bibliographic citations are omitted.

Pedro path. Ventura was then 77, and since the turn of the century had been setting broken bones not only for Pedranos but also for accident victims from many other parts of the republic and even from across the borders in El Salvador and Mexico. A decade later Ventura died, and a few years after that his daughter Rosario rather unexpectedly assumed the burden of repairing bone injuries. Because of her good results and widespread reputation, the town of San Pedro continued to attract sufferers from distant places. Rosario still practices today, but she is old and lacks the physical strength to mend some of the more severe fractures. But she is now only one of five or six bonesetters practicing in San Pedro. This is quite a change from the time old Ventura was the lone expert in a town of 2,000 people. The population of San Pedro now approaches 5,000, but the number of native bonesetters has increased disproportionately.

From the outsider's point of view, the healer resets bones by means of adroit manipulation, massaging the area with marrow extracted from beef bones, placing heated tobacco leaves against the bare skin, and applying a tight bandage. A splint of cardboard or slats may be used to immobilize the injured area. But the bonesetters and their clients see the process differently. In their view the work is not done by the human practitioner but by a special little bone concealed in the hand of the healer, who locates the precise point of the break by passing the bone back and forth over the general area of the injury. When the traveling bone finds the critical juncture it comes to a halt and stays clamped to the spot long enough to correct the break or dislocation. In describing the behavior of the searching bone, informants say it generates a force like an electric current that jumps in intensity when it reaches the injury, where it takes hold "like a magnet."

Any citizen of San Pedro can decide to become a carpenter or aspire to own a truck, but no one can simply choose to be a shaman, a bonesetter, or a midwife. To enter one of these sacred professions the individual must receive a supernatural call. To act on one's own initiative would be both ineffective and unsafe; the presumptuous individual would be stricken with death or misfortune. And so would the person who receives the summons and refuses to heed the mandate. The channels for communicating the divine will are multiple and marvelous. In his old age, Ventura recalled how he was induced to be a bonesetter. His story illustrates the complex process of persuasion.

THE CALL OF THE BONE

Not long after marrying at age 20, Ventura had a strange dream. A bone was hopping about. He woke up worried and went off early as usual to work in his distant cornfield. As he neared his destination he saw a curious object in the distance which turned out on closer inspection to be a very shiny bone. The bright object leapt toward him. He drew back in fright, but it jumped in his direction again, and then again. Fearful, and finding his way blocked, Ventura returned home, disguising the cause of his embarrassing retreat by feigning illness and going to bed.

During the night he had another curious dream. This time the visitor was a dwarf who asked Ventura, "Why didn't you pick me up? If you go on refusing you will die." In the morning he arose determined. On the way to work the bone reappeared. Again it jumped. This time Ventura was not afraid. He picked up the object, which measured an inch in diameter, wrapped it in his kerchief, and tucked it into his sash. On the way back he felt it move about. At home he put it in a shoulder bag and hung it in a corner. He did not know the bone's purpose, but instructional dreams followed. The same little man told Ventura that he was destined to aid humanity by caring for the afflicted, "because they are our children." The dwarf taught him a secret song, and at night Ventura would sing it.

In a dream one night the dwarf appeared with a skeleton. He handed Ventura a whip and told him to strike it down. Ventura obeyed and the skeleton collapsed into a heap of bones. Then the dwarf ordered him to put the skeleton back together, threatening to whip him if he failed. Ventura protested, "Señor, I cannot." The dwarf then said, "Where is the bone I gave you?" Ventura fetched the bone he had found on the path. With its help he began to recognize the different parts and to rebuild the skeleton, starting with the little toe bones and proceeding to the bigger bones. When Ventura had reconstructed the entire skeleton under the guidance of his magic bone, the dwarf said, "With this bone you will cure our children." Ventura still did not know just what he was to do, but he kept receiving instructions.

Ventura treated his bone with respect, placing it in a box of its own. When he closed the box he got on his knees and could hear the object making sounds as of people talking inside. He took it out, wrapped it in a silken cloth, blew on it repeatedly, and replaced it carefully. He was told never to let anyone touch the bone or else he or his children would die. The bone told him to guard it well because "I have work to do."

The bone announced that Ventura's young wife would give birth to a boy who would die. A boy was born and lived only a short while. Ventura experienced other misfortunes. He fell to quarreling with his wife, who expressed fear that because of his "fortuna" all their babies were destined to die. He replied that his call came from no human source but from God, that its true purpose was to give life, that they would live better and live longer on earth. But he made no use of the bone for a year. Meanwhile he got sick; his head and his heart began to ache, and he was on the point of death. Only by becoming a healer did he regain his health.

A boy he knew had broken a leg. In a dream the dwarf directed Ventura to use the bone. He complied; the break was mended and in three days the boy was able to walk again. Ventura told no one what he had done, but word spread and his practice grew. He never charged for his services, leaving it up to his patients to donate what they wished or to give nothing at all.

Some of the details of Ventura's experience are unique, but a comparison of his story and those of the other San Pedro bonesetters discloses a common pattern. The candidate encounters a small bone-like object that moves and he is instructed in his dreams to pick it up. He puts it away, and for a period of time, which may be short or last many years, he fails to act on any cryptic messages he receives. He usually suffers for this in some way until he begins to exercise his calling. He is trained by no one, only in dreams is he told how to cure, and in any case it is the secret bone that does the work. Since bonesetting is a hallowed duty the practitioner must not charge for his service.

Bonesetters earn little income from their part-time curing specialty in this money-conscious community. Sometimes they are called to attend an accident victim in another town, staying with the patient for several days or weeks in Chimaltenango or Antigua or wherever it may be. They receive meals and transportation costs and perhaps *"unos centavitos,"* but it is difficult to see what they gain for their time and labor beyond the satisfaction of knowing that they are carrying out God's humanitarian purposes and perhaps gaining a certain amount of immunity from accidents themselves. One bonesetter, who also heads a marimba band that travels to many towns, remarked significantly that he was in four road accidents without ever being injured.

Another bonesetter, who is also a leading midwife in San Pedro, had just been incapacitated with two injured ankles when word arrived that one of her patients was about to give birth. Despite her husband's protests she insisted on going out, and was able to walk after hastily doctoring her own ankles with the aid of a curing bone she had found long ago and had stored away without realizing its significance. The success of this emergency action launched her practice as a bonesetter and changed her luck. Previously prone to slipping and spraining her ankles, she now became nimble and sure-footed.

While all healers claim they acquired their special knowledge in dreams, their dream experiences differ in content and degree of specificity. Ventura had rebuilt the skeleton from the feet up; one of the newer bonesetters recalls beginning with the cranium and ending with the legs and feet. Others do not mention such a dream test at all. The man in Ventura's dreams was a dwarf. In another case he was a very large *ladino* with a beard, dressed completely in white from head to shoes. In the neighboring town of San Juan, which is nearly a suburb of San Pedro, a man destined to be a bonesetter was visited by someone he described as "a dwarf dressed in white like a doctor and with a suitcase." One Pedrano bonesetter described the visitor as a boy dressed in *ladino* clothes. Still another received his message from one of the two angels that guard Jesucristo. This same informant said that when he sets bones he begs forgiveness (*pedir un perdón*) just as Jesus did when he stumbled under the weight of the cross he was carrying.

The Zutuhil phrase describing a curer with supernatural connections is *k'o rxin*, meaning he or she has the gift, and the gift is understood as referring equally to the charismatic quality of the healer and to the object that embodies his power. In Spanish reference the power object, the bone in the case of a bonesetter, is variously called the healer's *suerte*, *fortuna*, or *virtud*. Bonesetters sometimes refer to the object as their instrument (*aparato*, *materiál*), although in their conception the mystic bone is the healer and its possessor the instrument.

The bone can alert its owner by moving or making a sound when a serious fracture occurs somewhere. Unaided, it can hop out of its box into the curer's shoulder bag or the folds of his sash when he leaves the house to travel or work in the field. If the owner drops the bone while mending a fracture, it can bring death to the patient. It can make itself invisible; a stranger might be looking directly at it and yet not see it. It can assume the guise of a man. It can disappear, as Ventura's bone did after that celebrated bonesetter died.

Normally the special objects belonging to sacred curers — shamans, midwives, bonesetters — accompany them in their coffins when they die. But according to Rosario, Ventura had a vision before dying that Rosario one day would become a bonesetter and that the bone should be kept in its usual box. Somehow it came into the possession of a man in San Juan who used it to cure his son's fractured limb, proclaiming that he had found his magic bone. He attracted patients and charged very high fees. This displeased the bone, and in a few weeks it came to Rosario in a dream. The bone told her it had returned because it was displeased by the Juanero's unconscionable behavior and would now remain with Rosario all her life. It said she was to become a bonesetter like her dead father and never charge for her services. In the middle of the night Rosario heard a noise and thought someone was tampering with the box that had belonged to her father. When she examined the box, she found the bone back in its usual place. She burned incense and two candles. Later, she had dreams and eventually, despite delay and reluctance, became a bonesetter, but only after a series of increasingly severe illnesses.

The bonesetter's bone is a sacred object, surrounded by taboos and credited with miraculous abilities. It is a repository of supernatural power, a potent cultural symbol binding patient and practitioner in a bond of faith and assurance. It partakes of the same mystique that draws pilgrims to the site of an enshrined relic. As a sign of the bonesetter's accreditation, it is the equivalent of the doctor's diploma.

Like the secular physician, the Pedrano bonesetter uses his hands to straighten fractures, however he may interpret the source of his dexterity and clinical judgment. In this respect he differs from his counterpart in Zinacantan where the most highly regarded bonesetters are those who "use prayers and other spiritual methods exclusively" while "a bonesetter who actually sets bones is considered far inferior."

In the native view, the bonesetter's medicine works because his bone is a conductor of supernatural forces. For Pedranos the manifest message of the magic bone is that religion empowers medicine. But the latent message reads in reverse: medicine empowers religion. Each instance of curing in the material world recharges faith in the existence of the spiritual world. Pedranos admire material progress. Tired of foot travel and back packs, they value the efficiency of trucks and buses acquired in increasing numbers. But greater mechanical efficiency brings greater human hazards. With more trucks there are more accidents and more need for bonesetters. If setting bones is seen in progressive San Pedro la Laguna as a sacred office, this may be because the very nature of the art — making broken parts whole — so graphically symbolizes and satisfies a profound human yearning to transform disorder into order, to convert chaos into cosmos.

X

Culture change

Nowhere in the world do human affairs remain precisely constant from year to year. Although others may speak of tradition-bound, conservative, changeless societies, new ways of doing things mark the history of even the most stable groups. Change occurs when an Australian aboriginal dreams about a new myth and teaches it to the members of his band; when a loader in a restaurant kitchen invents a way to stack plates more quickly in the dishwasher; or when a New Guinea big-man cites the traditional beliefs about ghosts to justify the existence of a new political office devised by a colonial government. Wherever people interpret their natural and social worlds in a new way, social change has occurred. Broad or narrow, leisurely or rapid, such change is part of life in every society.

    Culture change is extremely complex and is not well understood by social scientists. Although people may alter the way they live for variety or aesthetic pleasure, they most often change their behavior in response to problems or to better fulfill traditional goals. Most culture change begins with innovation or borrowing by one or more individuals. Many changes die early because they fail to gain acceptance by the society at large or even a significant segment of the group. For culture change to occur, innovations or borrowed elements must be accepted and eventually integrated into the existing culture pattern.

444

In the contemporary world the most important stimulus to change is contact among people with different cultures. All the processes of interaction, exchange of ideas, borrowing, and change under these conditions are called *acculturation*. A salient feature of acculturation situations that anthropologists investigate is the relative power over natural resources held by the groups in contact which often determines the course of change. Most non-Western tribal societies have been forced to change by the powerful onslaught of the emissaries of the West. Often this has meant serious cultural loss and social disorganization, conditions which may stimulate nativistic movements or movements for national liberation.

The articles in this section are studies of the effects of culture contact and people's attempts to cope with new and different objects, activities, and ideas. Often welcomed initially, such changes set off a chain reaction of consequences which themselves require adjustment or, if that fails, an entire reordering of world view.

33

Steel axes for stone-age Australians
LAURISTON SHARP

Technology and social structure are closely linked in every society. In this article, Lauriston Sharp shows how the introduction of an apparently insignificant, hatchet-sized steel axe to Australian aborigines can alter the relationship among family members, change patterns of economic exchange, and threaten the very meaning of life itself.

I

Like other Australian aboriginals, the Yir Yoront group which lives at the mouth of the Coleman River on the west coast of Cape York Peninsula originally had no knowledge of metals. Technologically their culture was of the old stone age or paleolithic type. They supported themselves by hunting and fishing, and obtained vegetables and other materials from the bush by simple gathering techniques. Their only domesticated animal was the dog; they had no cultivated plants of any kind. Unlike some other aboriginal groups, however, the Yir Yoront did have polished stone axes hafted in short handles which were most important in their economy.

Towards the end of the 19th century metal tools and other European artifacts began to filter into the Yir Yoront territory. The flow increased with the gradual expansion of the white frontier outward from southern and eastern Queensland. Of all the items of western technology thus made available, the hatchet, or short handled steel axe, was the most acceptable to and the most highly valued by all aboriginals.

In the mid 1930's an American anthropologist lived alone in the bush among the Yir Yoront for 13 months without seeing another white man. The Yir Yoront were thus still relatively isolated and continued to

Reprinted by permission of the author and the Society for Applied Anthropology from *Human Organization* 11(2), 1952.

live an essentially independent economic existence, supporting themselves entirely by means of their old stone age techniques. Yet their polished stone axes were disappearing fast and being replaced by steel axes which came to them in considerable numbers, directly or indirectly, from various European sources to the south.

What changes in the life of the Yir Yoront still living under aboriginal conditions in the Australian bush could be expected as a result of their increasing possession and use of the steel axe?

II. The course of events

Events leading up to the introduction of the steel axe among the Yir Yoront begin with the advent of the second known group of Europeans to reach the shores of the Australian continent. In 1623 a Dutch expedition landed on the coast where the Yir Yoront now live.[1] In 1935 the Yir Yoront were still using the few cultural items recorded in the Dutch log for the aboriginals they encountered. To this cultural inventory the Dutch added beads and pieces of iron which they offered in an effort to attract the frightened "Indians." Among these natives metal and beads have disappeared, together with any memory of this first encounter with whites.

The next recorded contact in this area was in 1864. Here there is more positive assurance that the natives concerned were the immediate ancestors of the Yir Yoront community. These aboriginals had the temerity to attack a party of cattle men who were driving a small herd from southern Queensland through the length of the then unknown Cape York Peninsula to a newly established government station at the northern tip.[2] Known as the "Battle of the Mitchell River," this was one of the rare instances in which Australian aboriginals stood up to European gunfire for any length of time. A diary kept by the cattle men records that: ". . . 10 carbines poured volley after volley into them from all directions, killing and wounding with every shot with very little return, nearly all their spears having already been expended. . . . About 30 being killed, the leader thought it prudent to hold his hand, and let the rest escape. Many more must have been wounded and probably drowned, for 59 rounds were counted as discharged." The European party was in the Yir Yoront area for three days; they then disappeared over the horizon to the north and never returned. In the almost three-year long anthropological investigation conducted some 70 years later — in all the material of hundreds of free association interviews, in texts of hundreds of dreams and myths, in genealogies, and eventually in

---

[1] An account of this expedition from Amboina is given in R. Logan Jack, *Northmost Australia* (2 vols.), London, 1921, Vol. 1, pp. 18–57.

[2] R. Logan Jack, *op. cit.*, pp. 298–335.

hundreds of answers to direct and indirect questioning on just this particular matter — there was nothing that could be interpreted as a reference to this shocking contact with Europeans.

The aboriginal accounts of their first remembered contact with whites begin in about 1900 with references to persons known to have had sporadic but lethal encounters with them. From that time on whites continued to remain on the southern periphery of Yir Yoront territory. With the establishment of cattle stations (ranches) to the south, cattle men made occasional excursions among the "wild black-fellows" in order to inspect the country and abduct natives to be trained as cattle boys and "house girls." At least one such expedition reached the Coleman River where a number of Yir Yoront men and women were shot for no apparent reason.

About this time the government was persuaded to sponsor the establishment of three mission stations along the 700-mile western coast of the Peninsula in an attempt to help regulate the treatment of natives. To further this purpose a strip of coastal territory was set aside as an aboriginal reserve and closed to further white settlement.

In 1915, an Anglican mission station was established near the mouth of the Mitchell River, about a three-day march from the heart of the Yir Yoront country. Some Yir Yoront refused to have anything to do with the mission, others visited it occasionally while only a few eventually settled more or less permanently in one of the three "villages" established at the mission.

Thus the majority of the Yir Yoront continued to live their old self-supporting life in the bush, protected until 1942 by the government reserve and the intervening mission from the cruder realities of the encroaching new order from the south. To the east was poor, uninhabited country. To the north were other bush tribes extending on along the coast to the distant Archer River Presbyterian mission with which the Yir Yoront had no contact. Westward was the shallow Gulf of Carpentaria on which the natives saw only a mission lugger making its infrequent dry season trips to the Mitchell River. In this protected environment for over a generation the Yir Yoront were able to recuperate from shocks received at the hands of civilized society. During the 1930's their raiding and fighting, their trading and stealing of women, their evisceration and two- or three-year care of their dead, and their totemic ceremonies continued, apparently uninhibited by western influence. In 1931 they killed a European who wandered into their territory from the east, but the investigating police never approached the group whose members were responsible for the act.

As a direct result of the work of the Mitchell River mission, all Yir Yoront received a great many more western artifacts of all kinds than ever before. As part of their plan for raising native living standards, the missionaries made it possible for aboriginals living at the mission to earn some western goods, many of which were then given or traded to natives still living under bush conditions; they also handed out certain useful articles gratis to both mission and bush aboriginals. They prevented guns, liquor, and damaging narcotics, as well as decimating diseases, from reaching the tribes of this area, while encouraging the introduction of goods they considered "improving." As has been noted, no item of western technology available, with the possible exception of trade tobacco, was in greater demand among all groups of aboriginals than the short handled steel axe. The mission always kept a good supply of these axes in stock; at Christmas parties or other mission festivals they were given away to mission or visiting aboriginals indiscriminately and in considerable numbers. In addition, some steel axes as well as other European goods were still traded in to the Yir Yoront by natives in contact with cattle stations in the south. Indeed, steel axes had probably come to the Yir Yoront through established lines of aboriginal trade long before any regular contact with whites had occurred.

III. RELEVANT FACTORS

If we concentrate our attention on Yir Yoront behavior centering about the original stone axe (rather than on the axe — the object — itself) as a cultural trait or item of cultural equipment, we should get some conception of the role this implement played in aboriginal culture. This, in turn, should enable us to foresee with considerable accuracy some of the results stemming from the displacement of the stone age by the steel axe.

The production of a stone axe required a number of simple technological skills. With the various details of the axe well in mind, adult men could set about producing it (a task not considered appropriate for women or children). First of all a man had to know the location and properties of several natural resources found in his immediate environment: pliable wood for a handle, which could be doubled or bent over the axe head and bound tightly; bark, which could be rolled into cord for the binding; and gum, to fix the stone head in the haft. These materials had to be correctly gathered, stored, prepared, cut to size and applied or manipulated. They were in plentiful supply, and could be taken from anyone's property without special permission. Postponing consideration of the stone head, the axe could be made by any normal man who had a simple knowledge of nature and of the technological skills involved, together with fire (for heating the gum), and a few simple cutting tools — perhaps the sharp shells of plentiful bivalves.

The use of the stone axe as a piece of capital equipment used in

producing other goods indicates its very great importance to the subsistence economy of the aboriginal. Anyone — man, woman, or child —
could use the axe; indeed, it was used primarily by women, for theirs
was the task of obtaining sufficient wood to keep the family campfire
burning all day, for cooking or other purposes, and all night against
mosquitoes and cold (for in July, winter temperature might drop below
40 degrees). In a normal lifetime a woman would use the axe to cut
or knock down literally tons of firewood. The axe was also used to
make other tools or weapons, and a variety of material equipment required by the aboriginal in his daily life. The stone axe was essential in
the construction of the wet season domed huts which keep out some
rain and some insects; of platforms which provide dry storage; of
shelters which give shade in the dry summer when days are bright and
hot. In hunting and fishing and in gathering vegetable or animal food
the axe was also a necessary tool, and in this tropical culture, where
preservatives or other means of storage are lacking, the natives spend
more time obtaining food than in any other occupation — except sleeping. In only two instances was the use of the stone axe strictly limited
to adult men: for gathering wild honey, the most prized food known to
the Yir Yoront; and for making the secret paraphernalia for ceremonies.
From this brief listing of some of the activities involving the use of the
axe, it is easy to understand why there was at least one stone axe in
every camp, in every hunting or fighting party, and in every group out
on a "walk-about" in the bush.

The stone axe was also prominent in interpersonal relations. Yir
Yoront men were dependent upon interpersonal relations for their stone
axe heads, since the flat, geologically recent, alluvial country over which
they range provides no suitable stone for this purpose. The stone they
used came from quarries 400 miles to the south, reaching the Yir Yoront
through long lines of male trading partners. Some of these chains
terminated with the Yir Yoront men, others extended on farther north
to other groups, using Yir Yoront men as links. Almost every older
adult man had one or more regular trading partners, some to the north
and some to the south. He provided his partner or partners in the south
with surplus spears, particularly fighting spears tipped with the barbed
spines of sting ray which snap into vicious fragments when they penetrate human flesh. For a dozen such spears, some of which he may have
obtained from a partner to the north, he would receive one stone axe
head. Studies have shown that the sting ray barb spears increased in
value as they move south and farther from the sea. One hundred and
fifty miles south of Yir Yoront one such spear may be exchanged for
one stone axe head. Although actual investigations could not be made,
it was presumed that farther south, nearer the quarries, one sting ray

barb spear would bring several stone axe heads. Apparently people who acted as links in the middle of the chain and who made neither spears nor axe heads would receive a certain number of each as a middleman's profit.

Thus trading relations, which may extend the individual's personal relationships beyond that of his own group, were associated with spears and axes, two of the most important items in a man's equipment. Finally, most of the exchanges took place during the dry season, at the time of the great aboriginal celebrations centering about initiation rites or other totemic ceremonials which attracted hundreds and were the occasion for much exciting activity in addition to trading.

Returning to the Yir Yoront, we find that adult men kept their axes in camp with their other equipment, or carried them when travelling. Thus a woman or child who wanted to use an axe — as might frequently happen during the day — had to get one from a man, use it promptly, and return it in good condition. While a man might speak of "my axe," a woman or child could not.

This necessary and constant borrowing of axes from older men by women and children was in accordance with regular patterns of kinship behavior. A woman would expect to use her husband's axe unless he himself was using it; if unmarried, or if her husband was absent, a woman would go first to her older brother or to her father. Only in extraordinary circumstances would she seek a stone axe from other male kin. A girl, a boy, or a young man would look to a father or an older brother to provide an axe for their use. Older men, too, would follow similar rules if they had to borrow an axe.

It will be noted that all of these social relationships in which the stone axe had a place are pair relationships and that the use of the axe helped to define and maintain their character and the roles of the two individual participants. Every active relationship among the Yir Yoront involved a definite and accepted status of superordination or subordination. A person could have no dealings with another on exactly equal terms. The nearest approach to equality was between brothers, although the older was always superordinate to the younger. Since the exchange of goods in a trading relationship involved a mutual reciprocity, trading partners usually stood in a brotherly type of relationship, although one was always classified as older than the other and would have some advantage in case of dispute. It can be seen that repeated and widespread conduct centering around the use of the axe helped to generalize and standardize these sex, age, and kinship roles both in their normal benevolent and exceptional malevolent aspects.

The status of any individual Yir Yoront was determined not only by sex, age, and extended kin relationships, but also by membership in one of two dozen patrilineal totemic clans into which the entire community was divided.[3] Each clan had literally hundreds of totems, from one or two of which the clan derived its name, and the clan members their personal names. These totems included natural species or phenomena such as the sun, stars, and daybreak, as well as cultural "species": imagined ghosts, rainbow serpents, heroic ancestors; such eternal cultural verities as fires, spears, huts; and such human activities, conditions, or attributes as eating, vomiting, swimming, fighting, babies and corpses, milk and blood, lips and loins. While individual members of such totemic classes or species might disappear or be destroyed, the class itself was obviously ever-present and indestructible. The totems, therefore, lent permanence and stability to the clans, to the groupings of human individuals who generation after generation were each associated with a set of totems which distinguished one clan from another.

The stone axe was one of the most important of the many totems of the Sunlit Cloud Iguana clan. The names of many members of this clan referred to the axe itself, to activities in which the axe played a vital part, or to the clan's mythical ancestors with whom the axe was prominently associated. When it was necessary to represent the stone axe in totemic ceremonies, only men of this clan exhibited it or pantomimed its use. In secular life, the axe could be made by any man and used by all; but in the sacred realm of the totems it belonged exclusively to the Sunlit Cloud Iguana people.

Supporting those aspects of cultural behavior which we have called technology and conduct, is a third area of culture which includes ideas, sentiments, and values. These are most difficult to deal with, for they are latent and covert, and even unconscious, and must be deduced from overt actions and language or other communicating behavior. In this aspect of the culture lies the significance of the stone axe to the Yir Yoront and to their cultural way of life.

The stone axe was an important symbol of masculinity among the Yir Yoront (just as pants or pipes are to us). By a complicated set of ideas the axe was defined as "belonging" to males, and everyone in the society (except untrained infants) accepted these ideas. Similarly spears, spear throwers, and fire-making sticks were owned only by men and were also symbols of masculinity. But the masculine values represented by the stone axe were constantly being impressed on all members of

---

[3] The best, although highly concentrated, summaries of totemism among the Yir Yoront and the other tribes of north Queensland will be found in R. Lauriston Sharp, "Tribes and Totemism in Northeast Australia," *Oceania*, Vol. 8, 1939, pp. 254–275 and 439–461 (especially pp. 268–275); also "Notes on Northeast Australian Totemism," in *Papers of the Peabody Museum of American Archaeology and Ethnology*, Vol. 20, *Studies in the Anthropology of Oceania and Asia*, Cambridge, 1943, pp. 66–71.

society by the fact that females borrowed axes but not other masculine artifacts. Thus the axe stood for an important theme of Yir Yoront culture: the superiority and rightful dominance of the male, and the greater value of his concerns and of all things associated with him. As the axe also had to be borrowed by the younger people it represented the prestige of age, another important theme running through Yir Yoront behavior.

To understand the Yir Yoront culture it is necessary to be aware of a system of ideas which may be called their totemic ideology. A fundamental belief of the aboriginal divided time into two great epochs: (1) a distant and sacred period at the beginning of the world when the earth was peopled by mildly marvelous ancestral beings or culture heroes who are in a special sense the forebears of the clans; and (2) a period when the old was succeeded by a new order which includes the present. Originally there was no anticipation of another era supplanting the present. The future would simply be an eternal continuation and reproduction of the present which itself had remained unchanged since the epochal revolution of ancestral times.

The important thing to note is that the aboriginal believed that the present world, as a natural and cultural environment, was and should be simply a detailed reproduction of the world of the ancestors. He believed that the entire universe "is now as it was in the beginning" when it was established and left by the ancestors. The ordinary cultural life of the ancestors became the daily life of the Yir Yoront camps, and the extraordinary life of the ancestors remained extant in the recurring symbolic pantomimes and paraphernalia found only in the most sacred atmosphere of the totemic rites.

Such beliefs, accordingly, opened the way for ideas of what *should be* (because it supposedly *was*) to influence or help determine what actually *is*. A man called Dog-chases-iguana-up-a-tree-and-barks-at-him-all-night had that and other names because he believed his ancestral alter ego had also had them; he was a member of the Sunlit Cloud Iguana clan because his ancestor was; he was associated with particular countries and totems of this same ancestor; during an initiation he played the role of a dog and symbolically attacked and killed certain members of other clans because his ancestor (conveniently either anthropomorphic or kynomorphic) really did the same to the ancestral alter egos of these men; and he would avoid his mother-in-law, joke with a mother's distant brother, and make spears in a certain way because his and other people's ancestors did these things. His behavior in these specific ways was outlined, and to that extent determined for him, by a set of ideas concerning the past and the relation of the present to the past.

But when we are informed that Dog-chases-etc. had two wives

from the Spear Black Duck clan and one from the Native Companion clan, one of them being blind, that he had four children with such and such names, that he had a broken wrist and was left handed, all because his ancestor had exactly these same attributes, then we know (though he apparently didn't) that the present has influenced the past, that the mythical world has been somewhat adjusted to meet the exigencies and accidents of the inescapably real present.

There was thus in Yir Yoront ideology a nice balance in which the mythical was adjusted in part to the real world, the real world in part to the ideal pre-existing mythical world, the adjustments occurring to maintain a fundamental tenet of native faith that the present must be a mirror of the past. Thus the stone axe in all its aspects, uses, and associations was integrated into the context of Yir Yoront technology and conduct because a myth, a set of ideas, had put it there.

IV. THE OUTCOME

The introduction of the steel axe indiscriminately and in large numbers into the Yir Yoront technology occurred simultaneously with many other changes. It is therefore impossible to separate all the results of this single innovation. Nevertheless, a number of specific effects of the change from stone to steel axes may be noted, and the steel axe may be used as an epitome of the increasing quantity of European goods and implements received by the aboriginals and of their general influence on the native culture. The use of the steel axe to illustrate such influences would seem to be justified. It was one of the first European artifacts to be adopted for regular use by the Yir Yoront, and whether made of stone or steel, the axe was clearly one of the most important items of cultural equipment they possessed.

The shift from stone to steel axes provided no major technological difficulties. While the aboriginals themselves could not manufacture steel axe heads, a steady supply from outside continued; broken wooden handles could easily be replaced from bush timbers with aboriginal tools. Among the Yir Yoront the new axe was never used to the extent it was on mission or cattle stations (for carpentry work, pounding tent pegs, as a hammer, and so on); indeed, it had so few more uses than the stone axe that its practical effect on the native standard of living was negligible. It did some jobs better, and could be used longer without breakage. These factors were sufficient to make it of value to the native. The white man believed that a shift from steel to stone axe on his part would be a definite regression. He was convinced that his axe was much more efficient, that its use would save time, and that it therefore represented technical "progress" towards goals which he had set up for the native. But this assumption was hardly borne out in aboriginal practice.

Any leisure time the Yir Yoront might gain by using steel axes or other western tools was not invested in "improving the conditions of life," nor, certainly, in developing aesthetic activities, but in sleep — an art they had mastered thoroughly.

Previously, a man in need of an axe would acquire a stone axe head through regular trading partners from whom he knew what to expect, and was then dependent solely upon a known and adequate natural environment, and his own skills or easily acquired techniques. A man wanting a steel axe, however, was in no such self-reliant position. If he attended a mission festival when steel axes were handed out as gifts, he might receive one either by chance or by happening to impress upon the mission staff that he was one of the "better" bush aboriginals (the missionaries' definition of "better" being quite different from that of his bush fellows). Or, again almost by pure chance, he might get some brief job in connection with the mission which would enable him to earn a steel axe. In either case, for older men a preference for the steel axe helped change the situation from one of self-reliance to one of dependence, and a shift in behavior from well-structured or defined situations in technology or conduct to ill-defined situations in conduct alone. Among the men, the older ones whose earlier experience or knowledge of the white man's harshness made them suspicious were particularly careful to avoid having relations with the mission, and thus excluded themselves from acquiring steel axes from that source.

In other aspects of conduct or social relations, the steel axe was even more significantly at the root of psychological stress among the Yir Yoront. This was the result of new factors which the missionary considered beneficial: the simple numerical increase in axes per capita as a result of mission distribution, and distribution directly to younger men, women, and even children. By winning the favor of the mission staff, a woman might be given a steel axe which was clearly intended to be hers, thus creating a situation quite different from the previous custom which necessitated her borrowing an axe from a male relative. As a result a woman would refer to the axe as "mine," a possessive form she was never able to use of the stone axe. In the same fashion, young men or even boys also obtained steel axes directly from the mission, with the result that older men no longer had a complete monopoly of all the axes in the bush community. All this led to a revolutionary confusion of sex, age, and kinship roles, with a major gain in independence and loss of subordination on the part of those who now owned steel axes when they had previously been unable to possess stone axes.

The trading partner relationship was also affected by the new situation. A Yir Yoront might have a trading partner in a tribe to the south whom he defined as a younger brother and over whom he would therefore have some authority. But if the partner were in contact with the mission or had other access to steel axes, his subordination obviously decreased. Among other things, this took some of the excitement away from the dry season fiesta-like tribal gatherings centering around initiations. These had traditionally been the climactic annual occasions for exchanges between trading partners, when a man might seek to acquire a whole year's supply of stone axe heads. Now he might find himself prostituting his wife to almost total strangers in return for steel axes or other white man's goods. With trading partnerships weakened, there was less reason to attend the ceremonies, and less fun for those who did.

Not only did an increase in steel axes and their distribution to women change the character of the relations between individuals (the paired relationships that have been noted), but a previously rare type of relationship was created in the Yir Yoront's conduct towards whites. In the aboriginal society there were few occasions outside of the immediate family when an individual would initiate action to several other people at once. In any average group, in accordance with the kinship system, while a person might be superordinate to several people to whom he could suggest or command action, he was also subordinate to several others with whom such behavior would be tabu. There was thus no overall chieftainship or authoritarian leadership of any kind. Such complicated operations as grass-burning animal drives or totemic ceremonies could be carried out smoothly because each person was aware of his role.

On both mission and cattle stations, however, the whites imposed their conception of leadership roles upon the aboriginals, consisting of one person in a controlling relationship with a subordinate group. Aboriginals called together to receive gifts, including axes, at a mission Christmas party found themselves facing one or two whites who sought to control their behavior for the occasion, who disregarded the age, sex, and kinship variables of which the aboriginals were so conscious, and who considered them all at one subordinate level. The white also sought to impose similar patterns on work parties. (However, if he placed an aboriginal in charge of a mixed group of post-hole diggers, for example, half of the group, those subordinate to the "boss," would work while the other half, who were superordinate to him, would sleep.) For the aboriginal, the steel axe and other European goods came to symbolize this new and uncomfortable form of social organization, the leader-group relationship.

The most disturbing effects of the steel axe, operating in conjunction with other elements also being introduced from the white man's several sub-cultures, developed in the realm of traditional ideas, sentiments, and values. These were undermined at a rapidly mounting rate, with no new conceptions being defined to replace them. The result was the erection of a mental and moral void which foreshadowed the collapse and destruction of all Yir Yoront culture, if not, indeed, the extinction of the biological group itself.

From what has been said it should be clear how changes in overt behavior, in technology and conduct, weakened the values inherent in a reliance on nature, in the prestige of masculinity and of age, and in the various kinship relations. A scene was set in which a wife, or a young son whose initiation may not yet have been completed, need no longer defer to the husband or father who, in turn, became confused and insecure as he was forced to borrow a steel axe from them. For the woman and boy the steel axe helped establish a new degree of freedom which they accepted readily as an escape from the unconscious stress of the old patterns — but they, too, were left confused and insecure. Ownership became less well defined with the result that stealing and trespassing were introduced into technology and conduct. Some of the excitement surrounding the great ceremonies evaporated and they lost their previous gaiety and interest. Indeed, life itself became less interesting, although this did not lead the Yir Yoront to discover suicide, a concept foreign to them.

The whole process may be most specifically illustrated in terms of totemic system, which also illustrates the significant role played by a system of ideas, in this case a totemic ideology, in the breakdown of a culture.

In the first place, under pre-European aboriginal conditions where the native culture has become adjusted to a relatively stable environment, few, if any, unheard of or catastrophic crises can occur. It is clear, therefore, that the totemic system serves very effectively in inhibiting radical cultural changes. The closed system of totemic ideas, explaining and categorizing a well-known universe as it was fixed at the beginning of time, presents a considerable obstacle to the adoption of new or the dropping of old culture traits. The obstacle is not insurmountable and the system allows for the minor variations which occur in the norms of daily life. But the inception of major changes cannot easily take place.

Among the bush Yir Yoront the only means of water transport is a light wood log to which they cling in their constant swimming of rivers, salt creeks, and tidal inlets. These natives know that tribes 45 miles further north have a bark canoe. They know these northern tribes can thus fish from midstream or out at sea, instead of clinging to the river banks and beaches, that they can cross coastal waters infested with crocodiles, sharks, sting rays, and Portuguese men-of-war without danger. They know the materials of which the canoe is made exist in their own environment. But they also know, as they say, that they do not have canoes because their own mythical ancestors did not have them. They assume that the canoe was part of the ancestral universe of the northern tribes. For them, then, the adoption of the canoe would not be simply a matter of learning a number of new behavioral skills for its manufacture and use. The adoption would require a much more difficult procedure; the acceptance by the entire society of a myth, either locally developed or borrowed, to explain the presence of the canoe, to associate it with some one or more of the several hundred mythical ancestors (and how decide which?), and thus establish it as an accepted totem of one of the clans ready to be used by the whole community. The Yir Yoront have not made this adjustment, and in this case we can only say that for the time being at least, ideas have won out over very real pressures for technological change. In the elaborateness and explicitness of the totemic ideologies we seem to have one explanation for the notorious stability of Australian cultures under aboriginal conditions, an explanation which gives due weight to the importance of ideas in determining human behavior.

At a later stage of the contact situation, as has been indicated, phenomena unaccounted for by the totemic ideological system begin to appear with regularity and frequency and remain within the range of native experience. Accordingly, they cannot be ignored (as the "Battle of the Mitchell" was apparently ignored), and there is an attempt to assimilate them and account for them along the lines of principles inherent in the ideology. The bush Yir Yoront of the mid-thirties represent this stage of the acculturation process. Still trying to maintain their aboriginal definition of the situation, they accept European artifacts and behavior patterns, but fit them into their totemic system, assigning them to various clans on a par with original totems. There is an attempt to have the myth-making process keep up with these cultural changes so that the idea system can continue to support the rest of the culture. But analysis of overt behavior, of dreams, and of some of the new myths indicates that this arrangement is not entirely satisfactory, that the native clings to his totemic system with intellectual loyalty (lacking any substitute ideology), but that associated sentiments and values are weakened. His attitude towards his own and towards European culture are found to be highly ambivalent.

All ghosts are totems of the Head-to-the-East Corpse clan, are thought of as white, and are of course closely associated with death. The white man, too, is closely associated with death, and he and all things pertaining to him are naturally assigned to the Corpse clan as totems. The steel axe, as a totem, was thus associated with the Corpse clan. But as an "axe," clearly linked with the stone axe, it is a totem of the

Sunlit Cloud Iguana clan. Moreover, the steel axe, like most European goods, has no distinctive origin myth, nor are mythical ancestors associated with it. Can anyone, sitting in the shade of a *ti* tree one afternoon, create a myth to resolve this confusion? No one has, and the horrid suspicion arises as to the authenticity of the origin myths, which failed to take into account this vast new universe of the white man. The steel axe, shifting hopelessly between one clan and the other, is not only replacing the stone axe physically, but is hacking at the supports of the entire cultural system.

The aboriginals to the south of the Yir Yoront have clearly passed beyond this stage. They are engulfed by European culture, either by the mission or cattle station sub-cultures or, for some natives, by a baffling, paradoxical combination of both incongruent varieties. The totemic ideology can no longer support the inrushing mass of foreign culture traits, and the myth-making process in its native form breaks down completely. Both intellectually and emotionally a saturation point is reached so that the myriad new traits which can neither be ignored nor any longer assimilated simply force the aboriginal to abandon his totemic system. With the collapse of this system of ideas, which is so closely related to so many other aspects of the native culture, there follows an appallingly sudden and complete cultural disintegration, and a demoralization of the individual such as has seldom been recorded elsewhere. Without the support of a system of ideas well devised to provide cultural stability in a stable environment, but admittedly too rigid for the new realities pressing in from outside, native behavior and native sentiments and values are simply dead. Apathy reigns. The aboriginal has passed beyond the realm of any outsider who might wish to do him well or ill.

Returning from the broken natives huddled on cattle stations or on the fringes of frontier towns to the ambivalent but still lively aboriginals settled on the Mitchell River mission, we note one further devious result of the introduction of European artifacts. During a wet season stay at the mission, the anthropologist discovered that his supply of tooth paste was being depleted at an alarming rate. Investigation showed that it was being taken by old men for use in a new tooth paste cult. Old materials of magic having failed, new materials were being tried out in a malevolent magic directed towards the mission staff and some of the younger aboriginal men. Old males, largely ignored by the missionaries, were seeking to regain some of their lost power and prestige. This mild aggression proved hardly effective, but perhaps only because confidence in any kind of magic on the mission was by this time at a low ebb.

For the Yir Yoront still in the bush, a time could be predicted when personal deprivation and frustration in a confused culture would produce an overload of anxiety. The mythical past of the totemic ancestors would disappear as a guarantee of a present of which the future was supposed to be a stable continuation. Without the past, the present could be meaningless and the future unstructured and uncertain. Insecurities would be inevitable. Reaction to this stress might be some form of symbolic aggression, or withdrawal and apathy, or some more realistic approach. In such a situation the missionary with understanding of the processes going on about him would find his opportunity to introduce his forms of religion and to help create a new cultural universe.

34

Cargo cults
PETER M. WORSLEY

When one cultural group becomes dominated by another, its original meaning system may seem thin, ineffective, and contradictory. The resulting state of deprivation often causes members to rebuild their culture along more satisfying lines. In this article Peter Worsley describes such a movement among the peoples of New Guinea and adjacent islands, an area where Western influence has caused cultural disorientation and where cargo cults have provided the basis for reorganization.

Patrols of the Australian Government venturing into the "uncontrolled" central highlands of New Guinea in 1946 found the primitive people there swept up in a wave of religious excitement. Prophecy was being fulfilled: The arrival of the Whites was the sign that the end of the world was at hand. The natives proceeded to butcher all of their pigs — animals that were not only a principal source of subsistence but also symbols of social status and ritual preeminence in their culture. They killed these valued animals in expression of the belief that after three days of darkness "Great Pigs" would appear from the sky. Food, firewood, and other necessities had to be stockpiled to see the people through to the arrival of the Great Pigs. Mock wireless antennae of bamboo and rope had been erected to receive in advance the news of the millennium. Many believed that with the great event they would exchange their black skins for white ones.

This bizarre episode is by no means the single event of its kind in the murky history of the collision of European civilization with the indigenous cultures of the southwest Pacific. For more than one hundred years traders and missionaries have been reporting similar disturbances

From "Cargo Cults," *Scientific American* 200 (May 1959) : 117–128. Reprinted with permission of W. H. Freeman and Company. Copyright © 1959 by *Scientific American*, Inc. All rights reserved. Illustrations are omitted.

among the peoples of Melanesia, the group of Negro-inhabited islands (including New Guinea, Fiji, the Solomons, and the New Hebrides) lying between Australia and the open Pacific Ocean. Though their technologies were based largely upon stone and wood, these peoples had highly developed cultures, as measured by the standards of maritime and agricultural ingenuity, the complexity of their varied social organizations, and the elaboration of religious belief and ritual. They were nonetheless ill prepared for the shock of the encounter with the Whites, a people so radically different from themselves and so infinitely more powerful. The sudden transition from the society of the ceremonial stone ax to the society of sailing ships and now of airplanes has not been easy to make.

After four centuries of Western expansion, the densely populated central highlands of New Guinea remain one of the few regions where the people still carry on their primitive existence in complete independence of the world outside. Yet as the agents of the Australian Government penetrate into ever more remote mountain valleys, they find these backwaters of antiquity already deeply disturbed by contact with the ideas and artifacts of European civilization. For "cargo" — Pidgin English for trade goods — has long flowed along the indigenous channels of communication from the seacoast into the wilderness. With it has traveled the frightening knowledge of the white man's magical power. No small element in the white man's magic is the hopeful message sent abroad by his missionaries: the news that a Messiah will come and that the present order of Creation will end.

The people of the central highlands of New Guinea are only the latest to be gripped in the recurrent religious frenzy of the "cargo cults." However variously embellished with details from native myth and Christian belief, these cults all advance the same central theme: the world is about to end in a terrible cataclysm. Thereafter God, the ancestors, or some local culture hero will appear and inaugurate a blissful paradise on earth. Death, old age, illness, and evil will be unknown. The riches of the white man will accrue to the Melanesians.

Although the news of such a movement in one area has doubtless often inspired similar movements in other areas, the evidence indicates that these cults have arisen independently in many places as parallel responses to the same enormous social stress and strain. Among the movements best known to students of Melanesia are the "Taro Cult" of New Guinea, the "Vailala Madness" of Papua, the "Naked Cult" of Espiritu Santo, the "John Frum Movement" of the New Hebrides, and the "Tuka Cult" of the Fiji Islands.

At times the cults have been so well organized and fanatically persistent that they have brought the work of government to a standstill. The outbreaks have often taken the authorities completely by surprise and have confronted them with mass opposition of an alarming kind. In the 1930's, for example, villagers in the vicinity of Wewak, New Guinea, were stirred by a succession of "Black King" movements. The prophets announced that the Europeans would soon leave the island, abandoning their property to the natives, and urged their followers to cease paying taxes, since the government station was about to disappear into the sea in a great earthquake. To the tiny community of Whites in charge of the region, such talk was dangerous. The authorities jailed four of the prophets and exiled three others. In yet another movement, that sprang up in declared opposition to the local Christian mission, the cult leader took Satan as his god.

Troops on both sides in World War II found their arrival in Melanesia heralded as a sign of the Apocalypse. The G.I.'s who landed in the New Hebrides, moving up for the bloody fighting on Guadalcanal, found the natives furiously at work preparing airfields, roads and docks for the magic ships and planes that they believed were coming from "Rusefel" (Roosevelt), the friendly king of America.

The Japanese also encountered millenarian visionaries during their southward march to Guadalcanal. Indeed, one of the strangest minor military actions of World War II occurred in Dutch New Guinea, when Japanese forces had to be turned against the local Papuan inhabitants of the Geelvink Bay region. The Japanese had at first been received with great joy, not because their "Greater East Asia Co-Prosperity Sphere" propaganda had made any great impact upon the Papuans, but because the natives regarded them as harbingers of the new world that was dawning, the flight of the Dutch having already given the first sign. Mansren, creator of the islands and their peoples, would now return, bringing with him the ancestral dead. All this had been known, the cult leaders declared, to the crafty Dutch, who had torn out the first page of the Bible where these truths were inscribed. When Mansren returned, the existing world order would be entirely overturned. White men would turn black like Papuans, Papuans would become Whites; root crops would grow in trees, and coconuts and fruits would grow like tubers. Some of the islanders now began to draw together into large "towns"; others took Biblical names such as "Jericho" and "Galilee" for their villages. Soon they adopted military uniforms and began drilling. The Japanese, by now highly unpopular, tried to disarm and disperse the Papuans; resistance inevitably developed. The climax of this tragedy came when several canoe-loads of fanatics sailed out to attack Japanese warships, believing themselves to be invulnerable by virtue of the holy water with which they had sprinkled themselves. But the bullets of the Japanese did not turn to water, and the attackers were mowed down by machine-gun fire.

Behind this incident lay a long history. As long ago as 1857 missionaries in the Geelvink Bay region had made note of the story of Mansren. It is typical of many Melanesian myths that became confounded with Christian doctrine to form the ideological basis of the movements. The legend tells how long ago there lived an old man named Manamakeri ("he who itches"), whose body was covered with sores. Manamakeri was extremely fond of palm wine, and used to climb a huge tree every day to tap the liquid from the flowers. He soon found that someone was getting there before him and removing the liquid. Eventually he trapped the thief, who turned out to be none other than the Morning Star. In return for his freedom, the Star gave the old man a wand that would produce as much fish as he liked, a magic tree and a magic staff. If he drew in the sand and stamped his foot, the drawing would become real. Manamakeri, aged as he was, now magically impregnated a young maiden; the child of this union was a miracle-child who spoke as soon as he was born. But the maiden's parents were horrified, and banished her, the child, and the old man. The trio sailed off in a canoe created by Mansren ("The Lord"), as the old man now became known. On this journey Mansren rejuvenated himself by stepping into a fire and flaking off his scaly skin, which changed into valuables. He then sailed around Geelvink Bay, creating islands where he stopped, and peopling them with the ancestors of the present-day Papuans.

The Mansren myth is plainly a creation myth full of symbolic ideas relating to fertility and rebirth. Comparative evidence — especially the shedding of his scaly skin — confirms the suspicion that the old man is, in fact, the Snake in another guise. Psychoanalytic writers argue that the snake occupies such a prominent part in mythology the world over because it stands for the penis, another fertility symbol. This may be so, but its symbolic significance is surely more complex than this. It is the "rebirth" of the hero, whether Mansren or the Snake, that exercises such universal fascination over men's minds.

The nineteenth-century missionaries thought that the Mansren story would make the introduction of Christianity easier, since the concept of "resurrection," not to mention that of the "virgin birth" and the "second coming," was already there. By 1867, however, the first cult organized around the Mansren legend was reported.

Though such myths were widespread in Melanesia, and may have sparked occasional movements even in the pre-White era, they took on a new significance in the late nineteenth century, once the European powers had finished parceling out the Melanesian region among themselves. In many coastal areas the long history of "blackbirding" — the seizure of islanders for work on the plantations of Australia and Fiji — had built up a reservoir of hostility to Europeans. In other areas, however, the arrival of the Whites was accepted, even welcomed, for it meant access to bully beef and cigarettes, shirts and paraffin lamps, whisky and bicycles. It also meant access to the knowledge behind these material goods, for the Europeans brought missions and schools as well as cargo.

Practically the only teaching the natives received about European life came from the missions, which emphasized the central significance of religion in European society. The Melanesians already believed that man's activities — whether gardening, sailing canoes, or bearing children — needed magical assistance. Ritual without human effort was not enough. But neither was human effort on its own. This outlook was reinforced by mission teaching.

The initial enthusiasm for European rule, however, was speedily dispelled. The rapid growth of the plantation economy removed the bulk of the able-bodied men from the villages, leaving women, children, and old men to carry on as best they could. The splendid vision of the equality of all Christians began to seem a pious deception in face of the realities of the color bar, the multiplicity of rival Christian missions and the open irreligion of many Whites.

For a long time the natives accepted the European mission as the means by which the "cargo" would eventually be made available to them. But they found that acceptance of Christianity did not bring the cargo any nearer. They grew disillusioned. The story now began to be put about that it was not the Whites who made the cargo, but the dead ancestors. To people completely ignorant of factory production, this made good sense. White men did not work; they merely wrote secret signs on scraps of paper, for which they were given shiploads of goods. On the other hand, the Melanesians labored week after week for pitiful wages. Plainly the goods must be made for Melanesians somewhere, perhaps in the Land of the Dead. The Whites, who possessed the secret of the cargo, were intercepting it and keeping it from the hands of the islanders, to whom it was really consigned. In the Madang district of New Guinea, after some forty years' experience of the missions, the natives went in a body one day with a petition demanding that the cargo secret should now be revealed to them, for they had been very patient.

So strong is this belief in the existence of a "secret" that the cargo cults generally contain some ritual in imitation of the mysterious European customs which are held to be the clue to the white man's extraordinary power over goods and men. The believers sit around tables with bottles of flowers in front of them, dressed in European clothes, waiting for the cargo ship or airplane to materialize; other cultists feature magic pieces of paper and cabalistic writing. Many of them deliberately turn their backs on the past by destroying secret ritual objects, or exposing them to the gaze of uninitiated youths and women, for whom formerly even a glimpse of the sacred objects would have meant the severest penalties, even death. The belief that they were the chosen people is further reinforced by their reading of the Bible, for the lives and customs of the people in the Old Testament resemble their own lives rather than those of the Europeans. In the New Testament they find the Apocalypse, with its prophecies of destruction and resurrection, particularly attractive.

Missions that stress the imminence of the Second Coming, like those of the Seventh Day Adventists, are often accused of stimulating millenarian cults among the islanders. In reality, however, the Melanesians themselves rework the doctrines the missionaries teach them, selecting from the Bible what they themselves find particularly congenial in it. Such movements have occurred in areas where missions of quite different types have been dominant, from Roman Catholic to Seventh Day Adventist. The reasons for the emergence of these cults, of course, lie far deeper in the life-experience of the people.

The economy of most of the islands is very backward. Native agriculture produces little for the world market, and even the European plantations and mines export only a few primary products and raw materials: copra, rubber, gold. Melanesians are quite unable to understand why copra, for example, fetches thirty pounds sterling per ton one month and but five pounds a few months later. With no notion of the workings of world-commodity markets, the natives see only the sudden closing of plantations, reduced wages and unemployment, and are inclined to attribute their insecurity to the whim or evil in the nature of individual planters.

Such shocks have not been confined to the economic order. Governments, too, have come and gone, especially during the two world wars: German, Dutch, British, and French administrations melted overnight. Then came the Japanese, only to be ousted in turn largely by the previously unknown Americans. And among these Americans the Melanesians saw Negroes like themselves, living lives of luxury on equal terms with white G.I.'s. The sight of these Negroes seemed like a fulfillment of the old prophecies to many cargo cult leaders. Nor must we forget the sheer scale of this invasion. Around a million U.S. troops passed through the Admiralty Islands, completely swamping the inhabitants. It was a world of meaningless and chaotic changes, in which anything was possible. New ideas were imported and given local twists. Thus in the Loyalty Islands people expected the French Communist Party to bring the millennium. There is no real evidence, however, of any Communist influence in these movements, despite the rather hysterical belief among Solomon Island planters that the name of the local "Masinga Rule" movement was derived from the word "Marxian"! In reality the name comes from a Solomon Island tongue, and means "brotherhood."

Europeans who have witnessed outbreaks inspired by the cargo cults are usually at a loss to understand what they behold. The islanders throw away their money, break their most sacred taboos, abandon their gardens, and destroy their precious livestock; they indulge in sexual license or, alternatively, rigidly separate men from women in huge communal establishments. Sometimes they spend days sitting gazing at the horizon for a glimpse of the long-awaited ship or airplane; sometimes they dance, pray and sing in mass congregations, becoming possessed and "speaking with tongues."

Observers have not hesitated to use such words as "madness," "mania," and "irrationality" to characterize the cults. But the cults reflect quite logical and rational attempts to make sense out of a social order that appears senseless and chaotic. Given the ignorance of the Melanesians about the wider European society, its economic organization and its highly developed technology, their reactions form a consistent and understandable pattern. They wrap up all their yearning and hope in an amalgam that combines the best counsel they can find in Christianity and their native belief. If the world is soon to end, gardening or fishing is unnecessary; everything will be provided. If the Melanesians are to be part of a much wider order, the taboos that prescribe their social conduct must now be lifted or broken in a newly prescribed way.

Of course the cargo never comes. The cults nonetheless live on. If the millennium does not arrive on schedule, then perhaps there is some failure in the magic, some error in the ritual. New breakaway groups organize around "purer" faith and ritual. The cult rarely disappears, so long as the social situation which brings it into being persists.

At this point it should be observed that cults of this general kind are not peculiar to Melanesia. Men who feel themselves oppressed and deceived have always been ready to pour their hopes and fears, their aspirations and frustrations, into dreams of a millennium to come or of a golden age to return. All parts of the world have had their counterparts of the cargo cults, from the American Indian ghost dance to the Communist-millenarist "reign of the saints" in Münster during the

Reformation, from medieval European apocalyptic cults to African "witch-finding" movements and Chinese Buddhist heresies. In some situations men have been content to wait and pray; in others they have sought to hasten the day by using their strong right arms to do the Lord's work. And always the cults serve to bring together scattered groups, notably the peasants and urban plebeians of agrarian societies and the peoples of "stateless" societies where the cult unites separate (and often hostile) villages, clans, and tribes into a wider religio-political unity.

Once the people begin to develop secular political organizations, however, the sects tend to lose their importance as vehicles of protest. They begin to relegate the Second Coming to the distant future or to the next world. In Melanesia ordinary political bodies, trade unions and native councils are becoming the normal media through which the islanders express their aspirations. In recent years continued economic prosperity and political stability have taken some of the edge off their despair. It now seems unlikely that any major movement along cargo-cult lines will recur in areas where the transition to secular politics has been made, even if the insecurity of prewar times returned. I would predict that the embryonic nationalism represented by cargo cults is likely in future to take forms familiar in the history of other countries that have moved from subsistence agriculture to participation in the world economy.

35

Highways and the future of the Yanomamö
SHELTON H. DAVIS

History is replete with examples of national expansion at the expense of less powerful neighbors. Scores of North American Indian nations, to say nothing of numerous groups in other parts of the world, have succumbed to more powerful neighbors. In this article, Shelton H. Davis describes how the Yanomamö, one of the last unacculturated groups in Brazil, face cultural extinction at the hands of intruders. Attracted by the discovery of uranium, geologists and miners travel along a new road that bisects tribal territory. Without an adequate reservation set aside for their protection, argues Davis, the Yanomamö have little chance to survive.

This is a promise that I can strongly make: we are going to create a policy of integrating the Indian population into Brazilian society as rapidly as possible. . . . We think that the ideals of preserving the Indian population within its own "habitat" are very beautiful, but unrealistic. — Sr. Mauricio Rangel Reis, Brazilian Minister of the Interior, March 1974.

The Yanomamö (also referred to as the Yanoáma, Shiriana, Xiriana, Guaharinbo, and Waika) are the largest unacculturated Indian tribe in South America. The tribe is estimated to number between 10,000 and 25,000 people, who live in hundreds of small villages skirting the border between Venezuela and Brazil. The Yanomamö men love to participate in highly ritualized chest-pounding duels, intervillage feuds, and warfare. The women of the tribe are expert gardeners, and cultivate magical charms to ward off the violence and the aggression of their men. Yano-

This article was written especially for this volume. Copyright © 1976 by Shelton H. Davis. Printed by permission. A revised version of this article will appear in the author's forthcoming book, *Victims of the "Miracle": Development against the Indians of Brazil* to be published by Cambridge University Press.

mamö shamans possess a vast knowledge of medical plants, many of which remain unknown to modern pharmacological science. During special curing ceremonies, these shamans blow an hallucinogenic drug called *ebene* in order to produce spiritual and visionary experiences.

For at least a century, the Yanomamö have been forced to retreat defensively into a vast jungle refuge area between the Orinoco and Marauia rivers. To the south, they were attacked by Brazilian rubber collectors and settlers. To the north, they fought off the expanding cattle frontier in Venezuela and the more acculturated and rifle-bearing Makiritare tribe. Until recently, however, the only major threats to the independence and territorial integrity of the Yanomamö came from inquisitive anthropologists, Italian priests, and North American evangelical missionaries. Unlike other Indian tribes of the Amazon Basin, the Yanomamö had successfully escaped the contamination of Western man, his civilization, his society, and his lethal diseases.

In 1974 and 1975, two events occurred that critically upset the former socio-environmental adaptations of the Brazilian section of the Yanomamö tribe. The first event was the construction of the 2,500-mile Northern Perimeter Highway (a major artery in the highly publicized Trans-Amazonic road system) through the tribe's territory. The second was the announcement in February 1975 that one of the world's largest uranium deposits had been discovered in Yanomamö territory. Both events have already had their effects on the physical and cultural well-being of the Yanomamö tribe. A narrative account of what has happened to the Yanomamö since these events should provide the reader with insight into the controversial question of Indian policy and development policy in the Amazon Basin region of Brazil.

THE ABORIGINES PROTECTION SOCIETY REPORT OF 1973

In the summer of 1972, a four-member investigating team of the Aborigines Protection Society of London (APS) visited the Amazon Basin on the invitation of the recently created National Indian Foundation of Brazil (FUNAI). One place visited by the APS team was the far northern territory of Roraima, the major home of the estimated 5,000 to 10,000 people who make up the Brazilian section of the Yanomamö tribe.

Initially, the APS team was impressed by the situation of the Yanomamö relative to other tribal groups in Brazil. Contacts with outsiders had begun only in the previous decade, and the Indians, according to the APS team, seemed to be "still largely insulated from the colonizing and commercial interests of Brazil." The Indians' main contacts during this period were with foreign missionaries (the Salesian Fathers, and the New Tribes and Unevangelized Field Missions of the United States) who had established several mission stations in the Yanomamö area, but who seemed to pose little threat to the integrity of the tribe. "The Yanomamö," the APS team wrote in their report published in 1973, "seemed to be content with their culture, and had proved strong enough to resist the converting zeal of missionaries."

The APS team was also impressed by the fact that FUNAI was planning to intervene in the Yanomamö area, and envisioned the creation of a federally recognized Indian reserve for the tribe. To the surprise of the APS team, however, it was discovered that the proposed reserve would only contain an area sufficient for 300 members of the tribe, and would exclude almost every Yanomamö village identified by FUNAI itself.

The APS team noted that none of the experienced missionaries in the Yanomamö area had been consulted about the reserve, and that its proposed limits would significantly endanger the tribe. "We consider," the APS team wrote, "that a major extension of this Reserve is both necessary and justified and furthermore that discussions should be opened with the Venezuelan authorities to see what forms of liaison and coordination of Indian policy are possible along the frontier."

In September 1972, meeting with the then-president of FUNAI, General Oscar Jeronimo Bandeira de Melo, the APS team suggested that negotiations should be carried out between the Brazilian and Venezuelan governments for the creation of an international Yanomamö reserve. The president of FUNAI responded to this suggestion by claiming that for reasons of "national security" it would be impossible for the government to create an Indian reserve or park along the borders of Brazil. In addition, he said that an international reserve established in collaboration with the government of Venezuela would be extremely difficult to create because it would have to be negotiated through the foreign offices of both governments, and might be taken advantage of by the Yanomamö for purposes of "smuggling gold across the frontier." Members of the APS team questioned these arguments, and when they left Brazil they had severe doubts about whether the physical and cultural integrity of the Yanomamö would be maintained.

THE NORTHERN PERIMETER HIGHWAY

In 1973, it became known that the Brazilian government was planning to build a major highway along its northern frontier. The new road was called the Northern Perimeter Highway, and was to be completed by 1975. Unlike the Trans-Amazonic Highway to the south which was built for purposes of agrarian colonization, the new Northern Perimeter Highway was to be the major minerals transportation link in the Amazon Basin of Brazil. It would begin on the Atlantic coast, and pass westward through the large manganese mining operation of Bethlehem Steel Corporation in Amapa. Then it would cut to the north, passing above the huge multimillion dollar bauxite project of Alcan Aluminum Company along the Trombetas River in Para. Finally it would proceed south and westward, skirting the borders of Colombia and Peru and passing through one of the potentially largest oil fields in Brazil. It was estimated that over 50,000 Indians were living in nearly a hundred isolated tribal groups along the path of the new road. Among these groups were the still hostile and unpacified Yanomamö, Waimiri-Atroari, and Marubo tribes.

In May 1974, Edwin Brooks, a member of the APS team, published a report indicating how this new highway network could affect the Yanomamö tribe. Brooks's report contained a series of recent Brazilian government maps which showed that two highways were being planned to pass through the proposed, but still to be demarcated, Yanomamö Indian reserve. One of these was the Northern Perimeter Highway. The other was a smaller territorial road that would join the mission stations at Catrimani and Surucucus. Both highways, Brooks claimed, would jeopardize the territorial integrity of the Yanomamö tribe. The construction of these highways, he predicted, would be as devastating in their effects upon Indians as the highly publicized BR-080 highway invasion of the northern part of the Xingu National Park, which in 1972 brought a measles epidemic and nearly destroyed the once safe and thriving Txukahamei tribe.

Uranium discoveries in 1975

In February 1975, the critical event occurred that would eventually determine the future of the Yanomamö tribe. At that time, Brazil's Minister of Mines and Energy, Shigeaki Ueki, announced the discovery of an immense uranium field in the Surucucus region of Roraima Territory. This was claimed to be one of the largest uranium fields in the world and it was located in the major territory of the Brazilian section of the Yanomamö tribe.

The existence of radioactive minerals in this region was known as far back as 1951, but exploration for uranium did not begin until 1970 when the Brazilian government allocated significant amounts of monies for development of the nuclear sector. By 1974, over 150 technicians were working in the Surucucus region of Roraima alone, including members of the military, Project Radam (the large aerial photographic and mineral reconnaissance survey of the Amazon), the state-owned mineral exploration company (CPRM), and Nuclebras, the new state-owned company created to promote uranium exploration and nuclear research in Brazil.

At the time of the announcement of the Surucucus uranium discoveries, it also became known that Brazil was holding secret negotiations with several European countries for the provision of long-term deliveries of natural uranium in exchange for the most advanced nuclear technology. In May 1975, these negotiations became public when it was revealed that West Germany would be constructing eight nuclear power plants in Brazil at a cost of four billion dollars in exchange for the development of new sources of uranium and the construction of several uranium enrichment and nuclear fuel recycling plants.

Most international observers viewed the nuclear deal between West Germany and Brazil in purely geopolitical and economic terms. Not unexpectedly, none of these observers noted the more immediate implications of the Surucucus uranium discoveries for the survival of the Yanomamö and neighboring Indian tribes.

ONCHOCERCIASIS STRIKES YANOMAMÖ TRIBE

In the weeks immediately following the announcement of the Surucucus uranium discoveries, reports about uprooting and contamination of the Yanomamö tribe began to appear. The most shocking of these reports was the revelation that a FUNAI medical team, headed by Dr. Jose Alfredo Guimarães, had found several new foci of the dreaded disease onchocerciasis (African river blindness) throughout the northwest Amazon region.

Onchocerciasis, which is carried by blackflies of the Simuliid family and whose symptoms include fibrous tumors on skin and eyes as well as blindness, was first reported in the Western Hemisphere in Guatemala in 1916. By 1965 the disease had spread to Colombia, and in the early 1970s the presence of the disease was reported in the Amazon region of Brazil. In 1973 several Brazilian doctors warned the government about the growing incidence of onchocerciasis in the Amazon, and cautioned against plans for the building of the Northern Perimeter Highway.

These warnings were repeated in a report by two American scientists, Drs. R. J. A. Goodland and Howard S. Irwin, published in October 1974. Goodland and Irwin noted that the only hope for containing the spread of onchocerciasis in the Amazon was to discontinue or reroute the Northern Perimeter Highway. Onchocerciasis, they claimed, was possibly the most serious health threat in the Amazon, and was spreading along the margins of the Northern Perimeter Highway. "If the road planned to pierce the main focus is not realigned," they wrote, "disaster as rife as in Africa must be expected."

Unfortunately, the report of the FUNAI medical team in early 1975 confirmed these predictions. According to this report, onchocerciasis, which was previously localized in the area surrounding the Venezuelan-Brazilian border, had now spread beyond Roraima, and was reaching as far south as Para, Acre, and the center-west of Brazil. In the state of Amazonas alone, in a sample of 310 people investigated, Dr. Guimarães found 94 (30.23 percent) to be infected with the disease.

The most serious incidence of the disease had occurred among the Indian tribes of the northwestern part of the Amazon Basin. Along the Marauia River, one band of Yanomamö Indians was found to have a 100 percent incidence of the disease. In the Upper Solimoes region, the Tikuna tribe revealed an incidence of 87.5 percent. Along the Demini and Mapulau rivers, five Indian tribes (the Uxi-u-theli, Waiho-ko-a-theli, Welihessipi-u-theli, Pakidai, and Tucano) were all reported to have been infected. Lower incidences of onchocerciasis were found among Tucano and Maku tribes of the Waupes River, and the Baniwa tribe of the Içana River region.

In revealing these statistics to the Brazilian press, the president of FUNAI, General Ismarth de Araujo Oliveira (nominated to replace General Bandeira de Melo in March 1974), claimed that control of onchocerciasis was extremely difficult because it involved the intervention of several ministries besides the Indian Foundation, and required an expensive movement of people involved in the execution of development projects along the Northern Perimeter Highway. Onchocerciasis, he went on to note, was virtually "flying on the wings of the fly," and the only combatant known was an expensive French remedy which, according to the General, when applied to Indians killed them because of lack of physical resistance.

INDIAN POLICY ALONG THE NORTHERN PERIMETER HIGHWAY

Following news of the epidemic, a picture of what Indian policy would be like along the Northern Perimeter Highway started to emerge. In March 1975, for example, a young Indian agent named Benamour Fontes revealed that he had abandoned his position as the leader of a FUNAI pacification expedition along the Yanomamö front. Speaking at a press interview in Manaus, Fontes explained his actions by claiming that he had not received the necessary strategic and financial support from the central offices of FUNAI in Brasilia. The salaries of his coworkers were not paid promptly, and hunters and lumbermen along with government geologists had already begun to invade the territory of the Yanomamö tribe.

In addition, Fontes revealed that all strategic support was being given to the more publicized Waimiri-Atroari pacification expedition to the south. He said that he wanted to avoid what happened to fellow Indian agent Gilberto Pinto, who had spent more than eight years asking for men and supplies and who was tragically killed by angered Waimiri-Atroari tribesmen in December of the previous year. A state of chaos,

Fontes concluded, existed along the route of the Northern Perimeter Highway, and this could only prove disastrous for the Yanomamö and other Indian tribes.

During this period, reporters increasingly sought an official statement of government Indian policy in the northern Amazon region from high authorities within FUNAI. The event which precipitated such a statement occurred on the same day as the resignation of Benamour Fontes, when the governor of Roraima Territory, Fernando Ramos Pereira, went before the Brazilian press and declared that in his opinion an "area as rich as this — with gold, diamonds, and uranium — could not afford the luxury of conserving half a dozen Indian tribes who are holding back the development of Brazil."

The governor's statement caused a sort of miniscandal in Brazil, and the president of FUNAI responded immediately by saying that there was nothing contradictory between the protection of the Indian tribes of Roraima, such as the large Yanomamö tribe, and the development of the country. Citing Article 45 of the new Brazilian Indian Statute, which gives the government the right to administer and lease Indian mineral resources, the president said that "the Indian can only benefit from the mineral wealth discovered on the lands which he inhabits." The Indian Statute, he claimed, calls for the "integration" of the Indians into the Brazilian economy, and provides for their "participation," as owners of property, in the exploitation of mineral resources contained on their lands.

At the same time, the president of FUNAI revealed that a contract had been signed with two anthropologists associated with the University of Brasilia for the creation of Project Perimetral-Yanomami, a far-reaching program for the integration of the Yanomamö tribe. The purpose of Project Perimetral-Yanomami would be to set the groundwork for the economic integration of the Yanomamö into the expanding penetration and colonization fronts in the far northern part of Brazil. The Indians, according to the president, would be inoculated against disease and provided with new economic skills to trade the products of their labor with colonists who were beginning to settle along the Northern Perimeter Highway. One of the anthropologists contracted by FUNAI said that the goal of Project Perimetral-Yanomami was "to implant a system of *direct integration* [italics added] that would permit economic advantages for both groups."

GENERAL IMPLICATIONS

To conclude, three points about the general significance of the foregoing events are important. First, the official government policy of integrating Indian tribes into the expanding economy, instead of protecting them in their aboriginal territories through the creation of closed Indian parks and reserves, has been tried in several other areas of the Amazon Basin, and has proved devastating for Indian tribes. The policy most recently failed with the Aripuana Indian Park in Rondonia, home of the 5,000-member Cintas Largas and Surui tribes. A brief description of conditions in the Aripuana Indian Park provides a forecast of what may happen to the Yanomamö tribe.

The Cintas Largas received considerable international publicity because of the brutal massacre at Parallel Eleven in 1963. In 1968, FUNAI proposed an Indian park for the Cintas Largas and neighboring Surui tribes, but then in 1970, it began to lease lands in the park to a large São Paulo colonization company, to seven international cassiterite (tin) mining firms, and to the state government for the purpose of building a series of interior roads.

By 1973, these encroachments on the Aripuana Indian Park had begun to take their toll on the Indians. Geologists from Project Radam and private companies were searching for minerals in every part of the park. Numerous landing strips were constructed in the area. Two roads effectively destroyed the territorial integrity of the park. Game was beginning to become critically scarce, and Indians were abandoning their gardens to outside settlers and colonists.

In 1975, under the auspices of the International Work Group for Indigenous Affairs, Dr. Jean Chiappino, a French physician who had recently spent several months in Aripuana Indian Park, published a report describing the conditions of the Cintas Largas and Surui tribes. These Indians received no effective protection from FUNAI, and were suffering from disease, hunger, and apathy. An epidemic of tuberculosis, carried by outsiders, had struck all age groups in one Surui band, bringing death to the Indians within the short space of two months. The initial symptom of the disease was a hoarse cough. This was followed by a "pussy expectoration . . . which exhausted the patient," and a "permanent fever." This syndrome developed fastest among Indian children, and "carried off its victims in terminal cachexia." The spread of the epidemic, Dr. Chiappino noted, "distressed, disoriented, and destroyed" Indian families and the social group. According to his calculations, over 60 percent of the Surui population observed was affected by this epidemic alone.

Most important, Dr. Chiappino claimed that this epidemic, as well as the general state of despair and disorganization among the Cintas Largas and Surui tribes, could be directly related to the "integrationist" policies of FUNAI. Although land protection is stipulated in the Brazilian constitution, these Indians were without any effective protection of their lands, and were suffering the worst effects of uncontrolled contact with outsiders. Economic integration was merely a convenient euphemism for hiding the nasty facts of physical and cultural death for these Indians. According to Dr. Chiappino, their survival could only be ensured through a concerted program of medical assistance and the creation of a closed and well-protected Indian reserve.

Second, Brazilian Indian policy must be seen within the context of the wider national program for the rapid economic development and occupation of the Amazon region. Despite the sincere and humanitarian intentions of some of its employees and the openness to outside suggestions and assistance from its present director, FUNAI is still an agency within the Brazilian Ministry of the Interior, and hence is substantially constrained in its protectionist functions by the larger developmentalist objectives of the federal government.

In certain recent cases, FUNAI has been able to protect Indian land and territorial rights, and there are some areas of central Brazil where Indian tribes are experiencing a demographic and cultural renaissance. However, in areas like the more populated northern part of the Amazon Basin, where Indian land rights conflict with the interests of large, multinational or state-owned mining companies, or with the plans of the National Highway Department, FUNAI has been unable to fulfill its constitutional mandate to Indian tribes.

Perhaps most significantly, the new Indian Statute passed in December 1973 provides FUNAI with the right to administer and lease Indian mineral resources. In the near future these mineral leasing provisions could provide the conditions for the total collaboration of FUNAI with powerful economic and developmentalist interests in Brazil. These provisions are particularly dangerous because of the recent discoveries of uranium and petroleum deposits in the Amazon Basin.

Third, Brazil alone must not be held responsible for the social and environmental consequences of the Amazon development program. What is taking place in the Amazon region today is a classic case of a high technology and dependency model of economic development being applied to one of the last and largest frontier regions of the world. For example, Project Radam, the huge aerial photographic survey that has been uncovering most of the mineral wealth of the Amazon, was substantially developed with technical assistance from government agencies and private corporations in the United States. Almost all heavy earthmoving equipment used to clear jungle for the Trans-Amazonic roads was supplied by European, North American, and Japanese multinational firms. The Amazon program received substantial financial inputs for hydroelectric and agribusiness development projects from international lending institutions such as the World Bank. Even more relevant to this discussion is the recent discovery of uranium on Yanomamö lands, which must be seen within the context of the entire global scramble for nuclear technologies, power plants, and fuels.

The tragedy of the destruction of the Yanomamö and other aboriginal tribes is that these unique peoples may provide an alternative and indigenous model for the socially and ecologically sound development of the Amazon region. By bringing pressure to bear for the creation of an international Yanomamö reserve, as suggested by the APS in 1973, we could provide the basis not only for the survival of these peoples, but also for the survival of the entire planet and ourselves.

36

Return to Manus
MARGARET MEAD

*Although relatively rare, community restudies are especially
valuable in analyzing culture change. By returning to the site of
an earlier field study, anthropologists can identify important
changes in the group's culture and more accurately identify
causal factors. In this article, Margaret Mead recalls nearly fifty
years of association with the people of a Manus village. During
her first visit in 1928, she learned to know the villagers intimately; she later watched them reject their traditional way of
life after World War II and then, within the last ten years,
attempt to revive it.*

"Did anyone remember you?" people asked me when, in 1953, I said I
had returned from Pere, the little Manus village in the Admiralty Islands
where my husband and I had spent seven months in 1928. "Did you
remember anyone?" they also asked, and I realized that either the
questioners had never lived in a village themselves or they knew little
about what anthropological field work was like. To the 210 people of
Pere village, we were the kind of event that would be talked about again
and again, and as long as I tried to think and write about anthropological problems, the memory of the people — especially the children, whom
I studied intensively — would be sharp and clear in my mind, each small
figure etched sharply against the background of the lagoon where their
pile houses were silhouetted.

Once in a while, as I went back and forth to the South Pacific, and
as members of other departments of The American Museum of Natural
History went on their separate expeditions, I would receive some scrap of
news. I heard that soon after we left — and they had beaten the death

Reprinted with permission from *Natural History* Magazine, June–July, 1976.
Copyright © The American Museum of Natural History, 1976. Illustrations are
omitted.

drums as our canoe pulled out of the village, for they were as sure as we
were that we had left forever — a Catholic missionary had established
himself in the village and had set up a school in our house, a house that
lacked the good lines of the native structures because it had been built to
let in more light. I once met a trader from Manus who told me reproach-
fully that several young men from Pere, who had been part of the
children's group that had run my household and made thousands of
drawings for my psychological study of child thought, had stolen a big
canoe and sailed away to the nearest large island. His voice suggested
that we had been a bad influence. But he had never stopped to think
about how 14,000 people, speaking some twenty different languages,
had originally reached that isolated archipelago, and that thousands of
years ago somebody doing some long-distance sailing had most likely
been blown off course.

Before glottochronology, a linguistic analysis that determines when
a language diverged from a mother tongue, was developed, we had no
way of estimating how long ago that trip took place, as no archeology
had been done. We were, however, able to get a pretty good idea of the
way the different language groups had specialized over the course of
centuries of growing coconuts and taro on the big and small islands,
trading sea products for land products along the shores, going on long
voyages to hereditary trade friends to exchange a turtle or a freshly
caught dugong for a large tree to be used as a housepost or a canoe.
They filled shelves in the rafters of their big houses with pots and
baskets made waterproof with gum (parinarium), spears with obsidian
points, spider web lures, ladles and bailers carved by peoples who were
both trade friends as individuals and enemies in sporadic warfare.

There was respect, contempt, envy, and hostility among the peoples
of this small world — the only world they had known until European
discovery of Papua New Guinea. First the Germans and then, after
World War I, the Australians had preempted the good, level land for
coconut plantations. They imposed a rough sort of law and order and
recruited young men to work on ships, on distant plantations, or as
wharf laborers at the ports.

In 1928 the adventures of going away to work as an indentured
laborer had replaced the adventures of warfare and the capture of
women. Iron had replaced obsidian and stone in knives and adzes. Beads
made in European factories had supplemented the beads made of shell
that were used in trade; for payments for small services; for the great
exchanges that surrounded and validated betrothals, marriages, births,
and deaths; for redistributing valuable imports within the villages; and
for keeping up the level of food production.

The system that kept men and women working unremittingly — to
meet obligations that lasted through generations after each marriage was

contracted — was stimulated by the addition of the new things brought by the Europeans. The traders paid in large packets of tiny beads for each packet of sago they took to feed the workers on plantations and the boat crews that joined the passenger ship that touched the port of Lorengau every six weeks or so.

As has happened in so many parts of the world, the first contact with the more complex technology and larger political system of the Europeans was stimulating. It improved the kind of fishhooks and tools people had to use; provided a wider occupational experience as boat crews, police, and child nurses; and offered new horizons for the future. They had already decided that some day soon they would become Christians. They would abandon the ancestral ghosts who hovered close to their preserved skulls, which hung in every house to discipline its occupants by making them sick and to protect them from the death-dealing malice of the ghosts of other households. Then they would learn to read and write and keep accounts to avoid the endless bickering over how many thousands of dogs' teeth and strands of shell money had changed hands and established indebtedness. European medicine was still respected for curing ringworm, cuts, and wounds, but the "doctor boys," as the medical assistants who were set up in each village by the Australian Mandate were called, had little effect among a people who believed that all illness and misfortune were the result of sin, either sexual or economic. In their scheme of things, theft, failure to pay a debt, and even looking lustfully at a woman were equated.

Their view of their future and our view were as divergent as their clothes and utensils, their beliefs and ceremonies were from ours. They saw the world the Europeans were bringing as one of wider opportunities for trade and adventure, within which their own lives would go on essentially unchanged. The entrepreneurial men and their entrepreneurial wives would go on initiating marriages in terms of which the young, the dependent, and the unenterprising would work for them, while a few sturdy individualists would opt out of the complex and exacting exchange system and simply fish and trade at the local market to keep their families in food.

But we, as anthropologists, foresaw a different fate. We saw a culture that would become impoverished, as young men accustomed to foreign ways would come to despise the authority and ghostly sanctions of their elders. The people would be transformed into a kind of native proletariat, working at low wages for foreigners, losing what they had developed over thousands of years and gaining very little in return. They would become economically dependent, subject to capricious outside authority, when they had once been masters of the seas they sailed.

One of these authorities, insensitive to local marriage customs, had a few years earlier lined up all the unmarried people in the village and indiscriminately married them to each other. It took several years of argument to regularize those marriages: to find fictional links so that these marriage arrangements could be attributed to the proper pairs of contracting cross cousins, the children of a brother-sister pair. The children of these marriages, who were free of property considerations, would grow up and live in the "middle," half in the old system and half in the new, neither here nor there. They would be like our schoolboy linguistic assistant who was the only boy in the village who had been taken away to school — to perfunctorily fulfill the demands of the League of Nations in Geneva.

So when we left, we neither expected nor hoped to see them again. But twenty-five years later, in 1953, I went back, accompanied by two student apprentices, Theodore Schwartz and Lenora Shargo, to investigate the enormous and unexpected changes that the Second World War had brought. Manus had been a major American base; great barracks had been built, surgeons performed miracles of patching up the wounded, as big ships and planes came and went. After the war, Manus was swept by a cargo cult, whose leader prophesied that if the people would throw away all their possessions, the ghosts of their ancestors would bring them large supplies of European goods — airplanes, modern drugs, and tons of food.

But while most Papua New Guinea cargo cults had petered out as a result of government disapproval and disillusioned believers, this political movement had thrived among the Manus people. Led by a man named Paliau, they had rebelled against the mission and set up a miniature government of their own, complete with schools, hospitals, "customs," "passports," parliament, and their own version of Christianity, in which the Lord God, despairing of his European representatives, decided to try the people of New Guinea themselves. The transformation had been so astonishing that my Australian colleagues insisted that I, who had known what they had been and projected what they might become, had to go back and find out what was really happening.

This was a new experience in anthropology. True, field workers had often returned to the site of their original work to follow up old leads, and field workers had studied in places where previous field workers had gone, to quibble over small points or to look at the people through eyes informed by new theories. But no one had studied children as I had, and so, no one had been able to return to find them as adults in charge. The world had never witnessed such rapid transformations from the end of the Stone Age to the Electronic Age, because there had never before been such vast technological gaps to traverse in so few years.

I found the people vigorously pursuing a course of modernization they felt to be their own — not imposed upon them — under a leader who was astute, imaginative, and farsighted. He had plans not only to eliminate the petty animosities of the Admiralty Islands but also to include the whole Bismarck Archipelago in a new federation of cooperation, modernization, and brotherhood. Like other recurrent Papua New Guinea responses to European political and religious ideas, it was to be a utopia constructed by adopting modern ideas — money instead of dogs' teeth, one God instead of ancestral ghosts and local place spirits, education instead of the trials of daring demanded by local warfare and headhunting, political unity instead of village feuds, and a rule of law instead of a rule of angry individual defense of rights and privileges. The European law — a law that would be substituted for feuds, supernatural curses, and sorcery, that would replace anger with good-humored friendliness — this was valued most.

A house was renovated for my use in their newly built land village, and my two young apprentices were set up in a nearby village. Again, I lived among the Manus for six months while recording the New Way. One of the reasons I had consented to go back, instead of exploring a new field as I had planned, was that I realized that the world was facing rapid social change, change in one generation instead of the more usual two- to three-generation shift from one way of life to another. We needed to know how this would work. In Manus I found perhaps the most successful model yet recorded. The Manus were practical, enterprising, interested in how things worked, willing to take chances with their children, confident of their own capacity to cope with new conditions. There was a good fit between the older system and the new, larger system into which they had no choice but to adjust.

It was possible to say that change such as had occurred there, in which a whole system was transformed, could release extraordinary amounts of energy. Old affinal exchange patterns, exploitative kinship patterns (in which young men slaved for their elders), and fear of illness as a principal sanction for good behavior were swept away in favor of the impetus provided by group achievement, cooperative action, and pride in mastering the institutions of the superordinate culture. It seemed that self-initiated, complete change was better and more efficient than piecemeal change in which people partly adjusted to partial change, as a man might limp on a sprained ankle, exacerbating the inflammation. From situations such as I had found in Manus in 1953, we could take new hope that the millions of people caught between the old and the new might make a smoother transition than we had expected.

When it came time to leave, they gave a big farewell feast for me the same night they received word that their new political system would have government recognition. This time the people bade me farewell with more depth of feeling, for now I had witnessed their successes, but again, neither they nor I expected we would meet again. "Like an old turtle, you are going out to sea to die," said old Pokanau, who was, he thought, older than I. Of course, nobody could be sure of this, for ages had only been kept since 1946, the year to which they trace their birth as a modern society.

In 1963 Theodore Schwartz decided he wanted to make an aerial survey of the twenty different language groups in the Admiralties, and so we organized a new three-year expedition. I went back three times to record still more change. The first new village had fallen apart; they had planned and built another one with a great open plaza into which a new government school had to be crowded. With the new school, all of their relatives and connections from a neighboring village moved in. Almost overnight the plagues of the modern world — crowding into cities, pollution from deposits of human waste in the sea, and juvenile delinquency — appeared, ten years out of the first proud modernization effort.

Paliau had built himself a large, ugly modern house out of tin and was now a member of the new Papua New Guinea Parliament. But his political génius was beginning to be compromised by his lack of English, which the younger generation of Papua New Guineans was rapidly mastering. The first student from Pere had entered the new university, and young Manus men and women were entering the educated sector in large numbers as teachers, nurses, clerks, interpreters, and accountants. Younger men were trying to take over from the Old Guard who had made the original successful social revolution and who thought everything should remain just as they had made it.

The people had still not realized much economic progress because the island has few resources. They were investing all their hopes in their children, gladly sending girls as well as boys to the school in Lorengau, and then on to higher education. Their version of Christianity was wearing a little thin with repetition without new vision. But Paliau had politically integrated the whole of the Admiralties so that in 1965 at Christmastime, which had traditionally been the political gathering point during the formation of the new society, people from all over the archipelago came to Pere. It was hard to get much anthropological work done that year because people were out in the bush working sago from dawn to dusk and everybody went to bed exhausted in the early evening, saving themselves and the fuel for their lamps for the big event.

The next year National Educational Television sent out a team to make a film of this small, vigorous society that had so blithely deserted the old ways for the new. The film ended with another "final farewell." These farewells were like Manus deathbed scenes: people gather around illness because they have no way of knowing whether or not someone who is sick will die. There was no way of predicting whether or not I would ever be able to come back.

But in 1971 I went back again with my colleague Barbara Heath, a physical anthropologist who had been following the entire population as children grew and the mature aged, showing us how odd traits, such as one blue eye, repeat themselves in the third and fourth generation. Things in Manus had taken another turn, as the people again condensed into a few years the learning that has taken other societies decades or even centuries. They were dissatisfied with schools; half their children were left in the village after finishing school, too small to work, too young to marry, with no place in society and no way of obtaining even pocket money, while their slightly more scholarly brothers and sisters had gone away for further schooling. With their usual energetic way of tackling problems, the parents discussed what was to be done, struggling with the old idea that the children's labor belonged completely to the parents until they could work their way free.

The dream of modernization was failing a little, and now, like people all over Papua New Guinea, they were beginning to ponder what was worth saving from the past before it was gone forever. The slit gongs, once abandoned for a gong made from a torpedo case, were back. Paliau had built himself a new house, beautifully constructed of thatch and bamboo. He hadn't even used a level — "just my eye, to teach the people," he said. The old dancers were back also, in old costumes worn over modern dress, which looked unesthetic to our eyes, but not to theirs. Paliau agreed that once the old exploitative economic order was gone, the "pleasures" of the past — dance, song, oratory, and costume — became acceptable. These changes echoed events in the wider world, as young people everywhere were beginning to turn from pollution and energy waste to the traditional pleasures of the outdoors and activities that neither pollute nor waste, where the imagination is neither sated nor deadened.

Last summer, 1975, we went back again, in overlapping visits — first Ted Schwartz, then Barbara Heath, then I. I stopped first in Port Moresby, the capital of Papua New Guinea, a new nation that attained independence in September 1975. A north coast Manus man was now the chancellor of the University of Papua New Guinea. There, I spoke to excited students who argued the pros and cons of the accounts that I, as an anthropologist, had written of one of their more than 600 different language groups, complaining that the customs of their own people had been different. I had a long talk with the son of Paliau's principal lieutenant, now minister of housing for the country. At a dinner party I met a young university instructor who came from one of the remote inland villages and was just leaving for the United States for a course in comparative literature. Twenty-five years before, it was the coastal and island people who had taken the lead in higher education, but now young men and women from all over Manus were responding to the high standards that had been set.

I heard that a daughter of one of the inland leaders was now a special adviser to the chief minister, and that she was in Manus helping to draft a regional contribution to the new constitution. When I reached Lorengau, the capital of Manus, I met her and we had long talks about the constitutional problems with which she was wrestling. The plans of the constitutional commission called for the establishment of electoral districts of equal size, which would have meant that villages that had been enemies for decades and possibly centuries would have had to choose a single representative. As an anthropologist who had studied Manus for almost half a century, I knew just what complications this plan would create. (Perhaps fortunately, this attempt to regionalize was abandoned at the last minute as politically inexpedient and too expensive.)

In Lorengau I also met the first young Manus poet who, after having traveled in Europe with the Moral Rearmament Movement for several years, was now teaching creative writing in the Lorengau high school. I met a theological student who returned to find a very poor reception for the brand of sophisticated theology he had learned at a seminary in Chicago. So he turned his energies to solving the problem of a polluted channel. He had persuaded his village to question the custom of allowing canoes from many villages to pass through the channel since the boats were now equipped with outboard motors going at full speed.

In the village my house had been renovated during our two-year absence. People had taken some of the floor boards out to reinforce their own floors, but now brought them back. The partitions had been improved by pieces of plywood taken from our friends' own houses, and the thatch had been mended. The village was seething with activity surrounding the preparations being made for two large exchanges. These exchanges restored some elements of the old style of validating marriages through the "side of the man" and the "side of the woman." The social transformation of 1946 had replaced this form with a new one called a "play," in which gambling winnings and European goods changed hands between principals who entered into these exchanges for pleasure. This differed from the traditional exchanges, which kept people working hard to provide the consumable parts of the exchange — sago, fish, pigs, and oil. But in the exchanges we saw last summer, the production of local food again played an important functional part, keeping the people busy producing food to meet their obligations.

Old Manus customs were also reappearing in a new set of sanctions placed on the young men by their elders. When the young men went away to work, the elders threatened them with curses if they failed to send remittances home, but the young also insisted that those elders should not dissipate the money; rather, they should put it to good use as investments for the younger men. And while the drop-out young boys were now away visiting their brothers and sisters in different parts of the country, some of the educated young men had returned to the village and were keeping records, making the local council more sophisticated, and resuming their hereditary occupations of fishing and trading.

The extreme emphasis on modernization and rejection of the characteristics of an earlier period were now gone. The society was still distinctively Manus, but with a new sense of identity, ready to combine the old and the new. I realized how little we had been able to learn when we used to study a people only once, and how illuminating and unique was this opportunity to follow the same population — a microcosm of the world — for forty-seven years, as they fanned out into the wider world, but retained the core of their culture at home.